Systems Approaches to Management

Systems Approaches to Management

MICHAEL C. JACKSON

University of Hull
Hull, United Kingdom

Kluwer Academic / Plenum Publishers
New York, Boston, Dordrecht, London, Moscow

Library of Congress Cataloging-in-Publication Data

Jackson, Michael C., 1951-
   Systems approaches to management / Michael C. Jackson.
     p. cm.
   Includes bibliographical references and index.
   ISBN 0-306-46500-0 -- ISBN 0-306-46506-X (pbk.)
   1. System analysis. 2. Management science. I. Title.

T57.6 .J33 2000
658.4'032--dc21

00-046623

ISBN 0-306-46500-0 (hardbound)
ISBN 0-306-46506-X (paperback)

©2000 Kluwer Academic / Plenum Publishers
233 Spring Street, New York, New York 10013

http://www.wkap.nl/

10 9 8 7 6 5 4 3 2 1

A C.I.P. record for this book is available from the Library of Congress.

Printed in the United States of America

For some people, when you say "Timbuktu" it is like the end of the world, but that is not true. I am from Timbuktu, and I can tell you we are right at the heart of the world.

Ali Farka Toure

PREFACE

It is nearly ten years since my book *Systems Methodology for the Management Sciences* was published. The intention at that time was to seek to recover for systems thinking the dominant role it had once played in the development of the management sciences; for example, in organization theory and operational research. That dominance had been lost, it was argued, for two reasons. Many academics continued to associate systems thinking with an unfashionable functionalism and rejected it for that reason. Many practitioners had lost faith because the systems movement seemed to be tearing itself apart as factions variously championed systems analysis, cybernetics, soft systems thinking, critical systems thinking and so forth.

Systems Methodology for the Management Sciences had modest success in rebuilding confidence in systems thinking in both the academic and practitioner communities. To academics it demonstrated that systems ideas had much to contribute in interpretive and radical, as well as in functionalist discourse. Systems thinking could exist in and support more than one paradigm and indeed had succumbed to its own disputes between paradigms - the source of the very infighting that troubled practitioners. To practitioners the book brought the message that diversity was a sign of strength in the systems movement and not an indication of weakness. It did this by demonstrating the complementary role that various systems methodologies could play in the overall task of managerial decision making and problem management.

Systems Methodology for the Management Sciences was a book that sought to develop the systems approach as a whole rather than to advocate a particular version of systems thinking against others. As such it contributed to the growing maturity of the systems movement. At the same time, of course, other developments have also impacted on systems thinking and helped to take the systems movement forward. The work of Maturana and Varela on "autopoietic systems" has become of increasing significance in a variety of different fields. Senge's combination of system dynamics with aspects of soft systems thinking, in *The Fifth Discipline*, captured the imagination of practitioners who helped propel it to the top of the best-seller charts. The impact of chaos and complexity theory has been felt in many disciplines and the insights that can be derived for management practice have started to be applied in organizations. And while these newer developments have appeared to monopolize the attention of commentators, it is true that significant progress has also been made in some of the already existing research programs in the field. Soft operational research became more widely accepted and "softer" versions of cybernetics and system dynamics were proposed. Soft systems methodology was reconceptualized to have a "Mode 2" as well as "Mode 1" usage, and was extended to the domain of information systems. Critical systems thinking came of age, severing its automatic connection to an emancipatory approach and further encouraging pluralism and multi-methodology use. Across much of the systems domain postmodernism forced a rethinking that began to effect practice as well as theory.

In these circumstances it is not surprising that there is a need for a new version of the book. This must take account of later arrivals in the systems arena, like chaos and complexity theory, chart progress over the last ten years in those research traditions which existed in 1991, and reflect on those developments in systems thinking that *Systems Methodology for the Management Sciences* itself had a modest part in bringing about.

In producing this new version I have tried to maintain and enhance what I believe are seen as the merits of the original book. These go back to the intention behind that volume. If systems thinking is to recapture a hegemonic role with respect to the management sciences it has to be theoretically and methodologically coherent in a world beyond functionalism, where a multitude of paradigms and discourses compete. If systems thinking is to be widely employed by managers and decision-makers then it must offer them clear and non-contradictory advice on how its findings can be put to use. The aims of the new book remain, therefore, to provide theoretical and methodological coherence to systems thinking, and to do so in a manner which enhances the practical relevance of the ideas.

Of course the new book also sees changes both to the material covered and its arrangement. The book has been thoroughly up-dated to offer an account of the main strands of systems thinking as they stand at the beginning of the new millennium. The structure of the book has also been altered so that, in line with changes in my understanding of the different systems approaches and what they can contribute to systems thinking generally, the significance of the material is more clearly and accurately represented. My guide to rearranging the structure has been the new account of critical systems thinking which I set out in Part III.

The book also has a change in name, reflecting some continuity with *Systems Methodology for the Management Sciences* but also the considerable rethinking and almost entire rewriting that has been necessary. It is certainly about "systems" and celebrates the power of systems ideas in both theory and practice. It remains much concerned with "methodology" as the way of ensuring a fruitful relationship between theory and practice. It is not only about methodology however. The social and systems theories, which have been incorporated in the variety of methodologies that exist, are documented at length and so are many of the models, tools and techniques which are made use of in systems methodologies. The phrase "Systems Approaches" is preferred to "Systems Methodology" to capture this more inclusive concern. The second part of the title of the original book could also prove misleading. To declare that the new book is "for the management sciences" would suggest that its audience is limited to that group of experts who seek to employ "science" in the service of managers. The readership of the original book was much broader than this as it was found to be accessible to students and informed practitioners as well as to academics and specialist consultants and management scientists. In the new book the scope is broader still and the aim is to appeal to a still wider audience. Systems thinking can be and is used by experts but much of it can be made available for managers undertaking their everyday tasks. The new name *Systems Approaches to Management* hopefully makes this clear. Even then it is necessary to insist that management is interpreted in the broadest possible sense. Systems thinking can be employed by radicals seeking to change the world and, given a particular postmodern tinge, by those seeking simply to have fun in organizations. This book caters for these individuals just as much as for managers seeking to improve the efficiency and effectiveness of large organizations. Whichever category you identify with, I hope you will find inspiring and helpful what *Systems Approaches to Management* holds in store.

The author is grateful to the following for their permission to reproduce previously published material:

Abacus, for Figure 4.5.

Harper Collins, for Figures 4.6, 4.7 and 4.8.

McGraw-Hill, for parts of *Critical Systems Thinking and Information Systems Research* (Jackson, in Mingers and Gill, eds., 1997), used in Chapter 12.

The Operational Research Society, for Figure 8.1.

Random House, for Figures 6.8 and 6.9.

Sage, for Figure 6.14.

Stockton Press, for parts of *Towards Coherent Pluralism in Management Science* (Jackson, 1999), used in Chapter 11.

John Wiley, for parts of *Creative Problem Solving: Total Systems Intervention* (Flood and Jackson, 1991), used in Chapters 10 and 11; and for Figures 2.1, 6.3, 6.6, 7.5, 7.15, 12.1, 12.2, 12.4 and 12,5.

Then there are some essential acknowledgements. Peter Checkland, Bob Flood and Paul Keys were mentioned in the previous book and their influence over the form and content of this book remains strong. As well as pursuing my research I have, over the last ten years, sought to build systems research groups, management departments, schools and faculties at Hull, and Lincolnshire and Humberside Universities; been editor of *Systems Research and Behavioral Science* and editor (and then associate editor) of *Systemic Practice and Action Research*; and acted as Chair of the UK Systems Society and President of the International Federation for Systems Research. Thanks to all who made these things possible and shared the endeavors - especially Russ Ackoff, Bela Banathy, Keith Ellis, Amanda Gregory, Gerald Midgley, Doreen Osuch and Zhu Zhichang. I am grateful to the students who helped me develop the ideas and worked on some of the projects reported in the book, particularly Mary Ashton, Alvaro Carrizosa, D.P. Dash, Steve Green, Giles Hindle, Luisa Garcia, Nasser Jabari, Bridget Mears-Young, Andres Mejia, Clemencia Morales, Maria Ortegon, Roberto Palacios and Gokhan Torlak.

Special thanks are due to Catherine Gaskell who did much of the basic research for the new material in the book and Alison Parker who finished the research and tidied up the text. Ted Geerling helped with the proof reading. Doreen Gibbs word-processed the manuscript and helped me organize and enjoy my working life. She is a model of efficiency, effectiveness and good humor.

I dedicate the volume to my wife Pauline and sons, Christopher and Richard, all of whom have made sacrifices so that it could be finished.

Mike C. Jackson
University of Hull

CONTENTS

Systems Approaches to Management

MICHAEL C. JACKSON

University of Hull
Hull, United Kingdom

1

INTRODUCTION

I intend, in this introduction, to say a few words about why systems thinking emerged and to give an account of the development of the systems tradition up to the present. The aim of the book can then be explained in terms of the state of systems thinking today. Finally some reasons are provided as to why you should bother to read the book.

1.1. WHY SYSTEMS THINKING?

Descartes (1968) writing in 1637, at the beginning of the age that was to give birth to the scientific revolution, argued that if he wanted to understand the world and its problems he should proceed by the method of "reductionism"

> to divide each of the difficulties that I was examining into as many parts as might be possible and necessary in order best to solve it [and] beginning with the simplest objects and the easiest to know ... to climb gradually ... as far as the knowledge of the most complex (p. 41).

The success of science in producing knowledge, and of its associated technologies in transforming our world, demonstrate that for certain classes of difficulties he was right. Problems occur with the use of reductionism and the natural scientific method (as it is usually understood), however, when we are faced with complex, real-world problems set in social systems (Checkland, 1981) - the very problems which we encounter in abundance today and which most threaten our organizations and societies.

Complex problems involve richly interconnected sets of "parts" and the relationships between the parts can be more important than the nature of the parts themselves. New properties, "emergent" properties, arise from the way the parts are organized. Even if the parts constituting a complex situation can be identified and separated out, therefore, this may be of little help because the most significant features, the emergent properties, then get lost. Further, although in the natural sciences it is often possible to test hypotheses by carrying out experiments in the laboratory into cause and effect among a limited number of elements, this proves extremely difficult with real-world problems. The significant factors involved do not easily identify themselves and the problem situation itself can seem to have no boundary. Another difficulty is that repeatable experiments are hard to carry out on real-world problems when initial conditions are impossible to replicate. Such experiments on people or social systems can in any case be ethically problematic. Finally, in seeking to understand and intervene in social systems, people are inevitably at the center of the stage. It is necessary to take into account different beliefs and purposes, different evaluations of the situation, the danger of self-fulfilling prophecies, and the sheer bloody-minded capacity of individuals to falsify any prediction made about them. For all these reasons, the attempt to apply reductionism, and the natural scientific method generally, to social and organizational problems has not been a happy one and has yielded only limited success.

Systems thinking, it is argued by Checkland (1981), can be seen as a reaction to the failure of natural science when confronted with complex, real-world problems set in social systems. Systems thinkers advocate using "holism" rather than reductionism in such situations. Holism does not seek to break down complex problem situations into their parts in order to study them and intervene in them. Rather, it respects the profound interconnectedness of the parts and concentrates on the relationships between them and how these often give rise to surprising outcomes - the emergent properties. Systems thinking uses models rather than laboratory experiments to try to learn about the behavior of the world and even then does not take for granted or impose any arbitrary boundary between the "whole" that is the subject of its attention, in the model, and the environment in which it is located. Instead, it reflects upon and questions where the boundary has been drawn and how this impacts on the kind of improvements that can be made. Contemporary systems thinking also respects the different "appreciative systems" (Vickers, 1965) that individuals bring to bear in viewing the world and making value judgements about particular situations. In order to contribute to an "holistic" appreciation of the problem situation at hand, different perspectives on its nature and possible resolution should be encouraged. Greater creativity will result and mutual understanding might be achieved about a way forward as appreciative systems become more shared.

1.2 THE SYSTEMS TRADITION

As we shall see in Chapter 4 the systems approach, or holistic thinking, has a very long history. It was not until the late 1940s and early 1950s, however, with the publication of Wiener's work on cybernetics (1948) and von Bertalanffy's on "general system theory" (1950, 1968), that it began to take on the form of a discipline. The approach was popular and immediately successful, and systems thinking from the 1950s to the 1970s was far and away the most important influence on the management sciences and a number of other fields. To give only a few examples, the systems approach dominated organization theory for over two decades while systems thinking was the often-stated theoretical justification behind practical methodologies such as operational research. Outside the management sphere sociologists were immensely influenced by general system theory and cybernetics through the work of Parsons, and French structuralists such as Levi-Strauss and Piaget acknowledged their debt to von Bertalanffy and Wiener.

The success of systems thinking in helping to develop other disciplines fuelled confidence in the systems movement about its own concepts and methods. In the Kuhnian (Kuhn, 1970) sense of the phrase, systems thinking was in a period of "normal science." By 1970 there was considerable agreement about how the notion of *system* should be understood and applied. The same could be said of the other key ideas in the systems dictionary - concepts such as *element, relationship, boundary, input, transformation, output, environment, feedback, attribute, purpose, open system, homeostasis, emergence, communication, control, identity* and *hierarchy*. Some systems people (those of the general system persuasion) put more emphasis on learning about the nature of real-world systems, while others concentrated on developing methodologies, based on systems ideas and principles, to intervene in and change systems. Nevertheless, there was a shared set of assumptions about the nature of systems and about the meaning and use of systems terms. Systems people, whether theorists or practitioners, operated from within the same paradigm. In summary, it was assumed that systems of all types could be identified by empirical observation of reality and could be analyzed by a simple enhancement (for example replacing laboratory experiments by the use of models) of the methods that had brought success in the natural sciences. Systems could then, if the interest was in practice, be manipulated the better to achieve whatever purposes they were designed to serve. Systems thinking at the beginning of the 1970s, therefore, was still dominated by the positivism and functionalism characteristic of the traditional version of the scientific method. This traditional type of systems thinking gave birth to strands of work such as "organizations as systems", general system theory, contingency theory, operational research, systems analysis, systems engineering and management cybernetics.

During the 1970s and 1980s, however, traditional systems thinking became subject to increasing criticism. In the theoretical domain there was an assault upon functionalism in disciplines such as sociology and organization theory. This was read by many as an attack on the systems idea itself. In the applied domain, approaches such as operational research seemed to content themselves with the piecemeal engineering of tactical problems. It appeared as though the systems approach it embraced was leaving this domain unable to deal with ill-structured and strategic problems, and so was hindering its development and influence. As a result of the apparent failings of traditional thinking, and the increasing criticism, alternative systems approaches were born and began to flourish. So, for example, in the late 1970s and early 1980s "soft systems thinking" and "organizational cybernetics" came to the fore, and in the late 1980s "critical systems thinking" was born. These new tendencies in systems thinking found themselves at war not only with the traditional approach but also with each other, for they were often opposed on fundamental matters concerning the nature and purpose of the discipline. They attracted different groups of adherents, put different emphases on the subject matter and key concepts of the field, and sometimes even harbored different interpretations of the role of systems thinking. They rested upon different philosophical/sociological assumptions. In essence, they were based on different paradigms. Systems thinking had entered a period of "Kuhnian crisis."

Inevitably, given the fundamental differences in orientation between the competing strands of the systems movement in the 1980s, even the notion of "system" came to acquire different uses and meanings. Nowhere is this more evident than in the shift achieved by Checkland in breaking from systems engineering and establishing soft systems methodology. In soft systems methodology, systems are seen as the mental constructs of observers rather than as entities with an objective existence in the world; systemicity is transferred "from the world to the process of inquiry into the world" (Checkland, 1983). Obviously, if the idea of "system" could be affected in this way, so could all the other systems concepts. This often led to considerable difficulties for systems writers, especially if they were sensitive enough to worry about whether terms tainted with positivist and functionalist implications could carry the new meanings that they were trying to give to them. Thus, Flood (1988) attests to the difficulty he found, after his own conversion from hard to soft systems thinking, in translating a manuscript written using traditional systems concepts, with their functionalist overtones, into a book privileging soft systems meanings and intentions.

Freed from an adherence solely to the functionalist paradigm, systems thinking continued to flower profusely in the 1990s. Senge's (1990) *The Fifth Discipline*, developed from system dynamics, became the basis for much work on "learning organizations." Maturana and Varela's work on autopoietic or self-producing systems (see Mingers, 1995) impacted on sociology (through Luhmann's comprehensive systems theory of society), law and family therapy. Soft systems thinking continued to develop and to gain ground, particularly in the field of information systems. Critical systems thinking called for the "radical" paradigms (in Burrell and Morgan's 1979 terms) to be opened up in systems thinking and attempted to reconstruct systems thinking upon pluralist foundations. Many people discovered or rediscovered a version of the systems approach through the popularization of chaos and complexity theory.

1.3 THE AIM OF THE BOOK

Despite all this endeavor, systems thinking overall enters the third millennium in a less secure position in the social sciences than it occupied thirty years ago. Many theorists, faces set against the evidence, still write it off as another version of functionalism, discredited in their eyes because of its inability to deal with the subtlety and dynamics of organizational processes and, in particular, power and conflict. Checkland (1994) and Galliers, Jackson and Mingers (1997) are still trying to convince organization theorists, in many senses the nearest of kin, of the relevance of recent developments in systems thinking to their concerns. Although they may buy into aspects of systems thinking presented as the latest management fad (as "the learning organization" or chaos and complexity theory), practitioners continue to see the approach as too theoretical to be helpful with their everyday concerns. The splintering of the systems movement into warring factions championing soft systems thinking against hard systems thinking and critical systems thinking against soft systems thinking may provide amusement to academics but is alienating to practitioners. Progress there might have been but the full potential of systems ideas still remains to be realized.

The aim of this book is directly related to the current state of systems thinking as an approach within the social and management sciences. Its purpose is no less than to reconstitute systems thinking as a coherent approach to inquiry and problem management so that it can again occupy a role at the leading edge of development in the applied disciplines. This is done (Part II) by demonstrating the power of systems ideas as a source of support and practical guidance to a variety of social theory perspectives - support that has been reinforced rather than threatened by the establishment of alternative soft, emancipatory and postmodern systems approaches. Second, I show (in Part III) how, in the context of critical systems thinking, the various systems approaches derived in Part II can help, as part of a pluralist rationale, to enhance the overall task of decision-making and problem management. Practitioners will then be able to recognize diversity as a sign of strength and not weakness in the systems movement.

1.4. WHY READ THIS BOOK?

It has been argued (Ackoff, 1974) that Descartes's reductionism was appropriate to the "machine age" of the industrial revolution and that systems thinking was born as a response to the dawn of the "systems age." At the beginning of the new millennium the systems age is well and truly upon us and is characterized, as we are all experiencing, by complexity, turbulence and a multiplicity of viewpoints about the direction we should be taking and how we should handle the difficulties we face. This is true whether we examine our personal lives, the organizations in which we work, the societies in which we live or the natural environment we are inhabiting. Wherever we turn we are confronted with problem situations constituted by innumerable, interconnected variables, which constantly change their shape and character because of apparently unpredictable interactions between the variables. The confusion this engenders can lead to a sense of meaninglessness prevailing, in which any way forward can seem as good or as bad as any other.

We have already noted that, in order to cope in this systems age, people are beginning to turn to systems thinking. This is especially the case with those who lead and co-ordinate business organizations but is also noticeable among those interested in broader social and environmental concerns. Managers of all kinds look to books like Senge's *The Fifth Discipline* (1990) for guidance on how to change their mental models so that they can better understand the underlying patterns of relationships (or systems archetypes) which, it is claimed, give rise to apparent variety and flux at the surface level. Others, aware of the limitations of traditional machine models for studying organizations in the new times, seek insights in the sciences of chaos and complexity. Successful organizations, they learn, need to be "dissipative structures" operating at the boundary between stability and instability (Stacey, 1993). Still others, especially those grappling with global problems such as poverty, population growth, pollution and forest destruction, follow Capra (1996) in calling for a new way of thinking, based upon a "deep ecological awareness", which responds to the fact that

> the more we study the major problems of our time, the more we come to realize that they cannot be understood in isolation. They are systemic problems, which means that they are interconnected and interdependent (p. 3).

This book seeks to capitalize on the renewed interest in systems thinking and to harness the new systems ideas being produced. It does so, however, in the context of an holistic tradition of inquiry which dates back centuries, and efforts to apply systems ideas in practice which can be traced back to at least the Second World War. This research tradition makes it possible for learning to take place and progress to be made. It allows us, for example, to understand the genesis of the new ideas and to evaluate their worth and originality. The result is, hopefully, a thorough and mature reading of what systems thinking has to offer in relation to managing the problems of the systems age.

Although many people seem to be natural systems thinkers, the current upsurge in the amount of literature on systems thinking suggests that they recognize the need to have these natural instincts further refined. This book is designed for those, whether academics, students or practitioners, with an urge to systems, who would appreciate a guide through the vast and diverse literature on systems thinking and would like the most relevant systems ideas and methods explained so that they can employ them. It might be used by consultants who want to gain expertise in systems thinking so that they can advise their clients on how to see and solve their problems using systems models and techniques. It can be used by revolutionaries to criticize the current social system and to propose alternative systemic arrangements. I suspect, however, that its main audience will be those without specific expertise and without, perhaps, a particular political agenda, but who simply believe that a systems approach might help them to cope better with the complex "messes" (Ackoff, 1981) they face in their everyday lives, in their organizations and in dealing with social and environmental problems. For these people, managers in the broadest sense of that term, it is worth concluding this introduction by setting out three reasons why the book you are reading might help you become a better decision-maker and problem-resolver.

The first applies to "commonsense" managers who now feel overwhelmed by the problem situations they are confronted with and are convinced that the "commonsense" solutions they have been employing no longer work or even make things worse. When you try to solve one problem another dozen pop up from somewhere else. You think you have dealt with a difficult situation by issuing some instruction or taking some action but, two months later, you recognize that where it matters things have not changed. Perhaps the problems you are facing are so entangled that you simply do not know where to start in trying to address them. Perhaps you are confronted by a superior who does not understand what you are trying to tell her and misinterprets your every action, or subordinates who say you never communicate with them although you believe you have set everything out as clearly as possible at least three times in the last month. All of these may be symptoms of problems that can be tackled using systems thinking. If you come to the book for this reason then you should find that the lessons you learn can help enhance the "commonsense" approach you have been employing to date and allow you to start to alleviate the "mess" you are confronting and move forward confidently again.

The second reason is relevant to "academic" managers who have absorbed all the lessons from the management gurus but now feel disappointed with the results. They have been through programs labeled quality management, lean manufacturing, downsizing, business process re-engineering, Investors in People, the learning organization, knowledge management and, because the holy grail seems as far away as ever, have become disillusioned with the apparently never-ending plethora of management fads. You might have seen expensive information technology investments fail because they do not connect to the strategy of the organization and bear no relation to the tasks that concern the users. Perhaps you have seen a total quality management initiative grind to a halt because it did not have sustained senior management support. Or a business process re-engineering exercise abandoned because of the resistance it built up among those it was supposed to be engineering for greater efficiency. Perhaps your attempt to become a learning organization floundered on the organizational politics engendered when middle managers felt their positions threatened. If so, maybe you have come to recognize that your organization has been playing, in a reductionist way, with "partial solutions." If the "boundary" had been drawn wider to consider people and strategy perhaps the I.T. investment would have succeeded. If the relationships between the parts of the organization had been given greater consideration and quality seen as an "emergent property" of all those parts functioning together, then that initiative, you feel, would have turned out better. If you come to the book for this reason then you should gain from systems thinking an understanding of the limitations of management fads, an ability to evaluate in systems terms the proposals of future management gurus, and insights that should help make future organizational change initiatives successful.

The final reason applies to "visionary" managers, who have a feeling that systems thinking is in tune with the times or is, indeed, the way to the future. Perhaps they have read predictions of what "tomorrow's company" will need to aspire to be. It will need to employ technology efficiently, but we no longer live in the machine age and, in order to compete in the knowledge-based world, it will have to involve its people more. It will need to be an inclusive company which looks after all its stakeholders - employees, suppliers, customers and local community, as well as shareholders. At the societal level you will have witnessed the collapse of state socialism and the failures of unbridled market capitalism, and perhaps be interested in some "third-way" to development. This third way (Giddens, 1998) has to envisage a new role for governance as power is both devolved down from the nation state to the localities and regions, and also up to transnational agencies. It has to respect interconnectivity in order to provide adequate responses to scientific and technological change, transformations in personal life and globalization. The third way itself needs to be inclusive in coping with cultural diversity and increasing ecological concerns. At both the organizational and the societal levels there is frequent talk of partnership, between stakeholders of organizations or between the public and private sectors. You will have noted how often the systems concept of "holism" gets an airing these days. If you come to the book because you believe systems ideas are in tune with the times, you will find herein a language and an understanding that enables you to make concrete proposals about how to create tomorrow's company and puts flesh on the bones of talk about the third way. Notions such as partnership, inclusiveness, stakeholding, governance, interconnectivity, globalization, and ecology all carry a systems ring about them and can be articulated and discussed more adequately in systems terms.

Most managers are a mixture of the commonsense, the academic and the visionary. For them it really is time to change their mental maps and to learn, understand and use systems approaches.

I

OVERVIEWS

2

ORIENTATION AND STRUCTURE

2.1. INTRODUCTION

In order to orientate the reader it is necessary to elucidate some of the terms used in this book. The word methodology will be regularly encountered. I first distinguish it from method and meta-methodology before explaining how it provides a link between theory and practice. It then becomes possible to examine different types of research and, in particular, to compare and contrast the strengths and weaknesses of the social science and systems traditions of work. The structure of Part I of the book falls into place and is briefly outlined. Another key term is obviously "system" itself. Reflections upon the value of this idea and other associated concepts, together with some thoughts on systems thinking and the systems movement, allow the structure of Parts II and III to be understood. The chapter ends with a table illustrating the argument of the book.

2.2. METHODOLOGY, METHODS, AND META-METHODOLOGY

Methodology concerns itself with the study of the principles of method use, in the sense that it sets out to describe and question the methods that might be employed in some activity. Methodology is, therefore, a higher-order term than methods and, indeed, than procedures, models, tools, and techniques, the use of all of which can be facilitated, organized and reflected upon in methodology. In systems thinking, for example, the Viable System Model (and there is often confusion over this) is simply a model employed to try to diagnose problems and to suggest how organizations might be designed. Methodology establishes the principles behind the use of such a model. As we shall see, the Viable System Model, the system dynamics method, etc., can all be used differently according to the methodology in which they are embedded. Meta-methodology is at a higher level still and explores the nature and use of methodologies. It is a term that is often employed in critical systems thinking where the relationship between methodologies is crucial and requires meta-methodological probing. The terms method, methodology and meta-methodology are, therefore, in a hierarchical relationship to one another. Part II of this volume details four types of systems methodology based upon the four most common research approaches found in the social sciences – functionalist, interpretive, emancipatory and postmodern. In each case the methods, models, tools and techniques most frequently associated with each methodology are also detailed. It is made clear, however, that there is usually the possibility of using such methods and tools in the service of the other methodologies as well. In Part III of the book the debate, focussing now on critical systems thinking, is often at the meta-methodological level.

2.3. METHODOLOGY, THEORY, AND PRACTICE

We can establish some further important distinctions if we consider the relationships between the concepts of methodology, theory and practice. A good starting point is Checkland's summary of the elements he sees as necessary in any piece of research (Checkland and Holwell, 1998). In Figure 2.1 we see three such elements. There must be a "framework of ideas" (F) in which knowledge about the situation being researched is expressed. This can be the current theory of a particular discipline although it might also be something much looser than this. Then there is a methodology (M) in which the F is embodied. The M marshals various methods, tools and techniques in a manner appropriate to the F and uses them to investigate the situation of interest. The third element is this situation of interest or "area of concern" (A). "A" might be a particular problem in a discipline or it can be some real-world problem situation. When we talk about practice in systems thinking we are usually referring to intervention in some real-world "A."

2.4. TYPES OF RESEARCH

It is worthwhile using these ideas to explore some of the different types of research that can take place. A first type might better be called "scholarship", although without the implication that this sometimes carries that the work is not original. With scholarship the research is essentially self-contained within a discipline and does not open itself to the real-world. F is the current appreciation of the nature of the discipline and the knowledge contained in the discipline and this is applied through M, which might embody what is

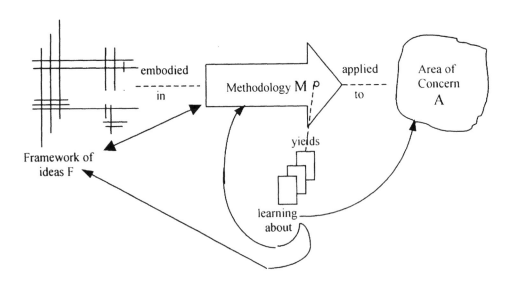

Figure 2.1. Elements relevant to any piece of research (Checkland, 1985, Checkland and Holwell, 1998, p. 13).

regarded as good practice in the discipline, to A which is a particular area of concern in the discipline. Much of the book by Checkland and Holwell (1998) engages in this type of scholarship. What is regarded as good knowledge and procedure in systems thinking is applied to a "confused" sub-area of the field, information systems, as an exercise in "conceptual cleansing." Once the conceptual cleansing has occurred, of course, the A can then be properly incorporated into the F of the field and employed to investigate the real-world with more chance of success. It is a common criticism of the social sciences that they are so busy revisiting their Fs that they rarely move onto applying their theories to the real-world.

A second kind of research is the positivist hypothesis testing which lies at the heart of the traditional account of the natural scientific approach. Here, hypotheses that purport to describe the behavior of a part of the real-world are derived from the F of the relevant science. The M of the science prescribes particular experiments and observations that need to be made and how they should be carried out in order that the hypotheses can be tested in the real-world. The experiments and observations are then applied to the A, that part of the real-world the behavior of which the hypotheses were meant to predict. The hypotheses either survive the test or are refuted. If rigorously conducted this procedure should lead to learning about each of F, M, and A. This kind of research is, of course, also common in the social sciences. In his book, *The Rules of Sociological Method*, Durkheim (1938) defines his F, which is his theory of the nature of social reality, and an M, which are the steps and procedures to go through in learning about aspects of that social reality. He applied this methodology in two classic texts in an attempt to understand the division of labor and suicide as sociological phenomena. In systems research, too, a version of the classic natural scientific approach is often employed. From F a systems model is derived that seeks to explain the behavior of some aspect of external reality. Methodological rules are applied to test the predictive capability of the model; to bring it into closer correspondence to A. Beer's (1966) "Yo-Yo Methodology" is an example of an appropriate M.

The kind of research process just described has been called "Mode 1" by Gibbons *et al.* (1994). It is a

> complex of ideas, methods, values and norms that has grown up to control the diffusion of the Newtonian model of science to more and more fields of enquiry and ensure its compliance with what is considered sound scientific practice (p. 167).

In Checkland's terms, in Mode 1 research the bias is very much towards the F rather than the A and knowledge production is controlled by the academic community that is guardian of the F. It is the academic interests of the particular scientific community that decide what problems are tackled. The needs of the discipline are paramount rather than the interests of possible users of the research outcomes and the results are, therefore, communicated through normal academic channels. The quality of the research produced is judged through peer review by other academics in the discipline.

Gibbons *et al.* argue that another form of knowledge production, Mode 2, is now establishing itself and complementing Mode 1. Mode 2 research (our third type of research) is governed by the A rather than the F. It is:

> Knowledge production carried out in the context of application and marked by its: transdisciplinarity; heterogeneity; organizational heterarchy and transience; social accountability and reflexivity; and quality control which emphasizes context-and use-dependence (1994, p. 167).

Elaborating a little, Mode 2 knowledge is produced to satisfy the demands of particular users. Research is organized around a particular A and is generated in negotiation with those who will find the outcomes useful. Because the research revolves around a real-world A, it is unlikely that any single discipline will be able to provide a suitable F. Mode 2 research is therefore "transdisciplinary." The F that is employed is likely to be "looser" than a theory or set of hypotheses and may be relevant to only one application. In Checkland's terms more attention is given to the M which becomes a kind of transferable problem solving capability. Diffusion occurs immediately at the point of production of the research and when this problem solving capability is applied in a new context. The organization of Mode 2 research has to be more flexible to respond to the changing and transitory nature of the problems it addresses. Tackling issues of real concern, Mode 2 researchers are also much more account-able to the public and the quality of the research must be judged on a wider set of criteria than simply contribution to the development of a discipline.

Tranfield and Starkey (1998) argue that management research should adopt a Mode 2 orientation, positioning itself in the social sciences as equivalent to engineering in the physical sciences and medicine in the biological sciences. In fact applied systems thinking, when its concern is social and organizational problems, has already occupied this space. From the first formulation of approaches such as operational research, systems analysis and systems engineering in the 1940s and 1950s, the emphasis has been on the client and his or her requirements. This has remained fundamentally the case, although "problem owners" apart from the client (in soft systems thinking) and "the affected but not involved" (in critical systems heuristics) also now fall into the embrace of systems thinking. In essence, applied systems thinking has always allowed itself to be governed by the A. It has em-ployed, for the most part, a rather weak, transdisciplinary F, consisting of various systems notions and concepts. On the other hand it has been strong on developing Ms, putting its systems ideas to work in ordered ways to tackle real-world problems. Operational research (as originally conceived), systems analysis, soft systems methodology, interactive planning and critical systems heuristics are all examples of well formulated Ms based on systems ideas. This is just what is required in Mode 2 knowledge production where the primary aim must be to develop a transferable problem solving capability. The other features of Mode 2 research are also easily recognizable in applied systems thinking; for example, the attention given in various systems approaches to the establishment of appropriate multi-disciplinary teams to undertake specific research projects.

2.5. ACTION RESEARCH

It is worth identifying a fourth type of research – action research. Action research originated in the work of Kurt Lewin who, in the late 1940s, recognized the problems inherent in trying to study complex social and psychological processes by breaking them apart (reductionism) and taking them into the laboratory. He advocated instead testing theory in action, in the process of implementation. Rapoport (1970) provides the standard definition of action research, viewing it as contributing

> both to the practical concerns of people in an immediate problematic situation and to the goals of social science by joint collaboration within a mutually agreed ethical framework (p. 499).

Depending where the action researcher puts the emphasis, on the theory (F) or practice (A) side, action research might be seen as a variant of either the second or third types of research that we have identified (Mode 1 or 2 in the language of Gibbons *et al*). In some of the literature on action research, however, there is recognition of another characteristic of the approach that clearly distinguishes action research from any of the other research processes we have considered. Checkland and Holwell (1998) call action research that emphasizes this aspect "interpretive action research." Interpretive action researchers make a clear virtue of the ability of the researcher, and the research process itself, to influence the situation being investigated. The radical nature of this step deserves further attention.

In the positivist account of the natural scientific method (if not in alchemy or modern quantum mechanics) it is assumed that the experimenter should ensure that she herself, and her research instruments, do not affect the outcome of the experiment. This guarantees the objectivity of the results and permits other researchers to carry out the same experiments and get the same outcomes. In the many parts of the social sciences that tried to copy this method the same assumption held sway. If the researchers, or the research itself, were in danger of affecting the behavior of the system being studied then this was seen to endanger the "objectivity" of the process. Genders and Player describe the situation in HM Prison Grendon. They were trying "to capture certain fundamental truths" about the institution but it fell into such a state of crisis that the research had to be abandoned lest it contributed to the problems, making "proper" scientific research impossible:

> The prevailing sense of crisis distracted staff from their usual business and, in some respects, distorted the processes which the research was designed to study. The air of despondency led to the expression of jaundiced views during the interviews, which marked a notable break with the earlier responses, and largely reflected a transient and ephemeral reaction to the issues of the moment. In consequence, interviews had to be halted until the institution regained a sense of equilibrium (quoted in Gaskell, 1997, p. 175).

The alternative, favored by interpretive action researchers, is to accept that any research on human or social systems will inevitably change them and to make a virtue of this fact. In making the same point, Checkland (in Checkland and Holwell, 1998) refers to conversations with Geoffrey Vickers:

> He used to point out that while Copernicus and Ptolemy offer very different hypotheses about the basic structure of our solar system, we know that, irrespective of whether the sun or the earth is at the center of the system, the actual structure is entirely unaffected by our having theories about it. Whereas when Marx propounds a theory of history this changes history! (p. 19).

The interpretive action researcher is under no illusion that he will be fully involved, with other participants in the problem situation, in a social process which will change that situation (Checkland and Holwell, 1998). He must, therefore, take some responsibility for any practical outcomes that arise and seek to ensure that these represent perceived improvements in the eyes of the participants. Of course, he must also declare in advance the F and the M brought to the real-world problem situation and, later, reflect on the learning achieved about this F and M, as well as about the A. This is his contribution to the research side of action research. The results will not be as clear cut as in the case of hypotheses confirmed or refuted, but the process of research and its outcomes will at least be "recoverable" to others in terms of the "research themes" embedded in the F and M.

2.6. SOCIAL SCIENCE AND SYSTEMS THINKING

The rationale of the book can now best be explained if we use the ideas and formulations developed to compare and contrast the relative strengths and weaknesses of the social science and systems traditions of research.

Methodology, as we have witnessed, is often subordinated to theory. In the first type of research which we considered, it is employed in a scholarly endeavor within a discipline to improve the conceptual armory available. In the second kind, it is the vehicle in which a discipline transports itself to the outside world but the focus of attention remains some problem in the discipline which, if solved, will allow it to progress. The social sciences are dominated by such research. As Gibbons *et al.* (1994) argue, it is only recently that another type of knowledge production, with priority given to the context of application, has attracted any attention. Action research has always been of very peripheral interest to social researchers. Not surprisingly, therefore, the social sciences are strong on theory, but relatively weak on practice. They rarely develop methodologies which are oriented to giving specific guidance to policy makers and problem solvers facing real-world difficulties.

The balance of advantage between social scientists and systems thinkers shifts when we consider methodology as a support to practice. Systems thinking has engaged in theory building but it is not where its main interest lies. Because of a more practical focus, the normal usage of the word methodology in systems thinking is to describe an organized set of methods and techniques employed to intervene in and change real-world problem situations. As we saw, the emphasis of systems methodology has been on dealing with the concerns of the client or problem-owner. Action research has always been regarded as possessing a healthy pedigree in systems circles, and soft systems thinkers in particular have embraced it whole-heartedly. The outcome is that systems thinkers can claim a lead over social scientists in terms of the practical usefulness of their methodologies. The downside is that, for the most part, they have tended to neglect theory, operating at best with weak Fs made up of poorly articulated systems ideas. It is not normally felt to be necessary for the advocate of a systems methodology to delve into its theoretical presuppositions even though it is obvious that any attempt to change the world rests upon taken-for-granted assumptions about the nature of that world. In not explaining these, systems thinking has failed to take full advantage of opportunities to learn from practice and to develop as a discipline (or more properly, perhaps, as a transdiscipline).

In this book the aim is to draw upon the respective strengths of the social science and systems traditions and to set out an agenda which will enable both working together to be further enhanced. I am concentrating on the systems tradition because my main concern is with the practical task of managing problems and bringing about change, and we have argued that systems thinking is very strong in this area. This will ensure that the emphasis is on the relationship between M and A, and on methodology serving practice. It is clear, however, that in order to understand fully and to be able to improve systems methodology, we shall have to link it to firmer theoretical anchorings, to some stronger Fs. Because systems thinking is weak in this respect, we have little option but to turn to ideas developed in the social sciences for the purpose of establishing some theoretical positions that can be used to further underpin systems methodology. The result of this linking should leave us with an improved capacity to learn about F, M and A, and to act in A.

2.7. THE STRUCTURE OF PART I

The above considerations have helped reveal some of the contributions this book hopes to make. Part I of the volume, as well as orientating the reader and introducing the structure of the argument (which I am doing now), contains Chapter 3, "Relevant Social Theory." This deals, in summary form, with the background social theory that systems practitioners need before they can adequately employ and improve upon existing systems methodology. Chapter 2 acts, therefore, as an introduction to some highly relevant social science for systems thinkers. Part I also contains Chapter 4, "Origins in the Disciplines", which traces the evolution of systems thinking in the disciplines, and its emergence as a distinctive area of study, and Chapter 5, which provides an introduction to "Applied Systems Thinking." Chapters 4 and 5 offer social scientists an examination of the history, development and main concepts used in applied systems thinking in terms they will understand, and therefore give social scientists access to the systems approaches which are presented more fully in Parts II and III of the book. Bridging the gap between systems thinkers and social scientists is another objective of the book and is, of course, central to its aim of improving the effectiveness of systems approaches.

2.8. SYSTEM, SYSTEMS THINKING AND THE STRUCTURE OF PARTS II AND III

I can now turn to "system" and seek to elucidate the way I employ that term and the value I attach to it. In doing this I set out the structure of the argument in Parts II and III of the book.

It was stated in Chapter 1, the "Introduction", that the common understanding that existed about the nature of systems thinking, and the meaning of the key concepts used, began to break down in the 1970s. A shared set of concerns was replaced by different factions championing hard, soft, critical and other perspectives. The systems movement had succumbed to the paradigm wars that had overwhelmed other disciplines such as sociology. It is now widely accepted, and must be the starting point for any contemporary study of systems methodology, that these various strands of the systems movement use the concept "system", and all the other important systems ideas, in different ways. Part II of the book picks out and investigates cases where systems concepts, models and methods have been brought together in unique ways and invested with a peculiar power for the purpose of intervening in the real-world. In the terms of this book, that means setting out and critically examining the most significant systems approaches. With the help of the social theory examined in Chapter 3, four such unique, distinct and effective ways of employing systems ideas, tools and techniques are identified. These correspond to functionalist, interpretive, emancipatory and postmodern versions of systems thinking. A chapter is devoted to each of these, with the theory or framework of ideas governing each approach considered (again with the assistance of relevant social theory), exemplar methodologies and their originators and advocates identified and a critique of the approach provided. As well as interrogating the theory and methodology of each approach, the methods, models and techniques usually associated with it are introduced. Examples of applications are always given when it is felt that these will contribute to understanding.

The structure of Part II reveals the primacy ceded to social theory at least during the current stage of development of the social sciences and systems thinking. It is the different paradigms in social theory – functionalist, interpretive, emancipatory and postmodern – that are allowed to provide the ordering mechanism. The various systems methodologies, methods and models are classified and clarified according to these paradigms. My assumption is that there is nothing about systems thinking that allows it to stand above the paradigms and to remain isolated from disputes between perspectives emanating from different paradigms. A better question to ask might be: Given the variety of systems methodologies and uses of systems ideas and models in Part II, what if anything is left of "system", and its associated concepts, that might lead anyone to want to construct a transdiscipline around it? What core systems notions remain and are held in common by the different tendencies in systems thinking? These are difficult questions. Nevertheless, I will offer three possible answers.

First, all systems approaches are committed to holism – to looking at the world in terms of "wholes" that exhibit emergent properties, rather than believing in a reductionist fashion that learning should proceed by breaking wholes down into their fundamental elements. The strength of this commitment varies from seeing holism as a replacement for reductionism to regarding it as simply complementary. And the meaning attached varies from a call (in functionalist approaches) to take into account and model all relevant aspects of the whole system to the injunction, in Ulrich's (1983) "critical systems heuristics", to reflect continually on the inevitable lack of comprehensiveness in our systems designs. Holism is, however, a distinctive feature of systems thinking and systems thinkers' advocacy of holism in their approaches provides a useful antidote to the prevailing emphasis upon reductionism in many disciplines.

Second, it might be argued along with Rescher (1979) that human beings inevitably organize their knowledge in "cognitive systems." These cognitive systems are structured frameworks linking various elements of our knowledge into cohesive wholes. They express certain intellectual norms – simplicity, regularity, uniformity, comprehensiveness, unity, harmony, economy – that people have found useful in thinking about and acting in the world. Rescher wants to argue that cognitive systems lie at the very heart of the scientific method itself, with a hypothesis becoming a scientific law not because of repeated observation and experiment but only when it can be integrated into a systematic body of scientific knowledge, a cognitive system. From this it could follow that science is much closer to the systems enterprise than has so far been believed.

Rescher also suggests that the success of the systematizing endeavor that is science in predicting and controlling the real world must mean that the world itself is orderly. With the continuing development of cognitive systems we should, therefore, get a growing conformity between our systems-based theories and the real-world. It is not surprising to Rescher that this should be so because he believes that there are evolutionary pressures that tend to assure a correspondence between our cognitive systems and the world. We do not have to follow Rescher in these later, somewhat "hard" systems conclusions. It is enough that his work provides some justification for using the concept of a system as the fundamental element in ordering one's epistemological endeavors. That alone supplies another powerful rationale for taking a systems approach in methodology construction.

The final, and most developed argument in favor of systems approaches (as opposed to any other kind of approach) must, however, rest upon the diversity, range, effectiveness and efficiency of the approaches themselves in relation to real-world problem management. Sir Geoffrey Vickers (see Checkland and Holwell, 1998), sitting down in retirement to write about his 40 years experience in the world of affairs, found little that could help him make direct sense of it all in the social sciences. In systems thinking, however, he found much of immediate value and was able to develop his sophisticated theory of "appreciative systems" as a result. It seems that systems ideas and concepts have a resonance with real-world practice which is sadly lacking in much social theory. For this reason systems methodologies can assist in the task of translating social theory into a practical form and encapsulating its findings in well-worked-out approaches to intervention. The systems notion of "boundary" is one which can have enormous significance during an intervention; for example in considering what to include as relevant during an information systems project. Checkland (1981) incorporates this notion in his soft systems methodology, which can be seen as an exploration of the consequences of drawing systems boundaries in different places according to alternative world views. Thus the concept of boundary is put to powerful use in the service of the interpretive paradigm. Part II explores the variety and use of available systems approaches and should provide compelling evidence to the reader for the capability of systems thinking to help us engage, in a theoretically informed way, with real-world concerns.

Part III takes up some unresolved issues about how systems thinking can develop as a transdiscipline given the variety of apparently competing perspectives, methodologies and methods that exist under its banner. It advocates "critical systems thinking" as the way forward, details the development of this approach and presents the theoretical, methodological and practical arguments in its favor.

Critical systems thinking accepts that the orthodoxy within the systems approach, and in management science, has broken down. Indeed, it played a significant role in this by campaigning for an "emancipatory" systems methodology to set alongside the functionalist and interpretive variants. To that extent, it agrees with Dando and Bennett (1981) that a "Kuhnian" crisis has arisen in systems thinking and management science. There is open competition between advocates of alternative approaches. Extradisciplinary considerations (of career and politics) play a significant part in motivating participants in the debate and are likely to influence its outcome. Critical systems thinking, however, points to a way forward from this position. It argues that, instead of seeing a crisis, systems thinkers should welcome an opportunity. The development of different versions of the systems approach can be presented as part of a process in which the transdiscipline is maturing theoretically and, at the same time, giving practitioners the opportunity to work, with a good chance of success, in a wider range of problem situations.

Of course, to sustain this position an argument has to be advanced that there are benefits to be gained from employing the variety of systems perspectives, methodologies, methods and models in a "pluralist" fashion, and it has to be shown that this can be done coherently. This "pluralist" vision of the future of systems thinking is put forward on the basis of evidence from Parts I and II and defended against the alternatives of isolationism, imperialism and pragmatism. It is argued that pluralism fits hand in glove with critical systems thinking to provide a basis for systems as a transdiscipline. Thus systems thinking, which has seemingly split into opposing tendencies, can be reconstituted on the much firmer foundations (as compared to the positivism and functionalism of traditional systems thinking) provided by pluralism and critical systems thinking. Systems thinking, in this guise, can again occupy a role at the leading edge of the development of the management sciences and of the applied disciplines in general.

One chapter in Part III is devoted to the "Origins of Critical Systems Thinking." Another considers more recent developments and outlines "Contemporary Critical Systems Thinking and Practice." Total Systems Intervention and other "multi-methodology" approaches are reviewed and a new form of critical systems practice is outlined. These chapters involve themselves itself very much with the meta-methodological as well as the methodological level of analysis. A final chapter considers three applications, following the guidelines provided by the new form of critical systems practice. Thus, Part III rounds off the book by considering the future prospects both for the theoretical development of systems thinking and for the practical use of systems ideas. There is then a short conclusion to the whole volume.

2.9. CONCLUSION AND STRUCTURE OF THE ARGUMENT

Table 2.1. The structure of the argument

Introduction	
Part I: "Overviews", in which there are 4 chapters	Chapter 2, orientating the reader and setting out the structure of the argument
	Chapter 3, outlining some relevant social theory
	Chapter 4, tracing the development of systems ideas in the disciplines
	Chapter 5, providing an introduction to applied systems thinking
Part II: "Systems Approaches", in which there are 4 chapters outlining different kinds of systems approach.	Chapter 6, presenting the functionalist systems approach
	Chapter 7, presenting the interpretive systems approach
	Chapter 8, presenting the emancipatory systems approach
	Chapter 9, presenting the postmodern systems approach
Part III: "Critical Systems Thinking", in which there are 3 chapters on the critical systems approach to the future development of systems thinking	Chapter 10, devoted to the origins of critical systems thinking
	Chapter 11, reviewing contemporary critical systems thinking and practice
	Chapter 12, detailing 3 critical systems applications
Conclusion	

This chapter has orientated the reader and set out the structure of the argument. In the next chapter, I consider some social theory that is highly relevant for a proper understanding of the role and usefulness of systems approaches. Table 2.1 outlines, in summary form, the structure of the book.

3

RELEVANT SOCIAL THEORY

3.1. INTRODUCTION

A reasonable starting point for looking for information on the key types of social theory would seem to be popular textbooks on sociology. Here one might expect to find, set out clearly for students, the agreed and established wisdom of the discipline. A quick glance at Craib's (1992) *Modern Social Theory: From Parsons to Habermas*, and Haralambos and Holborn's (1995) *Sociology: Themes and Perspectives*, soon shatters the hope, however, that there is any such accepted wisdom.

Craib divides social theory into three paradigms. An "action paradigm" embraces theoretical positions such as structural functionalism, conflict theory, symbolic interactionism, phenomenological sociology, ethnomethodology and structuration theory, and theorists such as Parsons, Schutz and Giddens. A "structure paradigm" covers structuralism (including structuralist Marxism), post-structuralism and postmodernism. A "structure and action paradigm" is identified with critical theory and the work of the Frankfurt School and Habermas. Haralambos and Holborn start with "functionalism", "conflict perspectives" and "social action and interpretive perspectives" as their three theories of society but, in a more detailed review later in the book, add structuration theory ("uniting structural and social action approaches") and "postmodernism." Craib's privileging of the distinction between "action" and "structure" leads him to combine four of Haralambos and Holborn's five categories into one. Parsons is in the functionalist paradigm for Haralambos and Holborn, to be carefully distinguished from phenomenologists and ethnomethodologists. Craib is able to see similarities between these traditions of work. For Craib, Habermas can bridge the "gap" between action and structure; for Haralambos and Holborn it is Giddens. It would be possible to go on but what is clear is that the most appropriate way of classifying different social theories depends on the perspective and the purpose of the reviewer.

Our perspective needs to be guided by the purposes of those who want to use and improve systems approaches. We need to highlight those social theories which, either implicitly or explicitly, provide "frameworks of ideas" to which existing systems approaches are related. On this basis we can hope to operate the theory - practice link; learning more about the adequacy of particular social theories and improving systems approaches as a consequence. Because of the practical orientation of systems thinking we must also be sure that the distinctions we draw point to significant differences between social theories when applied in practice in the world. Not all the fine theoretical distinctions made by social scientists do make a difference, but some are of considerable importance and must be regarded as crucial for systems thinking. It is eminently reasonable, therefore, to build our account of social theory on the basis of those accounts which, to date, systems thinkers have actually found relevant. I will however, at the end of the chapter, draw these accounts together using a recent classification of social research approaches that is finding much favor among organization theorists. We can then rest happy that the use we make of social theory does reflect current debates in the social sciences as well as the purposes of systems thinkers.

3.2. SOCIOLOGICAL PARADIGMS

We begin with a basic categorization of sociological orientations, drawing upon Burrell and Morgan's (1979) well-known classification of sociological paradigms but introducing a corrective to allow proper consideration of "structuralism." Burrell and Morgan's framework was constituted in order to relate work in the field of organizational analysis to a wider sociological context, and its success in that enterprise offered sufficient encouragement to others, including systems thinkers, who wished to take up their suggestion and apply the framework in other disciplines. Checkland (1981) employed it to uncover and differentiate from "hard systems thinking" the view of social reality implied by his "soft systems methodology." It was used by Jackson (1982) to demonstrate how the social theory implicit in all versions of soft systems thinking affected the capacity of the approach to intervene in and change social reality. The framework retains great popularity in the systems community.

It is Burrell and Morgan's thesis that theories about the social world can be conceived of in terms of four key paradigms. They employ the word paradigm, a usage derived from Kuhn (1970), to refer to the tradition of research regarded as authoritative by a particular scientific community. It is the set of ideas, assumptions and beliefs that shape and guide their scientific activity. Burrell and Morgan's four paradigms are constructed around the different assumptions social scientists make about the nature of social science and about the nature of society.

Assumptions about the nature of social science can be seen as either objective or subjective in kind. If a theory is underpinned by objective assumptions, it will have certain distinguishing characteristics. Social reality will be perceived as having a hard, objective existence, external to the individual (i.e., the theory adheres to a "realist" ontology). The theory will seek to establish the existence of regularities and causal relationships in the social world ("positivist" epistemology). Human behavior will be seen as being determined by external circumstances ("determinist"). Scientific tests and quantitative analyses will be the preferred techniques for acquiring detailed knowledge ("nomothetic" methodology).

If a theory is underpinned by subjective assumptions about the nature of social science, it will have quite other distinguishing characteristics. Social reality will be perceived as having a more subjective existence as the product of individual and/or shared consciousness ("nominalist" ontology). The theory will seek knowledge by attempting to understand the point of view of the people involved in creating social reality ("anti-positivist" epistemology). Human beings will be seen to possess free will ("voluntarism"). Getting as close as possible to the subject under investigation will be the preferred method of acquiring detailed knowledge ("ideographic" methodology). This distinction between objective and subjective assumptions about the nature of social science makes up the first dimension of Burrell and Morgan's framework.

Assumptions about the nature of society can be seen as emphasizing either regulation or radical change. The "sociology of regulation" concerns itself with understanding the status quo. Society is seen as being basically consensual, and the mechanisms by which social order is maintained are studied. The "sociology of radical change" concerns itself with finding explanations for radical change in social systems. Society is seen as being driven by contradictions and by structural conflict. Some groups in society benefit at the expense of others; any cohesion that exists is achieved by the domination of some groups over others. The sociology of radical change looks beyond the status quo. The distinction between these two sociologies makes up the second dimension of Burrell and Morgan's grid.

If we now combine the objective-subjective and regulation-radical change dimensions, we can produce a matrix defining the four key sociological paradigms. The four paradigms are labeled functionalist, interpretive, radical structuralist and radical humanist, as indicated in Figure 3.1. These paradigms, according to Burrell and Morgan, are founded upon mutually exclusive views of the social world. Each stands in its own right and generates its own distinctive analyses of social life.

Systems approaches are not social theories of the kind found inhabiting Burrell and Morgan's paradigms. They rarely provide explicit accounts of what the "real-world" is like, but concentrate instead on methodologies, methods and models systems thinkers can use when they seek to intervene in that world. Nevertheless, the designers of systems approaches will have either consciously or unconsciously incorporated assumptions about the nature of systems thinking (or social science) and the nature of social systems (or society). The Burrell and Morgan grid enables us to relate systems approaches to different sociological paradigms and to learn much about what they take for granted about social science and society in the "frameworks of ideas" they employ. This is the source of its popularity among systems thinkers and we shall ourselves use it for that purpose. For the moment I shall briefly explore the ways in which adopting the perspective of each paradigm affects the way we perceive systems and problem situations.

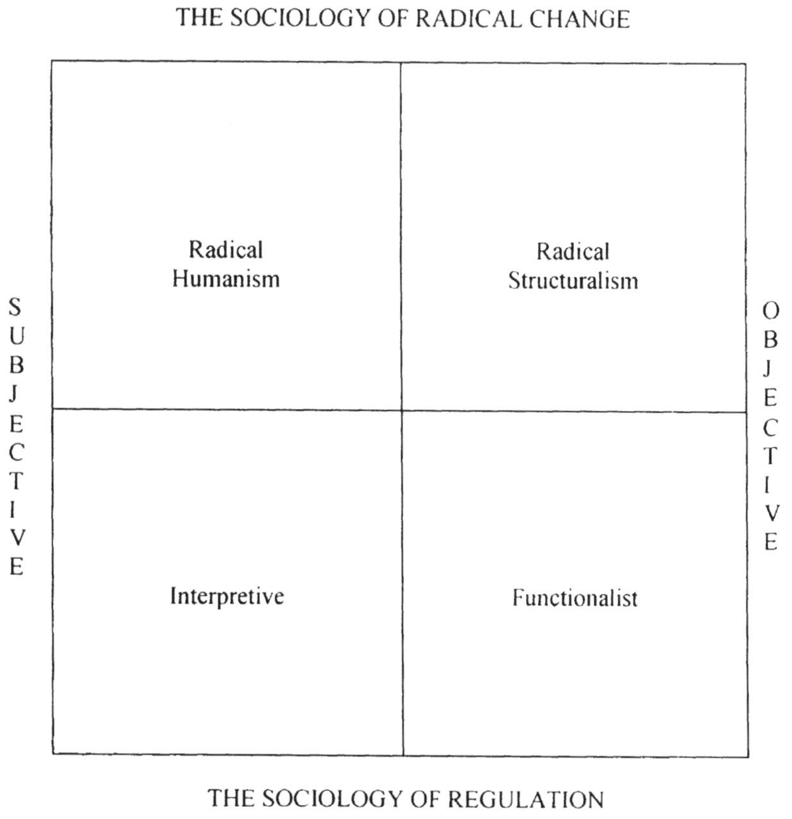

THE SOCIOLOGY OF RADICAL CHANGE

THE SOCIOLOGY OF REGULATION

Figure 3.1. Burrell and Morgan's four paradigms for the analysis of social theory

If we view systems from within the functionalist paradigm (objective, sociology of regulation), they seem to have a hard, easily identifiable existence independent of us as observers. We understand the workings of such systems if we can find regularities in the relationships between sub-systems and the whole. The human beings in the system present no more problems than do the other component parts. It is possible to construct a model of the system. The purpose of studying such systems is to understand the status quo better; this facilitates the prediction and control of the system.

If we view systems from within the interpretive paradigm (subjective, sociology of regulation) they seem to be much "softer", to elude easy identification and to possess a precarious existence only as the creative constructions of human beings. We can understand such systems by trying to understand subjectively the points of view and the intentions of the human beings who construct them. The presence in the system of human beings possessing free will makes a profound difference to the kind of analysis undertaken. It will not normally be possible to construct a model of such a system. We must acquire detailed information about it by getting involved in its activities; by "getting inside" it. The purpose of studying such systems is still to understand the status quo better so that prediction and control are facilitated.

If we view systems from within the radical structuralist paradigm (objective, sociology of radical change), they seem to have a hard existence external to us. We can discover causal regularities governing their behavior. We do not have to pay much attention, we believe, to human intentions. It is possible to develop models. However, the purpose of such study is to understand radical change. Emphasis is placed upon contradictions in the system and on conflict between different groups in the system. This facilitates the emancipation of people from presently existing social structures.

If we view systems from within the radical humanist paradigm (subjective, sociology of radical change), they seem to be the creative constructions of human beings. In order to analyze such systems, we have to understand the intentions of the human beings which construct them. The ability of people to transform the system they have created will be apparent. The way to learn about these systems is to involve ourselves in their activities. Emphasis is placed upon gaining understanding of the current social arrangements that are seen as constraining human development. This facilitates the emancipation of people from presently existing social structures.

The value of the Burrell and Morgan framework will now be clear in terms of the overall intention of this volume. There is one problem with it, however, which we must deal with here if we are to maximize the usefulness of social theory in helping us to understand the "functionalist" systems approach in Chapter 6 of the book. The trouble is that Burrell and Morgan's grid prevents us from identifying the nature, and appreciating the significance, of a distinct "structuralist" orientation in social theory (only "radical structuralism" is dealt with). This has important consequences for any analysis of systems thinking because it can be argued that cybernetics, for example, differs from hard systems thinking precisely in that it possesses structuralist (rather than positivist) underpinnings. We need to pursue this matter briefly in order to get clear the main characteristics of structuralism.

According to Burrell and Morgan, as we have seen, any objectivist approach to social science is defined as positivist in its epistemology, seeking to discover patterns and regularities in the social world. Keat and Urry (1975), however, argue that not all objectivists need to be positivists and that there are in fact very significant differences among objectivists based on the epistemologies they employ. In particular it is important to distinguish positivist and structuralist epistemologies. The following quotation highlights the differences:

> For the [structuralist], unlike the positivist, there is an important difference between explanation and prediction. And it is explanation which must be pursued as the primary objective of science. To explain phenomena is not merely to show that they are instances of well-established regularities. Instead, we must discover the necessary connections between phenomena, by acquiring knowledge of the underlying structures and mechanisms at work. Often, this will mean postulating the existence of types of unobservable entities and processes that are unfamiliar to us: but it is only by doing this that we get beyond the 'mere appearance' of things, to their natures and essences. Thus, for the [structuralist] a scientific theory is a description of structures and mechanisms which causally generate the observable phenomena, a description which enables us to explain them (p. 5).

Burrell and Morgan hide these differences by the vague way they use the phrase "positivist epistemology." For example, it is difficult to tell whether the patterns and regularities they discuss are at the surface of the social world (at the level of social facts) or whether we have to dig beneath the surface to discover "structures" (the patterns and regularities) that determine the arrangement of the social facts. Because they play down the difference between positivist and structuralist epistemologies, Burrell and Morgan give little attention to structuralism as a unified approach in the social sciences. Some theorists close to structuralism – such as the mature Marx and Althusser – receive attention because they are deemed to be "radical." Others not highlighted by the radical change dimension, however, such as Chomsky, Levi-Strauss and Piaget, get hardly a mention.

Structuralism originated with Saussure's linguistics but soon influenced a range of disciplines. Saussure insisted that the meaning of a linguistic sign was determined by its relationship to other signs. It is this emphasis on relationships, rather than on the nature of the elements themselves, which forges the link with some variants of the systems approach. The convergence between structuralism and, for example, cybernetics has long been apparent to structuralist writers. Levi-Strauss (1968) regards Wiener as having made an outstanding contribution to structural studies. Piaget (1973) is very complimentary about the achievement of cybernetics in synthesizing information and communication theories with guiding and regulatory theories.

Reviewing structuralism as a methodology, Craib (1992) recognizes a number of advantages. As well as emphasizing relationships between basic elements, it points us to the need to study structures, below the surface level, which are less observable but may have more explanatory power than those at the surface. The discovery of underlying relationships of this kind enables us to cut through the surface flux and to get at the core of what we should be studying. A major drawback, for Craib, is that structuralism can, in one sense, be seen as reductionist:

> The ability to distinguish an underlying structure or logic which has an explanatory importance can tempt the theorist to reduce the world to this level, and so to lose dimensions of meaning that exist at the surface level (p. 145).

Structuralism is infamous, for example, for promoting the "death of the subject." People are not the originators of their own thoughts and actions. Instead these are seen as resulting from the logic of underlying patterns of relationships.

We shall return to the distinction between structuralism and positivism in Chapter 6, when we are relating systems approaches to functionalist social theory.

3.3. METAPHORS OF ORGANIZATION

Burrell and Morgan regard the competing theories developed from within different paradigms as incommensurable. Scientists working in one paradigm are not understood by scientists committed to another. Moreover, there can be no measure, outside of the paradigms, which can be used as a basis for comparing and adjudicating between the claims to knowledge of theories produced from within different paradigms. There are, however, other vehicles for theory construction which have less severe consequences from the point of view of permitting debate between adherents of different positions and resolving disputes between them.

Pepper (1942), in a much neglected contribution to systems thinking, describes how a "root metaphor method" has, through "the traditional analogical method of generating world theories", led to a number of "world hypotheses" constituting the "principal metaphysical systems" which attempt to make sense of and explain the "world experience." This method is defined by Pepper in the following terms:

> A man desiring to understand the world looks about for a clue to its comprehension. He pitches upon some area of common-sense fact and tries to see if he cannot understand other areas in terms of this one. This original area becomes then his basic analogy or root metaphor. He describes as best he can the characteristics of this area, or, if you will, discriminates its structure. A list of its structural characteristics becomes his basic concepts of explanation and description. We call them a set of categories. In terms of these categories he proceeds to study all other areas as fact ... He undertakes to interpret all facts in terms of these categories (p. 91-92).

Pepper identifies six world hypotheses: "mysticism", "dogmatism", "formism", "mechanism", "contextualism", and "organicism"; although only the final four have proved capable of generating adequate world theories. Formism (or "realism" or "Platonic idealism") has "similarity" as its root metaphor. All specific objects of experience are seen as copies of ideal forms. Mechanism (or "naturalism" or "materialism") has "the machine" as its root metaphor. This world hypothesis sees the world as totally mechanistic, as operating under physical laws and thus being completely determined. Contextualism (or "pragmatism") presents the world as a complex characterized by change and novelty, order and disorder. The contextualist is concerned with "an act in its context." Acts are

> composed of interconnected activities with continuously changing patterns ... They are literally the incidents of life. The contextualist finds that everything in the world consists of such incidents (p. 233).

Within such a complex state of flux it is difficult to attain meaning and we have, therefore, to select "contexts" that organize and attribute meaning to the world. Successful contexts have "quality" and "texture." Organicism (or "absolute or objective idealism") has "organism" and "integration" as its root metaphors. The method of organicism can be summarized as

> noting the steps involved in the organic process, and ... noting these principal features in the organic structure ultimately achieved or realized (p. 281).

Less demanding than analogy, in terms of the requirement for developing and refining categories, is the use of metaphor in theory building. Metaphor is employed whenever we try to understand something in terms of a name or description which is not literally applicable to it. Football fans often liken a player from the opposing team who they regard as slow or clumsy to a "donkey." This will highlight for some spectators certain characteristics of this person when he is on the football field. It may not be difficult, however, to understand the point of view of the same player's girlfriend who refers to him as a "tasty dish." Far from being mutually exclusive, these different "readings" can provide us with insight into the ambiguity and complexity of life. Effective managers and professionals, according to Morgan (1986), can use metaphors to

> develop the knack of reading situations with various scenarios in mind, and of forging actions that seem appropriate to the readings thus obtained (p. 11).

Metaphors are not, therefore, incommensurable but can be used by a skilled manager, alone or with others, to enhance creative insight and develop critical thinking:

> Metaphor encourages us to think and act in new ways. It extends horizons of insight and creates new possibilities. As we gain comfort in using the implications of different metaphors in this way, we quickly learn that the insights of one metaphor can often help us overcome the limitations of another ... Metaphors lead to new metaphors, creating a mosaic of competing and complementary insights. This is one of the most powerful qualities of the approach (Morgan, 1997, p. 351-352).

The organization theory literature constantly reminds us that there are many different metaphors that can be used to look at organizations, each of which yields an alternative understanding of their character and functioning. Morgan (1986, 1997), in a text that has proved popular among systems thinkers, reviews the literature describing organizations as "machines", "organisms", "brains", "cultures", "political systems", "psychic prisons", "flux and transformation", and "instruments of domination", while making the point that these eight "images of organization" are only a selection of those possible. Choosing to look at an organization using any of these metaphors will obviously affect what we see as important and how we seek to change it.

Systems approaches, too, rest upon metaphorical understandings of the nature of systems, the most common being the organismic, "adaptive whole system" metaphor (Atkinson, 1984). And, because systems approaches are often used in the organizational context, it will obviously provide further insight into their nature, and how they might be improved, if we can uncover the image or images of organization embedded in each. To facilitate this process I shall review Morgan's eight metaphors here, paying particular attention to those aspects which are of significance for systems thinking.

Various strands of organization theory unite in treating organizations as if they were *machines*. The three most influential are administrative management theory, scientific management and a reading of Weber's bureaucracy theory. Henri Fayol (1949) can be credited with the creation of administrative management theory. In his book, first published in French in 1916, he advises managers to forecast and plan, to organize, to command, to coordinate and to control, and sets out 14 principles designed to guide managerial action; the most important of these being division of work, authority, scalar chain and unity of command. Frederick Taylor, the founder of scientific management, believed that the best way of doing each task in an organization could be established and that, on this basis, a fair day's pay for a fair day's work could be calculated (Taylor, 1947). Taylor's ideas, where adopted, tend to lead to an extreme division of labor and the shifting of control away from the point at which the task is carried out. Max Weber (Gerth and Mills, 1970) argued that bureaucracy is the most technically advanced organizational form because it is based upon an advanced division of labor, a strict hierarchy, government by rules and staffing by trained officials.

By putting together these three strands, it is possible to give a general account of the machine model. The organization is viewed as an instrument designed to achieve the purposes of the people who set it up or who now control it. It is constructed of parts combined according to management principles in a way that should enable maximum efficiency to be achieved. Decision making is assumed to be rational. Control is exercised through rules and a strict hierarchy of authority. Information is processed according to the arrangement of tasks and by exception reporting up the hierarchy.

The tendency to treat organizations as if they were *organisms* has been especially pronounced among advocates of the systems perspective in organization theory. This view portrays organizations as complex systems made up of parts existing in close interrelationship. Because they are like this, organizations can only be studied as wholes. The primary aim of organizations as systems is to ensure their own survival. Selznick (1948), Parsons (1956, 1957) and Katz and Kahn (1966) provide lists of needs that must be met by subsystems if organizations are to survive and be effective. Both formal and informal aspects of organizations are granted attention in the organismic model. Moreover, organizations are seen as open systems, having to take action in response to environmental changes if they want to maintain a steady state. If organizations are like organisms, it is clear what must be done to correct any malfunctions. The subsystems must be examined to ensure that they are meeting the needs of the organization, and the organization examined to see that it is well adjusted to its environment. A managerial subsystem is charged with this task.

Another strand of organization theory takes a neurocybernetic perspective and pictures organizations as being like *brains*. This metaphor emphasizes active learning rather than the somewhat passive adaptability that characterizes the organismic view. It has led to attention being focused on decision making and on information processing. The forerunner of the brain model was Herbert Simon (1947), who argued that individuals in organizations inevitably acted according to "bounded rationality", but that this could be compensated for by paying proper attention to organizational design and decision support. Later, J.R. Galbraith (1977) developed his view of organizations as information-processing systems. The best design of an organization was seen as contingent upon the uncertainty and diversity surrounding the basic task undertaken by that organization - since this determined the amount of information that would have to be processed. If task uncertainty was low, bureaucratic structures with their low information-processing capacities were adequate. But if task uncertainty was high, alternative structures would be required, based on strategies either to reduce the need for information processing or to increase the capacity for it.

In the new edition of *Images of Organization* (1997), Morgan expands his treatment of organizations as brains, giving much more attention to the idea of "learning organizations" and how they can be created. He is convinced that the brain metaphor raises many important possibilities if we can understand how to design complex systems that are capable of learning in a brain-like way. In considering the nature of learning organizations, Morgan draws upon cybernetics and upon the work of Senge (1990) - a case of systems thinking feeding into organization theory to provide greater conceptual clarity and practical usefulness. Organizations, if they are to learn, must scan their environments, relate relevant information to their operating norms, detect deviations from goals and objectives, and take corrective action if necessary. They must also possess the capacity for "double loop" as well as "single loop" learning. Single-loop learning allows the correction of deviations from goals and objectives established on the basis of existing norms. In double-loop learning there is questioning of the norms themselves. Organizations then become capable of "learning to learn", questioning the actual appropriateness of what they are doing.

To those who see organizations as *cultures*, managers who seek to promote the efficiency and effectiveness of their enterprises by concentrating their efforts on the logical design of appropriate structures (as recommended by proponents of the machine, organism and brain metaphors) are misplacing their energies. Social organizations can exist with and perform well while employing a host of apparently illogical structures. A far more important role for managers to play is as "engineers" of their organizations' corporate cultures. According to this cultural perspective, the essential character of organizations is conditioned by the fact that their component parts are human beings, who can attribute meaning to their situation and can therefore see in organizations whatever purposes they wish and make of them whatever they will. Organizations are processes in which different perceptions of reality are continuously negotiated and renegotiated. Their long-term survival depends therefore upon the achievement of shared values and beliefs.

This cultural view is a relatively modern approach spurred on by the popularizing efforts of authors such as Peters and Waterman (1982). The gist of the perspective is well captured by Thomas Watson, Jr., writing about his experiences with IBM:

> Consider any great organization, one that has lasted over the years - I think you will find that it owes its resiliency not to its form of organization or administrative skills, but to the power of what we call beliefs and the appeal these beliefs have for its people. In other words, the basic philosophy, spirit, and drive of an organization have far more to do with its relative achievements than do technological or economic resources, organizational structure, innovation and timing. All these things weigh heavily in success. But they are, I think, transcended by how strongly the people in the organization believe in its basic precepts and how faithfully they carry them out (quoted in Peters and Waterman, 1982, p. 280).

Looking at organizations through the *political* metaphor allows us to focus on how organizations are governed, on how different interests are reconciled, on the everyday politics of organizational life and on how power is obtained and used in organizations. To those whose working lives are blighted by petty bickerings, by squabbles between departments and other organizational sub-groupings, and by power struggles among senior managers, this can seem a refreshing and realistic perspective. In considering organizations as political systems, it is usual to draw attention to three frames of reference for describing the relationship between individuals and organizations - unitary, pluralist and radical. The unitary view represents the organization as a well integrated team pursuing common goals and objectives. The pluralist perspective emphasizes diversity of individual and group interests and sees the organization as a loose coalition. The radical view pictures organizations as "instruments of domination" used by some groups to benefit themselves at the expense of others. This view is considered separately below.

The idea that organizations are *psychic prisons* has been, perhaps, underused by systems thinkers. Morgan's account of the metaphor derives significantly from the work of Freud and other psychoanalysts. It concentrates on how our organizations might be reflections of the unconscious mind, of repressed sexuality, of a desire to protect ourselves from anxiety or fear of death. Another side of the metaphor looks at organizations as manifestations of ideologies which we consciously or unconsciously embrace and which trap us in alienating forms of life.

The *flux and transformation* metaphor is in such large part borrowed from systems thinking that we shall treat it in detail in the next chapter rather than in this. In the 1986 edition of his book, Morgan investigated the "logics of change shaping social life", the focus of this perspective, in terms of the theory of autopoiesis developed by Maturana and Varela, and the work of Maruyana on how interacting positive and negative feedback loops define system dynamics. The later edition updates the flux and transformation metaphor by concentrating much more on the "logic of chaos and complexity", a subject that has received considerable attention in many disciplines since the publication of the first edition. According to Morgan (1997):

> Using physical experiments and computer simulations as metaphors for understanding what happens in nature, [chaos and complexity theory] contribute important elements to a holistic theory of change (p. 261).

The view of organizations as *instruments of domination* is based upon Marx's (see 1961) account of the capitalist labor process, as brought up to date by Braverman (1974) and others. According to this frame of reference, organizations are hierarchical systems made up of different class and status groups whose interests are unbridgeable given the present structure of organizations and society. Organizations only hold together at all because of the power of some group(s) to control the activities of others. Relationships between the different classes are essentially exploitative. For example, in capitalist enterprises, workers receive wages, but the amount they receive does not represent an equivalent exchange for the labor power they expend. There is always some surplus value creamed off by the capitalist. Of course, it is always likely that conflict will break out, given that the only consensus that exists is an enforced consensus. It is the job of managers to keep such conflict in check and to control the labor process so that the powerful group(s) maximize their benefits. Using some ideas of Burrell and Morgan (1979), considered earlier, one can say that those who see organizations as instruments of domination concern themselves with issues of structural conflict, modes of domination, contradiction, and emancipation (radical change). This contrasts with those of a machine, organism, brain or cultural bent, all of whom emphasize the status quo, social order, consensus, social integration and cohesion (regulation).

In this section we have reviewed some of the key metaphors that researchers have employed, especially when they have been studying organizations. As we shall see in Part II of the book, systems approaches are heavily influenced by metaphors of organization. We can use our analysis to consider how metaphor, as part of the "framework of ideas" employed by each approach (implicitly or otherwise), affects the recommendations made about the best way to intervene in organizations to change them. Just as there exists knowledge on the strengths and limitations of different images of organization (Morgan, 1986, 1997), so shall we be able to start to build knowledge about the relative capabilities of different systems approaches, including the frameworks of ideas they employ. Pointing to finer distinctions than do the sociological paradigms, metaphors are particularly useful for distinguishing varieties of the functionalist systems approach. In Part III of the book, on critical systems thinking, metaphors will reappear as a device for encouraging creativity; in a process which Morgan (1993) calls "imaginization." We also have to revisit the paradigm incommensurability debate. Systems approaches can be related both to sociological paradigms and to metaphors. Are they incommensurable like the paradigms or can they be used together to probe ambiguity and complexity like metaphors?

3.4. CRITICAL THEORY AND HABERMAS

Those who view the social world through the radical paradigms, or perceive organizations as "psychic prisons" or "instruments of domination", are usually critical of what they see on the basis of some vision of how society might be much better. Marx, for example, criticized the alienating nature of labor in capitalist society by contrasting it with what free labor would be like in a classless, communist society. Marx's highly political exemplar of critical theory was taken up and reformulated into a research program at the Frankfurt Institute for Social Research which began its work in the 1920s. The three main contributors to the early work of the "Frankfurt School" were Horkheimer, Adorno and Marcuse. Craib (1992) summarizes their orientation as follows:

> the Frankfurt theorists are concerned with the way the system dominates : with the ways in which it forces, manipulates, blinds or fools people into ensuring its reproduction and continuation (pp. 210-211).

The most influential modern thinker of the critical theory persuasion, and owing a particular debt to the Frankfurt School, is the German political philosopher Jürgen Habermas. Habermas is a prolific and wide-ranging writer and, being very open to comment and criticism, is constantly adjusting and refining his arguments. It goes without saying that I cannot do justice to the complexity and sophistication of his thought in this brief exposition. What I need to do is concentrate on those aspects that have had the most impact on the development of systems methodology. I shall sometimes mix earlier with later formulations of ideas if it helps towards this purpose.

A number of important themes emerged in Habermas's inaugural lecture at the University of Frankfurt in 1965 (Habermas, 1970) and continued to be developed later (Habermas, 1974). According to Habermas, human beings possess two fundamental cognitive interests that direct their attempts to acquire knowledge: a *technical* interest and a *practical* interest. The two interests are "quasi-transcendental" because they necessarily derive from the sociocultural form of life of the human species, which is dependent on "work" and "interaction." Work enables human beings to achieve goals and to bring about material well-being. Its success depends upon achieving technical mastery over the environment of action. The importance of work for the human species directs knowledge towards a technical interest in the prediction and control of natural and social systems. Interaction requires human beings to secure and expand the possibilities for intersubjective understanding among those involved in social systems. Disagreement between different individuals and groups can be just as much a threat to the reproduction of the sociocultural form of life as a failure to predict and control natural and social processes. The importance of interaction leads the human species to have a practical interest in the progress of mutual understanding.

While work and interaction have, for Habermas, pre-eminent anthropological status, the analysis of power and the way it is exercised are equally important, he argues, if we are to understand past and present social arrangements. The exercise of power in the social process can prevent the open and free discussion necessary for the success of work and interaction. Human beings have, therefore, a third cognitive interest: an *emancipatory* interest in freeing themselves from constraints imposed by power relations and in learning, through a process of genuine participatory democracy, to control their own destinies. This interest is subordinate to the other two because it stems from derivative types of action, exploitation and systematically distorted communication. It aims at liberating people from these historically contingent constraints.

Corresponding to the three cognitive interests are three types of knowledge. First are the "empirical analytic" sciences linked to the cognitive interest concerned with the technical control of objectified processes. They aim to produce theoretical statements about the covariance of observable events from which law-like hypotheses can be derived. These sciences enable us, given initial conditions, to make predictions about future events. Second are the "historical hermeneutic" sciences that correspond to the practical interest. These sciences seek to access meaning and to gain an understanding of the creation of the intersubjective life world. They aim at maintaining and improving mutual understanding among human beings. Tied to the emancipatory interest are the "critical" sciences. These recognize the limitations of the other two types of knowledge (and the dangers when they are inappropriately applied) and attempt to synthesize and go beyond them in order to provide knowledge that will enable people to reflect on their situation and liberate themselves from domination by forces that they are involved in creating but that they cannot understand or control.

If we move now to Habermas's (1975) social theory, we find him arguing that, in advanced capitalist societies, the technical interest has come to dominate at the expense of the practical interest. The knowledge produced by the empirical analytic sciences (instrumental reason) has come to be regarded as the prototype of all knowledge, and the subsystems of society concerned with the development of the forces of production and oriented to the development of the "steering" capacities of society - the subsystems served by instrumental reason - have gained primary significance. The state apparatus in particular has increased its powers and sees its function as that of steering society and overcoming the periodic crises to which all capitalist systems are prone. The result is that practical problems about what ought to be done are defined as administrative problems, beyond the realm of public discussion, and tackled by experts from the scientific subsystem. Politics is defined as the task of ensuring that the social system runs smoothly. Luhmann's systems theory (to be discussed in the next chapter) is taken by Habermas (1976) as the prime ideological reflection of the predominance of instrumental reason:

> This theory represents the advanced form of technocratic consciousness, which today permits practical questions to be defined from the outset as technical ones, and thereby withholds them from public and unconstrained discussion (p. xxxii).

To Habermas, this dominance of the technical interest is anathema. The knowledge produced by the empirical analytic sciences is very necessary to the development of modern societies. It can guide "instrumental action" oriented to the development of the forces of production and "strategic action" oriented to the development of steering capacities. But social evolution depends as well upon "communicative action" (Habermas, 1984) related to the practical and emancipatory interests in the creation of mutual understanding free from domination and supported by the historical hermeneutic and critical sciences. The institutional framework of society has its own logic of "rationalization" different from that governing the subsystems of instrumental action (the economy, the state apparatus) that are embedded in the institutional framework. Rationalization in the domain of instrumental action concerns control over the forces of production and over the organizational forms that promote the steering capacity of society. Rationalization in the domain of social interaction, in the institutional realm of society, requires the development of communication free from domination. Questions of what norms should govern interaction (of what we should do, or might do) are logically independent of questions about the development of productive forces or about system integration and cannot be reduced to them.

Habermas, therefore, wants to set proper limits to the sphere of applicability of the knowledge produced by the empirical analytic sciences. At the same time, he is also careful to reject the claim of the historical hermeneutic sciences to be the sole method appropriate to studying human and social phenomena. Hermeneutics can only be universal if people make their history as knowing subjects free from the play of unconscious forces, and if actions have only intended consequences. However, because of the existence of power relationships that make mutual understanding based on genuine consensus difficult to achieve, and because of the complexity of modern societal arrangements, the results of human actions will often be different from what was intended by human actors. So they cannot be grasped, in the manner of hermeneutics, solely in terms of subjective intentions.

Both the empirical analytic and historical hermeneutic approaches must be complemented by a third type of inquiry, critical theory. To explain the relationship among the three kinds of knowledge, Habermas (1974) turns to the psychoanalytic encounter. Psychoanalysis is primarily hermeneutic. It attempts to understand what subjects say and to explicate the hidden meaning of what is said. But to achieve this the analyst cannot remain at the hermeneutic level. The analyst must get below the explanations offered by the subjects, to explain causally why they are distorted and conceal matters the subjects cannot bring to consciousness. This requires an empirical and analytic study of the systematic process through which patients deceive themselves about their conditions. The hermeneutic and empirical analytic elements of the psychoanalytic method are mediated by critical theory, for the whole stimulus behind the psychoanalytic encounter should be emancipatory. If successful, the analyst liberates subjects from unconscious forces that they could not control and increases the area over which they have rational mastery. Success is measured by the extent to which the patients recognize themselves in the explanations offered and become equal partners in the dialogue with the analyst.

This psychoanalytic model can, with care, be seen as relevant to society as a whole. Where possible, Habermas wants to reduce the area of social life where people act as things (and are therefore subject to instrumental reason) and to increase the realm of the hermeneutic (where rational intentions are realized in history). To this end, he needs to develop a theory that can ground the process of critique at the societal level. Here Habermas is at his most original. His elaborate theory of social evolution, forged in debate with Luhmann and linking the development of the forces of production, the organizational forms necessary to enhance the steering capacity of societies, and the institutional sector of society (the arena of politics and ethics), is one manifestation of this. Such a theory enables Habermas to argue for restricting instrumental reason to appropriate subsystems of society and for the need to pay separate attention to the creation of mutual understanding in the institutional sphere. His most famous contribution, however, is his attempt to provide a rational basis for a critique of the state of development of the institutional realm itself, through his theory of "communicative competence." This is the last part of Habermas's work that we need to consider.

Marx had concentrated on the economic base of society and on alienated labor. The theory of communicative competence reflects a recognition, in practical terms, of the growing importance of the institutional framework of society and the need, therefore, for a critique of a type of alienation that occurs in the socio-cultural life-world, what Habermas calls "distorted communication." It also represents what has been called a "communication - theoretic reformulation of critical theory" (Spaul, 1997). Communication now becomes the focus of attention as the means by which already socialized individuals can reach intersubjective agreement. Particular procedures and standards have to be established which, if properly employed in dialogue and debate, ensure that the outcome is rational. According to Habermas, appropriate procedures and standards can be built on a study of the normative assumptions entering into communication itself, since the commitment to mutual understanding through free and open debate seems to be prefigured in all speech and discourse:

> The idea of autonomy is given to us with the structure of language. With the very first sentence the intention of a common and uncompelled consensus is unequivocally stated (1970, p.50).

I will follow McCarthy (1973) in detailing the theory of communicative competence. In normal linguistic interaction, Habermas argues, participants naturally accept four different types of validity claim. These are that the utterance is intelligible; that its propositional content is true; that the speaker is justified, in terms of certain social norms, in saying what is said; and that he is sincere in uttering it. These last three claims relate to what Habermas refers to as the "three worlds" - objective, social and subjective. He argues that:

> By attending to the modes of language used, we can clarify what it means for a speaker, in performing one of the standard speech acts, to take up a pragmatic relation (1) to something in the objective world (as the totality of entities about which true statements are possible); or (2) to something in the social world (as the totality of legitimately regulated interpersonal relations); or (3) to something in the subjective world (as the totality of experiences to which a speaker has privileged access and which he can express before a public); such that what the speech act refers to appears to the speaker as something objective, normative, or subjective (1987, p.120).

If any of these claims is called into question it is necessary to enter into "discourse" to judge its truth, the correctness of the norm, or the sincerity of the statement. Habermas argues that it is a normal expectation in communicative interaction that participants are willing to enter into discourse to defend their positions, and that the outcome should reflect the better argument and not any constraints on discussion.

It is now necessary to describe the conditions for an "ideal speech situation" from which a true agreement can emerge. According to Habermas, the structure of communication is free from constraint when all participants have equal chances to select and perform speech acts, and there is an effective equality of chances for the assumption of dialogue roles. This general requirement is further specified into demands designed to ensure unlimited discussion and demands that insist that discussion is free from constraints of domination - whether their source is conscious strategic behavior by one or more of the parties or communication barriers secured through ideology or neurosis. So all participants must have the same chance to initiate and perpetuate discourse and to put forward, call into question, and give reasons for or against statements, explanations, interpretations, and justifications. And all participants must have the same chance to express their attitudes, feelings, and intentions, and to command and to oppose, to permit and to forbid, and so forth. Where these exacting conditions are met, an ideal speech situation pertains and any consensus emerging will be rationally motivated and genuine. Obviously such circumstances will be rare, but this does not detract from the usefulness of Habermas's conceptualization since it can equally be used to unmask "systematically distorted communication" in situations where unequal chances to participate in dialogue or an unequal distribution of power determine the nature of the false consensus reached. For Habermas, therefore, our progress towards a rational society is measured by the extent to which communicative competence is realized in society. This in turn depends on the establishment of certain social conditions relating to freedom and justice. Only then can the power for domination inherent in instrumental reason be made subject to full public control.

Although Habermas's social theory is at quite a high level of generality, we shall come to appreciate, as this book progresses, just how significant it has been for systems thinking. As well as helping to furnish critiques of functionalist and interpretive systems thinking, it was foremost in the development of both emancipatory and critical systems approaches.

3.5. MODERNISM VERSUS POSTMODERNISM

Almost all the theorists contributing to the sociological paradigms and metaphors of organization that we have reviewed, and to the development of critical theory, can be seen as working within the tradition of the Enlightenment. The Enlightenment, in general terms, was a European intellectual movement, with its origins in the eighteenth century, committed to reason and science as the means for building a better world and sweeping away the myths and prejudices that had bound previous generations. The philosopher *par excellence* of the Enlightenment was Kant who described it as the escape from self-imposed tutelage; the tutelage being the traditions which people had allowed to be inflicted upon themselves. According to Harvey (quoted in Haralambos and Holborn, 1995, p.908), the idea of the Enlightenment

> was to use the accumulation of knowledge generated by many individuals working freely and creatively for the pursuit of human emancipation and the enrichment of daily life. The scientific domination of nature promised freedom from scarcity, want, and the arbitrariness of natural calamity. The development of rational forms of social organization and rational modes of thought promised liberation from the irrationalities of myth, religion, superstition, release from the arbitrary use of power as well as from the dark side of our own human natures.

Habermas may have abandoned emancipation through the individual human subject for emancipation through communicative action, and has his concerns about how instrumental reason came to dominate the Enlightenment project, but he remains committed to the aims of the Enlightenment. Critical theorists want to see the full potentialities of the Enlightenment realized rather than abandoned. There is, however, another group of theorists whose work we must now consider, who regard the whole Enlightenment rationale as flawed and want to abandon the entire project. These theorists are often labeled "postmodernist" in contrast to the "modernists" who are in thrall to the ideals of the Enlightenment.

Postmodernism is frequently linked to supposed changes in culture and in society more generally, as well as to a new theoretical position. Thus postmodernist culture is variously associated with postindustrial society, consumer society, media society, knowledge- and information-based society, the dominance of multinational companies, a post-Fordist decentralization of enterprises, and a new stage in the development of late capitalism in which everything becomes a commodity. What is not in doubt is that postmodernism has had a significant effect on architecture, theater, literature and art, together with social theory. Obviously, I intend to concentrate here on the debate between modernists and postmodernists as it has affected social theory. To begin with, some of the main points of schism between modernists and postmodernists are outlined. A brief review of some of the contributions of postmodernist writers is then attempted, together with a summary of the main tenets of postmodernism. Finally, I seek to relate the discussion to systems approaches.

Modernism, as we remarked, seeks to consolidate and build upon the achievements of the Enlightenment. It upholds reason and believes that rationality is the most important vehicle for helping human beings perfect themselves and their societies. The world is seen as logical and orderly so that it can be probed by science to produce objective truth. Language is "transparent" so that it is capable of conveying truth and acting as a suitable means for arriving at consensus. History is seen as having a meaning based upon human purpose or, if not that, upon the rationalization of social systems. There is progress towards some unitary, predictable end state, which might be the emancipation of humanity or the perfect functioning of the system. Modernism essentially believes in the order of things and searches for unity, identity and consensus. It offers security through rational explanations of what is happening, centering on the human subject or the increasing complexity of society. Seriousness and depth are characteristics of modernism as it plans and charts the onward march of rationality and progress.

Postmodernism seeks to puncture the certainties of modernism, particularly the belief in rationality, truth and progress. It denies that science has access to objective truth, and rejects the notion of history as the progressive realization and emancipation of the human subject or as an increase in the complexity and steering capacity of societies. Language is not transparent, and it certainly does not offer the possibility of universal consensus. There are many different "language games", obeying different rules, in which speakers take part in order to defeat opponents or for the sheer pleasure of playing. We have, therefore, to be tolerant of differences and of multiple interpretations of the world, and we must learn to live with the incommensurable since there is no meta-theory that can reconcile or decide between different positions. Postmodernism offers little security. Rather, it thrives on instability, disruption, disorder, contingency, paradox, and indeterminacy. The image is more significant than "reality", and so postmodernism emphasizes superficiality and play instead of seriousness and depth.

Lyotard, in his book *The Postmodern Condition* (1984), recognizes two major manifestations of modernism in social theory. These can be labeled, following Cooper and Burrell (1988), "systemic modernism" and "critical modernism."

Systemic modernism, as its name suggests, is identified with the systems approach as a means of both understanding society and programming it for more effective performance. Parsons' work (considered in Chapter 4) represents an early, optimistic phase of systemic modernism, reflecting the managed resurgence of capitalist economies after World War II and their stabilization using, particularly, the mechanism of the modern welfare state. The latest phase is found in Luhmann's highly technocratic, all-embracing and despairing version of systems theory. In this, instrumental reason is completely triumphant as everything is subject to the rational requirements of the societal system. It is the system that is the vanguard of history and progress as it follows its own logic to increase "performativity" (in terms of input-output measures) and handle environmental uncertainty. Humanity is dragged in the wake of the system. Individual hopes and aspirations simply respond to the system's needs, and consensus is engineered to improve the system's functioning. Internal dissension, strikes and conflict represent the system readjusting to increase its viability and effectiveness.

Knowledge under systemic modernism, Lyotard argues, is completely subservient to system imperatives. First, science is privileged over the other less malleable forms of learning, and then science and technology are reduced solely to programming the system. Truth gives way to performativity. Only research relevant to the functioning of complex, large-scale systems is financed and only results that contribute to improving the input-output equation are recognized. The technocrats who subscribe to this knowledge have the power to implement the findings and so to verify their correctness. Thus a vicious circle is set up in which profit, power, and proof become indissolubly linked. Further, what is implemented also becomes associated with what is right and just. Power becomes the basis of legitimization. Questions about efficiency and salability replace those about truth or falsity and justice. Education, too, is turned to the same purpose.

The second form of modernism, critical modernism, is based upon Kant's program of enlightenment. It rests upon what Lyotard calls the power of "grand narratives" that seek to explain history in terms of progress. These grand narratives take two forms. First, there are philosophical "totalizations" that offer a unified view of all learning. Differences are overcome as previously irreconcilable sciences and knowledges are combined in one language game. A good example is Hegel's universal history of philosophy, celebrating the becoming of the "spirit." Second are those narratives that chart the emancipation of the human subject. History is seen as the progressive liberation of humanity from constraints so that it can assume mastery and take on responsibility for its own destiny. Marxism is, of course, the best example of this kind of grand narrative. The history of all societies can be explained as leading to a communist utopia in which all conflict and contradiction are overcome.

Not surprisingly, since his work combines elements of both types of grand narrative, Habermas is fingered by Lyotard as being the archetypal representative of critical modernism. Habermas proposes a unified theory of knowledge linked to different human interests, and aims his whole project at human emancipation directed by universal consensus arrived at in the "ideal speech situation", with participants presumably sticking to one language game. More surprising to the reader, perhaps, will be the idea that Luhmann and Habermas can be classified together as modernists - even if they are modernists of different varieties. For, as discussed previously, Habermas regards himself as an implacable opponent of Luhmann's systems theory and as setting out the grounds on which the imperialism of instrumental reason can be resisted. Lyotard, however, sees more similarities between their two positions than differences. Both Habermas and Luhmann believe that the world is logical and meaningful; that history has a subject - whether this is humanity or the system; that discourse can capture the order that exists "out there" in reality; and that human beings can understand and change, or at least influence, what happens in society.

Looking at the two kinds of modernism, Lyotard is convinced that systemic modernism is the most powerful. The grand narratives are no longer credible, as more "realistic" views of science and knowledge have prevailed. It is obvious, to Lyotard, that the language games people play are too numerous and complicated to be subsumed under any totalizing endeavor. Moreover, despite the commitment of critical theories to oppose the status quo, these theories are in fact easily incorporated into it. Indeed, the minor resistances they provoke actually provide a fertile source of renewal for the system.

While recognizing systemic modernism as the strongest adversary, Lyotard is firm in his opposition to all forms of modernism, whether emphasizing the functionality of the system or human emancipation. He wants to construct a postmodern alternative. The certainties encouraged by modernism, the metadiscourses pretending to provide objective understanding of the whole, can exact a high price in terms of a terrorism either of the systems or of the philosophical and political kind. For this reason it is necessary to "wage war" on totalizations, to emphasize dissension, instability, and unpredictability, and to activate "difference." The blind spot of modernism, those things rendered unpresentable and unspeakable in its narratives, must be brought to the fore.

This task is made easier because, although modernism is powerful, it is becoming clear that it is built upon fragile foundations. Science is seen to be only one kind of language game, with limited relevance to social affairs. Even within its sphere of relevance, the modernist account of science is prone to attack. The new physics, as in quantum theory, concerns itself with instabilities and with uncertainty and the undecidable. Put simply, science does not function as modernism would have it. Postmodern science, therefore, rejects performativity and asks questions about purposes. It sees systems not as stable but as subject to discontinuity and catastrophe. They are temporary islands of determinism within a sea of indeterminacy. The quest for precise knowledge about systems is misguided; more precision only reveals greater uncertainty. The attempt to limit individual initiative, according to systemic requirements, destroys exactly the novelty the system needs to adjust to its environment. Our new understanding of science provides no support, therefore, for modernism.

The possibility of developing a metalanguage that modernism could employ to legitimate its grand narratives is also open to attack. There is no one social subject that can be addressed using a universal meta-language and there are many language games, of which each of us knows only a few. Nor is it easy to sustain the modernist notion that language is oriented to achieving consensus. Language games are characterized by struggle and dissension, and this seems highly necessary in order to promote innovation and to energize and motivate human action and behavior. Communication should, therefore, be imbued with the capacity for innovation, change, and renewal, and refusal of conformity should be encouraged. Consensus can only be possible in localized circumstances and is only desirable if subject to rapid cancellation.

I shall now briefly discuss the contributions of Derrida and Foucault , two of the most famous postmodern theorists (see the chapters by Hoy and Philip in Skinner, ed., 1985). We need to be aware that their work emerged out of the "structuralism" which dominated French intellectual life at the time. Indeed, both are often referred to as post-structuralists. Structuralism, the reader will recall, originated with Saussure's linguistics. Saussure argued that the meaning of a sign was not related to some objective thing in the world nor to the intentions of the subject. Rather it was determined by its relationship to other signs. The point can be made in relation to the work of the structuralist anthropologist, Levi-Strauss (for example, see 1968). Levi-Strauss studied the myths used by various Indian tribes in central and southern America. If the myths were studied as a system, across the tribes, an underlying structure emerged based on the relationship between the different elements in the myths. The meaning of the myths was, therefore, to be found in the relationship between these elements. It did not relate to a correspondence between the myths and what existed in the natural world, nor could any individual or tribe grasp the meaning of the myths. Levi-Strauss, however, did seek to explain the structure underlying the myths; seeing it as an expression of problems all the tribes faced in arriving at and justifying particular kinds of social practices. It is in refusing this type of explanation that post-structuralist and postmodernists differ from structuralists. As Craib (1992) puts it:

> there is an absence [in postmodernism] of causal explanations which involves a rejection of the notion of ontological depth, and a concentration on appearances, representations, and a rejection of historical explanation (p.184).

Derrida accepts whole-heartedly the notion that linguistic meaning derives from the structure of language itself. Rather than simply mirroring objects, language creates objects. Craib (1992) states it neatly:

> The starting point is that meaning does not come in any way through a relationship to something outside language; there is absolutely nothing to which we can look to guarantee meaning, to assure us that we are right. Meaning, then, always lies elsewhere and it is not guaranteed by anything outside itself; and of course, the world we see is created in and by meaning (pp.185-6).

Once the relationship between signs and what is signified in the world is broken, it appears to Derrida that it must be possible to create an infinite number of relational systems of signs from which different meanings can be derived. To take the distinctions made in any particular discourse as representative of reality is an illegitimate privileging of that discourse which involves hiding other possible distinctions. Derrida's "deconstructive" method seeks to reveal the deceptiveness of language and the work that has to go on in any text to hide contradictions (which might reveal alternative readings) so that a particular unity and order can be privileged and "rationality" maintained.

The shift to the study of the structure of language and away from the intentions of the speaker, in Derrida, puts his work at the forefront of the attack upon "humanism"; this attack being another characteristic of postmodernism. In his view it is discourse that speaks the person and not the person who uses language. In the contemporary world, where there are many possible discourses, the notion of an integrated, self-determining individual becomes untenable. From this follows a rejection of the idea of historical progress, especially with man at the center of it. Finally, Derrida also shares the usual postmodern skepticism with regard to scientific progress.

Foucault's concern, in his early work (see Philip in Skinner, ed., 1985), is with discourse at the level of fields of knowledge. Every field of knowledge is constituted by sets of discursive rules which determine whether statements are adjudged as true or false within the context of that field. The particular discursive rules which operate within a field of knowledge, and the classificatory scheme offered by that discursive formation, will alter over time but there is no reason to believe that current classifications are any "truer" than earlier ones, in the sense that they mirror the world more closely. Each discourse supplies its own rules for determining truth. The idea of epistemological progress is, therefore, rejected by Foucault. So is the notion of the autonomous human being as providing a constant subject for history. Individuals have their subjectivities determined by the discourses that pertain at the time of their birth and socialization. Discourses not only structure the world but shape individuals for the world in terms of their social identity and way of seeing.

Foucault is particularly interested in the discursive formations that constitute the human sciences, such as medicine, psychiatry, psychology, criminology and sociology. In the modern era, he argues, these disciplines have created human "subjects" in such a way as to make them available for considerably stricter discipline and control by society. The human sciences support modern society, and are supported by modern society, in enabling the regulation of the population. The discursive rules in the human sciences produce classifications of what is normal behavior. Signs of disease, disturbance or deviance are then easily recognized and subjected to treatment.

For Foucault, however, discourses are not simply "free floating" as they may appear in Derrida. If his earlier work was an "archaeology", looking at the structure of discourses, his later writings emphasize the need to study the technical and material framework in which discourses arise. As is the case with the human sciences, discourses play a role in establishing patterns of domination; they are inextricably connected to power:

> Foucault argues that knowledge is a power over others, the power to define others. Knowledge ceases to be a liberation and becomes enslavement.....A discourse embodies knowledge ... and therefore embodies power. There are rules within a discourse concerning who can make statements and in what context, and these rules exclude some and include others. Those who have knowledge have the power to fix the flow of meaning and define others. The world is thus made up of a myriad of power relations, and each power relation generates a resistance; therefore, the world is a myriad of power struggles... (Craib, 1992, p.186).

His exploration of the power/knowledge relationship is Foucault's most valuable contribution to social theory. A claim to power is seen as present in any claim to knowledge. Discourses carry power in the way that they make distinctions and so open or close possibilities for social action. At the same time they depend upon power relationships. Bodies of knowledge can help to fix general patterns of domination, as in the human sciences. Because of the nature of power however, as omnipresent in social relations, their claims can always be contested.

Foucault gives the name "genealogy" to the accounts he offers of the power struggles involved as particular forms of discourse become dominant. Genealogy is undoubtedly critical in the sense that it is an unmasking of the pretensions of "totalizing discourses" to provide objective knowledge. It offers criticism directed at the power/knowledge systems of the modern age in favor of "subjugated" knowledge. In this way a space is opened up that makes resistance possible, albeit on a "local" basis and in response to specific issues. By paying attention to difference at the local level, to specific knowledge, to points of continuing dissension it might be feasible to give a voice back to those silenced or marginalized by the dominant discourses.

In seeking to set out some common themes among postmodern authors, Alvesson and Deetz (1996) highlight the following seven ideas in order to show their relevance to organizational research:

i)   the centrality of discourse
ii) the discursive production of the individual
iii) the discursive production of natural objects rather than language as a mirror of reality
iv) the loss of power of the grand narratives
v)   the power/knowledge connections
vi) research aimed at revealing indeterminacy and encouraging resistance rather than at maintaining rationality, predictability and order
vii) hyperreality - simulations replace the "real-world" in the current world order

We have covered all of these with the exception of the last, which is an idea due to Baudrillard (see Haralambos and Holborn, 1995). Baudrillard takes the postmodern notion that signs gain their meaning from their relationship to other signs, and not from their reflection of a reality, and uses it to interpret the contemporary world. In this world signs and images are everything, and reality counts for nothing. We live in "simulations", imaginary worlds which consist of signs that refer only to themselves. Disneyland is an exemplar but Los Angeles too offers a make-believe world with no connection to reality. It is "nothing more than an immense script and a perpetual motion picture" (Baudrillard, quoted in Haralambos and Holborn, 1996). Television is the culprit in much of this.

If the postmodernists are right there are, as Burrell (1989) and Jacques (1989) have noted, considerable implications for systems thinking. If history is no longer seen as unilinear and predictable, then there is little point in seeking to arrive at forecasts of the future. If there is a decline in belief in rationality and an optimum solution to problems, then the problem-solving techniques will lack legitimation. Deep analysis of systems in search of laws and regularities is unlikely to receive much support. It would be more productive to emphasize the superficial, to concentrate on image, to take note of accidents, and to respect arbitrariness and discontinuities. If there are no acceptable grand narratives to guide the idea of progress, then systems approaches can only hope to bring about temporary and contested improvements. Indeed, in a world of multiple truths competing for prominence, systems practitioners will be impotent unless they recognize power and the social and political contexts of their work. Finally, the postmodern world does not seem to value "seriousness" very highly; perhaps there is a need to introduce more humor, lightness, irony and sarcasm into the use of systems ideas.

All in all the fit between postmodern social theory and systems thinking may not look good. Postmodernists do, however, employ a number of systems ideas - Foucault was, after all, a Professor of Systems of Thought. For their part, some systems thinkers and management scientists have sought to respond to the challenges thrown down by postmodernism. In Chapter 9 we shall explore a possible closer collaboration; with systems thinking putting to use, in intervention, the various systems models, methods and techniques but in the spirit of postmodernism. Can this improve our capacity for intervention? Can it help us learn more about the value of the postmodern perspective?

3.6. CONCLUSION

We have sought, in this chapter, to identify and review the most relevant social theory for those wishing to use systems approaches. In particular we have concentrated on those social theory perspectives that have had an impact on systems thinking by providing either implicitly or explicitly the frameworks of ideas on which systems approaches have been constructed. To carry the argument forward, in Part II of the book, it is necessary now to identify those key types of social theory which will be used to order our analysis of the different systems approaches at that time. My view, looking backward to the review of social theory and forward, using my privileged access to what is to come, is that most value can be gained by concentrating on four key types of social theory and, in Part II, seeing how these types have been and can be enhanced by systems ideas. These four types are:

- Functionalist approaches
- Interpretive approaches
- Emancipatory approaches
- Postmodern approaches

The reader will only be able to judge the success of concentrating on these four types at the end of the book. Nevertheless, some preliminary arguments can be proffered here. The functionalist approach was identified as important by Burrell and Morgan, and the majority of Morgan's "images of organization" fit into this category. As we shall see it is also the case that a great deal of systems thinking can be categorized as functionalist in nature, often because of a commitment to the organismic analogy. Systems methodologies and models crowd the functionalist paradigm. We cannot ignore it. We do have at our disposal the distinction between "positivism" and "structuralism" in epistemology and the "metaphors" identified by Morgan as means by which we can make finer distinctions within this large category. The interpretive paradigm deserves our special attention because, as I have long argued (Jackson, 1982), it provides the theoretical home for soft systems thinking. The establishment of soft systems thinking as an alternative to the "hard" and "cybernetic", functionalist systems approaches, was an event of great significance in systems thinking. An appropriate response to Burrell and Morgan's "radical paradigms", and Morgan's "psychic prison" and "instruments of domination" metaphors, and to the impact of Habermas's work on the development of emancipatory and critical systems methodology, is to recognize "emancipatory approaches" as a third distinct category. With postmodernism, it is the challenge posed to systems thinking, perhaps more than the impact it has already had, which ensures that we grant it special attention. In Part II, therefore, there will be four chapters relating systems approaches to, in turn, functionalist, interpretive, emancipatory and postmodern social theory.

The classification we have adopted, dividing social theory into four types, does in fact have support in the organization theory literature. Deetz (see Alvesson and Deetz, 1996; Hardy and Clegg, 1997) has produced a grid similar to that of Burrell and Morgan but which, he believes, more adequately captures the similarities and differences between different "research positions", taking into account the recent work in critical and postmodern social theory. The dimensions he employs to arrive at his 4-celled matrix need not concern us here. However, the classes of research approach he arrives at are: normative, interpretative, critical and dialogic. These correspond neatly to our functionalist, interpretive, emancipatory and postmodern approaches - the differences in names reflecting the different purposes of our reviews. In order to make this point and to provide another insight into the

Table 3.1. Features of four research approaches (adapted from Alvesson and Deetz, 1996, p. 198)

Features	Functionalist	Interpretive	Emancipatory	Postmodern
Basic goal	Demonstrate law-like relations among objects	Display unified culture	Unmask domination	Reclaim conflict
Method	Nomothetic science	Hermeneutics, ethnography	Cultural and ideological critique	Deconstruction genealogy
Hope	Efficiency, effectiveness, survival and adaptation	Recovery of integrative values	Reformation of social order	Claim a space for lost voices
Organization metaphor	Machine, organism, brain, flux and transformation	Culture, political system	Psychic prison, instruments of domination	Carnival
Problems addressed	Inefficiency, disorder	Meaninglessness, illegitimacy	Domination, consent	Marginalization, conflict suppression
Narrative style	Scientific/ technical, strategic	Romantic, embracing	Therapeutic, directive	Ironic, ambivalent
Time identity	Modern	Premodern	Late modern	Postmodern
Organizational benefits	Control, expertise	Commitment, quality of work life	Participation, expanded knowledge	Diversity, creativity
Mood	Optimistic	Friendly	Suspicious	Playful
Social fear	Disorder	Depersonalization	Authority	Totalization, normalization

material covered in this chapter, I have adapted Deetz's classification as Table 3.1. The terminology for the approaches and the odd characteristic are changed, but otherwise I follow Deetz closely. There is obviously no attempt to incorporate any systems ideas in these approaches at this stage.

This preparatory theoretical work done, we can turn to the development of systems thinking. Systems thinking can put meat on the bones of different social theories, allowing them to be more adequately and effectively employed to intervene in the social world.

4

ORIGINS IN THE DISCIPLINES

4.1. INTRODUCTION

The primary purpose of this chapter is to provide an introduction to the origins of systems ideas in various disciplines; particularly in philosophy, biology, sociology, management and organization theory, control engineering and the physical sciences. In the course of this inquiry we note the birth of systems thinking *per se* in the form of general system theory and cybernetics. We also deal in detail with chaos and complexity theory, which many regard as the best candidate for a contemporary general system theory. Once systems thinking had established itself as a transdiscipline, in the 1940s and early 1950s, its influence soon began feeding back both into the disciplines from which it was derived and into other fields such as geography and political science. The aim of the chapter is to take systems thinking in the disciplines, and in terms of its own development as a transdiscipline, up to the point where it began to give rise to specific methodologies for intervening in the real-world to solve practical problems. The nature, development and status of such *applied systems thinking* then becomes a topic to be covered in Chapter 5.

The emphasis in this chapter is on those systems ideas which, aligned with relevant social theory, can be seen to have given rise to the systems approaches which are the focus of Parts II and III of the book. The point needs making, however, that we shall occasionally cover what may seem to be non-systemic ideas if they have had an impact, even if more indirect (demanding re-orientation perhaps rather than supplying concepts), on those approaches. This is the case, for example, with Husserl's phenomenology. I should also mention that, while "Origins in the Disciplines" covers a lot of ground, it cannot do everything. More detailed material, perhaps influencing only one approach, is covered in later chapters dealing with particular approaches.

It might seem to the reader that having been provided with an introduction to the origins of systems ideas, what she next needs is a summary of the main systems concepts and of their meaning in contemporary usage. Such a reader will need to be patient, I'm afraid. As was pointed out in the "Introduction" to the book, even the most basic concepts, such as "system" and "boundary", change their meaning according to the "language game" being played by the particular strand of systems thinking - functionalist, interpretive, emancipatory, postmodern - in which they are employed. The reader will be familiarized with the meaning of systems concepts, when it is common and when it varies across different systems approaches, in Parts II and III of this book.

We start our account of the emergence of systems thinking in the disciplines with a consideration of philosophy.

4.2. PHILOSOPHY

It is a commonplace of many Eastern religions that enlightenment comes when you are able to see the interconnectedness of everything and feel at home in the "One." Another kind of holistic thinking can be found among peoples, like the North American Indians, who recognize how entwined their way of life is with their natural surroundings and reflect upon the need to respect and nurture their environments. Beguiling as these ideas are to those of us brought up in the 1960s, I will spare you the quotable quotes and pass rapidly on to the Western philosophical tradition.

As with so much in the Western intellectual tradition, we owe the first attempts to think using systems ideas to the ancient Greeks. Aristotle employs systems thinking to elucidate the nature of body and soul and the relationship between individuals and the State (Russell, 1961). The soul is said to give the body its purpose and, therefore, its identity as a thing. The parts can only realize their purpose through this thing; for example, an eye can only see when it is connected to the body. Aristotle transfers this notion of an organic whole to his discussion of politics. Just as a hand can only fulfill its purpose, of grasping, when joined to a body, so an individual must be a part of a State in order to fulfill his purpose. In Aristotle's philosophy the whole is clearly prior to the parts and the parts only obtain their meaning in terms of the purpose of the whole - they are not separable. Implicit, as well, is the belief that the same systems "laws" apply whether it is the body and soul or society that is being considered.

That other great master in the Greek philosophical tradition, Plato, also found value in employing systems ideas across different domains of application. There is a Greek word, *kybernetes,* which means the art of steersmanship. The word referred principally to the piloting of a vessel but Plato used it to refer to steering the ship of State (see especially "The Republic", Book VI, Plato, 1999). Both usages imply regulation which was why, as we shall see, the name cybernetics was given to the new science of "communication and control" in the 1940s.

Given the importance of Plato and Aristotle, it is not surprising to find systems ideas dominating the writings of many later philosophers included in the usual pantheon of the Western tradition - Spinoza, Kant, Hegel and Marx, for example. Spinoza believed that the universe as a whole consisted of a single substance and that it was illogical to try to break this whole down into parts that could exist on their own (see Honderich, ed., 1995). Kant, we have already noted, was the philosopher of the Enlightenment eager to push rational thought to the limit in order to free man from prejudice and illusion. At the same time as being aware of the need for holistic understanding as the basis for science and ethics, he also reminds us of the limitations imposed on this quest by our own minds. His philosophy is a reflection on these restrictions in terms of the "categories" we have to use in thinking. Hegel (see Russell, 1961) believed that nothing was real except the whole. His whole, called "The Absolute", is however more complex than that of Spinoza. Separate things do exist but they are only aspects of a complex whole; a kind of organism, which we have to recognize they are part of if we are to see them truly. An appreciation of "The Absolute" can be approached through the "dialectical" method, which consists of a movement between "thesis", "antithesis" and "synthesis." Any statement about the nature of the whole, the thesis, can be shown to be limited by counterposing to it another connected statement, the antithesis. These can then be combined in a further attempt to describe the whole, the synthesis. This in turn however, as the new thesis, can be shown to be limited by introducing another antithesis. Eventually the dialectic can take us close to an understanding of the whole in which each of the superseded theses is understood in its proper place in relation to the whole.

Marx, as is well known, turned Hegel's dialectic on its head and saw it as operating not in the realm of thought but in history itself; specifically in the history of class struggle. He was a "dialectical materialist." His early work revolved around a critique of alienated labor in capitalist society and gave rise, eventually, to the critical theory of the Frankfurt School and Habermas. His later work concentrated on the nature of different social formations, with particular emphasis on the structure of capitalist society. The best known interpreter of the writings of the mature Marx is the French philosopher and "structuralist marxist" Althusser. For Althusser (who was Foucault's teacher), history is a "process without a subject." Every mode of production produces its own human nature and

> individuals must be seen as the agents of the mode of production, in the role of capitalists, workers etc., according to the positions to which they are assigned through the mechanisms reproducing the social formation (Callinicos, 1976, p. 70).

Of primary importance in Althusser's work is this idea of social formation or "social totality." The social totality consists of a number of separate but interrelated "instances" of which the economic, the political, the ideological and the theoretical are the most important. The three "superstructural" instances mentioned here are not simply reducible to the economic base. History is the result of the relations between "relatively autonomous" instances. It is determined (but not predetermined) by the contradictions internal to each instance and the uneven development of the distinct instances relative to one another in the social totality. This "complex" contradiction operating within and between instances (which Althusser calls "overdetermination") is the basic difference between the dialectic as envisaged by Althusser and the "simple" contradiction of thesis and antithesis in Hegel.

Althusser regards the various instances as related systemically within the social whole. The totality is to be conceptualized as a "structure in dominance." Which instance is dominant in any social formation will be determined by the contradiction within the economic instance between the social relations of production and the forces of production. The economy is ultimately determinant but it

> is never active in the pure state; in history, these instances, the superstructures, etc., are never seen to step respectfully aside when their work is done. From the first moment to the last, the lonely hour of the 'last instance' never comes (Althusser, quoted in Callinicos, 1976 p. 43).

The job of the economy is to allocate the other instances to roles in the social whole. It is for Marxist science, according to Althusser, to grasp theoretically the unity of necessarily related and yet necessarily uneven instances at any point in time – "the conjuncture."

Another school of philosophical thought, American pragmatism, contained ideas of a systemic nature which have had a clear impact upon the development of soft systems thinking. The experimentalism, or nonrelativistic pragmatism, of E.A. Singer has been particularly important. The main lines of influence have been traced by Britton and McCallion (1994). Singer's experimentalism is a kind of synthesis of rationalism and empiricism in which neither laws nor facts are granted primacy. They are necessarily intertwined as some laws have to be assumed to generate facts and vice-versa. There are no fundamental truths which can be taken as a sure starting point for inquiry, but a process of learning can be put in train by developing together sets of facts and laws. An approximation to the truth emerges as the outcome of this process.

This notion of inquiry as a process derives, of course, from Hegel and the dialectic plays a part in soft systems thinking. In pragmatism, however, inquiry is not in pursuit of an understanding of "The Absolute" but is oriented to "usefulness." Progress in science cannot be detached from other human interests and from objectives, goals and desires in society more broadly. The aim of science must be to assist with the pursuit of ideals. These will be the ideals of humankind generally rather than any particular sectional interest (this is nonrelativistic pragmatism). The various sciences, which offer different viewpoints on the same problems, need to be co-ordinated in a structure that it is reasonable to call a "systemic process of inquiry." The ideal, truth, is approached as a high degree of purposefulness is achieved and each person becomes able to realize his or her desires.

Another branch of philosophy, this time European, to have impacted on soft systems thinking has been phenomenology. This was first developed by Husserl, writing towards the end of the nineteenth century and at the beginning of the twentieth. The emphasis of his philosophy on "meaning", rather than on the causal explanation of human behavior, provided support to those who wanted to shift systems thinking in a softer direction. According to phenomenologists, the data individuals get through the senses would be entirely chaotic unless human consciousness brought some order to it. Philosophy should therefore seek to understand the structures and workings of the human mind and the way in which, by making classifications, it constructs the world around us and creates meaning (Haralambos and Holborn, 1995). The classifications employed are therefore simply products of the human mind and do not relate to objective reality. If we can suspend our belief that we have access to reality, "bracket" our common-sense assumptions, we can study the categories and distinctions humans employ and understand how the external world is really created.

In leaving this survey of philosophy and systems thinking we need just to remind ourselves of the contributions of postmodernist writers dealt with in the last chapter. Derrida, Foucault and Lyotard challenge many of the central tenets of the Western philosophical tradition.

We turn now, in this chapter, to our review of how systems ideas played a significant part in the development of the disciplines of biology, sociology, organization and management theory, control engineering and the physical sciences, and in the process were refined into a more precise form suitable for the purposes of intervention.

4.3. BIOLOGY

Philosophy, as we saw, yielded to systems thinking notions such as "holism", "the use of analogy", "restrictions on our capacity to comprehend the whole", "totality" and a "systemic process of inquiry." Biology has provided equally fertile ground for the development of systems concepts; contributing, amongst others, "complexity", "emergence", "hierarchy", "equilibrium", "adaptation", "homeostasis", "self-regulation", "open-system", "environment", "autopoiesis" and "autonomy."

The fruitfulness of biology as a source of systems ideas can be accounted for by the complexity of its subject matter. The organized complexity of the phenomena of interest to biology, particularly whole organisms, resisted attempts made by "mechanists" to explain them using nothing but the laws of physics and chemistry. Resistance to the reductionism of treating living systems simply as complex machines was initially led by "vitalists", who believed that there had to be present in an egg some kind of "vital spirit" that guided its growth into a whole organism. Checkland (1981) traces how this unsustainable form of holism was gradually replaced in the early twentieth century, as an alternative to mechanism, by the arguments of the "organismic" school in biology. Organismic biologists argued that while living systems might obey the laws of physics and chemistry, there was something more to them than that. A hierarchy existed in nature – molecules, organelles, cells, organs, organisms – and at certain points in the hierarchy, stable levels of organized complexity arose which demonstrated "emergent properties" which did not exist at levels below. An organism was such a level of organized complexity. It had a clear boundary, which separated it from its environment, and seemed capable of maintaining itself by carrying out transactions across its boundary. The emergent properties exhibited at the level of the whole organism called for a new language of description not available in physics and chemistry. Biology was necessary as the science corresponding to a new level of reality characterized by the autonomy of living systems.

Checkland (1981) discusses C.D Broad's *The Mind and its Place in Nature* (1923), J.C. Smuts's *Holism and Evolution* (1926), and J.H. Woodger's *Biological Principles* (1929), as significant milestones in the establishment of "organismic biology" and, therefore, in the early rise of systems thinking. Broad elaborated the theory of emergence which, he argued, explained the existence of different levels of reality. The fact that organisms, as wholes, had characteristics which were not reducible to their parts meant that biology was necessary. Smuts believed that it was organized complexity that gave rise to new levels of reality:

> Every organism, every plant or animal, is a whole with a certain internal organization and a measure of self-direction. A whole is a synthesis or unity of parts, so close that it affects the activities and interactions of those parts ... their independent functions and activities are grouped, related, correlated and unified in a structural whole (quoted in Checkland, 1981, pp. 78-79).

Woodger similarly studied the notion of "organization" and summarized the need for different types of explanation at the different levels of hierarchy produced by organized complexity:

> from what has been said about organization it seems perfectly plain that an entity having the hierarchical type of organization such as we find in the organism requires investigation at all levels, and investigation of one level cannot replace the necessity for investigations of levels higher up the hierarchy .. a physiologist who wishes to study the physiology of the nervous system must have a level of organization above the cell level to begin with. He must have at least the elements necessary to constitute a reflex arc, and in actual practice he uses the concepts appropriate to that level which are not concepts of physics and chemistry (quoted in Checkland, 1981, p. 79).

Of equal significance in discussing the contribution of biology to systems thinking is the work of L.J. Henderson and W.B. Cannon. Henderson, although originally a biochemist, became a systems thinker more generally and we shall have cause to come back to his writings when we look at systems ideas derived from sociology. For the moment, though, we can concentrate on his analysis of the living organism, which he saw as characterized by a high degree of complexity, by its durability and by the fact that it is constantly active. Central to the survival of the organism is its ability to maintain an equilibrium through self-regulating mechanisms. The achievement of this crucial stability requires the organism to be constantly responding to its environment and adapting to suit this environment:

> the fitness of organic beings for their life in the world has been won in whole and in part by an almost infinite series of adaptations of life to its environment, whereby, through a corresponding series of transformations, present complexity has grown out of former simplicity (Henderson, 1941-42, pp. 4-5).

Cannon's major work, *The Wisdom of the Body* (1932, revised 1939), was similarly taken up with the ability of organisms, and particularly our bodies, to persist over many decades while consisting of extraordinarily unstable material and being open to the environment. For Cannon, living systems are marvelous in that they

> may be confronted by dangerous conditions in the outer world and by equally dangerous
> possibilities within the body, and yet they continue to live and carry on their functions with
> relatively little disturbance (Cannon, 1939, pp. 22-23).

He refers to these states of stability as "equilibria." The processes that maintain the "steady state" are referred to as "homeostatic"; an example would be the self-regulating mechanism controlling body temperature.

The best known biologist of all to have influenced systems thinking was Ludwig von Bertalanffy. He brought together in one framework the relevant concepts derived from biology and extended them to other domains through "general system theory" (see next section). He thus became one of the founding fathers of the transdiscipline of systems thinking itself. For von Bertalanffy (1950, 1968), every living system is a "whole" made up of interrelated and interdependent parts, interacting to maintain that whole. These parts are both ordered in a hierarchy and differentiated to perform specific functions, helping the system to survive and adapt to its environment. In addition there needs to be some sort of "transformation process" inherent in the system whereby it takes in inputs, transforms them and produces outputs back into its environment. The key concept here is that of an "open system."

Conventional physics, and for a long time biology, von Bertalanffy argued, had only dealt with systems "closed" to their environments. However, many systems are "open systems" importing material, energy and information from, and exporting them to, their environments:

> We find systems which by their very nature and definition are not closed systems. Every
> living organism is essentially an open system. It maintains itself in a continuous inflow and
> outflow, a building up and breaking down of components, never being, so long as it is alive,
> in a state of chemical and thermodynamic equilibrium but maintained in a so called steady
> state which is distinct from the latter ... What now? Obviously the conventional formula-
> tions of physics are, in principle, inapplicable to the living organism *qua* open system and
> steady state (von Bertalanffy, 1968 p. 39).

Closed systems obey the second law of thermodynamics, gradually running down, increasing in entropy and reaching an equilibrium state where no energy can be obtained from them. Open systems can temporarily defeat the second law of thermodynamics. By living off their environments, importing complex molecules high in free energy, they can evolve toward states of increased order and organization. Organisms, for example, maintain themselves in a steady state and can increase their complexity, reversing the law of entropy, by exchanging materials with their environments. Many have argued (e.g. Emery, 1969; Lilienfeld, 1978) that Bertalanffy's famous article *The Theory of Open Systems in Physics and Biology* (1950), which first rigorously distinguished closed and open systems, established systems thinking as an intellectual movement.

Some of the primary characteristics of open systems identified by von Bertalanffy were "regulation", "feedback" and "equifinality." Regulation is necessary if the interrelated and interacting parts of open systems are not to give rise to chaos and disorder. An effective means of regulation is through feedback whereby a message is generated if part of a system's functioning is going awry and is transmitted to an "effector" which takes action to bring it back on course. von Bertalanffy notes, tellingly, that

> a great variety of systems in technology and in living nature follow the feedback scheme, and
> it is well-known that a new discipline, called Cybernetics, was introduced by Norbert Wiener
> to deal with these phenomena... It should be borne in mind, however, that the feedback

> scheme is of a rather special nature. It presupposes structural arrangements of the type mentioned [i.e. that of the open system] (von Bertalanffy, 1968, p. 44).

Equifinality is the ability to reach the same final state from different initial conditions and in different ways. It depends on the existence of feedback and regulation.

Before leaving the contribution of biology to systems thinking it is necessary to discuss the theory of "autopoiesis" formulated as a result of much research by the neuro-biologists Maturana and Varela. Autopoiesis is an ancient Greek word referring to self-production. At the time Maturana and Varela were beginning their research, in the 1960s, traditional biology (as we have seen) tended to look at living systems largely in terms of their relationships with the environment - as open systems. Maturana and Varela, by contrast, looked at living systems in terms of the "processes that realized them." In 1973 their first book, *Autopoiesis: The Organization of the Living*, was published. In what follows we shall concentrate on the concepts they developed to express their conclusions about biological entities. The epistemology employed to reach the conclusions will be picked up again in later chapters.

Maturana and Varela begin by posing the question "What is the necessary and sufficient organization for a given system to be a living unity?" (Varela *et al.*, 1974). They argue that such unities must be autopoietic systems: "Living beings are characterized by their autopoietic organization" (Maturana and Varela, 1992). Mingers (1995), in an excellent introduction to their work, explains that the autopoietic organization

> produces, and is produced by, nothing other than itself. This simple idea is all that is meant by 'autopoiesis'. The word means 'self-producing' (p. 11).

This simple idea gets considerably more complicated when Varela *et al.* (1974) get to work on a definition:

> the autopoietic organization is defined as a unity by a network of components which (i) participate recursively in the same network of productions of components which produced these components, and (ii) realize the network of productions as a unity in the space in which the components exist (p. 188).

Maturana and Varela (see Varela *et al.*, 1974) have, in fact, proposed a "six-point key" which can be used to ensure correct identification of autopoietic systems. For our purposes, however, it is sufficient that the reader grasps the importance of the "circular organization of the living system" and how an emphasis on this provides a rather different picture of organisms to that painted by biologists stressing organism - environment relations.

According to Maturana and Varela, autopoietic systems have both "organization" and "structure." Here organization denotes "those relations that must exist among the components of a system for it to be a member of a specific class" (Maturana and Varela, 1992). The organization must remain invariant if the unity is to maintain its identity. The structure of a unity, defined as the components and relations that actually constitute a particular unity, can, however, change without the unity ceasing to exist. In other words, two unities of the same class must have the same organization but may have different structures. Maturana (1986) concludes that "a dynamic composite unity is a composite unity in continuous structural change with conservation of organization."

Autopoietic systems are, therefore, closed systems in the sense that they seek to maintain their own organization as constant. They are also structure-determined rather than externally-determined systems. We already know that any change in a composite unity is structural change (rather than change in organization). Maturana (1986) argues further that the nature of any changes are determined internally by the structure of the unity and not by an "independent external agent":

> an external agent that interacts with a composite unity only triggers in it a structural change … nothing external to them can specify what happens to them … It follows from all this that composite unities are structure determined systems in the sense that everything is determined by their structure (pp. 335-336).

We can conclude our overview of the theory of "autopoiesis" in biology by drawing out two further implications.

First, Maturana and Varela recognize that those systems that exhibit autopoietic organization (i.e. living systems) are necessarily autonomous:

> Autonomy is the distinctive phenomenology resulting from an autopoietic organization: the realization of the autopoietic organization is the product of its operation. As long as an autopoietic system exists, its organization is invariant; if the network of productions of components which define the organization is disrupted, the unity disintegrates. Thus an autopoietic system has a domain in which it can compensate for perturbations throughout the realization of its autopoiesis, and in this domain it remains a unity (Varela *et al.*, 1974, p. 188).

Maturana and Varela go on to expand this idea, stating that

> what is distinctive about [autopoietic systems]… is that their organization is such that their only product is themselves, with no separation between producer and product. The being and doing of an autopoietic unity are inseparable, and this is their specific mode of organization (1992, pp. 48-49).

Second, if autopoietic systems are to continue to exist they must establish appropriate relationships with their environments. This is true even though autopoietic systems are organizationally closed and structure-determined. They must take from the environment those elements which "permit the processes of production of components to take place" (Maturana, 1975). The environment, as we know, does not specify or direct changes in the unity. Nevertheless, it does "trigger" events that bring about structure-determined changes. The same holds for the effect of the unity on the environment. So that the interactions between them can achieve stability over time it is essential, from the point of view of the unity, that its autopoietic organization selects a structure suitable for its particular environment. In this way, the unity and its environment, following mutual changes, become "structurally coupled." Structural coupling can also occur between two living systems sharing the same medium. In this way they produce a "consensual domain."

Von Krogh and Roos (1995) argue that

> since its introduction, autopoiesis theory has gradually evolved into a general systems theory. In our opinion, this has had an impressive impact in many fields … (p. 41).

The next section will help clarify what exactly they mean by this.

4.4. GENERAL SYSTEM THEORY

Ludwig von Bertalanffy's name is writ large in the short history of systems thinking because he sought to extend his original work in biology to establish an entirely new discipline, called "General System Theory":

> Its subject matter is the formulation and derivation of those principles which are valid for
> 'systems' in general (von Bertalanffy 1968, pp. 32-33).

Together with the work of Wiener on "cybernetics" (see later in this chapter), this contribution gave birth, in the 1940s, to systems thinking as a distinctive area of research. Alongside the writings of von Bertalanffy we need to consider, in setting out the main ideas of general system theory, contributions from Bogdanov and Boulding.

Bogdanov's three volume *Tektology* was published in Russia between 1912 and 1927. It anticipated many of the themes later identified with general system theory although, at the time, it had virtually no impact. The problem for Bogdanov was that his ideas were seen as being in opposition to Marxism, were heavily criticized by Lenin, and were suppressed by the Soviet authorities. It was fifty years later before Gorelik introduced the principal ideas of *Tektology* to the West (Gorelik, 1975). Available now are translations of Bogdanov's *Essays in Tektology* (Gorelik, 1984, second edition) and, overseen by Dudley (1996), of the first book of the *Tektology* itself. According to Gorelik:

> Tektology can be characterized as a dynamic science of complex wholes. It is concerned
> with universal structural regularities, general types of systems, the most general laws of their
> transformation and the basic laws of organization of any elements in nature, practice and
> cognition ... [It] is relevant today because it has much in common with such modern gener-
> alizing sciences as general systems theory, cybernetics, structuralism and catastrophe theory
> (1984, p. ii).

The word *tektology* derives from the Greek *tekton*, which means "builder." Both nature and human beings are involved in the building or creation of forms and systems, ranging from the most basic to the extremely complex and hierarchical, drawing on the organizing and disorganizing processes innate within them. Central to the natural and social worlds, therefore, is "organization." Everything exists as an "organization." In Gorelik's (1984) opinion, "this point of view is identical to the systems approach."

For Bogdanov an organization (or "complex") is constituted by elements and the inter-relationships between elements. Particular complexes arise when specific elements are combined in terms of specific relationships. When a complex exhibits organization, the whole will be greater than the sum of its parts. However, as was mentioned, man and nature also contribute certain disorganizing processes which can lead to a complex being less than the sum of its parts. Disorganization should not be seen as necessarily undesirable. If it leads to decomposition then it gives rise to opportunities for new combinations. Organization and disorganization always exist in nature side by side, complementing one another and, in cases where they are mutually balanced, giving rise to a "neutral" complex. Summarizing, Bog-danov states:

> Thus, for tektology, the first basic notions are those about elements and their combinations.
> Elements are activities and resistances of all possible kinds. Combinations result in three
> types: organized, disorganized and neutral complexes. They differ in the magnitudes of the
> practical sum of their elements (Bogdanov, in Gorelik, 1984, p. 47).

Tektology goes on to look at how organizational forms are created, regulated and destroyed. Two mechanisms are at work here. The "formulating mechanism" governs the joining and separating of elements and complexes. When two complexes join or come into "conjunction" there can be total co-operation, total resistance or, more likely, partial adding together and partial resistance. The usual outcome of conjunction is, then, "a system composed of the transformed conjugating complexes" (in Gorelik, 1984). The successful linking of complexes, their activities and elements, is referred to as "ingression." The "regulating mechanism" has as its basis the notion of "selection." By means of selection, a complex (which is perceived by Bogdanov as an "open system") assimilates or disassimilates requisite variety from the environment and is, in effect, regulated by it. Positive progressive selection, or a preponderance of assimilation, results in an increase in the number of elements in a complex; negative progressive selection leads to the reverse. These ideas are then employed by Bogdanov to investigate a variety of organizational outcomes - stability of forms, divergence of forms, centralist and skeletal forms and crises of forms.

Although it is clear to Gorelik (1975) that the "conceptual part" of general system theory (GST) had first been put in place by Bogdanov, for the reasons mentioned it is von Bertalanffy who is seen as the founding father. Von Bertalanffy had himself, in fact, been promoting an embryonic form of general system theory (GST) as early as the 1920s and 1930s, although it was not until the early 1950s that his ideas became more widely known in scientific circles. In the previous section we saw the development of his systems thinking in biology, culminating in a seminal article on open systems (von Bertalanffy, 1950). Here we trace his ideas on GST drawing particularly on a collection of his essays first published in 1968.

Von Bertalanffy conceived of GST as a new scientific doctrine concerned with the laws which apply to systems behavior in general. Such a science was possible because:

> there exist models, principles and laws that apply to generalized systems or their subclasses, irrespective of their particular kind, the nature of their component elements, and the relations or 'forces' between them. It seems legitimate [therefore] to ask for a theory, not of systems of a more or less special kind, but of universal principles applying to systems in general. In this way we postulate a new discipline called 'General System Theory' (von Bertalanffy, 1968 pp. 32-33).

He derived his own insights from biology but they could be transferred to other disciplines as well because the principles at work were not specific to biology. They were general system principles that applied to complex systems of all types, whether they were of a physical, biological or social nature. In order to ensure exact definition of the general system principles and ensure formal correspondence across disciplines, von Bertalanffy favored the use of mathematics:

> General system theory, therefore, is a general science of 'wholeness'...In elaborate form it would be a logico-mathematical discipline, in itself purely formal but applicable to the various empirical sciences (von Bertalanffy, 1968, p. 37).

According to von Bertalanffy GST was not only possible but it also fulfilled a real and urgent need. The sciences had become increasingly specialized and scientists in different disciplines found it difficult to communicate with one another:

> the physicist, the biologist, the psychologist and the social scientist are .... encapsulated in their private universes, and it is difficult to get word from one cocoon to the other (von Bertalanffy, 1968 p. 30).

GST made conversation possible between scientists many of whom were, in fact, studying systems but in terms of their own disciplines. Furthermore, GST could provide models capable of being transferred to and used in different fields, accelerating progress in the individual disciplines.

Having established the nature of GST, von Bertalanffy dedicated himself to promulgating this new science. In 1954 he gave institutional embodiment to his ambition by setting up, with Boulding (an economist), Gerard (a physiologist) and Rapoport (a mathematician), the Society for General System Research. This had four aims:

- To investigate the isomorphy of concepts, laws, and models in various fields, and to help in useful transfers from one field to another
- To encourage the development of adequate theoretical models in fields which lack them
- To eliminate the duplication of theoretical efforts in different fields.
- To promote the unity of science through improving the communication between specialists

The impact of GST on various disciplines was considerable over the following decades. In organization theory countless books were published looking at management from an open systems point of view (e.g. Koontz and O'Donnell, 1974; Kast and Rosenzweig, 1981). In the area of applied systems thinking, the socio-technical approach and much of operational research/management science relied on von Bertalanffy's conclusions. Van Gigch (1978) for example, in an influential contribution, succeeded in using GST to give coherence to a range of management science techniques. We shall have cause to examine these influences, as well as Miller's (1978) thoroughly researched attempt to integrate knowledge across biological and social systems, in Chapter 6. In a number of its intentions, therefore, GST met with some success. The hope that general laws could be discovered that hold across all system types has, however, not been fulfilled, despite the efforts of, for example, Weinberg (1975), Klir (1985), and Rapoport (1986). Partially because of the gap between its high ambitions and its actual achievements, GST has come in for some severe criticism (Berlinski, 1976; Lilienfeld, 1978). It is argued that the mathematical analogies purveyed lack any genuine empirical content. The recent interest in autopoiesis and complexity theory as "general system theories" suggests, perhaps, a reversal in fortunes for GST and for appreciation of the significance of what von Bertalanffy was proposing. Even the Society for General System Research, which staggered on through the 1980s and 1990s with a few hundred members and various name changes, is now, as the International Society for the Systems Sciences, benefiting from the revived interest in systems ideas.

Another angle on GST was provided by Boulding, a co-founder with von Bertalanffy of the Society for General System Research. In his well-known paper, *General Systems Theory - the Skeleton of Science* (1956), he argued that the aims of GST could be realized in two ways. Either you could seek to develop a theory of very general principles, which was von Bertalanffy's approach, or you could provide an ordering of different fields of study according to the apparent complexity of the basic "individual unit of behavior" each discipline concerned itself with. He chose the latter course and produced an intuitive hierarchy of levels of real-world complexity. This hierarchy, stretching from structures and frameworks at the simplest level to transcendental systems, at the most complex, is summarized in Table 4.1. Boulding notes that the characteristics of lower level systems can be found in higher level systems; for example aspects of all the levels 1-6 in level 7 - people. Each level, however, presents emergent properties that cannot be understood simply in terms of an understanding of lower levels - hence the need for a new discipline. He uses the hierarchy to point out gaps in our knowledge, especially our lack of adequate systems models much above level 4. He also points to the danger, for the purposes of explanation, of employing a level of theoretical analysis below the level of the empirical phenomenon that is of concern. The reader will remember von Bertalanffy's objection to the emphasis placed by cybernetics on using control mechanisms to study open systems. Boulding's warning, in this regard, will

Table 4.1 A summary of Boulding's (1956) hierarchy of complexity

1.	At level 1 are structures and frameworks which exhibit static behavior and are studied by verbal or pictorial description in any discipline; an example being crystal structures
2.	At level 2 are clockworks which exhibit predetermined motion and are studied by classical natural science; an example being the solar system
3.	At level 3 are control mechanisms which exhibit closed-loop control and are studied by cybernetics; an example being a thermostat
4.	At level 4 are open systems which exhibit structural self-maintenance and are studied by theories of metabolism; an example being a biological cell
5.	At level 5 are lower organisms which have functional parts, exhibit blue-printed growth and reproduction, and are studied by botany; an example being a plant
6.	At level 6 are animals which have a brain to guide behavior, are capable of learning, and are studied by zoology; an example being an elephant
7.	At level 7 are people who possess self-consciousness, know that they know, employ symbolic language, and are studied by biology and psychology; an example being any human being
8.	At level 8 are socio-cultural systems which are typified by the existence of roles, communications and the transmission of values, and are studied by history, sociology, anthropology and behavioral science; an example being a nation
9.	At level 9 are transcendental systems, the home of "inescapable unknowables", and which no scientific discipline can capture; an example being the idea of God

need to be taken seriously by us in considering the different systems approaches in Part II of this book.

The next section will show us that this was true but also that sociology had not waited for von Bertalanffy in order to begin working with systems ideas.

In reviewing the potential of GST, von Bertalanffy noted that:

> Concepts and theories provided by the modern systems approach are being increasingly introduced into sociology, such as the concept of general system, of feedback, information, communication, etc. (1968, p. 196).

4.5. SOCIOLOGY

The powerful notion of society as a system dominated the development of much of traditional sociology. It can be found in the work of Pareto, and his followers, in the belief that society is a system in equilibrium which, despite apparent surface changes, seeks to return to its original state. Durkheim, Spencer and many others favored the organismic analogy: society was viewed as a system made up of interconnected parts functioning to maintain the whole. Such a system was capable of evolving in response to environmental and other changes. It is worth putting in place the main elements of these two strands of sociological thought because they had such an important impact on management and organization theory.

According to Aron (1967), the essential criticism of the second part of Pareto's *Treatise on General Sociology* is that he

> is trying to work out a general system of interpretation that would represent a simplified model comparable to the simplified model of rational mechanics ... he thinks that with the cycles of mutual dependence he has defined the general characteristics of social equilibrium (pp. 174-175).

Aron is referring to Pareto's formulation of a general mechanism which underpins the movement of society. Four variables, called "interest", "residues", "derivations and "social heterogeneity", are seen as being in a state of mutual dependence. Each of the variables acts upon the other three and is, in turn, influenced by them. The movement of society is determined by the reciprocal action of the variables upon each other. At the surface of society significant change may appear to take place as different élite groups succeed one another in power. These changes are, however, merely the result of temporary fluctuations in the relationships between the key variables. Equilibrium will reassert itself sooner or later and social stability is, thereby, maintained. We may think we are seeing history in the making but, in fact, we are witnessing a repetitive process of readjustment between the variables. As Aron (1967) remarks, Pareto "implies that *plus ça change, plus c'est la même chose.*"

Of the utmost significance in helping to diffuse Pareto's ideas in the United States was the biochemist L.J. Henderson. From his Harvard base, Henderson created a "Pareto Circle" which heavily influenced thinkers such as Elton Mayo, Roethlisberger and Dickson, Barnard and Parsons. What each of these made of Henderson's systems thinking will be addressed as part of later sections and chapters. As for Henderson himself, we have already seen the importance to him of the concepts of equilibrium and stability in his analysis of the living organism. The same concepts dominated his sociological work. For Henderson, drawing on the work of Pareto, the social system, like any system, is made up of components which are mutually dependent or interactive. Each component

> is indeed more or less dependent upon all other factors and they, reciprocally, are dependent upon it. A change in one factor is, therefore, accompanied and followed by a long series of changes involving all the other factors of the system (Henderson, 1941-42, pp. 145-146).

The components of a social system, persons or sub-groups, are heterogeneous and exist, together with their properties and relations, in a "state of flux." This state, however, is not chaotic or random; rather, it is characterized by changes that are

> in general subject to connections and constraints of a kind that may be referred to, or considered as in a measure determined by, the condition of equilibrium (Henderson, 1941-42, p.88).

The connections and constraints resulting from the mutual interaction between components ensure that equilibrium reasserts itself and stability is maintained in the long run. This is important because systems are inevitably in a relationship with their environments and in danger of being disturbed by them. Henderson believed that when systems are interfered with from without "they then attempt to restore the state that would have existed if there had been no interference" (1941-42). They are, therefore, resistant to change. Like a boxer's punch-ball, you can hit it hard but eventually it returns to an equilibrium state.

As well as to the mechanical equilibrium model, traditional sociology owes a huge debt to the organismic analogy. The central figures who developed this analogy in sociology were Spencer (1820-1903) and Durkheim (1858-1917). Both saw social systems as made up of mutually dependent elements functioning in ways that contributed to the maintenance of the whole. Just as the human body has certain needs that must be met by its organs (heart, lungs, liver, etc.) if it is to survive, so societies possess "functional prerequisites" which have to be satisfied by their parts. The elements and institutions of a social system are, therefore, best understood in terms of the contribution they make to the whole. Spencer (see 1969), writing at about the same time as Darwin, was taken up with how societies evolved. In order to be successful in adapting to its environment, and therefore to survive in the long term, a society had to have specific characteristics. The particular mixture of races was an important factor for Spencer. So was the capacity of the most able to benefit from their efforts. Too much government regulation, in his view, would hinder a society in the battle of the "survival of the fittest." Durkheim (1933, 1938) similarly sought his explanations of "social facts" at the level of society rather than in the interactions between individual members of society. Social facts, whatever the original cause of their existence, had to serve some useful function for society as a whole if they were to persist. Social order is the most important functional prerequisite of society and has to be supported by various forms of the division of labor, by a "collective conscience", by religion, etc.

From sociology, the organismic analogy passed into anthropology and was given coherent theoretical expression by Malinowski and Radcliffe-Brown as "structural functionalism" (see Craib, 1992). In structural functionalist analysis, predictably, recurrent activities in a society are explained by the function they perform for the maintenance of that society's needs for survival. The organismic analogy also lent itself very well to the study of organizations. In the next section, on organization and management theory, we shall witness structural-functionalism in a pure form in the work of Selznick and, combined with insights from general system theory, in the account of organizations offered by Katz and Kahn.

In the 1940s and 1950s one version of sociological systems theory came to dominate American sociology. This was, as Buckley (1967) calls it, Talcott Parsons "equilibrium-function model." Parsons attempted to construct a systems model for analyzing all elements of the social world. This consisted, nominally, of a combination of the notion that social systems are made up of the interaction of individuals (drawn from Weber), the mechanical-equilibrium model and a form of structural functionalism concentrating on the functional prerequisites that must be met by social systems if they are to survive. In practice, in Parsons's theory, individual choice is so circumscribed by the "systems of action" people inhabit that it is the two analogies we have been considering to date that hold center stage. As Craib (1992) has it:

> Parsons sees a social system of action as having needs which must be met if it is to survive, and a number of parts which function to meet those needs. All living systems are seen as tending towards equilibrium, a stable and balanced relationship between the different parts, and maintaining themselves separately from other systems (p. 39).

The most famous part of Parsons's equilibrium-function model is the elaboration, with Smelser (1956), of the four functional imperatives that must be adequately fulfilled for a system by its subsystems if that system is to continue to exist. The first letters of these four imperatives - adaptation, goal attainment, integration, and latency (or pattern maintenance), make up the well-known AGIL mnemonic. Due to the recursive character of systems, this AGIL scheme can be employed to analyze and link the various levels of system right through from the individual personality system to the social system. The meaning of the terms that make up AGIL is as follows:

A = adaptation: the system has to establish relationships between itself and its external environment

G = goal attainment: goals have to be defined and resources mobilized and managed in pursuit of those goals

I = integration: the system has to have a means of coordinating its efforts

L = latency (or pattern maintenance): the first three requisites for organizational survival have to be solved with the minimum of strain and tension by ensuring that organizational "actors" are motivated to act in the appropriate manner

The elegance of Parsons's thinking can best be grasped if we turn now to his study of organizations as systems.

The defining characteristic of formal organizations for Parsons (1956, 1957) - that which distinguishes them from other types of social system - is their primacy of orientation to the attainment of a specific goal. The goals of organizations could, following the functionalist logic, be directly related to the needs of the wider society and organizations classified on that basis. So there are:

- Economic organizations, like business firms, oriented to the adaptive function
- Political organizations, like government departments, oriented to the goal-attainment function
- Integrative organizations, like those of the legal profession, oriented to the integrative function
- Latency organizations, like churches and schools, oriented to the pattern maintenance function

Within organizations (made up of interacting individuals), order was maintained by a value system that inculcated shared norms among organizational members. To ensure harmony, this value system had to be congruent with the central value system of society, internalized by individuals during the socialization process (e.g., education). Equilibrium should be easily maintained in this manner since organizations could legitimize themselves in their participants' eyes in terms of the function performed for society. The main source of strain for organizations occurred if the central value system of society began to change. In these circumstances, organizations exhibited "dynamic equilibrium", adapting in the direction of a new type of stability.

The structure of organizations was understood by Parsons through the use of his AGIL scheme. Like all social systems, organizations have to meet four functional imperatives to survive, and so require four types of subsystems to deal with the requirements set out in AGIL.

Parsons (1960) saw the management task in organizations as differing depending upon at which of three levels it operated. At the "technical system level", it was concerned directly with the transformation process; at the "managerial level", with integrating technical-level activities and mediating between these and the institutional level; and at the "institutional level", it integrated the organization with the wider community it was supposed to serve.

Parsons's equilibrium-function model was immensely important in the development of organization theory, influencing among others Katz and Kahn (1966), Thompson (1967) and Kast and Rosenzweig (1981). In his later work, Parsons consolidated his thinking further by incorporating cybernetic insights and certain general system theory formulations: a case of the general systems tradition feeding back into a discipline from which it had itself taken some inspiration.

One of the most highly regarded of recent European sociologists, Niklas Luhmann, makes even more use of modern systems ideas than did Parsons; in his case ideas drawn principally from cybernetics and the theory of autopoiesis. The stature of Luhmann as a thinker can be gauged by the quality of some of the opponents he has drawn into argument. To Habermas, as we saw, Luhmann is the archetypical representative of a type of systems theory that emphasizes "system integration" at the expense of individuals and their concerns and values. To Lyotard, as was mentioned, his work represents the continuation, in a more pessimistic form, of the "systemic modernism" of which Parsons's thinking represented an earlier, more optimistic phase. Even the briefest of introductions, therefore, can provide some benefits.

For Luhmann (1986), drawing on the work of Maturana and Varela but extending the scope of their claims, social systems are autopoietic systems. This means, as we know, that they are geared towards their own self-reproduction and this provides for their autonomy. Thus while they are "irritated" by their environments, they develop according to their own structural arrangements. It is Luhmann's understanding, and this is the most original and radical aspect of his thought, that the basic components constituting the autopoiesis of social systems are "communications." The individual members of social systems do not continually reproduce that system (as many suppose), rather, it is communications or "communicative events":

> The idea of system elements must be changed from substances (individuals) to self-referential operations that can be produced only within the system and with the help of a network of the same operations (autopoiesis). For social systems in general and the system of society in particular the operation of (self-referential) communication seems to be the most appropriate candidate (Luhmann, 1989, pp. 6-7).

Communicative events, therefore, make up "networks of communications" and are constantly referring to the previous communications and necessarily lead on to others. Mingers (1995) points out that Luhmann doesn't actually give any examples of communications to aid understanding of his ideas and has a stab himself:

> In the law, a legal communication might be the judgement of a court. It contains a particular selection of information; ... it is presented in a particular way; ... and it is interpreted in particular ways. The judgement as a whole leads to further communications both directly through its consequences and indirectly as part of case law (p. 143).

At the same time as autopoietic systems are engaged in their self-reproduction they are, through the same processes, defining themselves in relationship to their environment. In Luhmann's conception, therefore, the system or society must be considered not only as a "unity" but also in terms of "difference." This demands a significant readjustment in perspective for any theory of the system of society:

> The theory must change its direction from the unity of the social whole as a smaller unity within a larger one ... to the difference of the systems of society and environment .... More exactly, the theme of sociological investigation is not the system of society, but instead the unity of the difference of the system of society and its environment. In other words, the theme is the world as a whole, seen through the system reference of the system of society. Difference is ... a means of reflecting the system by distinguishing it (Luhmann, 1989, p. 6).

Luhmann uses the cybernetic idea of "requisite variety" to think through the relationship thus created between the societal system and its environment. In essence the problem is that the societal system has to cope with an environment that is much more complex than itself. In order to survive, a system tries to match its own variety to that of the environment, and achieve "requisite variety", by differentiating itself internally and so, simultaneously, restricting the way it perceives the environment. Social evolution, for Luhmann, is determined solely by the developing steering capacities of society as it seeks to manage environmental complexity by expanding system complexity at the same time as controlling that system complexity.

As a result of this internal differentiation, modern society becomes increasingly "function" oriented. Basically this means that "subsystems become established by the particular tasks that they carry out" (Mingers, 1995). With "functional differentiation" the subsystems become increasingly autonomous and eventually distinguish themselves from their environments "self-referentially." The subsystems themselves become "autopoietic unities", demonstrating organizational closure and self-reference:

> Every function system, together with its environment, reconstructs society. Therefore, every function system can plausibly presume to be a society for itself, if and in so far as it is open to its own environment. With the closure of its own autopoiesis it serves one function of the societal system (society). With openness to environmental conditions and changes it realizes that this has to occur in the societal system because society cannot specialize itself to one function alone (Luhmann, 1989, pp. 107-8).

The sociology we have been studying so far, which is all of a functionalist and modernist orientation according to the theoretical considerations of Chapter 3, has clearly been greatly influenced by systems ideas. The same is not the case with sociology that has based itself on alternative traditions such as the interpretive, emancipatory and postmodern. It is, nevertheless, worth briefly considering these traditions if only for the inspiration they provided for later systems thinkers determined to break with the functionalist and modernist orthodoxy.

In looking for affinities between his own soft systems methodology and social theory, Checkland (1981) finds the interpretive tradition much more relevant than the functionalist and identifies the writings of Weber, Dilthey and Schutz as significant. We covered the bare bones of interpretive thinking in Chapter 3 but it is worth adding a little flesh, from sociology, at this point.

Weber's work, along with that of Marx and Durkheim, is often seen as one of the three pillars upon which the sociological enterprise is built. Although there is continuing dispute about whether his complex and wide-ranging *oeuvre* leans more to the functionalist or the interpretive theoretical position, there is no doubt that he was the originator of the "social action" approach that has contributed so much to the latter. Rather than using "system" and "structure" as starting points, Weber argued, sociology should be based upon the study of social actions:

> Sociology ... is a science which attempts the interpretive understanding of social action in order thereby to arrive at a causal explanation of its cause and effects... Action is social in so far as, by virtue of the subjective meaning attached to it by the acting individual (or individuals), it takes account of the behavior of others and is thereby oriented in its course (Weber, 1964, p. 88).

The possibility of interpretively understanding the subjective meaning behind social action gives students of society, Weber thought, an advantage over those working in the natural sciences who can have only external knowledge of their subject matter. To model sociology on the natural sciences therefore, to the exclusion of this "inner-understanding" or *verstehen*, could only impoverish it. There are no social facts "out-there" whose existence can be demonstrated and whose nature can be analyzed by the methods of the natural sciences. "Social relationships" such as states, organizations, corporations and associations

> must be treated as solely the resultants and modes of organization of the particular acts of individual persons, since these alone can be treated as agents in the course of subjectively understandable action (Weber, 1964, p. 101).

It is illegitimate to reify such collectivities, to treat them as things capable of their own social action independent of the individuals who comprise them.

The procedure of *verstehen* could be used by sociologists to yield "meaningfully adequate" interpretations of social action. Weber felt strongly, however, that such interpretations ought to be complemented with considerations of "causal adequacy":

> even the most perfect adequacy on the level of meaning has causal significance from a sociological point of view only in so far as there is some kind of proof for the existence of a probability that action in fact normally takes the course which has been held to be meaningful (Weber, 1964, pp. 99-100).

Weber now faced a problem. This was, in Parsons's words,

> to define the kinds of generalized categories which met the logical requirements of this schema (of logical proof) and at the same time embodied the point of view peculiar to the historical-cultural sciences, the use of subjective categories (Parsons, Introduction, in Weber, 1964, p. 11).

The problem was solved by "ideal types" – Weber's basic theoretical category.

Ideal-types are theoretical constructs related to some finite portion of reality selected according to the sociologist's interests and her view of significance. They should be precisely and unambiguously defined, and reveal their "one-sidedness", in order that there can be no confusion between the theoretical construct and reality. Ideal-types can be theoretical formulations of both rational and irrational phenomena as long as they are adequate at the level of meaning, i.e. embody objectively possible forms of action. They need not relate to ideas which have actually existed in people's heads. They correspond only to the pure type of meaning attributed by the sociologist. Weber's work is replete with examples of "ideal-types" – bureaucracy, Calvinism, feudalism, capitalism. They are always used for one purpose in empirical investigation; for comparison with reality

> in order to establish its divergences or similarities, to describe them with the most unambiguously intelligible concepts, and to understand and explain them causally (Weber, 1969, p. 110).

Dilthey (1833-1911), working within the tradition of "hermeneutics", the theory of interpretation, had offered to sociology an alternative direction almost from its earliest days. He rejected the notion that human actions are governed by laws and are therefore intelligible, like natural events, through the use of the scientific method. To understand human behavior we must interpret it according to people's actual intentions. The method of *verstehen* is recommended as the means to gain such knowledge and to grasp how human intentions give rise, through a process of "objectification", to cultural artifacts. Checkland (1981), exploring Dilthey's thinking, is attracted by his notion of "the hermeneutic circle" – a circular process of enquiry relating parts to wholes, and vice-versa, which gradually leads to greater understanding of social reality being achieved. He also finds of interest Dilthey's use of the concept of *Weltanschauung*. *Weltanschauungen* are world-images constructed on the basis of our views of the world, our evaluation of life, and our ideals. Common types tend to recur and are therefore significantly implicated in the process of objectification.

The "phenomenological sociology" of Schutz can be seen as a synthesis of the work of Weber and of the philosophical originator of phenomenology, Husserl (see earlier section). Schutz's work did not result in the refutation of any of the basic concepts of Weber's interpretive sociology. It did attempt, however, to clarify some of them. Schutz felt that Weber had not stated clearly enough the essential characteristics of *verstehen*, of subjective meaning, or of action. Using the phenomenological method, pioneered by Husserl, Schutz (1967) gives an excellent account of what it is like to live in the world. Craib (1992) summarizes as follows:

> He attempted to show how we build our knowledge of the social world from a basic stream of incoherent and meaningless experience. We do this through a processes of 'typification', which involves building up classes of experience through similarity .... We build up what Schutz calls 'meaning contexts', sets of criteria by means of which we organize our sense experience into a meaningful world and stocks of knowledge, which are not stocks of knowledge about the world but, for all practical purposes, the world itself. Action and social action thus become things that happen in consciousness: we are concerned with acts of consciousness rather than action in the world, and the social world is something which we create together (p. 99).

If interpretive sociology provided significant theoretical assistance to soft systems methodology, Marxist sociology, as a representative approach from "radical" social theory, played a similar role for emancipatory and critical systems thinking. Systems thinkers with emancipatory concerns were able to find, in Marxist thought, guidelines for using systems methods and models in a radical manner. It helped, of course, as our overviews of the work of Habermas (Chapter 3) and Althusser (earlier section) showed, that there were systems ideas already at work in the Marxist tradition. Almost exactly the same argument can be made for postmodernism and systems thinking. The main impact was in providing systems practitioners with a reorientation of thought and practice, but this was assisted by "systemic" aspects of post-structuralism. We leave the full explication of these relationships until Part II.

It remains only to mention the work of those sociologists who have been seen as candidates for unifying the diverse strands of sociological theory. Giddens's theory of structuration is put forward by Haralambos and Holborn (1995) as possibly uniting structural and social action approaches. Structuration theory explores the "duality of structure" whereby structures both make social action possible and, at the same time, are created by social action. For example,

> just as every sentence in English expresses within itself the totality which is the 'language' as a whole, so every interaction bears the imprint of the global society (Giddens, 1976, p. 122).

During interaction individuals make use of facilities drawn from the global society (such as power) and at the same time as they apply them, in interaction, reproduce the structures of the global society. During the process of speaking a language and recreating structures, of course, some possibility for originality and change will be present to the individual or group. However, this is exactly where the problem arises. As Archer says:

> The theory of structuration remains incomplete because it provides an insufficient account of the mechanisms of stable replication versus the genesis of new social forms (quoted in Haralambos and Holborn, 1995, p. 907).

For Craib (1992) it is Habermas who is capable of bridging the "action paradigm" and the "structure paradigm." Certainly his attempt to reconcile hermeneutics, positivism and Marxism, and to see value in each, is original and monumental in its scope, but criticisms, especially from a postmodern perspective, remain. This matter of whether different sociological perspectives can be combined is not simply an academic one that can be left to social theorists. As we shall see in Part III, some critical systems thinkers favor looking for an all-embracing theory (such as provided by Giddens or Habermas) to guide their practice, while others accept "paradigm incommensurability" and prefer to work with a variety of competing positions. The choice has some significant implications for intervention.

4.6. MANAGEMENT AND ORGANIZATION THEORY

From the 1930s onward, three different models of management competed for precedence in organization theory: the traditional approach, human relations theory and systems thinking (Kast and Rosenzweig, 1981). The traditional approach was based upon Taylor's scientific management, Fayol's administrative management theory and Weber's bureaucracy theory, and encouraged the view that organizations were like machines. This view was considered briefly in Chapter 3 and has been subject to criticism from many commentators. Human relations theory grew out of the critique of the traditional approach, particularly its alleged failure to take account of human needs. Theorists such as Mayo, Maslow, Herzberg, and McGregor studied and drew conclusions about issues such as group behavior, individual motivation, and leadership. While it was a useful corrective to traditional theory to put humans and their needs at the center of organizational analysis, this could easily lead to the neglect of factors such as the market, technology, competition and organizational structure; factors that, it is arguable, have far more effect on organizational performance than decisions on how to manage people. Organizations have to take account of human needs, but not at the expense of everything else (Perrow, 1972).

Gradually, because of the weaknesses of traditional and human relations thinking and because of its superiority, the systems approach came to dominate management and organization theory. Systems thinkers argued that organizations should be seen as whole systems made up of interrelated parts. The trouble with other theories of management, according to the systems perspective, was that they concentrated on only one or two of the aspects of the organization necessary for high performance. The traditional approach concentrated on task and structure, and the human relations approach on people. The systems approach was said to be "holistic" because it believed in looking at organizations as wholes. The traditional and human relations approaches were "reductionist" because they looked at parts of the organization in isolation. Another significant advantage claimed for the systems approach was that it saw the organization as an "open system" in constant interaction with its environment. This was opposed to the limited, "closed" perspective of the traditional and human relations models, which tended to ignore the environment.

The systems approach first expressed itself in the form of the mechanical equilibrium model, originally derived from Pareto and popularized in the United States through Henderson's "Pareto Circle" (see previous sub-section). Barnard's book, *The Functions of the Executive* (1938), is the classic example but consideration of this will be saved until Chapter 6 because of its continuing contemporary relevance. Of equal importance historically is the work of Roethlisberger and Dickson (1956), who used this kind of thinking to explain the findings of the famous Hawthorne experiments and to consider what factors might cause the personal disequilibrium of workers.

Figure 4.1, taken from Roethlisberger and Dickson's *Management and the Worker* (1956), shows the kind of equilibrium analysis employed to understand what were, in simple cause and effect terms, the baffling results of the experiments. A key element in the figure is "Organism or Individual in Equilibrium" which, in this context, means presumed to be working effectively. If a worker is knocked out of equilibrium this will trigger complaints about his work situation and/or reduced work effectiveness. Such an outcome cannot be explained in terms of just one simple cause; rather, it comes about through the mutual influence of a whole variety of interconnected factors, ranging from those pertaining to the individual himself (e.g. personal history), to those concerned with work conditions (e.g. social milieu), to social conditions outside the factory. If equilibrium is disturbed then the complex relationships between the elements will eventually ensure that either the old order is restored or a new form of equilibrium is obtained. Also noteworthy is Roethlisberger and Dickson's attention to "Social Conditions Outside Factory." In their view this shifts their analysis beyond the "closed system" perspective. While this is true it does not make it an "open systems" approach in von Bertalanffy's sense. There is a vast difference between disturbance from the environment and the living off and with the environment that von Bertalanffy describes.

Indeed, it was not until the organismic analogy replaced the mechanical equilibrium analogy, as the basis for the systems approach to management, that systems thinking became of overwhelming significance in the organizational sciences. The organismic analogy lent itself very well, of course, to the study of organizations. Organizations could be represented as primarily geared to ensuring the survival and continuity of themselves as systems. The various parts of organizations could be understood in terms of the contributions they made to the maintenance of the whole organization. The variety of organismic systems models has

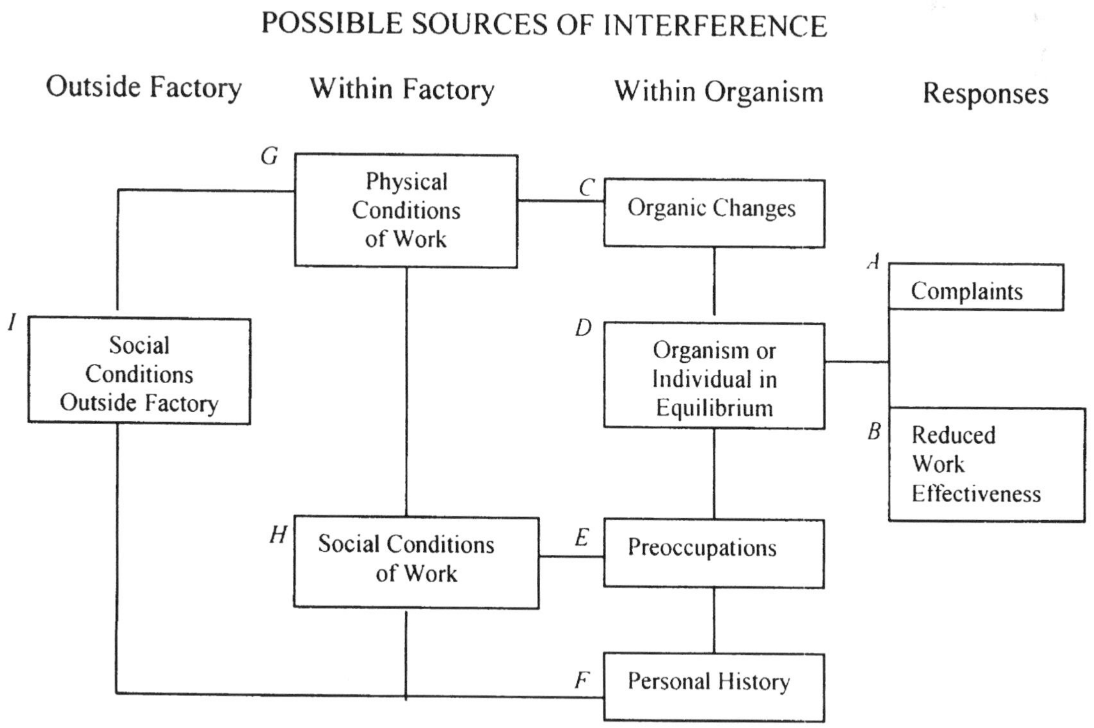

POSSIBLE SOURCES OF INTERFERENCE

Figure 4.1. Scheme for interpreting complaints and reduced work effectiveness (reproduced from Roethlisberger and Dickson, 1956, p. 327).

been so great that all I can do in this section is pick out two of the most important landmark – Selznick's adaptation of "structural functionalism" for the study of organizations and Katz and Kahn's marrying together of Parsonian ideas with a rigorous working out of the nature of "open systems" derived from von Bertalanffy. We covered Parsons's "equilibrium function" model in the previous section. The explicitly prescriptive side of the organismic systems approach is considered in the sections on socio-technical systems thinking and contingency theory in Chapter 6.

Selznick (1948), seeking to analyze what organizations were like, found himself diverging considerably from the traditional view that they were instruments of rational action. Following Barnard, he saw that they were cooperative systems with both formal and informal aspects; rational action embodied in the formal structure was modified by the social needs of individuals. Such cooperative systems were also subject to the pressure of their environments, to which some adjustment had to be made. Organizations were, therefore, "adaptive structures" that had to adapt their goals and change themselves in response to environmental circumstances. To Selznick it appeared that many of the adjustments made by organizations, in response to both internal and external determinants, took place independently of the consciousness of the individuals involved. Organizations were acting like organisms, reacting to influences upon them in ways best designed to ensure their own survival.

Selznick derived his insights from sociological systems theory and it seemed to him that, if organizations behaved in this manner, the best way of studying them was to use structural-functionalist analysis. Organizations were primarily oriented to their own survival. They had needs that had to be met if survival was to be ensured. For Selznick, organizations possessed the following stable needs, deriving from their nature as co-operative systems and adaptive structures:

- Security of the organization in relation to social forces in its environment
- Stability of the lines of authority and communication
- Stability of informal relations
- Continuity of policy and the sources of its determination
- A homogeneous outlook with respect to the meaning and role of the organization

Activity in an organization was best understood not in terms of conscious purpose, but by how it contributed to meeting these needs, or "functional imperatives", of the organization.

Sociological systems theory, through Selznick and Parsons, contributed to organization and management theory an understanding of the nature and role of organizational subsystems in meeting organizational needs. Further progress came from biology by way of general system theory. It was not long before von Bertalanffy's rigorous working out of the idea that organisms were open systems was transferred, in the manner of general system theory, to other disciplines. By the 1960s it had become thoroughly absorbed into organization theory, with the rich armory of concepts surrounding the open system notion complementing those of structural functionalism. Katz and Kahn's 1966 (second edition 1978) *The Social Psychology of Organizations* was the classic expression of this new development, the more so since it succeeded in integrating the open-systems notion with ideas from psychology and much from Parsons's sociology.

Katz and Kahn begin by pointing out the advantages of their approach. It is more "scientific" than the traditional view because it does not fall into the trap of identifying organizational purposes with the goals of individual members. Organizations are systems with their own goals. Further, the traditional and human relations approaches take a closed view of the organization. It is clearly advantageous to abandon this and to start looking at organizations as open systems. Organizations are best represented as entities in close interrelationship with their environments, taking in inputs and transforming them into outputs. These outputs, in the form of products, can provide the means for new inputs, so that the cycle can begin again. The main purpose is to maintain a steady state and to survive.

Reviewing and building on von Bertalanffy's findings, Katz and Kahn have it that ten characteristics define all open systems (including, of course, organizations):

- The importation of energy from the external environment
- The throughput and transformation of the input in the system
- The output, which is exported to the environment
- Systems as cycles of events: the output furnishes new sources of energy for the input so the cycle can start again
- Negative entropy: open systems "live" off their environments, acquiring more energy than they spend
- Information input, negative feedback and a coding process: systems selectively gather information about their environments and also about their own activities (so they can take corrective action)
- The steady state and dynamic homeostasis: despite continuous inflow and export of energy, the character of the system remains the same.
- Differentiation: open systems move in the direction of differentiation and structure elaboration (e.g., greater specialization of functions)
- Integration and co-ordination to ensure unified functioning
- Equifinality

Other significant aspects of the Katz and Kahn model closely follow Parsons's thinking. Five generic types of subsystem are recognized that meet the organization's functional needs:

- The *production* or technical subsystem, concerned with the work done on the throughput
- The *supportive* subsystem, concerned with obtaining inputs and disposing of outputs
- The *maintenance* subsystem, which ensures conformance of personnel to their roles through selection, and through rewards and sanctions
- The *adaptive* subsystem, ensuring responsiveness to environmental variations
- The *managerial* subsystem, which directs, coordinates, and controls other subsystems and activities through various regulatory mechanisms

The occasion when the "organizations–as–systems" approach yielded its unchallenged hegemony in U.K. organization theory can be precisely dated to 1970 and the publication of Silverman's *The Theory of Organizations*. In this book Silverman undertook a damning critique of systems thinking in management, at least in its functionalist form, and proposed as an alternative an "action frame of reference", ultimately deriving from the work of Weber. This alternative was presented as an "ideal-type" of action theory constituted by seven propositions which are summarized in Table 4.2.

This critique, and the alternative proposed by Silverman, were so persuasive to many organization and management theorists that they wrote off systems thinking for more than a generation. Following Silverman's lead, they explored phenomenological, ethnomethodological, Marxist and, eventually, postmodern approaches to organizational analysis without recognizing that systems thinkers were engaged in a similar exploration in their own discipline, albeit with practical action as the primary concern (Checkland, 1994; Galliers, Jackson and Mingers, 1997). In return, it must be said, systems thinkers largely ignored what was going on in organization theory.

A more fruitful relationship was established between the reflective practitioner Sir Geoffrey Vickers and systems thinking. Vickers found systems concepts and ideas of more use than those of any other discipline he came across for explaining what he had experienced in his long career as a manager and decision-maker. At the same time he rejected the simplicities of the goal-seeking and cybernetic systems paradigms that were dominant at the time he was writing, and extended his systems studies to embrace meaning and judgement, and how these were linked to the culture and history of society. For Vickers, achieving stability in social systems involves much more than establishing a goal from outside the system, monitoring performance and taking corrective action on the basis of feedback information. Multiple possible courses of action are generated from within social systems. Societies and organizations can only be governed through a complex process in which shared norms and values are established and maintained. This makes possible, but also depends on, the negotiation of relationships between different participants. The interpretive aspect in this account of social systems, and how they adapt and change, has provided sustenance to those interested in developing the soft systems perspective.

The most important notion employed by Vickers in developing his study of the "peculiarities of human systems" (Vickers, 1983) is that of an "appreciative system." Vickers argues that the components of human systems, active individuals attributing meaning to their situation, make it impossible to study such systems using the methods of the natural sciences. The only way to understand decision-making in human systems is to understand the different appreciative systems that the decision makers bring to bear on a problem (Vickers, 1965, 1970). Appreciative systems are "the interconnected set of largely tacit standards of judgement by which we both order and value our experience" (Vickers, 1973).

Table 4.2. Silverman's ideal type of action theory (adapted from Silverman, 1970, pp. 126-127)

1.	The social and natural sciences have entirely different types of subject matter
2.	Sociology is concerned with understanding action rather than observing behavior Action derives from meaning attached to social reality
3.	Meanings derive from society, become institutionalised and can be experienced as social facts
4.	While society defines man, man also defines society. Particular constellations of meaning have to be continually reaffirmed
5.	Through their interactions men can modify, change and transform social meanings
6.	Explanations of human actions must take account of the meanings of those involved in the social construction of reality
7.	Positivistic explanations asserting that action is determined by constraining forces are inadmissible

An individual's appreciative system will determine the way she sees (reality judgement) and values (value judgement) various situations and condition how she makes "instrumental judgements" (what is to be done?) and takes "executive action"; in short, how she contributes to the construction of the social world. It follows, according to Vickers, that if human systems are to achieve stability and effectiveness, the appreciative systems of their participants need to be sufficiently shared to allow mutual understandings to be achieved. Human systems depend upon shared understandings and shared cultures.

It should be pointed out that Vickers's social theory (as far as it can be pieced together from hints in his various writings - see Jackson, 1978) is not itself interpretive. For Vickers, developments in human society depend upon interactions between a "world of ideas" and a "world of events" as they intertwine in a "two-stranded rope." They do not depend solely upon changes in appreciative systems. Nevertheless, the interpretive element in his thinking does offer a useful starting point for anyone interested in producing interpretive systems theory and enriching soft systems methodology. It was Checkland who first recognized Vickers's significance in this respect, and he has since used Vickers's work as an important theoretical support for his own interpretive systems-based methodology for problem solving (Checkland, 1981, 1989; Checkland and Casar, 1986).

4.7. CONTROL ENGINEEERING AND CYBERNETICS

As was noted in the earlier section on "Philosophy", the nature and importance of control processes was known to the ancient Greeks. The Greek word *kybernetes*, meaning the art of steersmanship, was employed by Plato to refer both to the piloting of a vessel and to the steering of the "ship of state." From the Greek *kybernetes* came the Latin *gubernator*, and hence the English governor. This last word, of course, also has technical and political meanings, both relating to control. Watt's 1788 "governor" is perhaps the most famous of all automatic control devices. As part of a steam engine, it is the self-adjusting valve mechanism that keeps the engine working at constant speed under varying conditions of load. A governor in the political domain is a public steersman or political decision maker. In the nineteenth century, Ampère kept the word *kybernetes* alive in the discipline of political science. Claude Bernard, a physiologist writing in the 1860s and 70s, was fully aware of control processes taking place in organisms which were analogous to those operating in machines and politics. In the twentieth century, the study of the mathematics of control processes has given rise to the academic discipline of control theory and the application of the ideas in the profession of control engineering. Much of this work is highly technical and should not detain us here. We look at some more general applications of the ideas when we consider the systems engineering approach in Chapter 6. At the same time, however, recognition and attention to the ubiquitous nature of control processes in all fields of study gave birth to a new science - "cybernetics." Cybernetics is not itself a discipline. Rather it is a transdiscipline, the establishment of which, like general system theory, signaled the emergence of systems thinking in its own right. It is cybernetics as a transdiscipline that has provided the vehicle through which, as Checkland, 1981, remarks:

> ideas from control theory and from information and communication engineering have made contributions to systems thinking no less important than those from organismic biology (pp. 83-84).

During World War II scientists from different disciplines - physicists, electrical engineers, mathematicians, physiologists, etc. - were brought together to work on military problems. An interdisciplinary ferment was created and one group of scientists became aware of the essential unity of a set of problems surrounding communication and control whether in machines or biological entities. Norbert Wiener was at the center of this group, which also included J.H. Bigelow who had worked with Wiener during the war on improving the accuracy of anti-aircraft guns, and A. Rosenblueth, a medical scientist and a colleague of W.B. Cannon.

Wiener first used the name cybernetics for a specific field of study in 1947. In 1948 his book *Cybernetics* was published, bringing together contemporary ideas about control processes and establishing the famous definition of cybernetics as the science of control and communication in the animal and the machine. Almost as soon as it was coined, however, this definition appeared too limiting and Wiener himself (1950) applied the insights of cybernetics to human concerns. Cybernetics was to be a true interdisciplinary science. It had general applicability, Wiener argued, because it dealt with general laws that governed control processes, whatever the nature of the system under governance. The two key concepts elucidated by Wiener at this time were control and communication. In understanding control, whether in the mechanical, biological, or political realm, the idea of negative feedback was shown to be crucial. This allows a scientific explanation to be provided for behavior directed to the attainment of a goal. All such behavior depends upon the use of negative feedback. In this process, information is transmitted about any divergence of behavior from a preset goal and corrective action taken, on the basis of this information, to bring the behavior back toward the goal. Communication is equally significant, because if we wish to control the actions of a machine or another human being, then we must communicate with that machine or individual. Thus the theory of control can be seen as part of the theory of messages. Control involves the communication of information. In developing this aspect of their work, cyberneticians were able to draw on the 1949 volume *The Mathematical Theory of Communication*, by the communications engineers Shannon and Weaver.

The continuing growth of interest in cybernetics in the 1950s owed much to the work of W. Ross Ashby, who published his most famous book, *An Introduction to Cybernetics,* in 1956. As well as being a popularizing text it introduced the important notion of "variety" and the well-known "law of requisite variety." The book also demonstrated again how cybernetics could impact on many different areas of thought. Ashby noted how it should reveal numerous interesting and suggestive parallels between machine, brain and society. Interest in the new science was indeed spreading beyond engineers and physiologists to psychologists, sociologists, anthropologists and political scientists. In 1959 Stafford Beer published *Cybernetics and Management* and then, in 1961, J.W. Forrester's *Industrial Dynamics* appeared. As a result the list of those interested began to include management scientists and managers.

The names of Beer and Forrester continue to dominate management cybernetics to this day. Beer (1959a) was the first to apply cybernetics to management in any comprehensive fashion (in his book *Cybernetics and Management*), defining management as the science and profession of control. He also offered a new definition of cybernetics as the "science of effective organization" (Beer, 1979). Throughout the 1960s and early 1970s Beer was a prolific writer and an influential practitioner. It was during this period that his model of any viable system, the VSM, was developed. This could be used to diagnose the faults in any existing organizational system or to design new systems along sound cybernetic lines. Forrester (1961, 1969) invented system dynamics, which held out the promise that the behavior of whole systems could be represented and understood through modeling the dynamic feedback processes going on within them. Forrester's work found a great range of applications, from the study of industrial to urban to world dynamics. Using system dynamics models, decision makers can experiment with possible changes to variables to see what effect this has on overall system behavior.

To prepare the ground for detailed analysis of the work of Beer and Forrester and indeed of many other systems approaches, in later chapters, it is necessary at this point to introduce some of the key concepts developed in cybernetics. If we do so taking our examples largely from the managerial domain it will further assist our later studies and help to demonstrate the relevance of cybernetics to the concerns of this book.

According to Beer (1959a), systems which are worthy of being suitable subjects of concern for cybernetics (as opposed to statistics, operational research, etc.) are likely to demonstrate the characteristics of extreme complexity, self-regulation and probabilism. Cybernetics provides a way of analyzing each of these characteristics and tools to enable managers to cope. Simplifying considerably (since in fact the cybernetic tools represent an interrelated response to the characteristics of cybernetic systems), extreme complexity can be dealt with using the black box technique, self-regulation can be appropriately managed using negative feedback and probabilism yields to the method of variety engineering (Schoderbek, Schoderbek, and Kefalas, 1985). It is these three building blocks of cybernetic management that I shall now seek to elucidate in this section.

4.7.1. The Black Box Technique

Let us consider first the idea of complexity and what is meant by this. According to Schoderbek *et al.* (1985), the complexity of a system is the combined outcome of the interaction of four main determinants:

- The number of elements comprising the system
- The interactions among these elements
- The attributes of the specified elements of the system
- The degree of organization in the system (i.e., whether there are predetermined rules guiding the interactions or specifying the attributes)

It is extremely important to consider the last two of these factors in judging complexity. On the face of it, a car engine can look complex in terms of the number of elements and interactions, but in fact is relatively simple because of the limited attributes of the specified elements and the high degree of organization in the system. A two-person interaction may appear simple, but in fact can be very complex once we add in the diverse attributes of humans and the lack of specified organization in many such systems.

Considering these four determinants of complexity, it is obvious how complexity can soon proliferate alarmingly in organizations. Exceedingly complex systems, which are so complicated that they cannot be described in any precise or detailed fashion, will be common. These systems, it follows, cannot be easily examined in order to discover what processes are responsible for system behavior. In cybernetics, a system of this type is called a "black box." By contrast, a box within which all possible states are observable and can be understood is "transparent." Organizations and their environments are close to being black boxes. In order to cope with black boxes, managers and their advisers need to gain some knowledge of system behavior, even if they can never fully understand what causes the behavior. How can this be achieved?

According to Ashby (1956), the way *not* to proceed in approaching an exceedingly complex system - a black box - is by analysis. Reductionist analysis of each of the separate parts of the system will never enable whole interactions to be understood. If we take a complex system apart for analysis, we find that we cannot reassemble it in a way that produces the same pattern of behavior. Instead of analysis, therefore, the black box technique of input manipulation and output classification should be employed. By this procedure, an experimenter may discover some regularities that make the system more predictable. The black box technique is shown diagrammatically in Figure 4.2.

Managers of complex enterprises cannot hope to understand all the possible combinations of interactions within the systems under their control. They should not, therefore, seek to proceed by analysis, but should apply the black box technique of manipulating inputs and observing outputs. Faced with a black box, a manager does not have to enter it to learn something about it. Instead, the system is investigated by the collection of a long protocol, drawn out in time, showing the sequence of input and output states. The manager can then manipulate the inputs to try to find regularities in the outputs. Initially, if nothing is known about the box, random variations of input will be as good as any. As regularities become established, a more directed program of research can be conducted.

There are problems with the black box technique, as when a particular experiment changes a system to such an extent that it cannot be returned to its original state for further experiments (Ashby, 1956). It is also very important not to jump to conclusions about the behavior of a system without observing it for a sufficient length of time (Beer, 1979). Nevertheless, it is an important tool that managers *have* to use at all times, because only by working with black boxes can they avoid being overwhelmed by confusing detail. The more conscious they become of this, the more informed will be the way they break down their organizations into black boxes for control purposes. Once this level of sophistication is reached, the technique can be seen to have profound implications for organizational modeling and for the design of appropriate information systems.

4.7.2. Negative Feedback

Exceedingly complex probabilistic systems have to be controlled through self-regulation. The understanding of self-regulation that cybernetics can provide is important to

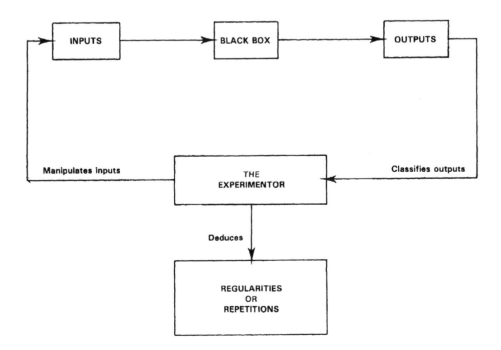

Figure 4.2. The black box technique (adapted from Schoderbeck *et al.*, 1985)

managers for two reasons. First, it is the existence of mechanisms bringing about self-regulation that gives a degree of stability to the environment of organizations. It is useful to managers to know how this stability comes about and how it might be threatened, especially by an organization's own actions. Second, if managers understand the nature of self-regulation they may be able to induce it in the organizations they manage. This is desirable because managers lack the "requisite variety" to intervene in all the decisions that will have to be made. It is also necessary because managers cannot accurately determine what types of environmental disturbance their organizations will have to face. They should therefore seek to make their organizations "ultrastable" (Beer, 1981a), capable of continuing to pursue the goal for which they were designed whatever the prevailing environmental conditions. This again requires self-regulation.

The work of Wiener (1948) has established that the way to ensure self-regulation is through the negative feedback mechanism. The feedback control system is characterized by its closed-loop structure. It operates by the continuous feedback of information about the output of the system. This output is then compared with some predetermined goal, and if the system is not achieving its goal, then the margin of error (the negative feedback) becomes the basis for adjustments to the system designed to bring it closer to realizing the goal. A simple closed-loop feedback system is represented in Figure 4.3. It seems that, for this system to work properly, four elements are required:

- A desired goal, which is conveyed to the comparator from outside the system
- A sensor (a means of sensing the current state of the system)
- A comparator, which compares the current state and the desired outcome
- An activator (a decision-making element that responds to any discrepancies discovered by the comparator in such a way as to bring the system back toward its goal)

This kind of control system is extremely effective, since any movement away from the goal automatically sets in motion changes aimed at bringing the system back onto course (Schoderbek *et al.*, 1985). It is the basis on which central heating and air-conditioning systems operate to maintain a constant room temperature. Homeostasis in the body is achieved by negative feedback, so that the body is able to maintain stability in spite of extensive shifts in outside circumstances. An example is the homeostatic process by which warm-blooded animals maintain their body heat at around 37°C. Cooling of the body stimulates certain centers in the brain, which "turn on" heat-generating mechanisms. Picking up a pen from a desk, constantly registering the discrepancy between the position of the hand and the pen, involves negative feedback. So, too, can managers achieve better regulation of social organizations by ensuring that appropriate negative feedback processes are in place.

A number of additional points should be made before we leave the concept of negative feedback. First, in designing feedback control systems, it is important that managers ensure that there is rapid and continuous comparison of actual performance against the desired goal, and similarly rapid and continuous taking of corrective action if necessary. If there are delays or lags in the system, attempted adjustments may only add to instability. We are all familiar with the situation where attempts to slow down an apparently still-overheated economy only send the economy into a slump because, in fact, the economy's slowing down of its own accord has not yet been registered.

Second, it should be noted that we have been discussing only simple, first-order feedback systems (see Schoderbek *et al.*, 1985). More sophisticated (second-order) systems are capable of considering and choosing among a variety of different responses to changes in an attempt to bring the system back toward its goal. Still more sophisticated (third-order) systems are capable of changing the goal state itself in response to feedback processes. In this case the goal is determined inside the system, and does not originate externally as in Figure 4.3.

Finally, it should be emphasized that feedback control alone may not be enough to achieve adequate regulation of organizations (see Strank, 1982). It is usually necessary to employ strategic control, based upon "feedforward" information that attempts to predict disturbances before they actually affect the organization. It may also be useful to try external control, attempting to intervene directly in the environment to make it more congenial to the organization.

4.7.3. Variety Engineering

Managers are unable to make accurate predictions either about the organizations they manage or the environments within which those organizations are situated. They are continually confronted by unexpected occurrences that they and their organizations must have the capacity to respond to if those organizations are going to be successful. They have to learn to live with probabilistic systems.

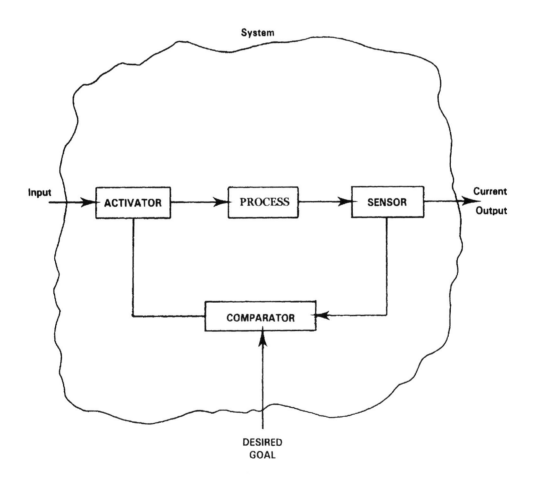

Figure 4.3. A closed-loop feedback system

Fortunately, cyberneticians have taken an interest in probabilistic systems and, thanks to Ashby (1956), can provide some understanding of the difficulties faced by managers and ways of dealing with them. Ashby takes the credit because of his invention of the key concept of *variety*. The variety of a system is defined here as the number of possible states it is capable of exhibiting. It is, therefore, a measure of complexity. Obviously, variety is a subjective concept depending on the observer. A football team's variety will be much greater if one is assessing it as the manager of an opposing team, compared to if one is assessing it for a draw on the football pools. Just as obviously, organizations and their environments are systems that possess massive variety from the point of view of managers.

The problem for managers, as Ashby's "law of requisite variety" has it, is that only variety can destroy variety. In order to control a system, we need to have as much variety available to us as the system itself exhibits. So, if a machine has 20 ways of breaking down, we need to be able to respond in 20 different ways to be in control of the machine. If managers are going to control their organizations and make them responsive to environmental fluctuations, they must command as much variety as these systems themselves exhibit. Sometimes exhibiting requisite variety is easy enough. If I am engaged in a game of noughts and crosses (tic-tac-toe) and I am reasonably skilled, I can always exhibit enough variety to prevent my opponent from winning. But what if we are faced (like managers) with systems exhibiting apparently massive variety? How can we cope with this?

The answer is that we must either reduce the variety of the system we are confronting (variety reduction) or increase our own variety (variety amplification). This process of balancing varieties is known as "variety engineering" (Beer, 1979). Since the variety equation initially seems to place managers at a huge disadvantage, they will require all the skills of variety engineering if they are to balance varieties and (following the law of requisite variety) achieve control. And this must be done in ways appropriate to the organization being considered and its goals. For example, if I am manager of a relatively low-variety football team that is facing a high-variety football team, such as Manchester United, and I want to win, I have to engage in variety engineering. I must amplify the variety of my team, perhaps by improving their tactics or by entering the transfer market. Alternatively, I could reduce the variety of the Manchester United team by allocating a player to take their best player out of the game, or by gaining information about their pattern of play (thereby making it more predictable).

Managers have to learn how to use variety reducers, filtering out the vast complexity of operational and environmental variety and capturing only that of relevance to themselves and the organization. And they have to learn how to use variety amplifiers, amplifying their own variety vis-à-vis the operations and the organizations's variety vis-à-vis its environment. Figure 4.4 (after Espejo, 1977) represents this managerial variety engineering.

We now have the three most important building blocks of cybernetics – the black box technique, negative feedback and variety engineering – in place. I want however, before moving on, to mention another aspect of feedback which it was necessary to understand before system dynamics could be developed. As well as negative feedback, which is deviation counteracting and therefore used as the basis for all control systems, there is also "positive feedback." This is deviation amplifying. The positive feedback process is one where the output is fed back to the input, but rather than reducing any divergence from the goal it produces a further movement in the direction in which the output is already moving. In a seminal paper written in 1963 (reproduced in Buckley, ed., 1968), Maruyama berated cyberneticians for focusing on deviation–counteracting relationships and all but ignoring mutual causal processes which are deviation amplifying:

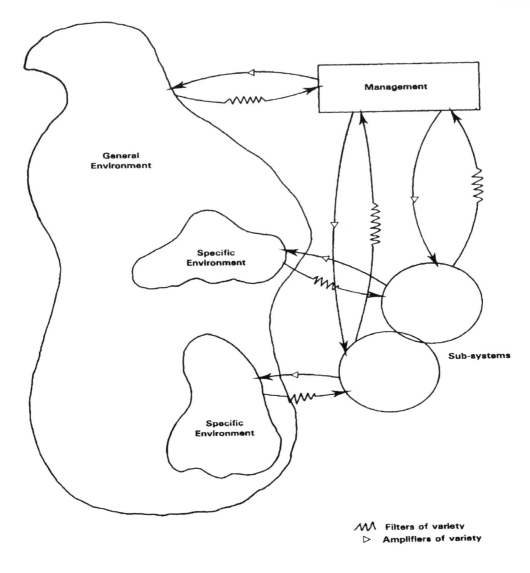

Figure 4.4. Managerial variety engineering (adapted from Espejo, 1977)

> Such systems are ubiquitous: accumulation of capital in industry, evolution of living organ-
> isms, the rise of cultures of various types, interpersonal processes which produce mental ill-
> ness, international conflicts, and the processes that are loosely termed as 'vicious circles' and
> 'compound interests'; in short, all processes of mutual causal relationships that amplify an
> insignificant or accidental initial kick, build up deviation and diverge from the initial condi-
> tion (Maruyama in Buckley, ed., 1968, p. 304).

Maruyama notes that the deviation–counteracting process is also called "morphostasis",
while the deviation–amplifying process is called "morphogenesis." Since they both involve
mutual feedback, they clearly fall within the domain of cybernetics. Because study of the
first type has been so predominant, he suggests calling this "the first cybernetics" and giving
the name "the second cybernetics" to the newer study of deviation amplifying relationships.

Having identified the need for "the second cybernetics" Maruyama, in the same article,
goes on to examine positive and negative feedback networks and the possible relationships
between the two:

A society or an organism contains many deviation-amplifying loops as well as deviation-counteracting loops, and an understanding of a society or an organism cannot be attained without studying both types of loops and the relationships between them (in Buckley, ed., 1968, p. 312).

Loops exist where each element has an influence, either directly or indirectly, on all other elements and each element influences itself through other elements. There is, therefore, no hierarchical causal priority involved. Maruyama begins to unpick the characteristics of loops involving both deviation-counteracting and deviation-amplifying relationships. Questions can then be asked about the behavior of systems containing many interacting loops with different qualities. Such questions, as we shall see in Chapter 6, are core concerns of system dynamics.

Our brief overview of the development of control engineering and cybernetics has concentrated on the control part of the definition of cybernetics: the science of control and communication. The importance of the second of these concepts must not, however, be overlooked. The recognition that it is information flows and communication links that, more than anything else, bind organizations together represents significant progress over the management and organization theory previously considered. Cybernetic models can provide the detailed understanding necessary for the effective design of information systems to aid managerial control.

4.8. THE PHYSICAL SCIENCES AND TOWARD SYNTHESIS

Fritjof Capra has for some time (e.g. *The Tao of Physics*, 1975) been pointing to similarities between the holistic understanding of the world supplied by Eastern philosophy and some of the findings of modern science. One part of the argument he has been developing is that in all of the disciplines of the natural sciences – physics, chemistry, biology – it has been necessary for scientists to abandon the mechanistic and deterministic assumptions underlying the Newtonian world view. In order to understand the nature of reality they have had to forge a new perspective which recognizes relationships and indeterminacy; in short, a perspective that is much more systemic in character. In a recent book (Capra, 1996), he makes it clear that, in his opinion, acceptance and enhancement of this new paradigm is essential to tackling the problems that we face in the world today. The major problems are all systemic problems and must be tackled from this new "holistic ecological viewpoint."

Capra's contribution highlights the value of holistic investigation, whether the phenomena studied are physical, biological or social. Systems thinkers should not, therefore, write off the physical sciences as having little interest for them because they are wedded to reductionism and determinism. Holistic explanation is playing an increasing role in these sciences as well. Indeed, some of the discoveries in the physical sciences, in quantum physics, thermodynamics and chaos theory for example, have significant value for systems thinkers more generally whatever their field of study. This opens up the possibility of a synthesis across all the disciplines, with certain key concepts of a systemic nature playing a significant role whether in physics, chemistry, biology, psychology, sociology or management. The opportunity for a new general system theory emerges. This time, rather than the physical sciences being excluded because von Bertalanffy despaired of their reductionism, they might, because of their sophistication and rigor, take the leading role in transferring adequate theories and models to those disciplines which lack them.

In this section we look at the work of some systems thinkers, particularly Jantsch, Wheatley and Capra, whose reading of the natural sciences suggests that a synthesis across all disciplines might be possible based upon holistic thinking. We also pick up on some of the systemic work in the physical sciences which we have not covered so far but which is starting to have an important influence on systems thinking generally; in particular Prigogine's Nobel prize winning study of "dissipative structures."

Jantsch, in his 1980 publication *The Self-Organizing Universe,* refers to the "new paradigm" he sees as relevant across the physical, biological and social sciences as the "paradigm of self-organization." His book is aimed at creating

> a new *synthesis*, at letting appear the contours of an emergent unifying paradigm which sheds
> unexpected light on the all-embracing phenomenon of evolution (Jantsch, 1980, p. xiii).

The view of "self-organizing evolution" presented is non-reductionist and directs our attention toward

> ... an increasing awareness of being connected with the environment in space and time
> (Jantsch, 1980, p.3).

To illustrate this idea and to formulate his new synthesis, Jantsch draws primarily upon Prigogine's theory of dissipative structures and the notion of autopoiesis introduced by Maturana and Varela. These scientists evinced

> profound concern for self-determination and self-organization, for openness and plasticity of
> structures and for their freedom to evolve (Jantsch, 1980, p. 1).

An appreciation of their work is crucial because

> biological and social systems need an understanding of phenomena such as self-organization
> and self-regulation, coherent behavior over time with structural change, individuality, com-
> munication with the environment and symbiosis, morphogenesis and space-time-binding in
> evolution (Jantsch, 1980, p. 6)

Summarizing his findings, Jantsch identifies three central aspects of the emerging paradigm of self-organization:

> [1] a specific macroscopic dynamics of process systems; [2] continuous exchange and
> thereby co-evolution with the environment; [3] self-transcendence, the evolution of evolu-
> tionary processes (1980, p 9).

A process view of systems replaces the traditional view of systems as being made up of "solid" components and making up solid structures. Systems instead appear as sets of coherent, evolving, interactive processes which may temporarily manifest themselves as stable structures. A view of evolution as merely "adaptation and survival" is replaced by a perspective focussing on co-evolution. As life evolves so, at the same time, does its environment adapt and evolve with it. The emerging paradigm offers "a non-dualistic perspective" which allows us to see the potential of co-evolution, and the interconnectedness of the human world with overall evolution, for realizing self-transcendence. A new sense of meaning emerges as we recognize the role we can play in creation.

Margaret Wheatley (1992) is preoccupied with the lessons we can learn from the "new science" about how organizations might be managed and led. It is a scientific worldview, Newtonian Mechanics, which currently dominates our thinking about these issues:

> each of us lives and works in organizations designed from Newtonian images of the universe.
> We manage by separating things into parts, we believe that influence occurs as a direct result

> of force exerted from one person to another, we engage in complex planning for a world that we keep expecting to be predictable, and we search continually for better methods of objectively perceiving the world (Wheatley, 1992, p. 6).

Unfortunately, the science has changed and so we are working with an outdated and inappropriate scientific worldview. In the new science currently emerging in the disciplines of physics, chemistry and biology,

> the underlying currents are a movement toward holism, toward understanding the system as a system and giving primary value to the relationships that exist among seemingly discrete parts. When we view systems from this perspective, we enter an entirely new landscape of connections, of phenomena that cannot be reduced to simple cause and effect, and of the constant flux of dynamic processes (p. 9).

Wheatley then proceeds to summarize the contributions made by each of the disciplines to the new science. Quantum physics lays stress on the idea of "relationship." In quantum mechanics, particles do not exist as independent things: "they come into being and are observed only in relationship to something else" (1992). In biology, new notions of evolution and co-evolution have come to the fore. Autopoietic systems are able to maintain their autonomy while being "structurally coupled" with their environments. The Gaia hypothesis represents the world as a living organism "actively engaged in creating the conditions which support life" (1992). The work of Prigogine on dissipative structures, in the field of chemistry, reveals that

> disorder can be the source of new order .... In a dissipative structure, things in the environment that disturb the system's equilibrium play a crucial role in creating new forms of order.... Disorder can be a source of order, and ... growth is found in disequilibrium, not in balance. The things we fear most in organizations - fluctuations, disturbances, imbalances - need not be signs of an impending disorder that will destroy us. Instead, fluctuations are the primary source of creativity (Wheatley, 1992, pp. 19-20).

Chaos theory brings together insights from a variety of disciplines, including chemistry, to provide a new way of understanding order and disorder. These two forces need to be seen as existing in an intimate relationship to one another:

> We have even found order in the event that epitomizes total disorder – chaos ... But as chaos theory shows, if we look at such a system long enough and with the perspective of time, it always demonstrates its inherent orderliness. The most chaotic of systems never goes beyond certain boundaries (Wheatley, 1992, pp. 20-21).

In Wheatley's view the new science has important implications for organization theory and for leadership. We need to concentrate on relationships between people and between people and their setting. We should facilitate process and encourage self-organization. Enterprises can be managed through concepts and a few guiding principles. We should not seek to rely on elaborate rules, task definition and structures. We can trust in chaos; organizations should be allowed to evolve. In Chapter 6 we shall spend more time elucidating these ideas and evaluating how useful they are for managers.

Capra, in his book *The Web of Life : A New Synthesis of Mind and Matter* (1996), firmly locates the "paradigm shift" he sees occurring in our study of natural and social phenomena within the holistic tradition of thought. Holistic investigation is "contextual thinking" which insists that parts of systems can only be understood in terms of their relationships with each other and with the whole. For the systems thinker, as Capra notes, relationships are primary. This type of thinking began with Aristotle, whom Capra calls the "first western biologist." Aristotle's was an organic perspective that likened the world and all it contained to a living being. This world view dominated Western philosophy for over two thousand years. Throughout this period nature and humanity were seen as existing on the basis of interrelationships.

In the seventeenth century, however, the Aristotelian world-view came under threat as the "Scientific Revolution" gained momentum. The philosophy that underpinned the Scientific Revolution was "Cartesian Mechanism." "Analysis" was now promoted as the means by which to gain knowledge. Broadly defined, analysis involves the division of a whole into separate parts for the purpose of understanding those parts. The behavior of the whole can then be deduced by studying the properties of the parts in isolation. This approach, of course, exists at the opposite end of the spectrum to holistic thinking. The success of the Scientific Revolution led to the dominance of Cartesian mechanism within the realm of science. Little opposition was possible in the mainstream, even from the field of biology which had previously championed holistic thinking. It was left to artists, writers, poets and philosophers, under the banner of "Romanticism", to keep holistic thinking alive during the eighteenth and nineteenth centuries. However, interestingly enough, Capra does point to some reflections of Kant on the nature of organisms as complex wholes. Kant went so far as to argue (apparently anticipating autopoiesis) that within the organism each part not only supports the other parts but also "produces" the other parts.

In the twentieth century, as we have witnessed, biologists again found themselves having to cast off the constraints of mechanistic thinking and returning to a holistic approach in order to advance their discipline. We studied the contributions made by Woodger, Cannon, and especially von Bertalanffy, to the birth of contemporary systems thinking earlier in this chapter. Von Bertalanffy's work seems particularly significant to Capra because he was the first to really emphasize "process thinking" alongside contextual thinking. He was concerned with the processes that occurred within systems.

It is from within the holistic tradition of thought, buttressed and enriched by some newer but compatible developments in science, that Capra sees the solution emerging to the serious global problems affecting us and our world today. We are all aware of problems of war, poverty, population growth, pollution, forest destruction, etc., but our methods for tackling such problems are proving largely ineffective. In particular, little or no attention is given to the systemic nature of the world and its problems. In Capra's opinion, problems are being treated separately, in isolation from other problems and their contexts. He argues that decision-makers must begin to view different problems as being interrelated and begin to see how our attempted solutions are affecting the prospects of future generations. If we are unable to shift our perceptions and values in this way, problems will persist and escalate and at some point the damage may become irreversible.

Capra is optimistic that our problems can be solved but to do so we have to alter our way of thinking. We must reject the old world view and adopt a perspective which can produce "viable solutions" to global problems. According to Capra "the only viable solutions are those that are 'sustainable'" (1996). These are solutions that address the whole network of global problems and meet the needs of future generations as well as our own needs. Makeshift solutions must be abandoned in favor of long-term problem solving.

Fortunately, Capra argues in *The Web of Life*, we are on the verge of seeing the emergence of a new scientific understanding of life. This breakthrough represents a "paradigm shift" that will usher in the necessary "new perception of reality." This perception is deeply systemic and marries earlier holistic thinking with some of the latest advances in the sciences. It encourages us to look at the world from a holistic viewpoint and to understand it as an integrated whole. It recognizes the fundamental interdependence of all phenomena and the fact that, as individuals and societies, we are all embedded in (and ultimately dependent on) the cyclical process of nature (1996, p. 6).

This new perspective can be called "ecological" because it sees life as being at the center of the set of relationships that make up the whole. The shift in perception it encourages is toward "deep ecological awareness":

by calling the emerging new vision of reality 'ecological' in the sense of deep ecology, we emphasize that life is at its very center ... If we have deep ecological awareness, or experience, of being part of the web of life then we *will* (as opposed to *should*) be inclined to care for all living nature (1996, p.12).

To Capra, then, it is clear that

a theory of living systems consistent with the philosophical framework of deep ecology ... and implying a non-mechanistic, post-Cartesian understanding of life, is now emerging (1996, p. 153).

Three concepts are central to this new theory – "pattern of organization", "structure of the system" and "process." The pattern of organization is the formation and arrangement of relationships between the system's parts. It determines the characteristics of the system, be it a living or a non-living system. The structure of a system can be defined as "the physical embodiment of its pattern of organization" (Capra, 1996). Process refers to the ever present flow of "matter" through living systems because they are in constant contact with their environments. To manage this flow the components of the system have to undergo continual change and transformation, giving rise to growth, development and evolution. An understanding of the process of life is vital as it is "the activity involved in the continual embodiment of the system's pattern of organization" (1996). The three concepts are therefore interdependent and, taken together, provide for Capra the "key criteria of a living system":

The *pattern* of organization can only be recognized if it is embodied in a physical *structure*, and in living systems this embodiment is an ongoing *process* (1996, p.156, my emphasis).

The conceptual framework thus created is best approached, Capra believes, by taking three theoretical viewpoints and using them to elucidate each of the three criteria of a living system. The pattern of organization is best understood through study of Maturana and Varela's work on autopoiesis; the structure of the system is best expressed through Prigogine's notion of "dissipative structures"; and the process of life can be grasped in terms of Bateson's theory of "cognition." Capra attempts to take key concepts from each of these strands of thought and to bring them together in the form of a "new synthesis."

We dealt at some length with the idea of autopoiesis earlier in this chapter. Capra's main focus is on the claim that living systems are circular networks which constantly produce themselves. The nature of the system, and its behavior, are determined through the relationships between the parts of the system; thus living systems are self-organizing systems. Their identity and existence depend upon autopoiesis, upon their ability to preserve their pattern of organization. It also depends upon them being able to continually renew themselves; adapting, developing and evolving in relationship with their environments. In Capra's words,

the central characteristic of an autopoietic system is that it undergoes continual structural change while preserving its web-like pattern of organization (1996, p. 213).

The notion of "dissipative structures" is due to Ilya Prigogine, a Russian scientist, who won the Nobel prize in 1977 for his work on the thermodynamics of systems far from equilibrium. For Prigogine, traditional science had focussed for far too long on systems in a state of "thermodynamic equilibrium" and largely ignored processes and structures occurring "far from equilibrium." These were "looked down on as nuisances, as disturbances, as subjects not worthy of study" (Prigogine and Stengers, 1984). This, however, is to miss the point of how open systems are able to change and evolve. Systems are continuously subject to fluctuations and, as a result of the effects of positive feedback, these fluctuations can be powerful enough to drive systems far from equilibrium. In this state a system may disintegrate. Prigogine showed, however, that under certain conditions chemical systems are able to pass through randomness and achieve a new level of order as "dissipative structures" – so called because they require energy from the outside to prevent them from dissipating. Rather than focussing on the inevitability of decay as systems run down to a state of maximum entropy, as classical thermodynamics does, the theory of dissipative structures highlights the capability of open systems to evolve towards greater complexity through spontaneous self-organization. Prigogine and Stengers (1984) provide the example of the "chemical clock" in an attempt to explain the nature of order far from equilibrium:

> Far from equilibrium we may witness the appearance of chemical clocks, chemical reactions which behave in a coherent, rhythmical fashion ... Every one of us has an intuitive view of how a chemical reaction takes place; we imagine molecules floating through space, colliding and reappearing in new forms. We see chaotic behavior similar to what the atomists described when they spoke about dust dancing in the air. But in a chemical clock all molecules change their chemical identity *simultaneously*, at regular time intervals ... Obviously such a situation can no longer be described in terms of chaotic behavior. A new type of order has appeared ... We can speak of a new coherence, of a mechanism of 'communication' among molecules. But this type of communication can arise only in far-from-equilibrium conditions (p. 13).

Dissipative structures are able, through self-organization, to maintain a stable state in unstable conditions far from equilibrium. They do this, as we mentioned, through the exchange of resources with their environments. Such exchanges require continual metabolic flows and changes. Dissipative structures, it follows, arise from "the interaction of a given system with its surroundings" (Prigogine and Stengers, 1984). It seems to Capra, therefore, that Prigogine's theory of dissipative structures can provide a solution to the problem of "the co-existence of structure and change, of order and dissipation" (1996). The characteristics of a dissipative structure mean that a system can maintain the same overall structure while experiencing a continuous flow and change of components. Moreover these are the very characteristics that ensure the survival of the system and the maintenance of life. Life itself must depend on the compatibility of what Prigogine refers to as "stillness and motion" in far from equilibrium conditions. Acceptance of the theory of dissipative structures provides Capra with an important building block in establishing his new understanding of life.

The third concept in Capra's synthesis is "process." Pattern and structure can only be fully understood if they are considered in terms of processes:

> the pattern of life is a set of relationships between processes of production; and a dissipative structure can only be understood in terms of metabolic and developmental processes (Capra, 1996, p. 167).

From the writings of Gregory Bateson, an anthropologist and psychiatrist much influenced by cybernetics, and from the work of Maturana, Capra derives the notion that "cognition" is central to the process of life. Bateson's theory of cognition suggested that mental processes are immanent in all kinds of living systems, from organisms to social systems and ecosystems (Capra, 1996). Systems that exist on the basis of mental processes can develop in much the same way as our minds develop. They are capable of exhibiting memory, learning and decision-making. In order to manifest these attributes, it follows that living systems will need to possess a common pattern of organization. For Capra this idea is important because it illustrates that understanding the process of mental activity is as significant for grasping the phenomenon of life as are "pattern of organization" and the "structure of the system."

Capra is convinced that his synthesis, of the three strands of thought that we have been considering, yields a new understanding of life and "evolution":

> the models and theories of self organizing systems discussed in this book provide the elements for formulating ... a new theory of evolution (1996, p. 221).

This synthesis will allow us to "reconnect" with the "web of life" by providing us with a theoretically informed conceptual framework. The new ecological awareness that we achieve through this framework will enable us to build sustainable communities which both meet our own needs and provide for those of future generations. Capra then proceeds to outline five principles which we must understand if we are to achieve "deep ecological awareness." Once this level of "ecological literacy" is attained we are well equipped to lead "an ecological lifestyle and for environmental activism" (1996, p. 8). These principles will be considered further in Chapter 8 on "emancipatory systems thinking."

4.9. CHAOS AND COMPLEXITY THEORY

Boulding, one of the originators of general system theory, saw it as exhibiting

> a prejudice in favor of system, order, regularity, and nonrandomness ... and a prejudice against chaos and randomness ... The whole, empirical world is more interesting ('good') when it is orderly. It is the orderly segments of the world, therefore, to which the general systems man is attracted (1965, p. 26).

It is somewhat ironic, therefore, that the aspect of systems theory that seems to be of most general application today is the study of chaos and complexity. Chaos and complexity theory is able to lay claim to being the science of the global nature of systems (Gleick, 1987), relevant as it appears to be to disciplines as diverse as meteorology, chemistry, geology, evolutionary biology, economics and management.

The early emphasis of general system theory on order and regularity was at one with classical science which can itself be characterized by its unceasing search for "fixed laws." Fixed laws and orderly, regular patterns of behavior, based on cause–effect relationships, enabled scientists to make predictions and forecasts. This emphasis, however, meant that classical science had to ignore what Gleick calls "the irregular side of nature, the discontinuous and erratic side ... these have been puzzles to science, or worse, monstrosities" (1987). However, some forty years ago a small number of scientists, for the most part working in isolation from one another, began to discover the "erratic side" of nature and to think along different lines. Two discoveries earned chaos theory an important place in scientific study. First, it was found that complex and unpredictable results could be produced in the behavior of systems from entirely deterministic equations. There was no necessity to introduce any probabilistic element at all. Second, it was a common finding of the early pioneers that there is in fact considerable order in chaos. Chaos, in the technical sense, should not therefore be seen, as in everyday language, as implying randomness, disorder and irregularity. In the zone between stability and instability, systems can be observed to demonstrate a general pattern of behavior even if their specific behavior is unpredictable. As Gleick (1987) suggests, given the apparent disorderly, irregular and unpredictable behavior of so many systems in the world, there was a dire need for some sort of "chaos theory." It now seemed that it could be supplied.

We have noted the importance attached by Wheatley to chaos theory as part of the "new science" that could transform thinking about management and leadership. Capra, as well, incorporates aspects of chaos theory into his "new perception of reality." Indeed Prigogine's dissipative structures can be seen as an example, from chemistry, of systems exhibiting chaotic behavior. We shall here, using Gleick (1987) as our main guide, take this important topic further by tracing the development of chaos and complexity theory and isolating its main contributors. In Chapter 6 we study the significance of this aspect of systems thinking for management.

Before proceeding, however, it is necessary to be a little clearer about definitions. Because it originated in a variety of fields of study there is no one single accepted "chaos and complexity theory." There are a variety of theories which show a family resemblance and therefore give rise to an aspiration for a more general theory. Besides this there is additional confusion surrounding the relationship between "chaos theory" and "complexity theory." Chaos theory was the first term to be used. It was employed to describe the similar results emerging from the study of chaotic behavior in different fields in the physical sciences. It is also, usually, the narrower in scope, referring to the mathematics of non-linear dynamic behavior in natural systems. The repeated application of a set of mathematical equations or fixed rules of interaction give rise to patterns of order or disorder which can be described in the language of chaos theory.

Complexity theory is wider in scope, used to describe the behavior over time of complex human and social, as well as natural, systems. The new name, complexity theory, reflects a recognition that complex social systems are able to change and evolve over time. They are not bound, therefore, by fixed rules of interaction and do not develop on the basis of the repetition of a mathematical algorithm. Trying to capture the distinction, it is sometimes said that chaos theory concerns itself with "complex adaptive systems" whereas the subject matter of complexity theory is "complex evolving systems." The term complexity theory is also favored, for obvious reasons, by those who study complex systems in their own right rather than as a result of their interest in a particular discipline. The Santa Fe Institute, established in 1984, is the best known research center specializing in the behavior of complex adaptive and complex evolving systems. Scientists from a range of disciplines have co-operated there to build computer representations of the behavior of a variety of biological, ecological and economic systems. In this book, the historical account of the development of the theory will be dominated by the term "chaos theory." When the primary concern is to extract general lessons for managers, however, I shall most often use the term "complexity theory." Do not expect consistency in the literature at large. Johnson and Burton (1994) describe the situation accurately when they state:

> Models that use concepts similar to those found in chaos theory, but that have relaxed some of the strict chaos theory restrictions, are loosely grouped under the heading of complexity theory ... but there is no institutionalized scientific discipline known as the science of complexity. Often, the term complexity theory is used interchangeably with chaos theory (p. 321).

Although Poincaré, a nineteenth century mathematician, is sometimes claimed as the founding father of chaos and complexity theory, it was only in the 1960s and 1970s that the serious investigation of unpredictable behavior in complex systems began. By the 1980s, however, a movement was taking shape that had the possibility of transforming the concerns of the scientific establishment, and Gleick (1987) was able to claim that "20th century science will be remembered for three things: relativity, quantum mechanics and chaos." What had happened in the interim?

Edward Lorenz, a metereologist working on the problem of weather prediction, is usually considered the pioneer in the development of chaos theory. Using his primitive computer, Lorenz had built a model of the behavior of the weather based on just twelve equations. The results seemed realistic in terms of actual behavior with the weather demonstrating familiar patterns although never repeating itself exactly over time. In this sense there was both order and disorder. Gleick takes up the story:

> One day in the winter of 1961, waiting to examine one sequence at greater length, Lorenz took a shortcut. Instead of starting the whole run over, he started mid way through. To give the machine its initial conditions, he typed the numbers straight from the earlier printout. Then he walked down the hall to get away from the noise and drink a cup of coffee. When he returned an hour later, he saw something unexpected, something that planted a seed for a new science. This new run should have exactly duplicated the old....Yet as he stared at the new printout, Lorenz saw his weather diverging so rapidly from the pattern of the last run that, within just a few months all resemblance had disappeared. Suddenly he realized the truth. There had been no malfunction. The problem lay in the numbers he had typed. In the computer's memory, six decimal places were stored: .506127. On the printout, to save space, just three appeared: .506. Lorenz had entered the shorter, rounded-off numbers, assuming that the difference – one part in a thousand – was inconsequential.... Yet in Lorenz's particular system of equations small errors proved catastrophic ... He decided that long-range weather forecasting must be doomed (1987, pp. 15-17).

Lorenz's findings showed that tiny changes in a system's initial state do not inevitably lead to small-scale consequences. On the contrary, this "sensitive dependence on initial conditions" that complex systems exhibit means that minute changes can alter long term behavior very significantly. This is often referred to by commentators on chaos theory as the "butterfly effect"; the idea being that the flapping of a single butterfly's wings, producing apparently insignificant changes in atmospheric conditions today, might have effects over time that would lead to a storm happening somewhere in the world that would not otherwise have happened, or vice versa.

The discovery he had made led Lorenz to search for equations which would express the notion that simple initial conditions can produce complex behavior. These equations were inevitably "non-linear." Gleick (1987) defines linear equations as "easy to think about ... solvable ... can [be taken] apart, and put ... together again – the pieces add up." Non-linear equations, however, "generally cannot be solved and cannot be added together." Traditionally scientists had sought quite indiscriminately to "linearize" non-linear systems. Capra (1996) points out the futility of this, arguing that

> non-linear phenomena dominate much more of the inanimate world than we had thought, and they are an essential aspect of the network patterns of living systems (p. 122).

The widespread presence of non-linearity makes prediction impossible over large swathes of the natural and social sciences.

Lorenz, however, had not only "found unpredictability, but he had also found pattern" (Gleick, 1987) in the behavior of the weather. As Rosenhead puts it:

> Every weather pattern, every cold front is different from all its predecessors. And yet ... the Nile doesn't freeze, and London is not subject to the monsoon (1998, pp. 2-3).

Unpredictability, it seemed, could also encompass a surprising degree of order. Lorenz now started experimenting with other sets of equations describing somewhat simpler systems. One set sought to capture the behavior of a convection system, another set turned out to mirror what happened with a waterwheel. In each case there was a sensitive dependence on initial conditions but also a recognizable pattern. When the behavior of the waterwheel example was put onto a graph, a remarkable result was observed. The output always remained within the limits of a double spiral curve. This was novel because previously only two types of behavior had been investigated mathematically - first, the steady state in which the variables never change and, second, periodic behavior in which the system infinitely repeats itself. Lorenz's simple sets of equations behaved like the weather system, in an "aperiodic" fashion, never settling down to a steady state and never repeating themselves exactly. At the same time they were clearly "attracted" to a particular pattern of behavior. For this reason, Lorenz called the image he had produced the "Lorenz attractor" (see Figure 4.5). Since Lorenz's experiments, aperiodic behavior has been thoroughly investigated and it has been postulated that all manner of natural systems are governed by what are now called "strange attractors." A strange attractor seems to keep the trajectory followed by an otherwise unpredictable system within the bounds of a particular pattern. It keeps a system to a pattern without requiring it ever to exactly repeat itself. This can be distinguished from a "stable attractor", which demands it returns to its original state. Strange attractors also produce "self-similar behavior", giving rise to the same pattern at whatever scale their effects are examined. Exploration of the nature of self-similar behavior and "fractal" patterns has played an important role in the development of chaos and complexity theory, as we shall see.

The publication of Lorenz's findings in a meteorological journal in 1963 is usually regarded as signaling the birth of chaos theory. The next decade or so, however, was marked more by individual scientists working on aspects of the theory, largely in isolation, than by the birth of a scientific movement. Stephen Smale focused his work on chaotic systems and, independently, came to conclusions similar to those of Lorenz. The mathematician, James Yorke, recognized the impossibility of prediction but insisted that problems of "disorder" should be at the center of the scientific enterprise. He provided the first proper mathematical definition of the term "chaos." A pioneer of particular importance to us here was Robert May, because he extended the application of chaos theory beyond simply physical systems.

May was a biologist particularly interested in predicting the behavior of biological populations over time. The equations describing such systems were clearly simple if populations were able to rise indefinitely. However, once predators and diminishing food supplies were included as important elements affecting such growth, behavior became impossible to predict. When attempting to study biological populations, "...the appropriate mathematical description involves non linear differential equations" (May, 1974). Experimenting with different inputs to his equations, May discovered that once growth rate passed a certain level there was bifurcation in his results indicating that the population could be in two different states. Raising growth rate still further led the outcome to jump between four different values. And if the rate was increased further, the predictions bifurcated again, yielding eight possible states. Bifurcations became quicker and quicker until chaos suddenly appeared and it became impossible to predict the outcome. Close inspection of a graph of the results did, however, show patterns of order emerging in the chaos. The graph also demonstrated the property of "self-similarity", having an exact copy of itself inside.

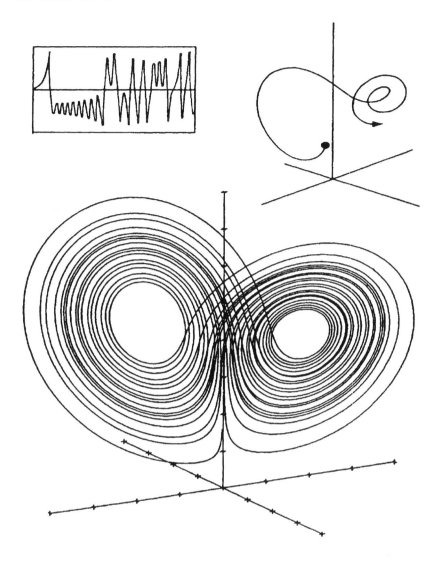

THE LORENZ ATTRACTOR (above). This magical image, resembling an owl's mask or butterfly's wings, became an emblem for the early explorers of chaos. It revealed the fine structure hidden within a disorderly stream of data. Traditionally, the changing values of any one variable could be displayed in a so- called time series (top). To show the changing relationship among three variables required a different technique. At any instant in time, the three variables fix the location of a point in three-dimensional space; as the system changes, the motion of the point represents the continuously changing variables.

Because the system never exactly repeats itself, the trajectory never intersects itself. Instead it loops around and around forever. Motion on the attractor is abstract, but it conveys the flavor of the motion of the real system. For example, the crossover from one wing of the attractor to the other corresponds to a reversal in the direction of spin of the waterwheel or convecting fluid.

Figure 4.5. The Lorenz attractor (reproduced from Gleick, 1987, pp. 28-29)

Benoit Mandelbrot, a mathematician and employee of IBM, also studied self-similarity and made discoveries that played a significant part in the further development of chaos theory. Mandelbrot pointed out that although many of nature's features may seem geometric, relatively simple in their construction and outward appearance, in fact most of nature is much more complicated. A cloud, for example, is indescribable in geometric terms. This led him to conceive of "fractal geometry", able to account for and analyze complex and irregular phenomena such as clouds:

> many patterns of nature are so irregular and fragmented that, compared with ... standard geometry ... nature exhibits not simply to a higher degree but an altogether different level of complexity ... Responding to this challenge, I conceived and developed a new geometry of nature... It describes many of the irregular and fragmented patterns around us, and leads to full-fledged theories by identifying a family of shapes I call *fractals* (Mandelbrot, 1983, p. 1).

Mandelbrot discovered that "fractal wholes" were made up of characteristic patterns and parts that demonstrated self-similarity. This means, in simple terms, that the parts of the whole are similar in shape to that whole. Mandelbrot uses the example of a cauliflower. His fractal geometry provided a mathematical language capable of describing this. Gleick summarizes his contribution to chaos theory as follows:

> Fractal dimension becomes a way of measuring qualities that have no clear definition: the degree of roughness or brokenness or the irregularity of an object. A twisting coastline, for example, despite its immeasurability in terms of length, nevertheless has a certain characteristic degree of roughness. Mandelbrot specified ways of calculating the fractional dimension of real objects, given some technique of constructing a shape or given some data, and he allowed his geometry to make a claim about the irregular patterns he had studied in nature. The claim was that a degree of irregularity remains constant over different scales. Surprisingly often, the claim turns out to be true. Over and over again, the world displays a regular irregularity (1987, p. 98).

Fractal structures have now been noted and explored in many different fields of knowledge.

Helge von Koch, another mathematician, constructed a mathematical curve to express this idea further. Capra gives a simplified explanation of this construction known as the "Koch curve" or "Koch snowflake":

> The geometric operation consists in dividing a line into three equal parts and replacing the center section by two sides of an equilateral triangle [see Figure 4.6]. By repeating this operation again and again on a smaller and smaller scale, a jagged snowflake is created [see Figure 4.7]. Like a coastline, the Koch curve becomes infinitely long if the iteration is continued to infinity. Indeed, the Koch curve can be seen as a very rough model of a coastline [see Figure 4.8]. With the help of computers, simple geometric iterations can be applied thousands of times at different scales to produce so-called 'fractal forgeries' - computer generated models of plants, trees, mountains, coastlines, etc., which bear an astonishing resemblance to the actual shapes found in nature (1996, pp. 138-139).

Figure 4.6. Geometric operation for constructing a Koch curve (reproduced from Capra 1996)

Figure 4.7. The Koch snowflake (reproduced from Capra, 1996)

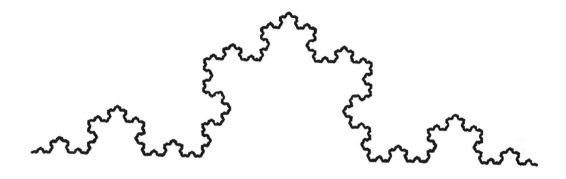

Figure 4.8. Modeling a coastline with the Koch curve (reproduced from Capra, 1996)

By the late 1970s and early 1980s, the chaos and complexity movement began to take shape. Feigenbaum discovered that bifurcations occurred at a constant rate and was thus able to predict the creation of self-similarity in complex, dynamic systems. In the late 1970s the Dynamical Systems Collective was formed at Santa Cruz College, headed by the physicist Robert Stetson Shaw. They found chaotic behavior in a dripping water faucet. Beyond a certain flow velocity the dripping no longer happened with an even regularity; nevertheless, when graphed, it could be seen that it did correspond to a pattern. The group carried out research into "strange attractors", making important contributions to information theory using this concept. A member of the Collective, the physicist and mathematician Norman Packard, is credited with inventing the notion of the "edge of chaos" - a narrow transition zone between order and chaos. This idea proved to have similar potential for the study of information management and information processing. As we shall discover, when we turn to the application of these ideas to management and organization, the concept of the "edge of chaos" proves to be perhaps the most powerful in the complexity theory lexicon. The concept was discovered, independently, by Chris Langton working at the University of Arizona. We noted that, in 1984, what became the most famous center for research into complexity theory was established. Known as the Santa Fe Institute it brought together scientists form a range of disciplines, including physics, biology, psychology, mathematics and immunology. The work of Kauffman, a medical scientist, using the edge of chaos idea and applying it to biology and evolution, has been one well-known output of the Institute. The important concept of "fitness landscapes" emerged from this work. Lewin provides a summary of Kauffman's idea:

> You have to think about the fitness of an individual in terms of different combinations of
> gene variants it might have. Now think of a landscape, in which each different point on the
> landscape represents slightly different packages of these variants. Lastly, if you imagine

some of the packages as being fitter than others, raise them up as peaks. The fittest of the packages has the highest peak. The landscape overall will be rugged, with peaks of different height, separated by valleys. Remember, this landscape represents fitness probabilities, places where individuals of a species might be, depending on the combination of genetic variants they have in their chromosomes. If an individual happens to be in a fitness valley, then mutation and selection might push it up a local peak, representing a rise in fitness. Once on the local peak it may, metaphorically gaze enviously at a nearby peak, but be unable to reach it because that would require crossing a valley of lower fitness (1992, quoted by Ortegon, 1999, pp. 18-19).

Kauffman extended the idea to two landscapes, representing predator and prey, and further still to consider multiple species. Such systems would eventually come to rest, poised at the edge of chaos and with average fitness optimized.

New applications for chaos and complexity theory are constantly being found - in astronomy, economics, geology, physiology, computer art, music, etc. Gleick is convinced that the movement is reshaping the fabric of the scientific establishment:

> Chaos is a science of process rather than state, of becoming rather than being. Now that science is looking, chaos seems to be everywhere... Chaos breaks across the lines that separate scientific disciplines ... because it is a science of the global nature of systems ... Chaos poses problems that defy accepted ways of working in science. It makes strong claims about the universal behavior of complexity (1987, pp. 4-5).

The importance of chaos and complexity theory as a "systems approach to management" will also be clear. It is certainly a systems approach, encouraging holistic explanations and eschewing reductionism. In chaos theory, as Begun puts it:

> Events are connected to other events – they occur in systems. Systems are subsystems of larger systems. Relationships among variables rather than single variables, become the primary object of study. Efforts to isolate single variables and their effects become feeble or even ludicrous (1994, p. 330).

Moreover, at least in Stacey's (1996) view, chaos theory offers a systems approach that is different to almost anything else that has been available before in systems thinking. In his opinion everything pre-dating the complexity revolution is stuck in the stable equilibrium paradigm. Stacey is one of a number of authors who have sought to apply complexity theory to management in interesting ways. The appeal of this will be obvious from what we have already learned. Complexity theory does not deal in repetitive and predictable behavior but embraces change and evolution in dynamic systems. It assumes that the systems it studies do not fit linear models. Despite this aversion to prediction and forecasting, it suggests that there may be some long-term patterns that underlie the behavior of complex systems. Also it may be possible to discover some simple rules that govern complex systems behavior. Mathematically at least, complex outcomes seem to be generated using simple equations. We take these ideas forward, in terms of their relevance to management and organization, in Chapter 6.

4.10. CONCLUSION

This chapter has seen us examining the origins of systems thinking in disciplines as diverse as philosophy biology, sociology, management and organization theory, control engineering, and the physical sciences. Even this is not complete. A study of psychology, for example, would have seen us having to give attention to Gestalt theory – our tendency to create order in the world around us by seeing it in terms of wholes. We have also witnessed the birth of systems thinking *per se* and considered some candidates for a general theory of systems – general system theory itself, autopoiesis, cybernetics, chaos and complexity theory. Once established, systems thinking began to feed its insights back both into the disciplines that produced it and disciplines that, lacking a developed theoretical framework, felt that they could make use of systems ideas. In the latter category would come geography (e.g. Chorley and Kennedy, 1971; Chapman, 1977; Bennett and Chorley, 1978) and political science (e.g. Deutsch, 1963; Easton, 1973; and Yon Pil Rhee, 1999). Essentially, with some gaps acknowledged, we now understand the main features of systems thinking as it developed in the disciplines and as a transdiscipline in its own right. We are at the point where it is possible to turn to the use that can be made of systems ideas. In the 1940s systems thinking began to give rise to specific methodologies for intervening in the real world to solve practical problems. It is this "applied systems thinking" that is the subject of the next chapter.

5

APPLIED SYSTEMS THINKING

5.1. INTRODUCTION

The focus of the chapter is on applied systems thinking, and we begin by distinguishing this aspect of the systems movement from others in which the main concern is either with developing "systems science" or with using systems ideas in particular disciplines. A second section seeks to describe the development of applied systems thinking over the past few decades from the 1940s to the present. Inevitably the discussion is in terms of systems methodology. Methodology, as we saw, looks at the principles behind the use of models, methods, tools and techniques to provide understanding and, usually in the case of systems thinking, to bring about change. The two dimensions of the "system of systems methodologies" are employed to reveal the transformations that have had to occur in the way systems ideas are conceived, and are used, in order that these ideas can be of maximum benefit to decision-makers and problem-solvers. These revolutions in methodology can be linked, through these dimensions, back to social theory and the need for systems thinking to escape its original functionalist orientation before it could become of more general significance for practitioners. Thus, this chapter draws upon Chapter 3 as well as on the exploration of the evolution of systems ideas in the disciplines presented in Chapter 4. The third section of the chapter offers some further clarification of the nature of systems thinking as a transdiscipline, of the contribution I think systems thinking can make to the applied disciplines, and of the meaning of certain terms employed in the chapters which follow in Parts II and III of the book. Finally, in a section on the status of applied systems thinking, I argue for the value and significance of systems ideas as a guide to practice as compared to the many other possible prescriptions that can be bought on the market. This amounts to my championing systems thinking, and justifying doing so, in the face of an increasing proliferation of management "fads" of one kind or another.

5.2. THE SYSTEMS MOVEMENT

Checkland (1981) finds it helpful, in placing order on the burgeoning literature of the systems movement, to make an initial distinction between work applying systems thinking in other disciplines and work concerned with the study of systems as such. The latter category of literature can then be divided further into that demonstrating a primary interest in the theoretical development of systems thinking and that where the main concern is with the "problem-solving" application of systems thinking to real-world problems. The problem-solving strand of work was then further sub-divided by Checkland into hard systems thinking, systems ideas used to aid decision-making, and soft systems thinking.

The utility of the basic distinction employed by Checkland was confirmed in Chapter 4. There we saw systems ideas developing and being employed in a variety of disciplines. We also witnessed the birth of systems thinking *per se*, with researchers becoming interested in the properties of systems themselves. Once this latter "general system theory" tendency was established, it became possible for general systems work to influence the specific disciplines and vice versa. Nevertheless, the systems movement can still be usefully divided according to whether it is primarily concerned with advancing a particular discipline or primarily interested in systems in their own right. The fact that systems thinking applied to "problem-solving" only emerges as a result of a secondary distinction in Checkland's formulation is, however, misleading today. Since 1981 this strand of work has become the most important achievement of the whole systems movement. The use of systems ideas in the "problem-solving" mode is worthy, as this and later chapters will show, of recognition as an independent endeavor of first ranking importance in systems thinking. A contemporary map of the systems movement, based upon this revision of Checkland's guidelines, must therefore show three initial distinctions, as in Figure 5.1.

It would perhaps be a mistake to try to take Figure 5.1 to a higher level of resolution, at least in the form of a rigid map. There will be various legitimate views of the disciplines on which systems thinking has had most impact and a number of different criteria that could be employed for classifying systems-based "problem-solving" approaches. Nevertheless, let us briefly consider each of the main categories to see what sort of divisions could be made.

In Chapter 4 we witnessed the impact of systems thinking in disciplines as diverse as philosophy, biology, sociology, management and organization theory, control engineering and the physical sciences. Some impact in other areas of work, such as geography and psychology, was also suggested. Each of the major disciplines in the social and natural sciences could probably be examined, as a research exercise, for the way it had given birth to or been influenced by systems ideas. As a general point, it is probably true to say that the influence of systems concepts has probably been less in the recent past than it was in the 1940s and 1950s. Undoubtedly systems thinking became discredited in the minds of many because of its association with an unfashionable form of functionalism. This is changing as it is recognized that systems ideas can contribute rigor and relevance to a variety of theoretical positions. It is one of the purposes of this book to demonstrate that a newly conceived form of systems thinking, what I call "critical systems thinking" in Part III, can again assume a leading role in the development of the applied disciplines.

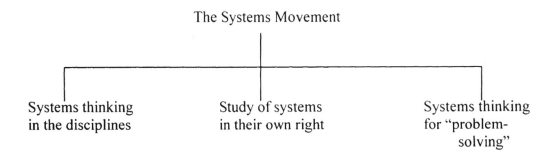

Figure 5.1. Contemporary map of the systems movement

In terms of the types of research encouraged in the disciplines by systems thinking, both "scholarship" and "hypothesis testing" (see Chapter 2) have been to the fore. In the case of scholarship, taking a systems approach has been seen as good practice by some theorists in each discipline and systems ideas have been applied to areas of theoretical concern in order to yield a more rigorous formulation and arrangement of the concepts of the discipline. In the case of hypothesis testing, systems models of the subject matter of the discipline provide hypotheses about the nature of a part of the world of interest to the discipline, and these hypotheses are tested through experiment and observation. The results, in the form of verification or falsification of the hypotheses, add to the theoretical knowledge stock of the discipline in relation to that part of reality. As newer forms of systems thinking, which place greater emphasis on methodology and an action orientation, become accepted, it is likely that they will push the disciplines towards a more "Mode 2" orientation in research and ensure they are user-centered.

The second main branch of the systems movement concentrates on the study of systems in their own right. Chapter 4 exposed a number of systems approaches offering themselves as candidates capable of providing a general theory of systems. The most significant of these would have to be cybernetics, autopoiesis, chaos and complexity theory and general system theory itself. Which of these might be regarded as possessing most generality and, therefore, as offering the "purest" form of general system theory must be open to debate. General system theory stated that ambition and seized the territory as its very *raison d'être*. Chaos and complexity theory, with its claim to embrace disorder as well as order, can be seen as the most potent challenger.

The kind of research indulged in by advocates of general system theories is best seen as a kind of "scholarship." It leads to a conceptual reordering sometimes of the general system theory itself and sometimes in the discipline to which the general system theory is brought. The impact of von Bertalanffy's general system theory on organization theory, autopoiesis on family therapy, and chaos and complexity theory on management thinking, are all examples of the latter. The use of general system theories to guide hypothesis testing, or research which is orientated to users, is more unusual. As Checkland (1981) pointed out: "The problem with GST is that it pays for its generality with lack of content."

In this book, henceforth, the primary concern will be with the third main branch of the systems movement - systems thinking for "problem-solving" or "applied systems thinking." It is in this area, I shall argue, that systems thinking has had it greatest successes and has its most distinctive contribution to make. Chapter 2 saw me arguing that, from its original formulation, applied systems thinking adopted a Mode 2 orientation to research and put its emphasis on serving the needs of the client. Since that time the manner in which "clients", "customers", "decision-makers", "problem-owners", "the affected but not involved", etc., can become part of the process of research and practice has been a dominating theme in applied systems thinking. The progress made in developing "interpretive action research" is just one important outcome of this endeavor.

Lane and Jackson (1995) sought to provide an annotated bibliography reflecting the "breadth and diversity of systems thinking." Since the bias was implicitly to applied systems thinking it is worth drawing attention here to the 8 strands identified. They were : general system theory, organizations-as-systems, hard systems thinking, cybernetics, system dynamics, soft systems thinking, emancipatory systems thinking, and critical systems thinking. This selection of books and papers remains useful to outsiders wishing to find out what systems thinking is and also to insiders interested in exploring areas of the systems movement other than their own. In this book, as already indicated, I take a step back and employ a broad classification of different types of social theory to order the variety of approaches in applied systems thinking. The four types identified in Chapter 3 as most relevant to this purpose were functionalist, interpretive, emancipatory, and postmodern social theory. Chapter 6, in Part II of the book, takes a look at those systems methodologies and the models, methods and techniques associated with them, which predominantly adhere to a functionalist rationale. In this category come operational research, systems analysis, systems engineering, system dynamics, mechanical equilibrium models, socio-technical systems thinking, contingency theory, living systems theory, cybernetics, autopoiesis and chaos and complexity theory. Chapter 7 examines applied systems approaches based upon an interpretive logic including interactive management, social systems design, interactive planning and soft systems methodology. In Chapters 8 and 9, respectively, possible emancipatory and postmodern varieties of applied systems thinking are explored. In each case, and within chapters as well, the social theory explained in Chapter 3 is used to differentiate between different ways of using systems ideas and to highlight the strengths and weaknesses of the various approaches. Before embarking on this analysis, however, it will help to provide a more general, historical overview of the way in which applied systems thinking evolved.

5.3. THE DEVELOPMENT OF APPLIED SYSTEMS THINKING

When interest first developed in examining the theoretical underpinnings of systems methodologies, Burrell and Morgan's grid of sociological paradigms was used as a point of reference (Checkland, 1981; Jackson, 1982). However, any way of seeing is also a way of not seeing, and that framework did not always cast the clearest light over some points of interest in the systems field. The language was foreign to those educated in the management and systems sciences, and a job of translation always needed to be done to make the analysis clear. The action orientation and problem centeredness of systems thinking posed additional complications in carrying over ideas. The failure of Burrell and Morgan to distinguish a positivist from a structuralist epistemology within functionalism, and the consequences of this for an analysis of systems thinking, has already been noted in Chapter 3. For all these reasons, Jackson and Keys (1984) sought to provide a "system of systems methodologies" - an alternative framework that would serve a similar purpose to Burrell and Morgan's grid in organizational analysis but would be more suited to the language, concerns and internal development of the management and systems sciences. It was designed to relate different systems methodologies to each other on the basis of the assumptions they made about the nature of problem situations or "problem-contexts." In fulfilling this role the system of systems methodologies (SOSM) had an important impact on the establishment of pluralism as an element in critical systems thinking, as we shall see in Chapter 10. It can also play a part, and this may be its most lasting legacy, in allowing us to visualize how management science and systems thinking have progressed and developed over the last half century. In order to understand this we need to consider the two axes upon which the SOSM is constructed (see Figure 5.2).

The horizontal axis establishes a continuum of increasing divergence of values and/or interests between those concerned with, or affected by, a problem situation. The terms unitary, pluralist, and conflictual are taken from the industrial relations literature to reflect this. So "participants" or "stakeholders" can exist in a unitary relationship to one another when they are in genuine agreement about their objectives, sharing values and interests. They can be in a pluralist relationship if their values and interests diverge but they share enough in common so that it is worthwhile their remaining members of the "coalition" that makes up the system or organization. They can, however, be in a conflictual or coercive relationship if their interests diverge irreconcilably and power comes to bear so that some group or groups gets its own way at the expense of those who are coerced.

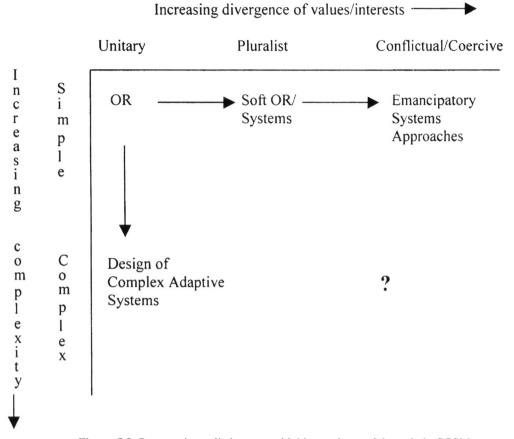

Figure 5.2. Progress in applied systems thinking understood through the SOSM

The vertical axis details increasing complexity on a continuum from simple to complex. It can best be understood by considering what makes problem-situations simple and complex. In simple situations, the systems of interest are characterized by having a small number of elements with few, or at least regular, interactions between the elements. Such systems are likely to be governed by well understood laws of behavior, to be closed to the environment, in von Bertalanffy's sense, and to consist of parts which are not themselves purposeful. At the other end of the continuum are complex situations where the systems of concern are characterized by having a large number of elements which are highly interrelated. Such systems are probabilistic, open to highly turbulent environments and have purposeful parts.

Although the separating out of these two axes of "complexity" – one associated with people, their values and interests, the other with the increasing complexity of "systems" – is, of course, artificial, it is a device which is frequently found in management thinking and has proved its utility. Organizations, for example, are often characterized as open socio-technical systems. This means that they have a technical aspect and are systems which seek to pursue goals efficiently and effectively in often volatile environments. They also have a human and social aspect and depend for their viability on the establishment of shared meanings among the personnel who make them up. Either social or technical characteristics may predominate in particular organizations, or parts or levels of organizations, but their successful development would seem to depend upon sufficient attention being given to both. Habermas's sociological theory, as we saw in Chapter 3, employs a related device. For him, the socio-cultural form of life of the human species is underpinned by "work" and "interaction." The importance of work leads humans to have a "technical interest" in achieving mastery over our natural and social environments. The importance of interaction leads humans to have a "practical interest" in expanding the possibilities of mutual understanding among all those involved in the reproduction of social life. Disagreement and conflict among individuals and groups can be just as much a threat to the reproduction of the socio-cultural form of life as a failure to predict and control natural and social affairs. The understanding of "power" and the cultivation of an "emancipatory interest" is also essential to ensure the open and free discussion necessary for the success of interaction. It follows that problems arise for the human species if the systems on which it depends become too complex to predict or control, or the values and interests of "stakeholders" become so divergent that genuine agreement about the objectives to be achieved is impossible.

Some independent justification for the utility of the two axes making up the SOSM can, therefore, be found. The main justification for us, however, will be if they allow us to better understand the evolution of applied systems thinking (taken to embrace operational research, management science, and related developments) over the last half century. The result of employing the two axes, for our purposes, is to produce a diagram in which problem situations can be seen as becoming more difficult to manage as one moves along a continuum of complexity or a continuum of increased divergence of values and/or interests. Let us now use this simple chart to explain progress in applied systems thinking.

Management science had its origins in Taylor's "scientific management", formulated before the First World War. But the attempt to devise methodologies, based upon systems ideas, as a means of solving problems did not get off the ground until around the time of the Second World War. It was during the Second World War that the approach known as "operational research" (OR) came into its own. It proved successful in helping the allied war effort in a variety of ways. Not long after the war the methodologies known as systems analysis and systems engineering also became established and, along with OR, were employed to assist reindustrialization generally in Europe, the USA and beyond following the war, and the military specifically in the build up to the "cold war."

All these approaches, together with others that will be mentioned in the course of this brief historical account, will be covered in depth in the next chapter. The detailed arguments presented can then be used to check the overview currently being presented. For the moment, however, we are simply concerned to chart progress in applied systems thinking according to the parameters of Figure 5.2. In these terms, the early approaches to applied systems thinking can all be located in the top-left hand corner of the chart, as based upon "simple-unitary" assumptions. Not surprisingly given the situation in which they were born, when objectives were clear, – we want to win the war and make our organizations more efficient as quickly as possible – all these early approaches assume that problem situations are unitary in nature. Indeed, they rely on there being a shared and therefore readily identifiable goal. Later in the 1960s and 1970s when these approaches were taken into the universities to be further "refined" by academics, an original bias towards quantification became an obsession with mathematically modeling the system of concern. This, of course, is only possible if the system is relatively "simple." So the underlying assumptions of textbook OR, and this is true, albeit to a lesser extent, of systems analysis and systems engineering, are simple-unitary. These methodologies are stuck in a particular area of the chart, assuming that people share values and that systems can be mathematically modeled. Despite these limiting assumptions, all three of the approaches mentioned had success in tackling technical problems; OR, for example, made considerable headway in solving queuing, scheduling, inventory and routing problems.

Unfortunately, difficulties arise when one seeks to extend the range of application of these approaches, exactly because of the assumptions embedded within them. They presuppose that one can begin an intervention by defining the desired goal, but this can be extremely difficult. Often problem situations seem to be pluralistic, in that there are different value positions and interests, or they appear conflictual. In either case there will be alternative goals. In these circumstances, methodologies of a unitary nature, which ask one to predefine the goal, cannot get started because they offer no way of bringing about any consensus or accommodation around a particular goal to be pursued. Similarly, if the system of concern is so complex that one cannot mathematically model it, then the approaches dealt with so far are again not a great deal of use. They assume that problem situations are simple enough to be modeled. If this assumption does not hold, any model that is produced can only offer a distorted view of reality from a particular perspective. The effects of these limitations in practical projects were documented by Hoos, in 1972, and had been theoretically diagnosed by Ackoff, for example, by the end of the 1970s (Ackoff, 1979a). In the 1980s came a general understanding of the lack of usefulness of these approaches for more complex problem situations, and in problem contexts which are pluralistic and/or conflictual. OR departments started being moved down and then out of organizations as their work was seen to be less relevant and significant.

Fortunately for applied systems thinking, and would-be problem solvers, the last 30 years have seen attempts to break out of the constraints imposed by employing simple-unitary assumptions. In the process the area of application of systems methodologies has been extended so that they can now cope with problem situations that are recognizably more complex and that are more appropriately defined as pluralistic or conflictual.

We shall consider the vertical axis first. The tendency in "hard systems" approaches, such as OR, was to try to include in a mathematical model the myriad interacting variables that appear on the surface of problem contexts and seem to be affecting the workings of the system of concern. The purpose of this was to optimize their contribution to the achievement of a fixed goal. The breakthrough came when a few pioneers abandoned this procedure in favor of approaches which were prepared to search beneath the surface to discover those key features that determine a system's viability. Once such key variables were determined, it became possible to learn how to design these into a system so that it can survive by continually regulating and self-organizing itself as its environment changes. Those who forced the pace of progress down the vertical axis, allowing systems thinking to be applied to more complex problem situations, gave up the attempt to mathematically model the surface features of systems. They began to dig below the surface to reveal the important design features that must be present in systems if they are to be viable and effective over time because they are capable of adapting in turbulent environments. There was a shift, in social theory terms, from a positivist to a more structuralist approach as the determining features of viability were researched. The systems approaches involved in making this breakthrough show a common concern, therefore, with the design of complex adaptive systems (as is indicated on Figure 5.2). System dynamics has gone part of the way. Socio-technical systems thinking, "organizational cybernetics" and "living systems theory" have more clearly and explicitly sought to produce models which try to help with the design of complex adaptive systems. More recently, some adherents of complexity theory have sought to lay claim, for themselves, to the whole area of research into complex adaptive systems. All these approaches aim to show what elements you have to design into systems to make them viable and effective over time.

Great progress has also been made along the horizontal axis, this time in the development and refinement of methodologies which assume that problem situations are pluralist and provide recommendations for analysis and intervention on this basis. The relevant methodologies within applied systems thinking tend to be referred to as "soft systems" approaches and include "interactive management", "interactive planning", "social systems design", "strategic assumption surfacing and testing", and "soft systems methodology"

(SSM). The tradition of work that has come to be known as "soft OR" has also given birth to approaches premised upon the significance of pluralism, most notably "strategic choice" and "strategic options development analysis."

Along this dimension, the breakthrough came when the aim of producing one single, objective model of a problem situation was abandoned. This was seen to be both impossible and undesirable given multiple values and interests. The trick was to make subjectivity central in the methodological process and to work with a variety of models of the world. In Checkland's SSM – a highly developed approach of this kind – systems models expressing different viewpoints and making explicit their implications are constructed so that alternative perspectives can be compared and contrasted. The purpose is to generate a systemic learning process in which the various participants in a problem situation come to appreciate more fully each other's world views and the possibilities for change, and a consensus or at least accommodation (however temporary) becomes possible between those who started with and may still hold divergent values.

Researchers on the horizontal dimension emphasize the importance of values, beliefs and philosophies; their primary concern is changing organizational culture and gaining commitment from participants to a particular course of action. In relation to OR the shift, sociologically, is from a positivist to an interpretive approach. Soft ORers and soft systems thinkers, in contrast to other operational researchers and those concerned with the design of complex adaptive systems, do not try to design models for use over and over again. This would be unproductive because of the widely different viewpoints which will be relevant in each problem situation. Instead, what is usefully replicated, as Checkland (1981) argues, is the methodology employed. The same approach to bringing about consensus and accommodation is tried out again and again and is gradually improved. Applications of Ackoff's "interactive planning", Checkland's SSM and Warfield's "interactive management" are now each in the many hundreds. A significant body of patiently derived research has been accumulated in this area. The result is that we know much better than before the process that needs to be gone through to bring about an accommodation between different value positions and to generate commitment to agreed changes.

If we move further along the horizontal axis toward conflictual or coercive situations, then the difficulties become magnified. Traditionally, applied systems thinking has not given as much thought as it should to these problem areas. Beer (1989) tells a relevant and insightful story. He relates how Ferdinand I, who reigned in Vienna in the 1840s, issued only one coherent order as emperor and that was "I am the Emperor and I want dumplings." Beer asks what you might do as the Lord High Chancellor for OR in Vienna at that moment. In seeking a solution he goes through linear programming (product-mix strategy), cost-benefit analysis and a consideration of OR's professional ethics (are dumplings morally reprehensible?). Beer suggests that OR could reach only one useful conclusion in these circumstances and that is "Bring the old devil lots of dumplings, p.d.q." Using management science, apparently, one either has to serve the powerful in organizations or leave their service.

More recently, attention has turned to the development of "emancipatory systems approaches" which address the particular problems of coercive contexts. Ulrich's (1983) "critical systems heuristics" is frequently cited as an emancipatory systems approachs because it allows one to ask who benefits from proposed changes or new systems designs in conflictual situations or where there is coercion. Critical systems heuristics also offers a means of empowering those who are affected by management decisions but not involved in them. In general, however, the difficulties of designing systems methodologies on the basis of complex-coercive assumptions have proved daunting. Unless one regards "postmodern systems approaches" as a kind of radical defiance in the face of complexity and coercion, there is little to be found. The question mark in the bottom right-hand corner of Figure 5.2 indicates that there is much work to be done in this area of the chart.

We have been tracing the development of applied systems thinking using the two dimensions which frame the chart in Figure 5.2; their concerns being with increasing complexity and increasing divergence of values and/or interests. It is possible to further illuminate the progress made by employing some of the social theory of Chapter 3. We have seen that the two axes reflect Habermas's "technical" interest, on the one hand, and his "practical" and "emancipatory" interests on the other. The increasing concern in systems thinking with the values/interests axis reflects a major re-orientation in these terms. Using Pepper's idea of "root metaphors", progress along the simple-complex continuum can be understood as a shift from mechanism toward a much greater interest in organicism and formism. Contextualism clearly provides the world-view governing soft systems approaches. Employing Morgan's "images of organization", it is easy to detect progress along the simple-complex dimension as being based on the successive exploration of the machine (OR, systems analysis, systems engineering), organism and brain (socio-technical systems theory, living systems theory, organizational cybernetics), and flux and transformation (complexity theory) metaphors. Progress along the values/interests dimension equates to the successive privileging of the culture, political, psychic prison, and instruments of domination metaphors.

In developing the analysis, we noted that a change in the "sociological paradigm" providing the theoretical backdrop for OR was necessary in order to make progress along the two dimensions. In the case of the simple-complex continuum it was an epistemological shift from positivism to structuralism which permitted a breakthrough to be achieved. With the values/interests dimension a break with both the ontology and epistemology of functionalism was required. Soft systems thinking rests upon the interpretive sociological paradigm. To understand the nature of conflictual and coercive contexts an appreciation of the radical humanist and radical structuralist paradigms was called for. I have not sought to position postmodern systems thinking on this chart, but any systems approach based on this type of social theory will, again, clearly be embracing another sociological paradigm.

The insights that can be gained from viewing different systems approaches in the light of social theory will provide the critique that is fundamental to each chapter of Part II of the book. The fact that different paradigms are involved, providing the theoretical assumptions of the different types of systems approach, means that we shall in Part III come up against the problem of paradigm incommensurability. Critical systems thinking, as we shall see, recommends using different systems methodologies together in a manner which takes advantage of the strengths and counteracts the weaknesses of individual methodologies. Just how is this possible when different systems approaches are based upon conflicting epistemological and ontological assumptions?

5.4. SYSTEMS THINKING AS A TRANSDISCIPLINE

The chapter began with our seeking to situate applied systems thinking within the context of the systems movement as a whole. It continued with a consideration of the development of applied systems thinking, with particular attention being given to the emergence of new systems methodologies able to guide problem-solving in a wider range of contexts. I want to summarize now the way I am using terms in this book to ensure sufficient clarity in the arguments still to be developed.

The phrase "systems movement" I take to refer to the various professional societies and academic groupings which advocate systems thinking, and the periodicals, newsletters etc., that promote systems thinking, as well as those who research or practice using a systems approach. Systems thinking is then a general term used to denote the theories, methodologies, models, tools and techniques, which are based on systems ideas and concepts and are employed by those who argue for a systems approach. The systems approaches discussed in Part 2 are particular expressions of theories, methodologies, and systems models and methods. Applied systems thinking refers to that part of the systems movement that has as its primary concern the use of systems thinking to promote "problem-solving". As we saw, this can be differentiated from systems thinking used in the disciplines and the study of systems in their own right. Applied systems thinkers are interested in systems research, in the development and enhancement of systems theories, methodologies and models, but in a "Mode 2" rather than "Mode 1" form. Systems research of this kind is designed to promote systems practice in the services of users. For this reason, applied systems thinkers are much concerned with systems methodologies. Systems methodologies reflect particular theoretical positions. They also provide principles for the use of the various systems models, methods, tools and techniques in practice. Systems methodologies represent to the applied systems thinker the kind of "transferable problem solving capability" that is essential in Mode 2 research.

Is it then possible to regard systems thinking as a discipline in its own right? The answer seems to be definitely no, because it does not seek to delimit a particular area of reality for study which it can call its own; at least not in the same way as do chemistry, geography or sociology. As we witnessed, systems thinkers can be found in a whole variety of disciplines. Systems thinking has not succeeded however, as was the hope of the founders of GST, in establishing itself as a meta-discipline. Whether and where it has proved useful in particular disciplines has depended on the nature of those disciplines and upon their state of conceptual development. Systems thinking is probably best regarded, therefore, as a transdiscipline or cross-discipline. Its theories, models and methods can add value in a variety of fields.

Both systems research and systems practice can be, but need not be, multidisciplinary. This term is probably best saved to refer to the personnel and practice, rather than the substance, of the research itself. Thus a multidisciplinary research project will bring together researchers from different disciplines, each bringing their own unique perspective to bear. Systems research can be interdisciplinary especially when it concerns itself with gaining knowledge of systems in their own right. It is legitimate to see cybernetics, GST, and complexity theory, for example, as working between disciplines, filling the gaps left by more conventional approaches. On the other hand, as we know, systems research can equally be found in the individual disciplines, providing sustenance for their development.

The arena in which systems thinking has had its greatest success, as I started to argue earlier, is that of problem-solving. There is a resonance between systems thinking and real-world practice. The range, and the efficiency and effectiveness, of systems approaches, in promoting problem management, are a testimony to that. This must have something to do with the encouragement that applied systems thinking gives to interdisciplinary practice.

Finally, just as systems thinking is not a meta-discipline, nor is it meta-paradigmatic. It does not exist "above" the paradigms; in fact, its main ideas are interpreted differently according to the paradigm from which they are viewed. Rather, systems thinking seems to possess a particular role, through the methodologies it is able to provide, in ensuring the findings of particular paradigms can be put into practice. It is transparadigmatic, serving each paradigm by enabling the social theory found within it to have practical relevance.

5.5. THE STATUS OF APPLIED SYSTEMS THINKING

It seems to be the case that the shelf life of management "fads" is diminishing. "Total Quality Management" (TQM) had a long run but was eventually overtaken by "Business Process Reengineering" (BPR), which had its day before being replaced by the "Learning Organization", which had its moment, and so on. It is also widely accepted that change programs based on TQM, BPR, "Rightsizing", "Knowledge Management", or whatever, fail, in the great majority of cases, to bring the benefits expected. Ackoff (1999a) provides a list of the literature on which such an evaluation can be based and is able to explain the reason for failure in systems terms. I have, elsewhere (Jackson, 1995), taken time to criticize the management fads and will not repeat the exercise here. I do intend, however, to set out a few reasons why systems thinking, of the kind propounded in this volume, should be seen as having a higher status than that of a "fad"; why it should be regarded as a serious and worthwhile attempt to develop management theory and practice. The process of justifying taking a systems approach began in Chapter 2, where I put forward arguments in favor of holism, of the value of organizing knowledge in "cognitive systems", and for the efficacy of systems thinking as a practical approach to problem-solving. That process will continue throughout the book. I am aware, nevertheless, that a full justification would require setting out a theory of knowledge and mounting a philosophical defense of "holism", at the very least; which is beyond the scope of our ambition here. I am content simply to move the argument forward by providing some more pointers as to why we should grant high status to applied systems thinking. There are five arguments we might reasonably make at this stage.

The first very general argument concerns the need to do careful research and over reasonably long periods of time. Before we go about proclaiming that we know the answers to all the problems facing managers, we have an obligation to undertake serious research. Systems thinking can reasonably claim that the progress it has made along the two dimensions framing the SOSM , allowing it to tackle more complex problems and problems involving values and interests, has been based on such research. Along the complexity continuum, for example, there have now been many applications of socio-technical systems theory, and of Beer's "viable system model" (a model within the "organizational cybernetic" tradition). These have enabled reflection and learning about the key design features that need to be present in complex adaptive systems. Mention was made of the hundreds of applications of "interactive management", "interactive planning" and "soft systems methodology" as the values/interests dimension was developed. I am most familiar with the research program, running at the University of Hull since the early 1980s, which gave birth to "critical systems thinking." In a disciplined way we sought to consider the contrasting strengths and weaknesses of the variety of systems approaches to problem solving. We looked at the theoretical underpinnings of the approaches and tried to ask what they assume about the problem situations in which they seek to intervene. We also tried out these approaches in practice. In other words, we investigated theoretically *and* practically the strengths of the array of systems methodologies and developed our own appreciation of the usefulness of each beyond the proclamations of their originators. As the following chapters reveal, there have been a number of well-founded "Mode 2" research programs running in systems thinking for a good number of years. In the best cases they have produced learning about the "framework of ideas" (F) brought to bear in the research, the methodology or methodologies (M) employed, and the area of application (A) that was being addressed.

A second main point involves the need to be open to learning during the research process. In order to do serious research it is necessary to set up strong hypotheses which you are willing to see refuted; which indeed you seek yourself to falsify. Those who propagate management fads often appear to know the answers before they actually do the research, which then amounts to little more than a self-fulfilling prophecy. This is often combined with a tendency, among management "gurus", to recommend solutions which they believe hold in all circumstances. Perhaps we thought that we had rid ourselves of universal panaceas in management when we abandoned the machine model of Taylor, Fayol and Weber. But with the "fads" we seem ready again to adopt models recommended for all circumstances. The touting of universal panaceas to managers leads to the kind of disaster diagnosed some time ago by Lorsch (1979). Looking back on human relations theory, which had many things in common with newer fads, Lorsch wrote:

> The behavioral sciences occasionally hum with enthusiasm about certain ideas ... Each ... becomes almost a fad with strong advocates to tout its early successes. Then, as a growing number of companies try the ideas or techniques and as reports of failures and disappointments mount, the fad quickly dies. This often repeated pattern has caused many managers to lose interest in trying other behavioral science ideas that could help them (p. 179).

Lorsch's strictures have been echoed more recently, almost to the letter, by John Harvey Jones (1993):

> The difficulty is that there can never be any single correct solution for any management problem, or any all-embracing system which will carry one through a particular situation or period of time ... the skill of the manager consists of knowing them all and .... choosing the particular ideas which are most appropriate for the position and time in which he finds himself (p. 2).

Such words are music to the ears of many systems thinkers. I often categorize the work in which I have been involved, within critical systems thinking, as being based upon ignorance. We have not pretended to know what makes organizations efficient and effective and what makes them reasonable places to work in. I still would not claim to be sure whether it is getting the structure right or the processes right, or managing the culture, or dealing with the politics. It seems to require something of all these but we need to carry out further research to be sure. Serious research is better based on an acknowledged ignorance than upon "truths" known in advance.

This brings me to a third point. Compared to the holism encouraged by systems thinking, the solutions to problems offered by other management thinkers often seem extremely partial. TQM has done a lot to improve process design but can be criticized for ignoring wider organizational structures and the politics of organizations. IT investments frequently fail because they are too technology based, ignoring the fit with business strategy and the very people who have to operate new systems as users. A piece in the *The Economist* (1993) argues for the significance of the variables of power and conflict, almost always ignored in "fad" writings, in preventing companies achieve efficiencies through management information systems. Too much management thinking is partial in what is regarded as crucial to business success. First it is culture, then flexibility, then structure. An overall, holistic vision is missing. You can see this easily enough if you ask what the relevant "guru" or management fad is taking for granted about what makes organizations effective. Are organizations being seen just as machines; or are they being thought of as organisms needing to adapt to their environments; or as cultures in which different value systems and political interests coexist? Propagators of new fads are continually finding new pieces of the jigsaw but failing to fit them in properly. Systems thinking, as I have tried to suggest, is able with its holistic view to see the broader picture and the true complexity of the management task. Systems thinking is also holistic in the sense that it entertains the perspectives offered on organizations and their management by various sociological paradigms. Its concern is to get the greatest benefit from each of these possible theoretical positions, adding its own contribution of rigor and relevance in each case.

My fourth point builds on the second and third. Applied systems thinking has invested much time in unearthing the philosophical and sociological underpinnings of the intervention methodologies it employs. It asks the question: what is being assumed about "systems" when intervening in this or that way? This necessary theoretical moment is often missing in the management literature. Fad writers do not, for the most part, explore the theories underlying their recommendations; they do not ask what they are taking for granted about organizations in intervening in them in particular ways. Underlying all prescriptions for intervening are various theories about the nature of social systems. For a host of reasons it is incumbent upon us to surface them.

We can begin to explain this by remembering a famous remark of Keynes made in the *Concluding Notes* of his book *The General Theory of Employment, Interest and Money* (1973, p. 383):

> Practical men, who believe themselves to be quite exempt from any intellectual influences, are usually the slaves of some ... academic scribbler of a few years back.

Fad writers are often the slaves of academic scribblers a few years back, but because they cannot recognize a theoretical orientation in previous work similar to that implied by their own efforts, they do not learn from previous research and simply duplicate it in an impoverished form.

The failure to reflect on the theory on which their recommendations are based also ensures that the advocates of fads cannot relate their experiences back to theory so as to learn why some interventions succeed while others fail. Unless one understands the assumptions one makes in doing things a particular way, one cannot really learn from an intervention so that one can modify those assumptions and improve one's chances of success on later occasions. There is a temptation to make the same prescriptions or try the same method out again and again, because it worked before; suddenly, one will try it out in circumstances where it does not work, with disastrous results. Charles Lamb helps us build on this argument with a story he told about the first tribe to discover cooking (retold in Kanter *et al.* 1992). While the tribe was away one day, gathering roots and berries, there was a fire in their village and one of the huts, built of wood and thatch, was burned down. Fortunately, the only casualty was a pig. When the villagers returned they liked the smell of the roast pig and some of the people dipped their hands in its still hot carcass. Putting their hands to their mouths to cool them off they encountered a delicious taste as well. They had discovered cooking. Whenever in the future the villagers wanted to replicate the experience of eating the beautiful roast pig, they would get a pig, tie it up in one of the huts, and burn the hut down. It is difficult to learn from trial and error, it seems, and it can be costly. Reasoned intervention based on theory can help us to learn and can reduce costs.

I could go on at length about the need for a theoretical moment, usually present in applied systems thinking and usually absent in the fads. If one does not know what one's theories are, one cannot make links with other disciplines or explain one's knowledge and pass it on to the next generation. One has to deliver insights as a guru. If one does not have a theoretical check, it is impossible to appreciate that the methods being used might be working for the "wrong" reasons - perhaps because they appeal to the powerful and lend themselves to authoritarian usage. As Bahro (1978) wrote of the old Soviet ideology: "It *appears* as 'true' and 'scientific' precisely to the extent that the compulsion functions effectively."

We are led onto my final point, which is about the purpose of management knowledge from the point of view of applied systems thinking. This is often given very little prominence in other management writings although it is surely not irrelevant to ask what are the consequences for organizations and societies of applying management theory. Are we doing the right things as well as trying to do things right? Are we questioning ends as well as means? What ideological commitment is embedded in management "knowledge"? Who benefits? These are the sorts of questions which, with its theoretical awareness and ethical commitment, critical systems thinking has been prepared to raise.

The argument of this section has been that it is necessary to engage in careful and considered research, both theoretical and practical, if we are to produce results of real use to managers. Such research is much in evidence in applied systems thinking which should, therefore, be accorded a higher status than skeptical managers might grant to management fads.

Chapter 5 completes Part I of the book, "Overviews." The reader should now have the necessary grasp of relevant social theory, and a sufficient understanding of the history and development of systems thinking, to cope with the detailed analysis of "Systems Approaches" given in Part II. Part II devotes a chapter to summarizing and critiquing each of four possible types of systems approach - functionalist, interpretive, emancipatory and postmodern.

II

SYSTEMS APPROACHES

In considering the various systems approaches, in Chapters 6-9. we shall be putting the emphasis on 'methodology'. This is in part because we have already spent much time outlining the social and systems theories which have been, explicitly or implicitly, incorporated into systems methodologies. The primary reason, however, is that it is methodology that is critical to applied systems thinking. From the point of view of practice, it is methodology that allows the translation of social and systems theories into guidelines that can be employed by practitioners to intervene in and change the world. According to the particular theoretical orientation imparted to intervention, through methodology, the practitioner will use methods, tools, models and techniques in a certain way. From the point of view of research, it is properly formulated methodologies that allow the translation back of what is learned in practice in order to influence theory. As we know, applied systems thinking can be seen as a kind of 'Mode 2' research. It is client orientated. On the other hand, it hopes, through each intervention, to stimulate learning about the theory, or 'framework of ideas', employed, about the methodology used, and about the area of application within which the intervention took place.

The overview of social theory, in Chapter 3, ended by identifying four generic research approaches - functionalist, interpretive, emancipatory and postmodern. We have already concluded that systems thinking is not 'meta' to these paradigms: it cannot stand above them. Rather, it serves them by adding greater conceptual rigor within their theoretical formulations and/or by enabling translation of these formulations into guidelines for practical action. In Part II, therefore, applied systems thinking is itself classified in terms of the same four approaches to research and intervention. The chapters take the approaches in turn and treat them in a similar way. The reader is first introduced to the general theoretical background that governs the approach. We then turn to the specific systems methodologies which reflect this theoretical background. There is always more than one existing methodology fitting in with each theoretical background. In the case of each methodology we fill in any new theory that is necessary, usually because it has proved of specific use to that methodology. Where possible, however, we concentrate on the methodology itself and the way that it is employed to turn theory into practice. Also set out are any models, methods, tools and techniques which are commonly associated with the particular methodology being considered. These may prove to be detachable and useable within other methodologies, but it is best to view them alongside the methodology they were designed to serve. Case studies are included as necessary. After each methodology, and any specific theory and any associated models, methods, etc., have been described, a brief summary of the strengths and weaknesses of that methodology is provided. Once the main variants of methodology associated with each theoretical position have been dealt with, a generic systems methodology for that theoretical position is established. This will, in fact, be an elaboration of the relevant part of Table 3.1 in systems terms and with the emphasis on methodology for the purposes of intervention and change. Each chapter concludes with a critique of the systems approach covered at a more general and theoretical level.

6

THE FUNCTIONALIST SYSTEMS APPROACH

6.1. INTRODUCTION

I need to remind the reader of what, on the basis of Chapter 3, it is like to look at systems from the functionalist point of view. When this perspective is adopted, systems appear as objective aspects of a reality independent of us as observers. Using the methods of the natural sciences, they are examined in order to discover the laws that govern the relationships between their parts or sub-systems. If knowledge about the behavior of a system can be gained in this way, the knowledge can be used by experts to improve the technical efficiency or efficacy of the system and/or its long-term ability to adapt and survive. The tenor of the functionalist approach is modernist. There is an optimism that progress in science will enable better prediction of natural and social events, and greater control over disorder and inefficiency.

The "root metaphors" of mechanism, organicism and formism hold sway within functionalism. In terms of Morgan's images of organization, we find the machine, organism, brain, and flux and transformation metaphors most commonly employed. We shall, however, in what follows, be able to identify variations within the functionalist tradition of thought according to the root metaphor or image of organization that is privileged. We should also remember that functionalists differ according to epistemology. Some take the positivist position that empirical observation of a system will reveal the law-like relations between parts governing its behavior. Others take the structuralist view that it is necessary to describe structures and mechanisms operating at a deeper level because it is these that causally generate the observable phenomena.

As we saw, for many decades in systems thinking functionalism and the systems approach were virtually synonymous. Functionalism supplied the philosophical and sociological ground on which systems thinking could grow, and systems thinking provided the concepts and models that enabled functionalism to blossom in the social sciences. Today it is still the case that much of systems thinking remains dominated by the functionalist paradigm. It is, therefore, impossible to cover everything. I have chosen, for inclusion in this survey of the functionalist systems approach, those areas of work within applied systems thinking that seem to offer most to the manager. Roughly, and according to the date of their emergence, I take for study the "organizations-as-systems" tradition, "hard systems thinking", "system dynamics", "organizational cybernetics", "living systems theory", "autopoiesis", and "complexity theory." It should be possible to recognize how all of these hold to the basic tenets of functionalism while differing in certain of the details, for example in terms of the metaphors they most frequently employ.

6.2. ORGANIZATIONS-AS-SYSTEMS

"Organizations-as-systems" thinking had its theoretical roots and developed within the disciplines of sociology and management and organization theory. It is not surprising, therefore, that it has two strands: one dominated by the mechanical analogy and the other by the organismic analogy. Pareto's sociology, which looked at society as a system in equilibrium, was popularized by Henderson and brought into the domain of management thinking by Roethlisberger and Dickson, and by Barnard. Barnard's work is taken as an example of this approach because of its contemporary relevance. The organismic analogy, employed in sociology by Durkheim and Spencer, sees society as an interconnected whole, capable of adaptation and evolution, and with the parts fulfilling the needs of the whole. Selznick and, with a heavy dose of von Bertalanffy's general system theory, Katz and Kahn transferred the analogy to the level of the organization. The organismic model of the nature of organizations provided the theoretical basis for the two most important research programs developed within the "organizations as systems" tradition - contingency theory and socio-technical systems theory. Equally important to the emergence of these two approaches, as we shall see, were various empirical studies of organizations and their performance, all of which tended to throw doubt on traditional and human relations thinking about management. The organizations-as-systems tradition, in the guise of contingency theory and socio-technical systems theory, is based upon a combination of these theoretical and empirical contributions.

The work of Barnard, contingency theorists and socio-technical theorists represents the most prescriptive side of the organizations-as-systems tradition, giving managers specific advice about how they should run their organizations.

6.2.1. Barnard's Systems Thinking

Barnard was an extremely experienced executive. Between 1927 and 1948 he was President of the New Jersey Bell Telephone Company and he also served on government agencies and in charitable positions. His introduction to academic thinking came as a member of Henderson's influential "Pareto Circle" at Harvard, mixing with the likes of Mayo, Roethlisberger, Dickson and Parsons. As a result of this intellectual exposure, and drawing on his practical experience, he produced in 1938 an early systems account of the nature of organizations, called *The Functions of the Executive*. This became one of the most influential books ever published in the field of management. Essentially, in this volume, Barnard uses a mechanical model to advise executives on how they should sustain organizations in equilibrium by the careful manipulation of inducements to stakeholders. I shall consider this work in two parts: looking first at his exposition of the nature of organizations as systems, then at his conclusions about how executives should behave to ensure that their organizations survive and are more efficient.

Barnard reasoned that organizations were "co-operative systems." When an individual tries to do something, she is subject to strict physical and biological constraints that determine what it is possible to achieve. In order to realize major tasks, therefore, individuals have to co-operate and this gives rise to the birth of co-operative systems.

Co-operative systems will persist, Barnard argues, as long as they are effective and efficient. Barnard links effectiveness to the success of the organization in accomplishing its purpose. Efficiency relates to the need to provide, to individuals who co-operate, a surplus of satisfactions over dissatisfactions. Unless these individuals receive such a surfeit, they will not continue to remain as members of the organization (in the case of employees), or to have dealings with it (in the case of other stakeholders). Effectiveness and efficiency are achieved through the interactions among people as managed by both the formal (studied by traditional theory) and informal (studied by human relations theory) structures of the enterprise. The formal structures are the consciously coordinated activities that define a common purpose, reward organizational members, and put individuals in communication with one another. The informal structures are those that arise without a common or consciously coordinated joint purpose. They are equally significant, Barnard argues, to proper organizational functioning, and executives of necessity should pay close attention to the informal as well as formal aspects of organizations.

From this analysis of organizations as co-operative systems, Barnard derives his conclusions about what executives should do in order to manage them properly. There are essentially three functions the executive must undertake. First, organizational communication must be maintained by creating a proper structure for the enterprise, selecting suitable people for the executive role, and securing an informal organization that backs up and supports the formal. Second, essential services must be secured from appropriate individuals by making them aware of the organization, bringing them into a co-operative relationship with it, and making sure they are motivated to work for or with the organization by offering them sufficient inducements in return for their contributions. Finally, the organization's objectives should be formulated and the idea of a common purpose inculcated at all levels of the enterprise.

Barnard believed his thinking was relevant to all forms and types of organization. His aim was to discover features common to executive functions in all organizations. What was significant was that he attempted to do this by considering, first, what kind of systems organizations are. Thus he did not simply produce a list of elements of the management process, as Fayol had done. He asked himself what organizations as systems were actually like and then derived from this analysis conclusions about what executives needed to do to manage them properly (to keep them in equilibrium). Barnard sought to capture, in his model of organizations as co-operative systems, the theoretical conclusions he had reached about the way organizations function, as supported by his own practical experience. His hope was that other executives could learn from this how best to control their own enterprises.

To critics there is obviously too much emphasis in Barnard's work on organizations being naturally co-operative systems. The mechanical-equilibrium model that underlies it cannot deal with internal conflict or, for that matter, with structure elaboration in response to a changing environment. Nevertheless, the idea of studying organizations as whole systems consisting of closely interrelated parts, the equal attention given to formal and informal aspects of organizational life, and the attempt to base a theory of management on the need to manage sensitively systems in equilibrium, remain lasting and important contributions. Today, indeed, it is extremely fashionable to see organizations as needing to serve the interests of all their "stakeholders" - not just the shareholders. To those who regard the performance and/or ethics of "tomorrow's company" as dependent on embracing all stakeholders, Barnard is the unrecognized intellectual pioneer.

6.2.2. Contingency Theory

6.2.2.1. Introduction to Contingency Theory

By about 1970 the contingency approach to the study of organizations and their management had become the established paradigm in organization theory. It remained dominant throughout the 1970s (Kast and Rosenzweig, 1981) and to some it still is. Writing in 1996, Donaldson states:

Our view is that while ... newer organization theories have something to contribute that supplements contingency theory it remains the core explanatory theory of organizational structure (p. 69).

Contingency theory, based upon the organismic analogy, views organizations as consisting of a series of interdependent subsystems, each of which has a function to perform within the context of the organization as a whole. Because of their importance to the survival needs of the organization, each subsystem is conceptualized as representing a functional imperative; an imperative that has to be met if the organization is to be viable and efficient. Contingency theorists are not in complete agreement as to which subsystems should be singled out as critical. For the purposes of this account, I will identify four subsystems of significance: the goal, human, technical, and managerial subsystems. The goal subsystem is concerned with overall purpose and objectives. The human subsystem embraces the people in the organization, their leadership, and their motivation. The technical subsystem is involved with the transformation of the inputs into the organization (matter, energy, information) into useful outputs (products, services, energy, information). The managerial subsystem must co-ordinate the other subsystems and look to the organization's relationship with the environment. In addition, management must consider the best structure for the organization in the light of the demands of the other subsystems. Contingency theory assumes that each of the subsystems is open to a range of variation. Each should be designed so that it is congruent with the others and corresponds to the environment with which it is faced. The size of the organization will also have an important effect upon the subsystems and the organizational structure.

Contingency theory additionally rests upon the open systems view that regards the organization as dependent upon the wider environment. The organization and environment are seen as being in a state of mutual influence and interdependence. The contingency theory of organizations is concerned to understand and represent the key relationships between the organization and its environment. It tends to be assumed that these can be understood in terms of the organization's need to survive; the organization must be adapted in certain ways if it is to survive in its environment. The economic performance of a firm decides whether it survives or not, and this is determined in turn by the way the organization manages its relationship with the environment. The theoretical background of contingency theory is represented in Figure 6.1, showing the primary subsystems of the organization as an open system.

As was stated, contingency theory depends equally on the conclusions emerging from the results of various empirical investigations, and I shall discuss these in the following. For the moment, however, let me establish the main hypotheses upon which contingency theory rests. There seem to be four of these.

First, there is no one best way to structure the activities of an organization in all circumstances. In this sense, contingency theory is a rebuff to traditional management theory and human relations theory, which pretended to produce principles of management applicable to all circumstances. According to the contingency approach, no such general principles exist.

Second, certain contextual factors determine the nature of the structure because of the constraints they impose. These constraints are assumed to have force because organizations must achieve certain levels of performance in order to survive. If organization structure is not adapted to context (technology, environment, etc.), then opportunities are lost, costs rise and the maintenance of the organization is threatened.

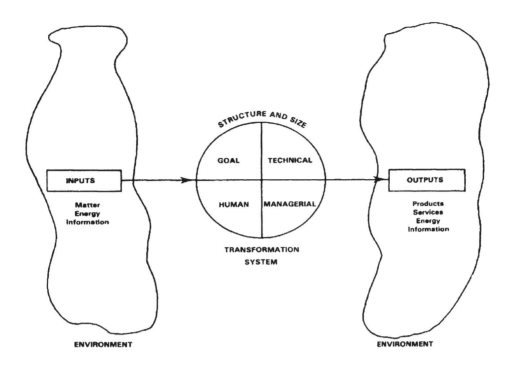

Figure 6.1. The primary subsystems of the organization as an open system

Third, it follows that depending on circumstances (i.e., on the context), some form of organization structure is likely to be more effective than others. Different organizing principles are appropriate to different contextual circumstances; it all depends on certain key strategic contingencies. This offers the prospect of reconciling earlier management theories, by establishing the domain to which each theory is apt. It shows the way forward by suggesting that the appropriateness of management principles depends on the nature of the situations in which they are applied. In some circumstances each of the earlier theories might be correct, even the much derided traditional approach.

Finally, empirical work can be conducted to establish what is the appropriate match between the organizational structure and the nature of the demands placed on it by humans, technology, environment and size.

I shall now consider, in turn, the key strategic contingencies and the effect these have upon each other and upon the most suitable organizational structure.

6.2.2.2. The Goal Subsystem

The goal subsystem obviously is closely interrelated to other internal subsystems. Choice of goal will have an effect on the technical, human, and managerial subsystems and also upon the best structure to employ. Similarly, each of the other subsystems will affect the nature of the goals pursued and the way they are pursued. Another important interrelationship will be with the environment. Goals must be chosen that ensure the legitimacy and the viability of the organization within the context of its wider environment. In a stable environment it may be possible to set static goals. In a highly uncertain and turbulent environment, goals will have to be more flexible and multiple, satisfying a variety of constraints. The organizational structure employed will have to reflect the need for flexible goals if the environment is uncertain. Fuller discussion of goals from the organizations-as-systems perspective can be found in Thompson and McEwan (1958),

Etzioni (1960), and Perrow (1961). Perhaps the most influential contribution, however, has been that by Chandler (1962) who was able to demonstrate historically the necessity of a fit between strategy and structure. Donaldson (1996) sums up his argument as follows:

> Corporations need to maintain a fit between their strategy and their structure otherwise they suffer lower performance. Specifically, a functional structure fits an undiversified strategy, but is a misfit for a diversified strategy where a multidivisional structure is required for effective management of the complexity of several distinct product markets (p. 61).

6.2.2.3. The Human Subsystem

The role of human beings in organizations is accorded a special status within most contemporary theories of management. Individuals are seen to possess certain needs that must be satisfied if they are to be attracted and encouraged to stay within the organization and if they are to be motivated to give of their best. In other words, human needs have acquired the status of a functional imperative. Theorists differ with regard to the nature of this imperative according to the "model of man" to which they subscribe (Schein, 1970). However, it is correct to see the human relations thinkers' emphasis upon the human desire for self-realization and self-actualization as legitimate concerns here (McGregor, 1960; Argyris, 1964). Thus human relations theory has its place (as does traditional theory) within the contingency perspective, but now it is recognized that human needs are only one of the various functional imperatives that have to be met. Given that proviso, human relations thinkers have shown that attention should be given to informal groups, to the proper design of jobs and to participation in decision making.

6.2.2.4. The Technical Subsystem

The type of structure one should choose for an organization, to get maximum efficiency, will depend also on the kind of technology employed to bring about the transformation process. The analysis of Woodward (1964) has been particularly influential here, and I shall concentrate on that. Perrow's (1967) work on the topic might also be consulted by interested readers, together with authors such as Blauner (1964) for the effect of technology on the human subsystem.

Between 1953 and 1957, Woodward led a research team in a survey of about 100 manufacturing firms in South East Essex in England. Her deliberate intention was to see if these firms were following the principles set out in traditional theory and, if so, whether this was bringing business success. In an investigation of certain specific features of the ways they were organized (division of labor, specialization, number of levels in the hierarchy, span of control, nature of communication taking place, etc.), Woodward found considerable variation among the firms. For example, regarding span of control, in some firms foremen had to supervise only a handful of personnel; in others, perhaps eighty or ninety workers. Obviously, the "one best way" traditional approach was not being applied. Furthermore, there seemed to be no connection between business success and what traditional theory considered to be the best organizational structure. This was very worrying.

Eventually, Woodward found a way of explaining the variations in structure among the firms. This involved relating organization structure to the technology or production system employed. Three broad categories of technology were identified:

- Unit and small batch (production largely to customer requirement)
- Large batch and mass production (assembly line)
- Process production (continuous flow production of liquids, gases, etc.)

These differences in technology appeared to account for many of the differences in structure found. Furthermore, it seemed that firms most nearly approximating the typical structure for their technology were the most successful. There appeared to be one form of structure most appropriate to each production system, and success, therefore, was a matter of getting the technology-structure fit right. If technology changed, structure should be changed in order to bring success. In fact, in the middle range of technologies, mechanistic structures seemed to be the best; so there were *some* circumstances in which traditional theorists were correct. Their view was simply limited. Woodward demonstrated, therefore, that particular technologies need particular structures to get the best performance.

6.2.2.5. Size

Pugh and a group of other researchers, originally based at what is now the University of Aston in England (Pugh and Hickson, 1976), have carried out a considerable amount of empirical research attempting to discover the link between contextual variables and various structural aspects of organizations. They wanted to know how variables such as origin, ownership, size, charter, technology, market, location, and dependence correlated with internal factors like specialization, standardization, formalization, and centralization. Scales were developed for each contextual and internal structural element; many organizations were examined to see where they fitted on the scales, and statistical analysis was undertaken with computer assistance. Stable correlations seemed to hold between contextual and internal factors across seemingly very different types of organizations. So, for example, if one knew an organization's score on the scales of size, technology, and so forth, one could predict its specialization score. Examining their results, the researchers surprisingly found only moderate correlations between technology and structure. This was, of course, contrary to Woodward's conclusions - although it is argued that the two bits of research can be reconciled on the basis that Woodward's organizations were generally smaller than those looked at by the Aston researchers (Hickson *et al.*, 1969). Instead, the latter found the strongest correlation between size and structure; depending on the size of an organization, a particular structural configuration seemed to be appropriate. So, for example, increased size seemed to bring about decreased centralization but increased structuring of activities (standardization, specialization, and formalization). It follows that size is a very significant variable that managers need to take into account when designing organization structures.

6.2.2.6. Environment

The survival of organizations as open systems depends upon some degree of exchange with outside parties. Different environmental conditions and different types of relationship will, contingency theorists argue, require different types of organization structure for high performance to be achieved and sustained. The usual conclusion is that the higher the degree of environmental uncertainty and turbulence, the more the structure of an organization needs to be adaptive, with fluid role structures, co-ordination achieved by frequent meetings, and considerable lateral communication. Examples of such theorists are Burns and Stalker (1961) and Lawrence and Lorsch (1967).

Burns and Stalker argue that different environmental conditions require different management systems in organizations. Some circumstances favor a mechanistic structure, others an organismic structure. The mechanistic, traditional organizational form is suitable for stable environments and, indeed, made possible the large increases in scale and efficiency of undertakings characteristic of the early twentieth century. This structure is, however, unsuitable in times of rapid technological and market change. The bureaucratic firm is incapable of accommodating the demands of large-scale research and development, and the new relationships with the market, required in these conditions. Uncertain and turbulent environments require more adaptive management systems, exhibiting greater flexibility and demanding more commitment from members; what Burns and Stalker call an "organic" or organismic structure. A survey of the Scottish electronics industry, which was at the time confronted with rapidly changing environmental circumstances, allowed Burns and Stalker to specify the nature of the organismic structure suitable to an unstable environment.

Mechanistic structures exhibit specialization, independence of tasks, strict rules, vertical communication, tight job descriptions, and a hierarchy with communication coming down from an omniscient leader at the top. Organismic structures need to show less formal task definition, greater task interdependence, continual redefinition of duties, horizontal as well as vertical communication, and greater decentralization of decision making. These two forms of structure represent ideal types from which actually existing organizations will, of course, diverge.

Burns and Stalker point, therefore, to the need to adjust organizational structure according to the nature of the environment faced. Unfortunately, as they also point out, this is far from easy to achieve because organizational participants develop vested interests in protecting existing organizational designs and procedures.

Lawrence and Lòrsch have extended this work and conclude that different sub-units within organizations (production, sales, research and development) will themselves require different structures because they each relate to different sub-environments (technical, market, and scientific, respectively). In certain kinds of environments, there will be a need for high differentiation in an organization as each sub-unit necessarily develops particular attributes in response to its own environmental segment. This will demand innovative strategies on the part of managers to ensure the overall integration of the system in the face of its total environment. Overall organizational performance demands a degree of differentiation among sub-units consistent with the requirements of their specific environments and a degree of integration consistent with the demands of the total environment.

6.2.2.7. The Managerial Subsystem

Management is clearly a functional imperative of efficient and effective organizations, since some management is needed to balance the pulls exerted by the other subsystems and to fit the organization into its environment. Thompson (1967) and Kast and Rosenzweig (1981) have elaborated upon Parsons's three-level division of managerial tasks (described in Chapter 4). Beyond this, however, the role of management was for some time seriously neglected by contingency theorists. The explanation is that it was seen simply as the element in the system that responded (or otherwise) to the determinations imposed on the organization by other variables. The work of Child (1972, 1984) changed that. Child has argued that managers possess "strategic choice." Managers can choose or influence some of the environmental factors that affect their organizations (e.g. employees, customers, location); they are not simply prey to environmental determinations. Organizations can also

THE FUNCTIONALIST SYSTEMS APPROACH

operate at less than optimum performance and still survive; this gives managers slack to exercise their judgement about what structure to employ. Finally, Child suggests, much the same performance may be obtained with different structures. So, again, there is room for choice. With Child's work the managerial subsystem was reinstated as an important and independent influence on the organizational structure. Although widely accepted, Donaldson (1996) has argued that recent research casts doubt on Child's conclusions:

> The argument of Child ... that the systems imperatives are weaker than pioneering structural contingency theory supposed has been examined and is not as valid as generally presumed ... the proportion of structural variance to be explained by choice is under 30 per cent at best. And it may well be less than 30% because of any other causes of structure that might exist .... The results support structural theory in its original form with the determinism intact (pp. 67-68).

Having reviewed the key strategic contingencies, I shall now briefly consider recent developments in contingency theory, the methodology of the approach and what criticisms might be leveled at it.

6.2.2.8. Recent Developments

One interesting development in contingency theory has been to see the best way to structure an organization as contingent upon the amount of information processing it has to do, which in turn is dependent on the uncertainty and diversity surrounding its basic task. This approach, as developed by Galbraith (1977), was mentioned earlier as an example of the employment of the "organizations as brains" metaphor. It helps to generalize a number of the more specific findings of contingency theory. It also extends the potential of the approach (which was previously heavily organismic in character) and brings it closer to the organizational cybernetic thinking discussed in a later section of this chapter.

In general terms, however, the pioneering work in contingency theory was published during the 1960s and, for advocates of the approach, the period from 1970 to the present has been what Kuhn (1970) would call a period of "normal science." The main emphasis for researchers has been on "puzzle-solving" and consolidation within the bounds of the paradigm. The Aston studies, for example, have been replicated many times and the main contingency-structure findings of the original work have been upheld. Moreover, generalization of the results has been possible. Donaldson reviewed thirty five studies, based in fifteen different countries, of the relationship between size and degree of specialization by function: all the studies found a positive correlation (Donaldson. 1996). As Donaldson (1996) states:

> The normal science that has been pursued within the contingency paradigm is probably the largest single normal science research stream in the study of organizational structure to date (p. 58).

In his view it has led to a confirmation and strengthening of contingency theory.

6.2.2.9. Methodology

As will be clear from the above, Donaldson, the leading contemporary advocate of the approach, regards the paradigm of contingency theory as providing a basis for research "leading to the construction of a scientific body of knowledge" (1996). The theory underpinning the approach is sociological functionalism:

Just as biological functionalism explains the way the organs of the human body are structured so as to contribute to human well-being, so sociological functionalism explains social structures by their functions, that is their contributions to the well-being of society (Donaldson, 1996, p. 54).

An organization is viewed by contingency theory as a center of mutual influence and interaction between four subsystems (goal, human, technical and managerial), the variables of size and structure, and the environment in which the organization is located. Contingency theory postulates that the effective performance of an organization is contingent upon the subsystems of the organization being designed in accordance with each other and the demands of the environment with which they interact. Attention has to be paid to getting an organizational structure appropriate to the demands of the subsystems and the environment. These ideas are represented in Figure 6.2.

The research approach adopted is positivist. Contingency and structural factors are defined and measured. Empirical evidence is sought across a number of organizations, which might reveal correlations between contingency factors and aspects of structure. Where associations are found, tests are carried out to confirm a "fit" between contingency and structure - do organizations that demonstrate such a fit perform better than those which do not? Humans, their viewpoints and beliefs, do not feature prominently therefore in the research.

The purpose of the research is twofold. Sociologists of organization add to their knowledge of what causes lie behind particular types of structure. On the other hand, those interested in practice are in a position to advise on what type of structure for an organization will lead to optimum performance in the context in which it finds itself. Quite specific proposals for the design of organizations can be made on the basis of the empirical studies conducted under contingency theory - as, for example, in Lawrence and Lorsch (1969). Of particular importance, perhaps, was the work of Woodward, and Burns and Stalker, which

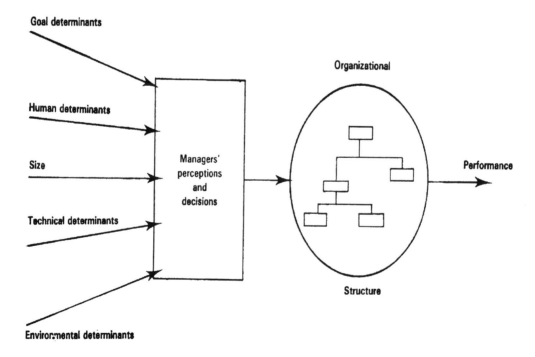

Figure 6.2. The contingency theory perspective

recommended "organic" rather than "mechanistic" structures to deal with rapid technological and environmental change. According to Donaldson (1996):

> The task of research and academic writing in this approach was to bring these models and findings to the attention of managers so that they could avoid the inefficiencies both Woodward ... and Burns and Stalker ... depicted, resulting from failure to adapt organizational structure to technological change rapidly enough (p. 60).

A business education based on contingency theory would allow managers to recognize system imperatives and adjust their organization structures rapidly to "fit" with strategic contingencies. This would ensure optimum performance.

6.2.2.10. Critique

Donaldson (1996) recognizes that:

> Much of the criticism from outside of the paradigm revolves around the perceived neglect of an action-level analysis in structural contingency theory research (p. 64).

He also notes concern about whether correlations between contingency variables and aspects of structure are able to prove the "direction of causality" and about the relative neglect of organizational politics in contingency theory. He is himself, however, in no doubt that progress in the "normal science" of contingency theory will be able to deal with these anomalies in the future as it has dealt with others in the past. We shall have to take up some of these issues again in our general critique of the "organizations-as-systems" approach.

6.2.3. Socio-technical Systems Theory

6.2.3.1. Introduction to Socio-technical Systems Theory

The second set of empirical investigations that helped shape the organizations-as-systems perspective were those carried out within the socio-technical systems tradition. Socio-technical systems theory is associated with the Tavistock Institute of Human Relations and particularly with the names of Emery, Rice and Trist. From the 1940s onward, these theorists attempted to transfer behavioral science and systems ideas to industry through the consultancy mechanism. Particularly important in the early development of the theory were the "Coal Mining Studies" (Trist and Bamforth, 1951; Trist *et al.*, 1963). In the next section I consider some of the important management concepts developed during the early stages of socio-technical systems thinking. The Coal Mining studies are then described. There follows a sub-section on later conceptual developments. Finally, an extended case study details a socio-technical intervention of the 1960s, Shell's New Philosophy of Management, which was ahead of its time and has considerable contemporary relevance.

6.2.3.2. The Early Stages of Socio-technical Systems Thinking

Socio-technical systems theory sees organizations as pursuing primary tasks that can best be realized if their social, technological, and economic dimensions are jointly optimized and if they are treated as open systems and fitted into their environment. We can consider this more fully by examining seven interrelated ideas or concepts that inspired or were developed during the early studies.

Of paramount importance is the idea that work groups or organizations should be regarded as interdependent socio-technical systems. They have interactive technological and social aspects, and in designing the structure of the group or organization both of these should be considered. If the structure of the work organization is designed with only the technology in mind, then it may be disruptive of the social system and not achieve maximum efficiency. If it is designed with only the social and behavioral aspects in mind, it is unlikely to make very good use of the technology.

This leads onto a second idea: In designing work organizations, their social, technological, and economic elements (the subsystems recognized in socio-technical theory) should be jointly optimized. The attainment of optimum conditions for any of the three elements may not result in optimum performance for the system as a whole. For example, the optimum structure to make use of the technology might not serve the social subsystem very well. Joint optimization means ensuring optimization of the whole, even if this requires a less than optimum state for each separate aspect.

Joint optimization is possible (and this is the third concept) because there is organizational choice. It is possible within the same technological and economic constraints to operate with different forms of work organization, with various social and psychological results. So, given the constraints, managers should exercise their choice over the type of work organization to adopt with the social system in mind.

The next concept is that of primary task. An organization's primary task is the task it has to perform in order to survive. It is for the purpose of realizing this primary task that the social, technical, and economic subsystems have to be jointly optimized.

The fifth notion is the by now familiar one that work organizations should be regarded as open systems. The socio-technical thinkers were very influenced by von Bertalanffy's conclusions and employed the usual open system, input-transformation-output model to understand production systems.

The Tavistock theorists also emphasized a sixth idea, the importance of group working. They considered that workers were more satisfied if they worked in groups. Groups could tackle whole tasks, and make work more meaningful for the individual. Socio-technical thinking encourages, therefore, the setting up of semi-autonomous work groups. These groups (which the studies showed could be forty or fifty strong) are supposed to act as self-regulating and self-developing social systems, capable of maintaining themselves in a steady state of high productivity. Control and decision making are exercised internally by the group and not externally by managers. Within the groups, great flexibility can exist with job rotation and workers being encouraged to become multiskilled. Each group can negotiate some of the details of its own labor contract with management. Many advantages are said to follow in addition to increased job satisfaction. The system should ensure more work is done because no individual is ever short of a job - if one finishes his own, he can always help with someone else's. Problems are dealt with quickly, as they arise, and as near to the point where they occur as possible. They do not require the intervention of management.

The seventh and final concept can be seen as a directly related consequence of setting up semi-autonomous work groups. Since the groups control themselves, they do not have to be controlled from the outside. This frees management for the much more important task of "boundary management." Instead of wasting time attempting to apply autocratic regulation, managers can invest their energies in relating the operating system (and the organization as a whole) to its environment; ensuring that the group doing the work in the operating system is supplied with the necessary input, and that its output is disposed of profitably on the market.

These concepts did not, of course, emerge all at once. Indeed, the reader studying Trist and Bamforth (1951) will find them working with a mechanical-equilibrium analogy rather than the later open system idea. The notion of primary task itself also underwent modification. Nevertheless, they made up the core of socio-technical thinking by the early 1960s.

6.2.3.3. The Coal Mining Studies

Most of the above concepts can be seen employed in the Coal Mining Studies. Trist and Bamforth (1951) and later Trist et al. (1963) used socio-technical ideas to study the mechanization of the British coal mining industry. In the traditional method of coal getting, the "hand-got method", small groups of skilled men worked in an essentially self-regulating and autonomous way on their own part of the coal face. The workers could choose who to work with, each developed multiple skills, they were responsible for their own pace of work and supervision was internal. Each group made its own contract with management. This form of work organization seemed to provide for a social system that suited the underground situation. With the advent of mechanization, however, the traditional form of work organization was abandoned, and the "conventional long-wall" method of coal getting was set up. This was a factory-like system of work organization with forty or fifty specialists, on different pay rates, all working together on a single long face. Furthermore, a three-shift system was introduced, with each shift doing a different part of the overall task. The whole system was coordinated by the constant involvement of management.

The conventional long-wall system was introduced to get the most out of the new technology and, indeed, looked optimum for that technology. However, it was introduced without a thought for the social system and had extremely dysfunctional social and psychological consequences. Productivity was disappointing, absenteeism and staff turnover were high, and there were constant problems for management, especially in handling the changeover between shifts.

In the later study, Trist et al. (1963) found that some miners, unable to tolerate the conventional long-wall system, had originated and won acceptance by management for what was called a "composite long-wall" system. This form of work organization was able to operate the new technology efficiently, but also paid attention to the needs of the social system. Demarcation between shifts disappeared and, on each shift, self-selected groups of forty or fifty men took on responsibility for the whole task. These groups allocated work, allowed individuals to become multi-skilled and were self-regulating. They were paid on a group bonus system. Where the composite long-wall form of work organization was introduced, the miners produced more, went absent less and were generally more satisfied with their work.

These studies consolidated the Tavistock researchers' belief in organizational choice (since different forms of work organization could operate the same technology); in the need to jointly optimize social and technical systems in pursuit of the primary task; in the usefulness of group working and the creation of semi-autonomous work groups; and in the view that managers were best employed in a boundary-spanning role, controlling the inputs and outputs of an open system.

6.2.3.4. Later Developments in Socio-technical Systems Thinking

In the 1960s, 1970s, and 1980s work based upon socio-technical ideas continued to burgeon, and the scale of intervention became extremely ambitious. The most important studies were probably the Norwegian Industrial Democracy Project (Emery and Thorsrud, 1969, 1976; Bolweg, 1976) and the various experiments carried out in Sweden, especially at Volvo's car plant at Kalmar which was designed and built around the concept of semi-autonomous group working (Gyllenhammer, 1977). In Britain there was Shell's attempt to establish a "new philosophy of management" using socio-technical concepts (Hill, 1971; Blackler and Brown, 1980). Alongside and in the course of these studies, at least six new ideas were added to the armory of socio-technical thinking. These were:

- Socio-technical theory as a means of promoting industrial democracy
- More attention given to appropriate job design
- Consideration of how technology could be redesigned to permit group working
- A greater appreciation of organization-environment relations
- Organizational goals added as an important subsystem
- The emergence of step-by-step methodologies for putting socio-technical thinking into practice

I shall take each of these new ideas in turn and explain its significance using examples from the key studies mentioned.

In a famous project conducted for the Norwegian Employers' Federation and the Norwegian Labor Organization, Emery and Thorsrud (1969) concluded that the attempt to extend industrial democracy should begin at the level of the shop floor, with control over the task itself. Allowing workers' representatives on the board had, on its own, little effect on levels of commitment and perceived involvement among the mass of workers. Socio-technical thinking and particularly the idea of semi-autonomous work groups showed how the process of democratization could be started at the bottom of the organization, where the benefits would be immediately registered, and then proceed upward. This conclusion was accepted and an ambitious project formulated, involving employers, unions, and gradually the government, to democratize Norwegian industry. There were even hopes that the lessons learned in industry would diffuse to other sectors of Norwegian society and beyond Norway itself. Four pilot projects were set up, positioned in key industries, as demonstration models from which the ideas could be spread outward (reported in Emery and Thorsrud, 1976). The pilot projects were a moderate success, but the expected widespread diffusion did not take place (Bolweg, 1976). The main payoff was actually in Sweden where, as a direct result of studying the Norwegian experiment, literally hundreds of projects began in the early 1970s.

Around the same time as the Norwegian project, earlier Tavistock research on job design was consolidated into a list of six requirements that jobs should meet if they are to be psychologically satisfying for workers (Bolweg, 1976). A job should be demanding and challenging in terms other than endurance. It should provide for continuous learning. The individual must possess a discrete area of decision making. The individual's need for social support and recognition in the workplace should be met. The task itself and the product should be related to the worker's life outside the factory. The job should also be seen as contributing to some desirable future.

The third new development concerned the redesign of technology to facilitate group working. In the early socio-technical studies, in spite of the notion of joint optimization, it was usually the case that the existing technology was accepted, with the real adjustments being made to the work organization and the social system. In the later work there was genuine redesign of technology in order to realize the true meaning of joint optimization. Volvo's car factory at Kalmar, for example, was especially designed to allow car manufacture by semi-autonomous work groups of around twenty people (Gyllenhammer, 1977). In this factory, opened in 1974, the assembly line had disappeared. A self-propelled vehicle (the "Kalmar carrier"), following conductive tape on the floor, transported the vehicles around the different areas of the factory controlled by the thirty or so work groups.

Each group could pace and organize its own work and was responsible for its own inspection. Each group made its own contract with management. Design changes made it possible for each group to be given responsibility for an identifiable part of the car. Kalmar was about ten percent more expensive to build than an equivalent ordinary factory, but Volvo regarded this as worthwhile given the better productivity and lower staff turnover and absenteeism that resulted.

The fourth innovation came in 1965 with the publication of Emery and Trist's article, *The Causal Texture of Organizational Environments*. Emery and Trist accepted von Bertalanffy's open system formulation, but felt that it neglected to deal with processes in the environment that are, themselves, among the determining conditions of organization-environment relations. They therefore added an additional concept - the causal texture of the environment. This refers to the degree of system-connectedness that exists in the environment itself. Emery and Trist isolate four ideal types of causal texture, forming a series in which the degree of causal texturing increases.

First, there are "placid-randomized" environments in which there is no connection between the parts of the environment, and the environment is homogeneous in character. Second are "placid-clustered" environments in which there is still no connection between environmental parts, but the environment is diverse, with certain resources in certain places (so the organization must know its environment). Third are "disturbed-reactive" environments. These are dynamic environments in which a number of organizations of the same type compete. Therefore, there is connection between environmental parts, and each organization has to take account of the others. Finally, there are "turbulent fields." With increasing interaction of organizations and interconnectedness of the environment, powerful dynamic properties arise, not only from the interaction of component organizations but also from the environment itself. The environment takes on its own dynamic. For example, timber enterprises, in the course of competing with one another, may overexploit the available timber, encouraging soil wash and erosion and making regeneration of timber resources impossible.

Emery and Trist argue that the environments in which organizations exist increasingly resemble turbulent fields. This makes management extremely difficult since uncertainty for organizations is increased as the consequences of their actions become unpredictable. Organizations must adopt flexible structures to increase their adaptive capabilities. But even this is not enough; individual organizations cannot expect to adapt successfully simply through their own direct actions. They will have to enter into joint collaboration with other organizations to seek solutions. The development of a set of values that can be shared by organizations will be important in this.

As these last points make clear, the arguments of Emery and Trist's paper took socio-technical thinkers beyond the mere reconsideration of organization-environment relations, and on to looking at the goals and values that organizations should adopt in turbulent field situations. This had immediate application because, as soon as the 1965 article was completed, the Tavistock researchers became involved in shaping a "new philosophy of management" for Shell UK (Hill, 1971; Blackler and Brown, 1980). Shell was certainly in a turbulent environment, faced with the beginnings of OPEC, rapid technological change, the birth of the ecological lobby and a difficult industrial relations climate. It therefore needed to rethink its traditional values and to move towards more flexible structures. A statement of "objectives and philosophy" (issued in May, 1966) saw the primary objective of the company, maximizing its contribution to the long-term profitability of the Shell Group, as subject to certain social objectives. For example, the statement declared that the resources the company used were community resources and must be used to contribute to the satisfaction of the community's need for products and services. More specifically, employee potential had to be enhanced, the safety of employees and the public given high priority, and pollution of the environment minimized. The document then went on to spell out the usual socio-technical requirement for joint optimization of the technical and social systems, and to detail the psychological requirements that related to the content of jobs. This intervention is described at length in the next sub-section.

The final new development was the emergence of procedures for operationalizing socio-technical theory. During the Norwegian project much attention was given to the need for collaborative research and to developing strategies to diffuse results. During the Shell experiment, a simplified nine-step method was produced for the actual socio-technical analysis of production systems (Hill, 1971). Perhaps the most widely known set of guidelines is Cherns's (1976) nine-principle checklist for socio-technical design. The nine principles are:

- Compatibility - the process of design must be compatible with its objectives (so if the aim is a participative organization, the design process must be participative)
- Minimal critical specification - of the way in which the work is actually carried out and who should carry it out
- The socio-technical criterion - variances from specifications are to be controlled as near to the point where they arise as possible
- The multifunction principle - to provide for flexibility and equifinality, each individual should be able to perform more than one function
- Boundary location - control of activities in a department should become the responsibility of the members, with the supervisor concentrating on boundary activities
- Information flow - information systems should be designed to provide information, in the first place, to the work teams who need it for task performance
- Support congruence - systems of social support should reinforce the organizational structure (so, if it is based on group working, payment should be by group bonus, etc.)
- Design and human values - high-quality jobs based on the six design characteristics
- Incompletion - design as an iterative process (once at the end, one must go back to the beginning again)

Cherns added a tenth principle in revising these guidelines in 1987. This principle, "power and authority", states that those who need resources to carry out their tasks should have the authority to command them and must accept responsibility for their proper use.

Socio-technical practice has had a major impact on industry and, apparently, brings satisfactory results (Pasmore *et al.*, 1982). This is true of the pure form of the theory and even more true if one takes into account its offshoot, the "quality of working life" movement. Some also see "quality circles" as having derived originally from socio-technical thinking and certainly many of the same principles are involved in quality circles, although in a less well-developed form. Those contemplating introducing any form of "group-working" or "empowerment" strategy could learn much from the socio-technical literature. Today socio-technical systems thinking continues to be developed in journals such as *Human Relations* and the *Journal of Applied Behavioral Science*. Writing in the second of these journals, in 1994, Shani and Sena proposed "socio-technical systems as a framework for examining the organizational implications of new information technology systems and as a tool for guiding the integration of change." Mumford has been engaged in a long and influential research program using socio-technical ideas in participative information-system design, culminating in her book of 1999. Fox (1995), reviewing socio-technical principles and guidelines, believes that they have a very important role to play in both contemporary organizational life and in research. His summary of the socio-technical process puts much emphasis on an initial "systems scan" stage. This stage, among other things, involves asking questions about the organization's mission, the managerial philosophy and values underlying the mission, and the relationship the organization has with its various stakeholders and the larger environment. An attempt has to be made to reconcile what the stakeholders most desire with what is viable in the current environment. As well as "technical analysis" and "social analysis", quality-of-working-life considerations are also crucial for Fox in any socio-technical intervention. He believes that action research can provide the means whereby organizational members and other stakeholders can participate fully to influence design outcomes. Their preferences must be accommodated "as far as is feasible." Fox is in full agreement with Cherns's principle that design should be an iterative process. It is never ending in the sense that the question "How can we improve upon the way we operate?" is always open. In Fox's view, "to a large extent, maintenance of this action-research-based process is more important than any given design solution." A thought which, if followed through, would turn him into a "soft" rather than a socio-technical systems thinker.

We can, I think, agree with Fox when he states that the socio-technical systems approach

> has more relevance today than ever before, as organizational personnel seek more fruitful means of empowerment and as their organizations strive for greater productivity and viability in increasingly turbulent environments (p. 91).

The following case study, while sounding a critical note, demonstrates this.

6.2.3.5. Case Study - Shell's New Philosophy of Management

This account comes from Hill (1971) and Blackler and Brown (1980). Some of the background has already been provided. Essentially, in the early 1960s, Shell UK was a company faced with some very pressing internal and external problems. Internally, the main problems were of an industrial-relations nature, with a multiplicity of unions complicating wage negotiations, frequent demarcation disputes, overmanning, excessive overtime working and supervisors who felt they were losing control to the shop stewards. A 1964 "rundown" of the company, including some dismissals, had created even more bad feeling among some employees. Shell was, therefore, hardly in a position to respond flexibly to the need for rapid technological change as required by the turbulent environment it faced. Neither was it likely to be adaptive enough to adjust to other external threats to companies in the oil industry in the era that followed Suez and saw the beginning of OPEC, as well as the birth of the ecological lobby. In 1965, a special study group headed by Hill proposed to top management some radical solutions for getting the company out of the difficulties it faced. These involved, firstly, promulgating a new philosophy of management throughout the company that would help change attitudes; and secondly, attending to the conditions of work of employees, improving these as part of productivity deals with the unions that would require greater flexibility and less demarcation on the employees' side. As soon as these recommendations were accepted by top management, socio-technical researchers from the Tavistock Institute were brought in to help develop the philosophy and to consider how it could best be diffused. To these researchers, the Shell problem situation was ideal for trying out their ideas on how organizations should be managed to deal with turbulent field environments. They were committed to the need to encourage new values, to introduce flexible structures, and to use particular methods of diffusion practiced during the Norwegian Industrial Democracy Project.

The philosophy of management sought to combine the pursuit of profit with various social objectives, such as treating Shell's resources as "community" resources, developing employee potential through appropriate job design, paying particular attention to employee and public safety, and minimizing pollution of the environment. It also embraced the principle of the joint optimization of the technical and social systems, although certain features of the technical system were regarded as fixed for the foreseeable future. The philosophy was diffused throughout the organization in a series of conferences held between 1965 and 1967 - first for top management, then for senior staff, and finally for lower staff levels: foremen, supervisors, and union officials. To give some indication of the effort that went into this, the philosophy conferences for senior staff were two-and-a-half-day events involving around 20 people from the same location. At the time, Hill believed that the conferences were getting across the message of the philosophy and its implications.

To complement and reinforce the lessons of the conferences, four further channels of implementation were opened. Three demonstration projects were set up aiming to show the power of socio-technical thinking in action. Success was patchy, but the simplified nine-step method of socio-technical analysis resulted and other experiments started on this basis. Departmental managers were charged with the task of acting as change agents. They were supposed to enthuse their staff with the philosophy and to encourage spontaneous job-design experiments. Early reports gave the impression of great activity in this area, but it seems that enthusiasm soon waned. One initiative, in the wax department at the Stanlow refinery, was played up to be a great success story of this part of the implementation process but came later, unfortunately, to be seen as something of a disaster and got the philosophy a bad name in certain quarters (Blackler and Brown, 1980).

The third leg of implementation was the productivity deals with the unions, which offered improvements in working conditions in tune with the philosophy (including staff status for all workers) in exchange for increased efficiency, greater flexibility and less demarcation. These were eventually successfully negotiated in 1968, the philosophy playing a very significant part in ensuring agreement and easing introduction. Finally, the design of a new refinery at Teesport was heavily influenced by socio-technical thinking. At this green-field site, genuine joint optimization of the social and technical systems was possible, the job design criteria for satisfying work were observed, and single-status employment was introduced.

Looking back at the experiment in 1980, Blackler and Brown concluded that earlier accounts of what happened at Shell (such as by Hill) were somewhat rosy. Accepting the enthusiasm of those involved, they nevertheless felt that the philosophy had only moderate success and in most important respects did not take off as expected. Nothing could be made of the notion of Shell stewarding "community resources", and so implementation turned out to be entirely inward looking. The conferences were very top-down events with at least implicit pressure on all present to conform and accept a philosophy developed by experts and ratified by senior management. The philosophy was sold rather than argued out. Many no doubt were convinced, but many others - especially at more junior levels - just went along with it as the easiest thing to do. The initial pilot projects, according to Blackler and Brown, raised and then dashed expectations and were not imitated. Activity at departmental-manager level soon declined, and a task force had to be sent in to sort out the wax plant at Stanlow. The philosophy helped passage of the productivity agreements, but the idea of collaboration gradually gave way to manipulation as negotiations proceeded, and management drove a hard bargain as the deals took on the character of ordinary bargaining over cash. By the time of the follow-up study, the pre-deal orthodoxy in terms of conditions for ordinary staff had largely returned. Even at Teesport, where more of the spirit of the philosophy survived, there was some return to traditional working conditions and arrangements.

In general, Blackler and Brown believe that the philosophy failed as an attempt to forge a new role for Shell in the world and as a means of creating a long-term partnership with its work force. However, from the point of view of top management, it succeeded in the short term since it did something to restore the legitimacy of the company in the eyes of its employees and helped the firm get through a period of industrial relations difficulties and negotiate new productivity deals. In this sense, Blackler and Brown see socio-technical thinking of this kind as manipulative - whatever the best intentions of those using the ideas. Such thinking appeals to managers because it presents all stakeholders as benefiting equally from company success. It neglects conflicts of real interest between, say, managers and unions, and fails to recognize the power of some groups over others. Socio-technical thinking is seen as misguided in believing that such problems can be overcome by better human relations. In reply (in Blackler and Brown, 1980), Foster, of the Tavistock Institute, and Hill defend the philosophy experiment. Foster regards it as remarkable for its day and as making a positive and worthwhile contribution. Hill sees Blackler and Brown's conclusions as negatively biased, narrow and academic. Although the philosophy was not sufficiently embodied in the organization to prevent setbacks, it brought many positive changes and provided great learning opportunities from which other projects benefited. For example, Shell Canada's Sarnia plant in Western Ontario was built, in 1978, on socio-technical principles after a "collective contract" had been agreed with the unions.

Reaching a balanced assessment of the Shell experiment is not easy. It certainly was remarkable for its time, both for the sophistication of the socio-technical ideas employed and the considerable and genuine enthusiasm generated among many involved. On the other hand, it seems true that a lasting transformation in management style and a permanent improvement in working life for ordinary employees were not achieved.

Bearing in mind what we have learned about socio-technical systems thinking, and the findings of this case study, we are now in a position to evaluate the "organizations-as-systems" approach as a whole.

6.2.4. Strengths and Weaknesses of Organizations-as-Systems

Viewing organizations as systems clearly provides a much richer picture of organizations than that supplied by the traditional and human relations models. In retrospect, it can be seen that the traditional model considered the goal subsystem and its effect upon structure, but largely ignored the human and technical subsystems and the issue of size. It was also a closed perspective, saying nothing about organization - environment relations. The human relations model considered the human subsystem, but neglected all the others. It, too, was a closed perspective. The organizations-as-systems approach looks at all the subsystems, their interrelationships, and the interactions between the subsystems (and the organization as a whole) and the environment.

According to early versions of the organizations-as-system approach (those governed by the mechanical-equilibrium analogy), organizations should be studied as systems of interdependent parts, and as having both formal and informal aspects. Later, as the organismic analogy began to dominate, it was seen to be appropriate, in addition, to view them as organisms striving for survival. They had needs, or functional imperatives, that had to be met by their subsystems. They had to adjust continually and adapt to internal and, especially, external forces because they were open systems dependent on their environments. Organizations had to take action in response to environmental changes if they wanted to maintain a steady state.

Although it is viewed as superior to the traditional and human relations approaches, the organizations-as-systems tradition has itself come in for some severe criticisms. A general charge is that it fails to deliver genuine scientific explanations for the statistical correlations discovered or the improvements supposed to follow from implementing its recommendations. The specific criticisms are that it downplays purposeful action in organizations; that it reifies organizations; that it cannot properly explain change and conflict; that it exhibits a managerial bias; and that its prescriptions for improving managerial performance are ill-founded and vague. I shall consider the criticisms in turn, drawing upon various sources (Lockwood, 1956; Gouldner, 1959; Buckley, 1967; Silverman, 1970; Burrell and Morgan, 1979; Clegg and Dunkerley, 1980). It will be recognized, however, that all the criticisms are interrelated.

As we have seen, the organizations-as-systems approach sees survival rather than goal attainment as the *raison d'être* of organizations. It also emphasizes the nonrational aspects of organizational functioning. Both these things can contribute to a neglect of the considerable amount of purposeful, goal-oriented activity that takes place in modern organizations. Rational planning activities are discounted. We saw in Donaldson's deterministic version of contingency theory, for example, that the power of managers was reduced to responding more or less quickly to system imperatives. If goals are to be achieved by organizations it is important to identify centers of command and control and to measure performance against goals. Little help is provided by organizations-as-systems thinking in this area.

There is also a tendency in the organizations-as-systems approach to "reify" organizations - to grant them the power of independent thought and action. When the organismic analogy is employed the organization is seen as best explained by its desire to meet functional imperatives and to adapt to its environment. Individuals are seen as subject to forces that are beyond their control and that they do not always understand. The conscious reasons they give for their actions are seen as no substitute for a scientific, functional explanation of what is occurring in the organization. Donaldson is happy to admit to the absence of an "action" perspective in contingency theory. And while the criticism may seem a bit harsh in relation to socio-technical thinking, it remains fundamentally true. Although attention is given to human beings, the tendency is to treat them mechanistically, as motivated if a series of psychological needs are met. All humans are supposed to respond favorably to appropriately designed jobs, group working, and an organization that provides them with a clear sense of purpose. People are not treated as self-conscious, autonomous actors capable of reading different meanings into the situations they face.

Internal tensions are admitted in the organizations-as-systems model but the main explanation provided for change is as an adaptive mechanism in response to environmental disturbances and pressures. Organizations seek as far as possible to maintain the status quo by preserving their existing structures. Structures are therefore seen as semi-permanent features of organizations that should form the main focus of analysis. Processes operate to support structures; structures are not temporary manifestations of process. Why organizations should wish to protect particular structures is not explained but such an emphasis might prevent necessary radical rearrangements of structure being contemplated.

The emphasis on social order in organizations, to the exclusion of conflict and instability, is also regarded as one-sided. With the mechanical-equilibrium model, equilibrium is maintained by the inculcation of shared norms and values into organizational participants. The organismic model pictures all the parts as functioning in cooperation to serve the whole. Unity and interdependence of parts are stressed. The idea that there might be different groups in organizations pursuing their own rationalities, based on competing social and economic interests, and frequently coming into conflict, is suppressed.

Many of the above points are brought together to justify the conclusion that the organizations-as-systems approach exhibits a managerial bias. The organization is seen as an integrated whole, the survival of which benefits all participants. The power of some group to control the organization is hidden since the organization is regarded as pursuing its own purposes. Conflict is disguised, or seen as a dysfunctional threat to the system and, therefore, all connected with it. In contingency theory and socio-technical theory, managers act paternalistically, for the good of all, by using their expert knowledge to adjust the organization in ways that will ensure its survival. Socio-technical theory even gets the workers to control themselves, relieving managers of one onerous chore, by convincing employees that they are getting a form of genuine control over their working lives. According to Blackler and Brown (1980), Shell's "new philosophy of management" was ideologically manipulative because it tried to cover real disputes with a gloss of common interest. In their view the conferences were top-down events at which the philosophy was handed down from on high, rather than subjected to thorough debate and discussion. The guiding ethos was indoctrination, not mutual understanding.

Finally, since organizations-as-systems developed primarily as an approach for understanding organizations, it is perhaps not surprising to find many of its remedies for changing and improving them accused of being vague and/or untested. In the case of all three of our examples - Barnard's systems thinking, contingency theory, and socio-technical systems thinking - the specific theory developed to support the approach is incorporated into a kind of "model" of how organizations should function. All these approaches believe that knowledge about organizations is being produced. When, however, we view organizations-as-systems as a methodology for bringing about change, rather than for producing knowledge, there is much less guidance. With the work of Barnard and contingency theory, managers are expected to learn how organizations should function, or should be structured, and to simply bring about the changes without further ado. Socio-technical thinking is much more specific about the need for change to be participative and guided by an action research process. Even here, however, the basic organizations-as-systems prescription remains: if an organization is not functioning effectively, examine its subsystems to see that they are meeting the needs of the organization and the organization to ensure it is well adjusted to its environment.

6.3. HARD SYSTEMS THINKING

At about the same time that Parsons, von Bertalanffy and others were perfecting the theory that was to dominate the "organizations-as-systems" tradition, other groups of systems thinkers were using systems ideas in a much more applied fashion to develop methodologies for real-world problem solving. The work of these systems thinkers gave birth to what has come to be known, following Checkland (1978, 1981), as hard systems thinking. Checkland originally included in this category only systems engineering and systems analysis (this incorporating additionally cost-benefit analysis and planning-programming-budgeting systems). It has become clear, however, that we can add to the list other approaches such as operational research (insofar as it embraces systems ideas at all), decision science, and management cybernetics (distinguished from organizational cybernetics in a later section). All these share the basic orientation, identified by Checkland (1978) as "the assumption that the problem task they tackle is to select an efficient means of achieving a known and defined end."

In this section, operational research, systems analysis and systems engineering are briefly described. There follows a critique sub-section in which the nature of hard systems thinking is firmly established; its strengths, when used appropriately, are stated; and a catalogue of the criticisms that have been leveled at the approach is provided. Acknowledgement is made that the criticisms are not always apt in respect of the best practitioners of the hard approach.

6.3.1. Operational Research

Operational Research (OR), or "operations research" as it is known in the United States, was for many years defined by the British Operational Research Society as

> the application of the methods of science to complex problems arising in the direction and management of large systems of men, machines, materials and money in industry, business, government and defense. The distinctive approach is to develop a scientific model of the system, incorporating measurements of factors such as chance and risk, with which to predict and compare the outcomes of alternative decisions, strategies or controls. The purpose is to help management determine its policy and actions scientifically.

The initial development of OR was in the United Kingdom, immediately prior to and during the second world war, from where it quickly spread to the United States. In both countries it soon found civilian application and played an important role in the postwar reconstruction of industrial production in the United Kingdom and in the increase in industrial efficiency in the United States. An excellent introduction to the "beginnings" of OR can be found in Keys (1991).

The first comprehensive textbook on OR appeared in 1957 and was written by Churchman, Ackoff, and Arnoff. It stresses the comprehensiveness of OR's aim as a systems approach responding to the overall problems of complex organizations. Interdisciplinary teams should use the most advanced scientific procedures to study all aspects of the system. The phases of an OR project are said to be:

- Formulating the problem
- Constructing a mathematical model to represent the system under study
- Deriving a solution from the model
- Testing the model and the solution derived from it
- Establishing controls over the solution
- Putting the solution to work (implementation)

Where certain classes of problems appear frequently in organizations, they are selected by OR for more intensive study. Churchman et al. (1957) identify those associated with inventory processes, allocating processes, waiting-time processes, replacement processes, competitive processes, and combined processes as problems falling into this category. The remaining two-thirds of the book is then taken up with describing the models and techniques relevant to solving these commonly recurring problems. Keys (1991) provides a summary.

Inventory processes are concerned with how great a "stock of resources" it is necessary to keep. To properly manage the inventory process a business needs to decide how much resource to order and when to order it. This all depends on the time taken for an order to be delivered, the rate at which resources are used and the cost of holding them in stock, and the cost of not having resources available. Many attempts have been made to mathematically model this process. In Keys's view, however, the assumptions built into such models are usually too simplistic to capture the real-world complexity of the situation.

Allocation problems are concerned with allocating scarce resources to carry out the range of activities that seem to be necessary. Keys gives an example from Glen:

> This example is concerned with the problem of how to manage an integrated enterprise which involves rearing cattle for beef and the production of crops to feed the animals ...the key management issue is how to balance the land use between cattle and crops, bearing in mind the need to purchase supplementary feed if insufficient is grown, the potential to sell excess crops, and the desirability of producing cattle of sufficient quality to meet regulations on its sale (1991, pp. 66-67).

Waiting-time processes require us to determine how to manage queuing systems effectively. This depends upon factors such as arrival time, number of servers, queue discipline and speed of service. Replacement processes involve questions of optimum replacement rates for resources that deteriorate or could fail altogether. Competitive processes occur in "games" and in bidding. In games different players adopt particular strategies, in order to win or lose, taking into account the strategy of others. How can benefit to all be optimized? In bidding situations there is a need to determine how to maximize return while ensuring the bid is higher than that of the competitors.

Another well-known OR text, Ackoff and Sasieni's *Fundamentals of OR* (1968), similarly emphasizes that OR should have a systems orientation, use interdisciplinary teams and apply the scientific method to problems of control arising in organized, man-machine systems. This book sets out the stages of the OR process in a manner similar to Churchman *et al*. It goes on to give in-depth treatment to those prototype, tactical problems that OR has developed some competence in tackling: problems of allocation, inventory, replacement, queuing, sequencing and coordination, routing, competition and search. The book is clear, however, that OR must also seek to develop competence with strategic problems.

Unfortunately for OR, the problems that the pioneers of the discipline had used as examples of those that OR was currently equipped to tackle came to be identified, especially in the universities of the United States, with OR itself. OR largely abandoned any pretence of taking a systems approach or of being interdisciplinary in nature. It failed to establish itself at the strategic level in organizations and became associated with a limited range of mathematical techniques. The practical result has been, according to Ackoff (1986), a decline in the significance of the profession. As the problems that OR defined as being within its compass during the 1950s and 1960s ceased to be of first-ranking importance to corporate management, OR moved down the organization. The intellectual result has been, in Churchman's (1979b) opinion, that the original intention of a holistic, interdisciplinary, experimental science addressed to problems in social systems has been betrayed, as OR has degenerated into little more than mathematical modeling. Thus two of the originators of OR as a discipline, Churchman and Ackoff, became two of the severest critics of the way the subject developed.

Summarizing his view of the state of classical OR, Keys (1991) writes:

> the classification into common processes and methods of modeling them leads to the view that OR is a set of techniques which can be applied to produce a solution to a given problem. There are cases where it is clear what the character of the problem is and application of standard techniques will yield useful information. However, in many cases this is not possible because the character of the problem is not clear or the assumptions necessary to apply standard methods may not apply. Then the operational researcher must develop methods particular to the case in hand. The view that OR is a set of techniques to be applied in a standard way omits the broader process of analysis in which they are embedded and the wider organizational context in which OR takes place (pp. 73-74).

Some operational researchers have taken the broader view that Keys favors. The contributions of Boothroyd (1978), Cook (1984), Eilon (1983, 1987) and Müller-Merbach (1984), in arguing for and keeping alive the original conception of OR as an interdisciplinary, problem-centered discipline with a necessary concern for process, should be acknowledged. It is also from within the OR tradition that one of the most interesting developments has taken place as a response to the perceived failings of hard systems thinking. We need to note here the emergence, in the United Kingdom, of what has come to be known as "soft OR." This is seen by its protagonists as complementary to hard OR and is now treated with increasing respect even within traditional OR circles. Soft OR is best regarded as an attempt to take the OR approach in an "interpretive" direction and will be considered in the next chapter.

6.3.2. Systems Analysis

Systems analysis was defined by Quade (1963) as

> analysis to suggest a course of action by systematically examining the costs, effectiveness and risks of alternative policies or strategies - and designing additional ones if those examined are found wanting (p. 122).

It was seen as representing an approach to, or way of looking at, complex problems of choice under uncertainty.

Systems analysis developed out of wartime military operations planning and during the 1940s and 1950s applications were mainly military, involving work on weapons systems and strategic missile systems. At that time the approach was closely associated with the RAND (an acronym for "research and development") Corporation, a non-profit body in the advice-giving business that was set up in 1947 and came to embrace systems analysis as its favored methodology. As set out by such as Hitch (1955) and Quade (1963), this methodology sought the broad economic appraisal of different means of meeting a defined end.

In the 1960s, systems analysis began to find broader industrial and governmental uses, the biggest breakthrough coming with the introduction of RAND-style systems analysis into the Pentagon by Secretary of Defense McNamara. In 1965 President Johnson ordered adoption of the principles of systems analysis, in the guise of planning-programming-budgeting systems, in all other departments of the federal government. Since that time, versions of systems analysis have been employed in numerous government departments and agencies, in local authorities, and in business, educational and health institutions all over the world.

In 1972 the International Institute for Applied Systems Analysis (IIASA), a non-governmental interdisciplinary research institution, was set up in Laxenburg, Austria, on the initiative of the academies of science (or equivalent institutions) of twelve nations. This Institute has been seeking to apply RAND-style systems analysis to major world problems of, for example, energy, food supply, and the environment. Three "handbooks" have been produced, edited by Miser and Quade (1985, 1988) and Miser (1995), which set out the IIASA approach. It is reasonable to turn to these for a detailed modern account of systems analysis.

According to the IIASA "handbooks", systems analysis aims to help public and private decision makers to resolve problems arising in complex socio-technical systems. It brings to bear the tools of modern science and technology, searching for regularities in systems behavior and seeking to provide evidence about the costs, benefits, and other consequences of various possible responses to the problem at hand. At the same time it tries not to neglect issues of social goals and values, matters of judgement and taste, and the need for craft knowledge to be employed alongside scientific technique. The methodology of systems analysis can be seen as consisting of seven major steps, as set out in Figure 6.3.

Miser and Quade (1985) provide, among other examples of problems to which systems analysis has been applied, the decision about how the Oosterschelde estuary in the Netherlands was to be protected from flooding. Three alternatives for this task were under review, and the consequences of adopting each of these were considered in terms of factors such as financial costs, degree of security from flooding, effects on jobs and profits in the fishing industry, changes in recreational opportunities, effects on the shipping industry and other sectors of the national economy, the ecology of the region, and social impacts. Given this wide range of factors, it is not surprising that each of the alternatives had weaknesses as well as strengths, and none turned out to be uniformly better than the other. The study succeeded, however, in clarifying the issues and thus informing the political process through which the final decision was made.

Miser and Quade, in compiling their "handbooks", declare their intention to restrict themselves to the known core of systems analysis. The type of problem that has mainly con-

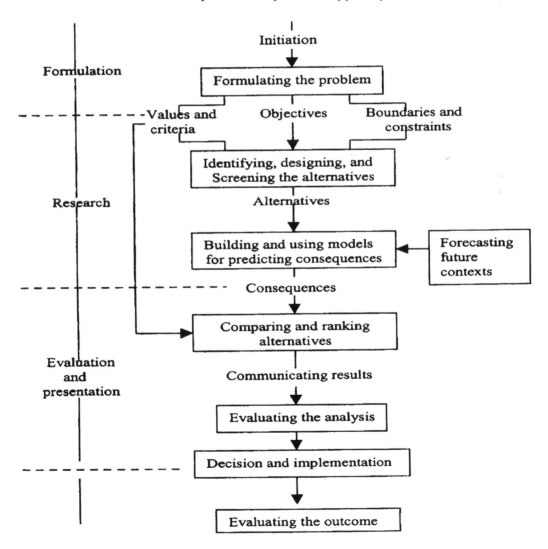

Figure 6.3. The systems analysis methodology (reproduced from Miser, 1995, p. 217)

cerned systems analysis in the past, Miser (1995) defines as being "relatively easy to structure and in which some important aspect is dominated by technology." In his comments on a case study for the New York City Sanitation Department, Miser provides insight into what can happen when this is not the case:

> ... the case study shows that there were many practical administrative difficulties involved in implementing what seems a relatively straightforward and uncomplicated program. Complications are especially likely to arise when there are many conflicting constituencies and interests that must be considered, and often responded to. Thus. this case is dominated by the time and effort that were needed to achieve a successful implementation of the final proposal (Miser, 1995, pp. 12-13).

Miser and Quade's hope is that systems analysis in the future can be extended to problems set in socio-technical systems where human behavior is much more important and, despite their declared intention, some of their contributors do move in this direction. A number of papers collected in Tomlinson and Kiss (1984) are more radical still. Some authors call for a profound reorientation - and a few for the complete abandonment - of the paradigm that has hitherto dominated systems analysis and hard systems thinking. Even in 1995, however, Miser is cautious. He points out that although "people-dominated" problems are now being explored within systems analysis, it is a relatively new idea. Therefore, he argues, it is still too early to include examples in the handbook. Miser's recognition of the limitations of systems analysis is much to be commended. A case study of the systems analysis approach in action follows.

6.3.2.1. Case Study - Improving Blood Availability and Utilization

The illustrative case for systems analysis is a study of blood distribution and utilization in the Greater New York area, reported in the literature by Brodheim and Prastacos (1979) and Prastacos (1980), and described by Miser and Quade (1985). Miser and Quade regard it as an outstandingly successful example of systems analysis in use, exhibiting all the main stages of a proper systems analysis approach.

The problem was essentially one of maintaining satisfactory levels of blood availability at hospitals so that it was there when and where needed, while attempting to reduce the high levels of blood that had to be discarded because it had passed its legal lifetime of 21 days without being used. At the time the study began, the "outdate rate" (the proportion of blood that had to be discarded) was around 20% of the total collected.

The socio-technical system of concern involved human donors, collection points such as Regional Blood Centers (RBCs) where the blood was collected from donors, Hospital Blood Banks (HBBs) that stored the blood in each hospital, the patients, and the medical and administrative staff engaged in various activities. The blood was collected at the RBCs, typed, screened, and processed (if necessary) before being distributed to the HBBs and used according to random patient demand. This system attained a degree of complexity due to the uncertainties of supply and demand; variations in the size of hospitals and therefore their blood banks; the uneven occurrence of the eight major blood groups in the population (ranging from 39% for the most common to 0.5%); the need for processed as well as pure blood; the difficulty of estimating some costs (e.g., costs of unavailability); the need to keep actors at both the regional and hospital levels happy; and fundamentally, of course, the requirement to maintain high levels of availability balanced against the desire to operate efficiently, cutting waste and maintaining the implicit commitment to donors to make the best use of their gift.

The management of the system as it existed was decentralized and reactive. HBBs placed daily orders with RBCs designed to keep their inventories at what each considered a safe level. Historically, inventories were high because emphasis was placed on ready availability and low utilization was accepted. The RBCs responded to orders placed, making on average 7.8 deliveries to each hospital per week, while attempting to keep their own buffer stocks. The outcome of the way the system was managed was satisfactory availability but high delivery costs and, as mentioned, high wastage rates.

The systems analysis began with a phase when the researchers familiarized themselves with the Long Island blood distribution system, which was to be the test bed for the analysis. Patterns of supply and demand were established by a combination of statistical analysis and Markov-chain modeling. Acceptable availability levels at hospitals were ascertained by asking HBBs to provide estimates of what they felt to be adequate stocks of each of the eight blood types. Relatively simple mathematical models were constructed simulating the system first at the hospital, then at the regional level.

In consultation with the HBBs, various alternatives for managing the system efficiently were then considered. Decentralized (as now) and wholly centralized options were entertained, but the optimum solution was obtained from a centralized management system combined with some rotation of stocks between HBBs. There was to be centralized management at the regional level with prescheduled deliveries to HBBs supplemented by emergency deliveries as necessary. In addition, blood would be collected from HBBs at the time of scheduled deliveries (if it looked as though it would not be used) and passed onto other HBBs where that type was in short supply. A final model was constructed that achieved set targets for availability and utilization, met all HBB requirements, and specified desired inventory levels for each HBB, frequency of necessary delivery to each HBB, and the size of the retention shipments to each. At the RBC level, inventory was evaluated and adjusted daily on the basis of anticipated regional blood flow. This programmed Blood Distribution System (PBDS) was implemented initially for four hospitals in the test region and later for others who volunteered to join the scheme. Finally, the analysts began adapting the PBDS to make it applicable to other regions.

The results of this systems analysis were impressive. Wastage of blood was cut from around 20% of the total collected to 4%. Instead of 7.8 unscheduled deliveries to each hospital per week on average, 4.2 deliveries were necessary, with only 1.4 unscheduled. This led to a reduction of approximately 64% on delivery costs, in part because the scheduled deliveries could be made at times of low traffic density. Availability of blood to patients was also improved, with the result that there were fewer cancellations in prescheduled surgery.

The success of the PBDS provides a good example of the ability of systems analysis to enhance prediction and control. Following research procedures based upon positivism, a model of the system was built that captured the interactions going on within it to such good effect that the system became predictable. Thus it was possible to conceive of a management system making use of prescheduled deliveries - the innovation from which most of the benefits were obtained. The fact that implementation brought the expected benefits can be seen to verify that the model accurately reflected the nature of the real-world system. It is taken for granted by the systems analysts, and by Miser and Quade, that what we have here is a legitimate use of hard systems thinking. The question of what ought to be done appears obvious, and so the problem is seen to be clearly defined, with adequate measures of performance available against which to judge system effectiveness. Such a stance is possible when, as in this case, the "client" is taken to be a relatively homogeneous group of decision makers, relatively free from political pressures and sympathetic to analysis. It is legitimate, as again in this instance, when the main concern is with the technical aspects of an agreed-upon transformation process. Impressively, there was constant reference back to the HBBs to check that the system would meet expectations.

6.3.3. Systems Engineering

Systems engineering has been defined by Jenkins as

> the science of designing complex systems in their totality to ensure that the component subsystems making up the system are designed, fitted together, checked and operated in the most efficient way (in Beishon and Peters, 1972, p. 82).

It developed, as the name suggests, out of the engineering discipline as the idea took hold that the engineering approach, previously used only to engineer components, could be extended to tackle systems made up of the interaction of many components. The term *systems engineering* was probably first used in the Bell Telephone Laboratories in the 1940s, and they remained the leaders in the field during the 1950s as the methodology of systems engineering was gradually refined.

A.D. Hall's (1962) classic account of the methodology was based on his experience with the Bell Telephone Laboratories. Hall sees systems as existing in hierarchies. In systems engineering, plans to achieve a general objective must similarly be arranged in a hierarchy, with the systems engineer ensuring the internal consistency and integration of the plans. The methodology itself ensures the optimization of the system of concern with respect to its objectives. This requires a number of steps, the most important being problem definition, choosing objectives, systems synthesis, systems analysis, systems selection, system development, and current engineering. With Hall, the system of concern is usually a physical entity. Later accounts, however, stress the general applicability of the approach. Jenkins (1972), for example, sees the same systems engineering approach as relevant to hardware systems, parts of firms, whole firms, and local government. In providing a more detailed description of the systems engineering methodology, I shall follow Jenkins's account.

For Jenkins, the purpose of systems engineering is to ensure the optimal use of resources, the main ones being men, money, machines and materials. This can be achieved through a methodology incorporating four basic phases - systems analysis, systems design, implementation and operation. In systems analysis, the real world is taken to consist of systems and is examined in systems terms. The problem is formulated and the systems in which it exists are defined and analyzed in terms of important subsystems. The interactions between the subsystems are studied. Definition of the wider system and its objectives leads to specification of the objectives of the system being studied. In the second phase (systems design), the future environment of the system is forecast. The system is then represented in a quantitative model that simulates its performance under different operational conditions. The particular design that optimizes the performance of the system in pursuit of its objectives is chosen. The model, therefore, is an aid in the prediction of the consequences that follow from adopting alternative designs. A control system must be incorporated into the design of the optimum system at this point. The implementation and operation phases involve the construction, operation and testing of the system in the real world. In carrying through this methodology, the systems engineer acts as a generalist inside an interdisciplinary systems team containing specialists as well as systems engineers, and focuses the team's attention on the efficient achievement of overall objectives. Jenkins draws his systems concepts indiscriminately from engineering, biology and cybernetics, highlighting particularly notions of optimization, hierarchy and feedback. The main contribution of systems engineering is in establishing a systematic methodology within which other systems methods and ideas can be employed.

An example of the various steps of Jenkins's methodology being used to design a petrochemical plant can be found in Jenkins (1969) and, reproduced, in Wilson (1984). Today systems engineering remains extremely popular and has many applications. Gartz (1997), of the Boeing Commercial Airline Group, regards it as "a problem-solving discipline for the modern world." In his view "the systems engineering discipline offers ways to manage size and complexity and assure resulting excellence in engineering." In an attempt to justify this claim he puts forward a paper which examines

> the subject of how the ... Boeing 777 is developed and outlines the advances that were made to the systems development process. Systems engineering concepts get tested to their limits ... many advances to the practice of systems engineering and systems development were introduced on this airplane, including new tools, processes, teaming arrangements, safety improvements and technology all designed to give the airline buyers and their customers, the flying public, increased comfort, features and dollar value (Gartz, 1997, pp. 632-634).

6.3.4. Strengths and Weaknesses of Hard Systems Thinking

Although, on occasions, protagonists of each of the strands of hard systems thinking have made claims for the superiority of their own perspective against the others, on grounds such as breadth of application and ability to engineer new as well as existing systems, the above analysis supports the contention that the similarities are more significant than the differences and that there is, indeed, a pretty unified hard systems paradigm within the systems approach. All three strands examined take *what* is required (the ends and objectives) as being easy to define at the beginning of the systems study. The job of the systems analyst is to find an optimum *how*, the most effective and efficient means to realize predefined objectives. Adapting another of Checkland's formulations (1978, 1981), the hard systems approach presupposes that real-world problems can be addressed on the basis of the following four assumptions.

1. There is a desired state of the system, S_1, which is known
2. There is a present state of the system, S_0
3. There are alternative ways of getting from S_0 to S_1
4. It is the role of the systems person to find the best means of getting from S_0 to S_1

We are now in a position to emphasize some of the positive achievements and features of hard systems thinking. It cannot be denied that the systematic approach to decision making and problem solving characteristic of hard systems thinking constitutes an advance over *ad hoc* thinking about the management task. The careful setting of objectives, the search for alternative means of reaching those objectives, and the evaluation of the alternatives in terms of a measure of performance made the efficient step-by-step control of projects feasible. This was perhaps particularly important in the domain of public spending, where no natural control mechanism (such as the market) exists. A further important achievement was to elaborate and popularize the use of mathematical models in order to aid decision making. Such models allowed predictions to be made about the behavior of real-world systems without the attendant risks and costs of intervening in the actual system of concern. For management scientists, constructing and working with mathematical and computer-based models stood in for the laboratory experiments of the physical scientists.

There was also a recognition in hard systems thinking of the interactive nature of system parts and of the need to draw the boundaries of any investigation wide so as to include all important influences on the system. This allowed the problem of suboptimization to be identified and avoided. It was recognized that optimizing the performance of each subsystem does not always lead to optimum performance of the whole. It also led to proclamations in favor of a comprehensive approach to problem solving even if such proclamations were then denied in the reductionist small print of the hard systems methodologies themselves.

Another feature of hard systems thinking that escapes some critics is that the practice has often been rather better than the precept. Indeed, this could hardly fail to be the case. For were OR, for example, to be simply the set of techniques described in many of the textbooks, it could hardly have survived in modern organizations; yet there are examples in British industry of very successful OR groups. This phenomenon of practice having stolen a march on theory, as aware practitioners deviated from the textbook representation of management science as an application of the natural scientific method, has led Tomlinson (e.g. 1984) to suggest that what is needed now is a rethinking of OR and applied systems analysis in the light of good practice. Appropriate precepts, paying much more attention to the social process of intervention, can then be constructed on the basis of successful practice. In fact, Tomlinson argues, such a rethinking is already under way and future practitioners should have the benefit of precepts that represent much more accurately what OR and system analysis are really about.

Finally, hard systems thinking insists that if it is to be useful it must be closely adapted to the interests and needs of its clients (Miser, 1995). This emphasis placed on clients and decision-makers took applied systems thinking along the path of Mode 2 research in which "knowledge production [is] carried out in the context of application" (Gibbons *et al.*, 1994). Appropriately more attention began to shift to methodology as the transferable problem solving capability. On this basis hard systems thinking was able to establish itself as a research tradition and recent developments, such as soft OR, are taking place that take account of some of the criticisms we shall now review.

The catalogue of criticisms that follow has been compiled from a wide variety of sources (Ackoff, 1979a, 1979b; Checkland, 1978, 1981, 1983; Churchman, 1979b; Hoos, 1972, 1976; Lilienfeld, 1978; Rosenhead, 1981, 1989). Often the same general criticisms can be found in the work of more than one commentator. I have not sought, therefore, to trace every criticism back to its source, but have broken the whole set of interrelated points down under five general headings.

First there are criticisms that suggest hard systems thinking has a very limited domain of applicability. Hard approaches demand the objectives be clearly defined at the very beginning of the methodological process. The machine metaphor is dominant. The goals of the controllers of the system are taken as given and the system parts are logically arranged to achieve maximum efficiency. This may be fine for engineering-type problems when ends are easy to specify and attention can be concentrated on means. In the vast majority of managerial situations, however, the very definition of objectives will constitute a major part of the problem faced. Involved parties are likely to see the problem situation differently and to define objectives according to their own world views, values and interests. This will give rise to many possible accounts of what the objectives of a particular system are, some of which might well be in conflict. In "softer" problem situations, therefore, it is not clear how hard systems methodologies can get started, since they lack the procedures for bringing about an accommodation between alternative definitions of what the objectives might be. Unfortunately, a common response to this difficulty from proponents of hard systems thinking is to distort the nature of the problem situation in order to make it fit the requirements of the preferred methodology. One objective or set of objectives will be privileged over others on the basis of the "expert" understanding of the system achieved by the systems analysts. A more appropriate response would be to admit that, outside the realm of engineering-type problems, hard methodologies are only useable in those circumstances where world views converge and unanimity is achieved about the need to maximize the performance of some relatively simple and easily separable subsystem.

A second kind of criticism relates to the failure of hard systems approaches to pay proper attention to the special characteristics of the human component in the socio-technical systems with which they sometimes aspire to deal. The system of concern is taken to exist in the world, the interactions within it are studied, and human behavior is fed with other data into a mathematical model that is then used to ensure improved regulation of the existing system. People are treated as components to be engineered just like other mechanical parts of the system. The fact that human beings possess understanding, and are only motivated to support change and perform well if they attach favorable meanings to the situation in which they find themselves, is ignored. This deterministic perspective in hard systems thinking, which puts the system before people and their perceptions, extends to the ability of humans to intervene in their own destiny. Hard systems thinkers take the future to be determined by factors outside the control of organizational actors. It is the job of the systems consultant to predict the inevitable future and help managers prepare for it. Thus the opportunity to mobilize people to design their own future is missed (Ackoff, 1979a, 1979b).

The third group of criticisms concerns the demand for quantification and optimization. Hard systems thinkers recognize that the systems with which they deal exhibit aspects of complexity, but still believe they are simple enough to be represented in mathematical models. When highly complex systems are involved, however, the building of a quantitative model is inevitably a highly selective process and will reflect the limitations of vision and biases of its creator(s). Far from recognizing this and demanding that the assumptions made in building the model be made explicit, hard systems thinking seems to treat the model too readily as synonymous with the reality. The model, which is of course far more easily manipulated than the real world, becomes the focus of attention and the generator of "optimum" solutions. It is convenient and cozy to play with the model, but the result is solutions that are out-of-date answers (since the model soon becomes an out-of-date representation) to the wrong questions.

Another consequence of the demand for quantification and optimization is the tendency to ignore those factors in the problem situation that are not amenable to quantification or, perhaps even more seriously, to distort them in the quest for quantification. Different aspirations or matters subject to differing value interpretations are forgotten or ground down on the wheel of optimization. It is this, together with the manipulation of models for their own sake, that has led to OR being characterized by Ackoff as "mathematical masturbation."

Fourth, the degree to which hard systems thinking offers succor to the status quo, and to the already powerful, is frequently noted. As I have already shown, in order to get going in softer problem situations, hard methodologies require the privileging of one objective or set of objectives over others. It goes without saying that the best way to ensure the continuance of a consultancy project, and the implementation of the proposals, is to privilege the objectives of the most powerful stakeholders. Having inevitably been forced into making such political choices, hard approaches seek to cover their tracks by encouraging "depoliticization" and "scientization" (Rosenhead, 1981). The complicated mathematical modeling discourages ordinary people from believing that they might have anything useful to contribute to decision making. It also suggests that differences of opinion and interest can be rationally dissolved by experts using the latest tools and techniques. Thus conflict is hidden. Since conclusions emerge from a computer model programmed by white-collar scientists, they take on an air of objectivity that is, of course, entirely spurious.

The naïveté of the hard approach to complex socio-technical problems (when it is so extended) can be accounted for, at least in part, by its roots in the engineering tradition and the "trained incapacity of engineers" (Hoos, 1976) to see systems as anything but things governed by predictable laws. The survival of such a naïve orientation - the subject of the fifth type of criticism - is more difficult to explain. Lilienfield (1978) argues that systems theory of this ilk should be regarded as an "ideology." It flourishes because of the service it renders to scientific and technocratic élites. Presenting, as it does, a view of systems as entities to be manipulated from the outside on the basis of expertise, hard systems thinking justifies the position and privileges of these élites.

Examining the points made above suggests that Keys (1987) and Jackson (1987a) are not too far wrong in summarizing the faults of hard systems thinking as arising from its inability to deal with subjectivity (criticisms one and two above), its difficulties in coming to terms with extreme complexity (criticism three) and its innate conservatism (criticisms four and five).

In short, hard systems thinking has been unable to make much progress either along the "participants" or "complexity" dimensions identified, in Chapter 5, as important for mapping progress in applied systems thinking. It has been left to other systems approaches to make these breakthroughs. Nevertheless, the hard approaches have registered some significant achievements. And, it must be continually emphasized, there will be some problem situations in which hard systems methodologies yield the most satisfactory results.

6.4. SYSTEM DYNAMICS

One of the first to react to the perceived failings of OR, and other management science techniques, was Forrester at the Massachusetts Institute of Technology. In Forrester's view the modeling techniques of OR were only able to deal with a small number of variables in a system and only then if the relationships between the variables were linear. Forrester had a background working with electrical circuits and servo-mechanism theory. He sought to bring together his knowledge of feedback control theory, his grasp of the potential of digital computers, and an experimental rather than analytical approach to modeling to develop methods to model and analyze problems in more complex systems. This approach was to be

> focused upon dynamic, systemic behavior in a way that is more akin to those of the practising manager than to the management science specialist (Forrester, quoted in Keys, 1991, p. 177).

Forrester and his team began work on inventory levels, at MIT, around 1956. Initially they called their approach "industrial dynamics." In 1958, Forrester published a paper in the *Harvard Business Review*, entitled *Industrial Dynamics - a Major Breakthrough for Decision Makers*, which announced the approach to the world. There followed a book on industrial dynamics in 1961. According to Collins, in a foreword to Forrester (1969), the aim of industrial dynamics was to

> isolate the dynamic characteristics of the system and to show how the behavior of the actual system might be modified using a digital computer to simulate the behavior of the system (p. viii).

Forrester continued to develop the principles and methods of industrial dynamics and to extend their area of application:

> The methods of 'industrial dynamics' were developed as a way to understand and to design corporate policy. From that work has developed a general viewpoint about the feedback-loop structure of systems and their subsequent dynamic behavior. The resulting principles and practices have been finding ever broadening applications (Forrester, 1971, p. ix).

Examples of dynamic systems studies included the processes of engineering systems, biology, social systems, psychology, ecology and "all those where positive - and negative - feedback processes manifest themselves in growth and regulatory action" (Forrester, 1969). Books on "Urban Dynamics" (1969), "Principles of Systems" (1969), and "World Dynamics" (1971) signaled an expanding ambition, and the need for a change of name from "industrial dynamics":

> The name has become a misnomer now that applications are becoming important outside the industrial corporation. Because the methods apply to complex systems wherever we find them, a better name is 'system dynamics' (Forrester, 1971, p. 13).

Since Forrester's pioneering work, system dynamics (SD) has spread from MIT to universities and consultancy organizations world wide, and there have been extensive applications in extremely diverse areas. Lane (1998) lists the collapse of the Mayan empire, the growth of a developing nation, the management of healthcare capacity in the Netherlands, oscillation in oil markets, the growth of a start-up company and a study looking at Shell's confrontation with Greenpeace over the proposed deep water disposal of Brent Spar as examples of such applications.

System dynamics in its broadest sense sees systems as "feedback processes" demonstrating a specific and orderly structure. It is this causal structure that gives rise to the system's dynamic behavior. In complex systems, problems arise because of the number of variables and their interrelationship through interacting feedback loops:

> The structure of a complex system is not a simple feedback loop where one system state dominates the behavior. The complex system has a multiplicity of interacting feedback loops. Its internal rates of flow are controlled by nonlinear relationships. The complex system is of high order, meaning that there are many system states (or levels). It usually contains positive-feedback loops describing growth processes as well as negative, goal-seeking loops (Forrester, 1969, p. 9).

From this it is clear that cause and effect are often not closely related in either time or space. In fact,

> in the complex system the cause of a difficulty may lie far back in time from the symptoms, or in a completely different and remote part of the system ... causes are usually found not in prior events, but in the structure and policies of the system (Forrester, 1969, p. 9).

It is essential, therefore, to obtain a deep understanding of the system's structure if we are ever to be able to make sense of its behavior and implement appropriate problem-solving measures. This requires us to construct a model of the system.

6.4.1. System Dynamics Models

Before the modeling process itself begins, we need an adequate representation of the system and its important elements. This will draw on available data, existing theories in the area of concern, and the capacity of the human mind to determine what is relevant to the system's behavior. Once this is achieved we can turn to modeling the system:

> To model the dynamic behavior of a system, four hierarchies of structure should be recognized: closed boundary around the system; feedback loops as the basic structural elements within the boundary; level variables representing accumulations within the feedback loops; [and] rate variables representing activity within the feedback loops (Forrester, 1969, p. 12).

In establishing the boundary of the system, the analyst needs to identify which elements are interacting to produce the behavior that is being investigated. The key is to include within the boundary all those interrelated components which have an influence on the problem situation and to exclude all those which do not affect behavior. Within the boundary, what happens - the dynamic behavior of the system - is generated by interacting feedback loops. This can be described with the help of the "signed digraph" approach, which is a causal loop diagram that expresses the "direction of feedback." A simple example is shown in Figure 6.4. Essentially a signed digraph enables us to express how elements influence and interact with other elements. In this example all the signs are positive because an increase (or decrease) in any of the elements will lead to a change in the same direction in the next element: a corresponding increase (or decrease). Additional problems would lead to more overwork and time pressure; less unfinished work would lead to fewer problems, etc. The harassed executive caught in this reinforcing feedback loop, in its vicious form, is heading for a nervous breakdown. If, however, a kindly boss were to insert, between "unfinished work" and "extra problems", the element "five extra staff", this could have a negative effect on extra problems, i.e. the extra staff would lead to a decrease in problems (which would be shown by a negative sign). This inverse relationship could help stabilize the loop. Signed digraphs can be extended to show how multiple loops impact upon each other and the whole system.

Once this conceptualization of structure has been attained, the model must be elaborated so that a digital computer can simulate the behavior of the system represented by the model. This is possible because, in Forrester's view, feedback loops are made up of two kinds of variables: "rate" variables and "level" variables:

> A feedback loop is a structure within which a decision point - the rate of equation - controls a flow or action stream. The action is accumulated (integrated) to generate a system level. Information about the level is the basis on which the flow rate is controlled (Forrester, 1969, p. 13).

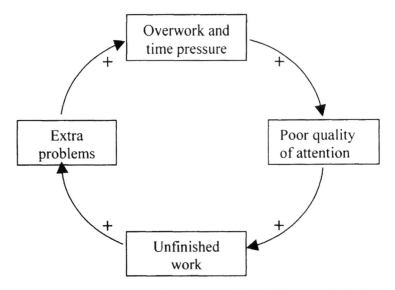

Figure 6.4 A Simple Signed Digraph (adapted from O'Connor and McDermott, p. 38)

A level, therefore, is a quantity of some element that can change over time. A rate is a flow, or relationship between elements, that contributes to that change per unit of time. Figure 6.5 illustrates the most simple feedback loop using these ideas. Flood and Jackson (1991) provide, as an example, the dynamics of stock control. This is represented, using system dynamics symbols in Figure 6.6. The manufacturing rate is a flow (like a valve) which adds to the stock level (a rectangular "vessel"). The delivery rate subtracts from the stock level. If this system is to be properly controlled, information about the demand must be fed back to increase the manufacturing rate. This allows the stock level to return to the desired level. In Figure 6.6 there are some additional symbols. The demand is an "auxiliary" and is represented by a circle; there is a "source" and a "sink" represented by clouds; and a "constant" looking like a small flying saucer.

Using a custom built computer programming language, such as DYNAMO, it is relatively simple to construct and manipulate models of this type. Computer simulation is

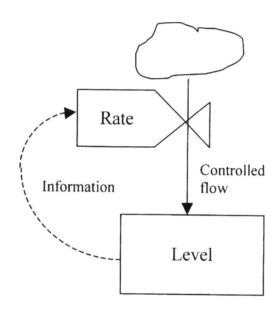

Figure 6.5 Simplest possible feedback loop having one rate and one level (adapted from Forrester, 1969 p. 74)

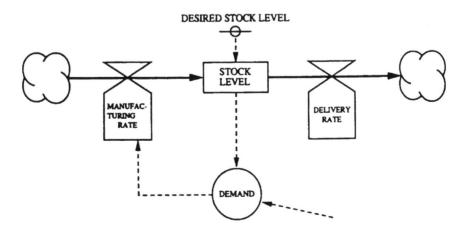

Figure 6.6. System dynamics representation of stock level (reproduced from Flood and Jackson, 1991, p. 69)

essential because, although humans can conceptualize the elements involved in a complex system, they are hopeless at predicting the dynamic behavior that ensues from their interactions; behavior that Forrester often finds is counter-intuitive:

> when the pieces of a system have been assembled, the mind is nearly useless for anticipating the dynamic behavior that the system implies. Here the computer is ideal. It will trace the interactions of any specified set of relationships without doubt or error. The computer is instructed by giving it a model … A computer model embodies a theory of system structure. It states assumptions about the system … The computer then shows the unexpected consequences that can lie within the assumptions (Forrester, 1971, pp. 15-16).

The computer simulation, therefore, captures the dynamic characteristics of a system conceptualized according to feedback loops and represented as a set of elements influenced by flows of material and information. Sophisticated models will also pay attention to the relative strength, or "dominance", of the different loops and to any time delays that could occur in the system. Also included in the model will be decision-points, where human actors can affect behavior. Experiments on the simulation make it possible to determine the results of changing decisions:

> By changing the guiding policies within the system, one can see how the behavior of the actual system might be modified (Forrester, 1969, p. 1).

Thus system dynamics can alert managers to the consequences of different actions and so assist them in decision making and problem solving.

6.4.2. System Dynamics Methodology

In Forrester's (1971) opinion the system dynamics approach combines the power of the human mind with the strengths of today's computers. The human mind is most useful in the early stages and in the final stage of the system dynamics methodology as set out by Forrester (1961). The early stages consist of defining the problem, identifying the factors bearing on the problem, and recognizing the feedback loops which relate materials, information and decisions. The final stage involves deciding on action to be taken to improve the behavior of the system. These steps require the human mind because:

> The human is best able to perceive the pressures, fears, goals, habits, prejudices, delays, resistance to change, dedication, good will, greed, and other human characteristics that control the individual facets of our social systems (Forrester, 1971, p. 15).

The other stages, however, need the computer because the mind is nearly useless for anticipating the dynamic behavior the system implies. These stages involve building the computer model, testing it to ensure its outputs correspond to actual system performance, modifying it if necessary, and experimenting using the model to explore the effects of different courses of action on system behavior.

It has been argued, however, that the absence of the mind of decision makers from certain crucial stages of the methodology, in Forrester's classic exposition, has had some unintended consequences. One of the most frequent criticisms of system dynamics is that it has difficulty getting its recommendations accepted and implemented. This is deemed to be due to the separation between decision makers and analysts while the latter are away building and testing elaborate computer models. According to the critics, this is not the way to ensure that recommendations have an impact. The analysts should be much more closely involved with the decision makers; working with them throughout the study so that the decision makers come to own the results. The need for mutual interaction with clients at all stages of the methodology is now much more widely recognized by advocates of system dynamics. Lane, for example, sees that involving decision makers throughout the methodological process is just as important to success as is the construction of an accurate model:

> Building on Forrester's ideas, system dynamics works closely with management teams to build transparent and comprehensible simulation models. The deliverable is not just the model but the process of building it and the learning experienced by the participating managers (Lane, 1995, p. 609).

Wolstenholme (1990) provides a methodology for system dynamics which seeks to get the most out of involving decision makers while, where appropriate, securing the benefits to be gained from computer simulation. He calls his overall approach "System Enquiry" which, he says, is a

> rapidly emerging field, which focuses on problem solving and analysis of complex real world systems by methodological means, where the emphasis is on promoting holistic understanding rather than piecemeal solutions (p. 1).

System dynamics provides a suitable methodology for "system enquiry" because it supplies managers with a "tool set" that they can use in systems design and problem solving. As Lane (1998) points out, "the aim is to work with managers to support debate regarding long term policy."

Wolstenholme's methodology has two phases, "qualitative system dynamics" and "quantitiative system dynamics." Table 6.1 sets out what is involved in each of the phases. The qualitative system dynamics phase is concerned with creating "cause and effect diagrams" of the signed digraph type. These system maps are deemed to be essential if any exploration or analysis is to be made of the systems under consideration. Wolstenholme stresses how important it is at this stage in the methodology to include and work with "system actors" every step of the way. Only then will the subsequent models truly represent the views and perspectives of those individuals working within the system:

> The diagrams create a forum for translating barely perceived thoughts and assumptions about the system by individual actors into usable ideas which can be communicated to others. The intention is to broaden the understanding of each person and, by sharing their perceptions, to make them aware of the system as a whole and their role within it; that is, to provide a holistic appreciation (1990, pp. 4-5).

Wolstenholme's "cause and effect" diagrams are, following the principles of system dynamics, made up of two fundamental components - the "process structure" based on resource flows and the "information structure" based on information flows. The process structure is derived by observing the system over a sufficient period of time. It is represented in a resource flow diagram, which takes account of delays and organizational boundaries. Once the process structure is mapped, information flows can be shown. These add "causality" and turn the diagrams from open loop models to closed loop models:

> The important idea in closed loop models is that information flows link knowledge about levels to rates and specify how the rates are to change in the future to change the quantities of the resources in the levels (Wolstenholme, 1990, p. 16).

Table 6.1. System dynamics – a subject summary (adapted from Wolstenholme, 1990, p. 4)

Qualitative System Dynamics	Quantitative Systems Dynamics	
(Diagram construction and analysis phase)	(Simulation phase)	
	stage 1	*stage 2*
To create and examine feedback loop structure of systems using resource flows, represented by level and rate variables and information flows, represented by auxiliary variables.	To examine the quantitative behavior of all system variables over time.	To design alternative system structures and control strategies based on (i) intuitive ideas, (ii) control theory analogies (iii) control theory algorithms, in terms of non-optimizing robust policy design.
To provide a qualitative assessment of the relationship between system processes (including delays), information, organizational boundaries and strategy.	To examine the validity and sensitivity of system behavior to changes in (i) information structure (ii) strategies (iii) delays/uncertainties.	To optimize the behavior of specific system variables.
To estimate system behavior and to postulate strategy design changes to improve behavior.		

Once completed, the system dynamics diagrams will reveal a lot about system behavior. One major use, for Wolstenholme, is the identification of information feedback loops:

> It is the analysis of such loops which facilitates understanding of how the processes, organizational boundaries, delays, information and strategies of systems interact to create system behavior (1990, p. 12).

The qualitative diagrams themselves might allow the managers and analyst(s) to

> explore alternative structures and strategies, both within the system and its environment, which might benefit the system (1990, p. 5).

However, it is always an option to construct a quantitative model on the basis of the qualitative representation.

Quantitative system dynamics involves "simulation modeling" through the use of computers and specially designed software. Taking the diagrams created in the qualitative phase, the analyst(s) and system actors attempt to identify and derive

> the shape of relationships between all variables within the diagrams, the calibration of parameters and the construction of simulation equations and experiments (Wolstenholme, 1990, p. 5).

Once a valid representation of the "real world system" has been achieved through normal testing procedures, the model can be used to

> facilitate experimentation and, hence, to design system structures and strategies for improved system behavior (1990, p. 59).

It will be noted that, even in the quantitative system dynamics phase, Wolstenholme insists that the managers should be involved. If the quantitative model becomes too complicated, it should still be possible to retain managerial commitment by referring back to, and amending as necessary, the qualitative representation.

The emphasis in the writings of Wolstenholme and Lane on involving managers, through methodology, in a process of learning might signal a reorientation in system dynamics from a "functionalist" towards an "interpretive" position. This, however, would require a shift from seeing system structure as the determining force behind system behavior, to seeing "system behavior" as being socially constructed as a result of individuals interacting on the basis of the meanings they attach to their situation. No such shift occurs. The primary rationale behind system dynamics remains gaining knowledge about systems, which are seen as existing in reality, by studying the interactions between their variables. Once this understanding is achieved, better prediction and control can be realized. It is wiser then, with Keys (1991), to see qualitative system dynamics as an attempt to overcome some of the limitations of hard systems thinking while remaining firmly within the same functionalist tradition. Another attempt to combine system dynamics with an acceptance of the importance of "subjectivity" will be considered in a later sub-section, when we look at Senge's "Fifth Discipline." In Chapter 7, when we review "Interpretive Systems Approaches", we shall also witness Vennix using system dynamics models in a more interpretive manner as part of "group model-building." At the moment, however, we require a case study illustrating system dynamics in action.

6.4.3. Case Study - An Accident and Emergency Department

Writing this in the winter of 1999/2000, at the height of a flu epidemic which is causing chaos in the UK National Health Service, I am attracted by a system dynamics study carried out in the health sector by Lane, Morefeldt and Rosenhead (1998).

The specific focus of the study is waiting times in Accident and Emergency departments where patients are brought in by ambulance or arrive by other means believing themselves to be in a crisis state. Although government and hospitals obviously seek to reduce waiting times in Accident and Emergency (A and E), the actual result of their actions is an increase in waiting times. Waits of eight hours or more in A and E, before a bed can be found, are not uncommon and occasionally A and E becomes so busy that it has to debar new arrivals by ambulance. This reality has to be set against the ambition in the Patient's Charter that patients admitted through A and E should receive a bed within two hours. The behavior of the system appears, therefore, to be counterintuitive given the best intentions of decision makers. Moreover, attempts to address the apparent causes of difficulties in A and E have the effect of simply displacing the problem elsewhere. Cause and effect in A and E cannot be treated in isolation. Many problems in the health sector are interconnected and an intervention in one area, say A and E departments, can have unintended consequences elsewhere. As Lane *et al.* say:

> Waiting lists, cost containment, cancellations of routine surgery, bed closures, bed blocking, community care … they queue behind each other and as action is taken to tackle the one at the front, the next one in line reveals itself. The …. merry-go-round of failed palliatives will continue until the interconnections between these issues are understood systemically (p. 2).

An example of the entanglement of causes is the impact of bed closures. This affects A and E directly, because it reduces the number of vacant beds, but also indirectly because it causes delay in admission of non-emergency cases potentially turning them into emergency cases, early discharge of current patients who may then require emergency readmission, and a reaction among GPs who can come to believe that sending patients to A and E is the only route to fast admission. Another example is the blocking of beds in hospitals by patients who cannot be discharged because not enough resource has been put into providing care for them in the community. Yet another is the effect of the politically driven campaign to reduce the maximum waiting time for non-emergency admission to eighteen months. Attempting to meet this target puts pressure on hospitals to treat non-serious cases as they near the deadline before serious cases earlier in the queue. Those serious cases may then require emergency admission.

Overall, then, the researchers concluded that this was a case for system dynamics. A system dynamics model was constructed based on the feedback loops controlling patient flow into and out of A and E. This had to take into account both internal and external factors. For example, whatever the situation in A and E itself, a patient could only leave that department for the ward when a bed became available. This obviously depended on the rate of non-emergency admissions and on patients being discharged. The "causal loop diagram" produced to capture these interactions is shown in Figure 6.7. Loop B1 takes patients out of A and E onto a ward once A and E procedure has been completed. Loop B2 shows such patients can only progress once a bed becomes available. B3 shows that non-emergency admission also depends on bed occupancy. B4 admits non-emergency ("elective") patients when there are free beds. B5 cancels elective admissions when bed occupancy is too high to accommodate the scheduled rate of admission.

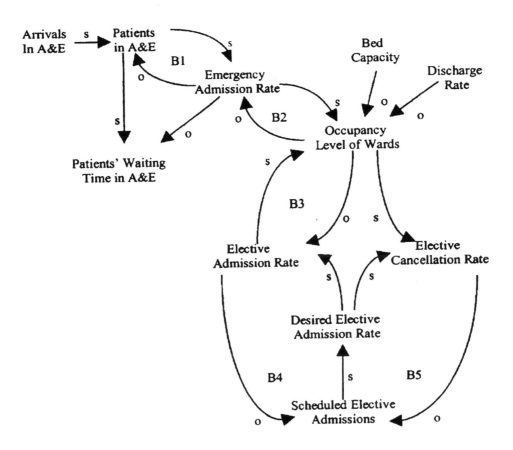

Figure 6.7. Causal loop diagram of the main effects determining waiting times in an A&E Department. The polarities of the causal links read as: s = variables move in the same direction, ceteris paribus; o = variables move in opposite directions, ceteris paribus (adapted from Lane, Morefeldt and Rosenhead, 1998, p. 6).

The next step was to build a "level" and "rate" diagram, that could be turned into a computer model, in order to explore the interconnections between the elements and the various feedback loops in more detail. The model was then validated by checking it for plausibility with some experienced practitioners who were collaborators in the project and checking its outputs for accuracy against the operation of a real-world A and E system as recorded in the databases of a major inner-London teaching hospital. Convinced of its conformity with reality, the researchers began to experiment with the model. An initial "base case simulation" involved running the model on the basis of data and parameters drawn from recent real world experience of the operation of such a system. Examining the results led to the conclusion that waiting time in A and E depended significantly on time of arrival. This was because of variations in arrival rate, but also reflected the number of A and E specialists on duty at particular times. Changing the staffing roster could, therefore, improve service.

There followed a series of "policy analytic runs" in which particular parameters or relationships were systematically changed in order to discover the impact on outputs. Perhaps surprisingly, reducing the number of beds available did not affect the average waiting time. Emergency patients were given priority for beds and the impact therefore fell on elective patients. As loop B5 suggests, scheduled admissions were simply cancelled. In fact reducing beds from 800, in the base case, to 700 almost doubled the percentage of elective cancellations. Increasing the demand from emergency patients, however, had a very different effect. An increase of 2% in demand led to little difference. With a further 2% increase, however, admission to a bed took three quarters of an hour longer even with the doctors working flat out. With a 5% increase in emergency admissions, the system goes out of control, with waiting times increasing from hour to hour. The researchers point out, ominously, that the most recent year-on-year increase at the hospital most involved in the study was 7%.

The researchers were able to conclude that, given the dynamics of the system, any further loss of beds would hit elective cancellations rather than the time emergency patients had to wait. There was little slack in the system, however, and, although some improvement could be brought about by adjusting duty rosters, any significant further increase in demand on A and E could, without more staff, threaten a catastrophic outcome. More generally, any attempt to improve just one aspect of a complex system under stress simply transfers the problem elsewhere. Policy makers often contribute to the problem by concentrating their efforts, for publicity purposes, on improving just one indicator:

> The next time the music stops, some other aspect of health service performance will be found wanting. Should reductions in A and E waiting times be bought at the expense of headlines such as 'Girl's Heart Surgery Cancelled Five Times'? There needs to be a coherent use of multiple indicators and a more sophisticated awareness, in practice, of their interconnections (Lane, Morefeldt and Rosenhead, 1998, p. 9).

6.4.4. Senge's *Fifth Discipline*

Senge's *The Fifth Discipline* (1990) is the most popular book that has ever been written on systems thinking, hitting the best seller lists throughout the world. The heady brew that Senge presents in this volume is a strange mixture of new age mysticism, the notion of organizational learning derived from Argyris and Schön (and covered briefly as part of the brain metaphor in Chapter 3) and system dynamics. The book is perhaps best known for promoting "the learning organization", an idea that has become extremely popular among practitioners. It is essentially a systems book, however, because the "fifth discipline' is systems thinking and this, as well as being the most important discipline in itself, underpins all the other four "disciplines" necessary for creating learning organizations. Senge conflates the "fifth discipline", systems thinking, with system dynamics when, as this book shows, systems thinking is a much broader enterprise. We shall therefore cover his account of this "fifth discipline" in this section on system dynamics. We shall have to return to the other four disciplines when we deal with interpretive systems approaches, and the entire book when we consider critical systems thinking - because it can be read as an attempt to combine different systems approaches. If the book fails in all its parts - as system dynamics, as an interpretive systems approach, and as a critical systems approach - there is no doubt that the whole has succeeded at least in bringing a lot of necessary attention to systems thinking.

Senge wants to destroy the illusion that the world is made up of separate and unrelated forces:

> we can then build 'learning organizations', organizations where people continually expand their capacity to create the results they truly desire, where new and expansive patterns of thinking are nurtured, where collective aspiration is set free, and where people are continually learning how to learn together (1990, p. 3).

To be capable of learning, organizations have to overcome certain "learning disabilities." This is possible once an organization masters the five disciplines essential to learning organizations. The five "disciplines" are "personal mastery", "mental models", "building shared vision", "team learning" and "systems thinking." Systems thinking is considered the "fifth discipline" because it is the underlying discipline which "integrates" all the others; for Senge, only through systems thinking can real organizational learning take place.

According to Senge,

> systems thinking is a conceptual framework, a body of knowledge and tools that has been developed over the past fifty years, to make the full patterns clearer, and to help us see how to change them effectively (1990, p. 7).

Examining this tradition, Senge identifies eleven "laws of the fifth discipline" which are integral to the developing learning organization. Most of these "laws" point to the counter-intuitive behavior of complex systems. The fact that nearly all are derived from system dynamics demonstrates just how partial Senge's reading of the systems tradition is. The eleven laws are as follows.

1.   "Today's problems come from yesterday's 'solutions'." Many so-called solutions merely shift the problem from one part of a system to another; as was the case when emergency cases were prioritized in our previous health service example.

2.   "The harder you push, the harder the system pushes back." Our attempts to improve organizations are often met by "compensating feedback" which we do not understand. The tendency then is to push even harder in the same direction but this only exacerbates the problem.

3.   "Behavior grows better before it grows worse." We are too easily encouraged by the fact that our "low-leverage" interventions can work in the short term. The trouble is that, after a time delay, the inevitable "long term disbenefit" appears.

4.   "The easy way out usually leads back in." Using our familiar solutions doesn't solve fundamental problems in the long-term. We need systemic thinking.

5. "The cure can be worse than the disease." Another problem with easy or familiar solutions is that, although they are ineffective in the long-term, they are "addictive",

> in the sense of fostering increased dependency and lessened abilities .... All 'help' a host system, only to leave the system fundamentally weaker than before and more in need of further help (Senge, 1990, p. 61).

Ill-conceived government interventions, for example, can lessen the ability of local people to solve their own problems.

6. "Faster is slower." Systems tend to have optimal rates of growth and, when growth becomes excessive, problems arise. The system seeks to compensate by slowing down and this can put its survival at risk.

7. "Cause and effect are not closely related in time and space." We tend to believe that cause and effect are close in time and space. We have to learn from system dynamics that, in complex systems, this is not the case.

8. "Small changes can produce big results - but the areas of highest leverage are often the least obvious." As we have seen, obvious changes do not usually bring long-term benefits. On the other hand, small, well focused actions can sometimes produce significant enduring improvements because they are in the right place at the right time. The trouble is that such changes are usually non-obvious because cause and effect are distant in space and time. System dynamics can help us find these points of "high leverage."

9. "You can have your cake and eat it too - but not at once." Dilemmas arise when we take a "snapshot" view and think of what is possible at a fixed point in time. For example, it may be impossible to have both high quality and low costs in three months time. Taking a process view however, as encouraged by systems thinking, we are able to recognize that both may be possible over time.

10. "Dividing an elephant in half does not produce two small elephants." Senge explains:

> Living systems have integrity. Their character depends on the whole. The same is true for organizations; to understand the most challenging managerial issues requires seeing the whole system that generates the issues .... Sometimes people go ahead and divide an elephant in half anyway. You do not have two small elephants then; you have a mess. By a mess, I mean a complicated problem where there is no leverage to be found because the leverage lies in interactions that cannot be seen from looking only at the piece you are holding (pp. 66-67).

11. "There is no blame." People tend to blame other people or outside circumstances for their problems. Systems thinking demonstrates that there is no "outside"; you and your enemies are part of the same system. Solutions must be found in managing relationships.

A learning organization must undergo a "shift of mind" if it is to understand and take note of these laws. Because of the increasing complexity of the world, it must take a systems perspective:

> Complexity can easily undermine confidence and responsibility ... Systems thinking is the antidote to this sense of helplessness that many feel as we enter the 'age of interdependence'. Systems thinking is a discipline for seeing the 'structures' that underlie complex situations, and for discerning high from low leverage change. That is, by seeing wholes we learn how to foster health. To do so, systems thinking offers a language that begins by restructuring how we think (Senge, 1990, p. 69).

The language of systems thinking allows us to describe complicated interrelationships and patterns of change in a relatively simple way. It relies on three concepts which can be seen as the "building blocks of systems thinking." These concepts are "reinforcing (or amplifying) feedback", "balancing (or stabilizing) feedback", and "delay."

Reinforcing feedback processes are "the engines of growth." In such processes whatever movement occurs is amplified to produce more movement in the same direction. A small change builds on itself as does the increasing size of a snowball as it rolls down a hill. In Chapter 4 we saw Maruyama arguing for a "second cybernetics" to study processes of this kind. Balancing feedback processes encourage stability. A system is brought back toward its goal by some self-correcting mechanism that is set in motion as a result of feedback about how far it is diverging from its goal. The study of such goal-oriented behavior was the subject matter of the "first cybernetics", as we also saw in Chapter 4. Reinforcing and balancing feedback processes are ubiquitous in organizations although, Senge argues, they often go undetected. "Delays" frequently go unrecognized as well. Delays occur when the impact of feedback processes take a long time to come through. They are present in almost all feedback processes and always "come back to haunt you in the long term" (Senge, 1990).

Using these concepts, managers begin to learn that there is an "elegant simplicity" behind the complexity of the issues they face, and it

> becomes possible to see more and more places where there is leverage in facing difficult challenges, and to explain these opportunities to others (1990, p. 94).

Moreover, even more assistance is available to managers because:

> One of the most important, and potentially most empowering, insights to come from the young field of systems thinking is that certain patterns of structure recur again and again. These 'systems archetypes' or 'generic structures' ... suggest that not all management problems are unique ... Once a systems archetype is identified, it will always suggest areas of high-and-low-leverage change (pp. 94-95).

If managers can master "systems archetypes", therefore, they can get most of the benefits of systems thinking. Diagrams of the system dynamics ilk are crucial for this.

Senge identifies two of the most frequently recurring archetypes as "stepping stones to understanding complex situations." These are the "limits to growth" and "shifting the burden" structures, both of which can be described in terms of the interaction of feedback loops.

In the "limits to growth" archetype:

> A reinforcing (amplifying) process is set in motion to produce a desired result. It creates a spiral of success but also creates inadvertent secondary effects (manifested in a balancing process) which eventually slows down the success (1990, p. 25).

Senge provides the example of work pressures being "solved" by working longer hours. Eventually, however, this builds up stress and fatigue which inevitably slows down our pace of work. The system is thus stabilized because even if we work longer hours we will get no more work done. The "limits to growth" idea is illustrated in Figure 6.8. This kind of "archetype" often frustrates attempts at organizational change. Things seem to be going well but then run out of steam. The all too natural reaction is to push harder using the same mechanisms. Unfortunately, this is futile. The management principle for this archetype, therefore, is "don't push growth; remove the factors limiting growth" (Senge, 1990). In limits to growth situations,

> leverage lies in the balancing loop – not the reinforcing loop. To change the behavior of the system, you must identify and change the limiting factor (1990, p. 101).

In the "shifting the burden" archetype:

> An underlying problem generates symptoms that demand attention. But the underlying problem is difficult for people to address … So people 'shift the burden' of their problem to other solutions … Unfortunately, the easier 'solutions' only ameliorate the symptoms; they leave the underlying problem unaltered (Senge, 1990, p. 104).

Somebody suffering stress at work should probably address the problem by reducing their workload or changing their job. These solutions can be difficult to implement, however, and delays may occur before any benefit is felt. An easier solution is to turn to drink for support. This can help alleviate the symptoms of stress but, of course, cannot address the fundamental problem. Having "shifted the burden" to drink the temptation is to stick with it. Ultimately this could have a deleterious effect on health and weaken the whole system. The "shifting the burden" structure is illustrated by a top circle, representing the symptomatic solution, interacting with a bottom circle, incorporating a delay, which represents the more fundamental solution. The example is shown diagrammatically in Fig. 6.9. The management principle for this archetype is "beware of the symptomatic solutions, … [they only] have short-term benefits at best" (Senge, 1990).

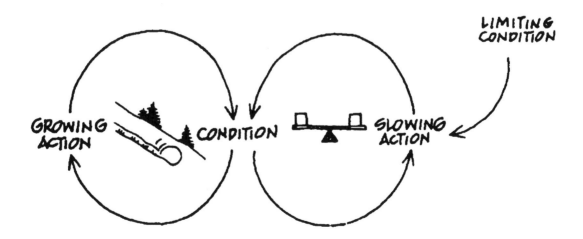

Figure 6.8. Limits to growth (reproduced from Senge, 1990, p. 97)

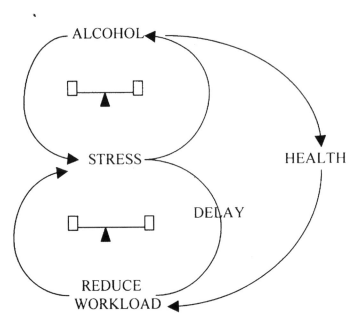

Figure 6.9. Shifting the burden (reproduced from Senge, 1990, p. 97)

According to Senge, researchers have now identified about a dozen systems archetypes. These are illustrated and further discussed in Senge *et al.* (1994) and Kim (1993). An appendix to *The Fifth Discipline* looks at seven archetypes apart from "limits to growth" and "shifting the burden", and we shall briefly describe these here.

"Balancing process with delay" occurs when behavior is adjusted in response to delayed feedback. Further corrective action is taken, which leads to the system overshooting its goal in the other direction and the response is repeated. Most people have had the experience of hopping about in showers when the water temperature changes slowly in relation to their aggressive actions with the control. "Shifting the burden to the intervener" occurs when an outsider succeeds in solving some obvious problems. The system becomes dependent on the outsider and the people within it becomes incapable of tackling their own problems. "Eroding goals" occurs when disappointments with corrective actions build up and the gap between goal and achievement is closed by lowering ambition rather than by taking other action. "Escalation" occurs when two people or organizations see themselves in competition and every action of one side is regarded as a threat by the other. When one side gets ahead, the other has to be even more aggressive, and so on. It is the "cold war" type of scenario. "Success to the successful" is the self-fulfilling prophecy type of structure where the apparent success of one activity, as against another, is rewarded by further resources in support of that activity, increasing its success further. "Tragedy of the commons" occurs when two systems operating in the same environment initially gain rewards from exploiting that environment. Because of a resource limit in the environment, however, the eventual result is exhaustion of that environment. In socio-technical systems terms, "turbulent field" environments have their own dynamics that can react back on the systems that depend on them. "Fixes that fail" are short-term solutions that worked in the past but, when used now, simply add to the problem. The temptation is to use the fix again rather than attempting to work through a long-term solution. "Growth and underinvestment" occurs when successful performance can only be sustained by increased investment. A delay occurs in making this investment and during this period performance may decline. This provides the justification for underinvestment.

For Senge,

> The archetypes start the process of mastering systems thinking. By using the archetypes, we start to see more and more of the circles of causality that surround our daily activity (1990, p. 113).

All that is required is the other four disciplines, themselves informed by systems thinking, to enable us to recognize and respond to systemic processes. We discuss this in the next chapter.

Popular though Senge's work is with managers, it is anathema to many system dynamicists. It is easy to see why. System dynamics started, let us recall, as a reaction against OR which tried to tackle the range of management problems using a limited set of models of a very specific type. Forrester thought of system dynamics as an approach that would allow analysts to model the full variety of management situations. Senge seems to have slipped back into the mistake of OR – believing that his "archetypes" are all that is necessary to assist with management practice. Furthermore, Senge's work appears as "unscientific" to hard-line system dynamicists. It is not necessary, apparently, to elaborate the models and to use computers to explore their behavior. Computer simulation was essential, in Forrester's view, because humans are so hopeless at predicting dynamic behavior.

6.4.5. Strengths and Weaknesses of System Dynamics

We shall complete this section by reviewing the strengths and weaknesses of system dynamics more generally.

The most important strengths of system dynamics are well captured in a quote from Forrester (1971):

> System dynamics could be the unifying framework and vehicle for interdisciplinary communication. Not only is system dynamics capable of accepting the descriptive knowledge from diverse fields, but also shows how present policies lead to future consequences (p. viii).

The versatility of system dynamics models arises because they operate at the "structural" level. As Senge (1990) recognizes,

> the art of systems thinking lies in seeing through complexity to the underlying structures generating change (p. 128).

> Ultimately, it simplifies life by helping us see the deeper patterns lying beneath the events and the details (p. 73).

System dynamics models manage complexity better than, say, hard systems models because the latter are constructed according to the positivist method and try to represent the surface detail. Furthermore, as Forrester suggests in the above, system dynamics lends itself well to the analysis of current policies and the exploration of alternatives; it makes easy the transition from model building to implementation. This is partly, obviously, because experimenting on models is easier, less dangerous and more ethical then experimenting on the real world. But, more particularly, it is also because system dynamics incorporates methods that can contribute well to each stage of the decision making process (see Meadows, 1980). Signed digraphs help us to develop a broad appreciation of the situation of concern and its dynamics. Next we have to acquire a deeper understanding of how to improve particular problem areas. The transition to a quantitative model allows this to occur. Finally, for implementation purposes, precision is absolutely vital. An exact mathematical model captured in a computer simulation can achieve the degree of precision required.

In considering the criticisms of system dynamics we need to be aware that it has been attacked by critics of very different persuasions. The following account is taken largely from Keys (1990) and Flood and Jackson (1991).

Attempts made by system dynamics to loosen some of the characteristics of the positivist version of the scientific method, in order to tackle problems of greater complexity, have left it open to the charge of having abandoned scientific rigor. System dynamics tries, through its general theory of systems behavior, to grasp the whole, even when this is difficult to model. Putting in place the feedback loops which constitute system structure and explain system behavior is held to be more important than exact representation achieved through reductionist methods. Obviously, this leaves system dynamics open to charges of being imprecise. It apparently jumps to conclusions about whole system behavior before the data have been collected, and the laws verified, which would make such conclusions justifiable. Far from building on the descriptive knowledge of diverse fields, in order to assist interdisciplinary understanding, these critics insist that system dynamics models are often based upon poor data, often ignore extant theories in the fields, and often do not undergo a rigorous enough validation regime. Of course, from the system dynamics point of view, it has to deviate from the traditional scientific method in order to tackle the complex problems it is interested in; problems on which sufficient data is difficult to obtain and about which laws are difficult to formulate.

Following on from the discoveries of chaos theory, another criticism of system dynamics is possible from a natural scientific perspective. Even if system dynamics models achieve sufficient precision and rigor, and are subject to proper validation procedures, surely they are rendered useless because of the "butterfly effect." It is a commonplace of chaos theory, as we saw, that tiny changes in a system's initial conditions can alter its long term behavior very significantly. Complex systems demonstrate a "sensitive dependence on initial conditions." It follows that even the best system dynamics models cannot give very accurate predictions of future states and so are of limited usefulness to decision makers, unless (a point not lost on complexity theorists, as we shall see) the "system archetypes" operate in the social domain in the manner of "strange attractors."

Interpretive and emancipatory systems thinkers (see Chapters 7 and 8) could forgive system dynamics its lack of precision in areas where precision is difficult to obtain – scientific exactitude must sometimes be sacrificed for practical usefulness. What they cannot forgive is its attempt to present itself as an objective and neutral approach in the domain of social systems where "objectivity" and "neutrality" are simply impossible to obtain.

Interpretive thinkers would question the underlying assumption of system dynamics that there is an external world made up of systems, the structure of which can be grasped using models built upon feedback processes. They regard social systems as much more intangible than this. Social systems are perceived as the creative construction of human beings whose intentions, motivations and actions play a significant part in shaping "system" behavior. It follows that the attempt by system dynamics to model social reality as though it were something external to humans is misguided. The subjective intentions of human beings, which are crucial, cannot be captured in "objective" models. Social systems are constituted through the interaction of humans acting according to their different values and conceptions of reality. Social structure emerges through a process of negotiation and renegotiation of meaning. It is an impossible task to model this process.

From the interpretive perspective, therefore, it is not appropriate to study social systems, as system dynamics would wish, from the outside. Rather it is necessary to respect the significance of human consciousness and to examine the world views and actions of the individuals who continually construct and reconstruct them. If we are to change social systems we must intervene in the process of meaning construction. This is why interpretive systems thinkers are content to build models which explicate particular world views and contribute to debate about the problem situation and possible changes to it. Models should seek to increase mutual understanding not try to represent external reality.

Because of subjectivity, many possible viewpoints on the nature and purpose of particular social systems are possible. The argument is that the richness inherent in social reality defeats system dynamics modelers. Their models must be selective accounts of "reality" constructed from one, often unstated, point of view. They therefore say more about the prejudices of the modelers than about the external world. Furthermore, system dynamics provides no means of questioning the world view underlying any model, for example by comparing it to another model constructed on the basis of an alternative world view. The criteria for deciding what is the optimal behavior of a system are similarly bound up with one model and one world view, and so are likely to go unquestioned. It is too easy for system dynamics modelers to privilege implicitly the aims of some groups over others.

This becomes very worrying from the perspective of emancipatory systems thinkers, especially when system dynamicists act as though they were élite technicians. They tend to see themselves serving decision makers as experts, providing objective and neutral advice. There is often little involvement of other "stakeholders." Ignoring other stakeholders in this way may seem to be ideologically biased and ethically unsound. This does not worry system dynamics experts who too often see their role as being limited to offering solutions before disappearing, leaving the decision makers to do the implementation.

The critics make some telling points, but system dynamics is not invalidated in all circumstances. If particular objectives have been decided upon, it may well be possible to use feedback models to carry out a rigorous study of physical flows and information links. System dynamics can then make a very real contribution to assessing different policy options. Beyond this, as Lane (2000) insists, the various craft skills developed by practitioners, and the willingness of some of its theoreticians to engage with the subjectivist wing of systems thinking, mean that system dynamics is less "austerely objective" than it is often painted.

6.5. ORGANIZATIONAL CYBERNETICS

When the cybernetic ideas detailed in Chapter 3 are combined together in attempts to assist managers, they are capable of yielding two different models of the organization, which we can label *management cybernetics* and *organizational cybernetics*. Management cybernetics represents little advance on hard systems thinking and is subject to the same criticisms. Organizational cybernetics, however, is based on a rather different epistemological orientation and is able to exploit fully the potential of the cybernetic building blocks. I shall introduce both management and organizational cybernetics before concentrating on the main vehicle for transporting the insights of organizational cybernetics to managers – Beer's "viable system model" (VSM).

The early pioneers of cybernetics frequently employed analogies in their work to illustrate particular insights. Not surprisingly, perhaps, a tendency grew up in the secondary literature to treat organizations as if they were actually like machines or organisms. This comes through in the great majority of books designed to teach managers about cybernetics (e.g. Strank, 1982). It is this kind of cybernetics – particularly that dominated by the machine analogy – that will be referred to here as management cybernetics.

The starting point for the management cybernetic model of the organization is the input – transformation – output schema. This is used to describe the basic operational activities of the enterprise. The goal or purpose of the enterprise is, in management cybernetics, invariably determined outside the system (as with a first-order feedback arrangement). Then, if the operations are to succeed in bringing about the goal, they must, because of inevitable disturbance, be regulated in some way. This regulation is effected by management. Management cybernetics attempts to equip managers with a number of tools that should enable them to regulate operations. Chief among these are the black box technique and the use of feedback to induce self-regulation into organizations. The latter is often supplemented by strategic control, based on feed-forward information, and external control. Management cybernetics makes little use of the more complex, observer-dependent notion of variety.

There is little to choose between this form of cybernetics and hard systems thinking. Conventional management scientists are able to take cognizance of its insights and to employ concepts such as feedback in their traditional analyses. Management cybernetics, therefore, offers no new direction in systems thinking. Whether based on a machine analogy or on a biological analogy, it can be criticized for exactly the same reasons as hard systems thinking – an inability to deal with subjectivity and with the extreme complexity of organizational systems, and for an inherent conservatism (see Jackson, 1986).

There is, however, another strand of cybernetics concerned with management and organizations that breaks somewhat with the mechanistic and organismic thinking that typifies management cybernetics, and is able to make full use of the concept of variety. This type of cybernetics is not obviously subject to the criticisms mentioned above (Jackson, 1986) and does represent a genuinely new direction within the functionalist tradition. It is labeled here *organizational cybernetics*. Beer (1959b, 1966, 1972) has been pushing organizational cybernetics (though he does not use this term) for some years and has worked hard at defining its relationship with hard systems thinking. In spite of this, and the respect accorded to Beer in the systems community generally, his work had little impact on the development of traditional management science; evidence, perhaps, that Beer's thinking is based upon different epistemological assumptions. It is, however, fair to say that organizational cybernetics can only be found in fully developed form in Beer's (1979, 1983a, 1984, 1985) later work. It seems to have emerged from management cybernetics as a result of two intellectual breakthroughs. First, in *The Heart of Enterprise*, Beer (1979) succeeds in building his VSM in relation to the organization from cybernetic first principles. This enables cybernetic laws to be fully understood without reference to the mechanical and biological manifestations in which they were first recognized. Second, more attention is given in organizational cybernetics to the role of the observer. Clemson (1984) makes a distinction between a first-order cybernetics appropriate to organized complexity because it studies matter, energy and information, and a second-order cybernetics capable of tackling relativistic organized complexity because it also studies the observing system. Organizational cybernetics is second-order cybernetics. This will become clearer in the next sub-section, which describes Beer's VSM; this model encapsulates all the most important features of organizational cybernetics.

6.5.1. Beer's Viable System Model

The traditional company organization chart is, for Beer (1981a), totally unsatisfactory as a model of a real organization. His aim in constructing the VSM is therefore to provide a more useful and usable model.

The VSM, as its name suggests, is a model of the organizational features of any viable system. In *Brain of the Firm*, Beer (1972) builds it using as an example of any viable system the workings of the human body and nervous system. His logic is that if we want to understand the principles of viability, we had better use a known-to-be-viable system as an exemplar. The human body, controlled and organized by the nervous system, is perhaps the richest and most flexible viable system of all. The result is a neurocybernetic model containing a five-level hierarchy of systems that can be differentiated in the brain and body in line with major functional differences. From this, Beer builds up a model – consisting of five subsystems – of any viable system. In *The Heart of Enterprise* (1979), the same model is derived from cybernetic first principles, demonstrating that it is perfectly general. It can, therefore, be applied to firms and organizations of all kinds. Indeed, in a one-person enterprise, all five functions will still have to be performed by that one individual. In *Diagnosing the System for Organizations* (1985), the model is presented in the form of a "hand-book" or "manager's guide", the intention being to aid application of the principles to particular enterprises. It is from these three sources (Beer, 1972, 1979, 1985) that the following account is primarily drawn. As will be seen, Beer makes full use of all the various concepts and tools devised by cybernetics to understand organizations and to make recommendations on how to improve their effectiveness. In the VSM, Beer encapsulates the cybernetic laws he sees as underpinning system viability and demonstrates their interrelationship.

6.5.1.1. Overview

For Beer, a system is viable if it is capable of responding to environmental changes, even if those changes could not have been foreseen at the time the system was designed. In order to become or remain viable, a system has to achieve requisite variety (at a level concordant with effective performance) with the complex environment with which it is faced. It must be able to respond appropriately to the various threats and opportunities presented by its environment. The exact level at which the balance of varieties should be achieved is determined by the purpose that the system is pursuing. Of course, amplifying organizational variety to balance environment variety, if that is the strategy pursued, causes problems for the managers of that system. In order to control their organizations they have to achieve requisite variety with the operations that they manage. There is variety engineering to be done between management and operations as well. Beer (1981a) sets out a number of strategies that can be used by managers to balance the variety equations for organizations in a satisfactory way.

In reducing the external variety confronting them, managers can use the following methods:

- Structural (e.g., divisionalization, functionalization, massive delegation)
- Planning (e.g., setting priorities)
- Operational (e.g., management by exception)

In amplifying their own variety, managers can employ the following methods:

- Structural (e.g., integrated teamwork)
- Augmentation (e.g., recruit experts, employ consultants)
- Informational (e.g., management information systems)

Essentially these strategies are designed to fulfill three requirements. First, the organization should have the best possible model of the environment relevant to its purposes. Second, the organization's structure and information flows should reflect the nature of that environment so that the organization can be responsive. Third, the variety balance achieved between organization and environment must be matched by an appropriate variety balance between managers and operations within the organization. With its emphasis on variety engineering, the VSM can legitimately be seen as a sophisticated working out of the implications of Ashby's law of requisite variety in organizational terms.

With these general comments about variety engineering in mind, it is now possible to elaborate more fully on the organization of the VSM. The model is made up of five elements (Systems 1 to 5 in Figure 6.10), which may be labeled implementation, coordination, control, development, and policy. It is essential that the functions handled by these five systems be adequately performed in all organizations. Great importance is also given to the design of the information channels that link the different functions with the system and its environment. As has already been said, this is a perfectly general model applicable to all systems. It will, however, be studied here with particular reference to organizations. I now take the five systems in turn before considering the overall structure of the model (and its recursive nature) and then the information that flows around the various communication linkages. Please refer to Figure 6.10 throughout this account.

6.5.1.2. System 1

The System 1 (S1) of an organization consists of the various parts of it directly concerned with implementation – with carrying out the task(s) that the organization is supposed to be doing. Subsidiaries A, B, C, and D in Figure 6.10 are all parts of System 1 of that viable system. It will be noted that each part has its own relations with the outside world, interacts with other subsidiaries and has its own localized management (1A, 1B, 1C, and 1D).

Each subsidiary (or part) of S1 is connected to the wider management system by the vertical command axis. Instructions for the subsidiaries arrive from higher-level Systems down this command channel. Each localized management, say 1B, therefore has a set of instructions received down the line that it interprets, instructing its operational element, B, what it should do (effector). What goes on in B is monitored (sensor) and transmitted back to 1B. 1B is then able to send this information about B's performance to higher levels along the upward communication channel. It is also, of course, able to compare actual performance with planned performance as it occurs and to adjust the behavior of B as necessary (the negative feedback mechanism).

It should be noted at this point that each part of System 1, or subsidiary of a firm, should be autonomous in its own right so that it can absorb some of the massive environmental variety that would otherwise flood higher management levels. If every aspect of the business had to be thought about consciously at the senior management level, the firm would soon grind to a halt. In order to make the parts of the System 1 autonomous, they must all be viable systems designed in accordance with the VSM. Indeed, if we had a more

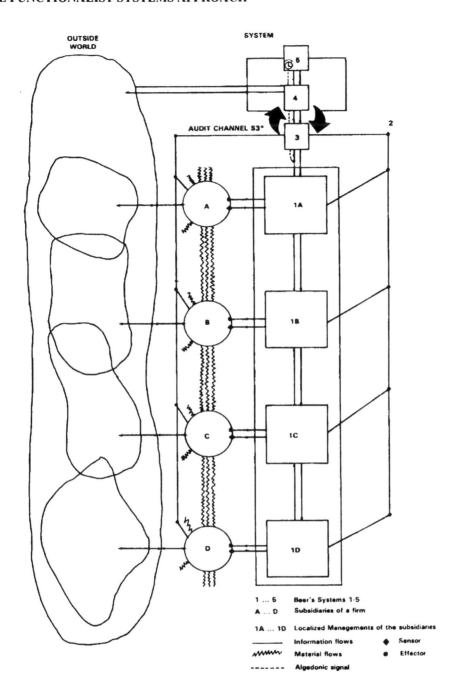

Figure 6.10. Beer's VSM

detailed version of Figure 6.10, in which the black box representations of the subsidiaries were opened up for viewing, we should find each subsidiary also shown according to the representation of Figure 6.10. This is the basis of the model's recursion, to be discussed later. If each subsidiary is made a viable system, it will be able to make its own decisions with respect to the external world and other subsidiaries.

A subsidiary should, then, be able to do what it likes. The only restrictions on the autonomy of the parts of System 1 stem from the requirement that they continue to belong to the whole organization. Their localized management levels use negative feedback to maintain performance and report back. Additionally, each part of System 1 must accept a degree of coordination and control by System 2 and 3, which are designed to facilitate the effective interaction and performance of all the divisions. Local management, say 1B, has only local facts to go on, and action that local management takes in an emergency may not be best from the overall corporate point of view. It must, therefore, be subject to limitation. Here, System 2 and 3 are particularly significant.

6.5.1.3. System 2

System 2 is a coordination function. Under normal circumstances, compatible instructions from higher management should ensure that the various parts of System 1 of an organization act in harmony. In an emergency, however, each part of System 1 will try to act in its own best interests, but based on only local information. The interactions set off among parts of System 1 in these circumstances might then lead to unpredictable and dangerous effects for the whole enterprise and for the subsidiaries themselves. There is a need, therefore, for a coordinating function as provided by System 2. System 2 consists of the control centers of the parts of System 1 linked to a corporate regulatory center. The corporate regulatory center receives information about the actions of the various subsidiaries and is able to prevent dangerous oscillations arising in the system created by all the subsidiaries.

Suppose that subsidiaries A, B, C, and D in Figure 6.10 all play a part in manufacturing the firm's major product, so that output from A is passed to B, from B to C, and so on. Now what happens if something goes wrong with the production program in B, for example? Local management, 1B, will try to adjust the B plan and take corrective action, but this may not be possible locally. It may require varying supplies received from A, and deliveries to C, in which case 1B must inform 1A and 1C of what is going on, and each will try to adjust accordingly. However, this is likely to send trouble reverberating throughout the system, creating violent oscillations. It is System 2's job to oversee these interactions and to stabilize the situation so as to obtain a balanced response from System 1. It sends feedback to the localized managements of System 1 to re-establish harmony, calling if necessary upon the resources of System 3.

6.5.1.4. System 3

Before passing on to System 3 itself, I must mention one other information flow, leading to System 3, which passes up the left-hand side of the model. This is the audit channel, or System 3*. It is there to give System 3 direct access to the state of affairs in the operational elements. Through this channel, System 3 can get immediate information, rather than relying on information passed to it by the localized managements of the subsidiaries. System 3 might want to check directly on quality, or on employee morale, or to see that maintenance procedures are being followed. Only System 3, with information provided to it by System 4, can know how essential any subsidiary is to the whole enterprise and therefore take action affecting its future; hence its need for direct access. System 3* is a vital function in any viable system.

We can now review the duties of System 3 itself. System 3 is a control function. It does not initiate policy but interprets it in the light of internal data from System 2 and 3* and external data from System 4. It is responsible for passing a coordinated plan down the line to System 1. It must oversee the effective implementation of policy and distribute resources to the parts of System 1 to achieve this. It has to monitor the performance of System 1 and take control action in accordance with information it receives up the information channel and also from System 2 and System 3*. Also it must report upward any information needed by the policy system above it. Particularly vital information has to be rushed through on the "algedonic" (or arousal) channel shown as a hatched line in Figure 6.10.

Three kinds of information system converge on System 3. First, System 3 is on the vertical command axis as part of corporate management. It transmits detailed interpretations of policy downward. It transmits information from the divisions upward, coalescing it into corporate information. It acts to send vital information upward extremely quickly. Second, it receives and acts upon information from System 2. It might send instructions downward on the basis of this, or consult upward. Finally, it responds to information received from System 3* advising on the fate of particular subsidiaries.

The three lower-level Systems, 1 through 3, make up what Beer calls the "autonomic management" of the organization. They are capable of optimizing the productive performance of the enterprise within an established framework and maintaining internal stability without reference to higher management levels. Autonomic management does not, however, possess an overall view of the organization's environment and it is therefore incapable of reviewing corporate strategy and reacting to threats and/or opportunities in that environment. This is where System 4 and 5 come in.

6.5.1.5. System 4

System 4, or the development function of the organization, has two main tasks. First it acts as what Beer calls the biggest "switch" in the organization. It switches instructions down from the thinking chamber of the organization, System 5, to the lower-level systems, and it switches upward, from Systems 1 and 3, information required by System 5 to take major strategic decisions. There is a constant danger of overloading System 5 with information that is not significant enough to warrant its attention. System 4 must prevent this by carefully filtering the information it passes upward. It will further operate on aggregate information collected by System 3 to put it in a form useful to top management. With regard to information passed by System 3 for urgent attention, System 4 will act as an "algedonode" - rapidly transmitting it upward or wholly suppressing it, according to its perceived importance (Beer, 1981a).

The second major task of System 4 is to capture for the organization all relevant information about its total environment. If the organization is to be viable and effective, it has somehow to match the variety of the environment in which it finds itself. To do this it must have a model of the environment that enables predictions to be made about the likely future state of the environment and allows the organization to respond in time. System 4 provides the organization with this model. The sort of model suitable would be one constructed according to Forrester's (1969) system dynamics approach. Having recognized relevant environmental threats and opportunities, System 4 filters the information and redistributes it downward or upward according to its implications. Information with immediate implications will be communicated to System 3 for speedy action. Information with longer-term implications will require the judgement of System 5.

System 4 is the point in the organization where internal and external information can be brought together. As such, activities like corporate planning, market research, operational research, research and development and public relations should be located there. Beer proposes that System 4 become the "operations room" of the enterprise, a real "environment of decision" in which all senior meetings are held.

6.5.1.6. System 5

System 5 is responsible for the direction of the whole enterprise. It is the thinking part of the organization, formulating policy on the basis of all the information passed to it by System 4 and communicating the policy downward to System 3 for implementation by the subsidiaries. One of its most difficult tasks is balancing the sometimes conflicting internal and external demands placed on the organization. The internal demands are represented by the commitment of autonomic management to optimizing ongoing operations, whereas the external demands are represented by System 4, which with its links to the environment tends to be outward and future oriented. System 5 must ensure that the organization adapts to the external environment while maintaining an appropriate degree of internal stability.

System 5 must also represent the essential qualities of the whole system to any wider system of which it is part, acting in this capacity simply as the localized management of a particular part of System 1 of the wider system.

Beer recommends that System 5 be arranged as an elaborate, interactive assemblage of managers - a "multinode." Decision making needs to be formalized and the effects of decisions monitored without threatening the freedom and flexibility of interaction allowed in the multinode.

The basic structure and processes of the VSM have now been described. What is further required is some discussion of two of the most important features of the model: its approach to corporate structure and to measures of performance.

6.5.1.7. Corporate Structure

It is worth discussing the idea of recursion on which the model depends. Recursion refers to the fact that the structure of the whole model is replicated in each of its parts. As was seen, the subsidiaries of an organization should be treated as viable systems in their own right and must, therefore, possess their own Systems 1 to 5. The organization, which is itself a viable system, might well at a higher level of recursion simply be an implementation subsystem or System 1 within another viable system. The generality of the model and its applicability to different system levels allows elegant diagrammatic representations of management situations to be constructed and acts as a great variety reducer for managers and management scientists. Lower-level systems that will inevitably appear as black boxes at higher levels of recursion can become the focus of interest in their own right with only a slight adjustment of attention.

6.5.1.8. Measures of Performance

Next, it is worth considering the nature of the information that flows around the various connections linking Systems 1, 2, 3, 4, and 5. This will often, given the importance of negative feedback for control, be information about how the different divisions of the organization and the organization as a whole are doing in relation to their respective goals. Achievement in most organizations is measured in terms of money, the criterion of success being the extent to which profits are maximized and costs minimized. This is not, however, regarded as satisfactory by Beer. It ignores how well the organization is doing in terms of preparing for the future by investing in research and development or in terms of more abstract resources like employee morale. It fails to reveal the cost-cutting manager who, in search of immediate profits, is damaging the organization's long-term future. Instead, Beer (1981a, pp. 162-166) advises adopting three levels of achievement (actuality, capability, and potentiality) that can be combined to give three indices (productivity, latency, and performance) expressed in ordinary numbers. These can be used as comprehensive measures of performance for all types of resources throughout the organization. These measures are able to detect the irresponsible cost-cutting manager.

6.5.2. Using the Viable System Model for Diagnosis and Design

Now that the VSM has been described, it is time to say how it can actually be used by managers and their advisers as part of a methodology for understanding and improving the performance of organizations. Obviously the VSM itself is a model and not a methodology, but it is based on such firm cybernetic principles that it is not difficult to extrapolate from those principles, and the model itself, exactly how to proceed in uncovering the faults of organizations. In essence, the methodology must center on looking at enterprises, or potential enterprises, to discover whether they obey cybernetic laws (in which case they will be viable and effective) or flout them (in which case they are likely to fail).

I will consider this in a little more detail. One use of the VSM, obviously, is to ensure that new organizational systems are designed according to the cybernetic principles elucidated in the model. The most ambitious attempt to use the model in this way - Project CYBERSYN, involving the regulation of the Chilean social economy under the Allende government - is described by Beer (1981a) in *Brain of the Firm* (second edition) and elsewhere (Beer, 1975, 1981b; Espejo, 1980). Other examples are given by Beer (1979) in *The Heart of Enterprise*. The model can also be employed as a diagnostic tool; the organization being analyzed can be compared to the VSM to check that its structures and processes are such as to ensure viability and effectiveness. Advice on how to proceed with diagnosis and examples can be found in various sources (Beer, 1984, 1985; Clemson, 1984; Espejo, 1979; Espejo and Harnden, eds., 1989; Espejo and Schwaninger, eds., 1993; Espejo *et al.*, 1996; Keys and Jackson, eds., 1985). To complete this account of the VSM, I set out a summarized procedure for using the model and then outline some common threats to viability that are always worth looking for while carrying out intervention using the VSM.

6.5.2.1. Detailed Procedure

The procedure for using the model to diagnose the faults of a proposed or existing systems design is quite complicated. However, it can roughly be divided into two parts:

- System identification (arriving at an identity for the system and working out appropriate levels of recursion)
- System diagnosis (reflecting on the cybernetic principles that should be obeyed at each level of recursion)

Various tasks have to be undertaken in each part as described below. This procedure was first set out in Jackson and Alabi (1986) and refined in Flood and Jackson (1991). In Flood and Jackson, a fully worked example is provided using the steps outlined. More detail on each of the tasks can be found in Beer's (1985) *Diagnosing the System for Organizations*, from which the procedure was originally derived. Espejo (1989) has done useful work on how the VSM can be used to help stakeholders examine possible organizational identities (for example, by considering the structural implications of alternative viewpoints). This enlarges our understanding of the first phase of system identification. I will now set out the procedure step-by-step.

A. System Identification

- Identify or determine the purpose(s) to be pursued
- Taking the purpose as given, determine the relevant system for achieving the purpose - this is called the "system in focus" and is said to be at recursion level 1
- Specify the viable parts of the System 1 of the system in focus - these are the parts that "produce" the system in focus and are at recursion level 2
- Specify the viable system of which the system in focus is part (wider systems, environments, etc.) - this is at recursion level 0

B. System Diagnosis

In general, this procedure draws upon cybernetic principles to:

- Study the System 1 of the system in focus
  - o For each part of System 1, detail its environment, operations, and localized management
  - o Study what constraints are imposed upon each part of System 1 by higher management
  - o Examine how accountability is exercised for each part and what indicators of performance are taken
  - o Model System 1 according to the VSM diagram
- Study the System 2 of the system in focus
  - o List possible sources of oscillation or conflict between the various parts of System 1 and between their environments
  - o Identify the elements of the system (various System 2 elements) that have a harmonizing or damping effect
  - o Ask how System 2 is perceived in the organization (as threatening or as facilitating)
- Study the System 3 of the system in focus
  - o List the System 3 components of the system in focus
  - o Ask how System 3 exercises authority
  - o How is the resource bargaining with the parts of System 1 carried out?
  - o Ask who is responsible for the performance of the parts of System 1
  - o What audit (or System 3*) inquiries into aspects of the parts of System 1 does Systems 3 conduct?
  - o What is the relationship between System 3 and the System 1 elements? Is it perceived to be autocratic or democratic? How much freedom do System 1 elements possess?
- Study the System 4 of the system in focus
  - o List all the System 4 activities of the system in focus
  - o How far ahead do these activities consider?
  - o Do these activities guarantee adaptation to the future?
  - o Is System 4 monitoring what is happening in the environment and assessing trends?
  - o Is System 4 open to novelty?
  - o Does System 4 provide a management center/operations room, bringing together external and internal information and providing an environment for decision?

       o Does System 4 have facilities for alerting System 5 to urgent developments?
- Study the System 5 of the system in focus
  - o Who is on the board, and how does it act?
  - o Does System 5 provide a suitable identity for the system in focus?
  - o How does the ethos set by System 5 affect the perception of System 4?
  - o How does the ethos set by System 5 affect the relationship between System 3 and System 4 - is stability or change emphasized?
  - o Does System 5 share an identity with System 1 or claim to be something different?
- Check that all information channels, transducers, and control loops are properly designed.

6.5.2.2. Common Threats to Viability

When one examines an existing or proposed social system design using the procedures outlined above, it is likely that a number of faults in its organization will be revealed. The following are some of the most common faults discovered by cybernetics. Discovery of any of these would be regarded by Beer as a threat to the organization's continued existence.

1. Mistakes in articulating the different levels of recursion, so that a system is not properly managed at each of its levels of operation. Often the importance of certain System 1 parts is not recognized. They are not treated as viable systems in their own right and therefore lack a localized System 1 management to attend to their affairs. In Beer's work in Chile (1981a), problems were encountered in regulating the social economy because the "allocation system" and the "people system" were not initially seen as independent viable systems at the same level of recursion as the production system. Another example is provided by Espejo (1979) in the context of a small firm.

2. The existence of organizational features that, according to the VSM, are additional and irrelevant to those required for viability. These are likely to hamper the organization in striving for effectiveness and may eventually threaten its ability to survive. These irrelevant features should therefore be dispensed with.

3. Systems 2, 3, 4, or 5 of an organization showing a tendency toward becoming autopoietic. An autopoietic system, as we know, is one that has the ability to "make itself" - to continue to produce those aspects of its organization that are essential to its identity. This is what makes systems viable and autonomous (Maturana and Varela, 1980). However, following the VSM, viability is a property that should be embodied only in the system's totality and in the parts of its System 1. A system developing autopoiesis in any of its Systems 2, 3, 4, or 5 is pathologically autopoietic, and this threatens its viability. In an organization, Systems 2, 3, 4, and 5 should serve the whole system by promoting the implementation function (System 1) and should not be allowed to become viable systems in their own right. If they do develop as autopoietic systems, it will inevitably be at the expense of the system as a whole. The faults typical of bureaucracies can be traced to these organizations becoming pathologically autopoietic (Beer, 1979, pp. 408-412).

4. Certain key elements are revealed by the VSM as being absent or not working properly in the actual organization. Corrective action should be taken to ensure that the functions concerned receive due attention. Beer (1984) particularly picks out Systems 2 and 4 as elements that are often weak in organizations. System 2 is frequently not fully established because the localized managements of the parts of System 1 resent interference from this relatively junior control echelon. Unless System 2 is able to assert itself, however, coordination between the various activities of the parts of System 1 will be put in jeopardy. System 4 is often weak in relation to System 3 because it is regarded in many organizations as being a "staff" function. For this reason, it may lack good communications with other parts of the organization, and its recommendations may frequently be ignored. If System 4 is weak, however, System 5 will lack the knowledge of the enterprise's environment necessary for it to give proper attention to development activities. It will forget its higher-level duties and will instead tend to get too involved with the work of System 3 or even try to intervene at System 1 level. Beer insists that System 4 must be a "line" function for its importance to be recognized, and it is represented as such in diagrams of the VSM. It will then prevent System 5 from "collapsing" into System 3, and System 5 will be able to perform its proper function, balancing the internal and external demands on the organization.

5. System 5 must represent what Beer (1984) calls "the essential qualities of the whole system" to the wider systems of which it is a part. Failure to do this will entail problems for the system's viability and effectiveness.

6. If the communication channels in the organization and between the organization and the environment do not correspond to the information flows shown to be necessary in any viable system. These channels must be carefully designed for the rapid transmission of information about how the system is doing in terms of the three indices of performance.

I have set out Beer's VSM as the most developed and useable expression of organizational cybernetics. The model has been described, a detailed procedure for applying it outlined, and six of the diagnostic points noted that often emerge when the VSM is employed to make a detailed check on the operational effectiveness of an organization. I now provide an example of the VSM in action. This is followed by a discussion of other work in organizational cybernetics and a critique of the tradition as a whole, with the VSM as its representative. The critique will enable us to draw out special features of the VSM to which it has been impossible to do justice in the description provided so far.

6.5.3. Case Study - Humberside Window Systems Ltd.

Humberside Windows is a leading Humberside and Lincolnshire window company manufacturing, selling and fitting PVC double glazed doors and windows. It grew dramatically after its foundation and was soon employing some 105 people, including 45 in the factory, 15 sales consultants and 25 fitters. At this stage the founder of the firm sold out to Spartan International Ltd. The new owners commissioned a study to look at the company's structure and information flows, which they felt could be improved. The systems consultants, with the agreement of management, decided to make use of Beer's VSM as a means of looking into the problems of Humberside Windows. Here I shall concentrate on the recommendations made for restructuring the firm in order to make it more viable and effective.

Having taken over the firm, Spartan International decided to rely, for the time being at least, on the skills of the existing technical director to manage its overall activities. This director had worked in several departments in Humberside Windows and understood the organization well, but inevitably found it difficult to adjust to his new role while continuing to fulfil his old duties overseeing purchasing, scheduling, fitting and manufacture. He began to experience considerable work overload, exacerbated by the tendency of all other managers to come to him for advice and guidance. The ex-owner's interventionist style of management had not encouraged others to make decisions for themselves and, indeed, there were no clear job descriptions that indicated individual spheres of discretion.

The most important roles in the organization directly responsible to the technical director were the works manager, the chief surveyor and the scheduling officer. The works manager controlled the factory making the PVC windows and doors and the glass shop. Things generally ran smoothly in this part of the business, although there were periods of considerable slack if the sales force could not sell enough of the product. The chief surveyor and his assistants were responsible for measuring openings for windows and doors and providing manufacturing specifications. His main concerns were the failure of many managers to take the initiative and make decisions, the tendency of sales people to try to please the customer even to the extent of selling items the company could not make and the failure to convey proper standards of work to the fitters. The scheduling officer had to schedule jobs for the 12 fitting teams working from headquarters. He also had to handle the numerous customer complaints and to deal with remedial work. His was a very stressful job, dealing with irate customers and often unable to find senior managers willing and able to take responsibility for problems and sort them out.

On the sales side of the business were a commercial manager and a sales director. The commercial manager's duty was to secure new large commercial contracts with local authorities, regional hospital boards, builders, factories and the like. Having recently been recruited from another company, he was acutely aware of just how chaotic management was in Humberside Windows and commented particularly on the lack of coordination between departments. The sales director's main responsibility was to increase sales to private householders. He had four sales managers under his control, each responsible for a showroom and salesmen in a particular geographical area. The sales director apparently made centralized decisions about such matters as advertising campaigns. He suffered from the same problem as all other senior managers, with other people in the firm constantly coming to him for advice about things that were not his concern.

Looking at this problem from the viable system point of view, it was possible to identify three levels of recursion (see Figure 6.11). Spartan International resides at recursion level 0. Recursion level 1 encompasses the headquarters of Humberside Windows and all its activities. Recursion level 2 embraces the three activities of Humberside Windows that can be regarded as viable systems in their own right - production, sales, and fitting. That these could all be viable systems is clear from the existence of firms in the window business making a living from each of these operations. Diagnosis began at recursion level 2.

Production has two System 1 operational elements - the factory and the glass shop. The basic internal management functions of the production subsystem, Systems 1 through 3, are handled well. However, this relatively efficient part of the business was not realizing its potential because it had no direct links with the external environment. Its only outlet was

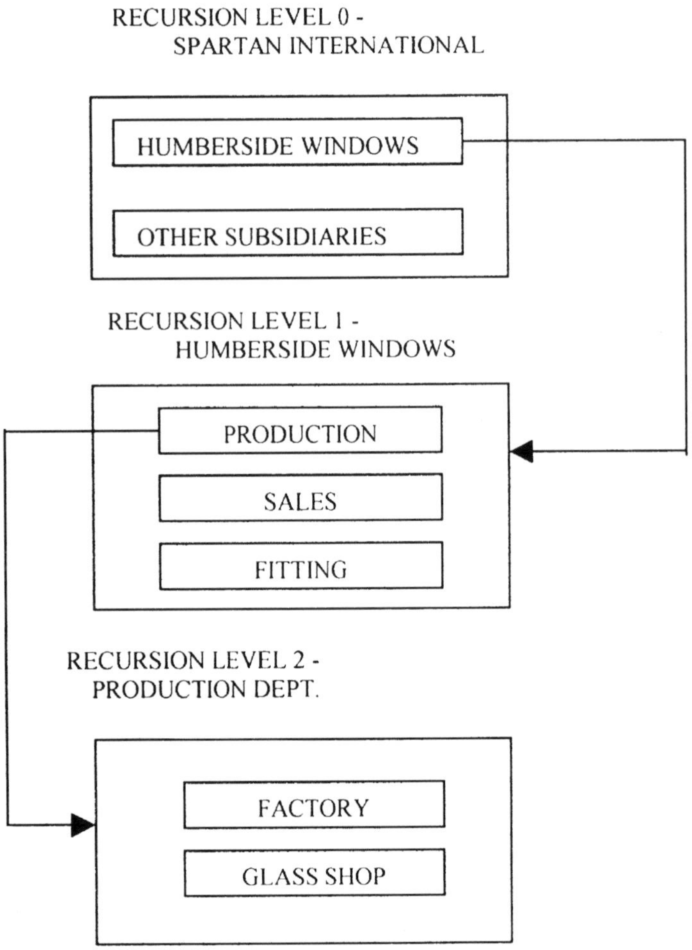

RECURSION LEVEL 0 -
SPARTAN INTERNATIONAL

RECURSION LEVEL 1 -
HUMBERSIDE WINDOWS

RECURSION LEVEL 2 -
PRODUCTION DEPT.

Figure 6.11. Recursion levels at Humberside Windows

through the sales arm of Humberside Windows. Recommendations were therefore made to capitalize on the viability of this part of the business by allowing it to sell its product to other organizations selling and fitting windows and doors; obviously, appropriate Systems 4 and 5 would have to be put in place.

Sales consists of the four geographical branches, which can be regarded as System 1 operations. Each of these has its own manager but is in reality controlled by the sales director. The sales director also fulfills the Systems 2 through 5 functions. The main problem here seems to be the lack of autonomy granted to the sales managers. Recommendations were made to the effect that each sales manager should become a local marketing manager responsible for promoting as well as selling the product in his or her region. The sales director would then be freed for overall marketing activities. Attention was also drawn to the need to provide adequate training to the sales force on which products and services Humberside Windows was actually capable of providing.

Fitting consists of 12 fitting teams as System 1 elements. It is poorly controlled. The scheduling officer performs the System 2 role, but Systems 3 and 3* hardly exist. The technical director is nominally Systems 4 and 5, and because of the lack of a System 3 even finds himself getting dragged into dealing with customer complaints, but as mentioned he has too many duties elsewhere to perform these functions adequately. It was recommended that proper attention be given to the meta-systemic functions 2 through 5 in fitting. What should follow is better training for the fitters, with proper standards of work being communicated and demanded from them. Fitting should be subject to checks on the quality of work. Customer complaints should be handled separately from the scheduling task. Additionally, thought might be given to appointing a senior fitter to head each team.

Turning to recursion 1, the recommendations centered on trying to establish appropriate Systems 2, 3, 4, ad 5 at the Humberside Windows level. Most of the managers who should have been concentrating on these functions (the sales director, the technical director) were otherwise engaged in activities at recursion level 2. To free them to operate at the proper level, a System 3 was necessary that would oversee but not interfere unnecessarily with the System 1 elements of manufacturing, sales and fitting. These System 1 parts should be granted greater autonomy to pursue agreed goals in their own way, using resources allocated in an annual budget. Adequate control could be maintained by System 3 if it institutionalized System 2 and System 3* coordination and audit channels and generally improved information flows. Freed from the need to interfere lower down in the enterprise, managers at recursion level 1 would then need to be educated, as a first step by providing them with appropriate job descriptions, to see themselves and act as managers of the whole of Humberside Window Systems Ltd. An adequate System 4 would need to be put in place. Humberside's planning was short term when it occurred at all. There was little time or effort put into market research or the future development of the business. Spartan International would need to ensure a System 5 existed that could achieve the right balance between ongoing activities and development efforts. Frequent meetings between Systems 3, 4, and 5 managers would initially be necessary to coordinate managerial exertions and to develop an identity for the company and an ethos to guide its actions. These needed careful planning and feeding with appropriate information.

In broad terms, the recommendations sought to make Humberside Windows more adaptive in the face of its environment while improving control of operations at all levels of the organization. Some were accepted and put into effect, others proved not to be feasible given the history and culture of the organization at that time. If they had been followed as a whole, they should have enhanced the organization's ability to be efficient and effective and its capacity to change in response to environmental requirements.

The recommendations were not reached solely on the basis of empirical observation of the dysfunctions of the existing system. The cybernetic principles encapsulated in the VSM highlight particularly problematic aspects of the organization of all systems and guide the investigator to consider how these are being handled in the system of concern. The model pinpoints systemic/structural constraints that have to be observed by any organization. Similarly, the recommendations emerge from ensuring that an underlying structure and system of relationships are established in the organization that obey cybernetic principles. The structuralist bias of cybernetic diagnosis and redesign requires that an organization be produced that respects cybernetic laws.

6.5.4. Organizational Cybernetics : Another *Fifth Discipline*?

Other sources for organizational cybernetics are the writings of two adherents of Beer's thinking, Clemson (1984) and Espejo (1977, 1979, 1987), and the collections of papers on the VSM (including many case studies) edited by Espejo and Harnden (1989) and Espejo and Schwaninger, eds., (1993). The "St Gallen School" of cybernetics (see Ulrich and Probst, 1984) also evinces similar concerns and tackles them from a compatible theoretical position. More recently, Yolles (1999) has provided a comprehensive introductory volume, *Management Systems : A Viable Approach*, which sets out a version of "viable system theory" and "viable inquiring systems" drawing heavily upon the work of Eric Schwarz as well as Beer. Perhaps the most extravagant claims for organizational cybernetics, however, have been made by Espejo, Schuhmann, Schwaninger and Bilello (1996), in a book on "organizational transformation and learning." This seems to want to establish organizational cybernetics as a kind of "fifth discipline", replacing but otherwise playing a role akin to system dynamics in Senge's schema. We shall concentrate on this contribution here.

Espejo *et al.* (1996) ask us to face up to the fact that change is confronting the world of business and management at a "dazzling rate." In these circumstances some of the new approaches to management are seen as "valuable":

> integrated management; ecological management; human resources management; total quality management; information management; organizational change; the learning organization; organizational architecture; the virtual corporation; business process redesign (p.1).

They need drawing together, however, so that the common thread running through them all can be recognized:

> Cybernetics - the science of communication and control - can and should be used to connect these various approaches by presenting them in a common language. Seen from such a perspective, the common purpose of these approaches boils down to the following issues: 'How can organizations cope with increasing environmental complexity? How can their action become more effective? (pp. 1-2).

According to Espejo *et al.*, their empirical research has uncovered eight major issues of concern to managers, areas which they feel are crucial to "good" and "effective" management:

- "identity": a clear vision, spread throughout the levels of the organization
- "adaptation - inventing the corporation": proactive adaptation is essential if an organization is to survive, develop and prosper
- "implementation - investing in the corporation": the need to foster quality and continuous improvement
- "structure and process": open and participative structures are necessary in order to encourage autonomy and enhance local variety
- "understanding organizations better": accepting that a variety of viewpoints is necessary in organizations
- "change, transformation and learning": organizations must learn how to reconfigure themselves continuously and discontinuously
- "human resource management - people in organizations": personal development will inevitably aid organizational development
- "ecological responsibility": organizations need to develop a sustainable ecological balance with their milieu

These issues can be tackled if we are willing to learn a "new language" through which we can more fully understand management action in organizations. This language has emerged from cybernetics and draws particularly on the work of Ashby, Bateson, Beer, and Maturana and Varela. The cynic, of course, will not be surprised that it is cybernetics that can provide answers to these issues. They might have been chosen deliberately as that sub-set of the range of management problems that cybernetics feels happiest talking about. Matters such as how exactly to bring about an accommodation between alternative viewpoints, or how to handle organizational politics and power, do not appear on the list. There follows a discussion of the basic concepts of cybernetics; the new language that can give rise to a "new paradigm" of management.

Effective action in organizations under the new paradigm requires breaking away from the "traditional model" of management, with its emphasis on the boss-subordinate relationship. We need to embrace instead "self-management network structures":

> Corporate survival depends on less well defined work patterns, supported by better communications and a greater recognition of interdependencies among the organization's members as they collaborate in teams that are often temporary and, to a large degree, self-regulating (Espejo et al., 1996, p. 71).

In many organizations this will require a culture change. People need to be flexible and self-regulating and to concern themselves with good communications. They need to change their relationships with others in the process of inventing and reinventing their organization in pursuit of its ascribed purpose. Fundamental to all this is "learning":

> Organizational learning implies behavior modification, including changes in relationships, in order to create the conditions for creating, acquiring and transferring distinctions and practices (p. 19).

A learning organization has employees who can overcome "defensive practices"; it evolves towards structures that encourage individual creativity; distributes problem-solving capacity; continues to learn; creates its own environment; and ensures that individual and organizational expectations are clearly defined. It depends on vision and commitment. According to Espejo et al. the VSM, a "model of recursive structures", is a suitable model for ensuring self-regulation and effective communications, and the complementarity of cohesive management and autonomy. Recursive structures

> are necessary for current trends in management and organizational practices to bear fruit. For instance, recursive structures and management are necessary for an effective implementation of total quality, business process re-engineering and just-in-time supplies (1996, p. 104).

Espejo's more recent writings (and not just in the 1996 book) add a "softer" element to organizational cybernetics. We noted his work (1989) showing how the VSM could be used to explore different organizational identities through explicating the structural implications of each. His cybernetic methodology (1989, 1990) seeks, after a fashion, to combine the VSM with aspects of soft systems methodology. Now, in Espejo et al. (1996), we have organizational cybernetics acting as a kind of "fifth discipline" in the same way that system dynamics does for Senge. It can bring about a paradigm shift to a more holistic view of management and integrate other "disciplines", such as human resources management and organizational learning, which are themselves in need of systemic awareness. This is all surface decoration, however. Deep down, Espejo remains as committed as ever to the VSM as a model which expresses laws of effective organization. If an enterprise does not respect the law of requisite variety, for example, it will not work as well as one that does and, indeed, its viability will be threatened. Even in his most "interpretive moments" (e.g. Espejo and Harnden, 1989) Espejo believes this. He wants to employ the VSM to reveal the cybernetics of the situation and "diagnosing communication problems leads to a discovery of the causes of operational problems, thus making it possible to improve the situation" (Espejo, 1990). Forced to choose between what his cybernetic diagnosis tells him and what the participants in a problem situation believe, Espejo would opt for his cybernetic diagnosis.

Espejo's failure to take the VSM out of the functionalist paradigm is not, however, the end of the matter. We need to remind ourselves that the VSM is only a model, if a very rigorous and useful one, and that it can be employed by different methodologies in the service of various paradigms. In the next chapter we consider Harnden's interpretive reading of the VSM and, in Chapter 8, its possible usage as an emancipatory tool, as well as Beer's development of cybernetics in "Team Syntegrity." The functionalist paradigm certainly does not exhaust the possibilities opened up by the VSM.

6.5.5. Strengths and Weaknesses of Organizational Cybernetics

A useful starting point in considering the many strengths of the organizational cybernetic model is to stress its generality. This stems from its very nature. The recommendations endorsed in the model do not tightly prescribe a particular *structure*; they relate more to a system's essential *organization*, to use a distinction drawn by Varela (1984). They are concerned with what defines a system and enables it to maintain its identity, rather than with the variable relations that can develop between components integrating particular systems. As a result, the VSM has been found to be applicable to small organizations (Espejo, 1979; Jackson and Alabi, 1986), large firms (Beer, 1979), training programs (Britton and McCallion, 1985), industries (Baker, Elias, and Griggs, 1977), local government (Beer, 1974) and national government (Beer, 1981a). I can testify that it was the only management model capable of integrating, in one volume, six diverse contributions to a seminar series about the management of transport systems (Keys and Jackson, eds., 1985). A number of other, very varied applications are set out in Espejo and Harnden, eds., (1989) and Espejo and Schwaninger, eds., (1993). From an analysis of all these cases, it is possible to pick out those features of the VSM that serve it most advantageously when it is used to assist management practice.

First, the model is capable of dealing with organizations whose parts are both vertically and horizontally interdependent. The notion of recursion enables the VSM to cope with the vertical interdependence displayed in, say, a multinational company that itself consists of divisions embracing companies, which embrace departments, and so on. The applicability of the VSM at different system levels acts as a great variety reducer for managers and management scientists. The idea of recursion is not unique to Beer's writings – Parsons's AGIL schema (see Chapter 4) is applied at different system levels – but only in the VSM is it incorporated into a usable management tool. Horizontally interdependent subsystems, the parts of System 1, are integrated and guided by the organizational meta-system, Systems 2 through 5. The hoary old problem of centralization versus decentralization is dealt with in the VSM by arrangements to allow the subsystems as much autonomy as is consistent with overall systemic cohesiveness. There are some close parallels between Beer's account of this issue and the contingency theory approach to differentiation and integration offered by Lawrence and Lorsch (see the section of this chapter on "Organizations-as-Systems").

Second, the model demands that attention be paid to the sources of command and control in the system. The relative autonomy granted to the parts within the VSM should again be noted. In the VSM, the source of control is spread throughout the architecture of the system. This allows the self-organizing tendencies present in all complex systems to be employed productively. Problems are corrected as closely as possible to the point where they occur. Motivation should be increased at lower levels in the organization. Higher management should be freed to concentrate on meta-systemic functions. The importance of encouraging self-organization and freeing management for boundary-management activities has been well documented in the literature of socio-technical systems theory (see "Organizations-as-Systems"). It is also one of the main planks of the "St Gallen School" of organizational cybernetics. Ulrich, Malik, and Probst all offer reasons why it should promote greater efficiency (Ulrich and Probst, eds, 1984). Some restrictions on autonomy are, of course, essential and these are imposed by Systems 2 and 3 (so as to ensure overall systemic cohesiveness) and by System 4 in its role as a development function collecting together relevant environmental information and, in the light of threats and opportunities, suggesting necessary changes to systemic purpose and consequent alterations of organizational structure. System 5 has overall responsibility for policy, and this will often involve balancing internal and external demands as represented in the organization by the desire of System 3 for stability and the bias of System 4 for adaptation. The System 3-4-5 interrelationship, as described by Beer, shows interesting similarities with Thompson's (1967) well-known discussion of the administrative process.

Third, the model offers a particularly suitable starting point for the design of information systems in organizations, as indeed has been convincingly argued by Espejo (1979), Espejo and Watt (1978), and Schumann (1990). Most designs for information systems are premised upon some taken-for-granted model of organization – usually the outdated classical, hierarchical model. It takes a revolutionary mind to reverse this, to put information processing first and to make recommendations for organizational design on the basis of information requirements, as revealed by the law of requisite variety; yet this is what Beer succeeds in doing with the VSM (see particularly Salah, 1989). As was mentioned earlier (see "Organizations-as-Systems"), Galbraith achieves a similar reversal with his model of the organization as an information - processing system.

Fourth, the organization is represented as being in close interrelationship with its environment, both influencing it and being influenced by it. The organization does not simply react to its environment but can proactively attempt to change the environment in ways that will benefit the organization. Morgan (1983) sees dangers in this proactive aspect of cybernetics because it might lead organizations to damage the field of relationships upon which they depend. He need not worry about the role of the VSM. There is as much emphasis in Beer's model upon surviving within and developing a set of relationships as upon goal seeking.

Fifth, the VSM can be used very effectively as a diagnostic tool to make specific recommendations for improving the performance of organizations. A system of concern can be compared against the model to check that its structures and processes support an underlying organization capable of ensuring survival and effectiveness. Advice on how to proceed with diagnosis was given in the earlier subsection on using the VSM.

Finally, having dealt with the role of the VSM in promoting organizational efficiency, I should also acknowledge the contribution it can make to helping the realization of human potentiality in enterprises. The model provides powerful cybernetic arguments for granting maximum autonomy to the parts of an organization and for the democratic definition of purposes. Beer advocates decentralization of control because of the implications of the law of requisite variety. The parts must be granted autonomy so that they can absorb some of the massive environmental variety that would otherwise overwhelm higher management levels. The only degree of constraint permitted is that necessary for overall systemic cohesion and viability, and this constraint facilitates the exercise of liberty rather than limits it. if less control were exercised, the result would not be greater freedom for the parts, but anarchy (Beer, 1979, Chapter 7). The constraints imposed on the parts of System 1 by the meta-system should be regarded as being like the laws enacted in a democratic society. We do not regard laws against assault and theft as infringements of our liberty because they increase our freedom to go about our normal business unhindered. The degree of autonomy granted to the parts by the VSM is the maximum possible if the system as a whole is to continue to exist.

The cybernetic argument for the democratic derivation of purposes effectively follows from this. For only with democratic involvement can the parts be convinced that the system is serving their purposes and that they stand to gain from its continuance. Only then can they be expected to accept meta-systemic constraints as legitimate and use the autonomy granted to promote efficiency rather than disruption. Just because System 5 is labeled "policy", therefore, does not imply that it is solely responsible for deciding the purposes of the enterprise. In Beer's (1985) view the board, as well as looking after the shareholders,

> also embodies the power of its workforce and its managers, of its customers and of the society that sustains it. The board metabolizes the power of all such participants in the enterprise in order to survive (p. 12).

If, then, the stakeholders in a system have agreed about the purposes to be pursued, and those purposes are embodied in System 5, the VSM offers a means of pursuing the purposes efficiently and effectively with only those constraints on individual autonomy necessary for successful operation.

Because of the link between efficiency and democracy, established cybernetically by Beer, it is clear that the model depends for its full and satisfactory operation on a democratic milieu – ideally perhaps on a president who, when System 5 is presented during an explanation of the workings of the VSM, can exclaim "At last, *el pueblo*" (Beer, 1981a). This, of course, is why Beer (1985) counsels us in *Diagnosing* on the unfortunate effects the exercise of power can have in viable systems.

Organizational cybernetics draws its strengths from three "world hypotheses" - mechanism, organicism and formism; and from the machine, organism and brain metaphors. This was evident in the case study. Humberside Windows was encouraged to improve the efficiency of its transformation processes, to become more responsive to its environment and to devolve responsibility "recursively" so as to increase its overall problem solving capabilities. It is not surprising, therefore, that organizational cybernetics provides a highly sophisticated organizational model. I have argued elsewhere (Jackson, 1985a) that it is superior to the traditional, human relations and contingency theory models – the alternatives commonly offered in organization theory. In the course of the analysis above, I have had reason to mention the work of well known organizations-as-systems theorists such as Parsons, Lawrence and Lorsch, Thompson, socio-technical thinkers and Galbraith. The principles encapsulated in the VSM fit well with the most advanced findings of modern organizational science (Flood and Jackson, 1988). Moreover, the model integrates these findings into an applicable management tool that can be used to recommend specific improvements in the functioning of organizations.

Perhaps even more significant, the VSM rests upon the science of cybernetics. This ensures that its use generates enormous explanatory power compared with the usual analyses carried out in organizational theory. The key here is the structuralist epistemology upon which organizational cybernetics is based. Structuralism, as the term is employed in this book (the reader is referred back to the discussion of this issue in Chapter 3), embraces a "realist" epistemology which is fundamentally different to positivism. Positivism encourages empirical observation, analysis, and classification of surface elements – the sort of approach we have witnessed being used by organizations-as-systems theorists and hard systems thinkers. Structuralists, by contrast, believe that these surface phenomena are generated by underlying structures that should be uncovered and understood. It is therefore incumbent upon scientists to provide explanations of the phenomena available to our senses in terms of the underlying, unobservable mechanisms that produce them. Structuralists seek to model the causal processes at work at the deep structural level that generate the surface phenomena and the relationships between them.

As was noted in Chapter 3, the convergence in approach between cybernetics and structuralism has long been apparent to structuralist writers. Cyberneticians have been much slower to recognize the similarity in concern. This is surprising given the number of concepts that are the common currency of both cybernetics and structuralism – concepts such as organized complexity, regulation, transformation, equilibrium, information exchange and feedback and control. It is even more surprising given some of Beer's (1966) comments in the relatively early text *Decision and Control*, in which he clearly demonstrates a structuralist orientation. He argues, for example, that scientific management should not be content simply with discovering the facts but should also seek to know what the facts mean, and how they fit together, and then seek to uncover mechanisms that underlie them. Ever since, of course, he has been shouting loud enough that the VSM is an attempt to set out, in terms of cybernetic laws, the necessary and sufficient conditions of viability for any autonomous system (e.g. Beer, 1979, 1990).

The link between cybernetics and structuralism is confirmed in other sources. Jackson and Carter (1984) demonstrate a correspondence between the function of myth in Levi-Strauss's structural anthropology and the way variety attenuation works in Beer's cybernetics. Molloy and Best (1980) argue that Beer's VSM can be used as an "iconic model" to reveal underlying mechanisms supporting surface system behavior and to provide explanations of observable phenomena. In general, there is little reason to doubt that cybernetics is based upon structuralist assumptions. It serves to develop explanations of observable occurrences in social systems based upon principles and laws governing the behavior of all systems under control. Even the emphasis placed in organizational cybernetics on the role of the observer has its corollary in structuralism. At least in Levi-Strauss's (1968) and Piaget's (1973) versions of the doctrine, the fundamental structures uncovered relate back to the basic characteristics of the human mind.

If Beer's VSM integrates the findings of the organizations-as-systems school, we can now understand that it goes beyond them as well. Underpinned by the science of cybernetics, and thus realizing a structuralist project, its use generates enormous explanatory power compared with the usual analyses carried out in organization theory. Organization theorists (at least those driven by positivism) cling to perceived relationships between surface phenomena as the source of their insights. Cybernetics allows an explanation of such perceived relationships to be extracted from consideration of processes at work at a deeper, structural level. For example, socio-technical thinkers find that delegating control to autonomous work groups improves the effectiveness and efficiency of organizations by improving performance in the groups themselves and by freeing managers for boundary management. The VSM can provide a scientific explanation of this in terms of requisite variety. It is not farfetched to see the whole history of positivist organization theory as an empirical commentary upon the cybernetic principles underlying the viability of systems as unearthed deductively by Beer.

The link between organizational cybernetics and structuralism also helps to explain why hard systems thinkers have had such difficulty absorbing Beer's work. Organizational cybernetics is based on an alternative epistemology and represents a genuinely new direction in systems thinking. Further, we can begin to grasp more fully the basis of the criticisms aimed at the VSM. Once we step outside structuralism and view the VSM using the assumptions of the interpretive and radical paradigms, as defined by Burrell and Morgan (1979), then doubts inevitably begin to appear. Perhaps too much emphasis is placed upon organizations as logically designed structures of communication and control, and not enough on organizations "as *processes* in which different perceptions of reality are continuously negotiated and renegotiated" (Checkland, 1980). Perhaps, if the social world consists of antagonistic class formations, with some groups exploiting others, the VSM does provide too convenient a vehicle for increasing the power of dominant groups. It is to these criticisms that we now turn.

Considerable effort has been made elsewhere in clarifying, classifying and debating the most frequent criticisms raised against Beer's model (Jackson, 1985a, 1986, 1988a; Flood and Carson, 1988; Flood and Jackson, 1988). Of the eight criticisms in general circulation, two (misplaced mechanical or biological analogy, and encouraging organizations to damage their field of relationships) have been answered above. Two other arguments, that variety is a "poor measure" (Rivett, 1977) or "unexceptional" in its implications (Checkland, 1980), and that cybernetics emphasizes stability at the expense of change (Ulrich, 1983), are misplaced in relation to the VSM, as the previous description of that model shows. A fifth criticism, that cybernetics is difficult to apply in practice (Rivett, 1977; Thomas, 1980), is gradually being addressed in the literature (Beer, 1985; Clemson, 1984; Espejo, 1989, 1990). In short, while these five criticisms may hold against management cybernetics, they cannot be sustained against organizational cybernetics.

That still leaves three interrelated, criticisms that are troubling about organizational cybernetics, and these we need to review more fully. It has already been argued that the VSM more than stands comparison with the most advanced theories produced by orthodox organization theory. Yet that word "orthodox" reveals a nagging doubt. Our standard of comparison for the VSM so far has been the functionalist, organizations-as-systems tradition. Consider the VSM from the point of view of another sociological paradigm – the interpretive, for example – and it does seem to capture only a subset of what is generally accepted as significant about organizations. For Checkland (1980), looking at things from the interpretive paradigm, the VSM is at best only a partial representation of what an organization is. It is a representation, moreover, that misses the essential character of organizations: the fact their component parts are human beings, who can attribute meaning to their situation and can therefore see in organizations whatever purposes they wish and make of organizations whatever they will. Because of this, it is as legitimate to regard an organization as a social grouping, an appreciative system, or a power struggle as it is to see it through the eyes of the VSM.

This links in to perhaps the most frequent criticism of the model: that it underplays the purposeful role of individuals in organizations. Morris (1983), while not agreeing with this criticism, captures its flavor nicely with his phrase "the big toe also thinks!" For Adams (1973), the VSM implies that man, the basic unit in organizational systems, is free only in the same way that the knee is free to jerk – as a reflex action. In Ulrich's (1981a) view, cybernetic models leave out perhaps the most important feature of socio-cultural systems; human purposefulness and self-reflectiveness. This charge has very practical consequences, for it suggests that the VSM could mislead managers into placing too much emphasis on organizational design and too little on the role of individuals in organizations. If the criticism is correct, managers seeking to promote the efficiency and effectiveness of their enterprises by concentrating effort on their logical design as adaptive goal-seeking entities (as recommended by the VSM) may be misplacing their energies. Social organizations can, perhaps, exist and perform well while employing a host of apparently illogical structures. The emphasis placed on organization design may preclude proper attention being given to the generation of shared perceptions and values (to "organizational culture"). The point can, of course, be overdone. In Beer's and Espejo's work, the tendency has been to pay increased attention to the perceptions and roles of individuals. In principle, the VSM does cater for the purposeful role of individuals in organizations. The model suggests that it is to the advantage of organizations to grant maximum autonomy to individuals. Nevertheless, the emphasis remains overwhelmingly on systemic/structural design to the neglect of the requirement to manage processes of negotiation between different viewpoints and value positions. In Humberside Windows, the consultants did not presume it was necessary to address the possibility that different values or conflict existed among the stakeholders of the enterprise. Neglect of the culture and political metaphors probably hampered the acceptance of some of the recommendations made.

Following very much from this point, a further criticism is that underplaying the role of individuals carries autocratic implications when cybernetic models are used in practice. This is an old criticism. Lilienfeld (1978) comments on a 1948 review of Wiener's *Cybernetics* in which a Dominican friar, Pére Dubarle, expresses his fear that cybernetic techniques might help some humans to increase their power over others. Against management cybernetics the criticism is fair enough. Models that treat organizations as simple input-transformation-output systems, with an externally defined goal, clearly lend themselves to autocratic usage by those who possess power. The criticism is also, however, leveled against the VSM (Adams, 1973; Rivett, 1977; Checkland, 1980). It is believed that, when applied, the VSM inevitably serves the purposes of narrow élite groups. Much of this criticism has to be misplaced. For Beer (1985), an organization's goal is not externally defined but emerges as a compromise from among the various internal and external influences on the organization. Further, despite the terminology of Systems 1 through 5, he insists that the VSM should not be seen as hierarchical – all five functions are dependent upon each other. What the VSM arguably achieves, when it is used in organizations, is an increase in efficiency and effectiveness. There is nothing to prevent the application of the VSM to democratic organizations in which all participate fully in the process of goal setting. The model might improve the efficiency and effectiveness of these organizations as well. Indeed, I have already rehearsed the argument that it requires only that degree of control over individual freedom necessary in order to maintain cohesiveness in a viable system – law and order for the benefit of all. It cannot therefore be argued that the VSM *inevitably* serves autocratic purposes.

Of course, the problem still arises of the model being misused by a powerful group. Ulrich (1981a) argues that Beer's VSM does in fact lend itself to this kind of usage. He insists that design tools should be so constructed that they are impossible to subvert for authoritarian use. Beer replies (1983b) that the risk of subversion does exist but that safeguards can be built into the system to minimize the danger.

This final argument can only be further elucidated if we move to a meta-level of analysis. I shall pick it up again at the end of this chapter when we engage in a critique of the functionalist systems approach more generally.

6.6. LIVING SYSTEMS THEORY

The most ambitious attempt to integrate knowledge across different system types, following the true faith propounded by von Bertalanffy, is Miller's theory of "living systems." In the huge tome dedicated to this theory (Miller, 1978), he presents his aim as to provide a general theory with the potential to unify the scientific study of living systems. Such a theory is crucial if knowledge about living systems is to grow and develop:

> Many scientists have expressed the need for a commonly accepted language, systematic theories, and basic laws to organize the huge volume of research findings and bridge the gaps of our knowledge about living systems ... [Such a theory] can also supply a fixed structure into which new discoveries can be fitted [and can] also provide common measurement units that make research at different levels comparable in a way they are not when each field has its own idiosyncratic measures ... Without such theory the scientist does not know how to decide which of an overwhelming number of possible observations are worth making (Miller, 1978, p. 5).

The considerable amount of work that has gone into elucidating and extending living systems theory, since its original formulation, has been reported primarily in the journal *Behavioral Science* (now merged into *Systems Research and Behavioral Science*). Here we take a look at the general theory before considering its application to organizations and reviewing methodology, case studies, and strengths and weaknesses.

6.6.1. The General Theory

Miller's general living systems theory is concerned with "concrete" systems which exist in "physical space-time." He defines a concrete system as

> a non-random accumulation of matter–energy in a region of physical space-time, which is organized into interacting interrelated subsystems or components (1978, p. 17).

This emphasis can be distinguished, for example, from Parsons' "abstracted analysis" which relied on concepts such as the social role. The advantage of studying concrete systems is that we can actually observe them, their structures and processes. We can be sure that they exist.

The "complex structures" that are living systems exist, for Miller (1978; Miller and Miller, 1990), at eight hierarchical levels:

- Cell
- Organ
- Organism
- Group
- Organization
- Community (added by Miller and Miller in 1990)
- Society
- Supranational Systems

These have in common that they are open systems with semi-permeable boundaries existing in certain environments; they have sub-systems which process inputs, throughputs and outputs; and they have purposes and goals directed at maintaining steady states of negentropy. Purposes are preferred internal states; goals are preferred external relationships. They derive from the system's original "template", which guides its development but can be modified by learning. The purposes and goals reflect a "hierarchy of values" which determines how the system acts, for example to deal with strain if all its needs cannot be met immediately. As one climbs the hierarchy, the structures and processes evident in systems become more complex:

> The larger, higher-level systems have emergent capabilities which enable them to accomplish things that systems at lower levels cannot achieve (Miller, 1978, p. 1025).

Living systems, at all levels, have 20 "critical subsystems" (the "timer" was a later addition to the 19 of 1978 – see Miller and Miller, 1990). These subsystems are "critical" because they carry out specific processes that are essential for life. As Tracy (1995) puts it:

> A living system must either possess each of these critical subsystems or have access to the processes through association (e.g. symbiosis, parasitism, or patronage) with other systems (p. 7).

Any living system must possess a "decider" subsystem which applies decision rules, according to the purposes and goals, and ensures they are enacted at all levels of the system. To do this, the decider subsystem depends upon a group of subsystems which process information through input, coding, internal transmission, association, storage and output. They ensure that the "decider" has all the information it needs from other subsystems and can transmit control information to those subsystems. A living system also processes matter and energy through input, distribution, conversion, production, storage and output. Another group of subsystems deals with these functions as well as providing for the support and movement of the system itself. Two subsystems, the reproducer and the boundary, process both information and matter-energy. Table 6.2 shows the complete list of 20 critical subsystems and the processes for which they are responsible. Figure 6.12 is Tracy's diagrammatic presentation showing some of the relationships between the subsystems. Here I list the subsystems again with, in brackets, examples from the level of the organization (examples from Miller and Miller, 1995): Reproducer (chartering group); Boundary (matter-energy - guards at entrance) (information - librarian); Ingestor (receiving department); Distributor (assembly line); Converter (operators of oil refinery); Producer (factory production unit); Matter-energy storage (stockroom personnel); Extruder (janitorial staff); Motor (crew of company jet); Supporter (building repair and maintenance personnel); Input Transducer (secretaries taking incoming calls); Internal Transducer (factory quality control unit); Channel and Net (all users of corporate phone network); Timer (people who operate factory whistles); Decoder (foreign language translation groups); Associator (people who train new employees); Memory (filing department); Decider (top executives, department heads, middle managers); Encoder (annual report writers); and Output Transducer (public relations department).

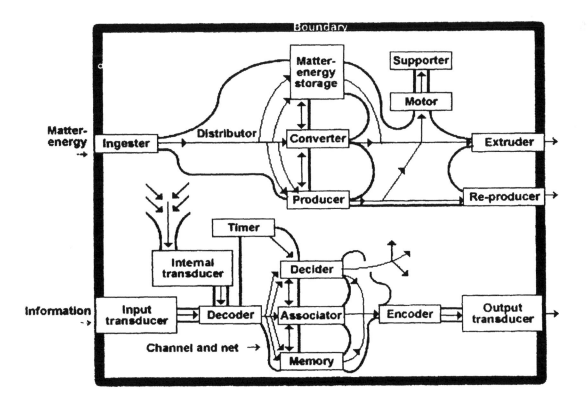

Figure 6.12. Simplified schematic of the critical subsystems (adapted from Tracy, 1994, p. 13)

Table 6.2. Critical subsystems and critical processes of a living system

Sub System	Process
Reproducer	Transmit template information for a new system.
	Assemble matter-energy to compose the new system.
	Assist the new system until it becomes self-supporting.
Boundary	Contain and bind together the system's components.
	Protect the components from environmental stresses.
	Exclude or permit entry to matter-energy and information.
Ingestor	Bring matter-energy across the boundary from the environment.
Distributor	Carry matter-energy around the system to each component.
Converter	Change inputs into forms more useful to the system.
Producer	Form stable, enduring associations among inputs.
Storage	Hold deposits of various sorts of matter-energy.
Extruder	Transmit matter-energy out of the system
Motor	Move the system or parts of it in relation to environment.
	Move components of environment in relation to each other.
Supporter	Maintain a proper spatial relationship among components.
Input transducer	Bring markers bearing information into the system.
	Change them into forms that transmit within the system.
Internal transducer	Receive markers from subsystems or system components.
	Change them into forms that transmit within the system.
Channel and net	Carry information-bearing markers around the system.
Timer	Generate and transmit timing signals to decider subsystem.
Decoder	Alter the code of information input into a private code.
Associator	Form enduring associations among items of information.
Memory	Store, maintain, and retrieve information-bearing markers.
Decider	Establish purposes and goals for the system
	Receive information inputs from all other subsystems.
	Analyze inputs, synthesize plans, and choose a plan.
	Transmit information outputs that implement the choice.
Encoder	Alter code of information from private to public code.
Output transducer	Change system's markers into other forms of matter-energy.
	Transmit markers bearing information from the system.

6.6.2. The Living Organization

Tracy (1994) has swallowed whole Miller's thesis that organizations are living systems. For him,

> organizations are, or should be, alive. They are living systems and should be treated as such. They are living because they derive many of their most important characteristics from the genetic makeup of their members. Because of their origins, organizations exhibit the same essential processes and structures that you and I display (p. xi).

Like cells, organs and organisms, therefore, organizations are comprised primarily of "protoplasm" and this gives them the distinctive character of being living systems. They also possess a template which governs their behavior, development and reproduction. Part of this template derives from the genetic make-up of their members but part also comes from what Dawkins calls "memes." Memes are "ideas" which carry information about the structure and processes of the system. A new business, for example, is organized according to its corporate charter, a franchise agreement, or the beliefs of its founders. The "memetic template" of an organization supplements the underlying set of instructions supplied by the genetic templates of the social system's members (Tracy, 1994, p.7)

Organizations, like other living systems, seek to sustain themselves and are capable of doing so indefinitely. They do this through the input - throughput - output process. For example they hire and fire personnel and seek to ensure the flow of resources necessary to provide their products or services. Within the bounds of their templates, organizations seek to actualize their potential. They also propagate through franchising or creating new divisions in their own image. Of course, like organisms, organizations must maintain a productive relationship with their environments. Managers have to ensure that their organizations adapt to the environment and act on the environment to make it more congenial for the pursuit of the organization's particular purposes and goals. To achieve all these things, organizations depend on the 20 critical subsystems identified by Miller.

Tracy insists that organizations should be viewed as "life-forms." Managers should behave towards them as parents, or stewards, or physicians; they must make decisions

> based on organizational values and for the sake of the organization. They must also attend to the health of the organization, protecting it from predators and invaders, keeping it well fed with resources, leading it into favorable environments, modifying its behavior, diagnosing its illnesses, and prescribing appropriate treatments ... [They] must understand that the organization has a life of its own, that it has a right to survive and develop its potential, and that it may well outlive them ... Their role, if they choose to accept it, is to make good decisions for the organization based on its values, purposes and goals (1994, p.4, emphasis in the original).

Tracy's book *Leading the Living Organization* has separate chapters on the detail of how this perspective can help manage the birth of an organization, motivation, resources and power, information flow, matter-energy flow, internal conflict and stress, environmental relationships, problems of leadership, change and the future. We return to the insights to be gained for managing change in our sub-section on applications of living systems theory.

6.6.3. Methodology and Living Systems Theory

Miller and Miller (1995) believe that living systems theory is a scientific theory which seeks to describe real phenomena and also that it implies an approach to solving problems.

As a scientific theory it has to subject itself to verification or falsification according to the normal rules of the traditional scientific method. Hypotheses must be derived from the theory and tested against reality. Because it is a general system theory, hypotheses derived from living systems theory can refer to commonalities between systems of the same type, systems at the same level or systems at different levels. Miller and Miller view cross-level research as the most powerful of these. Cross-level research seeks isomorphisms among systems at two or more levels which can be used to build models applicable to a variety of systems. *Living Systems* (1978) contains a list of 173 testable cross-level hypotheses and others have been postulated since. The first experimental test of a multilevel hypothesis, derived from living systems theory, concerned information input overload. Experiments at the levels of cell, organ, organism, group and organization were conducted by specialists in the appropriate fields. Miller and Miller (1995) report that:

> Data from all levels ... yielded information input-output curves alike in form ... These results confirmed the hypothesis of a formal identity in this aspect of information processing at these five levels (p. 24).

Other examples are provided in Miller and Miller (1995).

Living systems theory can also be used to improve the functioning of individual living systems. In the case of an organization, the consultant would approach problem diagnosis in the same manner as a physician would with a patient. Miller and Miller describe the appropriate methodology in more detail:

> It involves observing and measuring important relationships between inputs and outputs of the total system and identifying the structures that perform each of the [20] sub-system processes ... The flows of relevant matter, energy, and information through the system and the adjustment processes of subsystems and the total system are also examined. The status and function of the system are analyzed and compared with what is average or normal for that type of system. If the system is experiencing a disturbance in some steady state, an effort is made to discover the source of the strain and correct it (1995, pp. 25-6).

A set of symbols is available which represent levels, subsystems, and major flows in living systems and enable the use of diagrams and simulations in diagnosis. Miller and Miller (1991) have also provided a list of organizational pathologies, unearthed by living systems theory, that can help consultants with diagnosis. All this depends, of course, on there being measures of normal values and ranges for critical variables in organizations. Miller and Miller point out that while there are thousands of such measures for physiological variables crucial to humans, little effort has been put into developing indicators of organizational health.

6.6.4. Case Studies of the Application of Living Systems Theory to Organizations

Miller and Miller (1995) refer to living systems applications in hospitals, a psychiatric ward, public schools, a public transportation system, the US Army and IBM. Miller's ideas were introduced into Sweden and elaborated on by Samuelson. Holmberg (1995) lists and describes six areas of subsequent application: geoinformatic systems, urban management systems, sea rescue systems, system modeling and simulation, software engineering and living systems monitoring and tutoring. Swanson (1995) has applied living systems theory to accounting in the form of "concrete process analysis." Here we confine ourselves to reviewing Tracy's use of living systems theory to illuminate the management of change, and the US Army example.

According to Tracy (1994), change may occur in organizations for the purposes of maintenance, actualisation or propagation. It can be directed internally to the structure and processes of the organization itself or externally toward the environment. Sometimes it just happens to the organization or reflects the pattern of its template. At other times, however, managers, as the leading element in the "decider subsystem", are required to direct change either reactively in response to events or proactively. Tracy (pp. 183-4) lists seven types of managed change required to maintain the organization:

- Replacing assets lost through entropy
- Adding value sufficient to offset entropic losses
- Correcting process errors
- Adjusting to environmental changes to maintain equilibrium
- Influencing or controlling the environment from critical to less critical assets
- Shifting entropic losses from critical assets; and
- Shifting entropic losses from the system to its environment

The first four of these we can recognize as reactive; the final three as proactive. Four further kinds of proactive managed change are necessary if the organization is to actualize its potential:

- Adding components and resources in excess of system losses
- Increasing the complexity of the system in accordance with the increasing variety of its environment
- Increasing the complexity of the template and/or decider subsystem in accordance with increasing complexity of the system
- Recognizing the need for unprogrammed growth and elaboration of the system and coordinating it

Finally, propagating the organization requires managers to proactively influence the environment through dissemination to accept and incorporate important values of the organization.

The US Army project was a three year study of 41 battalions. It was the first large-scale application of living systems theory (Miller and Miller, 1995). The Army had come to the conclusion that some battalions were more effective than others in realizing their mission. The aim of the "living systems process analysis" conducted was to help understand how battalions function and see how their effectiveness was related to the quality and quantity of flows of matter-energy and information. Various data sources were employed, from standardized questionnaire results to interviews, in order to discover the importance of each matter-energy and information process and how well each was being handled. The living systems analysis confirmed the Army's findings on the relative effectiveness of different battalions, but was able to go much further in explaining why this was the case. For example, it was found that there was a close relationship between a battalion's appreciation of and ability to process information and its effectiveness:

> The information variables of meaning, lag, volume, cost, and distortion were repeatedly shown to be good indicators of unit effectiveness (Miller and Miller, 1995, pp. 38-9).

6.6.5. Strengths and Weaknesses of Living Systems Theory

There are widely differing opinions on the value of Miller's living systems theory. Mingers (1995) does not find it convincing or useful at all:

> for Miller's typology is purely descriptive and, indeed, begs the very question that it seeks to answer – How should we characterize living systems in the first place? (p. 121).

This is in sharp contrast to the value he puts on autopoiesis, which postulates the existence of a generative mechanism that could produce the observed characteristics of living systems; a genuine explanation, in other words. Mingers is commenting, however, on a book by Bailey (1994) which sees compatibility between living systems theory and autopoiesis, and seeks to combine the strengths of these two approaches with his own social entropy theory (SET) to overcome the weaknesses of traditional functionalism (inability to explain change or cover the full range of complex societies) while remaining firmly based within that tradition. Bailey states elsewhere (1996) that living systems theory "is a rich intellectual gold mine which deserves to be carefully mined for years to come." Of particular significance to Bailey are its elucidation of the eight levels, the twenty critical subsystems, the distinction between abstracted and concrete systems, the explications of stress and conflict, the concept of information overload, the notion of organizational pathology and the championing of cross-level research.

Moving beyond extreme reactions, Wilby (1995), in a review of Tracy's book, makes a number of points which any assessment of Miller's living systems theory needs to take into account. She questions whether anything other than a living organism can really be classed as a living entity. True, organizations contain people who are living systems but there are other components, such as social and political forces, at work in organizations as well. She asks whether we might be on safer ground regarding the idea that organizations are living systems simply as a metaphor. Although Tracy believes that organizations actually are "alive", it is not necessary to share his conviction in order to get something out of the book. Finally, Wilby doubts whether the treatment of power relationships in living systems theory is adequate. Power is seen as stemming from the control of excess resources and negotiation is seen as a satisfactory means of resolving problems arising from this. For Wilby power is much more complex and can involve coercion, intimidation, pressures and conflict from both inside and outside the organization.

Further possible criticisms of living systems theory will emerge when we develop our critique of functionalist systems approaches more generally. We can leave these aside for the moment while we turn to autopoiesis – the systems approach that Bailey finds compatible and Mingers incompatible with living systems theory.

6.7. AUTOPOIESIS

The reader will remember from Chapter 4 that the word autopoiesis means "self-production" and that what is distinctive about the organization of living systems is that their only product is themselves. Maturana and Varela derived their theory of autopoietic systems from biology and remain somewhat uncommitted to its application in subject areas other than the biological sciences. Varela, in particular, fails to see how autopoiesis could be used in social or organizational analysis; although he does put forward the much "looser" notion of "organizational closure" which he feels might be more easily applied to social systems. Maturana agrees that, strictly speaking, social systems are not autopoietic systems but points out that they may be considered as serving as "mediums" for autopoietic systems. Despite the reservations expressed by Maturana and Varela the power of the theory of autopoiesis, and its related concepts, means that the temptation is great to employ it in other domains.

We have already met, in Chapter 4, the work of the sociologist Luhmann. In Luhmann's view, as long as we see the basic components constituting the autopoiesis of social systems as "communications" rather than individuals, then we can extend the scope of the theory and properly claim that social systems are autopoietic systems. Zeleny and Hufford (1992) are equally keen to demonstrate that the human family (a "spontaneous social system") can be characterized as autopoietic. They see that:

> The family organizes its social domain and coordinates its social action in a spontaneous self-perpetuating fashion. It must also continually adapt, spontaneously, to the external challenges and interferences of society, social engineers, and reformers (p. 155).

It is therefore a suitable candidate for testing against Maturana and Varela's "six-point key" which can be used to ensure correct identification of autopoietic systems. In brief, the family system passes the test. It is a unity with a well-defined boundary; it is defined through its clearly identifiable and role-separable components; family members display system-derived properties that characterize them as family members; the boundary is defined and maintained by family members themselves; the components within the family are produced through family interactions; and all components of the family, boundary or otherwise, are produced through both biological and social production. Zeleny and Hufford (1992) conclude that

> based on the above evaluation, the six-point key being successfully applied, the family is an autopoietic unity defined in the space of its own components (p. 156).

In this climate it is not surprising to find authors eager to apply the insights of autopoiesis to the field of management and organizational studies where, as von Krogh and Roos (1995) point out, it is relatively unknown. In the opinion of von Krogh and Roos this is unfortunate because autopoietic theory could be

> instrumental in developing a new organizational epistemology: why and how knowledge, individualized or socialized, develops in organizations (pp. 34-35).

Unfortunately there remain very few examples of the use of autopoiesis to guide management practice. The most thoughtful of which I am aware is the attempt by Gregory (1994) to construct an evaluation methodology for organizations based upon the conclusions of autopoiesis. I describe this in the next sub-section. We will have to return to the debate about whether social systems are really autopoietic when reviewing strengths and weaknesses. For the record, von Krogh and Roos (1995) accept that not all processes can carry the label "autopoiesis" but that, since its formulation, autopoiesis has established itself as a general system theory with an impressive impact in many fields.

6.7.1. Methodology and Application

Gregory (1994) draws on previous work suggesting that what social organizations maintain through autopoietic processes is a distinctive corporate culture. Robb (1989a, b) is convinced that organizations can be regarded as autopoietic and that it is their cultures that are autopoietically generated and sustained. Humans, or at least certain relevant properties of humans, are components in the process:

> If humans come to believe that, through the organization, their perception of the world can be identified with that of their fellows in the organization and that they can realize themselves within the organization and only in that way, then they truly become 'components' of it (1989b, p. 249).

Gomez and Probst (1989) do not believe that organizations are truly autopoietic because they do not physically produce their own components – human beings. They feel able to advance an argument similar to Robb's, however, on the basis of "organizational closure." They claim that

> systems of corporate culture ... generate their own internal regularities and maintain their organization in a changing environment (p. 314).

For Gomez and Probst, the components of this process are the norms, values, aspirations and rituals self-produced within the culture and accepted by organizational members. These distinguish one organization from another. The set of shared beliefs, or corporate culture, also defines the system's boundaries. These are naturally very fuzzy but "all members belonging to the system as well as the relevant environment know intuitively where they are" (Gomez and Probst, 1989). According to this line of thinking, an organization retains its identity in a changing environment by maintaining its corporate culture. This set of beliefs is the "organization" that is kept invariant while the "structure", everything else about the organization, can change. Of course, it is also important to be "structurally coupled" to the environment in order to survive, and this requires the organization over time presenting the environment with suitable states from which it can select structures which enable autopoietic processes to be maintained.

Accepting, for the purposes of argument, that organizations are cultures and cultures are autopoietic systems, Gregory (1994) goes on to draw out the implications for managers. Because of the need for structural coupling, an organization must be capable of producing responses to change which provide a match to the demands of the environment. This means that an organization must develop its "variety", perhaps by attracting individuals and groups with diverse experiences and attributes to become members or by the training and development of existing members. At the same time it is important that the "identity" of the organization is not threatened. The integrity of the corporate culture must be maintained, therefore, by ensuring that, despite the diversity, there remains a unified commitment to some common set of core values:

> management must not only seek to ensure that the diversity attracted to the organization is of a kind which is purposive in enabling the organization to cope with its environment but, also, management must seek to harness that diversity. This harnessing process is more commonly referred to as socialization into the culture of the organization (Gregory, 1994, p. 60).

The loyalty of organizational members to core commitments can be assured by material incentives, providing a sense of identity, status and belonging, and by ensuring alignment of individual and organizational purposes. Of course, this should not go too far. It is only necessary that they have a general orientation in common. Ensuring both diversity and a consistent overall value system is a difficult balancing act. Go too far one way and things descend into chaos; too far the other and rigidity and lack of innovation set in. Summarizing her analysis of the autopoietic perspective on organizations, Gregory concludes that it pictures effectiveness as based on the organization's "ability to generate and perpetuate a culture which, by facilitating the development of its members, enhances the organizations own variety" (1994).

The purpose of Gregory's research was to examine different ways of evaluating organizations and she believes that, using the above definition, another form of "non-traditional" evaluation can be put in place. She notes Maturana and Varela's statement: "To grow as a member of a society consists of becoming structurally coupled to it", and suggests that the same principle must apply to individuals and the organizations of which they are part. Individuals must be enabled to realize their own potential in organizations in a manner that enhances organizations' long-term survival capability. She then sets out guidelines for an evaluation methodology that can judge individuals and organizations in this light. It is a six-stage procedure with a feedback loop to indicate that the evaluation is likely to proceed in an iterative manner (see Figure 6.13).

"Surfacing opinions and aspirations" details individual perceptions, strengths and weaknesses, and establishes what individuals want from the organization. Visioning requires forecasting the state of the environment and deciding what the organization needs to be like to succeed in the future environment. Analyzing the data means judging the capacity of individuals to move the organization forward and identifying any blockages that might prevent this. The career plans which are then developed should seek to capitalize on the

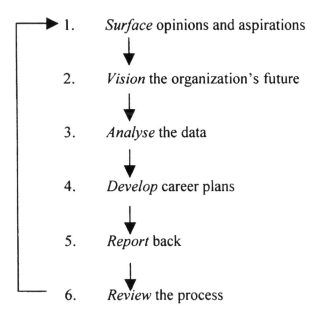

1.   *Surface* opinions and aspirations

2.   *Vision* the organization's future

3.   *Analyse* the data

4.   *Develop* career plans

5.   *Report* back

6.   *Review* the process

Figure 6.13. Conceptual model of culture based evaluation (adapted from Gregory, 1994, p. 203)

potential of individuals whilst developing them in directions that will benefit the organization. The information is then fed back to the individual who should be actively encouraged to undertake whatever training is necessary. The whole process is then reviewed in terms of whether the participants became involved in it and acted upon the reports they received. Gregory is aware that the evaluator's role in this type of evaluation can only be one of facilitator. She accepts Robb's view that intervention in autopoietic systems,

> in an attempt to design or adapt such systems by humans, themselves systems of a lower logical order, will be 'seen' by the organization simply as a perturbation from its environment which, if the organization is viable, can be dissipated (quoted in Gregory, 1994, p. 194).

Gregory describes an evaluation of "Goxwell Council for Voluntary Service" using this approach. It succeeded in getting participants to devote considerable thought to their own and others' strengths and blockages, and directing them to look at their potential.

6.7.2. Strengths and Weaknesses of Autopoiesis

It is clear that many academics are now attempting to develop autopoiesis in order to make it of some use to the study of social systems. Robb, Luhmann, Zeleny and Hufford, and Gregory are among them. Mingers (1995), however, feels that

> fundamental difficulties are involved in such an application ... there are obvious problems. Is it right to characterize social institutions as essentially processes of production and, if it is, what exactly is it that they are producing ... what is it that would constitute the boundaries of such systems and, moreover, how can it be said that such institutions act as unities? ... Overall, it seems difficult to sustain the idea that social systems are autopoietic, at least in strict accordance with the formal definition (pp. 123-124).

Let us take these points in turn.

Autopoietic systems are centrally concerned with processes of production so, if organizations are autopoietic systems, they must produce something – but what? If we take humans as the components, they are produced by biological processes - not by the organizations themselves. But what other possible components are there? Robb's (1989a) answer is that only those human properties which are required for the production of the autopoietic system need be regarded as components. The whole human is not involved but only a "mind-set" which guarantees compliance with the dominant culture so preserving the unity of the organization. The same thinking is employed to respond to Mingers's point that it seems impossible to identify the boundaries of social systems on the basis of a distinction between components produced by and producing the system, and components not involved in this process. After all people can choose whether to belong to or leave particular institutions. In Robb's (1989a) view, boundaries are exactly defined according to the mind-sets required by the system at a particular time. Such a boundary divides whole individuals from others and also those characteristics and properties of particular individuals necessary to operate within the system from those that are not. If the individual cannot supply the thoughts and actions necessary to the system, then he may be discarded and replaced, or the system may change its structure to accommodate the loss. Finally, Mingers finds it difficult to see how institutions can be said to act as unities – surely it is only people who can act? Robb (1989a) is convinced that in some organizations people do play the role of components, merging their identity with that of the larger unity in the process. Their "survival" comes to depend on the organization as they lose their individuality, and their capacity to act against the demands of the unity is curtailed.

Mingers (1989) is not impressed by Robb's answers, which he regards as too vague and contentious to provide any proof that social systems can be autopoietic. At the heart of his objections lies a fundamental ontological doubt:

> Namely, to what extent can the terms which we use in social description (e.g. middle class, organization, Warwick University) denote objectively existing entities as opposed to being constructs of the observer (1989, p. 175).

Because this doubt cannot be quelled, Mingers can never accept that social systems are autopoietic in the strict sense. He does, however, think that the concept can be of use metaphorically. Indeed, even if the idea does not transfer in any strict sense, it still seems useful to me as a corrective to the picture of organizations as open systems responding slavishly to their environments, as presented in the organizations-as-systems tradition of work.

We can conclude this section by noting that there is even considerable dispute about whether it is a good thing to encourage organizations to be autopoietic. Standing on one side of the argument are Zeleny and Pierre, whose views are summarized by Mingers:

> humans are autopoietic entities and, as such, autonomous and independent. Traditional types of organizations, however, treat them purely as components within the system, that is, they treat them as allopoietic. Not only is this wrong in a moral sense, but it is also not necessarily good systems design. Autopoiesis shows how systems can function in a decentralized, nonhierarchical way purely through the individual interactions of neighboring components (quoted in Gregory, 1994, p. 58).

On the other side is Robb (1989a), who declares that:

> To those who would see the achievement of autopoietic organization as a desirable objective in organizing, I warn that such an aim may result ultimately in the subordination of all

human aspirations and ambitions, values and welfare to the service of preserving the unity of such systems, and not to any human end. Once formed such organizations appear to be beyond human control, indeed, to be real-world living systems (p. 348).

What seems to be required is a dose of Gregory's sense of balance between diversity and integrity; together with an appreciation of Beer's insight that autopoiesis is all right in the whole system and in the component parts of System 1 but it is pathological when found in Systems 2, 3, 4 and 5.

6.8. COMPLEXITY THEORY

Remembering the distinction of Chapter 4, our concern here is with the "broader" complexity theory rather than chaos theory; the latter referring properly just to the mathematical study of non-linear dynamics. The reason for this, of course, is that our primary interest is systems approaches applied to management, and the complex social systems that managers have to deal with do not follow a set of fixed rules. These systems are capable of evolving and changing the rules of interaction on which their behavior is based. Despite this need to loosen some of the constraints imposed by a strict definition of chaos theory, many writers feel that the key insights, translated via complexity theory, remain of considerable import for management and organization theory. An early volume by Streufert and Swezey (1986) on *Complexity, Managers and Organizations* has been followed by numerous other books and academic papers, and there continues to be a considerable audience for work that seeks to show the relevance of complexity theory for managers.

A number of important "themes" emerge in all discussions of the application of complexity theory to management, and our account here is based upon an enumeration of these themes. This is somewhat artificial because the themes are highly interdependent. Nevertheless the procedure allows the main points to be clarified well enough. The themes are filled out with reference, particularly, to the work of Wheatley, Morgan and Stacey. We have already encountered Wheatley's (1992) view that complexity theory is fundamental in allowing us to move away from bureaucracy to the more fluid, organic, relationship-centered organizational structures that are appropriate today. In the new edition of *Images of Organization* (1997), Morgan finds that he has to considerably update his work on the "flux and transformation" metaphor in order to take into account the findings of chaos and complexity theory. In his opinion, the ideas of chaos and complexity theory have massive implications for modern management, especially in terms of what they offer to a holistic theory of change. Stacey (1992, 1993, 1996) has provided the most comprehensive reading of the potential of chaos and complexity theory within organization and management. He sees the "complexity revolution" as being so very important because, with some rare exceptions (system dynamics, Senge's "archetypes"), all previous applications of systems thinking to management have been dominated by the stable equilibrium paradigm. They have emphasized efficiency, effectiveness and control to the exclusion of everything else. Even where reference to disorder, unpredictability, chance, emergence, dialectical evolution, etc, is made, there is lack of a coherent theoretical framework within which these "erratic aspects of organization" can be appreciated and understood. Complexity theory can supply the necessary theoretical framework.

The next sub-section sets out the main themes of complexity theory. We then consider "methodology" and an application before introducing, in a "strengths and weaknesses" sub-section, the voice of those troubled by the transfer of non-linear dynamical theories to organizations. As Johnson and Burton (1994) say,

> unfortunately several practical as well as conceptual difficulties are present in this application of chaos theory [to social systems] (p. 323).

6.8.1. Complexity Theory and Management

In the book *Managing Chaos* (1992) Stacey expresses his aim as being to "change the way managers think about the route to business success." Managers need to adopt a "far-from equilibrium mindset", based on a dynamic systems perspective, in order to cope with the unknowable future of innovative organizations. To take the first step along this road requires "accepting that you really have no idea what the long-term future holds for your organization." This theme, that the specific future of organizational systems is inherently unpredictable, is a recurring one in complexity theory and derives, of course, from the properties of non-linear feedback systems as studied in chaos theory. As we know, even fixed inputs into deterministic rules can generate non-linear feedback loops giving rise to the inherently unpredictable pattern of behavior that is chaos. Because organizations are replete with such loops, any links between cause and effect, actions and outcomes, get lost in complexity and a radical unpredictability results. Furthermore, the "butterfly effect" shows that complex systems are extremely sensitive to small differences in initial conditions. Tiny changes in such conditions can escalate into major consequences. Complexity theory demonstrates, therefore, that the long-term future of organizations is "unknowable." Managers should not make assumptions about the future because prediction is impossible. This renders long-term planning equally impossible and suggests that the strategic planning processes, that so many managers engage in, are useless if not downright damaging. Short-term prediction is possible because the consequences of changes can take time to become visible, but long-term planning achieves nothing because:

> When the dynamics are chaotic, specific events will follow an unpredictable path over the long-term. There will be an infinite number of possible long-term outcomes. The probability of any single event occurring is then infinitely small and provides no assistance in making a decision (Stacey, 1993, p. 237).

Long-term planning can be dangerous because tying an organization to a particular "vision", which limits what it is prepared to do, is exactly the opposite of what is required in an uncertain and ambiguous world. Out with long-term planning must go all the statistical analyses and financial models on which managers are tempted to depend:

> organizational decisions based upon financial models which are almost always linear approximations to the feedback mechanisms of an organization can ... only have any validity for very short-term periods into the future. The very dynamics of the business organization render general qualitative models useless for real strategic control. (1993, p. 237).

The reader will recall from Chapter 4, however, that chaos does not imply complete randomness. Underlying chaos it is possible, over time, to recognize "patterns" occurring in the way the system develops. Stacey (1993) argues that:

> Although the specific path followed by the behavior [of complex systems] ... is random and hence unpredictable in the long term, it always has an underlying pattern to it, a 'hidden' pattern... That pattern is self-similarity, that is a constant degree of variation, consistent variability, regular irregularity ... a constant fractal dimension. Chaos is therefore order (a pattern) within disorder (p. 228).

Morgan (1997) agrees that chaos and complexity theory can help us to understand how pattern evolves. Wheatley (1992) insists that nature's predisposition toward self-similarity can be extremely useful to managers. It directs our attention to what is important at the deeper level and away from the fads that can influence current management practice. If we are able to observe the underlying simplicity of the fractal structures which give rise to complex dynamic patterns, then we will understand a little more what is going on and be able to make sensible choices. In Senge's (1990) terms, what we are trying to do, in unearthing these "patterns", is to discover the "system archetypes" which all organizations tend to repeat, although they may actualize them in different ways. This makes it possible to engage in change initiatives with a greater chance of success because, as the "fifth discipline" teaches us, we can learn how to use small changes to create large effects. For Morgan (1997), it follows

> that any person wishing to change the context in which they are operating should search for 'doable' high-leverage initiatives that can trigger a transition from one attractor to another (p. 271).

Organizations can be led to follow patterns of undesirable behavior because they are caught by "strange attractors" or stuck in "system archetypes." With sufficient awareness of points of maximum leverage we can, through making relatively small changes, break the cycle and enable them to realize more fruitful ways of functioning. This way of thinking about organizational change is represented in Fig. 6.14.

The ability to recognize patterns in the way that organizations and their environments are evolving critically depends upon "learning", especially systemic learning. Stacey (1993) argues that we have to hone our powers of intuition and reasoning by analogy in order to observe patterns and make creative choices in relation to them. Wheatley (1992) tells us that she tries hard

> to discipline myself to remain aware of the whole and to resist my well-trained desire to analyze the parts to death. I look now for patterns of movement over time and focus on qualities like rhythm, flow, direction, and shape... I know I am wasting time whenever I draw straight arrows between two variables in a cause and effect diagram, or position things as polarities, or create elaborate plans and time lines (p. 43).

As well as "learning to learn" systemically themselves, managers have to rethink their enterprises in order to create "learning organizations" which are also capable of "double-loop" learning. For Morgan (1997) complexity theory enables us to do this:

> Instead of seeing these qualities as states that can be externally imposed on a situation through hierarchical means, or through the predetermined logic that we bring to the design of bridges or buildings, managers are invited to view them as emergent properties. New order emerges in any complex system that, because of internal and external fluctuations, is pushed into 'edge of chaos' situations. Order is natural! It is emergent and free! But most interesting of all, its precise nature can never be planned or predetermined (p. 266).

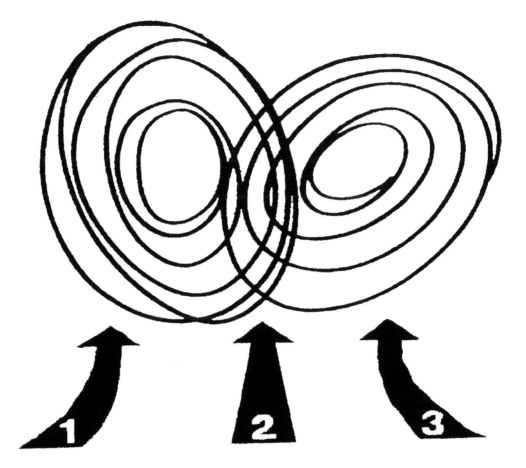

| What are the forces locking an organization into its existing "attractor" pattern? Structures? Hierarchies? Rules? Controls? Culture? Defensive Routines? Power relations? Psychic traps? Is the "attractor" appropriate? Should it be changed? | If change is required, how is the transition from one attractor to another to be achieved? How can small changes be used to create large effects? | What are the ground rules of the new attractor going to be? How can we manage through the "edge of chaos" of stage 2 while remaining open to emergent self-organization? |

Figure 6.14. Attractor patterns and organizational change (reproduced from Morgan, 1997, p. 268)

Managers, therefore, should be happy to live with continuous transformation and emergent order as a natural state of affairs. Wheatley (1992) makes the same point. We must stop being afraid that if we do not build "strong and complex" structures with "rigid chains of command" and "isolate departments", things will fall apart:

> It is time to take the world off our shoulders, to lay it gently down and look to it for an easier way. Lessons are everywhere ... Nature is abundantly littered with examples and lessons of order. Despite the experience of fluctuations and changes that disrupt our plans, the world is inherently orderly. And fluctuation and change are part of the very process by which order is created (pp. 17-18).

Managers need to rid themselves, therefore, of the notion that they can plan, organize and control their enterprises in order to attune them to chaos. But this does not mean that they can leave everything to chance. They have to propitiate favorable conditions for self-organization and learning. For Wheatley, this means shaping organizations through "concepts", not through elaborate rules or plans. It also requires us to pay attention to structures that encourage self-organization by facilitating relationships:

> I have come to expect that something useful occurs if I link up people, units or tasks, even though I cannot determine precise outcomes (1992, p. 44).

Morgan, similarly, emphasizes the need to manage through the creation of "new contexts" rather than through the details. By helping to shape emerging processes of self-organization, new contexts can emerge that enable a break to occur from an old, dominant attractor pattern. Being open to new metaphors can help managers to create new contexts.

Stacey agrees with Wheatley and Morgan that, although we should "trust" chaos, it also sometimes needs a helping hand. He wants to get us away from fixed, prescriptive models, toward developing "new mental models" for each new strategic situation. We also have to manage the effects of personality, learning behaviors and group dynamics to ensure that they support spontaneous self-organization. More than anything, perhaps, we must not let a strong, shared culture lead to a consensus which stifles innovation, damps down learning and prevents political interactions. An overwhelming consensus can only lead to stability and an incapacity to envision new strategic directions. Countercultures should, therefore, be encouraged because they ensure the emergence of new perspectives and an organization able to rethink its future; they are required "to sustain the dissipative structure far from equilibrium" (Stacey, 1993). A degree of conflict and contradiction is necessary, therefore, in any organization that wants to develop over time through "learning." Space must be made for dialogue and contention and the continual questioning of accepted ways of looking at things. To Stacey, the new approach offered by complexity theory is about

> sustaining contradictory positions and behavior in an organization . . positively using instability and crisis to generate new perspectives, provoking continual questioning and organizational learning through which unknowable futures can be created and discovered (1992, p. 17).

"Stable equilibrium organizations" are destined to relive their pasts. Organizations that operate "far-from-equilibrium", in the way described, can embark on exciting and unpredictable new journeys. It is, however, possible to court instability too passionately, in which case anxiety levels can rocket and the organization disintegrate.

In fact Stacey, developing another important theme, recommends avoidance of both extremes. According to complexity theory, all non-linear feedback systems can operate in a stable zone, an unstable zone or, in a phase transition between stability and instability, at the "edge of chaos." In the stable zone they ossify, in the unstable zone they disintegrate, but at the edge of chaos spontaneous processes of self-organization occur and novel patterns of behavior can emerge. This state of "bounded instability", at the edge of chaos, is difficult to define precisely. It is where disorder and order intertwine, so that behavior is irregular and unpredictable but has some pattern. Stacey states that:

> The conclusion we reach is that the dynamics of success are such that organizations have to strive to avoid attraction to equilibrium states of stability and instability. They have instead to strive to stay in a state of bounded instability or chaos. This is a very difficult state to sustain ... Scientists use the term 'dissipative structure' to describe a system held far-from-equilibrium ... A successful organization is a dissipative structure (1993, p. 231).

This is a desirable state for organizations to be in, and leads to success, because it is the place where they are able to display their full potential for creativity and innovation. According to Kauffman (1995) it is at the "edge of chaos" that systems exchange the greatest amount of useful information and interact most productively. In an actual organization at the "edge of chaos" we would expect to see different, and apparently opposing, ways of behaving occurring simultaneously. There would be "visible order" through attention to time and cost targets, consistent delivery of quality products etc., but also the existence of countercultures, political tensions, and contention and dialogue.

Stacey gives his most detailed account of what it means to operate at the "edge of chaos", and how to sustain this state, in *Complexity and Creativity in Organizations* (1996). The "edge of chaos" is a desirable state that exists at a phase transition between "stable" and "unstable" zones. It is attained when an appropriate degree of tension exists between an organization's "legitimate" system and its "shadow" system.

The legitimate system of an organization consists of the dominant rationality and those structures and planning processes that support the current primary task. It reinforces the existing corporate culture and favors existing power balances. The legitimate system promotes "ordinary management" and is essential for ensuring efficiency, constraining conflict and containing anxiety. If the legitimate system becomes too dominant, however, it prevents questioning of objectives, damps down conflict and stops all change. Double-loop learning becomes impossible. The organization will then ossify in the stable zone. A number of factors can lead to the legitimate system becoming dominant. The shadow system may support instead of challenge it, thus making the legitimate system even more powerful. There is often a general fear of change in organizations. Unconscious group processes can favor sticking firmly to bureaucratic routines and avoiding confrontation. The felt "need to belong" can mean that even spontaneous self-organization produces groups favoring co-operation and the status quo. Politics can be covert, rather than openly challenging, and so detract from proper dialogue. The tendency for all these things to occur becomes greater the longer the organization's "dominant schema" has held sway.

The shadow system of an organization consists of its various informal aspects. It can promote challenges to the legitimate system and is working well when it exists in tension with that system, seeking to replace at least parts of it. If the shadow system becomes too powerful, however, the situation in the organization can become anarchic. The legitimate system cannot contain the "psychotic fantasy" generated by the shadow system and is overwhelmed. The shadow system succeeds in sabotaging the pursuit of the organization's primary task. In these circumstances levels of uncontained anxiety rise and individuals cannot engage in creativity or double-loop learning. The organization enters the unstable zone and disintegrates. A number of factors can lead to the shadow system becoming too powerful. Unchecked positive feedback loops can magnify small changes into considerable alterations in the state of the system. These may result from the efforts of "extraordinary management", operating quite legitimately to encourage contradiction, conflict and change through the shadow system, getting out of hand. Vicious power struggles can be provoked and destabilization ensues. Alternatively, challenges to the status quo may arise spontaneously in the shadow system and, through positive feedback loops, produce too much tension and instability. Finally, the existence of competition and the need for an organization to continually adjust to its environment, can produce instability that cannot be managed by the legitimate system.

The preferable state, therefore, is the "edge of chaos", a balance between stability and instability brought about when there is just sufficient tension between the legitimate and shadow systems. There is a well functioning legitimate system consisting of clear structures and procedures, and capable of containing the anxiety that arises from creativity in the shadow system. At the same time, the shadow system should be characterized by diversity, tension and contention. Different groups will be engaged in dialogue and political maneuvering as they try out alternatives to the status quo. Some of these will become learning communities exhibiting group creativity and double-loop learning. If they become powerful enough they might start to challenge the legitimate system by acts of "creative tension." Innovation emanating from the shadow system starts to undermine the dominant schema. The legitimate system will then change, allowing the organization to perform primary tasks in novel ways or to pursue entirely new primary tasks. Creativity will have been unleashed which, once amplified to the organization, might allow it to climb higher up its "fitness peak" or even scale a new peak.

The "edge of chaos" is a paradoxical state where the legitimate system seeks to sustain the status quo and prevent anarchy, while the shadow system tries to change things. For Stacey (1996), ambiguity around, for example, the issue of centralization versus decentralization, should be ever present in organizational life and is best resolved through spontaneous self-organizing processes giving rise to new patterns of behavior. Organizations operating at the edge of chaos deal with such paradoxes the best. It is important, therefore, that managers know how to sustain organizations in this state. Stacey, of course, recognizes this and provides five control parameters which, if set at a critical point, should bring this about. Information about changes in the environment should flow at a rate to engage the shadow system as well as the legitimate system of the organization, but not so fast as to overwhelm both. There should be enough diversity in the shadow system to generate learning but not enough to induce anarchy. Connections between individuals and groups in the organization need to be set at some intermediate point, between weak and strong, ensuring sufficient stability but allowing some instability. Anxiety must be felt but must be sufficiently controlled by the legitimate system. Finally, a balance must be struck between extreme power differentials and an equal distribution of power. Authority contains anxiety but too much can prevent freedom of expression and creativity.

Through the control parameters, managers can help to ensure that their organizations operate at the edge of chaos. If this happy state is attained and sustained, then the legitimate system will enable ordinary management to plan for and control short-term performance. It will not be possible to plan for the long-term future, but an organization in the realm of bounded instability will exhibit archetypal behavior which managers can at least understand, even if they cannot predict how, in detail, the archetypes will be actualized. Moreover, creativity and learning will be enabled in such a way as to give the organization the best chance of recognizing those patterns that can be detected and responding to whatever remains unpredictable.

The last theme from complexity theory that we shall pursue is that of "relationships." In dynamic systems relationships are paramount. Wheatley (1992) stresses the importance of relationships between people and between people and their settings. For her:

> none of us exists independent of our relationships with others. Different settings and people evoke some qualities from us and leave others dormant. In each of these relationships, we are different, new in some way. If nothing exists independent of its relationship with something else, we can move from our need to think of things as polar opposites … What is critical is the relationship created between the person and the setting. That relationship will always be different, will always evoke different potentialities. It all depends on the players and the moment (p. 34).

We need to learn how to nurture such relationships.

The same is true of the relationship between the organization and its environment. Morgan (1997) argues that:

> It seems systemically wiser to view organization and environment as elements of the same interconnected pattern. In evolution it is pattern that evolves (p. 261).

Organizations evolve with their environments rather than simply adapting to changes in their environments: the two co-evolve. Kauffman's (1995) notion of a "fitness landscape" gives us a way of understanding the implications of this. Evolutionary biology suggests that species enhance their viability, compared to their competitors, if the adaptations they make allow them to reach "higher fitness peaks" in the "fitness landscape." Organizations, similarly, must change in ways which allow them to climb higher up their existing fitness peak or, if necessary, to switch to a higher peak. What complicates matters is the co-evolution of organizations with their environments. Any change an organization, or any of its competitors, makes will set off reverberations throughout the fitness landscape, represented perhaps by the whole industry. Depending upon the degree of connectivity between the elements in the landscape, the ecosystem may alter so radically that any particular organization can quickly become extinct. It is essential, therefore, that organizations react to changes in the fitness landscape. Unfortunately it is only on rare occasions, when the landscape is stable, that they have any chance of predicting the outcome of their or their competitors actions. To avoid getting stuck on an uncompetitive fitness peak, as the shape and structure of the landscape changes, Kauffman recommends strategies to organizations designed to increase the number of productive interactions between their parts and to enhance their information processing capacities. They are best broken up into networks of units which can act autonomously but are in continuous communication and interaction with other units. It is at the "edge of chaos" where living systems demonstrate the greatest capacity for efficiency and robustness.

6.8.2. Methodology and Case Study – Humberside Training and Enterprise Council

A strict interpretation of chaos theory would leave no room for managers to improve organizations, which would be seen as driven by deterministic forces into unpredictable behavior. Complexity theory, as we have seen, loosens many of the constraints of chaos theory and sees a role for managers in propitiating favorable conditions for self organization and learning. Stacey asks us to trust in chaos while identifying various control parameters that can be influenced to ensure the organization operates in a productive and innovative manner at the "edge of chaos." According to this reading, a methodology to intervene in organizations would draw lessons from the study of complex adaptive systems in the natural world and apply these lessons, through managerial action, to social organizations. Another possibility for using the ideas generated by complexity theory would arise if we were prepared to drop the pretence that they refer to anything in reality. We could suspend belief in the notion that organizations actually *are* complex adaptive or complex evolving systems. We could then judge the ideas purely on the basis of whether they were useful in helping actors to construct their social reality. If this line was taken, it would be possible to inform the use of complexity theory and learn about its value, by embedding it within an interpretive systems methodology (see next chapter). The case study I offer here shows some aspects of the kind of intervention implied by Stacey's work but is also suggestive of how complexity theory might be employed from an interpretive perspective.

Training and Enterprise Councils were established by government in order to promote local economic development. Within its region a Training and Enterprise Council (TEC) would seek to ensure the provision of appropriate training for businesses and encourage businesses to take advantage of the opportunities made available. In 1998 Humberside TEC had approximately 150 staff and a budget of around £30 million to achieve these purposes.

Under the leadership of its Managing Director, Peter Fryer, Humberside TEC determined that it had the best chance of achieving its objectives if it became a "learning organization." During the latter half of the 1990s, a number of activities were undertaken to bring this about. These included developing a deeper understanding of learning; using IT as an empowering rather than controlling technology; treating culture as an emergent property which all could influence; and applying what had been learned from complexity theory. An internal document (Storr, 1997) describes some of these initiatives and explains why complexity theory was seen as particularly appropriate in terms of the way the TEC wanted to change itself. Complexity theory encourages a shift from a command and control style of management to one suitable to an organization viewed as a complex adaptive or complex evolving system. It challenges the idea that organizations should strive for equilibrium and recommends instead that they should operate at the edge of chaos. When they are pushed away from equilibrium, self-organizing occurs naturally and organizations become capable of infinite variety and of responding more flexibly to their environments. This is essential because, as with fitness landscapes in biology, the business environment is constantly changing as a result of decisions made by the organizations inhabiting it. Only flexible organizations are able to take "adaptive" walks to "higher fitness points." In general, complexity theory was seen as a holistic rather than systematic approach to organization and as emphasizing dynamism and chaos rather than stability.

Translated into practical design principles, complexity theory meant to the TEC that it had to "make connections", "learn continuously", and "make processes ongoing" (Storr, 1997). Making connections involved ensuring all staff were highly interconnected, had opportunities for collaborative learning and saw networking as part of their job. The TEC had to learn continuously about its environment so that it could respond to and influence it and had to make learning integral to everyone's job, with mistakes seen as learning opportunities. A form was devised on which, each month, every employee could communicate to the Managing Director what he or she had learned. Making processes ongoing meant treating the TEC as a self-organizing system in which structures evolved as learning took place and new processes were established. To effect this fluidity, many controls were dropped and staff were trusted to use their own judgement and expected to exercise responsibility. Peter Fryer likes to compare rules and regulations to the stabilizers on a bicycle. Stabilizers may be useful when you are learning to ride but become a hindrance once you are able to cycle. A more open culture was introduced. As well as the forms recording learning, 360 degree appraisal was introduced and staff were made responsible for their own development. A couple of anonymous channels of communication were set up to enable the "shadow system" to flourish.

While all these changes were going on, a Ph.D. student of mine, Maria Ortegon, was invited to study how the ideas derived from complexity theory were affecting the people in the TEC and the way that they worked. Of particular interest was a self-managed team of consultants within the "Investors in People" Directorate. Over a period of around eight months the researcher involved herself in a series of "exploratory dialogues" or "oxygenation processes", as she came to call them, with these staff. She documented how they used complexity theory to understand their current organizational reality and to reflect on possible alternative ways of doing things. Inevitably this was a participative involvement because even by asking questions the researcher was helping the staff to clarify and reflect on the ideas they were discussing and using. She was under no illusion that she was researching, in some objective manner, a change that was occurring. Instead, she felt engaged in a process of mutual learning in which dialogue was enriched and organizational reality created. There were some important issues aired during the "oxygenation processes."

Undoubtedly, it was felt, the acceptance of complexity theory was eased because staff in the TEC had become so used to new ideas. As part of the drive to become a learning organization, they had been exposed to "action learning", soft systems methodology (see next chapter), 360 degree appraisal and methods of removing "defensive routines." An electronic bulletin board (CollabraShare) had been installed by volunteers to increase and enhance communication. There were numerous meetings, workshops and discussions, a "Computer Dinosaur Club" and the Managing Director's "Serious Thinking Sessions." People got used to appreciating alternative viewpoints and seeing "value in difference" because it can assist creativity.

The new "language" of complexity theory was, as a result, relatively rapidly absorbed; although it was interpreted differently in the various parts of the organization. People worked out the implications of the new concepts for themselves and, in the process, embodied them in their actions. Terms such as self-organization, self-management and "edge of chaos" became part of the jargon used by staff to understand their situation. In this way the language of complexity theory was assimilated into the culture of the organization. It began, not necessarily in a way that anyone was aware of, to affect values. Trust was put in people's potential, and in their ability to use their own judgement and take responsibility. Learning was seen as a continuous process and mistakes as offering opportunities for new learning. The nature of the language also meant that more emphasis was placed on dynamism and change, on "becoming" rather than "being."

Once absorbed, the language of complexity theory enabled discussion of important aspects of becoming a learning organization. Leadership style was one such aspect. Peter Fryer was seen as a facilitator of openness and questioning. He adopted a relaxed style which encouraged freedom of action but was always ready to give the right support to people to allow them to do their jobs and reflect on what they were doing. He delegated decision-making, insisting that organizations could not be controlled from the top and that the best ideas could emerge from anywhere in the enterprise. Peter Fryer had introduced the ideas of complexity theory into the TEC, and his management style and the attitudes he evinced were crucial to the success of the processes associated with complexity theory. People were led to wonder whether self-organizing processes really did happen spontaneously. It seemed that they actually had to be planned for and constantly stimulated.

The notion of working in self-managed teams was also subject to scrutiny. The teams had, in fact, been introduced in a rather abrupt fashion by senior management, and the impact that they had varied considerably during the critical period. Some staff found the new situation to their liking and grew in confidence. Others found taking on responsibility to be very demanding and remained confused for some time. Eventually most people started to enjoy the new working system. Collective decisions were taken and more commitment was felt towards them. Natural leaders emerged and the teams began to think more strategically about their roles in the organization. Looking back, some staff felt that creating self-managed teams meant, at first, a drop in level of performance. Focusing on team dynamics led to priorities being set aside and targets missed. Once critical problems were overcome, however, teams soon found themselves back in line in terms of performance. Beyond this, teams seemed to be more creative in tackling issues because their members were able to draw on each other's experiences. They began to learn how to learn as a team, reflecting on how the make up of the team and the way it worked impacted on performance. As they also convinced themselves of the value of working in self-managed teams, the TEC consultants were able to promote the new thinking in outside organizations. One team summarized the positive effect it has had on them as consultants as "getting people to think more, taking more risks, gaining more confidence in oneself, generating networks and processes that self-regulate and feedback on their own, etc."

Another issue which absorbed some attention was the apparent contradiction involved in trying to introduce self-organization and creativity in an institution like the TEC that is so subject to government regulation and auditing. There was a sense, it was felt, in which this regulation could be seen as representing the legitimate system espousing the dominant schema of the organization. The sources of instability introduced through complexity theory, and embedded in a shadow system, established the tension with the dominant schema that is necessary for creative outcomes to emerge. An "edge of chaos" situation was being sustained.

For those involved in the introduction of complexity theory into Humberside TEC, a number of questions remain to be answered. Storr (1997) wonders whether it is ever really possible to defeat hierarchy and to allow those in less powerful positions to challenge the more powerful. She is also concerned that the TEC, as a medium sized organization with a high degree of interconnectivity, might have provided a rather favorable environment for testing the ideas of complexity theory. How would they fare in large or multi-sited organizations? Maria Ortegon (1999) worries abut the paradox of the Managing Director, whose role was so crucial, needing to employ some "command and control" in order to get rid of command and control. She is also aware that dispute continues about whether concepts such as "bounded instability" actually describe something in organizational reality or whether they should be evaluated only in terms of the role they can play in enabling us to "enact" our own reality.

6.8.3. Strengths and Weaknesses of Complexity Theory

Rosenhead (1998) begins his enumeration of the problems associated with transferring the findings of chaos and complexity theory from natural to social systems, by stating that:

> It hardly needs saying that there is no formally validated evidence demonstrating that the complexity theory-based prescriptions for management style, structure and process do produce the results claimed for them (p. 10).

In the absence of reliable evidence, authors seeking to generalize complexity theory tend to rely on the "authority of science" and anecdote to make the case for them. In Rosenhead's view this means that a number of necessary links in the argument they need to make get overlooked.

First, they would have to demonstrate that chaos and complexity theory does apply to the natural systems that have been investigated. Rosenhead concedes that there is some solid evidence here – the weather, ecological cycles, chemical clocks etc. – but not enough to enable us to conclude that such results apply to all natural systems facing similar conditions. Many of the results cited are the outcomes of computer simulations rather than empirical observations. Such demonstrations are, of course, suggestive but cannot be proof that actual observed behavior is caused by the laws built into the computer program. In any case, not all non-linear dynamical systems do exhibit chaotic behavior. Depending on the equations and the relationship between and strength of the feedback loops, some do settle down to a state of stable equilibrium.

Stacey (1996) insists that the laws of complexity theory, originally derived for physical, chemical and biological systems, do apply equally strongly to the complex adaptive systems that managers have to deal with. While he is unable to discover any proof of this, Rosenhead accepts that an argument by analogy could demonstrate the genuine relevance of complexity theory to the social domain. Such an argument (following Brodbeck) would require:

> (a) that the natural scientific domain of complexity theory is better understood than that of management; (b) that there are concepts in the first domain which have been clearly put in one-to-one correspondence with similarly precise equivalents in the second; and (c) that connections (especially causal ones) between groups of concepts in the first domain are implicitly preserved between their equivalents in the second (Rosenhead, 1998, p. 14).

Rosenhead feels that complexity theory as a field is not yet mature enough to provide a reliable source for analogies and whatever equivalences are claimed; for example, the simple existence of non-linear feedback between elements is too general and undemanding to carry weight. Johnson and Burton (1994) share Rosenhead's view that the analogy does not work:

> Nothing about real social systems fits within [chaos theory] limitations ... all of the systems that organizational researchers study are complex and open to numerous outside influences (pp. 323-324).

There are at least two good reasons why this is so. First, as Rosenhead points out, the mathematical complexity theorists' primary concern is with *deterministic* chaos. Weather systems may be difficult to predict but meteorologists do know the basic structural equations that underlie them. In dealing with social systems, however, probabilistic elements abound. As Johnson and Burton put it:

> The complexity of the systems we deal with ... make it difficult, if not impossible, to identify all the variables and structural equations necessary to describe social systems with accuracy (1994, p. 323).

Under *stochastic* chaos, Rosenhead regrets, strange attractors do not manifest themselves. Further,

> human systems are remarkable, and different, because humans learn and consequently adapt both their own behavior and their environment (Johnson and Burton, 1994, p. 324).

The behavior of natural systems may be governed by laws but, because of the self-consciousness of humans, social systems are fundamentally different. Humans are quite capable of reacting against and disproving any law that is held to apply to their behavior (Rosenhead, 1997).

There remains the possibility that complexity theory can provide an illuminating metaphor for use in management and organization theory. Under this reading it loses any prescriptive force and must compete, on grounds of vividness and resonance, with other possible metaphors. If the insights it offers are as novel as are claimed, however, it should have no difficulty on this score. Begun (1994) puts the case for, arguing that

> chaos ... theory invite[s] us to explore the 95% of the organizational world that we have avoided because it is too dark, murky, and intimidating. Or, our theories and methods simply have not allowed us to see it. Integration of chaos ... theory into organization science will fertilize the soil of the discipline's weed patch of theories ... allowing some flowers and fruits to grow (p. 334).

In Rosenhead's view the metaphor is particularly instructive in its questioning of the need for a single "shared vision" and for its encouragement of an active organizational politics.

Shared vision can lead to "group-think", prevent the expression of alternative opinions and create a culture of dependency. The complexity metaphor reveals this. It also highlights the need to foster organizational politics as a way of ensuring the creativity and learning necessary for organizational survival. Rosenhead sees this as a useful antidote to the consensual regimes advocated in much management writing.

Carrizosa and Ortegon (1998), however, argue that the realities the complexity metaphor claims to highlight can be perfectly expressed and tackled using available organizational metaphors, indicating that, in a way, it has nothing new to say. Certainly, previous work on informal groups, group working, open-systems, emergence, organizations as information processing systems and "turbulent field" environments, seems to cover much of the territory that complexity theory wants to claim as its own. Stacey (1996) himself seems unclear on the point. Sometimes he argues for complete novelty, condemning all previous systems contributions pre-dating complexity theory as out-dated because they operate within the stable equilibrium paradigm. At other times, he suggests that the true value of complexity theory is in ordering, within the bounds of a single paradigm, previous comparable work. In general, once he gets down to the practicalities of recommending particular courses of managerial action, Stacey provides little that has not been heard before.

In assessing complexity theory as a metaphor for managers, we also have to consider the downsides of the particular vision it offers. Rosenhead (1998) is agitated by Stacey's explicit rejection of a role for analysis. In Stacey's version of the metaphor, "step-by-step analysis" is presented as "a caricature designed to show up complexity-based thinking to maximum advantage." This could lead managers to reject some tools which are useful if the world is as uncertain as Stacey portrays it. "Scenario planning", "robustness analysis", "group decision support systems" and "problem structuring methods" would have value even in a chaotic universe. The severity of the assault on analysis and planning leads Rosenhead to wonder whether chaos and complexity theory might have some ideological role linked to the social and economic circumstances of society today. Undoubtedly it shares with "postmodernism" a distrust of "rationality" as a vehicle for achieving social progress. Perhaps these ideas have such currency because they offer intellectual succor to the political argument that there is "no alternative" to the market for ordering our social affairs.

This point leads us to the final argument we must express in relation to complexity theory. What are we doing including an approach that says so much about conflict and change, and has elements in common with postmodernism, alongside functionalist versions of systems thinking? It is true that there are aspects of complexity theory that stretch the boundaries of the functionalist paradigm. Overwhelmingly, though, complexity theorists who apply their findings to management are convinced that there is enough "order" underlying the chaos they unveil in organizations to enable them to make prescriptions to managers about how they can improve their performance and increase their organizations' ability to adapt and survive. As Rosenhead puts it, referring to Stacey (1992):

> Indeed the strength and generality of the assertions based on complexity theory merge into a
> sense that its findings are non-negotiable (p. 13).

The words "manager" and "must" or "need to" are run together. There are certain actions managers "must take to be successful." Complexity Theory is telling Stacey something factual about the world of management and organizations that the rest of us might not know. In order to generate creativity, for example, we have to maneuver organizations toward the edge of chaos. Science tells us that this is essential whatever the consequences, in terms perhaps of anxiety, for the individuals involved. All this is in tune with the functionalist logic - as should be much clearer after the next section of this chapter.

6.9. A GENERIC FUNCTIONALIST SYSTEMS METHODOLOGY

We have, in the preceding pages, been discussing various systems approaches that stem from the functionalist theoretical orientation. Despite our declared intention to concentrate on "methodology", we have had to devote considerable space to the specific theories informing each approach and the methods and models most frequently associated with each approach. Functionalist systems approaches frequently take methodology for granted. There is an assumption that once some version of the scientific method has been used to determine exactly how the system of concern should function, it is a reasonably straightforward matter to redesign the real-world system to meet this blueprint. In this section, however, we concentrate entirely on methodology and seek to spell out exactly what is implied when we try to use functionalist systems approaches to intervene in social systems. As we have emphasized, methodology is crucial for applied systems thinking. From the point of view of practice, it allows the translation of social and systems theories into guidelines that can be employed by practitioners. From the point of view of research, it allows reflection back on the adequacy of the "frameworks of ideas" it employs, on its own appropriateness as a methodology, and on the nature of the problem situation being investigated.

In seeking to explicate soft systems methodology, Checkland (1981), and Checkland and Scholes (1990), establish some "constitutive rules" which "must be obeyed if one is to be said to be carrying out a particular kind of inquiry at all." The quotation is from Naughton (1977) who distinguished between these essential, constitutive rules and "strategic rules" which are more personal, which "help one to select from among the basic moves ... those which are 'good' or 'better' or 'best'" (Naughton, quoted in Checkland, 1981). The arrangement of constitutive rules, set out in Checkland and Scholes, can be built upon to provide the descriptions of generic systems methodologies that we are concerned with in this part of the book. In Chapters 6, 7, 8 and 9, having elaborated on the variety of systems approaches sharing a particular theoretical rationale, we develop the "constitutive rules" that must underpin any methodology adhering to that rationale. The procedure adopted is to develop the relevant constitutive rules in the form of a table and then to elaborate briefly on these, using examples from the systems approaches discussed in the chapter. We begin, therefore, with Table 6.3, which sets out the constitutive rules for a generic functionalist systems methodology.

I would wish to argue that, despite the variations we have seen between the "organizations-as-systems," "hard systems thinking," "system dynamics," "organizational cybernetics," "living systems theory," "autopoiesis," and "complexity theory" systems approaches, Table 6.3 captures the essence of the manner in which their key proponents would want to see them used. They all adhere to the functionalist theoretical rationale as described in Chapter 3 and at the beginning of this chapter. All are capable of generating research findings, indeed have given rise to long-lasting research traditions. Functionalist systems methodology can be adapted according to different circumstances and the preferences of different uses - the variety of the species demonstrates this. In terms of the guidelines adumbrated under 3, in Table 6.3, we can provide specific cases which should help the reader to carry out her further tests on the different approaches presented in the chapter. For example, Barnard assumes that organizations in the real-world are co-operative systems. In socio-technical systems thinking, analysis of the problem situation is conducted in systems terms. In hard systems thinking, models aiming to capture the nature of the situation are constructed enabling us to gain knowledge of the real-world. Organizational

Table 6.3. Constitutive Rules for a Generic Functionalist Systems Methodology

---

1. A functionalist systems methodology is a structured way of thinking, with an attachment to the functionalist theoretical rationale, that is focused on improving real-world problem situations.

2. A functionalist methodology uses systems ideas as the basis for its intervention strategy and will frequently employ methods, models, tools and techniques which also draw upon systems ideas.

3. The claim to have used a systems methodology according to the functionalist rationale must be justified according to the following guidelines:

    a. an assumption is made that the real-world is systemic;

    b. analysis of the problem situation is conducted in systems terms;

    c. models aiming to capture the nature of the situation are constructed enabling us to gain knowledge of the real-world;

    d. models are used to learn how best to improve the real-world and for the purposes of design;

    e. quantitative analysis is presumed to be useful since systems obey mathematical laws;

    f. the process of intervention is systematic and is aimed at discovering the best way to achieve a goal;

    g. the intervention is conducted on the basis of expert knowledge;

    h. solutions are tested primarily in terms of their efficiency (do the means use minimum resources?) and efficacy (do the means work?).

4. Since a functionalist systems methodology can be used in different ways in different situations, and interpreted differently by different users, each use should exhibit conscious thought about how to adapt to the particular circumstances.

5. Each use of a functionalist systems methodology should yield research findings as well as changing the real-world problem situation. These research findings may relate to the theoretical rationale underlying the methodology, to the methodology itself and how to use it, to the methods, models, tools and techniques employed, to the real-world problem situation investigated, or to all of these.

---

cybernetic models are used to learn how best to improve the real-world and for the purposes of design. In system dynamics, quantitative analysis is presumed to be useful since systems follow mathematical laws. Using autopoiesis, the intervention is systemic and is aimed at discovering the best way to enable the system to self-produce. In applications of living systems theory, the intervention is conducted on the basis of expert knowledge. With complexity theory, the recommendations made to managers primarily concern improving efficiency and efficacy (the means rather than the ends). In general terms, and with occasional explanation necessary, the names of any of the systems approaches discussed in this chapter can be used to head the sentences related to 3a – 3h in Table 6.3, replacing the particular examples provided above.

The functionalist systems approach is pervasive. The reader will be keen to discover what alternative uses can be made of systems ideas in the service of the interpretive, emancipatory and postmodern paradigms. Before moving on, however, we need to consider what we can, at this stage, say in general terms about the strengths and weaknesses of the functionalist systems approach.

6.10. CRITIQUE OF THE FUNCTIONALIST SYSTEMS APPROACH

We have covered many of the strengths and weaknesses of specific functionalist systems approaches within the body of this chapter. There remains the task of presenting a more generalized critique of functionalist systems thinking. This is done by first looking at the approach as a whole and, in its own terms, at some of its advantages; second, by stepping outside the paradigm governing the approach as a whole and viewing it from the perspective of alternative paradigms. In this chapter, therefore, this means considering functionalist systems thinking from the point of view of, in turn, interpretive, emancipatory and postmodern systems thinking. The same pattern, with a different type of systems approach as the focus of attention, is followed in the critique sections that round off Chapters 7, 8 and 9.

The basic claim made is that all the varieties of systems approaches studied in this chapter are fundamentally functionalist in nature. This applies therefore, to the "organizations-as-systems", "hard systems thinking", "system dynamics", "organizational cybernetic", "living systems theory", "autopoiesis" and "complexity theory" traditions. It can be confirmed by reference to the Burrell and Morgan (1979) criteria for identifying the functionalist paradigm. All the approaches we have looked at are "objectivist" and study systems from the outside. They seek the causal regularities or "structural mechanisms" that govern systems behavior; they believe that human beings can be understood scientifically and dealt with as component parts of the system; and they prefer quantitative techniques of analysis. They are also regulative in terms of their assumptions about social systems trying to understand how order arises and is maintained and aiming to facilitate better prediction and control. None of the approaches seeks knowledge of systems by aiming to understand subjectively the point of view and intentions of the human beings who construct them – the interpretive position. None emphasizes conflict, power, domination or radical change of social order – the emancipatory position. None has its primary focus on deconstruction, marginalization, irony, playfulness – the postmodern position.

A brief analysis of systems engineering on this basis will serve as an example to help clarify the argument. Jenkins's methodology for systems engineering clearly makes objectivist assumptions about the nature of systems thinking. Systems, subsystems, and wider systems are, apparently, all easily identified features of the real-world. The objectives of the system to be engineered can be ascertained. Understanding of the system is gained by breaking it down into its important subsystems and tracing input – output relationships. The presence of human beings in the system does not require any revision to the basic systems engineering approach. Jenkins (1972) wrote that

> the same systems thinking which can be applied to the design of hardware systems, such as space rockets, plants or shops, can also be applied, for example, to parts of firms, or whole firms, or to local government (p. 78).

Building a quantitative model of the system plays a very important role in this systems engineering. The assumptions made about social systems in the Jenkins methodology are just as clearly regulative. The purpose of systems engineering is to understand the current situation better with a view to facilitating prediction and control of the system of concern.

An overarching functionalist orientation is the most important feature of the various systems approaches we have considered so far. Of course, this should not lead us to underestimate the very real differences within the functionalist paradigm. We drew particular attention to a distinction of significance between those approaches that adopted a positivist epistemology compared with those employing a structuralist epistemology.

Jenkins's systems engineering methodology is an example of the former. It aims through empirical investigation to build up a systemic account of a real-world problem situation and the interactions that determine its nature. Hypotheses about how the system's performance might be improved are then incorporated into a mathematical model. The implementation and operation phases are the testing of the hypotheses. If the system performs according to plan, the systems concepts and tools employed in the earlier phases of the methodology are validated. Contingency theory, with its attempt to track the surface regularities that occur between contingency variables and structural aspects of organizations, offers another "ideal-type" example of postivism. System dynamics, by contrast, does not seek to provide general theory based on the specific content of what it examines. As Lane (2000) puts it, "the only universal law/theory on offer is a grand methodological, or structural theory, associated with a [feedback] representation scheme." Mingers and Bailey (see earlier in the chapter) would disagree about whether to ascribe positivist or structuralist underpinnings to living systems theory. Organizational cybernetics, autopoiesis, and complexity theory all adhere, with varying degrees of faith, to structuralism. I devoted some space to arguing, for example, that the VSM embraces structuralism and that this has some important consequences. One advantage is that it is able to find reasons behind the covariance of observable events which are noticed but not explained by contingency theory and socio-technical systems thinking. This enables organizational cybernetics, in the shape of Beer's VSM, to integrate the findings of the organizations-as-systems tradition into a coherent and applicable management tool. Another advantage of structuralist over positivist approaches is their greater ability to deal with "complexity." Taking the VSM as our example again, we find that it abandons the commitment to mathematical modeling and optimization which makes hard systems thinking inappropriate in complex problem situations. The VSM is about the design of goal-seeking, adaptive systems. It is claimed that organizations designed according to its cybernetic principles will be self-regulating and even self-organizing in the face of environmental perturbations. This is the best that can be achieved in situations where the systems of concern are exceedingly complex and probabilistic. In Craib's (1992) view, the strength of structuralism is that it has the ability to

> guide us towards the core, the most important and central aspect of what we are studying, beneath the surface flux. It categorizes not just the basic elements but also the relationships between them (p. 144).

On the other hand, as Craib also remarks:

> The ability to distinguish an underlying structure or logic which has an explanatory importance can tempt the theorist to reduce the world to this level, and so to lose dimensions of meaning that exist at the surface level (p. 145).

With regard to Pepper's "root metaphors" (see Chapter 3), functionalism incorporates "mechanism", "organicism" and "formism", with variations between different functionalist approaches arising from which of these they privilege. The influence of mechanism dominates Barnard's work and hard systems thinking. Organicism suffuses contingency theory, socio-technical systems thinking and living systems theory. Formism comes to the fore in autopoiesis and complexity theory. System dynamics draws on both mechanism and formism, and organizational cybernetics primarily on organicism and formism. Contextualism has a subsidiary role in complexity theory.

The various strengths and weaknesses of the different approaches within the functionalist tradition can also be related to the "images of organization" (see Morgan, 1987) on which they are based. Hard systems thinkers unite in treating organizations as if they were machines. This metaphor presents organizations as vehicles for realizing the goals of their founders or those who currently control them. The purpose of hard methodologies is to arrange the system parts so that these goals are reached with optimum efficiency. Decision making is assumed to be rational and strict control procedures are introduced to ensure conformance with rationally laid plans. Barnard relies on a conception of organizations as being in mechanical-equilibrium but other "organization-as-systems" approaches, such as contingency theory and socio-technical systems thinking, generally rest on the organismic analogy. They view systems as made up of functional sub-systems in close interrelationship, as open to the environment and as adapting and evolving over time. Living systems theory and autopoiesis also draw heavily on the organism metaphor. The VSM, as a model based upon organizational cybernetics, successfully combines the strengths implicit in viewing organizations as machines with what is to be gained by conceiving of them as organisms and brains. The arrangements at the operational level (Systems 1 through 3) ensure the optimum use of resources in carrying out transformation processes, while Systems 4 and 5 ensure adaptation to the environment and the institutionalization of learning. System 5 is charged with maintaining a balance between the "inside and now" and the "outside and then."

If the machine, organism and brain metaphors dominate in the functionalist paradigm, they do not entirely exhaust its possibilities. Culture is touched upon in socio-technical thinking, organizational cybernetics, autopoiesis and complexity theory. However, it is an attenuated version of the culture metaphor that is employed. It is assumed that the task is to engineer the culture of the organization in order to produce a "consensual domain." The "flux and transformation" metaphor, in a relatively rich form, has an impact on system dynamics and complexity theory. The overriding functionalist logic, however, insists that its influence is checked in order to enable decision makers in the "legitimate system" to predict and control. The political system metaphor has a walk-on part in socio-technical thinking and complexity theory. There is little sign anywhere of the "psychic prison" or "instruments of domination" metaphors.

In terms of Habermas's sociological theory (see Chapter 3), the primary orientation of the functionalist systems approach is toward serving the technical interest in prediction and control of natural and social systems. This is where the strengths lie of the different systems approaches that fall within this tradition. We must have considerable respect for the contribution made by, for example, hard systems thinking to showing how systems ideas could be used by managers to improve the technical aspects of transformation processes. The purpose of Jenkins's systems engineering is very obviously to facilitate prediction and control of the operations under surveillance. With contingency theory and organizational cybernetics the concern is not just with "instrumental action" to develop the forces of production but also with "strategic action" to improve the steering capacities of organizations. Contingency theory operates as an empirical analytic science aiming to derive and test law-like hypotheses about the link between various "external variables" and organization structure. These, if confirmed, could provide the foundation for better prediction and control of organizations. The VSM wants to provide knowledge, based upon cybernetic principles, that supports regulation in the social domain. Its aim is to increase the steering capacities of organizations and societies. It is a systems model of great generality, pinpointing various systemic/structural constraints that must be observed if an enterprise is to succeed as an adaptive goal-seeking entity. It is geared to tackling problems of differentiation and integration, providing insight into the proper arrangement of command and control systems, and into the design of appropriate management information and decision support systems, to treating organization-environment relations sensitively and yielding specific recommendations for improving the performance of organizations. All in all, it seems to lend itself to ready application by systems scientists and managers. A similar case could be made, to a greater or lesser extent, for all the varieties of the functionalist systems approach.

Even the severest critics of functionalist systems approaches agree that they can be useful in the right circumstances at an appropriate time. It would be valid and legitimate to use such approaches if the system of concern had a hard, easily identifiable existence independent of observers. The system should yield its most important secrets through study of the relationships among subsystems and between subsystems and the whole. If there are human beings in the system, they must agree upon ends and means and accept being treated like other component parts. It should be possible to construct a quantitative model. The aim must be enhanced prediction and control. The trouble is, these critics argue, that social systems rarely meet these criteria. The functionalist model, therefore, badly misrepresents the nature of most of the problem situations managers face. Social systems do not have an objective existence in the real-world, and it is not easy to discover what objectives they should pursue. Rather, they give rise to ill-structured messes in which the nature and role of people matters quite a lot. Others would want to claim that conflict, contradiction and power play a significant part in many social systems. Fundamentally, the dispute between the functionalist systems approach and its critics can be recognized as being about adherence to different sociological paradigms.

From the interpretive theoretical position it is seldom possible to extend functionalist systems approaches to social systems with any hope of success. A major problem is that functionalist approaches assume it is possible to arrive at a clear statement of the objectives of a system from outside the system concerned. But objectives, interpretive systems thinkers argue, originate from within social systems and different individuals and groups often vary considerably concerning the goals they wish to see pursued. Functionalist systems approaches have no means of bringing about a consensus or accommodation between the representatives of different world views or interests. Because the real issue is the creation of intersubjective understanding, functionalist approaches are ill-equipped to cope and will inevitably fail.

Even when, as with socio-technical systems thinking, autopoiesis and organizational cybernetics, there is support for the need to extend mutual understanding, functionalist systems approaches provide no substantive assistance. Little attention is paid to methods that might help, at the level of conscious meaning, to achieve and sustain shared understanding about purposes. Ulrich's (1981a) distinction between "syntactic" and "semantic-pragmatic" levels of communication helps to further establish this argument, particularly in relation to the VSM. The syntactic level is solely concerned with whether a message is well formed or not, in the sense of whether it can be "read." This matter can be dealt with by information-processing machines. The semantic and pragmatic levels are concerned, respectively, with the meaning and the significance of messages for the receiver – they inevitably involve people. Ulrich argues that the concept of variety, which underpins the VSM, operates only at the syntactic level. It is an information-theoretic measure of complexity referring "to the number of distinguishable states that a system or its output (the "message" it sends out) can assume at the syntactic level" (Ulrich, 1981a).

We can see that this is severely restricting as soon as we consider what criterion of "good" management must be entailed in the VSM (and the argument can be developed just as powerfully against other functionalist systems approaches). For Beer, apparently, good management can be no more than management that establishes requisite variety between itself and the operations managed, and between the organization as a whole and its environment. The lesson from the practical interest is that good management must also concern itself with the meaning and significance of purposes for participants in an enterprise and the creation of intersubjective agreement to pursue a set of purposes.

To interpretive systems thinkers, the fact that the functionalist systems approach misrepresents social systems means simply that it is not of much use for solving management problems. In Humberside Windows (see earlier in this chapter), for example, it was not presumed necessary when using the VSM to address the possibility that different value positions or conflict existed among the stakeholders in the enterprise. This neglect certainly hampered the eventual acceptance of some of the recommendations made. Furthermore the solutions, whether VSM, living systems theory or whatever, seem to come in advance and pass the real problems by. Solutions are brought ready-made to the problems. This is a weakness of the functionalist approach in the eyes of interpretive systems thinkers. To those of an emancipatory persuasion it is downright dangerous.

Emancipatory systems thinkers are worried by the fact that functionalist systems approaches do sometimes seem to work when applied to social systems. Logically this success must depend on there being either widespread agreement over objectives among the human beings who make up the system (which is likely to be quite rare) or an autocratic decision maker who can decide on the objectives of the system. This is the dangerous authoritarian implication of functionalist systems thinking when it is applied to many kinds of social system. Functionalist systems theorists as scientists offer "objective" knowledge about how systems should be organized. Their science enables them to prescribe the "best" solution irrespective of the values of the individuals in the system. Such an approach finds ready acceptance, as Lilienfeld (1975) has argued, among those

> contemptuous of the untidiness and irrationality of the political process [who] would prefer to replace the political process by an administrative world, a system which they as philosopher kings would manipulate from on high, from a position outside of and superior to the system they wish to control (p. 17).

For Habermas (1974), the risk is that of splitting human beings into two classes, "the social engineers and the inmates of closed institutions."

It follows, as well, that the predict-and-control criterion employed by functionalist systems theorists as a test of their procedures may not give a fair test of their methodologies when they are applied to social systems. Because of the existence of autocratic decision makers, the theory or model of social reality advocated by the analyst can be imposed upon other interests in the system – better enabling those decision makers to predict and control the workings of the system. The result is that functionalist systems methodologies do sometimes appear to work; although they are made to work only because of the existence of compulsion. This appearance of "working" is, however, an important reason for the functionalist systems approach still being accepted by many.

The analysis conducted here suggests that functionalist methodologies can only rarely be extended to social systems. They can be legitimately employed in that context only when there is agreement over ends and means among the human beings who make up the system. In that case, the purposeful character of the components of social systems becomes irrelevant, and social systems resemble hard systems. The knowledge produced by the critical sciences (tied to the emancipatory interest) is necessary in order to reflect on whether an encroachment of functionalist methodologies into the domain of interpretive thinking is, or is not, proper in any specific instance.

The argument from the emancipatory perspective needs to be pursued explicitly in relation to the VSM, because it is here that it is most difficult to sustain. The need for an emancipatory interest is actually accepted by Beer. Indeed, I have argued elsewhere

(Jackson, 1990a) that the VSM contains a "critical kernel." Beer seeks to demonstrate on cybernetic grounds that decentralization of control and democracy are necessary for viability and effectiveness. He also suggests some of the problems that existing social arrangements present to the proper operation of the VSM. At the top of the list are the existence of power relationships and our acquiescence in the concept of hierarchy (Beer, 1985). The implication is that we should redress power imbalances and abandon the hierarchical concept of organization. Acknowledgement of the unfortunate effects the exercise of power can have in viable systems is scarcely enough, however, in relation to such a pervasive aspect of organizational life. In an organization disfigured by the operation of power, many of the features of the VSM that Beer sees as promoting decentralization and autonomy instead offer to the powerful means for increasing control and consolidating their own positions. Even the granting of maximum autonomy to the parts can be interpreted, not as a step on the road to industrial democracy, but rather as the imposition of a more sophisticated (but equally compelling) management control technique. Workers are encouraged to believe they possess freedom, but this is only the limited freedom to control themselves in the service of someone else's interest.

Beer, as we said earlier in the chapter, accepts that there is a risk of subversion and that realistically, even if "immunological systems" are incorporated, the model can be used for good or ill. He goes on to suggest that, in this, "cybernetic approaches mirror advances in all other branches of science" (Beer, 1983b). The important question to ask, perhaps, is whether scientific advances that are to be applied in the management context to the design of social systems should mirror advances in other branches of science. According to Ulrich (1981a, 1983), it is exactly Beer's belief that this is the case that leads to problems. Beer conceives of his task as tool design rather than social systems design, and this directly determines that he will create a model that lends itself to autocratic usage. Certainly, at the present stage of development of the emancipatory dimension of the VSM, it does require the theoretical support of other critical sciences in order to ensure that its use is as liberating as its creator intends it to be. Beer has himself, as we shall see in Chapter 8, ventured outside the functionalist paradigm in order to try to provide the kind of support necessary.

In broad terms, the problem with functionalist systems approaches, from the interpretive and emancipatory perspectives, is that they do not restrict their advocacy of instrumental reason to where it might be appropriate - to deal with "technical" issues. Questions of what the organization should be doing are also defined as administrative problems to be decided by managers or experts on the basis of their knowledge about system needs. The practical interest in maintaining and improving mutual understanding, insofar as it is considered at all, is subordinated to the technical interest. Social integration is seen as wholly secondary to system integration. The emancipatory interest in freedom from alienation and domination is, meanwhile, almost entirely ignored.

From the postmodern perspective, the functionalist systems approach exemplifies the main (and worst) features of systemic modernism. It is modernist because it seeks objective truth by rationally probing for order in what is perceived as a logically constructed world. This is a case of systemic rather than critical modernism because progress is discerned in the rationalization of increasingly complex systems rather than in the emancipation of the human subject. Functionalist approaches seek to employ systematic and rational procedures to optimize the efficient and effective functioning of systems, thus maximizing their performance. Knowledge becomes identified with the means of programming the system. Truth is subservient to performativity. The élites that subscribe to this knowledge have the power to implement its conclusions and so validate its correctness. The vicious circle identified by Lyotard is set up as power becomes the basis of legitimation and vice versa. Complexity theory might give us pause in allocating all the systems approaches we have been examining to the modernist pantheon; it does after all, in the manner of postmodernism, reject the notion that the future is susceptible to forecast and gives some space to diversity, conflict and creativity. However, the emphasis on underlying order and uniformity, the lack of self-reflectiveness about purposes, and the managerial context in which Stacey situates the ideas, contribute convincing evidence that this is yet another version, if a slightly perverse one, of systemic modernism.

Given the criticisms that can be leveled against the functionalist systems approach, it is not surprising that in the 1970s disquiet with it began to grow. Complex problems that had social and political aspects and impacts assumed importance. Practitioners became frustrated because these problems should have been within the domain of systems thinking but seemed to elude or defeat the functionalist methodology that dominated the systems approach as it was then understood and practiced. At about the same time the intellectual landscape began to shift in systems thinking. Alternative systems approaches, challenging the traditional functionalist orientation in the field, began to appear. One of these was the interpretive systems approach as embedded in a variety of soft systems methodologies. This approach opened up a completely new perspective on the way systems ideas can be used to help with decision making and problem resolving. It is the subject of the next chapter.

The full benefit of interrogating the various systems approaches, in these critique sections, in terms of the social theory set out in Chapter 3 cannot, of course, be fully grasped until all four of the different approaches have been studied. This is because one of the primary aims of the book is to show the diversity and range of the various systems approaches. The practical usefulness of the theoretical investigations involved may not become clear until Part III of the book, where it is demonstrated how managers and their advisors can employ an understanding of the strengths and weaknesses of alternative approaches, as part of critical systems thinking, to address in a more holistic way the range of problem situations they confront. Nevertheless, I hope that something of the enhanced knowledge and capability that can be gained by working at a theoretical level will be apparent.

7

THE INTERPRETIVE SYSTEMS APPROACH

7.1. INTRODUCTION

The interpretive systems approach is frequently referred to as "soft systems thinking" because it gives pride of place to people rather than to technology, structure or organization. In contrast to the functionalist approach, its primary area of concern is perceptions, values, beliefs and interests. It accepts that multiple perceptions of reality exist, and sometimes come into conflict, and wants to help managers and consultants to work successfully in a "pluralistic" environment of this kind.

Interpretive theorists, as we know from Burrell and Morgan (1979), adopt a subjectivist approach to systems thinking and practice. They do not seek to study objective "social facts" or to search for regularities and causal relations in social reality. Systems possess a much more precarious existence as the creative constructions of human beings. It is necessary, therefore, to proceed by trying to understand subjectively the points of view and the intentions of the human beings concerned; hence the importance in soft systems thinking of probing the worldviews or *Weltanschauungen* (Churchman, 1979a; Checkland, 1981), or the "appreciative systems" (Vickers, 1970; Checkland, 1981), that individuals employ in understanding and constructing social reality. Models are used to explicate particular world-views rather than to capture some truth about the nature of "systems." People are seen as possessing free will, rather than as being subject to forces beyond their control, and this implies they must be centrally involved in any attempt to change and improve the systems they create. Methodology should be geared to getting as close as possible to what is going on, preferably by getting "inside" people's heads to find out and influence what they are thinking. Embracing "subjectivism" leads soft systems thinking to diverge from functionalism in many respects, but the two approaches do, it can be argued, share in common a commitment to regulation. The interpretive systems approach wants to tease out integrative values from multiple viewpoints and so assist managers predict and control outcomes.

Soft systems thinking is heavily influenced by the "root metaphor" of contextualism. Out of a complex flux of events, meaning can only be extracted by supplying appropriate "contexts." In terms of Morgan's metaphors, we find "culture" and "politics" most commonly employed in the interpretive systems approach. Individuals attribute meaning to their situation and can make of organizations what they will. Some engineering of corporate culture needs to take place to ensure that values and beliefs are sufficiently shared to ensure organizational survival and effectiveness. Politics will emerge as a result of different perceptions of the situation and different interests. Accommodations must be sought between different groups in the "coalition" that is an organization.

As we have seen, systems thinking is well served by functionalist systems theory. Indeed this led to a widespread belief that systems thinking is inevitably functionalist in nature. While this is not the case, it is true that those who have wished to develop interpretive systems methodologies, for intervening in and changing systems, have had to search much harder to find appropriate theoretical support. They have had to look beyond the philosophical mainstream, to pragmatism and phenomenology, to help explain and refine their endeavors. In sociology the more interpretive aspects of Weber's thought, together with the "hermeneutic" tradition, have proved of value. From organization and management theory, soft systems thinkers take comfort, ironically, from Silverman's (1970) assault on the functionalist systems approach, and sustenance only from Vickers's work, which again is rather peripheral in its discipline. We covered these influences in Chapters 3 and 4 and will add to those accounts as necessary in what follows.

For whatever reason, the lack of a coherent interpretive systems theory has not held back the development of systems methodologies for intervention based upon interpretive assumptions. The soft systems tradition of work is one of the most vibrant in the systems movement and provides managers with methodologies, methods, models and techniques which are extremely useful for resolving problems. This chapter covers the contributions made to the interpretive systems approach by Warfield, Churchman, Mason and Mitroff, Ackoff, Checkland and Senge. It then considers attempts that have been made to rethink operational research, cybernetics, and system dynamics within the context of the interpretive paradigm. The chapter concludes by setting out constitutive rules for a generic interpretive systems methodology and developing a critique of the interpretive systems approach as a whole.

7.2. WARFIELD'S INTERACTIVE MANAGEMENT

Interactive Management (IM), developed at the University of Virginia about 1980, is defined by Warfield and Cardenas (1994) as

> a system of management invented explicitly to apply to the management of complexity ... to enable ... organizations to cope with issues or situations whose scope is beyond that of the normal types of problem that organizations can readily solve (p. 1).

The predecessors of IM, Unified Program Planning and Interpretive Structural Modeling, arose from the systems engineering tradition (see Warfield, 1976). Today, however, IM has evolved into an approach which, although still rigorous, is oriented much more to dealing with the "softer" aspects of complexity. Central to the approach is the use of a highly trained facilitator working with a group of people knowledgeable about a particular situation. IM elaborates an organized process whereby the facilitator and the group collaborate to tackle the main aspects of concern, develop a thorough undertaking of the problem situation, and set out the basis for effective action.

IM is based upon a new science called the "Science of Generic Design." This science has given rise to and informs the three phases of the IM methodology: the Planning Phase, the Workshop Phase, and the Follow-up Phase. Within each phase various methods and techniques are used according to the logic provided by the methodology. This is particularly striking in the Workshop Phase. Here the different mental activities involved in problem solving are separated out and lent support by "consensus methodologies" (we would say "consensus methods").

Hundreds of applications of IM have been carried out to date in numerous locations and, as Warfield and Cardenas (1994) argue, it is one of the most heavily documented of systems approaches. Warfield and Cardenas list 115 significant applications, of great variety, between 1974 and 1994. Warfield (1994) details example applications in the areas of educational systems, economic development, human service systems, management in the U.S. Department of Defense and quality control of an industrial product. These are usefully organized according to a particular format providing, for each case, a summary, background, stages in the activity, use of the products and conclusions.

7.2.1. The Science of Generic Design

The Science of Generic Design (SGD) addresses the management of complexity through systems design. Complexity can take two forms: "situational complexity", arising from the nature of that which is under study, and "cognitive complexity", arising from the limited information processing capacity of human beings (so that they are easily "overwhelmed" by complexity). SGD must suggest how both forms of complexity can be managed through control of situational complexity, designed processes, designed working environments, provision of personal enhancers, etc.

SGD is underpinned, like all science, by "four universal priors" relating to the human being, language, reasoning through relationships and means of archival representation. These four are brought together by Warfield (1994), into the "Law of Universal Priors" which asserts that:

> The human being, language, reasoning through relationships, and archival representations are universal priors to science (i.e. there can be no science without each of them) (p. 16).

Warfield uses this law to establish the foundations of SGD. This means interrogating disciplines as diverse as mathematics, philosophy and social and behavioral science, guided by the four priors, in order to gather knowledge relevant to design. A number of the more important sources on which he draws will be predictable to readers of this book; for example, the laws of reasoning (dating back to Aristotle), American pragmatism (the work of C.S. Pierce) and the writings of Vickers.

Relevant knowledge of the human being, for the purposes of SGD, can be found in relation to rules, attributes (including limitations), individual and group behavior. For example, referring to attributes, it has been demonstrated that the human being can recall, from short term memory, only about seven items at a time. Examination of work on language, the second universal prior, needs to yield an appropriate language of design against which proposed languages may be evaluated. This specially designed language, it turns out, requires a mix of structural graphics and prose. It is this combination which provides the highest degree of "mind-compatibility." Allowing "reasoning through relationships" to guide the search for knowledge relevant to SGD, provides useful findings on types of inference, logic patterns, modes of definition, interpretive relationships, types of representation, gradation, validation, etc. Warfield (1994) devotes significant space to illuminating the six major categories of relationship found in English. A "definitive relationship" is one where A is a constituent or component of B; a "comparative relationship" assesses A and B in terms of some attribute held in common (e.g. weight); an "influence relationship" describes how B is affected by A; a "temporal relationship" involves precedence in time; a "spatial relationship" might state that A lies above B; and a "mathematical relationship" uses mathematical symbolism to express the relationship between A and B in terms of logic or function. The fourth universal prior, "archival representation", concentrates on the means by which the necessities of consensus in science and understanding of science can be met.

According to the "domain of science model" employed by Warfield (1994), the "foundations" of a science act as priors to its "theory", which guides its "methodology", which in turn governs "applications." Of course, these applications will yield results and evidence which can be used to support and enhance, or to reject, aspects of the foundations, theory and methodology. We are now at the stage of considering the theory employed in SGD.

Theory contains "Laws" and "Principles" consistent with the Laws. Its role is

> to explain the concepts and relationships so that the integrity of the Science as a body of
> coherent knowledge becomes plausible (Warfield, 1994, p. 113).

Theory, within SGD, is concerned with establishing laws and principles which are relevant to the management of complexity. The first element of the theory, as set out by Warfield, is "The Theory of Dimensionality." This establishes how contexts can be transformed, using the theory of relations, into logical spaces of a certain type, making it easier to handle information relating to them. The second element is the "Six Laws." Two of these, "the law of limits" and "the law of gradation", originate outside SGD and are of more general application. The other four, "the law of success and failure for generic design", "the law of requisite variety", "the law of requisite parsimony", and "the law of requisite saliency" are intrinsic to SGD. To give a flavor, the law of requisite parsimony indicates a need for "controlling the rate of presenting information for processing to the human mind, in order to avoid its overload during the Design Process" (Warfield, 1994). The "Principles of Generic Design" stem from the Laws and are the third element of theory. Warfield sets out sixteen principles, the first of which is the "Principle of Designing by Groups":

> Design should be carried out participatively by groups, the membership of which is chosen to
> help ensure that the requisite variety in the Design Situation is articulated (1994, p. 184).

This is supported particularly by the law of success and failure, the law of limits and the law of requisite variety. Other principles refer to the role of computer support in assisting various tasks, the need for speciality "roles" during the design process, the nature of the design environment, etc. On the basis of this theory, it is possible to derive a "methodology" to guide "applications."

7.2.2. The Interactive Management Methodology and Consensus Methods

IM is a true methodology, in our sense, because it is clearly based on theory and interprets this theory to provide guidelines for the use of methods and techniques in practice. An organization which has been trying to deal with a complex problem, but with little success, can take its concerns to an "IM Center" or IM expert. IM practitioners will then work with members of the client organization to plan an approach to the definition of the issue of concern and to the design of alternatives for resolving it. The clients will be led through three phases of activity; although it is always possible that passing through the sequence more than once will be necessary to achieve the greatest benefits.

The first phase is called "Planning" and its primary purpose is to ensure the most productive use of the time of every participant in an IM workshop. Five critical concepts are involved in this phase. There will be the "situation", involving at least one organization and including an issue (what others have called a problem or process) that has a scope which will become clear only as the process evolves. The "issue" is likely to be one that has bothered the organization(s) for some time and which has frustrated previous attempts to deal with it. The third factor is the "initial meeting goals" which arise out of an initial contact between a prominent member of the organization and the IM expert. The goals of this meeting should include scope and context statement writing, actor identification, state of definition assessment, and "white paper" investigation (a white paper is distributed to the participants prior to the workshop phase, and contains key information about the issue). There are then "second meeting goals" to be established at a meeting between the IM Broker, representing the client, and the IM Workshop Planner, or IM practitioner. Goals are formulated based on the scope and context statements proposed in the first meeting. The IM Broker needs to be familiarized with the roles involved in IM, the three phases of IM and the major outcomes of using IM. Following this, the IM Broker and the IM Workshop Planner can together draw up a detailed IM Plan covering the following components:

- context
- major outcome sought
- products sought
- process sequencing
- triggering questions
- generic questions
- workshop site
- participants
- IM staff
- other roles
- budget and schedule

The final critical stage during Planning is "communications." At this stage, the IM Broker will begin to identify " appropriate workshop participants." She will then meet these people to ensure that roles, schedules and responsibilities are all understood.

Phase 2 is the "Workshop Phase":

> In the Workshop Phase, participants will come together to work as a group. Their work will be governed by the IM Facilitator, based on the Workshop Plan. Three key concepts related to the issue are Context, Content, and Process. The *Context* will be set by the Scope Statement arrived at in the planning phase. The *Content* will be provided by the participants, who will be informed by the White Paper previously studied, if any. The *Process* will be provided by the IM facilitator (Warfield and Cardenas, 1994, p. 32).

Any IM Workshop will have certain generic goals regardless of the issue or the participant involved. These will consist of things such as "maximize the opportunity for high-quality contributions by every participant", "maximize treating the participants with much good will, thoughtfulness and respect" or "avoid sacrificing quality in order to meet an arbitrary time deadline." These generic goals are designed to facilitate IM processes. IM processes involve working with ideas and operating on ideas. The primary types of operation that can be carried out with ideas are as follows:

- generating ideas
- clarifying (interpreting) ideas
- amending ideas
- structuring ideas
- interpreting structures of ideas
- amending structures of ideas

In enabling these processes to take place successfully, and in the manner prescribed by the generic goals, the IM methodology coordinates the application of various "consensus" methods and techniques at appropriate times in the workshop. Seven such methods are recommended by Warfield (1994) as particularly suited for use within the IM methodology (with approximate frequency of use in IM studies in brackets): "ideawriting" (19%); "nominal group technique" (approaching 100%); Delphi method (5%); "interpretive structural modeling" (approaching 100%); "options field methodology" (40%); "options profile methodology" (25%); and "trade off analysis methodology" (2%). A number of these developed out of the "brainstorming" technique, often as a response to its failings. Warfield acknowledges that brainstorming pioneered the incorporation of behavioral science knowledge to promote group processes, specifically the avoidance of criticism during idea generation, but does not include it as one of his favored seven consensus methods.

Ideawriting or "brainwriting" is stimulated by a "triggering question." A small group of participants respond to a question by silently recording, on paper, their ideas. This may last for around 5 to 10 minutes before a first exchange of pieces of paper takes place. The page passed on will normally stimulate new ideas in the mind of the reader who writes them down on the paper. The process of exchange can then continue until all participants have examined all papers. The ideas can then be edited and organized for presentation.

Nominal Group Technique (NGT) also begins with individuals silently recording on paper their response to a carefully prepared trigger question. Once this process has finished, the facilitator asks each participant, in turn, for one of their ideas which he then writes down on a flip-chart which all can see. This continues until all the ideas have been displayed (or until three rounds have been completed). There follows a period, in which all are involved, of clarifying the ideas, editing, and adding any new ideas. No criticism of ideas is permitted. Finally there is a written ballot during which each participant is able to choose and rank, from all the ideas generated, the five of greatest priority for her. The facilitator then collates the results of the voting.

The Delphi method can be employed if there is clearly no benefit to be gained by bringing the participants into face-to-face communication. It is characterized by anonymity, controlled feedback and statistical treatment of the group response. A group of experts who know something about a relevant issue are contacted and the method is explained to them. They do not meet each other face to face. An initial questionnaire, bearing on the important aspects of the issue, is developed by the process leader and mailed to the group members. Replies are received and analyzed by the process leader. A revised questionnaire is devised and mailed to the participants. This questionnaire reveals the results of the earlier questionnaire and asks the experts to review their thinking and make new responses in the light of others' opinions. If their own views are "extreme" they may be asked to justify them. This process can continue iteratively until a reasonable consensus is reached about the matter of concern.

Interpretive Structural Modeling (ISM) was developed by Warfield himself and is a key feature of most IM studies. It is a computer assisted learning process which leads to the structuring of ideas and amending structures of ideas. A group of between 6 and 12 participants are led through the process by a skilled facilitator assisted by a computer operator and, possibly, other staff to document significant comments made by the participants. The starting point for ISM is a set of elements surrounding an issue of concern, which has been generated by some other technique, often NGT. A structuring theme is then identified, consisting of an appropriate relationship. For example, an "intent structure" is based on the relationship "A should help achieve B"; a priority structure on "A is of equal or higher priority than B"; a process structure on "A should precede B." The element set is entered into the computer which presents inquiries visually to the group based on the chosen relationship. If the "intent structure" was chosen, the computer will ask questions of the generic form: "Would accomplishing the objective A help to achieve the objective B?" Of course, the participants do not see the generic question but an actual question probing perceived interrelationships between the elements in the set. Participants discuss the questions as they emerge from the computer and provide reasons for the answers they would give. This will provoke an exchange of views and participant learning. Eventually, however, a vote is taken and the computer is informed of the majority opinion. The computer questioning and group discussion continue until the computer is satisfied that, according to logic, it can construct a map of the relationship between all the elements. The map displayed to the participants can itself become the object of discussion until the group is finally satisfied with the structure. Alternative types of structure can be generated using different structuring themes and relationships. Warfield (1994) provides, as one example, the "intent structure" produced by ISM, for the Department of Systems Science, City University, U.K., in response to the question "What should the Department of Systems Science be trying to achieve over the next five years?" This is shown in Figure 7.1.

Options field methodology involves structuring a set of options, often generated and clarified by NGT, into categories. ISM is employed to structure the set using the relationship "is in the same category as." A name is allocated to each category that this generates. The categories themselves can then be clustered and structured, with less important categories being eliminated. The options profile method can take off from an options field to provide an alternative design. Tradeoff analysis is a systematic means of choosing between different designs produced by options field methodology and the options profile method. It is important for Warfield that all of the seven consensus methods he recommends for the "Workshop Phase" are self-documenting.

The third phase of the IM methodology is the "Follow-up." It may well be that sufficient learning has already taken place, by going through the approach, that the issue of concern can be resolved by implementing the results obtained. On the other hand, another iteration might be necessary in order to reach a higher level of success.

We have noted Warfield and Cardenas's claim that IM is one of the most rigorously researched of systems approaches. A study of the comprehensive guides to SGD (Warfield, 1994) and IM (Warfield and Cardenas, 1994) supports this. As well as very detailed discussion of the foundations, theory, the three phases, and applications, a set of IM "Portfolios" are established which provide:

- a set of "success factors" for each of the 3 Phases
- a set of "failure modes" for each of the 3 Phases
- a set of five success levels
- a set of well-defined processes
- a set of well-defined roles

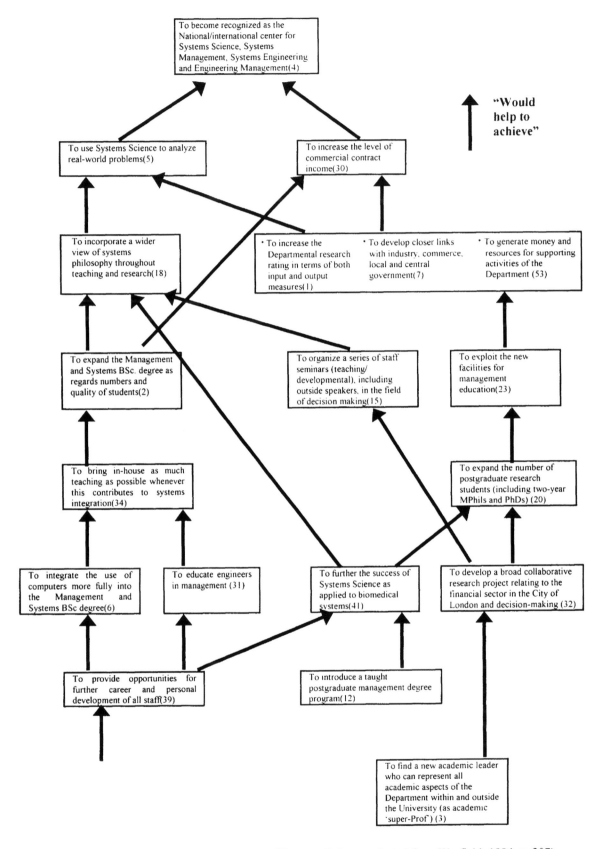

Figure 7.1. Intent structure for Department of Systems Science (adapted from Warfield, 1994, p. 307)

In addition, the appropriate environment for IM workshops (the "Demosophia Facility"), IM software, and approaches to IM documentation are all detailed.

Finally, Warfield and Cardenas are careful to reflect upon the possible outcomes from the use of the IM methodology. The tangible products come in the form of a more detailed and thorough definition of the situation, "logical structures" revealing significant aspects of the issue, alternative designs, and careful selection of one of the alternatives. On the other hand, it is important to emphasize also the more intangible outcomes connected to the process through which participants are taken. Here should be mentioned the learning that takes place among the participants, the commitment to the decision taken, and the documentation:

> The IM processes that are carried out involve substantial communication among the group members, and typically lead to significant learning about the issue or situation, as the participants learn from each other during the facilitated processes. All work is carefully documented (Warfield and Cardenas, 1994, p. 2).

7.2.3. Case Study - Community Council of Humberside

Early in 1994, Mike Jackson and Gerald Midgley from the Center for Systems Studies (CSS), University of Hull, were asked to run a one-day workshop for representatives of the Community Council of Humberside (CCH). The purpose was to examine possible improvements that could be made to the mode of operation of CCH in order to overcome current problems and ensure its relevance and effectiveness into the future. The "Planning Phase" of this study was conducted very informally and involved various communications between members of CSS and CCH, deciding who should be present at the workshop and fixing date, location, facilities, etc. It could have been improved by a closer adherence to IM recommendations. The rest of the study followed the IM methodology more faithfully.

The "consensus" approach used in the morning to structure the workshop phase was the "nominal group technique" (NGT). The participants, a group of eleven people, first formulated a "trigger question" which ended up as follows:

> What needs to be done to equip CCH to better stimulate action on rural issues in order to benefit it and its area of concern?

Participants then individually generated lists of ideas relevant to answering this question. These ideas were collected in a round-robin fashion and a composite list of 54 "possible improvements" to CCH was displayed on flip charts around the room. Following a classification stage, participants individually chose 7 of the ideas and ranked them on a scale of 7, for the idea most important to them, down to 1 for the idea least important to them. Over lunch the consultants calculated the group ratings for each idea.

The ideas were such a diverse set that it seemed impossible to structure them in just one hierarchy. After lunch therefore, using a variation of "options field methodology", the 54 possible improvements were structured into "categories" which, it was hoped, would inform decisions on what most urgently needed doing. Participants were asked to structure related ideas together into "decision areas." This process began with the most important ideas (those receiving 10 or more votes) and continued until all ideas which had attracted 3 or more votes had been fitted into the structure. During the course of this debate, the categories evolved and changed, before finally settling down to five. Table 7.1 presents the final structure of the decision areas, with the numbers in brackets representing the total votes cast for each of the "ideas" making up the decision areas.

A short period of time remained at the end of the day, which the consultants hoped would be used for deciding priorities for action and assigning responsibilities. However, probably because the participants were tired after a hard day, this time was not used effectively. The consultants decided that it would, therefore, be useful if they made their own recommendations as to what should happen next (see Jackson and Midgley, 1994).

The "Follow-up" consisted of the consultants' writing their report (easy because of the self-documenting nature of the techniques employed) and discussions following receipt of the report by CCH. The report recommended that CCH try for a higher "success level" through further use of systems methodologies. Since we were not wedded to IM, we were also able to suggest the possibilities available through "strategic assumption surfacing and testing", "critical systems heuristics", "soft systems methodology" and "viable systems diagnosis." In fact, work continued with CCH using viable systems diagnosis.

Table 7.1. The final structure of the decision areas (numbers in brackets are total votes cast for each "idea").

1) FINANCE AND FUNDING
Guaranteed funding for 3 years (33)
Charge realistic prices for services and introduce some services for profit (11)
Secure medium-term funding, plus reserves and liquid assets (5)

2) MISSION & POLICY
Drop all pretence to urban brief in Grimsby, Scunthorpe and Hull, and include rural in the name (13)
Change our name (12)
Introduce a relevant constitution (11)
Keep the high ground (4)

3) PLANNING
To focus our efforts on themes to a greater degree (17)
Clearer action plan, once focused as a result of an assessment of community need, to formulate a specific action plan over a definite time scale with definite outcomes (19)
Choose a specific number of "campaigns" and ensure they are well publicized and well targeted (7)
Clearer action plan – long and medium term (6)
Required to find out what issues are affecting people (3)

(4) MANAGEMENT AND ADMINISTRATION
Free the Director of every task not required by law in order to oversee and co-ordinate the work of the staff team and the voluntary management structure (10)
Someone to put the list into effect (10)
Rely much less on the written word and reduce at once by 50% the number of written words leaving CCH (8)
Introduce management accounts (5)
Set up an effective monitoring system (5)
Consider an organization managed by a voluntary executive but with the work carried out by professionals (3)
Restructure Committees, representation, plus training (3)
Try to compartmentalize our work in response to community need (4)
Separate off Parish Council work, and give service approximating to income (4)
Clarify the role of the Executive Committee (4)
Ensure good ways of creating a team spirit (3)

5) ACCESSIBILITY AND IMAGE
Move to more suitable prominent premises, i.e. make ourselves more accessible to the public (24)
Improve our publicity/public profile (17)
Be more assertive in recognizing and publicizing our strengths (6)
Choose a specific number of "campaigns" and ensure they are well publicized and well targeted (7)
To have an accessible user-friendly base of operations (3)

In general the consultants felt that the group had worked well with the methodology used to structure the workshop and considerable progress had been made. Since the group had participated democratically in generating the possible improvements and structuring the decision areas, it was hoped that they would feel ownership of the results. Also every individual in the group had learned about the significance for CCH of a much broader range of problems than they had, individually, initially recognized.

7.2.4. Strengths and Weaknesses of Interactive Management

There is no doubt that IM is a well formulated methodology according to the criteria established in Chapter 2 of this book. It is based upon clearly defined "foundations" and "theory." It allows translation of these into application and, through an action research process, seeks both improvement in the area of application and learning about the foundations, theory and methodology. The methodology is ordered, in its "Workshop Phase", according to stages of mental activity involved in working with ideas – generation, clarification, structuring, interpretation, amendment. The separation of these stages of mental activity helps with assigning appropriate consensus methods to each stage. The amount of detail on how to manage group discussion, which is so essential to the success of the interpretive systems approach, is greater than that provided in any other strand of soft systems thinking. The benefits of using IM are well documented in terms of the various tangible outcomes, as well as the learning and commitment generated among the participants.

It is possible to argue with some of the details of the approach. The need to work with a small group, usually of 8 to 12, is obviously limiting. The process can be cumbersome and time consuming as anyone who has sat through a computer assisted ISM session will testify. If too much emphasis is placed on the mechanics (which Warfield, to be fair, warns against), IM can lose the interactive, dialectical effect of brainstorming and produce less original ideas. It may still tend to cow minority views into submission. There must also be real doubts about whether the relational logic, on which ISM is based, adequately represents the way we process information about social reality. It is often difficult to be precise about social issues and with too many vague definitions the process of IM breaks down. Circumstances may not necessarily be structured and stable enough to guarantee that if we prefer A to B to C, we will always prefer A to C. More attention also needs giving to how the IM process translates into implementation. Cardenas (2000) provides useful guidance on improving IM in this respect.

The most telling arguments against IM, however, will come from those who question its interpretive philosophy. This is no guarantee that the design arrived at through the IM process is itself "viable" in functionalist terms. How does IM deal with conflict and power? I remember being part of an IM workshop during one of the Aegean seminars on the "socio-technical design of island ecosystems" (see Jackson, 1993a). The process stalled because a group of economists saw all other issues, whether ecological, cultural or about communications, as being part of the economics category set. All other participants thought the other issues should form their own category sets. With regard to power, Warfield (1994) states:

> The processes that are described in this book inherently invoke at least a modest redistribution of power in the social group within which they are applied. The direction of this redistribution is toward more participative formulation of designs (p. xxvii).

It is not clear how, if this redistribution is resisted, IM suggests dealing with the matter. In general terms there is a neglect of the "contextual" aspects of group work – what baggage the participants bring with them. Some of these issues will surface again in the general critique section of the chapter.

7.3. CHURCHMAN'S SOCIAL SYSTEMS DESIGN

C.W. Churchman was, the reader will remember, among the most influential pioneers of operations research in the postwar period in the United States. During the 1960s and 1970s, however, he became increasingly disillusioned with OR. The original intention to develop a holistic, interdisciplinary, experimental science addressed to problems in social systems was, in his view, being betrayed (Churchman, 1979b). Churchman's educational program in "social systems design" at Berkeley was an attempt to keep the original dream alive. He worked closely with Ackoff (see later section) for many years and influenced, among many others, Mason and Mitroff, whose approach is considered in the next section, and Ulrich, whose emancipatory systems approach features in the next chapter.

7.3.1 Philosophy and Methodology of Social Systems Design

Churchman's perspective on systems thinking, social systems design, is the result of careful and profound philosophical speculation. It is difficult to separate his philosophy from his methodology and so I discuss these together. Perhaps a reasonable summary of his approach can be provided by taking the four aphorisms that close his book *The Systems Approach* (Churchman, 1979a) and expanding on each in turn.

The systems approach begins when first you see the world through the eyes of another.

One implication for Churchman is that the systems approach begins with philosophy, which allows the world to be viewed from the radically different perceptions of opposed philosophical positions. *The Design of Inquiring Systems* (Churchman, 1971), in many respects his most important book, considers the different ways in which five important philosophers might design systems for finding things out. This first aphorism contains lessons from Kant and Hegel. We are reminded that whatever view of the world we hold is inevitably based on certain taken-for-granted, *a priori* assumptions (Kant). It is wise for systems designers to recognize, following Hegel, that there are many possible worldviews, constructed upon alternative sets of taken-for-granted assumptions. Once we appreciate this, it becomes clear that subjectivity should be embraced by the systems approach. Systems designers must accept that completely different evaluations of social systems, their purposes, and their performance can and do exist. The only way we can get near to a view of the whole system is to look at it from as many perspectives as possible (Churchman, 1970).

The systems approach goes on to discovering that every world-view is terribly restricted.

In *The Design of Inquiring Systems*, Churchman shows that each of the five designs for finding things out is incomplete in itself, resting upon assumptions that cannot be proved using its own logic. Increased sophistication in inquiry comes with recognition of the limitations of whatever inquiring system is employed. This opens the way, for Churchman, to a different understanding of objectivity. Subjectivity is not to be rigorously excluded (in practice it can't be, anyway), but must be included in any definition of objectivity – so that by bringing together different subjectivities, the restricted nature of any one worldview (W) can be overcome. A further point is that although individual worldviews are terribly restricted, they are also usually highly resistant to change. Worldviews cannot be seriously challenged just by exposing them to apparently contrary "facts", which they will simply interpret according to their fixed presuppositions: "No data can ever fatally destroy a W" (Churchman, 1970).

The conclusion of these ruminations is that we need a dialectical approach to objectivity such as suggested by the philosopher Hegel. In practice, Churchman charges systems designers with the task of making those responsible for social systems (decision makers) aware of the restricted nature of their own worldviews. This concept of *Weltanschauung*, or worldview, is an important one in soft systems thinking. It carries the implication that an individual's interpretations will be far from random; they will be consistent in terms of a number of underlying assumptions that constitute the core of that individual's worldview. We can therefore examine them systemically. This is best done, according to Churchman (1970), through a process of "dialectical debate." The worldview that makes the decision makers' proposals meaningful should be unearthed. This prevailing worldview (thesis) should then be challenged by another "deadly enemy" worldview based on entirely different assumptions and giving rise to alternative proposals (antithesis). Whatever facts are available can then be considered in the light of both worldviews. This should help to bring about a richer (i.e., more objective) appreciation of the situation, expressing elements of both positions but going beyond them as well (synthesis). The dialectical process advocated by Churchman can, therefore, be represented as consisting of the following steps:

Thesis
- Understand decision makers' proposals
- Understand the *Weltanschauung* (W) that makes these proposals meaningful

Antithesis
- Develop an alternative W (a "deadly enemy")
- Make proposals on the basis of this W

Synthesis
- Evaluate data on the basis of both Ws
- Arrive at a richer appreciation of the situation

There are no experts in the systems approach.

This admonition should be taken to heart most strongly by systems designers themselves. When it comes to matters of aims and objectives (and appropriate means), which inevitably involve ethical considerations and moral judgments, there can be no experts. Systems designers, because they seek to take on the whole systems, may become arrogant in the face of opposition from apparently sectional interests. It is incumbent on them to listen to all "enemies" of the systems approach (such as religion, politics, ethics, and aesthetics) since these enemies reflect the very failure of the systems approach to be comprehensive (Churchman, 1979c).

The systems approach is not a bad idea.

The attempt to take on the whole system remains a worthwhile ideal, even if its realization is unattainable in practice. From this arises the need for the systems designer to pursue his or her profession in the "heroic mood." This is the spirit advocated by

Churchman's mentor, the pragmatist philosopher E.A. Singer. Increasing purposefulness and participation in systems design, through the process of dialectically developing world views, is a never-ending process:

> Hence, the Singerian inquirer pushes teleology to the ultimate, by a theory of increasing or developing purpose in human society; man becomes more and more deeply involved in seeking goals" (Churchman, 1971, p. 254).

There is a need to help bring about a (Lockean) consensus around a particular worldview so that decisions can be taken and action occur. Before this worldview can congeal into the status quo, however, it should itself be subject to attack from forceful alternative perspectives (Churchman, 1971).

The extent to which Churchman's methodology comes as a shock to those reared on hard systems thinking is well illustrated by a story he tells in *The Systems Approach and Its Enemies* (Churchman, 1979c). During the 1960s, NASA was in the middle of the Apollo space program to put a man on the moon. It was thought a good idea to have various groups of scholars come to study the innovative methods NASA was using to manage this complex project. Churchman's was one such group. They, however, went far beyond NASA's intentions and began asking challenging questions and debating about the purpose of the Apollo program, which from a systems point of view did not obviously contribute to the betterment of the human species. A NASA group was monitoring the groups monitoring them, and graded the approaches used in terms of both relevance to NASA's mission and interdisciplinarity. Churchman's group received an F for the first category and an A for the second.

7.3.2. Strengths and Weaknesses of Social Systems Design

We have previously recognized Churchman's contribution to operations research. Let us now develop a number of points that have emerged, in our discussion, in order to do justice to the huge influence social systems design has had on the interpretive systems approach and the emergence of emancipatory systems thinking.

First there is the shift proposed by Churchman in our understanding of objectivity in the systems approach. In the organizations-as-systems, hard, and cybernetic traditions (the alternatives available when he was writing), objectivity is perceived to rest on the accuracy and efficacy of some model of the system of concern. Either the model is taken to represent the system of concern directly (as in organizations-as-systems and hard approaches) or it is held to suggest, because of the scientific laws it encapsulates, how the system of concern operates (as with the VSM). In both cases the objectivity of the model is demonstrated, and the results of the systems study "guaranteed", if the implemented solutions derived from the model work in practice. For Churchman, systems and whether they work or not are in the mind of the observer rather than in the real world. A model can only capture one possible perception of the nature of a system. Objectivity, therefore, can only rest upon open debate among holders of many different perspectives. And the results of a systems study can only receive their guarantee from the maximum participation of different stakeholders, holding various worldviews, in the design process. This is a fundamental shift indeed, and it is one that is necessarily adhered to (in theory at least) in all soft systems methodologies. Once the claim to be modeling some real world "out there" is abandoned, the only possible reason why anyone should want to follow the prescriptions of systems methodologists is that they can provide the means of better organizing open and free debate about the value or otherwise of existing and proposed systems designs.

A further point derives from Churchman's desire to strive for "whole system" improvement. Because decision makers inevitably have a restricted worldview (as does everybody else), following their worldview could lead to suboptimization in terms of the whole system. The systems designer's first obligation in carrying out a systems study, therefore, is not to the decision makers, even if they are paying the bills; rather, it is to the "clients", customers, or beneficiaries of the system (Churchman uses various words to describe this group). This is a very broadly defined set of people, all of whom have an interest in the system and whose objectives should, in view of this, be served by the system. In the case of an industrial firm it will include employees, stockholders, customers, suppliers and interested sections of the public. The purpose of social systems design must be to help social systems serve their clients. Its role, therefore, is to identify the interests of the clients and to influence the decision makers in the system to realize those changes that benefit the clients of the system. If a systems designer becomes convinced that the decision makers are serving the wrong clients, then he or she has a professional obligation to change the decision-making process (Churchman, 1970). The decision makers must be persuaded to confront their most cherished assumption with plausible counter-assumptions.

The final point also stems from Churchman's insistence that social systems design (originally OR) has to take on the whole system. To some (e.g. Bryer, 1979), this makes Churchman's work appear hopelessly idealistic and impractical. All that Churchman is doing, however, is pointing out the fate of all the applied sciences, which have no option but to live with the prospect that localized actions based on limited information can have disastrous consequences in terms of whole-system improvement. As Ulrich (1981b) argues, all such critics are doing is "blaming the messenger for the bad news." What Churchman does, following Ulrich's (1985) reading, is to use the theoretical indispensability of comprehensive systems design as an ideal standard to force us to recognize the requirement to reflect critically on the inevitable lack of comprehensiveness in our actual designs. So Churchman is not asking for the impossible, but is suggesting a way of proceeding, given that what is necessary, if we are to be sure our designs are justifiable - that we should understand the whole system - is, in fact, impossible. We need to make the lack of comprehensiveness of our designs transparent so that we can easily reflect on their limitations. A good way of doing this it to expose our designs to the "enemies" of the systems approach and learn from what they have to say about them.

The insistence that social systems serve their "true" clients, and that we constantly reflect upon the lack of comprehensiveness of our proposals for systems design, are aspects of Churchman's thinking that have inspired emancipatory and critical systems thinkers. So too is the deep moral commitment that is in evidence throughout the corpus of his work. For Churchman (see, for example, 1982) "wisdom" only emerges when we combine thought with a concern for ethics. He insists that the systems approach should address serious problems such as hunger, poverty and war, and that systems practitioners take responsibility for the social consequences of their work (see Flood, 1999).

Churchman ends *The Design of Inquiring Systems* (1971) with the question: "What kind of a world must it be in which inquiry becomes possible?." It is his failure to properly address this question, however, which provokes the severest criticism of his work. Social systems design, like other soft systems approaches, is criticized for its "subjectivism" and its "idealism", and for its consequent failure to come to terms with "objective" features of social reality. The highly structured, resistant social world studied by functionalist and radical structuralist social scientists is foreign to Churchman. His book *The Systems Approach and Its Enemies* surprises one reviewer (Sica, 1981), because in a book supposedly about social systems we are told remarkably little about what they are actually like. Because for Churchman there are no objective aspects of social systems to worry about, bringing about change means simply changing the way people think about the world - changing their *Weltanschauungen*. But there are problems here. From the point of view of objectivist social science, Ws are not so easily changed. They are closely linked to other social facts in the social totality. Changing Ws may depend crucially on first of all changing these other social facts. If we really wish to bring about change, we need some understanding of the laws that govern the transformation of the social totality. Only then can the real blockages to change (which may not be in the world of ideas) be located and pressure applied. To functionalist systems thinkers, therefore, Churchman can easily miss the real leverage points for bringing about change. From the perspective of some emancipatory systems thinkers, while he confines himself to the world of ideas, all that Churchman can guarantee by the process of dialectical inquiry is a continual readjustment of the ideological consensus.

Another criticism of Churchman's work, from the emancipatory position, is that it seems to be underpinned by a consensus worldview. He assumes that genuine participation in dialectical debate can be arranged and that there is a possibility of achieving synthesis. To those who see the social world as characterized by asymmetry of power, structural conflict, and contradiction, these are pious hopes indeed.

7.4. MASON AND MITROFF'S STRATEGIC ASSUMPTION SURFACING AND TESTING (SAST)

SAST is undoubtedly an example of soft systems thinking because it focuses managers' attention on the different assumptions, beliefs and worldviews involved in a problem situation rather than on the efficient design of systems. The human and political aspects come to the fore, while the issue of organizational structure slides into the background. There are a number of versions of the SAST approach that differ in their precise details. The substance, however, is the same. The account of SAST given here is drawn from the main sources with which either R.O. Mason or I.I. Mitroff, or both, have been associated (Mason and Mitroff, 1981; Mitroff and Emshoff, 1979; Mitroff, Emshoff, and Kilmann, 1979). It is an attempt to present the substance of the methodology in the clearest possible way and may not correspond to the detail of any one account. The methodology itself is approached through the underlying philosophy and principles on which it is based. The reader will recognize in SAST a profound debt to Churchman's work. This debt continues to be reflected in Mitroff's more recent writings, with Linstone (1993), on "unbounded systems thinking." Elements of SAST and Linstone's "multidimensional systems approach" (see Chapter 10) are combined to produce a new form of systems thinking which, they claim, is appropriate for the information/knowledge age.

7.4.1. Philosophy and Principles of SAST

SAST is designed for use with complex systems of highly interdependent problems, with problem formulation and structuring assuming greater importance than problem solving using conventional techniques. It is argued that most organizations fail to deal properly with such "wicked" problems because they find it difficult to challenge seriously accepted ways of doing things; policy options that diverge considerably from current practice are not given systemic consideration. SAST aims to ensure that alternative policies and procedures are considered. This necessitates the generation of radically different policies or themes since data alone, which can after all be interpreted in terms of existing theory, will not lead an organization to change its preferred way of doing things. An organization really begins to learn only when its most cherished assumptions are challenged by counterassumptions. Assumptions underpinning existing policies and procedures should therefore be unearthed, and alternative policies and procedures put forward based upon counterassumptions. A variety of policy perspectives can be produced, each supportable by the data available in an organization.

It is recognized that tensions may well ensue, since the success of the process depends upon different groups being strongly committed (initially at least) to particular policy options. However, to believe that ill-structured problems can be adequately tackled in the absence of such tensions is thought to be naïve. Organizations are arenas of conflict between groups expressing alternative worldviews. This offers great potential for developing alternative strategies and policies, but it must also be managed. SAST attempts to surface conflicts and to manage them as the only way, eventually, of achieving a genuine synthesis.

This philosophy is incorporated in a number of clearly articulated principles (Mason and Mitroff, 1981). SAST is adversarial, based on the belief that judgements about ill-structured problems are best made after consideration of opposing perspectives. It is participative, seeking to involve different groupings and levels in the organization, because the knowledge needed to solve a complex problem and implement a solution will be widely distributed. It is integrative, on the assumption that a synthesis of different viewpoints must eventually be sought so that an action plan can be produced. It is also "managerial mind supporting", believing that managers exposed to different assumptions will possess a deeper understanding of an organization, its policies and its problems. These principles are employed throughout the phases of SAST.

The idea that an approach can be both adversarial and integrative may appear perverse to some. That it is not was strongly brought home to me by one particular intervention in a firm that was in the process of introducing a quality-management program (see Ho and Jackson, 1987). In that firm there was an apparent consensus around the need for the kind of quality program proposed. However, this apparent consensus was founded upon very varied interpretations of the key concepts in the program. Only through a process of adversarial debate could these very significant differences be highlighted and the ground prepared for a more soundly based consensus built upon common understanding (see the case study later in this section).

7.4.2. SAST Methodology

The SAST methodology itself can be regarded as having four major stages: group formation, assumption surfacing, dialectical debate and synthesis. The aim of group formation is to structure groups so that the productive operation of the later stages of the methodology is facilitated. As wide a cross-section of individuals as possible who have an interest in the relevant policy question should be involved. It is important that as many possible perceptions of the problem as can be found are included. The participants are divided into groups, care being taken to maximize convergence of viewpoints within groups and to maximize divergence of perspectives between groups. A number of techniques, such as personality-type technology and vested-interests technology, are suggested as means to accomplish this. Each group's viewpoint should be clearly challenged by at least one other group.

During the assumption surfacing stage, the different groups separately unearth the most significant assumptions that underpin their preferred policies and strategies. Two techniques assume particular importance in assisting this process. The first, "stakeholder analysis", asks each group to identify the key individuals or groups on whom the success or failure of their preferred strategy would depend. This involves asking questions such as: Who is affected by the strategy? Who has an interest in it? Who can affect its adoption, execution, or implementation? And who cares about it? For the stakeholders identified, each group then lists what assumptions it is making about each of them in believing that its preferred strategy will succeed. Each group should list all the assumptions derived from asking this question of all the stakeholders. These are the assumptions upon which the success of the group's preferred strategy or solution depends. The second technique is "assumption rating"; for each of the listed assumptions, each group asks itself:

- How important is the assumption in terms of its influence on the success or failure of the strategy?
- How certain are we that the assumption is justified?

The results are recorded on a chart such as that shown in Figure 7.2. Each group should now be able to identify a number of key assumptions - usually in the most important/least certain quadrant of the chart - upon which the success of its strategy rests.

The groups are brought back together to begin a dialectical debate. Each group makes the best possible case for its preferred strategy while clearly identifying the most significant assumptions it is making. Points of information only are allowed from other groups at this time. There is then an open debate focusing on which assumptions are different between groups, which are rated differently, and which of the other groups' assumptions each group finds most troubling. Each group should develop a full understanding of the preferred strategies of the others and their key assumptions. After the debate has proceeded for so long, each group should consider adjusting its assumptions. This process of "assumption modification" should continue for as long as progress is being made.

The aim of the synthesis stage is to achieve a compromise on assumptions from which a new, higher level of strategy or solution can be derived. Assumptions continue to be neg-

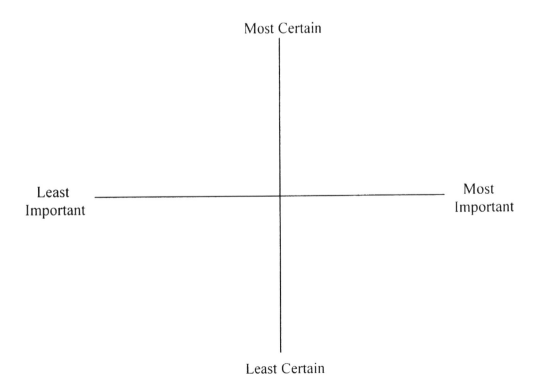

Figure 7.2. An assumption rating chart

otiated and modified. A list of agreed assumptions should be drawn up. If this list is sufficiently long, then the implied strategy can be worked out. This new strategy should bridge the gap between the old strategies and go beyond them as well. The assumptions on which it is based can be evaluated as it is put into effect. If no synthesis can be achieved, points of disagreement are noted and the question of what research might be done to resolve those differences is discussed. Meanwhile, any strategy put into effect can be more fully evaluated.

Examples of SAST in action can be found in Jackson (1989a), Mason (1969), Mason and Mitroff (1981), and Mitroff, Barabba and Kilmann (1977). I take as an illustrative case study for SAST an intervention in Thornton Printing Company that has been reported more fully in Ho and Jackson (1987).

7.4.3. Case Study - Thornton Printing Company

Thornton Printing Company engages in the printing of labels for other companies products and the printing of tickets. It also manufactures label-application machines for other companies. In recent years Thornton's business environment has changed very rapidly. Printing technology has been in a state of flux, with new products frequently coming onto the market. Many small and efficient firms have managed to take advantage of this situation to establish themselves and to gain a reputation for producing and delivering labels quickly and cheaply to exact customer specifications. Thornton has been unable to adapt satisfactorily to changing circumstances, and this has shown in disappointing financial returns. It does little research and development and, in fact, has no separate department for this. Inevitably it has fallen behind its competitors in product innovation. The firm has poor communications with its market and plays no role in trying to nurture its environment. Thornton's marketing has been far too passive in the face of aggressive tactics from competitors. Its sales force lacks proper training and professionalism, and does not seem motivated to establish and develop customer relations. Sales personnel are unable to service customers properly because of a simple lack of knowledge about what the company can offer. Internally, communication between sales and production planning is weak, and this causes difficulties in scheduling and in maintaining proper utilization of the diverse high-technology machines.

The situation within the production function itself was also at crisis point. Traditionally, managers and supervisors felt that employees did not work hard enough and imposed close supervision and control on subordinates. This had degenerated into management by threat, as market pressure had led to very high targets for output being set and detailed work routines and procedures being enforced. There were many errors and mistakes, leading to high levels of waste, spoiled work and low-quality products. This led to excessive overtime being worked to correct problems, and this in turn increased costs. Morale was extremely low. Workers felt they were being blamed for poor-quality work that in fact often resulted from the poor-quality materials with which they were supplied. They refused to collaborate with their supervisors and industrial-relations problems between management and unions or shop stewards were frequent.

In the face of these external threats and internal problems, Thornton obviously could have done with a well-trained and highly aware management team. In fact this was lacking. Management jobs were specialized and there was little team spirit. A number of senior managers failed to see the scale of the difficulties facing Thornton and were reluctant to change.

The managing director of Thornton Printing Company, alarmed by the situation, determined to put things right by introducing a comprehensive quality-management program into the company. He and his executive team formulated their own quality proposals based first and foremost on the notion of "conformance to requirements." A strong corporate culture was to be propagated and introduced from the top, emphasizing the importance of quality and conformance to requirements. There was to be a "quality coordinator" to act as a champion for the program and as a troubleshooter. The program was to be introduced with quality-management sessions for top managers and then cascaded down to the shop floor, where workers would demonstrate that they had absorbed the principles by applying them in their day-to-day work. It was recognized that for implementation to work, managers and supervisors would have to change their conception of their roles and become leaders, creating excellence and quality by motivating and educating their subordinates rather than by tightly controlling and threatening them.

"Conformance to requirements" was to apply both to relationships with customers and suppliers and to all work-related activities in the organization. With regard to customers, the aim was to learn their needs more accurately and to provide them with the best possible service. The company should innovate in cooperation with customers, developing an "enhancing" relationship with them. Suppliers were expected to contribute to quality by supplying "zero-defect" products and materials. In terms of internal activity, quality requirements were to be made clear and specific and communicated effectively. Quality targets for each process were to be set and used to establish a "prevention" approach to quality. The aim was to "get things right first time" in order that there would be zero defects. If there was a deviation from output requirements, that should be regulated immediately. Non-conformance to requirements was to be eliminated. In order to ensure that employees got it right the first time, it was important that they develop the right attitude. Employees were to be motivated to "own" quality themselves in order to ensure this. Inevitably there would have to be changes in work organization to make jobs more interesting and meaningful. The managing director was convinced that if conformance to requirements could be achieved, the organization would become more adaptive, morale would improve, there would be fewer mistakes and problems, and productivity and profits would increase.

The intervention in Thornton Printing Company began when the systems consultants were invited to observe some of the early quality-management sessions arranged for senior managers at which the program was supposed to be fully debated. Observation of these sessions revealed, alarmingly, that very little real discussion took place. There was an unstated assumption that quality management was right for Thornton and that it fitted in with the corporate culture. Managers spent most of the time trying to justify the validity of the various principles proposed, rather than challenging them. Furthermore, because the assumptions underlying the ideas put forward were not debated, different interpretations of key concepts remained. With the terminology employed continuing to mean different things to different people, no genuine communication could occur and no real consensus could be reached.

In these circumstances, the consultants were worried that the program might flounder on various fundamental weaknesses in the company that it did not address. These could be remedied by other methods in due course, but the first task was to convince the managing director of the validity of the consultants' immediate concerns. To achieve this, SAST was chosen as a methodology that could reveal the shaky assumptions upon which the quality management program was based.

Outsiders were not able to contribute actively at the sessions (one of the problems, of course). However, it was possible to present top management with a report that was critical of the quality-management program in its existing form. First, all the stakeholders – all those with an interest or concern in the program – were identified. Second, it was asked in relation to each of these stakeholders: What is being assumed of this stakeholder in believing that the quality management program will be successful? It was then a relatively easy matter to demonstrate how shaky many of these assumptions were. For the stakeholder "senior management", it was assumed that they had a shared vision of where the company was going and could communicate this to subordinates with ease. In fact, no clear vision existed. It was expected that sales staff would play a key role in nurturing customers. It was doubtful, in reality, whether they had a full understanding of what Thornton could offer to customers. Workers were assumed to be motivated to do things right first time simply by remembering the core concepts of quality management. Workers in fact seemed unlikely to do things right first time unless they knew something of corporate strategy and trusted their supervisors. Suppliers, it was hoped, would supply zero-defect raw materials, but the incentive for their doing so remained unclear.

This critique of the assumptions underpinning the existing program led to suggestions for an enhanced quality-management program based on different assumptions, and a comparison of how the existing and enhanced versions would address the problem situation confronting the firm. Suggestions were also made to Thornton about how other systems approaches might help alleviate problems not dealt with in the quality-management program. Specific uses were proposed for cognitive mapping, Checkland's SSM, dialectical debate, the VSM, and the system of systems methodologies (Ho and Jackson, 1987). Thus the study anticipated the informed use of different approaches in combination, which is now a hallmark of critical systems thinking (see Part III).

7.4.4. Strengths and Weaknesses of SAST

Mason (1969) has detailed what he sees as the advantages of a dialectical approach to strategic planning over the alternative expert and devil's-advocate methods. In the expert approach, some planner or planning department simply produces an "objective" plan, based upon the "best" evidence, for managerial consumption. The planners' assumptions remain hidden, and the opportunity is lost to produce plans premised upon other points of view. In the devil's-advocate approach, managers and planners produce a planning document that is then subject to criticism by top management. The criticism may uncover some assumptions. However, this approach often encourages top management to be hypercritical with the added problem that, if they are too destructive, the suggested plan disintegrates with no alternative to replace it. In these circumstances, planners may be tempted to produce "safe" plans to protect themselves from severe criticism. Again, with the devil's-advocate approach, the chance is lost to develop alternative plans constructed on different world views. A dialectical approach, such as SAST, is seen as overcoming all the weaknesses of the other two methods.

In more general terms, SAST is a useful addition to the armory of soft systems thinkers who see their primary role as being to promote intersubjective communication in organizations. SAST privileges the culture metaphor and the purpose of its use in Thornton was to create a stronger and more uniform corporate culture. The quality management sessions taking place were not being very successful in securing mutual understanding. It was felt that introducing an element of dialectical debate would help draw out different interpretations of the concepts of quality management, and different perspectives on the purpose of the program, so that the discussion would become richer and the consensus reached would be more soundly based. To this end SAST worked well. It handles pluralism effectively, first sustaining and making use of it to generate creative discussion and then managing its resolution in a new synthesis.

Of course, from the functionalist and emancipatory perspectives, SAST can be criticized for what it does not do well. SAST rests upon subjectivist rather than objectivist assumptions about systems thinking. As can be seen from the Thornton intervention, the concern is with understanding and engineering the way people view the world. If the way people perceive things alters, then it is assumed they will have the ability to bring about desired changes to social systems. There seems to be an unwarranted (for functionalists) assumption that once problems arising from the existence of different worldviews have been dissolved, then the difficulties stemming from situational or systemic complexity will disappear as well. Thus Mason and Mitroff (1981) support Rittle's conclusion that "every formulation of a wicked problem corresponds to a statement of solution and vice-versa. Understanding the problem is synonymous with solving it." This seems to miss the daunting problems concerned with organizing large-scale complex systems. The "cybernetic" dimension of problem solving is downplayed and the metaphors of organism and brain are ignored. In Thornton, the consultants had to suggest other systems approaches to deal with problems of organizational structure in a changing environment.

From a radical viewpoint, SAST is inhibited in the support it can offer because of its failure to recognize the effect of structural inequalities and power relationships on the kind of debate that takes place. It lacks an emancipatory dimension. In coercive situations, it can be argued, it will be impossible to achieve the adversarial and participative debate necessary for the proper application of SAST. Integration is achieved in such contexts by power and domination rather than through consensual agreement. Any employment of SAST is likely to get distorted and to provide benefit only to those possessing power in the organization. Mason and Mitroff (1981) see the main weakness of SAST as being its dependence upon the "willingness of participants to lay bare their assumptions." Kilmann (1983) points out that assumptional analysis "assumes that the participants want their assumptions exposed." In coercive contexts, the powerful are unlikely to want their assumptions revealed. SAST is most appropriately used, therefore, in pluralist rather than coercive contexts. In such contexts it can assist in structuring the exploration of different world views and help to bring about a synthesis, or at least accommodation, among participants so that action can be taken.

7.5. ACKOFF'S SOCIAL SYSTEMS SCIENCES (S³)

Like his friend and sometime colleague, Churchman, Ackoff has been much influenced by the pragmatist philosophy of E.A. Singer. I described in an earlier section how Churchman's interpretation of that philosophy produced a new understanding of objectivity in the systems approach. Ackoff has endorsed and contributed to that new understanding. For him, the conventional view that objectivity results from constructing value-free models that are then verified or falsified against some real world "out-there" is a myth. Purposeful behavior cannot be value free. Objectivity in social systems science must be seen as "value full" not value free:

> Objectivity cannot be approximated by an individual investigator or decision maker; it can be approached only by groups of individuals with diverse values. It is a property that cannot be approximated by individual scientists but can be by science taken as a system (Ackoff, 1999b, p. 312).

If his "non-relativistic pragmatism" led Ackoff to become, as we saw, one of the most influential pioneers of operations research in the post-war period in the United States, it also led him out of operations research again when that discipline became wedded to its mathematical models ("mathematical masturbation" as he described it) and lost touch with the real issues that concerned managers. In Ackoff's (1977) view, those who continue to work in the vein of hard systems thinking, with its emphasis on optimization and objectivity, inevitably opt out of tackling the important social issues of the age. To cling to optimization in a world of multiple values and rapid change is to lose one's grip on reality. The emphasis has to be upon learning and adapting. Objectivity has to be rethought as resulting from the "open interaction of a wide variety of individual subjectivities" (Ackoff 1974b); hence the need for wide participation and the involvement of all stakeholders in planning and design. Disillusioned with operations research, Ackoff gave the name "social systems sciences" (S^3) to the educational and consultancy activities he initiated at the University of Pennsylvania.

Ackoff's work has had a colossal impact on the wider OR and systems communities. As leader of the "reformist" (see Dando and Bennett, 1981) strand in OR, he went into battle against, and massacred (intellectually at least), the forces of the status quo (Ackoff, 1974a, 1979, a, b), while defending himself against advocates of the "revolutionary" tendency in OR and systems thinking (Ackoff, 1975, 1982). The terrain mapped in these debates remains central to any attempt to reconstruct the management sciences. The influence of his writings on corporate planning (Ackoff, 1970a), applied social science (1972), management information systems (1967), and management education (1968), has also been considerable. Recently (Ackoff, 1997, 1999a), he has been using his intellectual pre-eminence to warn managers against the "panaceas, fads and quick fixes" with which they are assailed:

> Today's generation of managers is panacea prone ... They get sucked into all these fads and panaceas that don't work. Two national studies have shown that two-thirds of the efforts to introduce quality programs have failed. Three-quarters of the programs in process re-engineering have failed, and so on and so on. But we don't seem to learn from this. We simply look for the next panacea instead of trying to rethink why the panaceas are failing. The answer is fundamentally very simple, the panaceas are anti-systemic (1997, p. 27).

The impact of his writings has had wide geographical, as well as disciplinary, spread. Carvajal (1983) has discussed the influence of Ackoff and his work on the development of the management sciences in Mexico. In the United Kingdom, he was "marriage broker" between the Tavistock Institute and the Operational Research Society when they worked together to form the Institute for Operational Research (later the Center for Organizational and Operational Research (see Friend *et al.*, 1988). He was prominent at the influential "OR and the Social Sciences" conferences held at Cambridge in 1964 and 1989 (Lawrence, ed., 1968; Jackson *et al.*, eds., 1989). His research work with the black ghetto in Mantua (1970b) gave birth to early attempts at "Community OR" in Birmingham, in the United Kingdom, and more recently have helped inspire the full-scale Community OR initiative in the U.K.

One could go on, but it is time to turn to what it is in the nature and detail of the work itself that has exercised such power.

7.5.1. The Changing Nature of the World and the Need for Interactive Planning

Ackoff's general philosophical orientation takes on precise form when it is related to the profound changes he believes advanced industrial societies are undergoing. About the time of World War II, he argues (Ackoff, 1974a, 1974c, 1981a), the "machine age" – associated with the industrial revolution – began to give way to the "systems age." The systems age is characterized by increasingly rapid change, interdependence and complex purposeful systems. It demands that much greater emphasis be put upon learning and adaptation if any kind of stability is to be achieved. This, in turn, requires a radical reorientation of worldview. Machine-age thinking – based upon analysis, reductionism, a search for cause-effect relations, and determinism – must be complemented by systems-age thinking, which proceeds by synthesis and expansionism, tries to grasp producer-product relations and admits the possibility of free will and choice.

Ackoff starts Chapter 1 of a recent book with a quote from Albert Einstein:

> Without changing our patterns of thought, we will not be able to solve the problems we created with our current patterns of thought (in Ackoff, 1999a, p. 3).

Those who manage corporations in the systems age need to alter the way they think about their enterprises. In the past it has been usual to regard corporations either as machines serving the purposes of their creators or owners, or as organisms serving their own purposes. Today, organizations must be considered as social systems serving three sets of purposes. They are themselves purposeful systems and have their own goals, objectives and ideals that should be taken into account. But they also contain, as parts, other purposeful systems: individuals, whose aspirations need to be met. And they exist, themselves, as parts of wider purposeful systems whose interests also should be served. Corporations therefore have responsibilities to themselves (control problem), to their parts (humanization problem), and to the wider systems of which they themselves are parts (environmentalization problem). Managers should seek to serve all three sets of purposes, developing all the organization's stakeholders and removing any apparent conflict between them:

> A socially-systemically conceptualized enterprise has 'development' as its principal objective: its own development, that of its parts, and of the larger systems of which it is a part (1999a, p. 38).

If this is achieved, internal and external stakeholders will continue to pursue their interests through the organization and ensure that it remains viable and effective.

Social systems scientists, who want to support managers in the systems age, must be very careful how they classify systems. Ackoff identified four different types of system and four different types of systems model (1999b, pp. 28-33). "Deterministic" systems have no purposes and neither do their parts (although they can serve the purposes of other purposeful systems). "Animated" systems have purposes of their own, but their parts do not. "Social" systems have purposes of their own, contain purposeful parts and are usually parts of larger purposeful systems. "Ecological" systems contain interacting mechanistic, organismic and social systems, but unlike social systems have no purposes of their own. They serve the purposes of the biological and social systems that are their parts. Problems arise if a model of one type of system is applied to a system of a different type. A particular problem has been the tendency to apply deterministic or animate models to social systems:

> The effectiveness of any model used to describe and understand behavior of a particular system as a whole ultimately depends on the degree to which that model accurately represents that system. Nevertheless, there have been and are situations in which application of deterministic or animate models to social systems have produced useful results for *a short period of time*. However, in a longer run, such mismatches usually result in less than desirable results because critical aspects of the social systems were omitted in the less complex model that was used (1999b, p. 34).

Drawing upon his philosophy, and reflecting upon these changing conceptions of the world and of the corporation, Ackoff sets out a new approach to planning that, he believes, is more appropriate to our current predicament. This "interactive planning" is the main operating tool of Ackoff's S³. Its aim is to confront "messes" – systems of interdependent problems (Ackoff, 1981). Interactivist planners do not want to return to the past (like reactivist planners), keep thing as they are (like inactivists), or accept some inevitable future (the "predict and prepare" approach of preactivists). They take into account the past, the present and predictions about the future, but use these only as partial inputs into a process of planning aimed at designing a desirable future and inventing ways of bringing it about (Ackoff, 1979b, 1981). Interactivists believe that the future can be affected by what organizations and their stakeholders do now, and that what they should do is reach out for ideals. If inactivists satisfice in seeking to resolve problems and preactvists aim to optimize through solving problems then interactivists idealize and thus hope to dissolve problems. They change the system and/or the environment in which the problem is embedded so that the problem simply disappears. A good example of the dissolving approach at work in a large machine-tool manufacturing company is provided in Ackoff (1981).

This company was faced with abrupt changes in demand for its products and tended to respond by alternately hiring and firing personnel, many of whom were skilled workers. This policy led to low morale, poor productivity and bad labor relations. Management sought to "resolve" the problem, tackling symptoms as they arose on the basis of experience and common sense. Because the problem only seemed to get worse, however, it was decided to use the skill of some operational researchers to "solve" it once and for all. They defined the problem as one of production smoothing. Data were collected and the relevant systems identified and modeled. Optimum solutions were suggested on the basis of the performance of the model. Unfortunately, the results obtained were only slightly better than those yielded by the managers' feel for the situation. Obviously the success of the simulation depended crucially on accurate forecasts of demand being incorporated into the model, but the dynamics which gave rise to demand were just too complex to model. Finally, a problem "dissolving" approach was tried. The problem was formulated as one which required a reduction in the fluctuations in existing demand (rather than simply a response to these) and the organization was redesigned to achieve this. It was found that demand for road-building equipment was counter-cyclical to that for machine tools and, furthermore, production of road-building equipment required much of the same technology, marketing and distribution skills and some of the same parts and sub-assemblies. Adding road-building equipment as a product line reduced combined fluctuations in demand to a small fraction of the fluctuations from machine tools alone. Stable employment was achieved with a consequent improvement in productivity, cash flow difficulties and the industrial relations climate.

Interactive planning, therefore, is the specific approach recommended by Ackoff to translate his general philosophy and theory into practice. We now consider the principles and methodology of interactive planning.

7.5.2. Principles and Methodology of Interactive Planning

Three principles underpin interactive planning. These are the participative principle, the principle of continuity and the holistic principle. The participative principle rests upon two related ideas in Ackoff's thought. The first is that the process of planning is more important than the actual plan produced. It is through involvement in the planning that stakeholders come to understand the organization and the role they can play in it. It follows, of course, that no one can plan for anyone else – because this would take away the main benefit of planning (Ackoff, 1970a). The second idea is that all those who are affected by planning should be involved in it. This is a moral necessity for Ackoff, but it also stems directly from the philosophical argument that objectivity in social systems science is "value full."

The participative principle states, therefore, that all stakeholders should participate in the various stages of the planning process. If top management is reluctant to permit full participation, stakeholders can often gain admittance as "consultants." It is usually then possible to increase their involvement over time. It should be noted here that professional planners are by no means excluded from the interactive planning process; it is simply that their role has changed. They now use their expertise not to plan for others, but to help other plan for themselves. Thus the benefits of the solving approach (and the resolving, supplied by managers, as well) can be included in an essentially dissolving orientation. Perhaps the major paradox of the professional planner's existence – how to quantify quality of life so that it is possible to plan well for others – is also removed, once it is recognized that people should plan for themselves. All that is needed is a planning methodology that people can use, with the aid of professional planners, but ensuring that it is their own ideals and values that are paramount.

The second principle is that of continuity. The values of an organization's stakeholders will change over time and this will necessitate corresponding changes in plans. Also, unexpected events will occur. The plan may not work as expected, or changes in the organization's environment may change the situation in which it finds itself. No plan can predict everything in advance, so plans, under the principle of continuity, should be constantly revised.

The final principle is the holistic; we should plan simultaneously and interdependently for as many parts and levels of the system as it possible. This can be split into a principle of coordination, which states that units at the same level should plan together and at the same time (because it is the interactions between units that give rise to most problems), and a principle of integration which insists that units at different levels plan simultaneously and together (because decisions taken at one level will usually have effects at other levels as well).

With these principles in mind, we now consider the interactive planning methodology itself. This has five phases. These phases should, however, be regarded as constituting a systemic process and so may be started in any order. Also, none of the phases, let alone the whole process, should ever be regarded as completed. The five phases are (Ackoff, 1981, 1999a):

- Formulating the mess
- Ends planning
- Means planning
- Resource planning
- Design of implementation and control

Formulating the mess involves analyzing the problems and prospects, threats and opportunities facing the organization at present. This requires three types of study. A "systems analysis" is needed, giving a detailed picture of the organization, what it does, its stakeholders and relationships with its environment. An "obstruction analysis" sets out any obstacles to corporate development. "Reference projections" are prepared, which extrapolate on the organization's present performance in order to predict the future the organization would be faced with if it did nothing about things, and if developments in its environment continued in entirely predictable way. Synthesizing the results of these three types of study yields a "reference scenario", which is a formulation of the mess in which the organization currently finds itself.

Ends planning concerns specifying the ends to be pursued in terms of ideals, objectives and goals. It involves five steps. First, a mission statement is prepared. This should outline the organization's ultimate ends (its "ideals") and aim to generate commitment among all stakeholders. Second, planners should help the stakeholders to specify the properties that they would ideally like the organization and its actions to have. Thirdly, an idealized design of the organization should be prepared. Fourthly, the closest approximation to this design that is believed to be attainable should be formulated. Finally the gaps between the approximation and the current state of the system should be identified.

Idealized design is both the unique and most essential feature of Ackoff's approach. It should incorporate the "vision" that the stakeholders have for the organization. An idealized design is a design for the organization that the relevant stakeholders would replace the existing system with today, if they were free to do so. The notion that the organization or system involved was destroyed "last night", no longer exists and can be designed afresh today, is meant to generate maximum creativity among those involved. Using this notion as a premise, two kinds of design are then desirable - "bounded" and "unbounded." A bounded design allows a complete rethinking of the organization that it is assumed has been destroyed, but not of its environment. An unbounded design can see changes in the containing systems as well; as long as such changes would improve the performance of the organization being designed. In Ackoff's view, designers will find that most organizations can be considerably improved within the context of a bounded design. Unbounded design usually only points to some additional improvements that can be made. This is because most of the barriers to change are in the decision makers' own minds and in the organization itself.

The success of idealized design depends upon marshaling creativity. To ensure this, only three constraints upon the design are admissible. First, it must be technologically feasible and not a work of science fiction. In other words, it must be possible with known technology or likely technological developments. Second, it must be operationally viable. It should be capable of working and surviving if it were implemented in what would be its environment now. Thirdly, the design must be capable of being improved continuously from within and without. The aim of idealized design is not to produce a fixed, utopian design that seeks to specify what the system should be like for all time. This would not be sensible since the values and ideals of stakeholders are bound to change. Nor would it be possible, because the designers cannot have at their disposal the information and knowledge necessary to settle all important design issues or to predict the state of the organization's environment far into the future. For all these reasons it is essential that the designed system be capable of modification and of rapid learning and adaptation. It must be flexible and constantly seeking to improve its own performance. In short, what is intended is the design of the best "ideal-seeking" system that the stakeholders can imagine. This will not be static, like a utopia, but will be in constant flux as it responds to changing values, new knowledge and information, and buffeting from external forces. Beyond these three constraints everything is open. Constraints of a financial, political, or similar kind are not allowed to restrict the creativity of the design.

An idealized design should cover all aspects of an organization and Ackoff (1999a, p. 90) provides the following as a typical list:

- Products and services to be offered
- Markets to be served
- Distribution system
- Organizational structure
- Internal financial structure
- Management style
- Internal functions, such as:
    Purchasing
    Manufacturing
    Maintenance

          Engineering
          Marketing and sales
          Research and development
          Finance
          Accounting
          Human Resources
          Building and grounds
          Communications, internal and external
          Legal
          Planning
          Organizational development
          Computing and data processing
- Administrative services (e.g. mail and duplicating)
- Facilities
- Industry, government and community affairs

The remaining three stages of interactive planning are directed at realizing the idealized design as closely as possible. During means planning, policies and procedures are generated and examined to decide whether they are capable of helping to close the gap between the desired future, the idealized design, and the future the organization is currently locked into according to the reference scenario. Creativity is needed to discover appropriate ways of bringing the organization toward the desirable future invented by its stakeholders. Alternative means must be carefully evaluated and a selection made.

Resource planning sees five types of resource being considered: money; plant and equipment (capital goods); people; consumables (materials, supplies, energy and services); and data, information, knowledge, understanding and wisdom. For each of the chosen means, suitable resources have to be acquired. It must be determined how much of each resource is wanted, when it is wanted and how it can be obtained if not already held.

Design of implementation and control looks at procedures for ensuring that all the decisions made hitherto are carried out. Who is to do what, when, where, and how is decided. Implementation is achieved and the results monitored to ensure that plans are being realized. The outcome is fed back into the planning process so that learning is possible and improvements can be devised.

The advantages said to follow from pursuing interactive planning are many. In particular, Ackoff claims (1979b, 1981) that the methodology:

- Facilitates the participation of all stakeholders
- Allows incorporation of aesthetic values into planning
- Generates consensus
- Generates commitment and mobilizes participants
- Releases suppressed creativity and harnesses it to individual and organizational development
- Expands the participants' concept of feasibility
- Eases implementation

7.5.3. Models Used in Interactive Planning

There are five things that Ackoff (1999a) feels that corporations must do to function as effectively as currently is possible:

> plan effectively, learn and adapt rapidly and effectively, democratize, introduce internal market economies, and employ a structure that maximizes their flexibility but minimizes the need for frequent restructuring (p. 43).

We have covered the interactive planning that is so essential to a social-systemically conceptualized organization, and the reader of Ackoff's books and papers will find him using many methods, tools and techniques in support of the interactive planning process. She will also find four models, each of which is designed to assist with the other four things corporations must do. Ackoff is clear that these four models are only compatible with the social-systemic conceptualization. They can, therefore, be employed to help shift from an "organismic" to a social-systemic form of organization. In achieving this, however, transformational leadership is also required (Ackoff, 1999a). The four models are of a "learning and adaptation support system", a "democratic organization," an "internal market economy," and "a multidimensional organizational structure."

An ideal-seeking system obviously requires a very particular kind of organizational design; one that encourages rapid and effective learning and adaptation. Ackoff (1999a, 1999b) supplies an outline for such a design which he variously calls a "responsive, decision system," a "learning and adaptation support system," a "management system" and a "decision support system." This usually contains five essential functions:

- Identification and formulation of threats, opportunities and problems
- Decision making - determining what to do about these
- Implementation
- Control - monitoring performance and modifying actions
- Acquisition or generation, and distribution of the information necessary to perform the other functions

Ackoff's model of a "learning and adaptation support system" is built upon an array of feedback controls, takes account of the work of Argyris and Schön on organizational learning and emphasizes the necessity of "double-loop" learning. Another feature that I particularly like is Ackoff's insistence that, if an organization is going to learn from its mistakes, it must detect errors of omission as well as errors of commission. An error of commission occurs when something is done that should not have been done. Most corporations, especially bureaucracies, only look for this type of error and punish those who make it. Errors of omission occur when something is not done that should have been done. Although such errors can have disastrous consequences, few organizations pick them up. It follows that if you want to minimize your chances of being punished, it is best to do nothing.

The need for a "democratic organization" arises from the fact that managers, to ensure proper co-ordination and integration, need to focus on the interactions of parts rather than on controlling the parts directly; from the rising level of educational attainment among the workforce; and from dissatisfaction, in democratic societies, of working in organizations "that are as autocratic as fascist dictatorships" (Ackoff 1999a). Ackoff's design for a "democratic hierarchy" or "circular organization" rests on the fundamental idea that every manager within the organization should be provided with a "board." At the top level this will involve external stakeholders as well:

> It is through its board that the interests of an organization's various stakeholders can be brought into consideration in discussions leading up to decisions (1999a, p. 181).

Figure 7.3 is a representation of the basic circular organization, which will need to be varied wherever it is applied.

Each manager's board should minimally consist of the manager whose board it is; the immediate superior of this manager; the immediate subordinates of this manager; and any others invited to participate in a way defined by the board. Thus every individual should have a say in decisions that affect him. The functions of the board are defined as planning for the unit whose board it is, policy for that unit, co-ordination, integration, quality of work life, performance improvement, and approval of the boss. The last point means what it says. Ackoff argues that each board must be able to remove the manager whose board it is. Making her position subject to collective authority, in this way, is what democracy is about.

Ackoff has come face-to-face with many organizational problems which he describes as involving "internal finance." In such cases he has found that the solution involves

> replacing a centrally planned and controlled corporate economy with an internal market (1999a, p. 207).

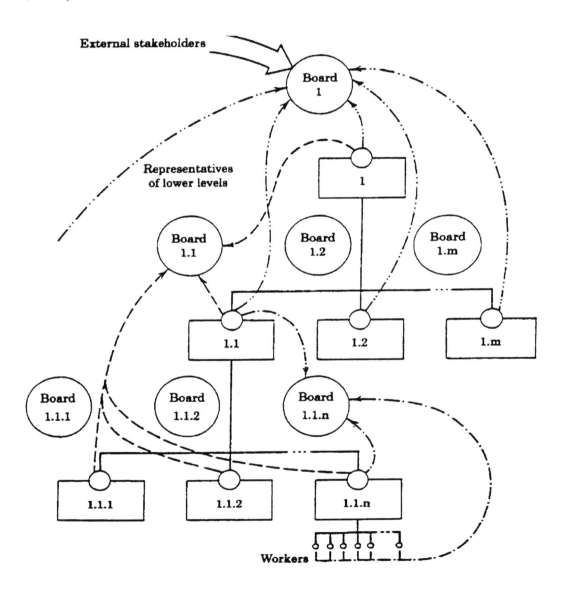

Figure 7.3. A circular organization (reproduced from Ackoff, 1999b, p. 336)

Every unit within an organization, including the executive office, must become a profit center, or a cost center for which some profit center is responsible. It should then be permitted to purchase goods and services from any internal and external supplier it chooses, and sell its output to any buyer it wishes. Higher authorities can override such buying and selling decisions but, if they do so, they are required to compensate the unit for any loss of income or increased costs due to the intervention. Ackoff (1999a, pp. 209-210) gives the example of Mobil's corporate computing center. This center was budgeted for and subsidized from above and, because none of the internal users paid for its services, there was no measure of the value of its services. All that was known was that the computer center itself was overloaded and its customers complained of the service they received. A new CEO agreed with Ackoff that it be made a profit center, charging what it wanted and selling externally if it wished. Internal users of the center were permitted to seek similar services outside. The costs of the computer center were reduced dramatically because, now they had to pay for its services, others used it more sparingly. At the same time the center became profitable by improving its service and gaining a substantial amount of external business.

A "multidimensional organizational structure" is to be recommended because it makes an organization more flexible and eliminates the need for continual restructuring. Organizations divide their labor in three ways and, in so doing, create three types of organizational unit:

- functionally defined units whose output is primarily consumed internally
- production- or service-defined units whose output is primarily consumed externally
- market- or user-defined units defined by type or location of customers

Reorganizations occur when the relative importance of the three ways of dividing labor changes and the system adjusts the level in the hierarchy at which different types of unit are manifested. Ackoff argues that time and effort can be saved if units of each type are placed permanently at every level. Restructuring can then be replaced by reallocating resources.

7.5.4. Case Study - A Black Ghetto's Research on a University

Ackoff (see especially 1999a, b) provides many examples of interactive planning in use, and at the Center for Systems Studies, University of Hull, the approach has been successfully employed, often in combination with other methodologies, in a number of projects; for example, in a diversion from custody project for mentally disordered offenders (Cohen and Midgley, 1994), in developing services for the improvement of housing for older people (Midgley, Munlo and Brown, 1996) and to develop services with young people missing from home or care (Boyd, Brown and Midgley, 1999). Here I take an earlier example describing work in the Mantua ghetto in Philadelphia in the late 1960s. This was one of the studies that gave rise to, rather than resulted from, interactive planning. It enables us to see how a properly designed action research program can produce learning of relevance for the community concerned and about the methodology and theory used in the project.

The project is described in an article by Ackoff (1970b) titled *A Black Ghetto's Research on a University*. It begins by complimenting OR on its technical development during the 1950s and 1960s but argues that, if OR is to continue to thrive, it will have to increase its relevance to important social issues and to strategic problems. OR will also have to enlarge its stock of concepts, its methodology and its philosophy. A good opportunity to begin the process, arose when, in 1968, Ackoff's group at the University of Pennsylvania received a request for assistance from the Mantua Community Planners (a coalition of neighborhood groups).

The Mantua ghetto in Philadelphia had, at the time, a population of about 22,000, which was 98% black. It was an area of critical underdevelopment and its population suffered from considerable poverty and disadvantage. The approach adopted by Ackoff's group was to insist that, while help could be provided, the ghetto community had to solve its problems in its own way. To get the benefits of planning, the ghetto community had to plan for itself. Three people from the ghetto community (soon to be joined by a fourth) were, therefore, employed at the university to work on the development of their community, taking advantage of university facilities (office space, secretarial aid, a graduate student assistant) but using these only as *they* saw fit.

Over the first weekend of the project, the team of three developed a program for their activities and proposed regular weekly meetings with the relevant university faculty. Soon requests for assistance from the ghetto community were flooding in, and a full-time senior member of the university staff had to be appointed to coordinate the requests for aid and the many offers of help from university personnel. After 6 months, further funding was received from the Anheuser-Busch Charitable Trust and additional money secured from the Ford Foundation to guarantee the project for 2 years.

During the course of the project, the Mantua Community Planners and the Young Great Society (another important ghetto group involved) increased their influence in ghetto affairs considerably and significant achievements were recorded. Manufacturing firms were set up and coordinated with other business enterprises in an industrial complex. Employment services were offered. A Mantua Community Federal Credit Union was established offering low-interest loans. An Architectural and Planning Center and a Joint Workshop (with university staff and students) produced neighborhood development plans. Two weekly newspapers and a newsletter were launched, and public meetings organized to discuss plans and issues of importance affecting the ghetto. Educational and recreational facilities were provided. A comprehensive list of what the "Mantuans [have] done for themselves, in which we have been of some help" is given by Ackoff (1970b).

Drawing out implications from the success of the Mantua project, Ackoff makes, perhaps, five points. First, the methodology adopted in the Mantua project offers a better way of carrying out research. University staff learned far more about the ghetto by being directly involved in it, under the guidance of its members, than they could have done using traditional research methods. Further, their knowledge was recognized by the relevant client, the ghetto leaders.

Second, the consultancy relationship was enhanced by not specifying to the client what skills the university faculty could offer. The ghetto leaders had to carry out research on the university to see how it might be useful. This is recommended as a useful way forward for OR in other contexts. OR has been relegated to the solution of technical and tactical problems because of its own propaganda, which boasts of its success in tackling these.

Third, because the ghetto could not rely on receiving resources to fund its planning proposals, its planning efforts constantly had to consider and respond to the wider system of which it was part, in order to generate the new resources necessary. It had to develop in tandem with the wider community to secure support for ghetto activities.

Fourth, planning had to be participative. Plans could not be imposed from above because of the complete dependence of the ghetto leaders upon their constituents. The ghetto leaders had continually to respond to the wishes of the "subsystems" that made up the systems they were trying to manage. It would be good practice in industry, Ackoff argues, if leaders were made subject to the authority of those controlled by their authority.

Finally, the approach to planning which simply predicts change in the environment and attempts to respond to it (predict and prepare) has to be abandoned. Most of the trends in the larger systems of which the black ghetto was part were detrimental to it. The future could not, therefore, be allowed to run its course. Active intervention in the wider environment was required in order to change the trends – what Ackoff describes, elsewhere, as designing a desirable future and finding ways of bringing it about.

Most of these five lessons find expression in the motto of the Mantua Community Planners: "Plan or be planned for." Blacks had to plan for themselves. They had to learn how to use available resources, such as those at the university and teach the university staff how to help them. They had to engage in continuous, adaptive and participative planning, involving the wider systems and all the subsystems in their plans. Most important of all, they had better not sit back and hope that nothing detrimental would happen to them. Unless they got out and designed a desirable future for themselves, they would become prey to somebody else's plans. They should not, therefore, predict and prepare but engage in idealized design of their own future.

The lessons of the Mantua research were given full expression in the book *Creating the Corporate Future* (Ackoff, 1981), subtitled "Plan or Be Planned For." In this volume Ackoff sets out the detailed methodology through which desirable futures can be planned and pursued. This "interactive planning" has as its operating principles, as we saw, that planning should be continuous, holistic, and participative and has, as its most original element, the idea that the phases of the planning process should be centered on the design of an "idealized" future. It is a methodology which effectively realizes the insight of "plan or be planned for" by endorsing it in its philosophy and providing a set of practical procedures through which the philosophical message is empowered.

The black ghetto example inspired later "Community OR" work in the U.K. In particular, the aims of extending awareness of OR to new sections of the community, while enriching OR methodology through involvement in novel situations, are central to the initiative (see Rosenhead, 1986), just as they drove the Mantua project. The Mantua project stands as an inspiring demonstration of the potential of Community OR for achieving these aims.

7.5.5. Strengths and Weaknesses of Interactive Planning

Ackoff's development of S^3, with its commitment to the notion that messes should be dissolved by designing a desirable future and inventing ways of bringing it about, has taken him a long way from some of his erstwhile colleagues stuck in the predict-and-prepare paradigm of hard systems thinking. To cope adequately with the complexity and turbulence found in and around organizations in the systems age, the emphasis has to shift to learning and adapting. The diverse values of different stakeholders are harnessed by interactive planning and managed by the participative involvement of the stakeholders at all stages of the planning process. Idealized design seeks to minimize petty differences of opinion between individuals and groups by focusing their attention on the ultimate ends they would like to see an organization pursuing. At the same time, it allows different stakeholders to incorporate their own aesthetic values into idealized design. Models such as the "learning and adaptation support system" provide guidance on how to improve decision makers' control over what can be controlled, while increasing responsiveness to what is uncontrollable.

One of the undoubted strengths of Ackoff's approach is that he does not see systems-age thinking as simply replacing machine-age thinking. Rather, he sees them as complementary and allocates space for the solving and resolving approaches within his basically dissolving orientation to social systems science. Much of the power of interactive planning stems from its ability to respond to diverse aspects of messes as revealed by a number of images of organization. Ackoff emphasizes that organizations are purposeful systems containing other purposeful systems and are part of wider purposeful systems. This inevitably brings the culture and political systems metaphors to the fore. The aim of idealized design is to enthuse the participants with a vision of what their organizations might be like and to endow them with a mission to create a desirable future on this basis. The process is meant to generate consensus, mobilize the stakeholders with a crusading zeal, and reveal that only the participants' limited imaginations prevent them getting the future they most desire right here, right now. This is all about developing a strong organizational culture that is shared by all the participants and yet encourages creativity. It needs remembering, however, that though Ackoff distances himself from the machine and organism metaphors, and builds interactive planning on more sophisticated views of the organization, he is still willing to make use of what the earlier thinking had to offer in support of his own preferred approach. S^3 seems to combine much of the best that can be gleaned from the culture and political system metaphors with considerable input from the machine, organism and brain metaphors as well. The idea of the organization as a brain leads to and supports the emphasis upon learning and adaptation as encapsulated in the "learning and adaptation support system." It is interesting that his chapter on this subject in *Ackoff's Best* (1999b) is headed by a quotation from Stafford Beer – a friend, but someone with whom he profoundly disagrees about the fundamental nature of social systems.

Given the violence of his assault upon hard systems thinkers, it is perhaps surprising that the main criticisms of Ackoff's work do not come from that source but from advocates of other more radical theoretical positions, anticipating what would now be called emancipatory systems thinking. In Dando and Bennett's (1981) terms, proponents of the "official" position in OR and systems have been unable to defend themselves against "reformist" soft systems thinkers and have been intellectually routed. It is a group of "revolutionary" - minded thinkers in systems and OR who took up the reformist challenge and sought to advance the debate further. What Ackoff misses, according to these critics, is what he would see if he were willing to view organizations as "psychic prisons" or "instruments of domination." According to these metaphors, organizational stakeholders do not share common interests, their values and beliefs conflict fundamentally and they are unable to agree upon ends and means, or reach a genuine compromise, under present systemic arrangements. If the system continues to hold together, it is because of coercive forces binding the less powerful to it.

It is Ackoff's inability to look at organizations from the emancipatory perspective that has led to a persistent line of critical attack launched at his work (see Jackson, 1982, 1983). First, interactive planning is accused of adopting a consensus worldview. Ackoff seems to believe that there is a basic community of interest among stakeholders that makes it likely they will participate freely and openly in an idealized design. If any conflict of interest does arise between system, supersystem and subsystems, it can apparently be dissolved by appealing to this basic community of interest at a higher level of desirability (Ackoff, 1975). To the critics this does not give serious enough attention to the deep-seated conflict and coercion they see as endemic in organizations and society (Chesterton *et al.*, 1975; Rosenhead, 1976). If irreconcilable conflict between stakeholders is frequent, as the critics assert, then Ackoff's approach is impotent because no agreement can be reached in such cases concerning the idealized future. Ackoff (1975), it is argued, tries to fix the argument in his favor by defining irreconcilable conflicts as those that involve logically incompatible ends. Since his methodology is oriented to the world of ideas, to expanding individual conceptions of the feasible, it is always going to be open to him to claim that a conflict is resolvable at a higher level of desirability. As Bryer (1979) argues: "It is an axiom of Ackoff's systems view that a 'higher' system can always be found as the only limits to systems boundaries are the subjective conceptualizations of the analyst." In the real world, however, it is easy to see that a social structure can operate such that it is impossible for all different groups to achieve their ends. Rosenhead (1976) argues that "only by abolishing the sweat-shop owner as a social category can his interest and those of his laborers be made compatible." From this perspective we need to talk about the social incompatibility of ends, not their logical incompatibility.

Second, it is argued by the critics that Ackoff's one-sided appreciation of social reality, a consensus rather than conflict view, leads him to take the possibility of participation for granted and to overestimate it as a remedy for organizational problems. Participation is essential to interactive planning, philosophically because it provides the justification for the objectivity of the results and practically because it generates creativity and ensures implementation. Perhaps because of its significance, Ackoff plays down the obstacles to full and effective participation. To get started, his interactive planning depends on all the stakeholders being prepared to enter into participative planning about the future. But will the powerful be willing to forgo their dominant position and submit their privileges to the vagaries of idealized design? Even if interactive planning can be started, another problem will be encountered. The methodology depends for the objectivity of its results on free and open discussion between stakeholders, but planning is complex and time-consuming. We cannot realistically expect that less privileged stakeholders will be able to participate equally in the planning process. Whatever help the analyst can give to less fortunate groups, the various stakeholders will enter the interactive planning process with widely divergent informational, political, and economic resources. The less privileged may additionally feel threatened by the massive resources that can be mobilized by the powerful, and limit their demands to what is "realistic" (Rosenhead, 1984). The organization will already represent a "mobilization of bias" against them in a way that requires no representation or advocacy (Bevan, 1980). The less privileged may even find themselves under the sway of a dominant ideology, through the mists of which they fail altogether to recognize their own true interests. Any discussion or debate among stakeholders can only, therefore, be exceptionally constrained.

Third, it is said that the belief of Ackoff in a consensual social world, and in the efficacy of participation, is only sustained because he artificially limits the scope of his projects so as not to challenge his clients' or sponsors' fundamental interests. In his research, Ackoff will only go so far as "circumstances permit." No matter, as Rosenhead (1976) argues:

> These circumstances are not facts of nature, but are the 'consequences' of particular social institutions (especially the project's sponsors) and their purposes. The circumstances 'permit' acts of social engineering which appear to resolve social conflicts; they do not 'permit' analyses or acts which challenge the sponsors' interests (p. 76).

If Ackoff were to truly challenge the sponsors' interests he would soon provoke conflicts that revealed deep status, economic and other inequalities in organizations that could not be spirited away by soft approaches.

Finally, related to the other points (at the root of the other points according to Mingers, 1984), soft approaches, such as interactive planning, can be criticized for their "subjectivism" or "idealism" and for their consequent failure to come to terms with structural features of social reality such as conflict and power. For Ackoff, it can be argued, conflict is always at the ideological level and is essentially dealt with by ideological manipulation. Perhaps it is possible to alleviate conflict temporarily at the ideological level by getting people to believe they have interests in common. But the subjective beliefs of groups about their interests do not necessarily coincide with their objective interests. Permanent reconciliation of conflicts between stakeholders might need to be in terms of objective and not merely subjective interests. To Rosenhead (1984), the fact that Ackoff ignores conflict and power is attributable to his "idealism" – the fact that he ascribes "prime motive power to the force of ideas." Another consequence of this idealism is that it limits his ability to understand how change comes about and hence the ability to promote change.

Unlike hard systems thinkers, Ackoff (1975, 1982) has responded vigorously to the charges leveled against his approach. He does not think much of any of the critics' arguments. If his work appears consensual to the critics, Ackoff believes it is because they are obsessed with the notion of irresolvable conflicts (as they would be from their emancipatory perspective). Ackoff (1982) has never encountered one of these in more than 300 projects on which he has worked. All the conflicts he has met, he has been able to address with the interactive planning approach. He suspects that the critics merely assert that such conflicts exist; if they went out and tried to use interactive planning on conflicts they see as irresolvable, they might find out differently.

With regard to participation, Ackoff (1975) accepts that it might meet with some resistance from powerful stakeholders. But there are ways around this, such as by introducing stakeholders first as consultants and then gradually increasing their role. The ability of low-level stakeholders to participate can, of course, be aided by professional planners. The idea that such stakeholders might not recognize their own true interests is elitist. In any case, just because full and equal participation cannot immediately be realized is a poor reason for not making whatever progress can be made. Better incremental change, Ackoff argues, than waiting for some judgment day when all wrongs will be corrected. Nor does Ackoff (1982) feel constrained by spending much of his time working with managers as his sponsors. They are often the most enlightened social group, he finds, and can see that benefiting other stakeholders will also benefit themselves. Finally, Ackoff (1975, 1982) simply does not accept the existence of the structural aspects of social reality that the critics discuss. The chief obstruction between people and the future they most desire is the people themselves and their limited ability to think creatively and imaginatively. Provide people with a mission, with a mobilizing idea, and the constraints on their and their organization's development will largely disappear.

In the exchanges between Ackoff and his critics we are witnessing a war between sociological paradigms; as we shall see even more clearly when we come to the general critique of interpretive systems approaches at the end of this chapter.

7.6. CHECKLAND'S SOFT SYSTEMS METHODOLOGY (SSM)

In the United Kingdom, in 1969, Peter Checkland and his colleagues at Lancaster University began an action-research program designed to extend the usefulness of systems ideas to ill-structured management problems. The aim was to produce a systems methodology capable of intervening in "soft" problem situations and of sharpening up, under special circumstances, to tackle more structured problems. Initially they used the systems engineering methodology of Jenkins. This demanded well-structured problems and clearly defined objectives and measures of performance. Obviously, these demands had to be loosened and the methodology radically adapted to make it appropriate for dealing with the complexity and ambiguity of the softer contexts in which it was now to be applied. What eventually emerged after considerable project work and reflection upon the experience gained was an entirely different kind of approach – Checkland's "soft systems methodology" (Checkland, 1976, 1981; Checkland and Scholes, 1990; Checkland and Holwell, 1998).

In the first full account of the methodology (Checkland, 1976), Checkland describes three of the most significant early project experiences that led to the formulation of SSM. In all three it was clear that serious problems existed, but the clients simply could not say what these were in precise terms. Each of the problem situations was, therefore, vague and unstructured. One of the projects, in a textile firm, gave rise to at least a dozen candidates for the role of "the problem." Generalizing from the three projects, Checkland was able to specify what the key features of SSM had to be and how these differentiated SSM from hard approaches.

First, in confronting softer problems, the analysis phase of a methodology should not be pursued in systems terms. In the absence of agreed goals and objectives, and an obvious hierarchy of systems to be engineered, using systems ideas too early can only lead to distorting the problem situation and to jumping to premature conclusions. Analysis, in soft systems approaches, should consist of building up the richest possible picture of the problem situation and not of trying to represent it in a systems account. Second, given that it is not obvious which system needs to be engineered, it is more appropriate to draw out of the analysis a range of systems relevant to improving the problem situation, each expressing a particular viewpoint of it. These notional systems can be named in "root definitions" and developed more fully in "conceptual models." The use of SSM will therefore lead to the construction of a number of models to be compared with the real world, rather than just one as in hard methodologies. Finally, while the models produced by hard approaches are blueprints for design, conceptual models are contributions to a debate about change. Hard methodologies, therefore, lead to the design of systems, SSM to the implementation of agreed changes.

Checkland likes to insist that SSM was derived and has developed as a result of experiences such as those encountered in these early projects. If this is meant to downplay the role that theory has played in the evolution of SSM, then it is misleading and hardly does justice to the strong theoretical element that has always been present in the research side of his action-research program. It is clear in fact that soft systems methodology had benefited all along from being theoretically informed; early on by the work of Churchman and Vickers, later by the interpretive philosophical and sociological theories of Dilthey, Husserl, Schutz and Weber, and the social theory classification of Burrell and Morgan. Certainly it is because he has been able to theorize so thoroughly his break with hard systems thinking that his writings do not betray the "tensions" between hard and soft positions that, as we shall see, he identified in Ackoff's and Churchman's work. Checkland is the purest of the interpretive systems thinkers because he recognized the theoretical direction in which soft systems thinking was heading, made this explicit and consciously constructed SSM on the basis of new, interpretive theoretical foundations. It is because of this, more even than because of the methodology itself, that his writings have had such a great impact on systems thinking and practice. We begin by examining this theoretical contribution.

7.6.1 Soft Systems Philosophy and Theory

In reflecting upon the shift of perspective achieved by SSM, Checkland (1983) suggested that whereas hard systems methodologies are based upon a paradigm of optimization, his own methodology embraces a paradigm of learning. Hard methodologies are concerned with achieving objectives. They are modeled on the natural scientific method and so aim to provide generalizable knowledge about structured occurrences. They seek this knowledge in management science by concentrating on the "logic of the situation" in organizations seen as driven by the official goals. Thus the world is taken to contain systems whose performance can be optimized by following systematic procedures. Unfortunately for the hard approach, in social systems the logic of the situation is usually much less significant in terms of what happens than the cultural interconnections forged from the meanings attributed to the situation by individuals and groups. SSM, recognizing this, seeks to work with the different perceptions of the situation, setting in motion a systemic process of learning in which different viewpoints are discussed and examined in a manner that should lead to purposeful action in pursuit of improvement.

Checkland's approach takes reality to be problematical and ceases to worry about knowing it ontologically; instead it concentrates on using a systemic methodology to investigate problems arising from the existence of different accounts of the reality. Put concisely (Checkland, 1989), it shifts "systemicity from the world to the process of enquiry into the world." Because hard systems thinking depends on objectives and purposes already being agreed (or imposed) – the very thing SSM concentrates on engineering – hard methodologies are a special case of the soft. They become relevant when learning reduces to optimizing because, given agreement over goals, only one system appears relevant and problem resolving turns on the best way to design that.

Using slightly different terminology, Checkland (1985a) argues that hard systems methodologies are predicated on the goal-seeking model of human behavior as exemplified in Herbert Simon's work, while SSM reflects a model of human behavior oriented to "relationship-maintaining" as set down in the writings of Vickers. This is demonstrated by the concern of hard systems thinkers with *how* we should achieve known goals, with prediction and control and with optimization. In soft systems thinking the emphasis is, rather, on *what* we ought to do and on participation and learning.

Checkland (1981) judges other systems thinking according to how far it has managed to rid itself of the goal-seeking and optimizing orientation. Hard approaches, as we have seen, stand irredeemably condemned, suitable for only a small subset of the difficulties that confront managers. The work of the socio-technical thinkers and of Beer is seen to rest firmly in the hard tradition. These authors each offer only one model of the whole system, which they take to encapsulate the optimum organizational arrangements for an enterprise intent on goal seeking. SSM prefers to generalize the methodology rather than the content of models. Ackoff's interactive planning is taken to resemble soft systems methodology in some respects, but too much use of the goal-seeking model is made, as with the emphasis put on the idealized design of the future. For Checkland, attempting to define an ideal future and get consensus on it presents immense difficulties. There is also evidence that Ackoff continues to believe in systems "in the world." Even Churchman does not escape completely from the hard paradigm. His work, Checkland believes, remains wedded to the notion of design, the main concern being with the design of goal-seeking systems in a systemic world (1981, 1988).

What Checkland (1981) knows he has achieved at a still deeper theoretical level, and what all the above arguments announce, is a complete break with the functionalism that has traditionally dominated the systems approach. SSM is closer to the interpretive sociology of Weber than the functionalism of Durkheim, and to the pheno-menology of Husserl and Schutz, and the hermeneutics of Dilthey, than to the positivism of Comte and Durkheim. It has more in common with the action theory Silverman (1970) constructed, in opposition to the dominant "systems" approach to organizations, than to the functionalist, organizations-as-systems approaches he attacks. Checkland rightly argues, therefore, that the social theory implicit in his methodology is interpretive rather than functionalist, and that its underlying philosophical base is in phenomenology rather than positivism. In soft systems methodology, systems are seen as the mental constructs of observers in the world. Different descriptions of reality, based on different worldviews, are embodied in root definitions. These root definitions are turned into conceptual models that are explicitly one-sided representations expressing a *Weltanschauung* – in other words, they are Weberian ideal types. A debate is then structured around the implications of these different perceptions of what reality could be like. Systemicity is transferred from the world to the process of inquiry into the world.

On completion of this section on Checkland's SSM, the reader may wish to refer back to the brief accounts provided in Chapter 4 of the work of Vickers, Weber, Husserl, Schutz, Dilthey and Silverman, in order to satisfy herself about Checkland's argument. Table 7.2 (from Atkinson, 1984, p. 17) gives a specific comparison between Checkland's SSM, Vickers's theory of appreciative systems, and Schutz's phenomenology, for guidance.

Checkland (1981) draws together his theoretical arguments by referring to Burrell and Morgan's (1979) grid of sociological paradigms (see Chapter 3). He argues that the implied social theory of hard systems approaches is functionalism. They are clearly regulative and objectivist in orientation. SSM, however, is more subjectivist in character and extends somewhat toward the radical change axis (refer to Figure 3.1), so

Table 7.2. Mappings between Checkland's soft systems methodology, Vickers's notion of appreciative systems and Schutz's phenomenology (reproduced from Atkinson, 1984, p. 17)

CHECKLAND'S SOFT SYSTEMS METHODOLOGY	VICKERS'S THEORY OF APPRECIATIVE SYSTEMS	SCHUTZ'S PHENOMENOLOGY OF THE INDIVIDUAL ACTOR
Problem situation	Worlds of events and ideas	Life-world
"Concern"	"Mismatch"	"Shock" "Act of attention"
1. Rich picture building 2. Problem theme development	Appreciation of situation via fact and value judgments	Meaning attribution
3. Root definitions 4. Conceptual model building	Instrumental judgments regarding strategies-source, appreciative world and schemata	Identification of projects-source, stocks of knowledge and life project, gives in-order-to motives
5. Comparison of the models with real world 6. Debate over systemic desirability and cultural feasibility	Reference back to appreciative world for executive decision on action to change course in the milieu	Selection of an appropriate project and course of action in line with our genuine-because motivation
7. Take action to improve the problem situation. This produces a new problem situation, the cycle begins again.	Take executive action to alter the course in the milieu to achieve stable relationships. This in turn produces new change in the worlds of events and ideas which can be problematical	Perpetrate the act in line with the project selected. This produces changes in one's life-world which in turn produces a new start and the demand for meaning attribution

the social theory implicit in soft systems methodology ....would lie in the left-hand quadrants with hermeneutics and phenomenology, although the position would be not too far left of the center line because the methodology will over a period of time yield a picture of the common structurings which characterize the social collectivities within which it works. Also given the analyst's complete freedom to select relevant systems which, when compared with the expression of the problem situation, embody either incremental or radical change, the area occupied must include some of the `subjective/radical` quadrant (Checkland 1981, pp. 280-281).

In support of his claim that the implied social theory of SSM embraces aspects of radical humanism (the subjective/radical quadrant), Checkland refers to a paper by Mingers (1980) that reveals some apparent similarities between the social theory of Habermas and SSM. This matter will require further attention in the "critique" section of this chapter.

As a final argument, closing the theory/practice loop, Checkland suggests that the failure experienced by himself and his colleagues when trying to use systems engineering, in their action research program, to solve problems in social systems discredits the functionalist account of social reality. In contrast, the success of SSM suggests that the phenomenological version of what the social world is like is correct. This alternative approach views social reality as

> constantly being constructed and reconstructed in a social process in which meanings are negotiated .... an `organization` does not exist as an independent entity but is part of sense making by a group of people engaged in dialogue (Checkland and Holwell. 1998, pp. 40-41).

Checkland and Holwell (1998), seeking to develop a richer concept of organization for the purpose of guiding information systems work, are brave enough to set out the model of "organization" that SSM has come to adopt as a result of the action research. Any such model, they state, must capture the tension between the willingness of individuals to organize for the rational pursuit of goals and the "sheer cussedness and irrationality" that they sometimes display. "Organization" arises from discourse between two or more individuals, out of which may emerge: a degree of agreement on purposes; social processes to pursue the purposes; and criteria for evaluating success in relation to the pursuit of those purposes. This, in turn, may lead to the definition of organizational "roles" and the establishment of "norms" and "values." These roles, norms and values are constantly renegotiated as part of the ongoing discourse. According to this analysis,

> an organization is clearly an abstraction: it is a social collectivity concerned with some collective action, and there are associated social practices which relate to this. But what causes it, as an entity, to exist? The answer can only be : the readiness of some people, usually large numbers of people, members and non-members alike, to talk and act as if there were a collective entity which could behave like a conscious being, with the ability to do things and then make them happen .... This way of thinking about an organization is rather abstract, but it is necessary to make sense of what we all know from observation and experience, namely that members of organizations are not necessarily simply quiescent contributors to the achievement of organizational goals (Checkland and Holwell. 1998, pp. 80-81).

Figure 7.4. expresses pictorially this rather "slippery" concept of an "organization." The notion of "organization" is treated as much more problematical; as depending for its very existence on the readiness of members and non-members to engage with it as if it were an entity capable of purposeful action in its own right. Despite their willingness to conform in this way, there will be many different conceptualizations of the nature and aims of the organization, based on the different values and interests of various individuals and sub-groups, apart from the "official" version of its purpose. Because the different values and

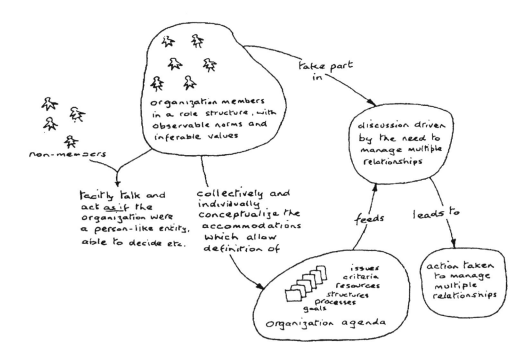

Figure 7.4. A richer model of the concept "an organization" (reproduced from Checkland and Holwell, 1998, p. 83)

interests will rarely coincide exactly, the "organization" depends upon the establishment of temporary "accommodations" between individuals and sub-groups which can provide a basis for action. And,

> following Vickers, the action is here expressed [in Figure 7.4] more richly as managing a (changing) set of relationships, rather than taking rational decisions to achieve goals. Philosophically this is a phenomenological model, sociologically an interpretive one (Checkland and Holwell, 1998, p. 84).

SSM helps to manage relationships by orchestrating a process through which organizational actors can learn and find out what accommodations are feasible and desirable.

7.6.2. Soft Systems Methodology

One problem with describing SSM is that it can still lead to multiple interpretations of how it should be used. Indeed, even those who might be regarded as familiar with the methodology and practiced with it seem to use it in rather different ways (Atkinson, 1986). Checkland would want to retain considerable flexibility for practitioners but needs to be able to say that some examples are simply not proper uses of SSM. This is a significant point because many declared uses of the methodology turn out, on closer examination, to be following "hard" reasoning, although dressed in soft language. In order to judge whether SSM is being employed correctly or not requires reference to the philosophy on which it is based. This is why it is even more important for those learning how to use SSM to become completely familiar with its underlying philosophy than it is for them to be adept at the techniques that support its various stages. Checkland has spent considerable time and effort explicating this philosophy as described in the last sub-section. He also provides lists of "constitutive rules" (Checkland, 1981; Checkland and Scholes, 1990) which prescribe certain principles that have to be followed in any genuine soft systems study. We are adapting the Checkland and Scholes version of the constitutive rules to arrive at our generic functionalist, interpretive, emancipatory and postmodern systems methodologies. The rules act as a kind of bridge to ensure that the philosophy is carried over into the practice.

Another, less significant, difficulty in describing SSM is that it has changed over time in response to the learning gained from its use in action research. I will outline three variants of the approach in chronological order – Mode 1, Mode 2 and SSM for information systems developments - before highlighting some of the most important features of SSM.

7.6.2.1 Mode 1 SSM

Although Checkland no longer uses it, the representation of SSM as a seven-stage learning system, which appeared in 1981 in *Systems Thinking, Systems Practice*, is still the best known today. It is shown in Figure 7.5. and reference should be made to this representation throughout the following discussion.

In the first and second stages a problem situation is entered and expressed and a "rich picture" of the situation is built up. As was mentioned earlier, it is important not to impose a definition on the problem at this early stage, by viewing it in systems terms. The aim is not to delimit particular problems "out there" in the real world but to gain and disseminate an understanding of a situation with which various participants feel a degree of unease. The early guidelines offered, for gathering information to express in a "neutral" rich picture, emphasized finding out about "structure" and "process" and thinking about the relationship between them – the "climate." Not long after, it became clear that a good way of doing the

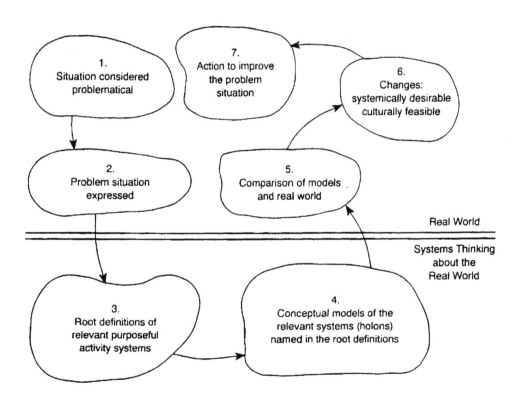

Figure 7.5. The learning cycle of soft systems methodology (adapted from Checkland, 1989, p. 84).

expression stage was to take the notion of rich pictures literally, and to draw pictorial, cartoon-like representations of the problem situation which highlight significant and contentious aspects in a manner likely to lead to original thinking later in the methodological cycle. The drawing of rich pictures has proved to be one of the most successful and frequently used of the methods and techniques that have come to be associated with SSM. Rich pictures aid creativity, allowing the easy sharing of ideas between organizational actors, are able to show interrelationships better than linear prose, and act as an excellent memory aid. Figure 7.6 is an example of a rich picture, drawn by Maria Carolina Ortegon (1999), of the "edge of chaos" state in complexity theory as described by Stacey.

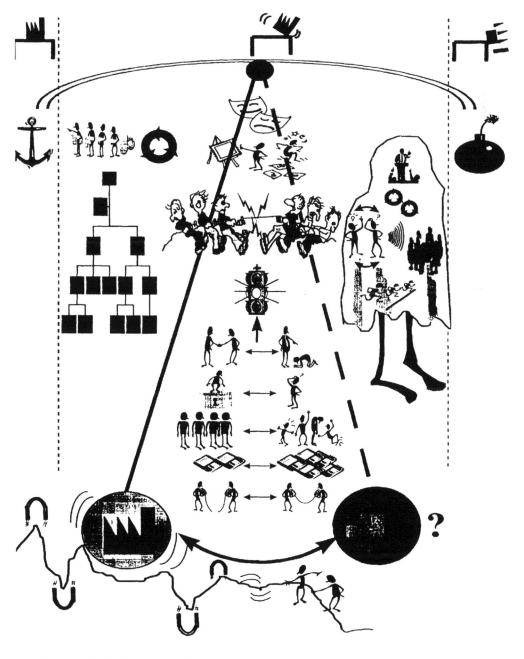

Figure 7.6. Rich picture of the "edge of chaos" (reproduced from Ortegon, 1999, p. 39)

The third activity involves choosing relevant human activity systems, offering insight into the problem situation, and preparing "root definitions" from these relevant systems. A root definition should be a condensed representation of a system in its most fundamental form. To ensure that root definitions are well formulated, they should be constructed giving consideration to all the elements brought to mind by the mnemonic CATWOE (customers, actors, transformation process, *Weltanschauung*, owners, environmental constraints). As an example of a well-formulated root definition, Checkland (1989) provides the following: "A professionally-manned system in a manufacturing company which, in the light of market forecasts and raw material availability, makes detailed production plans for a defined period." This is, in fact, a primary-task root definition setting out an official, explicit task to be performed. Issue-based definitions should also be put forward at Stage 3, designed to address particular issues of consequence in the problem situation (e.g, conflict between two departments). As the W in CATWOE indicates, each root definition reflects a different way of looking at the problem situation. For example, in considering a prison, it might be helpful to consider it as a punishment system, a rehabilitation system, a system for taking revenge, a system to protect society and as a system that constitutes a "university of crime" (Checkland, 1987). It follows that there are no correct or incorrect root definitions, only more or less insightful ones.

Stage 4 involves the construction of conceptual models of the systems defined in the root definitions. Conceptual models consist initially of seven or so verbs, structured in logical sequence and representing those minimum activities that are necessary to achieve the purpose enshrined in the root definitions. They can be developed to further levels of resolution by taking any of the activities as the source of a new root definition, which can then itself be modeled in more detail. Conceptual models do not seek to describe the real world or some ideal system to be engineered, but are merely accentuated, one-sided views of possible, relevant human activity systems. For this reason it is important that they are derived primarily from their root definitions so that a complementary pair of artifacts is produced: the root definition expressing what the system *is*, the conceptual model what it *does*. Once constructed, conceptual models can be checked against Checkland's (1981) "formal system model" to ensure that they are not fundamentally deficient. This is also the point in SSM where other systems thinking can be introduced as appropriate. For example, an analyst modeling a whole institution might produce a conceptual model reflecting the logic of Beer's VSM. The general structure of conceptual models is shown in Figure 7.7.

Conceptual models, developed if necessary to a higher level of resolution, are then brought back "above the line" (see Figure 7.5) to be compared with what is perceived to exist in the problem situation according to the rich picture produced at Stage 2. Four different ways of doing such a comparison have been developed (Checkland, 1981, 1989). Whichever method is used, the aim is to provide material for debate about possible changes among those concerned with the problem situation. Thus SSM facilitates a social process in which Ws are held up for examination and their implications, in terms of human activities, are made explicit and discussed. Stage 6 should see an accommodation developing over changes that are both desirable and feasible. Changes that appear desirable on the basis of systems models may still not be feasible given the history of the situation, the power structure, or prevailing attitudes. For example, it may seem desirable to implement a quality control system but it may only be feasible to set up procedures for dealing with customer complaints. When accommodations are found, the analyst (Stage 7) helps with action to implement the agreed changes. The conclusion of the methodological cycle does not see a "solution" to the original problem but merely the emergence of another, different problem

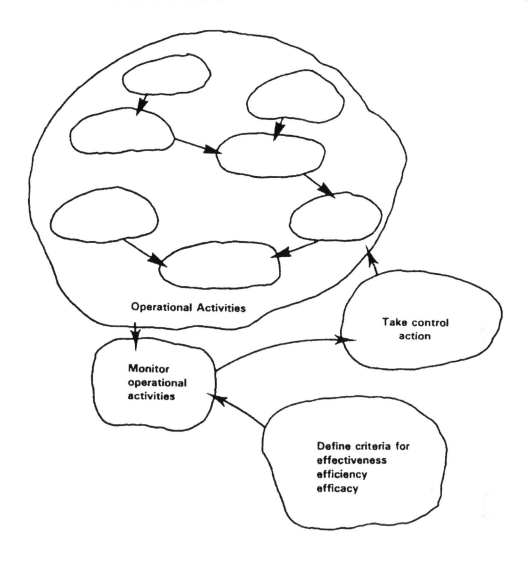

Figure 7.7. The general structure of a purposeful activity system (adapted from Checkland, 1989, p. 91)

situation. Problem resolving in social systems is, for Checkland, a never-ending process of learning, in which participants' attitudes and perceptions are continually tested and changed, and they come to entertain new conceptions of desirability and feasibility.

As experience of using SSM accumulated, Checkland began to find the original seven-stage presentation too limiting. It had always been stressed that the learning cycle could be commenced at any stage and that SSM was to be used flexibly and iteratively, but the seven-stage model still seemed to contribute to a systematic, step-by-step (rather than systemic) understanding of the process and one, moreover, in which use of the methodology appeared cut off from the ordinary day-to-day activities of an organization. In an attempt to overcome this and to demonstrate that SSM in use required constant attention to the interrelationships between "situational logic" and "situational culture", a new representation of the methodology was developed (see Figure 7.8). This "two strands model" gives equal space to the cultural stream of analysis and to the logic-based stream, and indicates some enhancements to the former which were added during the 1980s. The cultural stream is seen to depend upon three types of inquiry – referred to as Analysis 1, 2, and 3. Analysis 1 con-

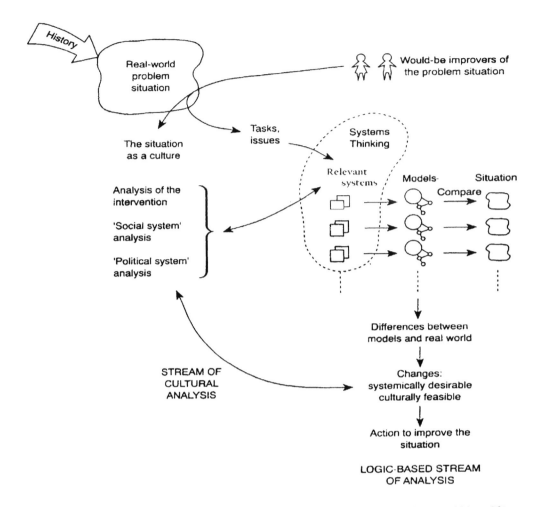

Figure 7.8. The "two strands" version of SSM (reproduced from Checkland and Scholes, 1990, p. 29)

siders the intervention itself and the roles of client(s), problem solver(s) and problem owners. Analysis 2 takes a cultural view of the social system, looking at social roles, norms of behavior and what values are used in judging role performance. The work of Davies (e.g., 1988), who has argued that the practice of SSM would benefit from a more explicit analysis of culture, has contributed here. Analysis 3 (a response to criticisms of SSM's lack of attention to issues of power – see later sub-section) examines the politics of the problem situation and how power is obtained and used. Stowell's (e.g., 1989) thoughts on power as manifest in various "commodities" (e.g., command of resources, personality, talent) that are exchanged or otherwise used in organizations have had an impact on this. Understanding of how power is disposed might make it possible to assuage some of its more baneful effects. The output of this analysis in three stages can be incorporated in the rich picture and must be continually updated and developed throughout an SSM study. Recognition of cultural and political aspects of the situation can assist the task of choosing suitable relevant systems and the process of arriving at recommendations that are "feasible."

Checkland's second major work on SSM (with Scholes, 1990) presented this "two strands model" of the methodology together with some modifications to the methods and modeling techniques supportive of SSM. There was no more mention of the "formal system model" or of the use of other systems thinking at Stage 4 of the methodology. Any residual role for functionalist systems thinking was thereby excised. Indeed, one is left wondering why so much emphasis is still put in SSM on building elegant conceptual models accurately derived from well-formulated root definitions. The most important feature of the new book was, however, the series of detailed case studies of SSM in action that it contained, and its most original contribution the reflection on those case studies, including a new distinction between Mode 1 and Mode 2 uses of the methodology.

7.6.2.2. Mode 2 SSM

The concept of Mode 2 SSM arises from reflection on how SSM is most easily and productively used by managers in their daily working lives. In practice Checkland and Scholes (1990) reasoned, managers are absorbed by the pressures and concerns of their immediate environments. They act and react according to their personalities, knowledge, instincts and so on and are unlikely, on an everyday basis, to operate according to the rules of a methodology. Rather than being methodology driven, they are situation driven. They may wish however, from time to time, to step outside the hurly-burly of ongoing events to try to make sense of what is happening or to apply some structured thinking to proposals for change. In these circumstances, if SSM's procedures and methods have become internalized sufficiently, a manager or group of managers can refer to the approach to help them think through the situation they are experiencing and the possibilities that it opens up. This, Checkland and Scholes would call a Mode 2 use of SSM. Figure 7.9 sets out how Mode 2 use differs from Mode 1 in terms of the F, M, A framework with which we became familiar in Chapter 2. In Mode 2 the methodology is taken as the framework of ideas employed to enable rigorous, systemic reflection upon the everyday flux of events and ideas. This process of making sense of what is going on is then the methodology which yields learning for the person in the problem situation carrying out the reflection.

As set out in *Soft Systems Methodology in Action*, Mode 2 SSM is not meant to replace Mode 1. Rather they represent a spectrum of possible uses. Mode 1 "interventions" are methodology driven and prescribe certain activities that need to be carried out. Mode 2 "interactions" are situation driven and allow managers to make sense of what is going on. In Mode 1, SSM is external and dominates proceedings. In Mode 2 it is internalized and only

	Mode 1	Mode 2
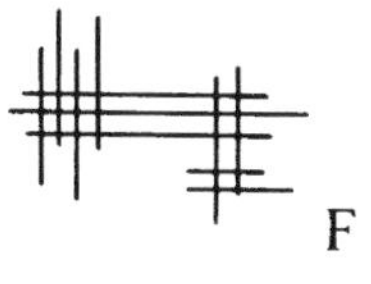 F	Systems ideas	SSM as in the 7 stages or 2 streams version
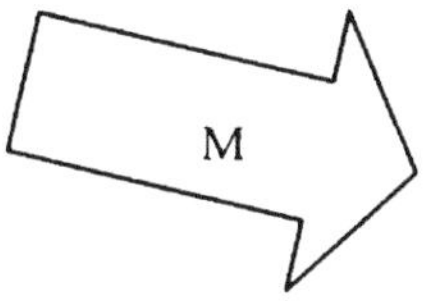 M	SSM as in the 7 stages or 2 streams version (intervention)	Reflection upon the everyday flux of events and ideas using SSM to make sense of it (interaction)
 A	Some part of the real world e.g. NHS, a company, the civil service, etc.	The learning of whoever does 2. above

Figure 7.9. Mode 1 and 2 defined in terms of the conceptualization of intellectual work (adapted from Checkland & Scholes, 1990, pp. 283 and 284).

occasionally breaks the surface of ongoing events. It is not easy to capture SSM in a way that does justice to both Mode 1 and Mode 2, and the rather sparse representation of Figure 7.10 is the currently preferred diagram for this purpose.

7.6.2.3. SSM and Information Systems

The field of study in which SSM has made its greatest impact, outside systems itself, is information systems (IS). The idea that Checkland's methodology could help with some of the problems (failure to deliver on objectives, resistance from end-users) which plagued the design and implementation of such systems, was attractive to some of his collaborators at Lancaster (e.g. Wilson 1984) as well as to many concerned with information technology applications elsewhere. Checkland has now turned his own attention to the field of information systems and regards the insight that purposeful activity models can be used in IS work as crucial to the recent history of SSM.

A third Checkland book appeared (1998), written with Sue Holwell who worked in both IS and IT in the Australian Government Service for twenty years. The book, *Information, Systems and Information Systems*, is an ambitious attempt to "initiate conceptual cleansing in the IS area." Checkland and Holwell begin by discussing the field of IS as it stands today. They describe it as being "crucial but confused": crucial because of the significant impact information technology can have on people and organizations, but confused because, in their view, the whole idea of IS is ill-defined and ambiguous. It is necessary to bring intellectual clarity to confusions about such concepts as "data", "information" and "knowledge." The out-dated model of the organization as a machine, which has traditionally underpinned work on information systems, must also be replaced. Experience demonstrates in the authors' view the inadequacy of such a model and they offer instead, as we have seen, a richer model

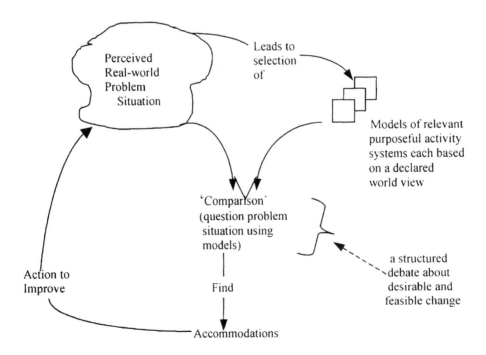

Figure 7.10. The currently preferred representation of SSM (adapted from Checkland, 1999, p. A9)

of the concept of "an organization" (see Figure 7.4). This richer model emphasizes meanings and purposes, and the processes involved as purposeful action is formulated. Once such action has been decided and understood it becomes possible to see what information needs exist among those involved and to provide appropriate information systems to support action:

> Formally organized 'information systems' will exist to support directly those taking the action which results from the formed intentions ... The main role of an information system ... is that of a support function; such systems do not exist for their own sake ... Any and every 'information system' can always be thought about as entailing a pair of systems, one system which is served ... the other a system which does the serving (Checkland and Holwell, 1998, p. 110).

Since it is the role of SSM to facilitate the exploration of meanings and purposes, to seek accommodations about purposeful action, and to express possible action in "human activity system" models, it provides the perfect basis for the development of information systems that truly meet users' needs.

The book endeavors, as did it its two predecessors, to provide a more adequate match between theory and actual experience, in this case of IS design, so that the two can be brought into a mutually informing relationship. A set of case studies of SSM at work shows how this can be realized and the effect it could have on the more productive employment of information technology.

7.6.2.4. Important Features of SSM

Before leaving the methodology itself, and providing an example of its use in practice, it is worthwhile highlighting some of its significant features. Most of the points I shall make in doing this can be linked to Checkland's (1985a) assertion that the methodology is doubly systemic; combining a cyclic learning process with the use of systems models within that process. They also refer more explicitly to Mode 1 rather than Mode 2 usage.

The cyclic learning process that SSM seeks to articulate builds naturally upon the complex social processes, including processes of management, that normally occur in organizations – worrying about the present situation, postulating alternatives, and seeking accommodations which allow change to happen. As we know organizations, for Checkland, are made up of different individuals and groups possessing different evaluations of the situation they are in. Their evaluations will overlap to some extent (otherwise, the organization could hardly exist), but there will usually be sufficient difference among world views to give rise constantly to issues that have to be managed. SSM takes as its task the management of the "myths and meanings" (Checkland, 1989) that are so central to the functioning of organizations, because they are the means by which individuals make sense of their situations. The aim, therefore, is to structure a debate, among different individuals and groups, in which different assumptions about the world are held up for examination and discussed. This debate does not lose touch with the facts and logic of the situation, since the models used to help structure it are systems models relevant to the real-world problem situation. But it is made clear that the "facts and logic" can be interpreted differently from different perspectives. If successful the debate will lead, if not to the creation of shared perceptions, at least to an accommodation between conflicting viewpoints and interests so that desirable change can be implemented.

The participants in a soft systems study learn their way to a new conception of feasibility as attitudes and perceptions are tested and changed. Changes that could not be conceived of because of the culture of the situation before the study began can seem obvious by the time it has finished. In order for this to occur, of course, the process of using SSM must be as participative as possible, including all interested parties. It is also essential that participants come to "own" the study by being involved in using the methodology. The soft systems practitioner is as concerned to give away this approach to making decisions as to provide a set of recommendations for action.

The notion that the methodology is a cyclic learning process draws upon Vickers's account of the process of appreciation and the way appreciative systems originate, develop and change in organizations. SSM is said by Checkland (1985a) to articulate in a formal way the process Vickers calls appreciation. Also explicit (Checkland, 1981) is the connection with Churchman's work on inquiring systems. The methodology searches for a possible Lockean consensus through a Kantian and Hegelian route in which different assumptions about reality are counterposed. SSM is Singerian in that it accepts that learning is never ending and should be sought in the heroic mood.

The methodology is doubly systemic in that it uses systems models as part of the systemic learning process just described. Checkland (1981) is prepared to make an "epistemological commitment" to systems models as a means of seeking to understand the world outside ourselves, because that world does appear to be densely interconnected and to reveal a degree of coherence and interrelatedness. Systems models are constructed during the formal systems thinking stages (4 and 5) of SSM and input into the real world to help structure a debate in which different perceptions of the facts and logic of the situation and different value positions are revealed and discussed. Appropriate models for this had to be invented; thus the "human activity system" concept was born. The idea was that pure models of purposeful activity (human activity system models) could be built, each expressing explicitly a particular viewpoint on the problem situation. These would contain sets of logically linked activities that when combined together produced, as an emergent property, a purposeful whole. As we know, SSM seeks to assist learning by making a comparison between these models and what is perceived to be taking place in the real world.

7.6.3. Case Study – Humberside Training and Enterprise Council

This case study examines work involving the use of SSM within Humberside Training and Enterprise Council (TEC) and is based on Hindle and Jackson (1997). TECs seek to foster economic growth and contribute to the regeneration of the local communities they serve. This is to be achieved through strengthening the local "skill-base" and assisting enterprises to expand and compete effectively. An important aspect of this work involves "contracting", i.e. a process of developing formal agreements between the TEC and a variety of local training suppliers. These contracts usually specify a number of specific "outputs" which will be required from a particular training program and, therefore, are fundamental to the TEC's ability to meet its aims. The contracts are also the focus of attention for funding bodies which aim to secure the appropriate use of the public funds administered by TECs. The project described here sought to inquire into, and develop actions to improve, the process of formulating contracts.

The importance of the contracting process for the TEC was the main driver of the project. There was a feeling in the Human Resources and Quality Department that the TEC's contracting activities might be made more effective and efficient by taking a holistic perspective on the process and making improvements as necessary. Although many TEC staff had considerable experience of contracting, the situation still presented a number of difficult aspects. First, the complexity of the overall process made it difficult for contracting staff to appreciate the whole picture and, hence, form a balanced perspective concerning the major actors, such as senior management, TEC contracting teams, internal and external audit groups, government bodies, training providers and the local community. Second, the formal nature of the contracts between the TEC and training suppliers generated a significant amount of detailed paperwork for the TEC and involved both internal and external audit. Finally, there was a need to develop a shared understanding between different TEC groups within the contracting process as they often performed different jobs separately. These aspects of the problem situation, together with the TEC's commitment to being a "learning organization" (based on Senge, 1990), led to the selection by the TEC of SSM as an appropriate methodology for the project. Some of the TEC staff possessed a basic appreciation of SSM from a previous study in which they had been involved, but it was felt that experienced facilitators would be needed to introduce the methodology and guide the initial learning process. This approach would enable the TEC to apply the approach themselves when appropriate in the future. Another objective of the project, therefore, was to enable TEC staff to become more familiar with SSM as a way of tackling ill-structured problem situations. The project team involved around a dozen TEC staff plus two facilitators, Giles Hindle and myself. The TEC project group was to include personnel involved in the contracting process, senior management, the Finance Director and the Human Resources and Quality Team.

The study utilized the "traditional" seven stage form of SSM as described by Checkland (1981), but incorporating rich pictures as a technique for structuring and expressing the problem situation (Stage 2 of the seven stage version). Also, due to time restrictions, the initial facilitated learning process involved a single iteration of the learning cycle of SSM. Further iterations, involving the implementation of decisions taken, were planned by the TEC group, but would take place outside the bounds of the project described here. Table 7.3 shows the structure of the project in terms of the activities of the TEC staff and facilitators. It was useful to think of the project as consisting of six phases. Also, it is worth noting that the TEC project team was split into four sub-groups, of around four participants each, in order to enable effective group-work during the production of rich pictures and models.

Table 7.3 describes the project in terms of the 6 phases.

7.6.3.1. Phase 1

The opening day of the project took place at a local hotel and was split between periods of introduction to SSM, periods of group-work by the four TEC sub-groups and periods of discussion between the project team as a whole. A reiteration of the project objectives was given by the Human Resources and Quality Director, explaining that, because the TEC's contracting process concerned several groups (internal to the TEC) involved in various different activities, it would be beneficial to develop an overall picture of the process and take action to improve it. This was followed by a general introduction to SSM.

First, it was stressed by the facilitators that a genuine appreciation of the interpretive philosophy of SSM was important for the participants if some form of unconscious reversion to, or blending with, traditional positivist thinking was to be avoided. Hence, if we were to use Morgan's (1986) various metaphors for describing organizations, the use of SSM was described as being most appropriate to the view of organizations as *cultures*. It was emphasized that SSM takes seriously the notions of participation and team learning, and the view that the most effective way to change an organization is to change the way people think within it.

Table 7.3. Structure of the Project

PHASE	ACTIVITIES	GROUP INVOLVED
1. Opening day (full day)	- introduction to SSM - building rich pictures - selecting relevant systems - introduction to modeling	- whole project team - in 4 sub-groups - whole project team - whole project team
2. Group work (over 6 weeks)	- modeling relevant systems	- each sub-group
3. Workshops (4 half days)	- modeling relevant systems	- each sub-group + facilitators
4. Final day (full day)	- presentation of relevant systems - debate regarding action to improve the situation	- whole project team - whole project team
5. Future work (ongoing)	- action to improve the situation - further iterations of SSM - evaluation of the project	- whole project team - whole project team - HR and Quality Manager
6. Initial Evaluation (½ day)	- evaluation of initial facilitated learning process - evaluation of SSM	- HR and Quality Manager + facilitators

After morning coffee, the introduction moved on to the seven stages version of SSM. The aim of the first day was to *introduce* Stages 2 to 4 of the methodology, expressing the problem situation (Stage 2), formulating root definitions of relevant systems (Stage 3) and developing conceptual models (Stage 4); and to *perform* the first iteration of Stages 2 and 3. The technique used to express the situation and generate relevant systems was rich picture drawing. A demonstration rich picture was provided by Giles Hindle to get things going (see Figure 7.11). With a touch of hesitancy, each of the four sub-groups began to develop their pictures. The pictures were "rich" in that they covered many issues and expressed many contrasting points of view. Groups appeared to enjoy the process, with lively discussion and playful laughter being common to all groups and an encouraging number of creative pictorial representations of issues.

Following the drawing, each sub-group presented their rich picture to the whole project team and from each of the groups' rich pictures it was possible to extract several issues which could form possible relevant systems to be taken forward to Stages 2 and 3. Table 7.4 gives a brief list of the relevant systems produced by each of the groups. We can see that, whilst many of the groups had picked up on similar issues, each group had its own perspective on the contracting process. For example, groups containing senior staff tended to concentrate more on the management of strategic issues and the relationships between the TEC and government bodies, whereas groups containing HR and Quality staff were primarily interested in raising contracting skills and meeting government quality standards.

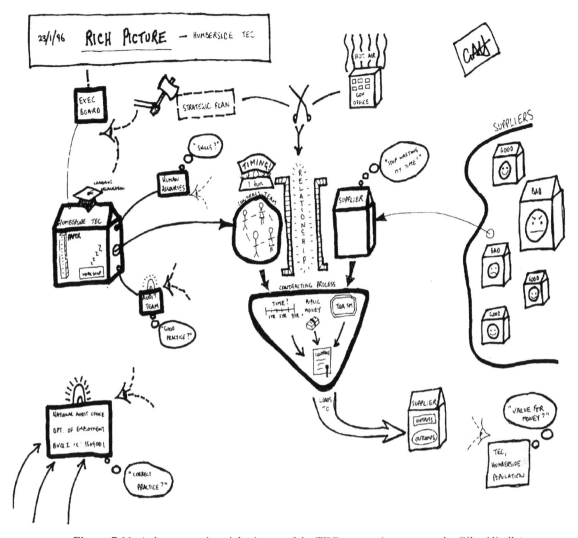

Figure 7.11. A demonstration rich picture of the TEC contracting process (by Giles Hindle)

The day continued with an introduction to Human Activity System (HAS) modeling. The introduction to HAS included the significant distinction between "hard" and "soft" systems thinking according to Checkland. Hence, participants were asked to relinquish the assumption embedded in everyday language that systems exist in the world, as when we speak of "the health care system" or "the education system." Without such a distinction the comparison of Stage 5 between the real world and the conceptual models would tend to be like with like. Each sub-group was left with the task of developing three or four of their relevant systems during phases 2 and 3.

Table 7.4. Relevant systems generated by the four sub-groups

SUB-GROUP 1
- a system to:
- change staff perceptions of government quality standards
- change the contribution of internal audit
- educate staff to do contracting "properly"
- integrate the roles involved in contracting
- make contractors aware of government quality standards requirements
- balance suppliers' requirements with those of the government

SUB-GROUP 2
- a system to:
- improve communication between teams
- streamline bureaucratic aspects of the job
- balance flexibility with regulatory requirements
- improve contracting with government
- ease contracting process for suppliers
- schedule contracting process to avoid time pressures

SUB-GROUP 3
- a system to:
- ensure contracting delivers desired outcomes
- cope with less able suppliers
- manage contracting with limited resources
- co-ordinate evaluation of contracting process
- reduce confusion about contracting
- co-ordinate the procedures of contracting
- ensure original intentions of contracts are met
- enable over-arm bowling whilst wearing a straight jacket

SUB-GROUP 4
- a system to:
- reduce bureaucratic nature of contracting
- ensure contracts deliver desired outcomes
- cope with variety of suppliers
- develop shared vision with suppliers
- alter suppliers' perceptions of contracts
- discover suppliers' views of contracting
- use contracts to ensure good practice
- improve understanding of contracting throughout the different levels of the TEC

7.6.3.2. Phases 2 and 3

The output of phase 1 included the project team's appreciation of the process of SSM together with a list of several relevant systems for each of the four sub-groups. Over the following six weeks the groups were charged with the task of developing three to four of their relevant systems into root definitions and conceptual models. This activity would be facilitated through four ½ day workshops, one with each group. The workshops allowed the groups and facilitators to go through the models in detail and develop new ideas where necessary. This proved vital to the project as it became clear that all the groups were having difficulty with the technical aspects of the modeling. The facilitators were also able to give general help and advice on the style of thinking used within SSM. Following the workshops, the facilitators produced technically correct versions of the groups' models which were then returned to the groups.

7.6.3.3. Phase 4

The final day saw a return to the aforementioned hotel and sought to bring together the logical stream of analysis undertaken in the preceding three phases. All groups were present. Each group was asked to present their chosen relevant systems and the subsequent root definitions and models. Following each group's presentation, a discussion took place regarding the feasibility and desirability of the ideas. From this discussion it was possible to make improvements to some of the models and also take account of some overlapping of ideas between the groups. From the dozen human activity systems presented, it was possible, through discussion, to distinguish four relevant areas where the group felt action needed to be taken. These were:

- Reduction of time pressures in the contracting process
- Appreciation and development of effective contracting skills within the TEC
- Change from annual to a three year flexible contracting process
- Development of mature and constructive relationships with training suppliers

As an aside to the above activity, a presentation was given by the facilitators illustrating some craft skills of SSM. The presentation included a root definition and conceptual model developed by the facilitators of the third relevant system above (see Figure 7.12) and an example of a HAS expressing an alternative *Weltanschauung* ("a system to make the contracting process as frustrating as possible for suppliers" - see Figure 7.13). The alternative HAS was used to underline how models in SSM can look at issues in a variety of ways and ought not to be restricted to perspectives existing in the real world.

7.6.3.4. Phase 5

The project was intended to be the start of ongoing activity at the TEC relating to the improvement of the contracting process and the use of SSM. Formal appraisal of the project including an assessment of the resultant changes was also due to continue indefinitely.

7.6.3.5. Phase 6

Although a comprehensive evaluation of the project from the TEC's point of view had been planned (phase 5), it proved useful for a facilitator to spend half a day with HR and Quality staff in order to capture initial reactions to the project and discuss the use of SSM.

Details of the evaluation of the project undertaken can be found in Hindle and Jackson (1997). In general terms, rich pictures (RPs) turned out to be the most popular technique with participants and have subsequently been used in other projects within the TEC. They appear popular for a number of reasons: "They are good fun and get everyone involved. They are technically easy, and hence *accessible*, and allow everyone's views to be expressed, whatever they are" (HR and Quality Manager). RPs were appreciated for their unprescriptive nature, i.e. participants were invited to express aspects of the TEC's contracting process which were of importance to *themselves*, rather than being told to address certain aspects in a prescribed way. This encouraged a broad project as the four groups displayed notably different perspectives on the contracting process and, consequently, tended to pick up on contrasting issues.

The modeling aspect of SSM, however, turned out to be more problematic, especially the CATWOE mnemonic used to help structure the HAS. People felt they would need more time to learn this aspect of SSM and it was clear that the TEC did not warm to what they saw as a technical, disciplined approach. There was a strong feeling that people would need to be confident about the technique if the TEC were to use HASs in the future and there was no doubt that the groups struggled initially. Participants did not feel confident they understood the technical aspects of HAS modeling after the first day, and they still did not at the end of phases 1 to 4. Despite this aversion to the technical aspects of SSM, the discussion generated by producing root definitions (RDs) was felt to be valuable. There was a feeling that simply using SSM as a problem structuring technique, without using HASs to develop ideas for feasible action, would have been less effective. Participants valued the emphasis on taking action within SSM as the relationship between problem structuring and

Full Root Definition:

A system, owned by the Executive Board and staffed by a steering group, to introduce a three year flexible contracting process in order to facilitate both TEC and supplier contract planning and management while ensuring Government Office satisfaction, minimizing the risks involved and in the context of existing staff experience

CATWOE Analysis:

C   TEC contracting staff and suppliers
A   Steering Group (Executive Board and Contract Managers)
T   Rigid Annual   Flexible 3 year
     contracting process   contracting process
W   A 3 year flexible contracting process will facilitate both TEC and supplier contract planning and management
O   Executive Board
E   Government Office, existing staff experience, risks involved, suppliers, contract planning, TEC culture.

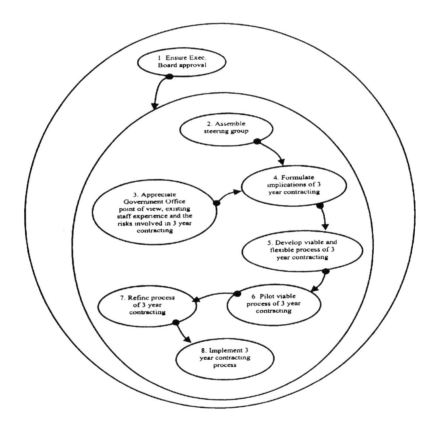

Figure 7.12. Root definition, CATWOE analysis and conceptual model of "a system to introduce a three year flexible contracting process"

taking action was seen as important. It was felt that many "problem solving" approaches concentrate on structuring the situation in some way and then leave it at that; there is no requirement within the methods to formulate actions to improve the situation and actually do something. This tends to promote the separation of thinking and action and can lead to the feeling that such methods are just about words and ideas, and not part of one's *real* work. Despite the technical problems with the modeling, participation was felt to be good and the project was seen as a success overall.

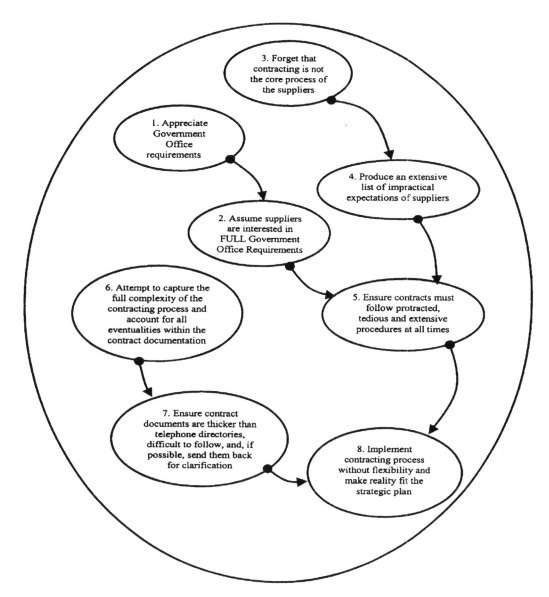

Figure 7.13. Conceptual model of "a system to make the contracting process as frustrating as possible for suppliers"

We were, of course, using SSM as a research tool as well as an action tool during this project. The interested reader can judge the success of this by referring to the reflections on the methods and techniques used as part of SSM, the methodology itself, and the underlying assumptions of the methodology, in Hindle and Jackson (1997). Some interesting conclusions emerged, particularly about the "sustainability" of SSM as a learning system in an organization that had work practices like the TEC and in which employees face constant time pressures.

7.6.4. Strengths and Weaknesses of Soft Systems Methodology

In an early paper, Checkland (1976) declared his intention to take systems thinking beyond the abstractions of general system theory and the constraints of specialized techniques. The story of SSM reveals the success of this enterprise. Contemporary SSM is based on some clearly stated principles or "constitutive rules" which guide the process of intervention in ill-structured problem situations. At the same time as it sets out these principles for method use, it does not determine that use. It provides a different response in each situation depending on the user and the nature of the situation. It is this flexibility that ensures its relevance in so many managerial situations. Checkland (1999) regards four intellectual breakthroughs as crucial to this success. These were the delineation of the notion of a "human activity system"; the use of models as epistemological devices rather than representations of the real world; the use of models to provoke debate and learning rather than for the purpose of design; and the extension of SSM to the domain of information systems. These breakthroughs occurred because of the establishment of an action research program that ensured lessons could be learned from experience and incorporated into SSM, that reflection could occur and enhancements could take place on the philosophical underpinnings of the methodology, and refinement could be made to supportive methods and techniques. A virtuous circle of interaction between ideas and experience became possible and was fully exploited by Checkland and his co-workers at Lancaster. The result was a paradigm revolution in systems thinking which liberated the discipline from the intellectual straightjacket in which it had been locked and, at the same time, made it much more obviously relevant to managers. Today SSM is used by both academics and practitioners, is important well beyond the confines of the systems discipline and has spread its influence to many countries outside the U.K.

Checkland has attracted most criticism on the issue of the theoretical alignment of the principles underpinning SSM. The constitutive rules openly embrace an interpretive position which provokes those coming from functionalist or more radical sociological paradigms. To put it at its simplest, functionalists believe that there is something in the various models produced by experts in management science and organization theory which managers must take seriously. To Checkland such models may merit a place at the debating table but they certainly cannot provide any objective truth about how organizations should be designed and managed. Radicals argue that the social world is characterized by asymmetry of power, structural conflict and contradiction, and that the failure of interpretive thinkers such as Checkland to grasp this means that their methodologies become distorted in use and are ineffective in bringing about significant change for the better. We shall examine this radical critique in a little more detail here but always remembering that the issue is one of a fundamental difference in paradigmatic orientation. This will be explored more fully in the final, critique section of this chapter.

It is argued by the critics that SSM is based upon a consensus world view which plays down conflicts of real interest and promotes the belief that if any conflicts do exist they can be resolved, temporarily at least, through a debate structured around root definitions and conceptual models (Thomas and Lockett, 1979). The alternative position, that deep-seated conflict is endemic in organizations and societies does not seem to be given serious attention by Checkland. As with Ackoff, this leads to an exaggerated commitment to participation as an appropriate and apparently sufficient mechanism for achieving mutual understanding on purposes. Radicals make the point, on the basis of their view of social reality, that the context in which the methodology is used, often in hierarchical settings, means that genuinely participative debate, on which the success of SSM seems to depend, must be severely constrained. Thomas and Lockett (1979), for example, suggest that power must inevitably shape which world views come to the fore and influence change in SSM. Jackson (1982, 1983) has argued at length that the debate about feasible and desirable change at Stages 5 and 6 of SSM will be crucially inhibited by power imbalances deriving from the structure of organizations and society. In the usual case, therefore, it seems that the results obtained by SSM will favor the powerful. It is impossible for SSM, in many circumstances, to bring about the conditions necessary for unconstrained discussion. Checkland, while taking more notice of power in the "two strands" version of SSM, remains largely silent on how it affects the supposed "neutrality" of his methodology. He feels that his experiences with SSM support an interpretive account of the social world in which power is a "commodity" rather than an element inextricably entwined with the structures of the social system. Others wonder whether his research program has been sufficiently well designed to properly justify this conclusion.

Burrell (1983) is convinced that the reason why Checkland is never faced with incommensurable worldviews, or any other anomalies that might lead him to question his interpretive perspective, is that he works primarily with a community sharing similar interests, i.e. managers. This is a community, moreover, that usually has the power to impose agreement on any other groups involved in the proceedings. Thomas and Lockett (1979) can quite easily see how working for powerful clients will restrict the emergence of alternative, radical world views in SSM and lead only to reformist recommendations for change. The client can restrict the information fed into the project at the analysis stage. If the soft systems practitioner wants to continue working for the client, he or she will quickly abandon any radical root definitions as not being "culturally feasible" given the realities of the problem situation. The choice of which changes to implement will be subject to existing decision-making processes in which the client is dominant. If the position of powerful stakeholders is not threatened by soft systems studies because significant issues can be kept off the agenda for debate, then the powerful might be willing to let other groups participate and it might seem that all stakeholders share common interests. If, however, soft systems practitioners were to challenge the hierarchical nature of organizations, the ultimate decision-making rights of powerful stakeholders, or the unequal distribution of organizational resources to different stakeholders, they would soon provoke conflicts that reveal the deep status, economic and other inequalities that emancipatory thinkers see as such fundamental aspects of social reality.

Finally, SSM is criticized for its "subjectivism" or "idealism", which is seen to prevent it coming to terms with structural features of social systems such as conflict and power (Mingers, 1984). Burrell (1983), for example, notes that Checkland always sees conflict as related to a clash of values and not to a difference in material interests. The social world may very well be created by people, the criticism runs, but it is not necessarily created by them in the full awareness of what they are doing. Further, it is created by people who have conflicting aims and intentions and who bring different resources to bear when the social construction is taking place. It follows that the social world escapes the understanding and control of any one person or group of people. It takes on the form of a highly complex and structured external reality that exercises constraint on the individuals who make it up. A sophisticated social theory is necessary in order to unmask "ideologies" and provide an understanding of how emancipation can be brought about.

What the critics of SSM are essentially arguing is that just as hard systems thinking has a limited domain of effective and legitimate application, so too does SSM. If it is impossible to achieve genuine consensus through open and free participation, if there is fundamental conflict, if *Weltanschauungen* refuse to shift, if power determines the outcome of debate, then SSM cannot be properly employed in these situations. It is obviously of importance to Checkland to resist this conclusion and he seeks to do so.

In Checkland's (1982) view, the critics assert rather than demonstrate the existence of objective and constraining features of social reality. Checkland's experience (unlike that of Rosenhead, 1984) is that *Weltanshauungen* are amenable to change and do alter – sometimes incrementally, sometimes radically. Instead of making "utopian" demands for the legitimate use of SSM, the critics should try to employ it to bring about the changes they deem desirable. Since it is a learning system it might, given the chance, assist in changing things in a manner that can contribute to realizing the aspirations to which the radicals subscribe. Checkland accepts that SSM has tended in practice to be used in a rather managerialist and conservative way, but he argues that because it is impossible to know in advance what learning will be generated by the methodology, it must in principle be capable of bringing about emancipatory/radical changes as well as regulatory/conservative results.

7.7. SENGE'S SOFT SYSTEMS THINKING

In the previous chapter we saw Senge trying to represent a somewhat impoverished version of system dynamics as "systems thinking." This "fifth discipline" has to be mastered by organizations if they are to become "learning organizations" because it reveals the systemic structures which govern the behavior of organizations. It is also the most important of the five disciplines necessary to the learning organization because it underpins all the other four. It is to these other four disciplines, dealing with the "softer" aspects of organizational learning, that we now turn.

7.7.1. Four Other Disciplines of the Learning Organization

The four other disciplines are "personal mastery", "mental models", "building shared vision", and "team learning."
"Personal mastery" is defined by Senge as

> the discipline of continually clarifying and deepening our personal vision, of focusing our energies, of developing patience, and of seeing reality objectively. As such, it is an essential cornerstone of the learning organization – the learning organization's spiritual foundation (1990, p. 7).

There are two central aspects here. First personal mastery endows people with purpose. An individual striving to attain personal mastery must continually clarify what is important to him and keep in mind why he is following a particular path. Second, the individual must learn to see current reality clearly. Although we must have aims and goals, it is immensely important that we "know where we are now." This gives us the ability to work with and not against the current situation. It ensures that the "gap" between our aspirations and the reality gives rise to "creative tension" rather than "emotional tension" and anxiety. Personal mastery depends on creativity, is an ongoing and infinite thing, and leads the individual to feel part of a larger creative process. It is a key discipline for Senge because individuals with personal mastery learn faster, are more committed to their work and are instrumental in creating an effective learning organization. Individuals cannot be forced to embrace personal mastery, but the organization can

> work relentlessly to foster a climate in which the principles of personal mastery are practiced in daily life. That means building an organization where it is safe for people to create visions, where inquiry and commitment to the truth are the norm, and where challenging the status quo is expected (1990, p. 172).

Senge defines "mental models" as

> deeply ingrained assumptions, generalizations, or even pictures or images that influence how we understand the world and how we take action (1990, p. 8).

Problems arise for organizations if such models go unquestioned because they can easily limit our vision, restrain learning and lead to inertia. Learning organizations need to ensure that the "mirror is turned inwards" and that mental models are frequently unearthed, brought to the surface and scrutinized. The discipline of managing mental models through facilitative organizational practices is, therefore, essential to building learning organizations.

In *The Fifth Discipline Fieldbook* (Senge *et al.*, 1994), a number of methods are introduced to support the five disciplines of the learning organization. Very important to the discipline of "mental models" is "creating scenarios." In a scenario planning exercise the maximum imagination must be employed to produce a variety of potential futures. The purpose is not accurate prediction of the future but the generation of awareness about where you stand in the present in relation to possible futures. A successful scenario exercise will help organizations to refine their sense of purpose, understand the forces acting upon them and recognize how well prepared they are for each of the potential futures. Kees van der Heijden (1996) describes the scenario work undertaken in the Royal Dutch/Shell Group of companies. Explicitly the purpose of this was to change the mental maps of managers and to allow them to undertake their own strategic thinking. In his view:

> Scenario planning succeeds, when an organization manages to adapt itself, such that it 'gains the high ground', i.e. maximizes its chances of achieving its purpose, in whatever environment it finds itself, through a process of organizational learning (van der Heijden, 1996, p. 53).

"Shared vision" refers to the pictures people throughout the organization come to have in common and feel a commitment to. It is an essential building block of the learning organization because it provides a focus for the work of individuals and for their generative learning. The practice of shared vision

> involves the skills of unearthing shared 'pictures of the future' that foster genuine commitment and enrolment rather than compliance. In mastering this discipline, leaders learn the counterproductiveness of trying to dictate a vision, no matter how heartfelt (Senge, 1990, p. 9).

While shared vision may start with visionary leadership therefore it must, through a process of "intensive dialogue", turn into widespread, collaborative, co-creation of the organization's future.

"Team learning" enables individuals to act as a collective and fosters enhanced discussion and dialogue. Dialogue is particularly important:

> The discipline of team learning starts with 'dialogue', the capacity of members of a team to suspend assumptions and enter into a genuine 'thinking together' (Senge, 1990, p. 10).

Learning organizations must foster team-based decision-making to ensure synergy from the learning of the whole team.

As we mentioned, the "fifth discipline", systems thinking, is important not only in its own right but also as the basis for these other four, softer disciplines. It can illuminate subtler aspects of personal mastery such as our connectedness to the world; help improve our mental models; provide a firmer basis for shared vision by revealing the forces shaping current reality; and enables team learning because it permits us to manage complexity.

7.7.2. Strengths and Weaknesses of Senge's Soft Systems Thinking

Midgley has, on occasion (1992, 1996), sought to build a pluralist version of systems thinking upon Habermas's communicative-theoretic reformulation of critical theory and, in particular, on the four validity claims said to be inherent in communication. The fourth of these, that the speaker is sincere in uttering what he says, relates to the "internal world" of the speaker. It might be argued that this world, unlike the natural and social worlds to which the other claims relate, has been much neglected in systems thinking. Midgley struggles to relate "personal construct theory" and "cognitive mapping" (see next section) to it. There is no doubt that Senge's work on "personal mastery" extends the scope of systems thinking in this area of concern. Beyond that, another strength of Senge's soft systems thinking could be that it complements the functionalist nature of his "fifth discipline", system dynamics.

Flood (1999), in *Rethinking the Fifth Discipline*, argues that Senge's work can be made more useful and empowering if it is enhanced by the contributions of other systems gurus, such as von Bertalanffy, Beer, Ackoff, Checkland and Churchman. This seems to be a rather kind way of saying that, as it stands, Senge's version of systems thinking is severely limited. This is indeed the case and, compared to Warfield, Ackoff, Checkland and Churchman, Senge adds little of originality to interpretive systems thinking. Indeed, he must be criticized for writing a book on "systems thinking" that pays so little attention to previous research by these and other systems writers. Weak in terms of the soft tradition to which it belongs, Senge's soft systems thinking inevitably also leaves itself open to the same "radical" critique attracted by Ackoff, Checkland and others. Finally, although Senge sees aspects of both functionalist and interpretive systems thinking contributing to the development of learning organizations, he fails to recognize, let alone think through, the possible theoretical contradiction arising from this and the problems it can pose. We shall return to this when we discuss critical systems thinking in Part III.

7.8. SOFT OPERATIONAL RESEARCH, SOFT SYSTEM DYNAMICS, SOFT CYBERNETICS

The difficulties encountered in trying to use functionalist systems approaches, arising from pluralism, complexity and power, have led to attempts by some theorists to modify them in an interpretive direction. In some cases, as for example with Wolstenholme's qualitative system dynamics or Espejo's organizational cybernetics, the result is little more than some soft appendages added to the prevailing functionalist rationale. On other occasions, however, a genuine shift in paradigm occurs and models, methods and techniques normally associated with the functionalist approach get genuinely embedded in a soft systems methodology drawing upon interpretive thinking. In this category come the soft operational research, soft system dynamics and soft cybernetics that we shall be considering here. This, of course, does not exhaust the possibilities. It is feasible to extract any tool, technique, method or model from its usual role serving the functionalist paradigm and to employ it in an interpretive manner. How successful it can be in the new role must be subject to research in each case. In the previous chapter we saw features of complexity theory successfully employed in an interpretive fashion to add to the "languaging" capabilities of staff in Humberside TEC. In considering in turn soft OR, soft system dynamics and soft cybernetics, we need to be aware, in each case, of what is being retained from the previous functionalist incarnation and whether this helps or hinders interpretive usage.

7.8.1. Soft Operational Research (OR)

For Rosenhead it became clear during the 1970s and 1980s that hard OR, an example of rational comprehensive planning, was both "socially undesirable" and "practically unfeasible" when extended to strategic problems:

> the methods which had seemed to work well on more limited problems fell apart when given a chance to show their paces on more ambitious projects (1989, p. 4).

Fortunately, writing in 1989, Rosenhead was able to identify a new generation of methods, complementary to hard OR, which were much better equipped to deal with complex decision problems. These soft OR approaches retained some of the defining characteristics of classical operational research, such as rational analysis and modeling, but in the context of an orientation much more suited to social reality. Rosenhead argues that they have in common an emphasis on structuring decisions and problems rather than solving them. They are decision aiding, and in support of this, are transparent to users, involve participation as a key component and are capable of incorporating conflict between different stakeholders. A useful collection of papers by leading figures in soft OR has been put together and edited by Rosenhead (1989). The methodologies discussed and illustrated in detail are "strategic options development analysis' (SODA), "soft systems methodology", "strategic choice", "robustness analysis", "metagame analysis" and "hypergame analysis."

The inclusion of Checkland's highly subjectivist soft systems methodology, among the set of approaches examined in Rosenhead's book, indicates the type of shift in orientation aimed at in soft OR. Soft OR methodologies accept the need to work with a plurality of world views, to pay attention to how perceptions alter during the process of intervention, and to construct coalitions and build a consensus in favor of change through open discussion and debate. Although only Checkland's is explicitly a systems approach, the majority of soft OR writers seem to accept the conclusions of soft systems thinkers, to embrace the interpretive paradigm, and aspire to construct methodologies based on the same beliefs about people and organizations. We shall review "strategic choice" and "SODA" in this regard.

OR, the reader will recall, came to prominence during the second world war as a kind of interdisciplinary, open-ended form of scientific inquiry into operational problems. After the war however, especially in academic circles, it rapidly became associated with the mathematical modeling of a set of well-defined problems. This was of concern to a number of OR practitioners who in response, and at Russ Ackoff's suggestion, sought a link with social scientists at the Tavistock Institute - the home of socio-technical systems thinking. An Institute for Operational Research (IOR) was established within the Tavistock framework. The strategic choice approach was born out of one of the early projects carried out, under the auspices of the IOR, on local government planning (Friend and Jessop, 1969).

The strategic choice approach is basically concerned with "coping with complexity." It

> deals with the interconnectedness of decision problems in an explicit yet selective way. The most distinctive feature of this approach is the way it helps users in making incremental progress towards decisions by focusing their attention on alternative ways of managing uncertainty (Friend, 1989, p. 121).

Strategic choice recognizes three types of uncertainty, each of which calls for a different response. Uncertainties within the working environment (UE) can be dealt with by analysis. Uncertainties pertaining to guiding values (UV) demand political responses aimed at clarifying objectives and, perhaps, conflict management. Uncertainties pertaining to related decision fields (UR) require exploration of the structural relationships between the decision currently in view and those with which it appears to be interconnected. Decision makers, confronted with complex problems, need to learn how to manage this uncertainty, responding appropriately to the different pressures according to the requirements of the moment. The aim of strategic choice is to

> provide foundations for the development of a set of relatively open, participative methods for representing the structure of interrelated decision problems and the various sources of uncertainty - technical, political, structural - which make them difficult to resolve (Friend, 1989, p. 122).

The framework used by strategic choice to order these methods suggests that there are four complementary modes of decision making - shaping, designing, comparing and choosing. In the shaping mode, the decision area is mapped in order to arrive at an agreed problem focus and problem structure. The designing mode sees various possible courses of action identified. In "comparing", the possible courses of action are evaluated against explicit criteria developed for the purpose. Choosing involves gaining commitment to immediate actions and planning future action. At each stage specific techniques are employed to help manage the complexity and uncertainty. For example, the "Analysis of Interconnected Decision Areas" (AIDA) is used during the designing mode to explore and examine the available courses of action within the selected problem focus. The attention given by strategic choice to the shaping and choosing stages, and to the process of incremental decision making, contrasts with many management science approaches which emphasize only designing and comparing.

SODA is an approach which aims to help OR consultants assist their clients to work with complex, messy problems. It requires of consultants that they develop excellent facilitation skills, so that they can manage "process" and ensure efficient and effective group decision making, and also that they have the ability to handle the complexity of the "content." In the latter case they require the traditional OR skills of model building and analysis. Eden (1989) identified four aspects which interact to produce the SODA methodology. These are particular perspectives held on the individual, the nature of organizations, consulting practice, and the use of technology and technique.

The theoretical perspective brought to the study of individuals and organizations is explicitly interpretive in nature. The emphasis is upon making use of the client group by paying particular attention to each personal, subjective view of the "real" problem:

> It is because of the complexity and richness that arises from attention to subjectivity, that a focus for SODA work is on the managing of process as well as content ... Individuality is legitimate and allowed to blossom within a SODA project. Protecting individuality is designed to ensure that the outcome of the project is both creative and also consensual (Eden, 1989, pp. 23-24).

Organizations, according to SODA, are negotiated orders made up of individuals who are constantly striving to make sense of their world. The "theory of personal constructs", due to Kelly (1955), is used to tap into this process of meaning construction and to facilitate the negotiation of a common perspective and agreement on action. Within organizations problem solving is best done in teams. SODA requires that teams are created in a way that ensures an adequate number of individual perspectives are brought to the issue under consideration.

The third perspective, on consulting practice, rests upon the theoretical viewpoint taken of the nature of individuals and organizations. It becomes the job of the consultant to concentrate on the role of "negotiation" in effective problem solving. She must employ excellent facilitation skills in order to manage negotiation between different perspectives and to ensure consensus and commitment emerge. The final perspective, technology and technique, brings the first three together:

> Through appropriate 'technology and technique' these building blocks come together through the concept ... 'a facilitative device'. Our approach is aimed at providing a device which can be used to facilitate managing the messiness of deciding on action. In this way we are attempting to create an analytically sound method of dealing with both content and process. In the case of SODA the technique is 'cognitive mapping', and the technology to help manage complexity is computer software called COPE (Eden, 1989, p. 26).

Cognitive mapping assumes that language is the basic currency of organizational problem solving. Initially a cognitive map is constructed for each member of the client group, representing the way he or she sees the problem situation. A map is built by listening to what an individual says and capturing this in a model consisting of a network of that person's ideas linked by arrows. The ideas are specified in comparison to their opposites e.g. government support for profit sharing schemes versus ambivalence towards profit sharing schemes. The arrows point to how one idea might lead to, or have implications for, another idea. The chains of cause and effect so produced can be signed positively or negatively to show whether an idea leads to the first or second pole of another. Such maps are amenable to formal analysis with the help of the COPE software. Once individual maps have been produced and agreed, they can be gathered together and merged to form a "strategic map":

> The aim is to produce a 'facilitative device' to promote psychological negotiation amongst team members so that, in the first instance, a definition of the problem can be established (Eden, 1989, p. 33).

The aggregated map or maps are analyzed to provide an agenda for a SODA workshop. At the workshop understanding of key goals, options and assumptions, and of the interrelated problems, will be negotiated.

The theory and concepts guiding SODA, according to the four perspectives, are summarized in Figure 7.14.

In a more recent text, Eden and Ackerman (1998) have applied many of the insights encapsulated in SODA to strategy making. They see the purpose of strategic management as being to "create and mould the future":

> It is a pro-active process of seeking to change the organization, its stakeholders ... and the context, or environment, within which it seeks to attain its aspirations (p. 3).

This can be accomplished through JOURNEY making – the journey being a process of "JOintly Understanding Reflecting and NEgotiating strategY." The journey must be carefully facilitated in order to encourage creativity and arrive at shared meaning about strategic intent and strategic direction. Eden and Ackerman offer a number of examples of this process at work including a comprehensive account of strategy development with the Northern Ireland Prison Service.

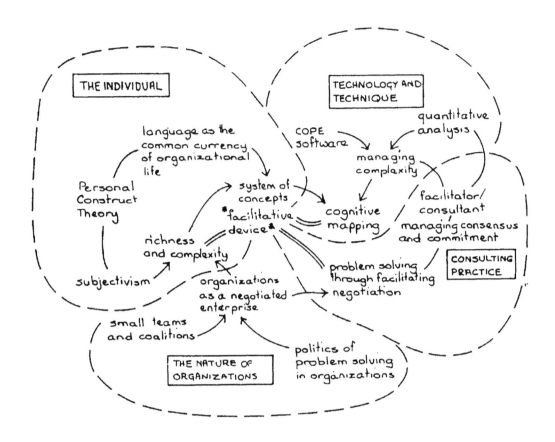

Figure 7.14. Theory and concepts guiding SODA (reproduced from Eden. 1989, p. 24)

7.8.2. Soft System Dynamics

Lane (2000) has argued convincingly that system dynamics is very different from hard systems thinking. Even on the basis of the classic texts of Forrester it is less austerely "objective" than is often represented. If one considers recent work by Wolstenholme, Senge and Lane, and the various craft skills that have grown up around the modeling, then it simply cannot be considered as "hard", or "optimizing", or "deterministic." At the same time, Lane makes no pretence, and would not wish to, that system dynamics is a "soft" method in the style of SSM. The system dynamics we examined in the previous chapter may be very different to hard systems thinking but it is still demonstrably functionalist in character, seeing system structure as the determining force behind system behavior. In this section, however, we shall consider another use of system dynamics models which does point the way to how they need to be employed if they are to support an interpretive methodology. This use is described in the work of Vennix (1996) on "group model building."

Vennix's work centers on building system dynamics models with teams in order to improve their performance when tackling strategic, messy problems. As problems become more complex it is clear that any individual can have only a limited view of their nature and causes. Group model building seeks to build on the natural tendency people have to think in terms of causal processes in order to systematically elicit and integrate the limited individual mental models into a more holistic view of the problem. As the result is a shared system dynamics model, this can then be used to explore the dynamics of the holistic view.

The client is involved throughout the model building process. The first step is to construct a preliminary system dynamics model on the basis of individual interviews of participants or the study of research reports and policy documents. This model is then further refined, in consultation with the individuals involved, before being presented at a group session. During the group session the team seeks to elaborate the model to bring it to a point where the dynamic complexity of their view of the problem situation can be explored. This process depends crucially upon the facilitator. This facilitator needs a thorough knowledge of system dynamics and must also exhibit the right attitudes, skills and tasks. If all goes well, the model building process will lead to the team learning their way to a shared social reality. A consensus will develop around the nature of the problem and a commitment arise behind potential solutions. In summary, group model building

> focuses on building system dynamics models with teams in order to enhance team learning, to foster consensus and to create commitment with a resulting decision (Vennix, 1996, p. 3).

Vennix is not entirely clear whether the resultant system dynamics model is supposed to reflect some pre-existing reality or whether it is simply the coming together of different appreciations of the situation in such a way that social reality can then be created. This distinction becomes largely irrelevant in practice, however, where the requirement to arrive at a consensus shifts the emphasis firmly in the direction of the interpretive aspects of his approach. This does, of course, mean that "group model building" lays itself open to all the criticisms constantly aimed at this position. Vennix's view that consensus will "almost automatically emerge" when group model-building has been conducted properly (1996, p. 5) would provoke questions, as would his attention to involving in the process all those with the power to implement change, but not necessarily those who could suffer from change (p. 138). An example of the use of group model building to address the problem of the declining size of the Dutch-registered merchant marine (1996, pp. 174-186) sees him having to go to extreme lengths to make his approach work in the context of genuinely divergent views about the causes of the problem and the likely future consequences. Nominal Group Technique and a variety of well developed consulting skills have to be brought in to assist group model building in order to keep the show on the road. On the other hand, he is convinced that, at the end of the process, restructuring the existing but scattered knowledge of the individuals concerned, and putting it into a systemic perspective, have allowed new insights to emerge. The quality of communication in the group was improved and a high level of consensus and commitment to the final decision generated. This is despite the fact that the system dynamics model remained far from complete and Vennix's account betrays little suggestion of the belief that it is attempting to model "reality."

7.8.3. Soft Cybernetics

The account of the viable system model (VSM), presented in the previous chapters, pictured it as a structuralist instrument. According to structuralist rationality, the VSM can be used as a tool to consider the implications of different system identities, but once a particular identity and purpose have been chosen, certain structural laws need to be obeyed. It is therefore incumbent upon the systems practitioner to understand these cybernetics laws. This knowledge permits a trained analyst to diagnose pathologies which give rise to faults at the surface level and to suggest how these can be corrected. Alternatively, it can inform the design of a new organizational system able to achieve its purpose effectively and efficiently and so maintain its identity.

The ascription of structuralist underpinnings to organizational cybernetics, and the setting out of particular procedures for using the VSM in accordance with this ascription, were based upon what the reader will hopefully regard as logical and coherent extrapolation from Beer's writings and from the way he and his followers have employed the model. It must be acknowledged, however, that other readings are possible. Even if the reading provided is seen as true to the spirit of Beer's books, it is still possible to argue that the VSM *should* be interpreted and employed differently. This is Harnden's (1989, 1990) position in aligning the VSM with interpretive theory and methodology. Harnden would class the interpretation of the VSM, provided in Chapter 6, as "representational" in that it pictures the VSM as trying to express certain fundamental laws governing the organization of complex systems – laws that we ignore at our peril. Harnden wants to attach the VSM to interpretive thinking; to him it is best regarded as an "hermeneutic" enabler. Organizational models should be seen not as seeking to capture objective reality, but as aids to orienting ongoing conversations about complex social issues. The VSM is a particularly good model, Espejo and Harnden (1989) argue, because it permits an extremely rich discourse to unfold about the emergence and evolution of appropriate organizational forms. It provides an "umbrella of intersection" for different perspectives and this should help us to coordinate our interactions in a "consensual domain."

Harnden has been convinced by the work of von Foerster, and Maturana and Varela, of the need to "bracket" objectivity. The early work in cybernetics, by Wiener, Ashby, *et al*, concerned itself with the regulation and control of systems perceived to exist in the world. More recently, however, cyberneticians have become interested in "constructivist epistemologies" which emphasize, instead, the purpose of the modeler, self-regulation and autonomy, and the interaction between observer and observed (see Umpleby, 1990). Von Foerster, a pioneer in these newer developments, called the early work "first order cybernetics", and distinguished the later work with the appellation "second order cybernetics." For him, while first order cybernetics was the cybernetics of observed systems, second-order cybernetics is the cybernetics of observing systems (von Foerster, 1981). As part of their studies on autopoiesis, and influenced by von Foerster, Maturana and Varela have similarly concluded that attention needs to be shifted to observers and the "distinctions" that they make. For them, cognition is an organizationally closed system and we must therefore give up any claim to have direct access to the phenomena around us. According to Maturana, before we can give any explanation about anything it is first necessary to make an "observation." This observation is made by an "observer" who, according to Maturana, is

> a human being, a person; someone who can make distinctions and specify that which he distinguishes as an entity (a something) different from himself (1975, p. 315).

The act of distinction is critical if we are to be able to identify what makes a living system a living system, different to other types of system:

> The act of indicating any being, object, thing or unity involves making an act of distinction which distinguishes what has been indicated as separate from its background (Maturana and Varela, 1992, p. 46).

The focus of study needs, therefore, to shift to these distinctions and how they are developed and sustained through language and in social systems - the "consensual domain." Harnden regards the VSM as an excellent "hermeneutic enabler" because it supports the making of distinctions which have been found useful by individuals discussing particular organizational forms and their possible transformation.

Ragsdell and Warren (1999) provide an excellent example of the use of the VSM as an "hermeneutic" enabler in a project with Hull Community Radio (HCR). An initial rich picturing exercise (not conducted by the authors) seemed to reveal that the most important problems confronting HCR concerned organizational structure and how it could cope with growth. HCR were worried that rapid growth in response to listener demand would lead to failures in communication and control. The fact that they used terms such as communication, control and feedback in their conversation, encouraged the analysts to introduce a simple version of the VSM into the discussions. This was followed up later by sending more detailed reading material to the HCR group. HCR soon became comfortable with notions such as recursion, feedback loops and primary tasks and gained commitment to the VSM. They were attracted by its relevance to their problem situation, by its non-hierarchical nature, and by the fact that it allowed them to discuss various responsibilities without, simultaneously, assigning particular individuals to these tasks. The VSM encouraged bonding within the HCR group, and between HCR and the analysts, because of the common language it provided. The authors conclude:

> Prior to the work with HCR, we had not appreciated the flexibility of the VSM. We had been somewhat biased towards it being a 'hard' approach to organizational design and had not associated it with facilitative, participative intervention. Our willingness to use it in a 'soft' way showed a fresh side to the model. Not only was it a vehicle for coming up with 'an answer' to the problem, but it gave us a common language through which we could relate to HCR. It gave us a medium to 'say a lot in a few words' (Ragsdell and Warren, 1999, p. 20).

7.8.4. Strengths and Weaknesses of Soft OR, Soft System Dynamics, Soft Cybernetics

One danger of employing methods, models and techniques to support a methodology and paradigm which is not their normal home is that it can leave them theoretically underpowered. Eden's SODA gains theoretical support from the notion that organizations are "negotiated orders" and from Kelly's "personal construct theory", but a case along these lines could be made regarding the rest of soft OR. There is a vague shared commitment to respond to the individual understandings of organizational actors, but the soft OR tradition generally seems unable to specify exactly what new paradigm is being opened up by its endeavors. Soft system dynamics could certainly benefit from a clearer recognition of the paradigm shift necessary to use system dynamics models to support mutual understanding according to the interpretive logic. Soft cybernetics is able to draw upon the conclusions of "second order cybernetics." However, the notions that we need to pay attention to the observer and that we have no direct access to "reality" are hardly startling or original given the history of philosophical debate on this issue and the fact that this point is taken for granted in soft systems thinking. It would pay those operating at the soft end of OR, system dynamics and cybernetics to research and draw more heavily on the theoretical resources of the interpretive paradigm itself.

The next question to ask is whether the methods, models and techniques extracted from the functionalist paradigm actually help or hinder the application of an interpretive approach. A case can be made, for soft OR, that the retention of rational analysis and modeling is beneficial even in a "problematic world." Soft system dynamics builds upon an, apparently, natural tendency in human beings to think in terms of causal processes. Soft cybernetics is seen as enriching the debate we are able to have, if we use only ordinary terms and concepts, about organizational structure and transformation. On the other hand it is easy to see that the particular steers these approaches impart, towards rationality, causality and organizational communication and control respectively, may severely limit our ability to grasp the complexity of social reality and the range of problems to which social systems give rise.

Another issue is the extent to which functionalist models, methods and techniques become denatured and lose sight of their "true vocation" when employed to serve the interpretive paradigm. Lane (1999, 2000) sees this danger clearly in relation to system dynamics. In his view, system dynamics can appease subjectivism to some extent but, if it moves too far in that direction, it will lose what is distinctive and effective about it:

> Indeed, if the placation of subjectivists involves the denial of the relevance of causal laws, causal explanations and the grand structural claim of system dynamics then the field should stop placating and start declaiming. While it is useful to clarify exactly what the system dynamics position is, there comes a point where criticisms must be turned on their head and worn as badges of pride (Lane, 2000, p. 15).

The same argument tells against the interpretive use of the VSM. Ultimately, Harnden (1989) believes that it is a matter of choice whether we adopt a representational view of the VSM or see it as an hermeneutic vehicle for orchestrating diverse viewpoints. However, this in itself is an interpretive conclusion. For those who see the VSM as expressing in a coherent and usable form the cybernetic principles of effective organization (and all the evidence of his writings suggests Beer is one of these), there is no choice about the cybernetic laws expressed in the VSM. If an enterprise does not respect the law of requisite variety, for example, it will not work as well as one that does and, indeed, its viability will be threatened. If their conversations lead participants to ignore the lessons of the law of requisite variety, with that result, then I suppose they have made a choice, but such a choice hardly respects the history of cybernetics or Beer's endeavors, and they will be punished for it when their organization ceases to be viable. Giving up on cybernetic laws relegates the VSM to becoming an optional addendum to the soft systems approach - possibly at stage 4 of Checkland's methodology, as another model worthy of debate. However, this is a depressing and unnecessary conclusion. The structuralist reading of organizational cybernetics provides it with its own domain for exploration and its own field of application: dealing with problems of communication, control, and organizing in complex systems. It could also be a damaging conclusion to reach for the overall strength of the systems movement, because soft systems thinking is certainly not equipped - in the way that organizational cybernetics is - to enhance the steering capacities of organizations and societies, and this is central to their successful evolution. I have called this kind of debate a battle for the "soul" of the VSM (Jackson, 1992) and we shall see it continuing in the next chapter on the emancipatory systems approach.

Becoming "softer" in their approach starts to expose users of previously "hard" or "cybernetic" methods, models and techniques to the wrath of unreformed functionalists. Perhaps there is some compensation in protection gained from the criticisms of emancipatory systems thinking? Unfortunately not. If we take soft OR as an example, we find Rosenhead (1989) having to admit his own embarrassment at the "manipulative - reformist" stance of the contributors to his collection of soft OR approaches. Soft OR methodologies are, one imagines, designed to be of use to any client; that is, to be "neutral." But any organization represents a particular mobilization of bias in which some participants will possess more power and receive more benefits than others. There surely should be more discussion of when such approaches can be legitimately employed. In fact Rosenhead's (1989) contributors, for the most part, avoid this kind of issue. Having embraced subjectivity in their methodologies, it becomes apparently impossible for them to decide whether the Nicaraguan *contras* can best be described as terrorists or freedom fighters (p. 81) or whether the U.S. leaders or the North Vietnamese had the right world view during the

Vietnam War (p. 301). It is easy to see how the lack of guidance provided by soft OR approaches about which "side" to take, when translated down to the level of managing organizations, is likely to produce soft OR studies serving powerful managers and maintaining the existing balance of forces in organizations. The arbitrary taking of sides produces good OR for managers (in the metagame analysis) and for the English "Albatross" Sailing Association (in the hypergame analysis) but, presumably, bad OR for workers and for the Welsh "Albatross" Association.

7.9. A GENERIC INTERPRETIVE SYSTEMS METHODOLOGY

We have in the preceding pages been discussing various systems approaches that take their lead from the interpretive theoretical orientation. In doing so we have had to devote some attention to the specific theories associated with the particular systems approaches but, in general terms, we have been able to emphasize methodology. Because as Checkland has it, soft systems thinking shifts systemicity from the world to the process of inquiry into the world, soft systems thinkers put a great deal more effort into explaining how the "frameworks of ideas" they employ are to be applied in order to generate "learning." There is an advantage for practitioners in that they receive much clearer guidelines setting out how soft systems methodologies should be used. For researchers it may seem that the theoretical formulations employed by soft systems thinkers are often hopelessly vague compared to those developed within functionalism. On the other hand, the tight specification of methodologies, and how they should be employed in practice, permits more rigorous research into methodology itself and into the nature of the problem situation under investigation. In Checkland's terms, the M replaces the F as the primary object of research. In Mode 2 research terms, the M rather than the F provides the transferable problem solving capability. An advantage for us, in terms of what we are seeking to achieve in this section, is that it becomes relatively easy to draw upon the various well defined soft systems approaches in order to arrive at a generic interpretive systems methodology. This is set out in Table 7.5, again building upon the constitutive rules elaborated by Checkland and Scholes.

I would wish to argue that despite the variations we have seen between Warfield's, Churchman's, Mason and Mitroff's, Ackoff's, Checkland's, and the others' work, Table 7.5 captures the essence of the manner in which these key proponents would like to see their contributions used. They all adhere to the interpretive theoretical rationale as described in Chapter 2 and at the beginning of this chapter. The guidelines adumbrated under 3, in Table 7.5, are crucial in this respect and we can provide specific cases which should help the reader to carry out her further tests on the different approaches presented in the chapter. Checkland makes no assumption that the real-world is systemic in carrying out rich picture analysis. In Warfield's work the analysis of the problem situation is designed to be creative and may not be conducted in systems terms. Idealized designs in interactive planning can be seen as possible human activity systems. Mason and Mitroff use models to interrogate perceptions of the real-world and to structure dialectical debate. Quantitative analysis is rarely found, except in soft OR and soft system dynamics, and then only to clarify the implications of world views. Churchman sees the process of intervention as systemic, never-ending and designed to promote learning which will alleviate unease. Vennix regards group problem solving as best conducted on the basis of participation. Changes are evaluated according to how effective they are in achieving stakeholder satisfaction. To this are added

Table 7.5. Constitutive rules for a generic interpretive systems methodology

---

1.   An interpretive systems methodology is a structured way of thinking with an attachment to the interpretive theoretical rationale that is focused on improving real-world problem situations.

2.   An interpretive systems methodology uses systems ideas as the basis for its intervention strategy and will frequently employ methods, models, tools and techniques which also draw upon systems ideas.

3.   The claim to have used a systems methodology according to the interpretive rationale must be justified according to the following guidelines:

   a.   there is no assumption that the real-world is systemic;

   b.   analysis of the problem situation is designed to be creative and may not be conducted in systems terms;

   c.   models are constructed which represent some possible "human activity systems";

   d.   models are used to interrogate perceptions of the real-world and to structure debate about changes which are feasible and desirable;

   e.   quantitative analysis is unlikely to be useful except to clarify the implications of world views;

   f.   the process of intervention is systemic, is never-ending, and is aimed at alleviating unease about the problem situation and generating individual and organizational learning;

   g.   the intervention is best conducted on the basis of stakeholder participation;

   h.   changes that might alleviate the feelings of unease or contribute to learning are evaluated primarily in terms of their effectiveness, elegance and ethicality.

4.   Since an interpretive systems methodology can be used in different ways in different situations, and interpreted differently by different users, each use should exhibit conscious thought about how to adapt to the particular circumstances.

5.   Each use of an interpretive systems methodology should yield research findings as well as changing the real-world problem situation. These research findings may relate to the theoretical rationale underlying the methodology, to the methodology itself and how to use it, to the methods, models, tools and techniques employed, to the real-world problem situation investigated, or to all of these.

---

concerns about how aesthetically pleasing the changes are and, sometimes, how ethical they might seem from other points of view. In general terms, and with occasional explanation necessary, the names of any of the systems approaches discussed in this chapter can be used to head the sentences related to 3a - 3h in Table 7.5, replacing the particular examples provided here. Furthermore, all these soft systems methodologies are flexible and they all provide the basis for generating a variety of research findings.

We must now consider the strengths and weaknesses of the interpretive systems approach as a whole.

7.10. CRITIQUE OF THE INTERPRETIVE SYSTEMS APPROACH

The same pattern for this critique is followed as for that in the previous chapter. The interpretive systems approach, and the advantages it brings, are first discussed in its own terms. It is then subject to a broad critique from the points of view of functionalist, emancipatory and postmodern systems thinking.

The basic claim made is that all the varieties of soft systems approach discussed in this chapter have made a significant break from functionalist systems thinking and established their own theoretical home in the interpretive paradigm as defined by Burrell and Morgan. It is now time to justify this and to work through the consequences. One defining feature of the interpretive paradigm, according to Burrell and Morgan, is its subjectivist approach to social science. Let us therefore look for evidence of a nominalist ontology, anti-positivist epistemology, a voluntarist approach to human nature and ideographic methodology in the writings of the soft systems thinkers.

Systems are perceived by adherents of the soft systems approach as having a subjective existence as the product of individual consciousness. Checkland (1981) argues that the emphasis of SSM "is not on any external 'reality' but on people's perceptions of reality, on their mental processes rather than on the objects of those processes." Ackoff does countenance an analysis of the systemic characteristics of messes ("formulating the mess") as a way of probing the future we are in. However, the way messes are interpreted depends very much on the point of view of the analyst: "Problems are products of thought acting on environments; they are elements of problematic situations that are abstracted from these situations by analysis" (Ackoff, 1974). Thereafter, interactive planning concentrates on people's perceptions of a desirable future. Churchman (1979c) sees the social world as the product of individual consciousness acting on what is "given" in experience. It is not external to the individual, imposing its structure on the consciousness of the individual. Rather, the structure is imposed by the concepts and labels used by individuals.

Theorists of a subjective orientation seek knowledge by attempting to understand the point of view of the people involved in creating social reality. Checkland's methodology explores the different Ws relevant to a system of concern by encapsulating them in root definitions and then elaborating them in conceptual models. Ackoff hopes to involve all the stakeholders of a system in the design of a desirable future for that system. For Churchman (1979a), "the systems approach begins when first you see the world through the eyes of another." Even the points of view of the enemies of the systems approach - politics, morality, religion, aesthetics - should be "swept in" in order to make the approach as comprehensive as possible (Churchman, 1979c).

Theorists with a subjective orientation see human beings as possessing free will rather than as being determined in their behavior by external circumstances. In Checkland's methodology, the various actors are presumed capable of learning and of making whatever changes to the system they deem to be both desirable and feasible. The latter word is introduced by Checkland to suggest that the realities of the problem situation may impose *some* limits on what is possible. It is an axiom of Ackoff's interactive planning that the stakeholders of a system do not have to accept the future that has been designed for them as inevitable; they can plan a desirable future for themselves and seek to bring this about. Churchman's systems approach rests on the power of decision makers to change social systems. The systems designer seeks to make this decision making rational by ensuring that it benefits all the customers of systems.

Theorists with a subjective orientation seek detailed information about systems by getting as close as possible to the subjects under investigation, rather than by the quantitative analysis of data. Checkland's SSM is designed to allow clients to engage in a learning process themselves so that they change their appreciative systems. He employs conceptual rather than quantitative models; these conceptual models are elaborations of different Ws relevant to the system of concern. Ackoff uses quantitative techniques only as subsidiary aids in the interactive planning process. Churchman (1979c) argues that the best method of inquiry for planning calls for "observing a lot of human behavior."

In spite of Ackoff and Churchman's occasionally functionalist language, and although they claim that their philosophical mentor E. A. Singer has overcome the objective-subjective dichotomy, it seems apparent that the social theory to which soft systems thinking corresponds is subjectivist in Burrell and Morgan's terms. This is an argument, of course, that Checkland enthusiastically embraces with respect to his own methodology. To those such as Burrell (1983) who might question whether Checkland's commitment to phenomenology was pure enough, one can reasonably respond by asking what a problem-resolving methodology based on a "pure" subjectivist social theory would look like. I find it difficult to see how it could be much different to what Checkland has produced.

It is relatively easy to argue, therefore, that the soft systems approaches we have considered in this chapter are subjectivist in nature. The unity of the soft systems tradition, in this respect, is supported if we consider it in terms of "root metaphors", images of organization, and Habermas's theory of human interests. The dominant root metaphor is the "contextualist", which has a concern with attributing meaning in order to give context to an "act." The "culture" and "politics" metaphors of organization are emphasized. An application of Habermas's schema reveals the main value of soft systems approaches to be in the support they offer to the practical interest in promoting intersubjective understanding. All the methodologies considered offer effective means of securing and expanding the possibility of mutual understanding among individuals in social systems - whether through interactive management, dialectical debate, focusing attention on an idealized design, engaging in a cyclic learning process, or learning through group problem solving. It is indeed a significant achievement that the systems approach associated in the minds of many, including Habermas, with the functionalism of Parsons, and the "advanced technocratic consciousness" displayed in Luhmann's work, should be the source of methodologies providing such effective assistance to the practical interest.

This common allegiance to the interpretive paradigm comes through in the detail of the methodologies we have been studying in this chapter. The writers taken to be representative of the interpretive systems approach do have their differences, to which the reader has seen Checkland alluding, but it is the similarities in their various methodologies that are most significant. All are concerned to cope with ill-structured problems, or messes, at the strategic level. All are opposed to tackling messes by the method of reductionism. Rather than attempting to identify and analyze systems in the real world, the approaches prefer to work with the different perceptions of systems that exist in people's minds. Multiple perceptions of reality are admitted and explored. Values are included explicitly rather than being excluded (in theory) from the methodological process. The privileged role of experts in the systems approach is questioned. The aim in each case is to encourage learning so that an accommodation can be reached among participants involved with a problem situation. Since many of our examples are coming from Churchman, Ackoff and Checkland, it is useful to have Cardenas's confirmation in Table 7.6 that Warfield's interactive management has all of the characteristics of soft systems thinking that I have identified.

Taking all this into consideration, it is clear that the functionalism underpinning the organizations-as-systems approach, hard systems thinking, organizational cybernetics, system dynamics, chaos and complexity theory, etc., has been abandoned in soft systems thinking. An epistemological break (in the sense of a shift between paradigms) has occurred, and a new direction in systems thinking has been opened up based upon other philosophical/sociological foundations. The interpretive systems approach opens up a completely new perspective on the way systems ideas can be used to help with decision making and problem solving. It arguably brings within the scope of proper treatment all

Table 7.6. IM as a soft systems approach (adapted from Cardenas, 2000, p. 69)

CHARACTERISTICS OF SOFT SYSTEMS THINKING ACCORDING TO JACKSON	CORRESPONDING CHARACTERISTICS OF IM
"All are concerned to cope with ill-structured problems, or messes, at the strategic level. All are opposed to tackling messes by the method of reductionism …"	Concern for dealing with complex situations and the emphasis on identifying relationships between elements
"…Rather than attempting to identify and analyze systems in the real world, all … approaches prefer to work with the different perceptions of systems that exist in people's minds …"	The cognitive orientation found in the concept of complexity on which IM is based
"… Multiple perceptions of reality are admitted and explored. Values are included explicitly rather than being excluded (in theory) from the methodological process …"	The emphasis on a participative approach through which the different perspectives and interests of stakeholders are considered
"… The privileged role of experts in the systems approach is questioned …"	Relevance of the direct participation of stakeholders in addressing complex situations
"… The aim in each case is to encourage learning so that an accommodation can be reached among participants involved with a problem situation"	Model development as a learning process and the meaning of consensus involved in IM group work

those wicked, messy and ill-structured problems that either escape or are distorted by the functionalist methodologies, considered earlier, because of the strict prerequisites that need to be met before those methodologies can be employed. The result has been a massive extension of the area within which systems thinking can be used to help with real-world problem management.

Of course, we cannot expect functionalist systems thinkers to see the embrace that soft systems thinking gives to subjectivism in quite such a positive light. The functionalist systems approach is concerned with the design of complex systems; in Habermas's language with supporting the technical interest in prediction and control. To functionalists, soft systems thinking has little to offer in this respect. Churchman, along with Mason and Mitroff, only sees a role for hard systems thinking once ill-structured problems have been tamed by softer approaches. There is no recognition that the organizations-as-systems tradition, system dynamics or organizational cybernetics could offer useful advice on the design of complex adaptive systems. Ackoff allocates space for the "machine" and "organism" models within his social systems sciences, but it is clear he regards the "purposeful systems" orientation as the most sophisticated. Checkland, however, is the *bête noire* for functionalists. He sees hard and cybernetic approaches as usable only in the "special case" when worldviews have coalesced to such an extent that there is consensus about what system to design. It is soft systems thinking which must be employed in the huge majority of cases when these special circumstances do not pertain. To functionalists this is anathema. They believe that it is possible to provide knowledge which can guide action in large areas of social and organizational life. Within these domains it is their own rationality, as witnessed by their ability to increase prediction and control, that must hold sway. What is the best queuing system for a particular supermarket or what would be an effective information-systems design for a particular organization are, for functionalists, not simply matters of intersubjective agreement.

If functionalist systems thinkers get frustrated with the subjectivism of the soft approach and its failure, as they see it, to provide knowledge about how to design complex adaptive systems, it is another aspect of the interpretive rationale underpinning soft systems thinking that emancipatory systems thinkers get angry about. The interpretive paradigm, as defined by Burrell and Morgan, is oriented toward regulation rather than radical change. Interpretive sociologists and organization theorists are said to be interested, at the expense of anything else, in how order and cohesion are achieved and maintained. Emancipatory critics argue that soft systems thinking, based as it is in the interpretive paradigm, must similarly be more suitable for preserving the status quo than going beyond it.

Much of the argument relates to the nature of the consensus or accommodation that soft systems thinkers are able to bring about and upon which agreements for change are founded. Following Habermas, emancipatory critics argue that appropriate rationalization in the sphere of social interaction demands not just any kind of consensus or accommodation, but genuine understanding based upon communication free from distortion. Methodologies, if they are to have any emancipatory potential, must pay attention to the possibility that systematically distorted communication might jeopardize the emergence of genuine shared purposes. To what extent do soft systems methodologies give consideration to this matter?

The answer is not very much. We have seen the critics arguing that Churchman fails to take account of any of the objective features of the social world that might lead to distorted communication, and that Ackoff's interactive planning can only lead to exceptionally constrained discussion or debate among stakeholders. I offer detailed argument now in relation to Checkland's methodology. The argument centers on two of the key stages in SSM - Stages 5 and 6, the discussion stages. It is here that the various relevant systems, expressed in root definitions and conceptual models, are examined and compared with what is perceived to exist in the real world and that agreed changes emerge. If these changes are to reflect a true consensus or accommodation among the actors, the discussion stages must conform as far as possible to the model of communicative competence proposed by Habermas. All actors must be willing to enter into discourse and this must be conducted in conditions that approximate the ideal speech situation. All participants must have equal chances to select and employ speech acts and to assume dialogue roles. There must be unlimited discussion that is free from constraints or domination, whether the source of these is the behavior of other parties or communication barriers secured through ideology or neurosis. The ability of some participants to impose sanctions on others (because they are more powerful) must not affect the outcome of the discussion.

Only if such conditions are met, will the consensus at the end of the debate reflect the strength of the better argument and not simply various constraints on discussion. Of course, in organizations and societies characterized by great inequalities, the kind of unconstrained debate envisaged here cannot possibly take place. The actors bring to the discussion unequal intellectual resources and are more or less powerful. The result of the unequal intellectual resources is that the ideologies of the powerful are imposed upon other actors who lack the means of recognizing their own true interests. The result of the inequalities in power is that the existing social order from which power is drawn is reproduced. As Giddens (1976) writes:

> The use of power in interaction involves the application of facilities whereby participants are able to generate outcomes through affecting the conduct of others; the facilities are both drawn from an order of domination and at the same time as they are applied, reproduce that order of domination (p. 122).

SSM, to the critics, merely facilitates a social process in which the essential elements of the status quo are reproduced - perhaps on a firmer footing, since differences of opinion will have been temporarily smoothed over. In doing so it supports the interests of the dominant group or groups in the social system. Checkland (1981) does seem to take the point that the debate at Stages 5 and 6 can be crucially inhibited by society's structure, but he concludes rather weakly from this that "it is the nature of society that this will be so." This is not at all helpful. It tells us nothing about the degree of constraint on discussion imposed by particular social arrangements and institutions or about the possibility of changing such institutions and arrangements in order to facilitate communicative competence. The social environment in which the methodology has to operate nullifies, therefore, its attempts to bring about changes based on a true consensus. The methodology is culpable in that it is prepared to accept for implementation changes emerging from a false consensus, or accommodation, produced by distorted communication.

In order to counter the arguments of emancipatory critics, soft methodologies would have to use Habermas's conceptualization of the ideal speech situation to unmask cases of systematically distorted communication and would then have to challenge those social arrangements that produce distorted communication. Unfortunately, emancipatory critics argue, there is a major deficiency in soft approaches, stemming from their adherence to interpretive theory, that prevents them doing this. Craib points out what this is in relation to interpretive approaches generally and symbolic interactionism specifically:

> The most regular criticisms you are likely to come across in the rapidly growing literature on symbolic interactionism are that it ignores the wider features of social structure and therefore cannot say anything about power, conflict and change, that its theoretical formulations are hopelessly vague, and that it provides an incomplete picture of the individual (1992, p. 90).

Wilmott (1989) uses the same argument against SSM:

> Its major shortcoming lies in its unnecessarily limited capacity to promote reflection upon the possibility that the content and negotiation of *Weltanschauung* are expressive of asymmetrical relations of power through which they are constructed and debated .... Phenomenology, and SSM in particular, simply lacks a social theory capable of accounting for why particular sets of perceptions of reality emerge, and why some perceptions are found to be more plausible than others (p. 76).

So soft methodologies lack any social theory that might allow them to understand, let alone challenge, the social arrangements that produce distorted communication. That this is so is starkly revealed by Checkland's (1981) attempts to get to grips with what he calls the "common structurings" found in social reality - what a functionalist thinker would take as the objective aspects of the social world. This acceptance of common structurings is rather surprising given the overall subjectivist orientation of the methodology. The notion that social systems are not completely malleable has, however, been a theme running through Checkland's work. At one time it found expression in the special position accorded social systems in the "systems map of the universe" (Checkland, 1971). As well as being the context for human activity systems, they also had to be seen as natural systems. They reflected the human need for community life. This created difficulties for those who were concerned to "engineer" social systems. In the fully worked-out version of the methodology, the word *feasible* (as we have seen) draws our attention to the need to arrive at changes that take into account the realities of the problem situation. The kind of change that can be considered will be limited by the historically determined attitudes and behavior patterns of the actors in particular social situations.

A more recent development is based upon Dilthey's concern to discover the common types of *Weltanschauung* that occur. It is, of course, the nature of such Ws that sets the limits to change for SSM. They operate at every important stage - embodied in root definitions, structured into conceptual models and brought to bear again at the discussion stages. The methodology can be used, according to Checkland, to reveal any recurrent Ws and it opens up the prospect of discovering "the universal structures of subjective orientation in the world" (Luckmann, quoted in Checkland, 1981). This search for common structurings is an admirable aim and one that the methodology is well suited to pursuing. It echoes the concern of interpretive sociologists to understand the social world as it is - to understand how order and cohesion are achieved. However, to go beyond regulation and to challenge the status quo, one would have to possess some theory of the origins of such common structurings. For example, which of the common structurings are historically contingent (and therefore amenable to change), and which are physiologically determined attributes of the human race (and therefore not amenable to change)? One would also have to put such a theory to the test in challenging the social institutions that carry what are regarded as the historically contingent structurings.

The Checkland methodology, tied as it is to subjectivism, has no such theory. There are odd references to "historically determined behavior patterns", "genetic inheritance", and "previous experiences" as placing limitations on the capacity of human beings to change, but nothing much is made of this and, as mentioned earlier, rather than challenge those structures that are historically based, the methodology prefers to deal in changes that are feasible given the existing social situation.

For all these reasons, emancipatory thinkers conclude that the interpretive foundations of soft systems thinking condemn it to regulation and severely limit its ability to bring about any radical change. To summarize, a key weakness lies in its failure to take account of the possibility of systematically distorted communication. There is a tendency to accept at face value, and work with, existing perceptions of reality. No attempt is made to unmask ideological frames of reference or to uncover the effects of "false consciousness." There is also a willingness to take as given compromises and accommodations achieved within the confines of prevailing power structures. This weakness is not easily remedied because of another problem inherited from the interpretive paradigm. Soft systems thinking might seek to seize upon and use Habermas's theory of communicative competence as a critical standard, but this would require in addition an appropriate social theory. The development of such a social theory, which would unearth contradiction and conflict, and the operation of power (according to those who follow the sociology of radical change), is currently precluded by soft systems thinking's attachment to subjectivism. For other compatible accounts of the relationship between soft systems thinking and interpretive social theory the reader can consult Mingers (1984) and Oliga (1988).

This conclusion is a disappointing one for many soft systems thinkers who harbor radical aspirations. We noted earlier, for example, Checkland's claim that the social theory to which his methodology corresponds is not simply interpretive (subjective/regulative) but must occupy as well some of the radical humanist (subjective/radical) quadrant of Burrell and Morgan's map. There is nothing therefore, according to Checkland, preventing the methodology being used as an instrument for radical change. Checkland bases this claim on an article by Mingers (1980) that reveals some apparent similarities between the social theory of Habermas and SSM. If these similarities are fundamental, Checkland's argument that his methodology can be used as a radical social instrument is greatly enhanced. Unfortunately, as I have argued elsewhere (Jackson, 1982), despite the similarities, the differences between the work of Habermas and Checkland are more significant. The major difference is theoretical and lies in Habermas's willingness to accept the usefulness, on appropriate occasions, of "objective" social theory. Habermas recognizes that although the social world is created by the interaction of people, it is not transparent to them. It escapes human beings, takes on objective features and constrains them. Humans are still in the grip of unconscious forces and their actions still have unintended consequences. In these circumstances, hermeneutics cannot be the sole method appropriate to the social sciences. There must also be a moment in social inquiry in which the objective features of the social world - when people do appear to act as things - can be studied. There is a need, too, for a critical moment (corresponding to the emancipatory interest). The hope is to reduce the area of social life where people act as things and to increase the realm of the hermeneutic, where rational intentions become realized in history. Though the major difference is theoretical, it *does* have a political result. Habermas's work opens up the possibility of political action to accomplish real change; it is potentially radical. Checkland's methodology confines itself to working within the constraints imposed by existing social arrangements; it is regulative.

Atkinson (1984) has argued that almost all systems thinking rests upon an "adaptive whole system" metaphor; a sort of amalgam of organismic, brain, and cultural thinking, and he and Checkland (1988) have shown an interest in extending the metaphor system and building models of "combative", "contradictive", "syndicalistic", "host/parasite" and other systems to map onto reality. No doubt the hope is that such conceptions will lead to more challenging root definitions and more radical changes. This work cannot, however, change the essentially regulative nature of SSM because it remains locked in interpretive thinking and leaves untheorized and unchallenged prevailing power structures. The same might be said of attempts to strengthen SSM by including references to culture and power in Analyses 2 and 3, respectively (see the earlier section on SSM). Only impoverished notions of culture and power can survive in the dominant interpretive climate of the methodology. It is not possible with interpretive ideas to think that culture might be engineered to serve the interests of a dominant group or that power is differentially distributed according to sex, race, status and class. That would require looking at organizations using the "instruments of domination" metaphor and adopting the assumptions of another sociological paradigm.

Having noted the functionalist and emancipatory critiques of soft systems thinking we must, finally, consider it from the perspective of postmodernism. From that viewpoint, soft systems thinking can be identified as a rather underdeveloped form of critical modernism, based upon Kant's program of enlightenment and seeking the progressive liberation of humanity from constraints. Churchman and Ackoff are the most effusive contributors to this tendency in the soft approach. The reader will remember Churchman's Singerian inquirer pursuing teleology to the ultimate in the heroic mission of increasing or developing purpose in human society, so that man becomes more and more deeply involved in seeking goals. Ackoff (1974) wants to change the future through the idea of interactive planning. He wants man to take over God's work of creating the future. Even Checkland (1981) has his moments, seeing SSM as "a formal means of achieving "communicative competence" in unrestricted discussion which Habermas seeks." At the same time, because it is so underdeveloped a version of critical modernism, for all the reasons we have been detailing in this section, soft systems thinking is particularly prone to slipping back into becoming no more than an adjunct of systemic modernism, readjusting the ideological status quo by engineering human hopes and aspirations in a manner that responds to the system's need and so ensures its smoother functioning. Somewhat ironically soft systems thinking seems incapable of grasping the nature of the system that it actually serves. Clarke and Lehaney (1999) provide an example of the use of Checkland's SSM, alongside brainstorming, to help with the development of a new community information system for a major health services trust. Under the leadership of the Director of Information Services the project was conducted in a very participative manner, involving consultation with a wide variety of stakeholders. With the appointment of a consultant to the project, funded by the regional head office, the power structure changed. Participants were still consulted but in the context of an intervention that had now become functionalist in character. It became the priority to use a structured approach to provide a technical solution, employing appropriate hardware, to a predefined problem. As a result, Clarke and Lehaney argue, the system that was eventually designed failed to meet the requirements at which it was targeted.

I have analyzed and assessed the interpretive systems approach at length and with good reason. Soft methodologies represent a genuinely new direction in systems thinking. Theoretically, a new paradigm has been opened up for exploration using systems ideas. In practice, Churchman, Ackoff and Checkland have massively extended the area within which management science can be used to help with real-world problems. Work on messes and ill-structured problems can be confidently undertaken using the approaches outlined in this chapter. Because of some of the claims made for soft systems thinking, however, it is vital to emphasize the weaknesses as well as the strengths of the soft approach. Soft systems thinking has a limited range of problem situations for which it is clearly the most appropriate approach, just as do all the other strands that make up the systems movement. The hope is that what soft systems thinking can achieve and what it cannot achieve are both now much better understood.

8

THE EMANCIPATORY SYSTEMS APPROACH

8.1. INTRODUCTION

The concept of "emancipation" is a much contested one in systems thinking, as it is in social theory more generally. There are arguments about whether we should be seeking human emancipation or individual emancipation or, indeed, whether non-human elements such as other species or the environment should be considered as well. Within Burrell and Morgan's category of the sociology of "radical change" there are subjectivist approaches (radical humanism) which see emancipation as coming about as individuals rid themselves of some form of "false consciousness", and objectivist approaches (radical structuralism) that picture emancipation as becoming possible because of changes in the structure of society. There are "modern" and "postmodern" versions of emancipation; the difference often resting on how "universal" or "local" the emancipation is supposed to be. Given this degree of complexity, it is probably best to introduce the topic by saying what all the approaches to emancipation we shall discuss in this chapter have in common and then to be clear about the distinctions employed to provide order to our discussion of the emancipatory systems approach.

All emancipatory systems approaches are suspicious of the current social order and seek to radically reform it. They see society, as presently constituted, as benefiting some groups at the expense of other groups which are suffering domination or discrimination. The divides in society which lead to inequality may be along class, race, gender, sexual orientation, age, capability or other lines. Whichever of these are chosen as the main foci of attention, the aim is to emancipate those who are suffering as a result of current social arrangements. Usually the process of emancipating the oppressed can also be seen to have benefits for the oppressors in the new social order. The job of emancipation requires more or less work on the part of the disadvantaged and their advisors depending on the degree to which contradictions in society are working in favor of change. In general, however, some sort of critique of the current order is required which unmasks the way in which it operates to promote benefits to some and oppression for others. Often this critique has to be combined with some sort of "therapeutic" procedure to overcome "false-consciousness" which prevents the disadvantaged from seeing the reality of their situation and rebelling against it. Critique points out the way that ideology and power function to sustain the status quo and the contradictions in the existing social order that can be exploited to change it. It is also, in most cases, conducted on the basis of some vision of a better state of affairs that can be brought about by social action. That is to say, it is premised upon some "ideal" such as a classless society, a world in which people live in harmony with nature, or a world in which people are free to determine their own future free from the constraints imposed by the operation of power. Emancipatory systems thinking draws upon various "root metaphors" either to describe and condemn the existing social order or to propose alternative social structures. The "images" of organization most frequently found in emancipatory writings are those of organizations as "psychic prisons" and as "instruments of domination"; the former signaling a more subjectivist path to emancipation, the latter a more objectivist route.

As Munro (1997) points out, the idea of emancipation may for many people, both within and outside management science, seem an odd notion to associate with operational research and systems thinking. Nevertheless, during the 1980s and 1990s, it is the case that a number of theorists and practitioners working with these ideas and methodologies became dissatisfied with the systems approach used, unreflectively as a technical instrument or as a vehicle to promote debate, without reference to whose interests might be served by the intervention. Drawing upon a variety of sources from the critical tradition in philosophy and social theory, they put up a standard for emancipatory systems thinking and started to produce significant work which seeks to provide a much broader social role for OR and systems thinking.

Brocklesby and Cummings (1996) suggest that there are two competing philosophical underpinnings for emancipatory systems thinking (they say critical systems thinking). The first is a tradition of thought starting with Kant, and stretching through Hegel and Marx, to Habermas. The primary concern of this tradition is with human emancipation. It defines emancipation in terms of collective, sometimes universal, emancipation from false consciousness and power relations. The second also derives from Kant but takes a postmodern turn, via Nietzsche and Heidegger, to its culmination in the work of Foucault. The dominant theme here is self-emancipation. As Munro (1997) suggests this second theme actually undermines the whole notion of human emancipation as conceived of in the other tradition. Munro adds a third possible emancipatory theme drawing its inspiration from the writings of McIntyre. This defines emancipation in terms of virtuous practices and the kinds of organizations and societies that can provide scope for individuals to develop themselves through virtuous practices. He admits that this has not yet been explored in OR and systems thinking.

I intend to explore three forms of emancipatory systems thinking in this chapter. The first looks to the tradition that reached its apotheosis with Marx and much influenced Habermas's early work. Its defining feature is some social theory which allows critique of the existing social system and indicates some alternative, improved social arrangement. I call it "emancipation as liberation." The second rests upon the same tradition but follows Habermas along the road which leads to a new critical standard - communication free from domination. I call this "emancipation through discursive rationality." Thirdly, there are those who take on the basic emancipatory rationale of this tradition but wish to combine it with more traditional systems methodologies or methods, taking advantage of their "critical kernel" (Jackson, 1990a). I call this, following Flood and Romm (1996), "emancipation through the oblique use of systems methods." I shall not, here, deal at length with the postmodern perspective on emancipation. Postmodernism does not, as Munro hints, lead necessarily to emancipatory practice and we shall deal with the complexities of the relationship between emancipation and postmodernism in the next chapter.

8.2. EMANCIPATION AS LIBERATION

Munro (1997) helpfully explains that the concept of emancipation derives from the Latin word *emancipo*, which was originally used in Roman Law to refer to the release of a child from the legal control of the family head to act in his own right. The concept entered the English language around the seventeenth century and become increasingly used in connection with freedom from slavery. In 1863 Abraham Lincoln inaugurated an "Emancipation Day" in the United States.

We pick up the story leading to emancipatory systems thinking, however, with Kant. In Chapter 3 we identified Kant as the preeminent philosopher of the Enlightenment, eager to push rational thought to its limit in order to free man from prejudice and illusion. In an essay, "What is Enlightenment?", Kant (1784) challenged the citizens of his day to break free from the chains of superstition and "dare to know." Traditional opinion did not have to be taken as given, it could be criticized and new knowledge built on the firmer foundations of reason. Foucault notes that after Kant's critical revolution "the world appears as a city to be built, rather than as a cosmos already given" (related in Brocklesby and Cummings, 1996). Of course, Kant was also aware of the limitations imposed upon reason by the categories the mind uses to order experience. Being critical also meant reflecting upon the nature of the restrictions imposed by these categories.

In Hegel's view, the categories of thought that Kant had treated as atemporal did, in fact, change over time. Progress occurred in the realm of ideas through the workings of the dialectic of thesis, anti-thesis, synthesis, thesis and so on. Eventually the contradictions present in thought would be overcome as "Absolute Knowledge" was obtained. Once this state had been reached, humans would be able to take control of their own destiny. Marx, as we saw (Chapter 4), turned Hegel's thinking around and located the dialectic not in the progress of human consciousness but in the material world:

> With (Hegel, the dialectic) is standing on its head. It must be turned right side up again, if you would discover the rational kernel within the mystical shell (Marx, 1961, p. 20).

History was governed not by changes in the world of ideas but by changes in the economic base of society.

Marx's account of alienated labor in the *Economic and Philosophical Manuscripts of 1844* had a major impact upon the development of emancipatory and critical thought. The main concern of Marx in this document is alienation in the economic realm of society. According to Marx, under the capitalist mode of production, both the proletariat and the bourgeoisie are alienated by worship of a "wordly god" - money. Man does not involve himself in the labor process for its own sake, because it is in his nature to do so, but because of a need "outside" - in order to survive or to amass wealth. It is the worker who represents the hope of the "repressed", creative potentialities within man, if only because his conditions are so bad that he sees the "actuality of an inhuman existence." The worker's estrangement from himself, from his own true nature, is not yet complete. Here "alienated" man is in revolt against greed, because the worker resents the state to which he has come.

Let us look more closely, then, at the "alienation" of the worker in capitalist society. Marx distinguishes four aspects of alienated labor. First, the worker is alienated from the product of his labor which he does not own. Labor produces wonderful things for the rich, but deprivation for the worker. Indeed, the more the worker labors, the more his deprivation increases and the "object" world opposing him grows, confronting him as an alien power. Second, there is self-estrangement in the production process. Work is alienating in itself since the worker's labor time is no longer his own but has been bought by the capitalist. This is demonstrated by the worker having to be coerced to labor and shunning work if no compulsion exists. Third, and stemming from the other two, the worker is estranged from his essential nature - the productive life. Work is as natural to man as rest or play and, in fact, more truly human. Work, the productive life, is the life of the human species. A worker should work because he realizes himself in the process and because he is able to contemplate his own being in the world of things he creates. Under capitalism, however, he works to maintain his physical existence and the objects he creates become a power over him. Finally, and as a product of the previous three aspects, man is estranged from his fellow men. Social relations are not free relations between individual and individual but are conditioned by the position of individuals in the market situation; relations between worker and capitalist, etc.

What is worth noticing about all this is the way Marx closely ties in his account of alienated labor with a critique of the wider society and, in particular, the system of private ownership of the means of production. Alienated labor is the specific result of a specific form of social and economic organization. If the product does not belong to the laborer it is because it belongs to someone else. If the worker is estranged during production it is because the labor time is owned by someone else and he is coerced to work. If he is estranged from his species-being, it is because of both these things; and his estrangement from other men is because of peculiarly capitalist relations of production. Alienated labor is, therefore, at the center of capitalist property relations. Under capitalism, the bourgeoisie owns the means of production and sells the fruits of the workers' labor as commodities on the market. Labor power, too, is bought on the market and is not fairly rewarded.

Also central to the critical method is the establishment of a point from which critique can be launched. For Marx this is a vision of man's essential being, total, all-sided, and unalienated, fully realizing his potential through labor. Marx believed that in a rational and good society, a communist society, man himself would be rational and good. He would reveal his wide range of creative potentialities as an inner necessity, a need. The following passage is illustrative:

> It is therefore in his fashioning of the objective world that man really proves himself to be a species-being. Such production is his active species-life. Through it nature appears as his work and his reality. The object of labor is therefore the objectification of the species-life of man: for man reproduces himself not only intellectually, in his consciousness, but actively and actually, and he can therefore contemplate himself in the world he himself has created (Marx, 1844, p. 329).

The critical method, therefore, relates particular "contradictions" to the broader social context and tries to establish a critical base from which to analyze both the contradictions and the wider context.

This early work of Marx on alienated labor heavily influenced the thinking of the so-called Frankfurt School of critical theorists, operating from the Institute for Social Research founded in 1923 at the University of Frankfurt. Craib (1992) and Brocklesby and Cummings (1996) provide brief summaries of the contributions of Horkheimer, Adorno and Marcuse, the main players in this version of critical theory. Their aim was to expose the manner in which "domination" expresses itself in instrumental reason, one-dimensional culture and through socialization. In summary Craib argues:

> The Frankfurt theorists are concerned with the way the system dominates: with the ways in which it forces, manipulates, blinds or fools people into ensuring its reproduction and continuation (pp. 210-211).

Habermas, in more recent times, has become the leading figure of the Frankfurt School, drawing upon both the early writings of Marx, the work of his predecessors at the Institute for Social Research, and some aspects of Marx's later work. In his later work Marx's vision became less humanistic and more objectivist and determinist in nature. In the three volumes of *Das Kapital* (Marx, 1961), he provided a "scientific" explanation of how the economic base of society conditioned the social, political and ideological superstructure. The capitalist mode of production also led to class struggle between the capitalist class, and their allies, and the exploited working class, and this was seen as inevitably leading to the overthrow of capitalism by the workers in a revolution that would give rise to a communist system. The determinism of the later Marx has been blamed by some for the "distortions" of socialism and communism found in the Soviet system. A more recent theoretical expression of this objectivism and determinism can be found in the work of Althusser (discussed in Chapter 4). As Althusser's student, Foucault also seems to have inherited some of the pessimism of this tradition about the capacity to achieve emancipation through human agency.

We can now discuss in turn the main strands of work that can be seen as contributing to the "emancipation as liberation" theme. These are labeled "Critical Operational Research/Management Science", "Habermas and the Critical Systems Approach", "Interpretive Systemology", and "Freire's Critical Pedagogy." I shall also discuss "MacIntyre and the Moral Community" and "Capra's Ecological Sustainability" because they share certain "emancipatory procedures" with the other approaches, although drawing on different theoretical positions - communitarian and environmental, respectively, rather than Marxist. Community OR will then be reviewed as an example of the practice of "emancipation as liberation." Finally, the strengths and weaknesses of this tendency will be considered.

8.2.1. Critical Operational Research/Management Science (OR/MS)

The point has been made (e.g. Rosenhead, 1989; Mingers, 1992a) that a good number of the founders of OR/MS had socialist or communist leanings. To them the role of science, and therefore of OR/MS, was to act as a progressive force in the construction of a better society. Mingers quotes Bernal from an influential text, *The Social Function of Science*, published in 1939:

> Science, conscious of its purpose, can in the long run become a major force in social change (Bernal, quoted in Mingers, p. 92).

Blackett, in the same book, wrote that

> socialism will want all the science it can get ... Scientists have ... to make up their minds on which side they stand (Blackett, quoted in Mingers, p. 92).

The radical potential of OR/MS began to surface again in the 1970s inspired by the new left thinking of the 1960s. Inevitably, the first steps in this rebirth consisted of attacks upon other forms of management science. Traditional OR/MS, already under fire from the soft systems thinkers, came under further attack from Marxist inclined scholars such as Hales (1974), Rosenhead and Thunhurst (1982), and Tinker and Lowe (1984). The thrust of this assault, as Wood and Kelly (1978) summarized it, was that traditional management science accepted existing structures of inequality of wealth, status, power and authority as given and thereby helped to buttress the status quo. Wood and Kelly thought that any critical management science should consider the origins of values, the historical development of organizations, the relations between organizations and society and the relationship between OR/MS and developments within capitalism.

According to Hales, management science under capitalism takes on a profoundly ideological character. It misrepresents the nature of the systems with which it deals, seeing them as consisting of objects to be controlled and denying the possibility of their free development as the conscious expression of the social nature of their members. This misrepresentation takes place primarily because of the social, political and economic pressure under which the discipline evolved. Management science must be understood as an ideology in relation to the development of the capitalist society that it is its major concern to serve. Essentially, it has evolved in response to the changing demands imposed on twentieth-century capitalism by the need to control the workforce.

Rosenhead and Thunhurst offer, specifically in relation to OR, a similar "materialist" analysis. OR is studied not simply in terms of the internal development of the subject; this internal development is further related to wider social processes and to the history of capitalism as a whole. In particular, the rapid growth of OR after World War II is seen as resulting from the demands of the postwar crisis of British capitalism. OR assisted the more efficient extraction of surplus value from the workers and so helped overcome the crisis. Furthermore, as one element of scientism, OR contributed to the mystification of the work-force. It was presented as the only source of rational answers to organizational problems. Thus it contributed to the subjective as well as the objective subjugation of the workers.

For Rosenhead and Thunhurst, as for Hales, the ultimate solution to management science's problems lies largely outside its own sphere of influence. Only by joining the wider struggle of labor against capital can management science hope to overcome its contradictions and speed the day when it becomes "self-management science", aiding active decision making by all rather than helping an élite to maintain control. Having said this, Rosenhead and Thunhurst do see some role for a critical OR in advancing the wider struggle and suggest some tasks it could perform. They also hint at the form the new self-management science, or "workers' science" (Rosenhead, 1987), might take after the necessary transformation in society has taken place.

Tinker and Lowe accused traditional OR/MS of being dominated by a technocratic consciousness and of having created a one-dimensional discipline. They advocated a "two-dimensional" management science that recognized the social as well as the technocratic side of the discipline. They also saw the need to understand the dialectical interplay between the technocratic and social aspects. It is necessary to grasp the social and institutional pressures that allow technocratic thinking to dominate.

The radical OR strand of work, nourished by Rosenhead, turned from critique to practical action in the 1980s with the "Community OR" initiative. In 1986 the Operational Research Society (U.K.), inspired by Rosenhead who was then its president, launched this initiative which was designed to extend awareness and use of OR to new sections of the community and to enrich OR methodology as a result of bringing it into contact with novel problem types (Rosenhead, 1986). The Community OR initiative and its links to emancipatory systems thinking are more fully discussed in a later sub-section.

8.2.2. Habermas and the Critical Systems Approach

Early calls for an emancipatory systems approach, based on the work of Habermas, can be found in the work of Jackson (1983, 1985b). The primary purpose of the paper *Social Systems Theory and Practice: The Need for a Critical Approach* (1985b) was to argue in an emancipatory manner for an appropriate systems approach to be fashioned for social systems in which there are great disparities in power and resources between participants, and that seem to escape the control and understanding of the individuals who create and sustain them. In constructing such a methodology, Jackson advocated following some suggestions of Habermas on the relation of theory and practice. In explicating the relationship between theory and practice, Habermas (1974) wrote:

> The mediation of theory and praxis can only be classified if to begin with we distinguish three functions, which are measured in terms of different criteria: the formation and extension of critical theorems, which can stand up to scientific discourse; the organization of processes of enlightenment, in which such theorems are applied and can be tested in a unique manner by the initiation of processes of reflection carried on within certain groups towards which those processes have been directed; and the selection of appropriate strategies, the solution of tactical questions, and the conduct of the political struggle (p. 32).

Jackson discusses these three functions and relates them to systems thinking. The first function involves professional scientists in the formulation of explicit theories about the social world. These theories must be corroborated according to the usual rules of scientific discourse. The construction of explicit social theories must therefore be an essential part of any social systems science. The second function involves the authentication of the knowledge produced by the first stage. Theoretical validation is not enough; knowledge must be validated by the social actors at which it is aimed in a process of enlightenment. Only if the theory helps these actors to attain self-understanding, and they recognize in it an acceptable account of their situation, can the theory be said to be authenticated. To explain this phase, Habermas turns to the psychoanalytic encounter (readers will remember a discussion of this in relation to Habermas's work in Chapter 3). The actors in the social world, Habermas believes, are very often in the same position as the neurotic patient undergoing psychoanalysis: they suffer from false consciousness and do not truly comprehend their situation. It is incumbent, therefore, on the critical theorist to employ a social theory capable of explaining the alienated words and actions of oppressed groups in society:

> The theory serves primarily to enlighten those to whom it is addressed about the position they occupy in an antagonistic social system and about the interests of which they must become conscious in this situation as being objectively theirs (Habermas, 1974, p.32).

This, of course, is the point of the first function outlined by Habermas - the formation and extension of critical theorems. If the social actors involved come to recognize themselves in the interpretations offered, that theory is then authenticated. The social actors previously deprived of self-understanding in the course of distorted communication are able to take an equal role in the dialogue. The conditions for an ideal speech situation are approximated in respect of this particular enlightened social group. This is a precondition for Habermas's third function - the selection of appropriate strategies. A rational consensus can be reached over the appropriate strategies to be adopted. As with the soft systems approach, the "clients" have complete autonomy in the matter of what changes to make to the system and its objectives. Now, however, they possess a social theory that enables them to comprehend fully their position in the social world and the possibilities for action that this affords. Jackson argues, therefore, that Habermas's suggested approach is more appropriate for a certain class of social systems than hard or soft systems methodologies. These are social systems characterized by inequalities of power and resources among the participants and by conflict and contradiction. They are the products of thinking and acting human beings, but at the same time are not transparent to them. These systems can escape both the understanding and the control of humans and take on objective features that constrain them.

Much of Oliga's work can also be seen as making an important contribution to emancipatory systems thinking by fulfilling the requirements of Habermas's first function and supplying social theories to support social systems science. This is true of his critical exegesis of the many conceptions of power as a social phenomenon (Oliga, 1989b). Ten faces of power are examined, the ideological understandings of power contained in hard and soft systems thinking are critiqued and a "contingent, relational" view of power appropriate to emancipatory systems practice is presented. Another paper (Oliga, 1989c) proceeds similarly to set out nine conceptions of ideology, to highlight a critical view of ideology suitable for the project of enlightenment and to use this analysis to unmask the ideological underpinnings of the different systems approaches. A third article (Oliga, 1990) examines systems stability and change as the outcome of an interaction between power and ideology.

Readers may be interested in work on accounting systems, by Laughlin (1987) and Power and Laughlin (1992), which similarly draws inspiration from Habermas to forge critical thinking in that discipline.

8.2.3. Interpretive Systemology

Interpretive systemology (Fuenmayor, 1991; Fuenmayor and Lopez-Garay 1991) is critical of the way that soft systems approaches easily fall prey to instrumental reason and end up, just like hard and cybernetic approaches, colluding in an unreflective attempt to improve organizational performance through regulation. Fuenmayor and Lopez-Garay, working from the University of Los Andes in Venezuela, seek to employ the same phenomenological foundations as the soft systems thinkers, and more especially the work of Husserl and Heidegger, to build an alternative interpretive systems approach with an emancipatory flavor.

The phenomenology they embrace requires the interpretive systemologists to start with the way that individuals make sense of the world. They do this by making "distinctions" which identify a portion of reality and separate it from the surrounding "scene." The search for truth then rests on a never-ending "de-becoming" process of unfolding the scene of phenomena. Contrasting perceptions of the reality that is "presenced" and the scene are explored through different "contextual systems", as the search for truth is

> orchestrated within a multiple interpretive process which bases a debate among different interpretations according to their diverse contextual systems (Fuenmayor, 1991, p. 485).

Mingers summarizes the methodology that arises from this epistemology:

> Briefly, this consists of (i) developing a number of possible interpretations ... of what the phenomena might be, (ii) comparing the phenomena with those different interpretations, and (iii) conducting a debate between the various interpretations, given the results of the comparison. This all leads, not to some particular result or agreement, but to a richer understanding and the possibility of further and deeper interpretations (1992b, p. 338).

Probing a little more, we find that the inquiring process takes on a recursive two-phase form. In one phase, the phenomena under study are highlighted through a "thematic contextual system" which guides critical exploration, but only so as to reveal other possible interpretations. Some of the other interpretations are then worked up into contextual systems and, with the thematic contextual system, are used in "thematic understanding" to interpret the phenomena under study, each according to its own concerns. This yields "thematic interpretations" which are the results of interpreting the phenomena in the light of each context of meaning. In the other phase, the various contextual systems and the interpretations yielded are brought together under another conceptual framework, so that an explicit debate can be orchestrated around them. This is called "thematic comprehension." The result of interaction between the two phases should be

> a state of enriched consciousness about the possibilities of the phenomenon under study and its insertion into a general conceptual framework (Fuenmayor, 1991, p. 487).

In a study of the University of Los Andes (Fuenmayor *et al.*, 1991), three contextual systems are initially employed, each of which offers a plausible interpretation of the mission of the University according to Venezuelan University Law. The University is considered as a research university, a technological university, and a paideutic university. In the "thematic interpretation" stage, however, it is discovered that the "actual workings and happenings" of its management and power systems provide little support for any of these interpretations. The actual "facts" of the situation seem to speak against the three contextual systems. As a result it is necessary to broaden the investigation and to consider a wider interpretive context. In this fourth interpretive possibility, the role of Venezuelan universities can be seen

> as social institutions that support and maintain the political and economic equilibrium of 'democratic' Venezuela within a situation of profound social injustice. Thus, universities constitute a mechanism of domination and oppression at the service of the country's ruling classes (p. 519).

In the light of this "supramodel" many unexplained workings and happenings, brought to the surface by the other three models, are said to make sense.

The initial stages of the methodology, when the interpretive systemologists remain true to phenomenology, differ little from those found in other soft systems approaches. They allow the construction and exploration of different contexts of meaning. Indeed, according to their own philosophy, the interpretive systemologists should simply continue for ever "unfolding the scene" and providing new interpretations. This would hardly be emancipatory however. Because of their emancipatory commitment, in practice Fuenmayor and Lopez-Garay are led to abandon their phenomenological pretensions and to promote one particular context of meaning as more accurately capturing the facts of the situation. As in the case of the university investigation, this privileged "context of meaning" is Marxist in character and has as one of its elements the belief that

> in Venezuela ... organizations and institutions tend to support the power structure that controls and maintains the uneven distribution of wealth, education, health and the unfair administration of justice (Fuenmayor *et al.*, 1991, p. 416).

Interpretive systemology is emancipatory, therefore, because it demonstrates the oppressive role that organizations play in the power structure of society. In doing so it should help

> to enrich the state of awareness of communities and people in general affected by these public institutions and to trigger and enrich public debates with regard to them (Lopez-Garay, 1991, p. 399).

Closing the scene, using Marxist explanations, allows the interpretive systemologists to assert their emancipatory credentials but only at the expense of the phenomenology they claim to embrace.

8.2.4. Freire's Critical Pedagogy

According to Cornel West, in his preface to *Paolo Freire: A Critical Introduction*,

Paolo Freire is the exemplary organic intellectual of our time ... His classic work, *Pedagogy of the Oppressed*, was a world-historical event for counter hegemonic theorists and activists in search of new ways of linking social theory to narratives of human freedom (quoted in McLaren and Leonard, 1993, p. xiii).

Freire was much influenced by the early writings of Marx and by critical theory more generally. At the center of the humanistic vision he inherited from these sources is the belief that individuals can only be fully human once they become capable of acting as knowing subjects to transform the world. Currently it is impossible for individuals and collectivities to realize their potential in this way because the masses suffer oppression at the hands of minorities. Freire saw his project, therefore, as one of helping the masses to liberate themselves. In the process, the oppressors would also be freed from their role of slaves to the system. In Freire's view, therefore,

the great humanistic and historical task of the oppressed [is] to liberate themselves and their oppressors (1970, p. 21).

The oppressed can only fulfill their historical task of humanization if they become aware of the social, political and economic contradictions that exist in social reality. They need to critically appreciate how these contradictions lead to their own exploitation. The oppressed must also recognize that the current state of affairs is not inevitable. It is something that they can transform through their own actions. Awareness of their exploitation and of their own ability to change things does not come easily to the oppressed. This is because the state of oppression acts upon men's consciousness and gives rise to "false perception" about the state of the world and the possibilities for transformation.

Although the oppressed must ultimately liberate themselves there is a role, therefore, for critical pedagogy. Critical pedagogy is a form of democratic dialogue conducted by those aware of oppression with those actually oppressed, through which the latter become aware of structures of domination and of the need for political involvement. By engaging in such dialogue the oppressed become demystified and see social reality as it actually is. The process that the oppressed go through is called "conscientization" by Freire. Conscientization is a kind of pedagogical politics of conversion

in which objects of history constitute themselves as active subjects of history ready to make a fundamental difference in the quality of the lives they individually and collectively live (McLaren and Leonard, 1993, p. xiii).

Freire was himself involved in many educational projects with economically poor communities in Brazil, where he was born, and elsewhere. These were usually adult literacy programs, although, for Freire, literacy is about more than simply the ability to read and write. It is important at the same time as imparting this technical skill to oppressed groups to provide them with the capacity to carry out a political reading of the way society is organized and of their own exploitation. In *Pedagogy of the Oppressed*, Freire explains that those engaged in delivering the program should first, through observation and conversations, seek to gain an understanding of the nature of the reality lived by the oppressed. The aim is to grasp the contradictions present in social reality and to gain an awareness of the extent to which people understand these contradictions. "Themes" are then chosen, relevant to the real situation faced by the oppressed. These should be familiar to them but sufficiently challenging to enable them to see their own circumstances in a new light. The literacy program is then based on words which relate to the chosen themes. The result should be that the oppressed learn to read their world more accurately at the same time as they learn to read books. Controversially, in the case of an adult literacy program in Guinea-Bissau, Freire is able to claim a degree of success because it raised people's awareness of their situation, even though it failed in terms of the numbers that were taught to read and write (see Freire and Macedo, 1987).

There are similarities in this to Habermas's account of the relationship between theory and practice in emancipatory interventions. In Habermas, oppressed groups are enlightened about their social situation through a kind of psychoanalytic procedure; in Freire this is replaced by a pedagogy designed to give rise to the process of conscientization. Freire also shares with Habermas (in Habermas's early work) and with the interpretive systemologists a certainty that Marxist theory, or something very akin to it, has already discovered the true nature of social reality. Because of this, the democratic dialogues undertaken with the oppressed can easily be represented by critics as fraudulent. Since the theorists know the truth in advance, "liberation" takes the form of coming to agree with the theorist. If the oppressed fail to recognize that they are the objects of class oppression and fail to seize their opportunity for emancipation or liberation, then they are deemed in need of further ideological cleansing. Freire was very aware of the dangers of appearing to impose knowledge, and was critical of those less scrupulous than himself in this respect, but the tension between wanting people to develop their own understanding of social reality and providing them with ready made answers remains in his work.

Another frequent criticism of Freire, also deriving from his commitment to Marxism, is the priority he gives to class oppression as compared to other forms of oppression, based perhaps on race or gender. It seems, even in his later books where he does acknowledge the existence of other forms of oppression, that these can all be reduced to class oppression. On the other hand, the alternative he offers to the Eurocentric world view of most critical theorists earns the praise of commentators. Finally, and refreshingly after our encounter with the interpretive systemologists, Freire is insistent that liberation cannot be achieved simply in idealistic terms. His own summary of the position is that:

> In order for the oppressed to be able to wage the struggle for their liberation they must perceive the reality of oppression, not as a closed world from which there is no exit, but as a limiting situation which they can transform. This perception is a necessary, but not a sufficient condition by itself for liberation; it must become the motivating force for liberating action (1970, pp. 25-26).

8.2.5. MacIntyre and the Moral Community

Munro (1997) has suggested that the work of MacIntyre could make a significant contribution to the development of an emancipatory approach in OR and systems thinking. MacIntyre notes the absence, in modern society, of any shared moral framework which would allow ethical disputes to be rationally resolved. A moral incommensurability exists between the positions taken by different groups and, as a result, power rather than rational argumentation has to be used to bring disputes to a close. In MacIntyre's view, addressing this situation demands a break from Kant's system in which ethics depends purely on reason and a renouncing of the passions. What is required instead is a return to the Aristotelian framework with its emphasis on "teleology" or the study of purposes or ends. In the Aristotelian ethical system, an act is judged ethical not in terms of its relationship to the individual will but in terms of its contribution to the ultimate purposes of communities or societies. People are born into societies in an untutored state but their ethical potential can be cultivated and realized in the context of society and its "telos" or ultimate ends. It is through community and an involvement with community that moral action becomes possible.

As Munro argues, this leads MacIntyre to ask what has gone wrong with modern society that makes it impossible to contain moral disputes and what must be done to correct this situation. What MacIntyre finds is that economic rationality so pervades the modern world that the very notion of "good" has been appropriated to refer to a commodity. The most valued goods, such as wealth, status and power, are "external goods", the attainment of which does not depend upon a relationship between a person's character and the goods pursued. These goods can be contrasted with "internal goods" which can only be attained by following a particular style of life. Moreover, with internal goods, the very practice of the appropriate way of life is regarded as a good in itself. Thus for the excellent painter, teacher, doctor or architect, the practice of the profession itself constitutes a good regardless of the external rewards of wealth and status that might follow.

In modern society, where economic rationality prevails, the whole emphasis turns to money as the means of access to consumer products. Other avenues to fulfillment receive little recognition and are not valued. People are interested in having rather than being. The individual is the poorer because the development of character is detached from the pursuit of a central life activity. Society is the poorer because the link between the individual good and the common good is broken. For MacIntyre what is required is a new social order and new institutions which allow individuals to flourish and develop their character in the pursuit of internal goods. Emancipation is about individuals perfecting themselves through a life project in communities and societies which encourage them to be "noble" or "virtuous." As Munro has it:

> This alternative form of emancipation has the moral community as its primary focus because it is only in terms of this community that the development of 'human potential' can be realized through the pursuit of those goods which are internal to that community's particular social practices (1997, p. 580).

Reviewing the traditional, hard systems approach, Munro concludes that the methods employed have no conception of an internal good. Soft systems thinking and certain other emancipatory approaches take into account a broader range of values but lack sufficient awareness of how values are bound up with one's whole way of life and the historical and material conditions which impact upon individual purposes. Community OR seems to offer the best prospect for incorporating MacIntyre's thinking into practice:

> For example, the moral community is of primary importance under MacIntyre's framework, just as it is in Community OR. It is this community which defines the objectives of their system and not some manager who happens to be a superior in the organizational hierarchy ...Often, the relationship between the professional and client in Community OR does not involve the exchange of money, indicating that the pursuit of some kind of 'internal good' is at stake. Community OR can make space for the pursuit of such internal goods because the other more measurable goods, such as money, need not be pursued as the ultimate objectives and need only be satisfied (Munro, 1997, p. 580).

8.2.6. Capra's Ecological Sustainability

Capra's *The Web of Life* opens, as we saw in Chapter 4, by drawing our attention to the seriousness of the "global problems" affecting us and our world at the present time; problems such as poverty, pollution, animal extinction and forest destruction. He then launches into a critique of how those responsible for decision-making currently address these problems. They tend to look at them separately and give little consideration to other problems which affect and are affected by the one they are considering. In Capra's view we must redress the ways in which we attempt to solve our problems by facilitating a shift in our perceptions and values. We must reject the old, reductionist world view and encompass a way of thinking which can produce "viable solutions" to global problems. According to Capra, "the only viable solutions are those that are sustainable" (1996). We must come up with solutions that address the whole network of global problems and ensure that, as well as meeting our own needs, they also meet the needs of future generations of life on our planet.

Fortunately, in Capra's opinion, science is on the very verge of witnessing the emergence of a new scientific understanding of life which will usher in a new perception of reality. The new paradigm, embraced by such as Maturana and Varela, Bateson, and Prigogine, views the world as an integrated whole and puts life at the very center of all things. It offers us access to a "deep ecological awareness." This sort of thinking also offers a new set of values. We can begin to believe that we are just one small part of the massive web of life, but with an awesome responsibility to work towards its maintenance. Capra tells us that

> deep ecological awareness seems to provide the ideal philosophical and spiritual basis for an ecological lifestyle and for environmental activism (1996, p.8).

In the manner of the "emancipation as liberation" procedure, therefore, Capra provides a critique of our current approach to "social ecology" and of the world view that sustains it. He then provides us with a new theory of living systems that will allow us to "reconnect" with the web of life and build sustainable communities which meet our current needs without diminishing the chances and opportunities of future generations. This critique allows him to propose new social arrangements which promote "maximum sustainability" by learning from the principles that he sees as forming the pattern and structure of the ecological system. These principles are five in number.

The first is "interdependence." For Capra, we have to understand that each element of the ecosystem is interrelated in an extremely complex "network of relationships", and we have to look at problems and issues not only as they affect ourselves now but also as they affect others now and could affect future generations. The second principle relates to the "cyclical nature" of ecological processes. Waste for one species is food for another and so there is no waste in the whole. This is seen as offering an extremely valuable lesson to human communities and should lead us to question the current state and functioning of businesses and the economy. The "flow of energy" to ecosystems originates from the sun. This third principle indicates that this is the only form of energy that can maintain our human communities without pollution and to ignore solar energy would be disastrous. Within the ecosystem "co-operation and partnership" are essential as each element within the web of life contributes to the sustenance of its community. This fourth principle points out that, in human communities, co-operation and partnership have become secondary values to those of competition, expansion and domination. Taking a lesson from ecology will help us value co-operation and partnership more highly and help conservation of the global community as a whole. Finally, we must recognize that ecosystems are "flexible" and encompass "diversity." Because of this they can adapt to environmental fluctuations. Human communities would do well to learn from this principle. In short, it is Capra's argument that

> the survival of humanity will depend on our ecological literacy, on our ability to understand these principles of ecology and live accordingly (Capra, 1996, p. 295).

8.2.7. Emancipation as Liberation : The Case of Community OR

It is not necessary that Community OR be practiced in the form of "emancipation as liberation." It can also be pursued with the aim of improving the efficiency and effectiveness of voluntary and community organizations, thus contributing to overall economic well-being. Or it can be seen as providing a forum through which marginalized groups can be given a voice and thereby integrated back into the mainstream. To an extent, what practitioners do with Community OR depends upon what role they see generally for "the community" in society – as contributing to it, enhancing it or challenging it. This point has been well made, using interpretive systemology, by Weedon (1992), and by Midgley and Ochoa-Arias (1999) who explore liberal, communitarian and Marxist options for Community OR. Many of the case studies illustrating Community OR (e.g. in Richie, Taket, Bryant, eds., 1994) can be seen to adhere to a "regulative" rather than "radical change" perspective, and will be evaluated differently according to whether a functionalist, interpretive or emancipatory theoretical position is adopted.

I accept also that, even among those who want to give Community OR an emancipatory twist, "emancipation as liberation" may not be the preferred option. "Emancipation through discursive rationality" or "emancipation through the oblique use of systems methods" or some postmodern version of "emancipation" could be chosen instead. My justification for including Community OR here, and giving it the particular emancipatory reading I do, is simply that a number of the thinkers discussed as part of the "emancipation as liberation theme", such as Rosenhead, Thurnhurst and Jackson, were significant in the early days of Community OR; and the work of the interpretive systemologists, Freire, and MacIntyre, is easily accommodated within the original purposes of Community OR. Further, I intend to concentrate on the origins of Community OR when the link with emancipation as liberation was clearer, rather than on the later directions in which it has been taken – which are too diverse to be followed in this book. That said, let us now describe the nature, background and early purposes of Community OR (COR).

COR aims to make appropriate operational research/management science expertise available to organizations whose main purpose is to serve the community rather than to make a profit or to perform some government function. Community organizations are often small, lack a clear managerial hierarchy, show a commitment to participative decision making, and possess few tangible resources. They pose different challenges to OR methodology. Indeed, given the usual impression of classical OR as a hard systems approach that seeks to use quantitative techniques to solve tactical problems in pursuit of goals specified by management in large organizations, we must wonder whether OR could ever provide a suitable approach in the different context of community and co-operative organizations. It is as well to be aware, therefore, that OR began not as a mathematical but as an interdisciplinary science and that the creation of interdisciplinary teams was seen as one of the most important elements of OR practice in the early textbooks (Churchman et al., 1957; Ackoff and Sasieni, 1968). I should also note that these same textbooks emphasize that OR is a "systems approach", aiming to be relevant to strategic as well as tactical problems. And we have already noted that many of the pioneers of OR were socialist scientists who believed that OR should be used for public rather than sectional interests, and that only under socialism could science realize its full potential for increasing human well-being (Rosenhead, 1987).

Given the aspirations of early OR theorists and practitioners, the way the discipline and profession actually developed and was employed came to many as a major disappointment (as discussed in Chapter 6). Some within OR, however, did keep faith with its original intentions. Cook (1973), for example, lamented that its current methodology had led OR to move from the position of "science helping society" to that of "science helping the establishment", and sought to develop new methods with clients outside the normal power structure. Others remained true, but felt obliged to change the disciplinary banner under which they worked – Ackoff, Beer, and Churchman, for instance. We can, therefore, reasonably talk in terms of an "enhanced OR" based on the spirit of the early pioneers of OR and drawing upon the work of those (either in OR, or on the fringe of the subject) who have continued to develop the discipline according to its original intentions. This kind of OR is an interdisciplinary science employing rational methods to alleviate ill-structured and strategic (as well as tactical) problems arising in social systems, for the benefit of society.

On the basis of enhanced OR, the idea of Community OR begins to look much more plausible. Furthermore, a long tradition of thought upon which COR can build is identified. Of particular significance, from this point of view, must be Ackoff's work with the leaders of the black ghetto of Mantua (Ackoff, 1970b, 1974a), work carried out under Cook's guidance with inner-city community organizations (Luck, 1984), Beer's project with the Allende government in Chile (Beer, 1981a) and various projects undertaken from Bath University in the United Kingdom with charitable and community groups (Jones and Eden, 1981; Sims and Smithin, 1982).

A recent surge in COR activity in the United Kingdom – including the setting up of the Community OR Unit at Northern College, Barnsley (now unfortunately closed); the Center for Community OR at Hull University: and a national COR network (see Carter et al., 1987) – can, however, be more immediately traced to the Community OR initiative launched by the Operational Research Society in 1986 and inspired by its then president, Jonathan Rosenhead. In his presidential address to the society, Rosenhead (1986) set out the route he believed OR had to follow if it was to carve out for itself a significant role in society and if future progress in the discipline was to be facilitated. This involved expanding the range of OR's clients beyond the managements of large organizations and, on the basis of the challenges arising in assisting "alternative" clients, developing available methodologies and methods to make them more appropriate to new problem situations. Rosenhead's preferred vehicle for traveling this route turned out to be COR and the announcement of the Operational Research Society initiative followed.

During the course of inviting proposals from institutions to house a Community OR unit, the steering group for the Operational Research Society initiative stated (Steering Group, 1986) the aims of COR to be:

1. To extend awareness of OR to new sections of the community, thus broadening the range of clients
2. To demonstrate the relevance of OR to a wider range of problem situations
3. To enrich OR methodology and revitalize intellectual life through involvement in novel types of problems
4. To contribute to improving the quality of discussion and decision making in society at large

It is also possible to interpret COR as having a more emancipatory dimension. This interpretation will be followed here and can be summarized under two more headings:

5. To help redress the resource imbalance that exists under capitalism by assisting those underprivileged in this respect
6. To develop decision-aiding and problem-solving methods appropriate to a more democratic and socialist milieu

The implications of these purposes will now be explained.

(1) The intention to broaden the range of OR's clients implies that the present set of customers is seriously limited. Rosenhead (1986) argues that the customers of OR have been

> almost exclusively ... the managements of formally established and legally entrenched organizations disposing of substantial resources (capital, equipment, buildings, supplies), including the labor power of their employees (p. 37).

Following Rosenhead's writings and Cook (1973), with some additions, the list of excluded groups will number, among others, patients' associations, community health councils, trade unions, consumer groups, political parties, charitable bodies, citizen groups, residents' associations, Councils for Voluntary Service, voluntary organizations and workers' cooperatives. As Rosenhead (1986) suggests, some of these have been ignored because they lack the funds to pay for OR consultants, whilst others, such as trade unions, have been neglected because of mutual suspicions regarding aims and intentions and because of fears of alienating OR's traditional clientele of managers.

In order to extend the range of organizations served, OR consultants have to accept the enhanced version of OR, be prepared to sympathize with the more varied concerns exhibited by "alternative" clients and be willing to provide services at reduced cost to needy clients – as suggested long ago by Ackoff (1974b). To extend awareness of the usefulness of OR to new groups entails publishing relevant work done through the various networks that link non-traditional clients. It will also help if methods and techniques suitable for Community OR are taught in degree courses and as a specialist provision to alternative clients.

(2) As has already been suggested, to demonstrate the relevance of OR to a wider range of problem situations requires a commitment to the development of "enhanced OR", drawing upon the spirit of the original pioneers of the discipline and upon the work of those who, whether calling themselves operational researchers or not, have developed OR or "systems" according to that spirit. The kind of OR that became the norm in the 1960s, and which still remains in the ascendancy, is unsuitable for the great majority of problems found in the community context. In large part this is because, as Rosenhead (1986) argues, it evolved and was fashioned according to the needs of large bureaucratic organizations with a tendency toward centralization, an emphasis on controlling their members' activities and an interest in deskilling their workers. Traditional OR methodology reflects the need for a hierarchically organized decision-making system that can dictate the goals to be pursued and can ensure implementation of recommended procedures using autocratic control devices. In these circumstances, human elements could be regarded as passive, and quantitative and optimizing techniques employed.

In doing Community OR, there are fewer situations where a clearly defined goal can be agreed upon or can be enforced through the managerial hierarchy, and many more situations where debate and consensus building are necessary before action can be taken. Wide involvement of personnel in decision making is necessary if satisfactory results are to be obtained and implementation achieved. Fortunately, during the 1970s and 1980s a number of "softer" approaches were developed in OR (e.g. Eden *et al.*, 1983) and systems thinking (Ackoff, 1981; Checkland, 1981; Mason and Mitroff, 1981) that encourage and facilitate participation and debate. An enhanced OR can utilize these methods in assisting alternative clients to come to terms with the "messes" (Ackoff, 1981) with which they are constantly confronted.

(3) Just as the OR methods wrought in the service of large corporations took on a specific form tuned to the needs of these enterprises, so the OR fashioned in the community context must take on characteristics that will make it adept in these circumstances. Thus the

experience of doing OR for alternative clients should enrich OR methodology and revitalize the intellectual life of the discipline and profession. The organizations that Community OR will serve usually lack the resources of traditional clients, may be wedded to democratic decision-making procedures, and may lack a clear managerial hierarchy that can delimit preferences and ensure the implementation of recommended changes. The usual props supporting the success of classical OR will therefore be missing, and practitioners will be forced in a different direction if their work is to prove useful. Rosenhead (1987) has listed some of the characteristics that an "alternative OR" has to take on. Six features of alternative OR are arrived at by taking each of six characteristics he sees as underpinning "managerialist OR" and replacing it by its opposite or "deadly enemy." The dimensions of alternative OR are then:

- A "satisficing" approach that permits different objectives to be measured in their own terms
- The use of analysis to support judgement with no aspiration to replace it
- The treatment of human elements as active subjects
- An acceptance of conflict over goals and the development of transparent methods that clarify conflict and facilitate negotiation
- Problem formulation on the basis of a bottom-up process in which decisions are taken as far down the hierarchy as there is expertise to resolve them
- The acceptance of uncertainty as an inherent characteristic of the future, and a consequent emphasis on keeping options open

A number of soft OR and soft systems thinking approaches already demonstrate some of these characteristics and can provide a good foundation for the future enrichment of OR methodology.

(4) The tools and techniques developed to aid alternative clients should, of course, contribute to improving the quality of discussion and decision making in the sectors of society in which these clients operate. This, however, is not the only benefit to emerge for society. It can be argued that in many other sections of society, too, methods capable of alleviating "messes" will be welcomed. For example, strategic problems in organizations and social issues facing governments are of a type with those confronting COR's clients - ill-structured, involving many stakeholders with multiple perceptions, and embedded in an uncertain environment. The work conducted by Ackoff (1970b) and his colleagues with leaders of the Mantua black ghetto (see Chapter 7) illustrates the point. The project revealed the need for continuous, adaptive, participative planning in the situation faced by the ghetto leaders - a situation characterized by uncertainty, lack of hierarchy and the need for active intervention. The idea that planning should be continuous, adaptive and participative later became the cornerstone of the interactive planning methodology recommended by Ackoff (1981) to corporate executives facing turbulent environments. So, in exposing itself to alternative clients and learning from the experience, OR becomes more relevant to the strategic and social concerns from which it has been effectively excluded because traditional OR is only deemed suitable for resolving tactical questions.

(5) It has been argued by Ackoff and Churchman that OR has a social responsibility to serve all the stakeholders of the systems in which it intervenes, and all segments of society. For Ackoff (1974b) OR practitioners, if they are to deserve the title "professional", must ensure that the interests of those not participating in a decision but affected by it are considered. They should also make provision for all those who might benefit from OR but cannot afford it. Ackoff has given detailed consideration (1974a, 1981) to how planning can

be made more participative, involving all of the interested parties, and how resources to assist with planning can be made available to the more underprivileged of these groups. Churchman (1970) similarly argues that the primary responsibility of OR as a profession must be to serve all the "customers" of the system it is supposed to be benefiting and not just the powerful decision makers.

From an emancipatory perspective, however, both Ackoff and Churchman seem to believe that the resource imbalances that are admitted to exist under capitalism - and that prevent full participation by those underprivileged in this respect - can be sidestepped by good OR practice that persuades the powerful that they, too, have something to gain by admitting the powerless into decision making (Ackoff, 1982; Jackson, 1982, 1983). While this is worth a try, self-respecting Community OR practitioners on occasion will have to take sides. They will come across conflicts of interest that cannot be simply resolved through debate with the powerful. To challenge resource imbalances, the Community OR practitioner may be called upon to help develop methods of struggle against the advantaged group or groups.

(6) Rosenhead (1986) has argued that there is nothing inherently capitalist about OR and that

> despite the market/control bias of the dominant methodology which it has actually accreted
> ... it could be argued that OR prefigures a planning mechanism for a society whose impetus
> does not come from the dynamic of capital accumulation (p. 48).

Community OR workers of an emancipatory persuasion will be hoping to show the truth of this and will certainly content themselves with the opinion that the tools and techniques perfected with alternative clients are those that will be most useful in some democratic, non-exploitative, socialist society of the future. Various methods already developed in the tradition of enhanced OR show potential in this respect.

Enough has been said to link the early development of COR to the "emancipation as liberation" theme. Jackson (1991) sets out the theory that guided the early practice of COR at the Center for Community OR, Hull University, and provides some examples of the work undertaken. Interested readers can follow the later development of COR in books of case studies edited by Richie, *et al.*, (1994), Bowen (1995), and in publications emanating from the Center for Systems Studies at Hull University (e.g. Cohen and Midgley, 1994; Midgley *et al.*, 1996; Boyd *et al.*, 1999).

8.2.8. Strengths and Weaknesses of "Emancipation as Liberation"

We can begin to sketch out at this point some of the main objections that can be leveled at the "emancipation as liberation" theme. The reader should bear in mind, however, that there will be a much fuller discussion of these issues in the critique of emancipatory systems thinking, as a whole, at the end of this chapter.

It is not difficult to see that those primarily interested in efficiency and effectiveness, in pursuit of economic growth, will be distrustful of the aspirations of "emancipation as liberation" thinkers. They would be far from impressed with Freire's claim that his adult literacy program in Guinea-Bissau could be claimed as a success even though it failed in terms of the numbers taught to read and write. Similarly they would be suspicious of MacIntyre's emphasis on internal goods when it is external goods that give rise to measurable improvements in the standard of living and greater freedom to pursue leisure activities. Craib (1992) summarizes the argument:

> From the point of view of more conventional social scientists, critical theory has no foundation in the real world - it cannot be tested and confirmed or refuted against any external measurement; it is often put in deliberately obscure terms which indicate not so much profundity of thought or the complexity of the problem under examination as the self-indulgence of the authors; much of it is logically meaningless, even when we can translate it into intelligible terms (p. 223).

A similar point has been made by soft systems thinkers (see Chapter 7) in defending their position from criticism by the emancipatory school. Checkland believes that emancipatory thinkers simply assert rather than demonstrate the existence of objective and constraining features of social reality; Ackoff argues that they are obsessed by "irresolvable conflicts" that he is unable to locate when he conducts his own studies using interactive planning. If emancipatory thinkers were able to set aside the preconceptions they bring to the study of social reality, and tried using soft systems approaches, they would find it far more amenable to change than they suppose. In any case, soft systems thinkers ask, is it not better to pursue meaningful piecemeal change than commit to revolutionary ventures which may never happen and which, as history shows, bring unpredictable and dangerous results for all concerned?

Emancipation as liberation seems to some critics to be élitist in character. The critique it offers rests upon a social theory, often Marxist in character, which it is claimed offers a superior perspective on social reality to that possessed by those living the social reality. This theory purports to offer genuine knowledge which can be used to unmask ideologies and liberate the oppressed from "false-consciousness." The critics want to know how the emancipatory theorists are able to step outside their own social situation and gain this privileged viewpoint. As Munro (1997) puts it, every therapist must also seek therapy and every judge can also be judged. Furthermore, from the perspective of Foucault, any claim to knowledge is also a claim to power over others:

> Foucault argues that knowledge is a power over others, the power to define others. Knowledge ceases to be liberation and becomes enslavement ... A discourse embodies knowledge ... and therefore embodies power (Craib, 1992, p. 186).

Emancipatory thinkers may be inviting the oppressed simply to enter into new relations of domination.

A final argument is raised by Mingers (1992a) against Laughlin's adaptation of Habermas's methodology and concerns how an "emancipation as liberation" approach can ever get started. Laughlin suggests that the researched, in his methodology, should be "those who have power to effect change in the phenomena being investigated" (quoted in Mingers). Mingers argues that this group is far more likely to want to protect the status quo rather than change it. If, however, the researched became those without power then it is difficult to see why an organization would ever submit itself to this kind of emancipatory study.

8.3. EMANCIPATION THROUGH DISCURSIVE RATIONALITY

In Chapter 3, I outlined how Habermas, in later writings, moved away from the notion of emancipation stemming from the mediation of theory and practice, and developed instead the idea of critique based on the theory of communicative competence. According to this theory, emancipation becomes associated with the "ideal speech situation" in which citizens determine their true interests free from "distorted communication." In the ideal speech situation it is the better argument that prevails and not the ideology of the powerful. This theory remains in the Enlightenment tradition of Kant and the younger Marx but also differs from it in some important respects. It breaks from the "philosophy of consciousness", adhered to by Kant, which placed emphasis on the individual subject and her relationship to objective reality. It is now the individual as a social being bound-to-others through language that is the center of attention. Marx's critique was directed at alienated labor in the economic sphere of society. Habermas is more concerned with the institutional realm and with communicative action. Craib (1992) summarizes the results that follow from giving priority to communicative action:

> First, rationality in this sense is not an ideal plucked from mid-air, but is there in our language itself ... Second, there is an implicit ethics which Habermas attempts to draw out - a universal ethics ... It is often referred to as a procedural ethic which directs not to the content of a norm but to the way it is arrived at. It is arrived at through free rational discussion ... Third ... is the implication of a radically democratic society, in which each has access to the tools of reason, the opportunity to contribute to the argument, to be heard and to be included in the final decision (pp. 234-235).

The critical standard employed in the emancipation as liberation tradition was a social theory explaining what was wrong with current society and outlining a better social system. In the "emancipation through discursive rationality" theme, the critical standard is found, by Habermas, to lie in the idea of autonomy given in the very structure of language itself. This provides the basis on which "distorted communication" can be identified and criticized and on which social arrangements can be promoted which allow the "ideal speech situation" to be approximated.

Forester (1992) has gone furthest in trying to show how Habermas's theory of communicative competence can be fruitfully used in fieldwork situations for "empirically rich, politically acute, social research." He argues that

> Habermas's sociological analysis of communicative action, has a vast and yet unrealized potential for concrete social and political research, for critical ethnographic analysis (pp. 47-48).

There is nothing as clearly linked to the detail of Habermas's work in systems thinking. There is, however, a strong emancipatory stream in systems thinking which prioritizes the achievement of democratic debate and has provided some useful approaches for actualizing this ideal in practice. Examples are "Search Conferences" and Banathy on "authentic systems design."

Search Conferences (Emery, 1993) emerged from socio-technical systems theory and aim to involve people in the creation of their own future. They promote the development of democratically self-managed groups and insist that all those directly involved in a situation should participate. In the case of groups exceeding the recommended fifteen to thirty people for a single Search Conference, parallel multisearch conferences are organized. Search Conferences work within organizational and community contexts to "rationalize conflict", provide a thorough understanding of environmental issues and constraints, and to promote learning. In Cardenas's (2000) view:

> The single major emphasis of Search Conferences lies in promoting and providing the means for actualizing a democratic ideal through participative group processes (p. 36).

Banathy's work is central to the soft systems tradition in the United States, of which Churchman, Ackoff and Warfield were pioneers. In his book, *Designing Social Systems in a Changing World* (1996), Banathy summarizes and builds on a number of soft systems approaches to reach his recommendations for how "evolutionary design communities" can collectively envision their ideal future and steer themselves towards it. His ideas are incorporated in "design conversations" which have taken place all over the world, in the past twenty years, but are most closely associated with Fuschl in Austria (a biannual meeting sponsored by the International Federation for Systems Research) and Asilomar in California (an annual meeting sponsored by Banathy's International Systems Institute). Important to the success of these events are some well-worked out procedures which are followed by participants in preparation for the conversations themselves. Also significant is the learning that has taken place around the roles and responsibilities that need to be assigned to group members to ensure productive and democratic discussion. "Guardians" are appointed for participation, keeping focus, following the selected group technique, documentation, accepting and honoring all contributions, implementing values, keeping the fire burning, and coordinating the task of the group. The conversations are structured around themes which are interrelated by a common concern to answer the question: "How can we use the insights from systems science for the improvement of the human condition?" (see, for example, M. Beneder and G. Chroust, eds., 1998; also the IFSR website, www.ifsr.org).

We shall concentrate further discussion in this section on Beer's "Team Syntegrity", Ulrich's "critical systems heuristics" and, extending the latter, on Ulrich and Midgley's writings on "the theory and practice of boundary critique."

8.3.1. Beer's Team Syntegrity

The origins of Team Syntegrity lie in Beer's thinking about how to locate rich and productive debate at the point, in an enterprise, where information about its internal state (generated by System 3) is brought together with information about the external environment (generated by System 4); a point known as the "operations room" in VSM parlance (see Chapter 6). As currently conceived (Beer, 1995), Team Syntegrity provides a theory and a set of procedures designed to promote non-hierarchical, participative and effective decision making around issues wherever they arise in organizations or, indeed, in non-organizational or multi-organizational settings. In White's (1994) opinion, it is an approach that answers to the "New Times" of the post-industrial age where democracy and decentralization are valued more highly than hierarchy and centralization:

> In response to the need for democratization of the workplace, to enable the possibility of self-management of teams, and to promote a participatory or inclusive management, there is the need to develop appropriate processes (p. 13).

Team Syntegrity is one such response.

Essentially, Team Syntegrity is a process for group decision making which centers on an "Infoset" consisting of 30 people who share an interest in addressing an issue of particular concern to them. White describes syntegrity sessions which debated the questions "How can we, sovereign world citizens, govern our world?" (1994) and "How should we run London?" (1998). The individuals who make up the Infoset agree to share information on the issue and debate it while occupying roles of equal status. Democracy, and the robustness and effectiveness of the process, are guaranteed by organizing discussion according to a particular geometric structure – the icosahedron. To understand the theory underlying Team Syntegrity, therefore, we have to understand the peculiar properties of the icosahedron.

The icosahedron has 30 edges, 12 vertices and 20 faces. Beer derives his interest in this particular polyhedron from the work of the American architect Buckminster Fuller who built "geodesic domes" based upon his "principle of structural relationship":

> According to this, the wholeness, the INTEGRITY, of the structure is guaranteed not by the local compressive stresses where structural members are joined together, but by the overall tensile stresses of the entire system. Hence came the portmanteau term for Tensile Integrity: TENSEGRITY (Beer, 1995, p. 13).

Buckminster Fuller regarded the icosahedron as the most interesting of the structures exhibiting tensile integrity. In Beer's view, and following cybernetic logic, the properties exhibited by geodesic domes could be transferred to group decision making to ensure democracy and effectiveness. Taking the 30 edges of the icosahedron to represent the members of the infoset, a protocol could be developed which would balance the tension between members in a way that ensured that no individual could dominate any of the others. At the same time, group discussion could be organized around the closed structure represented by the 12 vertices, so that maximum creativity and robustness was achieved. As Beer puts it:

> the views that we hear consolidate, gain or lose adherents, subtly change ... these views are REVERBERATING around the closed system ... This concept of Reverberation came to mean to me the instrumentality of tensegrity within the INFOSET: it generates *synergy* (Beer, 1995, p. 13, emphasis in the original).

The word Syntegrity derives from the dual notions of synergy and tensegrity.

A syntegration exercise follows "The Protocol"; a set of procedures designed to take maximum advantage of the qualities of the icosahedron. There are three distinct stages. The "Problem Jostle" sees "Statements of Importance" generated and refined through the "Hexadic Reduction." This produces 12 topics for debate related to the overall issue. The "Topic Auction" establishes teams from the 30 members of the infoset and allocates them to topics. Finally the "Outcome Resolve" involves three "syntegrity iterations" at which the topics are discussed. The whole process minimally takes four periods of four hours but can last up to 5 days.

Having determined the exact title of the Infoset's task, the 30 players and the facilitators assemble in a large room with extensive wall space, to which documents can be affixed, and containing 12 tables with a few chairs around each. The Problem Jostle begins with each player submitting to the facilitators at least one "Statement of Importance" (SI) which he feels is particularly relevant to the issue under discussion. An SI should be a concise, one or two sentence assertion. The facilitators scrutinize the SIs, eliding any that say similar things, type them up and make them available to the players. Any player who then regards a particular SI of extreme importance can move to one of the 12 tables (called "Hours" because they are arranged around the room in the pattern of a clock), name the SI and start a discussion group around that topic. Other players are free to champion alternative SIs in this way, join existing discussion groups or simply wander around the room. When, at a given table, enthusiasm develops around a particular topic, its advocates can write the topic down and seek further adherents to their cause. Any topic which can gain five signatories is classed as an "Aggregated Statement of Importance." While this self-organizing process is taking place, the facilitators assist by pointing out similarities between certain Aggregated Statements and seeking to position "polar opposite" statements at polar opposite "Hours," e.g. 12 and 6. The first session of the Problem Jostle should end with all 12 Hours having Aggregated Statements of Importance beside them. The aim of the Problem Jostle is to arrive at agreement on 12 agenda items well defined as "Composite Statements of Importance" (CSI) and arranged according to polarity. The next three sessions of the Problem Jostle, therefore, are designed to promote further reflection on existing Aggregated Statements of Importance, the emergence of new Aggregated Statements, and the reduction and refinement of these to just 12 Composite Statements arranged according to the prescribed pattern. This is known as "Hexadic Reduction." If necessary, a rating system can be employed to decide on the best CSIs. Open discussion and creativity are to be given maximum encouragement but it is also clear that the facilitators have a significant role to play.

In the syntegration on "How should we run London?", described by White (1998), the Infoset of 30 members included politicians, journalists, voluntary sector leaders, health experts, think-tank researchers, and other experts and citizens. The first stage of the Problem Jostle produced 25 Aggregated Statements and following a difficult Hexadic Reduction these were reduced to 12 topic areas, as follows:

- Strategic Planning
- Transport
- Children of the City
- Sustainability
- Exclusion and Inclusion
- Money/Finance
- Serious Media Coverage
- Arts and Education
- Demographic Diversity
- Representation
- The complexity of London
- Community involvement in governing London

The second stage of Team Syntegrity is the "Topic Auction" which allocates each of the 30 players into different teams according to the logic of the icosahedron. White (1994) describes this logic:

> From the icosahedron, 30 people can be organized into 12 self-managing teams. Since an edge is connected to two nodes, each person is a member of two teams … From the icosahedron, each node conjoins five edges, hence there are five members of a team. Each node can also be connected to five other nodes through the internal space of the structure (excluding the connection to the node directly opposite it, which represents a directly opposed topic). The five edges that can be connected internally from a node represent the critics to that node. Hence for each node (team or topic) there are five members and five critics (p. 14).

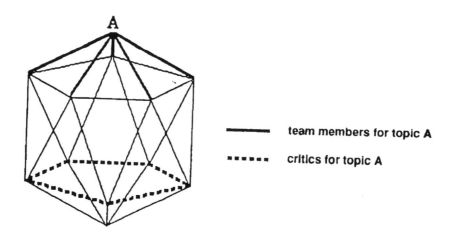

Figure 8.1. Team members and critics in the icosahedron structure (reproduced from White, 1994, p. 14)

This is shown diagrammatically in Figure 8.1. Individuals are asked to rank their preferred topics and an algorithm is employed to ensure that the highest level of satisfaction is obtained while respecting the constraints imposed by the structure of the icosahedron. Each player ends up assigned to two groups defined by a strut on the structure. The structure then determines which other topics she will be a critic of. Overall, there are 12 teams each discussing a topic and consisting of 5 members and 5 critics. The "Topic Auction" maximizes lateral communication and, in Beer's view, enables "reverberation" to be set up throughout the closed system represented by the icosahedron such that participants feel ideas rebounding back to them in a different and enhanced form.

The third stage, the "Outcome Resolve", sees further discussion around the CSIs. There are three rounds of discussion involving different configurations of team members and critics. The end result is meant to be convergence on 12 "Final Statements of Importance" (FSI) with which the whole Infoset is in agreement. The teams seek to work up their thinking into insightful FSIs. The critics within each team must remain silent while this process is going on but may then join in with relevant comment. Their role is to maximize internal tension at the same time as aiding creativity by transmitting reverberation throughout the structure. Examples of statements, provided by White (1994), are shown in Table 8.1.

Those who have worked with Team Syntegrity (White, 1994, 1998; Pearson, 1994) attest to the fact that participants feel that the process is open, self-organizing and non-hierarchical. They were also able to experience the power of "reverberation." In the London syntegrity exercise, this led to considerable cross-referencing between the 12 FSIs. Real progress seemed to be made in getting a diverse set of individuals to connect their goals and aspirations in a synergystic way. White (1998) concludes:

> The implications of such an approach are that it can help develop wider involvement in decision-making, improve the quality of decisions, build consensus around controversial (local) issues and encourage participation more generally (p. 16).

In practical terms, critics will seize upon the apparently arbitrary constraints imposed by Team Syntegrity. 30 people have to be found interested in the topic and able to take considerable time out of their normal working lives. They are then limited to discussing 12

Table 8.1. Example of statements (from White, 1994, p. 17)

Aggregate Statement of Importance

Personal responsibility is a crucial ingredient of good world citizenship

Final Statement

Responsibility pre-supposes that there is some consensus morality (guidelines NOT rules) available to us. Unfortunately we don't yet know what this consensus morality is. In our present state of ignorance people need rich accurate feedback about the consequences of their actions. This initiates a process of bringing into focus the implicit moral values which already tell us that some consequences are good, some are bad, and some are intolerable.

If we accept that different groups may have moral consensus which differ significantly, then there is a need for higher level moral guidelines which would enable these different groups to coexist amicably.

e.g. moral audits, after the fashion of "green audits."

---

topics. If 30 people cannot be found, as was the case with the syntegrity exercise on "governing the world" (White, 1994), the process can be organized around other regular polyhedra; the cube and octahedron require only 12 participants (because they have 12 edges). The effectiveness of such sessions remains to be researched however. Furthermore, it is argued (Pearson, 1994) that the process depends heavily on the participants "wanting to play" and being at the same level in terms of grasping meaning. White (1994) notes the lack of specific mechanisms to involve the silent or inarticulate, and (1998) the danger that discussions can degenerate into "networking sessions" rather than being topic focused. Finally, although participants may gain a greater understanding of each other and of the issue, there is currently a lack of research on how this is translated into action. Good intentions delivered in the context of a democratically organized Infoset can soon dissolve when they encounter power relationships and hierarchy in the real world. Theoretically, it seems to me at least, that the cybernetic logic which through the VSM so clearly connects organisms and organizations, is stretched to the limit in seeking links between geodesic domes and participative decision making processes.

8.3.2. Ulrich's Critical Systems Heuristics

Beer's work on Team Syntegrity can be seen as a demonstration, in systems terms, of how difficult it is to establish a basis for "communicative competence" and how artificial the process can become. Ulrich recognized these difficulties earlier on and sought to drive Habermas's thinking in an altogether more practical direction. Drawing heavily on Kant and Habermas, and combining insights from their writings with a recognition of the radical potential in Churchman's "social systems design" (see Chapter 7), Ulrich's *Critical Heuristics of Social Planning* (1983) stands as a landmark in the systems literature. This is because it described for the first time a systems approach that responded to the possibility that societies and organizations could resemble "psychic prisons" or "instruments of domination." The aim of the book was nothing less than to set out an appropriate philosophy for emancipatory systems thinking and to develop a methodology that could be used by planners and concerned citizens alike to reveal the "normative" content of actual and proposed systems designs. By normative content, Ulrich meant both the underlying value assumptions that inevitably enter into planning, and also the social consequences and side effects for those at the receiving end of planning. Critical systems heuristics was designed as a practically oriented, emancipatory systems approach.

In setting out this approach, Ulrich distances himself from the currently dominant use of the systems idea in what he calls "systems science" (OR, systems analysis, systems engineering, cybernetics). In systems science, which is based on limited mechanistic and organismic analogies, the systems idea is used only in the context of instrumental reason to help us decide *how to do things*. It refers to a set of variables to be controlled. Ulrich's purpose is to develop the systems idea as part of practical reason, to help us decide *what we ought to do*. To this end he argues for "critical systems heuristics", using each of these three words in the sense given to them by Kant. To be *critical*, one must reflect upon the presuppositions that enter into both the search for knowledge and rational action. A critical approach to systems design means planners making transparent to themselves and others the normative content of designs. All designs and proposed designs must be submitted to critical inspection and not presented scientistically as the only objective possibility.

Ulrich takes the *systems* idea in Kant to refer to the totality of the relevant conditions upon which theoretical or practical judgments depend. These include metaphysical, ethical, political, and ideological aspects. In attempting to grasp the "whole system", we are inevitably highly selective in the presuppositions we make. Ulrich follows Churchman ("every world view is terribly restricted") in seeing Kant's systems idea as an admonition to reflect critically on the inevitable lack of comprehensiveness and partiality of all systems designs. It is by reference to the whole systems concepts entering into these partial presuppositions that critique becomes possible. Finally, *heuristics* refers to a process of uncovering objectivist deceptions and of helping planners and concerned participants to unfold problems through critical reflection. It also signals that Ulrich is not going to attempt to ground critical reflection theoretically, but to provide a method by which presuppositions and their inevitable partiality can be kept constantly under review.

These arguments are further developed in a debate with the ideas on social systems design present in or inferred from the writings of Popper, Habermas, and Kant. Popper's primary concern is with the logic underpinning theoretical reason - with how we find out what is. The only rational application of theoretical reason, for Popper, is in instrumental reason, which helps us to decide how to do things. As far as social systems design is concerned, therefore, reason can only help us with technical questions such as the most efficient means to achieve predetermined ends. Rational discussion about ends, and even about the value content of means, is apparently not possible. The central question of practical reason – "What ought we to do?" - is placed by Popper beyond the scope of critical reflection. It is therefore left to "decision" and enacted without rational guidance. Practical reason, as far as it is admitted at all, is reduced to instrumental reason. This same attitude still pervades systems science. The goals served by systems science go unexamined as all the effort is put into finding the most efficient means for achieving predetermined ends. Ulrich wishes to make the question of what we ought to do subject to critical reflection.

Habermas's work is much more useful to Ulrich's enterprise because he recognizes that instrumental reason is not the only legitimate application of reason. Practical reason and emancipatory reason (aiming at freedom from oppression) are, as we know, equally important to Habermas, and each possesses its own proper object domain. All three forms of reason are capable of being critically reflected upon. In order that questions such as what ought to be done may be properly decided, according to Habermas, a process of rational argumentation must be established. All citizens, or at least all those affected by a planning decision, must be allowed to participate in the argument surrounding that decision. And the debate must be so arranged that all ideological and institutional constraints on discussion are eliminated, so that the force of the better argument persists. Through an analysis of the structure of actual speech situations, Habermas determines, as discussed earlier, what this ideal speech situation free from all constraints must be like - a theory of undistorted communication.

Ulrich regards Habermas's work as providing a useful theoretical boundary experiment but as having little practical application. In order to enter into Habermas's debate, speakers must be willing and able to exhibit communicative competence. This tends to presuppose the very rationality the debate was designed to ensure. Habermas, in attempting to ground his critical reflection theoretically, cuts himself off from the real world in which personal and group interests inevitably contaminate any such debate. Far better, Ulrich argues, to ground critical reflection on practice *heuristically*; to provide a method by which practical judgements can be constantly reflected upon and their partiality revealed by ordinary everyday accounts of the nature of social experience.

It is on a reconstruction of Kant's philosophy that Ulrich attempts to build his critical heuristics on a systems basis. Kant hoped to justify the kind of knowledge we have about the world; he was particularly concerned about what he called *synthetic a priori* concepts. These concepts are deeply implicated in the production of knowledge but are little understood and difficult to justify. Kant proceeded critically to reflect upon the necessary conditions for thought. He attempted to show the *theoretical* necessity of three sets of *synthetic a priori* concepts. First are two "pure forms of intuition" - space and time - present in the very possibility of things as appearances. Second are the twelve "categories", pure concepts of understanding necessary to connect perceptions together. Finally, there are three "transcendental ideas" - the World, Man and God. These transcendental ideas reveal to us the necessarily conditional character of our understanding of the totality. Kant then tried to show that these *synthetic a priori* concepts contributed valid knowledge about the world.

Ulrich builds on Kant's work but subtly transforms it in order to make it applicable to planning and systems design. Certain presuppositions, in the form of boundary judgments, inevitably enter into any social systems design. These boundary judgments reflect the designer's "whole systems judgments" about what is relevant to the design task. They also represent "justification break-offs" since they reveal the scope of responsibility accepted by the designers in justifying their designs to the affected. Thus boundary judgments provide an access point to the normative implications of systems designs. The task is to find a means of interrogating systems designs to reveal the boundary judgments being made. Ulrich proceeds by reflecting on which of the *synthetic, relatively a priori* concepts inevitably entering into a social systems design have heuristic necessity. Concepts are heuristically necessary if only by making them explicit does it become possible to reflect critically upon the presuppositions entering into planning and social systems design.

The concepts meeting this criterion are arranged according to the pattern set out by Kant. To Kant's space and time, the concept of purposefulness is added as an extra dimension necessary to map social reality. Twelve critically heuristic categories are established around a fundamental distinction between those involved in any planning decision (client, decision maker, planner) and those affected but not involved (witnesses). Three quasi-transcendental ideas are developed - the systems idea, the moral idea and the guarantor idea - as critical standards against which the limitations of particular social system designs can be compared. These concepts should enable any existing social system to be examined with a view to discovering the norms, values and so forth that went into its design. They should enable any potential systems design to be interrogated as to its presuppositions.

The 12 critically heuristic categories are the most important for our purposes here. They arise from four groups of questions based on the client, decision maker, planner and witnesses distinctions. The questions relating to the client concern the sources of motivation flowing into the design; they are about its "value basis." The questions relating to the decision maker examine sources of control; they are about the design's "basis of power." The questions relating to the designer seek the sources of expertise employed in the design; they concern its "basis of know-how." And the questions relating to the witnesses reflect on the sources of legitimation considered in the design; they ask for its "basis of legitimation." There are three questions asked of each of these four groups, giving the complete set of 12 boundary questions. The first question is about the social roles of the involved or affected; the second refers to role-specific concerns; and the third refers to key problems surrounding the determination of boundary judgments with respect to that group.

The power of the 12 questions to reveal the normative content of systems designs is best seen if they are put in both an "is" mode and an "ought" mode, and the answers are contrasted. For example, compare the answer to the question, "Who is the actual client (beneficiary) of the systems design?" with possible answers to the question, "Who *ought* to be the client of the systems design?" The 12 questions in the "is" mode can be summarized (after Ulrich, 1987) as follows:

1. Who is the actual *client* of the systems design?
2. What is the actual *purpose* of the systems design?
3. What is the built-in *measure of success?*
4. Who is actually the *decision maker?*
5. What *conditions* of successful planning and implementation of the system are really controlled by the decision maker?
6. What conditions are not controlled by the decision maker (i.e., are in the *environment*)?
7. Who is actually involved as *planner?*
8. Who is involved as *expert*, and of what kind is the expertise?
9. Where do the involved seek the *guarantee* that their planning will be successful?
10. Who among the involved *witnesses* represents the concerns of the affected? Who is or may be affected without being involved?
11. Are the affected given an opportunity to *emancipate* themselves from the experts and to take their fate into their own hands?
12. What *world view* is actually underlying the design of the system? Is it the view of (some of) the involved or of (some of) the affected?

Ulrich has shown the heuristic necessity of certain concepts for understanding social systems design. He now has to demonstrate how, making use of these concepts, particular social system designs can be validated and accepted for implementation. Here, Ulrich follows Habermas rather than Kant and requires some sort of participative debate to provide the final justification for practical knowledge. He regards Habermas's forum of speakers exhibiting communicative competence, however, as being impracticable. Ulrich suggests instead a dialectical solution to the problem. It is not enough that the involved, making use of the heuristically necessary concepts, be self-reflective about the partiality of their social systems designs. They must be subject also to a dialogue with the witnesses – in practice, representatives of those affected but not involved.

In order to put recalcitrant planners into a position where they have to enter into dialogue, Ulrich advocates the "polemical employment of boundary judgments. This idea stems from Kant's discussion of the "polemical employment of reason." For Kant, an argument is polemical if it is used with a solely critical intent against a dogmatically asserted validity claim. Affected citizens can employ boundary judgments against planners in this sort of way. They can assert alternative boundary judgments in the full knowledge that these reflect only personal value judgments. This is quite good enough to shift the burden of proof onto the planners and to leave them floundering to prove the superiority of their own boundary judgments. It should become clear that only agreement among all affected citizens can finally lead to conclusions about what ought to be done. Ulrich's dialectical solution, therefore, is to bring the systems rationality of the planners directly into contact with the "social rationality" of those who have to live in and experience the social systems designs.

The originality and significance of critical systems heuristics as a methodology for guiding emancipatory systems practice, has now been explained and an example of its use, from Cohen and Midgley (1994), is provided in the next sub-section. There are also some significant criticisms of the approach. First, it ignores the possibilities offered by theoretical and methodological pluralism; second, it adopts a limited notion of critique; third, it rests upon utopian assumptions; and fourth, it suffers from methodological immaturity.

The first point can be illustrated by considering Ulrich's criticisms of systems science and its usefulness in social systems design. These criticisms are somewhat overplayed, and the important role that instrumental reason (for example, in the guise of organizational cybernetics) can play in planning tends, therefore, to get neglected. This is unfortunate since rational social action will depend on what it is possible to do and on the choice of efficient means (matters of instrumental reason) as well as upon what we ought to do (a matter of practical reason). I should not labor this point; experts do have a role in Ulrich's systems approach. It may simply be a matter of emphasis. Nevertheless, the impression is conveyed that systems science approaches are more dangerous than useful when applied to questions of social systems design. Perhaps a better view, which is endorsed in critical systems thinking, is that systems science is all right in its place, and it does have a place in social systems design. In developing the role of the systems idea as part of practical reason, Ulrich forgets just how essential and useful it is as part of instrumental reason.

Ulrich takes his notion of critique from Kant and fails to enlarge it by drawing upon any of the conclusions reached by Marx. Critical systems heuristics is, therefore, critical in terms of the idealism of Kant, Hegel, and Churchman, but is not critical in terms of the historical materialism of Marx and the Frankfurt School sociologists. Ulrich's work allows us to reflect upon the ideas that enter into any social systems design, but it does not help us to reflect upon the material conditions that more objectivist thinkers believe give rise to those ideas and that lead to certain ideas holding sway. Obviously, an analysis conducted according to Ulrich's recommendations will help point to such material conditions. What it cannot do is provide an examination or explanation of the nature and development of those conditions. Material conditions that lead to particular ideas prevailing and to particular designs winning acceptance have to be introduced by Ulrich as "commonsense" explanations of what is occurring. Flood and Jackson (1991) summarize this criticism by suggesting that, while critical systems heuristics can respond to simple cases of coercion, it is useless in the face of complex-coercive situations where, for example, power might find its expression through a mobilization of bias expressed in the very structures of society or in the existence of "false-consciousness."

This same neglect of the structural aspects of social systems leads directly to our third criticism – Ulrich's recommendations are ultimately just as utopian as Habermas's. The question remains: Why should the involved bother to take account of the views and interests of those who are affected but not involved? The issue of which class, group or agency has the power, the will and the interest to bring about a rational society has bothered critical theorists throughout the twentieth century (e.g. Marcuse, 1968). No consensus has been reached, but at least it has been treated as an important question. Ulrich rather neglects this type of issue, a neglect that provides Willmott (1989) with grounds for doubting the efficacy of his methodology as an emancipatory approach. Midgley (1997), in the course of a review of 11 publications between 1985 and 1996 that have offered critiques of critical systems heuristics, is able to add to this. In his opinion the successful use of critical systems heuristics depends on there already existing a situation in which participative debate is possible. Since, however, coercion is best defined as the closure of debate, critical systems heuristics can hardly, as previously thought, be able to tackle problem situations in which coercion reigns. Furthermore, there is the danger that, even in conditions where open debate is possible, critical systems heuristics can introduce its own forms of coercion because those who are inarticulate, lack confidence or suffer from learning disabilities might be unable to engage effectively in rational argumentation.

Finally, Flood and Jackson (1991) accuse critical systems heuristics of methodological immaturity. Only recently have practitioners started to use the approach and there are few case studies from which inspiration can be drawn. Nor have methods, tools and techniques been developed to specifically aid critical systems heuristics in the way, for example, that they have been refined to serve soft systems methodology.

In the next sub-section we witness attempts to address some of these criticisms.

8.3.3. The Theory and Practice of Boundary Critique

In his more recent writings (e.g. 1998), Ulrich has been propounding a research program called "Critical Systems Thinking for Citizens." His aim is to contribute to the revival of civil society by developing and pragmatizing systems ideas so that they can be used by so-called ordinary citizens to help them participate fully in decisions over matters of public concern. This project becomes possible once we recognize the "critical kernel" at the heart of the systems idea. In Ulrich's view

> the systems ... message is not that we actually need to achieve comprehensive knowledge and understanding of whole systems, rather it admonishes us to reflect on the ways in which we may fail to consider the whole relevant system (1998, p. 6).

We are unable to comprehend the whole system whatever degree of expertise we have. In the matter of making boundary judgments, therefore, ordinary citizens can challenge the partiality inherent in the apparent rationality of professional planners and need not feel at a disadvantage. Emancipatory systems thinking must be brought into the reach of citizens by translating its concepts into everyday language:

> It is the goal of my critical systems heuristics ... to develop such an emancipatory systems approach ... readers will probably anticipate that one of its core concepts for achieving its end is a process of systematic boundary critique, and that the main vehicle driving this critical process is the critical employment of boundary judgments (1998, p. 7).

In a similar vein, Gerald Midgley and co-workers at the Center for Systems Studies, University of Hull, are seeking to extend and pragmatize the early work of Churchman and Ulrich on boundary critique. This has involved theoretical innovation as well as the use of critical systems heuristics, alongside other systems methodologies and methods, in an increasingly impressive list of live projects.

Midgley *et al.* (1996) recognize Churchman's contribution as establishing the fundamental idea that, in systems studies, the drawing of boundaries is crucial for determining how improvement is to be defined and what action can be contemplated. He was also the first to argue that justifying systems interventions requires continually redrawing the boundaries to "sweep in" stakeholders previously excluded from consideration. An early paper (Churchman, 1970) ends with him asking whether women have been involved in a set of proposed systems designs. Ulrich, of course, was influenced by Habermas's work on discursive rationality and argued that appropriate boundary judgments could only be established through dialogue between those involved and affected by a systems design. Midgley (1992) suggests that conflict between groups often arises when they possess different ethical positions on some issue and thus repeatedly make different boundary judgments. These boundary judgments can become stabilized by social rituals which reinforce stereotypical attitudes. The narrower boundary judgment gives rise to a "primary" boundary, and the wider to a "secondary" boundary. Between the two lies a "marginal" area. If the primary boundary is privileged, elements in the marginal area can be disparaged and become "profane." If the secondary boundary attracts attention and is reinforced then the marginal elements become the focus of attention and are made "sacred." Midgley (1992) provides the profane status often accorded to the unemployed, and the sacred status usually associated with the customer, as examples.

The tendency to unreflectively accept stabilized boundary judgments and so buttress the status quo needs addressing, Midgley believes, at the beginning of a systems intervention. It is necessary to challenge whatever consensus exists on boundaries by seeking to involve all those who might have an important perspective on the issue of concern. Thus it is often important (Midgley, 1994) to introduce an ecological perspective in order to counter the culture of "humanism" which leads to the environment being neglected and makes it subject to abuse. Of course, particular attention also has to be paid to involving groups who are directly affected by an intervention but are in danger of being marginalized. Projects conducted on this basis, from the Center for Systems Studies, have sought to engage elderly people in the process of developing housing services for older people (Midgley *et al.*, 1996); the young people themselves in developing services for young people missing from home or care (Boyd *et al.*, 1999); and members of the actual client group in a diversion from custody project for mentally disordered offenders (Cohen and Midgley, 1994). Having addressed issues of marginalization through boundary critique, and ensured the "sweeping in" of a wide variety of viewpoints, Midgley (1997) recommends proceeding by the "creative design of methods." In negotiation with the various stakeholders, research questions are identified, each of which may demand resolution using a different method or part of a method. Inevitably the research questions will be "systemically interrelated" and it is necessary, therefore, to achieve a synthesis among the methods employed to address them - at the same time as ensuring the continued involvement of marginalized groups. The "creative design of methods" is represented by Midgley as a form of critical systems thinking embracing "pluralism" and we will need to refer to it again in Part III. For the moment we shall content ourselves with illustrating the approach using the diversion from custody project which, at the same time, will demonstrate how critical systems heuristics can be employed.

The aim of the "North Humberside Diversion from Custody Project" was to try to prevent offenders suffering from mental health problems and/or learning disabilities ending up remanded in custody or sent to prison. The underlying rationale was, of course, that prisons could not provide the kind of treatment and rehabilitation regime needed by such individuals and would, indeed, exacerbate the problems they had (Cohen and Midgley,

1994; Midgley, 1997). Cohen and Midgley provided process consultancy support for the project over a one year period. It would have been possible to conceive of an "expert driven" study engaging only with the particular professionals concerned with the criminal justice system. Enlarging the boundaries of the project however, Cohen and Midgley determined that service users (those with mental health problems and/or learning disabilities, and caught up in the criminal justice system) should also be involved. During the course of discussions with both service users and professionals, a number of research questions came to the fore. These included: How should we evaluate current practice? If against some "ideal", how do we involve users in the design of the "ideal"? How do we deal with issues of power and expertise? How can we address people's needs more systemically? On the basis of these research questions, the "creative design of methods" produced a synthesis of methods that could address them as a whole:

> It reflected a synthesis of the emancipatory principle from Critical Systems Heuristics (concentrating on the identification of power issues) with the participative principles from both Critical Systems Heuristics (supporting competence in participation through the use of boundary questions) and Interactive Planning (supporting competence in participation through the constitution of planning groups reflecting different needs and expertise) (Midgley, 1997, p. 314).

Concerned that service users might be wary about contradicting professional opinion in an open forum involving both parties, Cohen and Midgley arranged for their approach, reflecting the synthesis of methods, to be operationalized in two, separate one-day events. Both followed the same format. First the participants were interrogated, using the 12 questions of critical systems heuristics, about the desired properties of a diversion system. They were asked, for example, Who should benefit from the system? What should the measures of success be? Who ought to design the system? Who should be considered expert and what are their roles? Using the list of desired properties, participants were then asked to design an "ideal" diversion system. They could make changes to any agency they wished as long as the design remained "technologically feasible", "viable", and "adaptable" (see the account of "interactive planning" in Chapter 7). Finally, participants were required to produce a more restricted "ideal" design working with current resources.

The responses to the 12 questions revealed many similarities between the views of clients and professionals, but also some important differences. Examples of the latter were the emphasis placed by clients on the detailed procedures employed by some agencies, notably the Police, and the need for all parts of the system to treat them as human beings. The professionals tended to talk at a more general level about these issues while being concerned with detailed funding arrangements. Also clients heavily prioritized their own expertise, accepting no other groups as "experts", while the professionals felt all agencies, as well as the clients, had some expertise to contribute. Given the similarities in responses to the 12 questions, it was not surprising that the "idealized designs" of the ideal diversion system also shared the same vision and had much in common. In this case, therefore, the consultants were able to provide a report expressing the similarities while pointing to areas where further discussion and accommodation were required. Table 8.2 provides, by way of example, the clients' design of the diversion service given the possibility of wide-ranging change.

Midgley's strictures on involving marginalized voices at the beginning of a systems design, and the practical demonstrations he and his co-workers have provided, offer a useful complement to the "idealism" of Ulrich's reflections. Nevertheless, it is arguable that the

Table 8.2. Clients' design of service given possibility of wide-ranging change

---

People should be able to call in a Psychiatric service 24 hrs a day. However, the person called should be a CPN or social worker rather than a psychiatrist.

Assessment
People should be transferred to a safe community from police custody.

Police
Need training. Basic training for new officers should include a week in a mental hospital.

Special Unit
Decision needs to be made whether a person should go to court.
If yes, a person goes into alternative to custody.

Court Case
Should be a court case, if appropriate, but offender can be absent.
Mental health problem <u>must</u> be raised.
A "hearing" instead of normal court case.

Alternatives to Custody
Not Rampton type places. A prison hospital which is more hospital than prison.
Psychiatric hospital
Community hostel.
Training programs should be offered to people in bail-hostels.
People should be bound over and given support such as probation, CPN etc., and should be kept near their family.
Employment Schemes, Training, Job Club, College, Job Placement.

Other Needs
Meeting place in community center for people who have been through the criminal justice system.
Bill through parliament to enforce diversion.
Public Campaigns (Like MIND initiatives) should be tried.
Continual review needed by all those involved to ensure on-going improvement.
A monitoring team (both external and from the system) to evaluate diversion.

Select Committee

What sort of balance? 50-50 ex-users/professionals.
Ex-Users should be volunteers and elected by other ex-users.

"creative design of methods" remains caught in the same trap as critical systems heuristics – it depends on there already being the possibility for participative involvement and debate. Midgley (1997) has sought to answer this by arguing that where there is closure of debate we must widen our definition of systems practice to include direct political action and campaigning. In other words, we should take sides with those deemed to be marginalized and engage in direct action in order to create the conditions under which genuine debate becomes possible. This, of course, addresses a difficulty in the emancipation through discursive rationality approach but opens itself up to a criticism of the "emancipation as liberation" tradition. On the basis of what social theory do the campaigners justify their ability to recognize marginalized groups and privilege their interests? Midgley's work, although most clearly identified with the "emancipation through discursive rationality" approach, draws upon the strengths of both of the other emancipatory traditions discussed in this chapter – at the same time, of course, as inheriting any associated weaknesses.

8.3.4. Strengths and Weaknesses of "Emancipation through Discursive Rationality"

The "emancipation through discursive rationality" tradition seems to overcome a significant weakness of many other emancipatory approaches in that it does not require privileged access to a particular social theory in order to ground its critique. On the other hand, in examining that tradition, we have repeatedly come up against the objection that it presupposes the very thing it seeks to bring about – a society in which decisions in the public sphere are taken on the basis of discursive rationality. It seems to require that the conditions for communicative competence are already present in society and that all citizens are equipped equally to take part in participative debate. To critics this is an unrealistic picture of the nature of our current social systems. We have seen MacIntyre arguing, for example, that in modern society there is a lack of any shared moral framework which would allow ethical disputes to be rationally resolved. Because of this moral incommensurability it is power rather than rational argumentation that is used to settle disputes.

There is a still more fundamental criticism that comes from the poststructuralist and postmodern stable. This questions the role Habermas assigns to language as offering the possibility of universal consensus. Derrida, as we noted in Chapter 3, sees language as deceptive rather than transparent, and as seeking, over the heads of its users, to maintain its own unity and order and to hide contradictions that might reveal the partiality of discourse. In Lyotard's view, we live in a world of multiple truths which give rise to incommensurable interpretations and we should be tolerant of difference rather than seeking to subsume it in the quest for universal consensus. Language reflects difference in that there are many "language games", obeying different rules, which are played by speakers. Language, therefore, is not oriented to achieving consensus, rather it is an arena for struggle and dissension in which speakers seek to defeat their opponents, often for the simple pleasure of the game. To Lyotard, communication has to be like this in order to promote renewal, innovation and change, and to challenge conformity. Consensus is stultifying, can be dangerous and should only be encouraged in localized circumstances and if subject to rapid cancellation.

We are getting close to a basic challenge to the whole of the Habermasian problematic. Habermas, firmly within the tradition of the Enlightenment, seeks progress and human emancipation through reason. It is essential, therefore, that the better argument triumphs in discourse and any inequalities of power which might prevent this happening are swept away. In the world of multiple truths inhabited by the postmodernists there is, by contrast, no objective station on which to stand from which the better argument can be judged. Humans are too different to share a common ground. Their individual subjectivities are shaped by discourses which are themselves connected to power structures. Any claim to knowledge is at the same time a claim to power over others. The "better argument" will emerge as a result of power struggles, not from rational debate, and itself represents just another claim to power. Power therefore, cannot be excluded from debate in order to ensure communicative competence. It is always already present. Craib (1992) describes Foucault's views on the matter:

> Discourses and institutions are both 'fixed' by the power relations inherent within them ... Foucault argues that knowledge is a power over others, the power to define others. Knowledge ceases to be liberation and becomes enslavement ... A discourse embodies knowledge ... and therefore embodies power. There are rules within a discourse concerning who can make statements and in what context, and these rules exclude some and include others. Those who have knowledge have the power to fix the flow of meaning and define others. The world is thus made up of a myriad of power relations. and each power generates a resistance; therefore, the world is a myriad of power struggles (p. 186).

8.4. EMANCIPATION THROUGH THE OBLIQUE USE OF SYSTEMS METHODS

The systems approaches we have considered so far in this chapter have depended upon the importation of ideas from other disciplines to establish their emancipatory credentials: on Kant's philosophy and Habermas's sociology, for example. I have suggested elsewhere (Jackson 1990) that an interrogation of modern systems thinking can, independently of any other tradition, yield emancipatory conclusions and an emancipatory methodology. To demonstrate this, I sought to take Beer's VSM and Checkland's SSM as highly developed examples of two strands of modern systems thinking (the cybernetic and the soft systems) and to expose the "critical kernel" in each. This required asking of each approach:

(i) What possible grounds exist in this approach for a critique of existing social arrangements and the "contradictions" that underpin them?

(ii) What hints are provided about alternative social arrangements in which existing problems of power and domination could be resolved?

Let us repeat the argument here.

Beer's aim, the reader will recall from Chapter 6, was to unearth the cybernetic laws underpinning complex organization so that we can understand how systems are capable of viability. There are two aspects of his account which appear to possess emancipatory potential. First, Beer advocates decentralization of control as essential for effectiveness and efficiency. This follows from the implications of the "law of requisite variety." The parts must be granted autonomy so they can absorb environmental variety that would otherwise overwhelm higher management levels. This is an important step on the road to empowerment in its own right. Furthermore, it can be argued that if the parts are to use this autonomy to promote efficiency rather than disruption, they must also have a say in what overall purposes are pursued. This takes us on to the second critical aspect. Beer argues that System 5 must represent the essential purposes of the whole system to ensure viability. The arrangement of the Systems, 1-5, should not be regarded as hierarchical. In Beer's view, "the board", as well as looking after the shareholders,

> also embodies the power of its workforce and its managers, of its customers, and of the society that sustains it. The Board metabolizes the power of all such participants in the enterprise in order to survive (Beer, 1985, p. 12).

The model depends, therefore, for its full and satisfactory operation, on a democratic milieu – ideally perhaps on a president who, when System 5 is represented during an explanation of the workings of the VSM, can exclaim "at last, *el pueblo*" (Beer, 1981).

Beer, therefore, provides cybernetic grounds for a possible critique. Decentralized control and democracy are necessary for viability and effectiveness. He also suggests some of the problems existing social arrangements present to the "proper" operation of the VSM. Top of the list here are the existence of power relationships in organizations and our acquiescence in the concept of hierarchy:

> System Three is not constructed as a box to house people with better suits and bigger cars than anyone else. That they do have these things is simply the result of a general acquiescence in the hierarchical concept (Beer, 1985, p. 92).

The implication is that we should redress power imbalances and abandon the hierarchical concept of organization. For a fuller discussion of these issues see Jackson (1988a).

Walker's (1990) account of how a large workers' co-operative restructured itself according to the proposals contained in Beer's VSM is also instructive.

Checkland's SSM, as we saw in Chapter 7, grew out of the frustration experienced by consultants trying to use hard systems methodologies in soft problem situations. The methodology embraces a paradigm shift, basing itself on interpretive rather than functionalist assumptions, and shifting the emphasis from attempting to model systems "out there" in the world toward using systems models to capture possible perceptions of the world. What emancipatory potential exists in SSM? In hard systems thinking, the "guarantee" for the results obtained is that the systems model accurately represents the world and that this has been verified (or not falsified) through normal scientific procedures. In SSM the attempt to model the world is abandoned and so this guarantee no longer exists. The only possible justification for implementing the results of a soft systems study must therefore be that the results and their implementation have been agreed upon after a process of full and genuine participatory debate among all the stakeholders involved or affected. Soft systems thinkers should therefore be critical of all social arrangements which prevent the kind of open, participative debate that is essential for the success of their approach and is the only justification for the results obtained. In fact, despite Checkland's (1981) assertion that SSM could be used in an emancipatory way of which Habermas would approve, this critical kernel of SSM has been little developed and soft systems thinkers have been content to fly in the face of their own philosophical principles and acquiesce in proposed changes emerging from limited debates characterized by distorted communication. SSM continues to be employed uncritically in problem situations where the mobilization of differential power resources by different interest groups makes genuine participation impossible (see Jackson, 1982). Still less has Checkland addressed the question of alternative social arrangements within which SSM could be "properly" employed. Responding to a hypothetical critique from Habermas, he weakly argues:

> What I hear Habermas arguing is that the debate at stages 5 and 6 of the soft systems methodology will be inhibited by society's structure. I think that it is the nature of society that this will be so (Checkland, 1981, p. 283).

Whatever has or has not been made of SSM, that explosive critical kernel remains and the way to develop it is clear from Habermas's thinking.

The argument of my 1990 paper was, therefore, that inside modern systems thinking could be found a justification, independent of any other tradition, for adopting an emancipatory systems approach. In Beer's work the grounds for critique are cybernetic and the particular focus of attention is power and hierarchy. The VSM requires a democratic milieu in which to operate properly. With Checkland's SSM the grounds for critique must be the "ideal speech situation" and the target institutional arrangements which lead to distorted communication. The philosophy of SSM demands communicative competence as the foundation for the process it orchestrates. It was argued that modern systems thinking becomes coherent when liberated from its regulative shell and interpreted from the emancipatory position.

Flood and Romm (1995, 1996) have taken this further and indicated that, whether it possesses a critical kernel or not, any systems method, model, tool or technique, can be employed for an emancipatory purpose:

> The given and immediate purpose of any method can be dominated by the given and immediate purpose of some other method so that, for example, with astute and careful handling a cybernetic or soft systems method can be employed to tackle emancipatory issues in a way which undercuts and redirects its original theoretical underpinning (1995, p. 378).

They provide examples (1995, 1996) of the VSM being employed in this way to deal with corruption and coercion, and Ackoff's interactive planning being used to establish fairer social relationships.

As Flood and Romm recognize, this employment of systems methods designed for other purposes to pursue emancipatory ends is a special case of what they call the "oblique" use of systems methods. When systems methods and models are used "obliquely" they are put to use in the service of a paradigm foreign to the one with which they were originally associated. Research is needed in the case of particular tools and techniques to see just how flexible they are when employed in this way. Nevertheless the approach is pretty general as we saw in the last chapter, with the use of "functionalist" models to serve interpretive purposes. We can support this attempt to give sustenance to the emancipatory paradigm, therefore, and indeed, in the next section, set out the constitutive rules for a generic emancipatory systems methodology which should make using systems methods obliquely, in this way, easier and more productive.

As an example of the oblique use of methods in the service of the emancipatory rationale, I shall refer to Flood's (1990) project of "liberate and critique" as set out in *Liberating Systems Thinking*. In this book, Flood argues that some of Foucault's postmodern arguments and methods are necessary to support the Habermasian position in realizing an emancipatory rationale. Habermas provides a basis for accepting three types of rationality (technical, practical, critical), for promoting the development of each of these, and for criticizing the limitations of each. However, he is naïve in the way he conceptualizes power; believing that power can be made to follow knowledge (to issue forth from the force of the better argument). Foucault sees power as immanent in all aspects of social life and as intimately linked to knowledge; so that, for example, it determines what the better argument is. Various localized forces, which cannot be grasped through some grand narrative such as Habermas's social theory, decide which discourses should be dominant and what knowledges subjugated.

Flood argues, therefore, that in order to achieve the maximum diversity in systems approaches, so that the fullest support can be provided to Habermas's emancipatory rationale, it is necessary first to follow Foucault's method to reveal subjugated knowledges. Emancipatory analysis must focus as much on revealing lost or suppressed knowledges as on the examination of those that have survived and become dominant. Foucault provides the understanding and the means, "oppositional thinking", necessary to liberate suppressed knowledges so that a diversity of approaches is achieved. Such thinking is for "fighters and resisters" rather than those who already know the answer, and it focuses on the extremities and the non-routine. Once suppressed discourses have been restored to attention, they can be subject to critique according to the principles set out by Habermas for assessing the theoretical and methodological legitimacies and limitations of different knowledges. An "adequate epistemology for systems practice" (Flood and Ulrich, 1990; Flood, 1990) can be established on essentially Habermasian foundations, but with support from Foucault's conceptualization of power.

As an example of a subjugated knowledge in systems thinking, Flood and Robinson (1989) provide general system theory (GST). GST has lost favor in the systems movement, but the reasons can hardly be entirely scientific, they argue, because the criticisms leveled against GST (which have become generally accepted) simply do not stand up to close examination. Presumably, we are supposed to gather from this that GST has had power withdrawn from it in the course of various non-discursive engagements. However, Flood and Robinson provide no analysis of how or why this might have happened and so the example is ultimately unconvincing. This does not detract from Flood's conclusions about the usefulness of Foucault's writings for emancipatory systems thinking. Oppositional thinking needs developing as a means of liberating both people and knowledges, even if we should choose to guide its use with a modernist emancipatory rationale.

This case of using an aspect of postmodernist thinking to support an emancipatory systems approach demonstrates how general the oblique use of methods can become. When properly guided by the generic emancipatory methodology presented in the next section, it adds considerably to the flexibility of the emancipatory systems approach and the armory at its disposal. We must not forget, of course, that depending upon the nature of the emancipatory perspective served by the oblique use of methods, the approach can find itself subject to the kinds of criticisms already raised against the "emancipation as liberation" and "emancipation through discursive rationality" traditions.

8.5. A GENERIC EMANCIPATORY SYSTEMS METHODOLOGY

We have in the preceding pages been discussing various systems approaches that take their lead from the emancipatory theoretical orientation. In general, emancipatory approaches provide a critique of current social arrangements, the way they benefit some groups at the expense of others, and a vision of a better state of affairs that can be brought about by social action - a rational society governed by communicative competence, a classless society, a society free of racial and/or gender oppression, etc. There is inevitably, therefore, a good deal of theory to be grasped in order to appreciate the emancipatory rationale. It might be argued that the emancipatory systems approach has favored theory rather than methodology and practice. This is certainly the position of champions of the soft systems cause, such as Ackoff and Checkland. It is also an opinion held by an otherwise sympathetic reviewer of emancipatory and critical operational research/systems (ORS) (Mingers, 1992a):

> A space has been created for Critical ORS but this space has yet to be painted in with practical critical methodologies (p. 109).

This is probably unfair to the efforts of such as Fuenmayor and colleagues, Beer, Ulrich, Midgley, and those working in Community OR and the Center for Systems Studies at Hull. Nevertheless it has a ring of truth in that the connections between the "framework of ideas" (F), the methodology (M), and the "area of application" (A) are rarely developed as fully as they should be in emancipatory systems studies. There may be various reasons for this. Mingers (1992a) suggests that the main difficulty is an inadequate treatment of power; and perhaps, here, there is something to be learned from the postmodern perspective as set out in the next chapter. There are also fundamental difficulties in declaring an emancipatory rationale up-front when working in organizations and a society where, as emancipatory thinkers would see it, hierarchy, inequality and privilege are so firmly embedded. Whatever the reasons, making these connections is essential to the future health of the emancipatory systems approach. As we have been arguing throughout the book, a clear methodology for linking theory to practice is essential if this is to be done and it is in this spirit that I now set out proposals for a generic emancipatory systems methodology.

I would wish to argue that, despite the variations we have seen in and between the "emancipation as liberation", "emancipation through discursive rationality", and "emancipation through the oblique use of systems methods" traditions, Table 8.2. captures the essence of the manner in which the key proponents would wish to see their approaches used. They all adhere to the emancipatory theoretical rationale as described in Chapter 3 and at the beginning of this chapter. Examples can be provided to show how the different approaches fulfil the conditions set out in 3a - 3h of Table 8.3. It is a fundamental of any emancipatory approach based on Marxism that the real world can exhibit features, derived from its systemic arrangements, that alienate and oppress particular individuals and social groups. Ulrich and Midgley see "boundary critique" as essential to discovering who is disadvantaged by current systemic arrangements. Freire's "radical pedagogy" assists the oppressed to build accounts of reality expressing their disadvantaged status. Habermas provides the psychoanalytic encounter as an analogy for the process that needs to be undertaken to enlighten the oppressed about their current situation. Although we have provided few examples, quantitative analysis can clearly be employed torecognize discrimination against racial minorities, women etc. Community OR is an example of a practice designed to improve the position of the disadvantaged. One of Ulrich's 12 questions in "critical systems heuristics" asks: "Are the affected given an opportunity to emancipate themselves from the experts and take their fate in their own hands?" Beer's Team Syntegrity

Table 8.3. Constitutive rules for a generic emancipatory systems methodology

1. An emancipatory systems methodology is a structured way of thinking, with an attachment to the emancipatory theoretical rationale, that is focused on improving real-world problem situations.

2. An emancipatory systems methodology uses systems ideas as the basis for its intervention strategy and will frequently employ methods, models, tools and techniques which also draw upon systems ideas.

3. The claim to have used a systems methodology according to the emancipatory rationale must be justified according to the following guidelines:

   a. an assumption is made that the real-world can become systemic in a manner alienating to individuals and/or oppressive to particular social groups;

   b. analysis of the problem situation is designed to reveal who is disadvantaged and how they are disadvantaged by current systemic arrangements;

   c. models are constructed which reveal the sources of alienation and oppression and propose alternative social arrangements in which these disappear;

   d. models are used to enlighten the alienated and oppressed about their situation and what they can do about it;

   e. quantitative analysis may be useful especially to capture particular biases in existing systemic arrangements;

   f. The process of intervention is systemic and is aimed at improving the problem situation for the alienated and/or oppressed;

   g. the intervention is conducted in such a way that the alienated and/or oppressed begin to take responsibility for their own liberation;

   h. changes designed to improve the position of the alienated and/or oppressed are evaluated primarily in terms of ethicality and emancipation.

4. Since an emancipatory systems methodology can be used in different ways in different situations, and interpreted differently by different users, each use should exhibit conscious thought about how to adapt to the particular circumstances.

5. Each use of an emancipatory systems methodology should yield research findings as well as changing the real-world problem situation. These research findings may relate to the theoretical rationale underlying the methodology, to the methodology itself and how to use it, to the methods, models, tools and techniques employed, to the real-world problem situation investigated, or to all of these.

is frequently evaluated positively because participants feel that the process is open, self-organizing and non-hierarchical. In general terms, and with occasional explanation necessary, the names of any of the systems approaches discussed in this chapter can be used to head the sentences related to 3a - 3h in Table 8.3 replacing the particular examples provided here. Moreover, emancipatory systems methodologies are flexible in the face of the peculiarities of the circumstances in which they are employed (users, problem situation, etc.); and are capable of yielding research findings.

We need now to consider the strengths and weaknesses of the emancipatory systems approach as a whole.

8.6. CRITIQUE OF THE EMANCIPATORY SYSTEMS APPROACH

The same pattern for this critique is followed as for those in the two previous chapters. The emancipatory systems approach, and the advantages it gives, are first discussed in its own terms. It is then subject to a broad critique from the point of view of functionalist, interpretive and postmodern systems thinking.

From the discussion that has taken place, it is apparent that the concerns addressed by emancipatory systems thinking include some that are entirely foreign to other systems approaches of a functionalist or interpretive nature. Let us recall Wood and Kelly's contention, mentioned at the beginning of the chapter, that the common thrust of the emancipatory challenge lies in a refusal to accept as preordained existing inequalities of wealth, status, power and authority, and in a refusal to act simply as legitimization and support for the status quo. To take this stance, emancipatory systems thinking must be based on entirely different assumptions about the nature of society from those accepted in more traditional approaches. Other systems approaches rest on a belief in social order and consensus and aim to promote integration so as to improve existing social systems, from which all are seen as benefiting. They help buttress the status quo. Emancipatory systems thinking specializes in identifying contradictions in social systems, the existence of conflict, and the domination of some groups over others. The aim is to promote radical change and to emancipate the deprived majority. These differences amount in Burrell and Morgan's terms to a difference between adherence to the sociology of regulation and adherence to the sociology of radical change. This distinction is a fundamental one that means that emancipatory systems thinking operates from a different paradigm to functionalist and interpretive forms of systems thinking. The result is that emancipatory systems thinking has a unique contribution to make in highlighting and assisting us to address oppression and disadvantage. Issues of inequality between classes, genders, races, people of a different sexual orientation, etc., which are easily brushed under the carpet by other systems approaches, come to the fore when problem situations are confronted using the emancipatory perspective. Some of the most significant questions that bother humankind today, such as world poverty, destruction of the environment and the future we are leaving to later generations, can at last get serious attention from systems thinkers. This is the significant contribution that the emancipatory systems approach makes to systems thinking, and is one that makes it worthy of the most serious attention from all those interested in the holistic resolution of important problems.

The gaze that the emancipatory systems approach directs towards coercion and oppression, and its dependence on the "psychic prison" and "instruments of domination" metaphors for exploring organizations and society, inevitably means that it can appear to offer a one-dimensional view of the nature of problem resolving. Ulrich, for example, rails against the limitations of the machine and organismic analogies that dominate systems science and, in the process, downplays the importance of the "technical interest" that humans have in securing better prediction and control. To those critical systems thinkers, aware of what functionalist, interpretive and postmodern systems approaches can deliver, it seems that the emancipatory systems approach has a limited domain for which it is appropriate. We shall now seek to delimit that domain from the functionalist, interpretive and postmodern perspectives.

Functionalists would want to point to the role that increasing efficiency and effectiveness have had in improving the standard of living of large segments of the world's population. The functionalist systems approach, in assisting with this, seems to have made a much more direct contribution to liberating men and women from backwardness and "slavery" than does the emancipatory systems approach. The emancipatory systems approach is rather vague in the way it defines "emancipation" and "liberation." Perhaps it wants to define these in terms of the achievement of some aspirations of the human spirit other than the availability and pursuit of consumer goods, but such a position can seem élitist and irrelevant to the mass of the population. Hence, the suspicion felt by functionalists of Ulrich's neglect of "instrumental reason" and for the claim by Freire and his supporters that a literacy campaign can succeed even if it does not teach many people to read and write. Pearson (1994) is making a related argument when he suggests that technical expertise must be protected by responsible authorities from "simplistic democracy":

> Perfect democracy empowers equally the incompetent, the ignorant, the evil, the foolish, and the stupid, along with the decent (p. 316).

The functionalist argument is that the knowledge and expertise contained in the hard and cybernetic systems approaches can bring real, verifiable improvements in the efficiency and effectiveness of organizations. This risks being ignored by emancipatory systems thinkers who emphasize equal participation at all costs and seek to orientate systems in pursuit of ill-founded conceptions of what human beings are capable of becoming.

The arguments of interpretive systems thinkers, such as Ackoff and Checkland, against the emancipatory systems approach were summarized in the previous chapter and repeated earlier in this. Interpretive thinkers believe that those adopting the emancipatory perspective too readily assume the existence of "irresolvable conflicts" and of constraints on social improvement. If they left their theoretical ivory towers, they would find that, in practice, reform can be brought about. Emancipatory thinkers, the criticism runs, are themselves constrained by their desire for utopian change which ensures all wrongs are righted at once. If they became involved in piecemeal improvement strategies they could achieve much of what they claim to want. Wedded as they are to impossible standards, such as those imposed by the requirement for communicative competence, they are rendered powerless. Furthermore interpretive thinkers are nervous of the utopian aspirations of emancipatory systems thinkers, which have brought disaster in the past, and contemptuous of the élitist notion of "false-consciousness." It seems that those who do not share emancipatory views can be dismissed as being ideologically contaminated.

Postmodernists share the distrust that interpretive thinkers feel toward the "grand narratives" of emancipation embraced by some emancipatory systems thinkers. In the absence of any objective standards against which to judge "knowledge", or any shared moral framework to provide a generalizable account of what is justifiable, such narratives are simply claims to power over others and can easily lead the oppressed into new relations of domination. We should, therefore, seek to challenge totalizing discourses. Consensus, rather than being a desirable state of affairs, needs to be overthrown. Postmodernists reject the notion that there can be progress toward some state of universal emancipation or betterment. The particular experiences we have, caught in our own webs of historical and cultural determination, are too complex and diverse to be reconciled. Furthermore, there is no common human essence that through emancipation can be brought to perfection. As Munro (1997) puts it, the postmodernist position

> seriously challenges whether there is truly anything lying dormant, either hidden or repressed, which can be emancipated. Such a position would suggest that talk of an emancipatory OR methodology ultimately lacks any real content (p. 580).

There is no true "self", or genuine human nature, that can be rescued from the myriad of interlocking power/knowledge relationships into which we are thrown and which constitute our being.

All this, of course, throws doubt on the role of "experts" in the emancipatory systems approach. Such experts are important because they can, on the basis of the social or systems theory they have mastered, recognize sources of alienation and domination and lead the oppressed to see the true nature of their situation and how they might overcome their oppression. Postmodernists ask how such experts can arise, apparently stepping outside of their own social situation and the power games that involve everyone else, in order to acquire such superior knowledge. Postmodernists reject expertise based on "objective" knowledge and respect only local expertise gained in the heat of local struggles.

There is debate in the systems community as to whether the postmodernist perspective simply undermines the notion of an emancipatory systems approach, as Munro suggests, or whether it provides an alternative, if very different, foundation for emancipatory and critical practice in systems thinking, as Brocklesby and Cummings (1996) argue. This will be taken up as an important issue in the next chapter.

9

THE POSTMODERN SYSTEMS APPROACH

9.1. INTRODUCTION

The basic thrust of post-structuralist and postmodern thinking (referred to here simply as postmodernism) is aimed at the totalizing and normalizing tendencies of the discourses that dominate in modernism. All "grand narratives", whether referring to maximizing the efficiency and effectiveness of "systems" or to the possibility of universal emancipation, are subject to debunking. As displayed in Table 3.1 of Chapter 3, the postmodern approach seeks, through methods such as deconstruction and genealogy, to reclaim conflict and to ensure that marginalized voices are recognized and heard. It adopts an ironic and playful disposition in order to ensure diversity and encourage creativity.

As all of Burrell and Morgan's four paradigms are modernist in orientation, postmodernism cannot be related to that framework except in an oppositional manner. It does, however, correspond quite closely to Pepper's "root metaphor" of "contextualism" (or "pragmatism"). Contextualism presents the world as a complex of continuously changing patterns made up of the incidents of life. This complex is characterized by change and novelty, order and disorder. There is no "depth" to explore and meaning is difficult to obtain. We noted that the interpretive systems approach was also influenced by this root metaphor; but whereas the interpretive response is to seek order through consensus and accommodation, the postmodern response is to emphasize and promote novelty and disorder and to refuse meaning. Morgan (1993) sees commonalities between postmodernism and chaos and complexity theory:

> The postmodern world view, which, of interest, is paralleled in aspects of the new science emphasizing the chaotic, paradoxical and transient nature of order and disorder, requires an approach that allows the theory and practice of organization and management to acquire a more fluid form (pp. 282-283).

This allows him to link postmodernism with his "flux and transformation" metaphor. As we saw in Chapter 6, however, the flux and transformation metaphor, as expressed in complexity theory, reduces too readily to a search for pattern underlying the disorder. Postmodernism is more radical than this. Alvesson and Deetz (1996) suggest that the metaphor of "carnival" may be more appropriate.

Brocklesby and Cummings (1996) trace the postmodern tradition back to Kant and his admonition that we should have the courage to use our own reason and "dare to know." This, of course, was the same source that gave rise to the emancipatory systems approach. Postmodernism diverged from the Enlightenment tradition when it followed Nietzsche and

Heidegger in pursuit of self emancipation rather than Hegel, Marx and the Frankfurt School in the quest for universal or collective human emancipation. Nietzsche provided the first questioning of Hegel's view that there is progress in history and of the emphasis placed on the human essence and individual rationality. The self, for Nietzsche, is a contingent product of various physical, cultural and social forces. To be free, an individual has to re-style himself by critically questioning all received opinion and accepted ways of doing things. People need power in order to do this and, therefore, people's "will-to-power" is something to be celebrated. Taking his lead from Nietzsche, Heidegger sought, through critical questioning, to undermine the whole direction taken by western philosophy as it had evolved from Plato and Aristotle to Hegel. He wanted to reorientate philosophy around the study of *Being*, concentrating particularly on the uniqueness of each person's "being-in-the-world." As Brocklesby and Cummings summarize:

> Critical thinking and emancipation for Heidegger is very much a personal matter. One gets free by confronting the real, stark question that confronts one's self, but is at once all too easy to avoid: Why am I Being and not nothing?' No person can ask this question for, or of, another. One gets free by recognizing that all Being, all the structures and categories that surround us, are based on nothing but our thrown-ness, and confronting the existential angst that this promotes. No shared utopia, or resolution of this predicament, is on offer (p. 748).

We cannot take comfort, therefore, in the idea that history has a purpose or in the acceptance of any inherited concepts. To be authentic, it is necessary to face up to the contingency of our own existence and make of it what we will. For existentialists like Heidegger, existence precedes essence.

Brocklesby and Cummings see a direct line from Nietzsche and Heidegger to Foucault:

> The genealogy to Foucault ... concerns itself ... with providing tools which individuals can use themselves as they see fit, to free their minds to alternatives by highlighting the way in which power within systems subjugates them. This approach seeks to bring into play, to make visible, the unwritten categories and rules of the system(s), so as to enable individuals to develop responsive strategies to them, rather than collectively build shiny new systems (p. 741).

Looking at the practical aspects of Foucault's work, Brocklesby and Cummings argue that it enables individuals to understand the extent to which they are determined by existing structures of power and knowledge. It also allows them to grasp some of the mechanisms by which the current order is sustained and offers them tools and techniques to use as, they see fit, in local strategizing and subversion to undermine the current system. They cannot hope to proceed on the basis of consensus and must accept that difference will prevail but, in Taket and White's (2000) terms, they may be able to achieve "consent to act."

The reader will recall, at this point, our own discussion of the work of Lyotard, Derrida and Foucault in Chapter 3, which offers a useful complement to the Brocklesby and Cummings account by emphasizing the important influence that structuralism had on the development of postmodernism. It is also worth repeating here the seven ideas that Alvesson and Deetz suggest postmodern thinkers share in common:

- the centrality of discourse
- the discursive production of the individual
- the discursive production of natural objects rather than language as a mirror of reality
- the loss of power of the grand narratives
- the power/knowledge connection

- research aimed at revealing indeterminacy and encouraging resistance rather than at maintaining rationality, predictability and order
- hyperreality – simulations replace the "real-world" in the current world order

While acknowledging the influence of structuralism on postmodernism, and Foucault's title as a Professor of Systems of Thought, we ended our account, in Chapter 2, suggesting that it might prove difficult to manage the fit between the systems approach and postmodern thinking. Certainly we must recognize that postmodernism does not offer us a systemic conceptual framework or even a systemic manner of proceeding in intervention. Foucault was insistent that there was no unity even in his own work, and that his texts were a toolkit, elements of which could be used, or otherwise, by anyone as they saw fit:

> If people are willing to open them and make use of such and such a sentence or idea, or analysis or other, as they would a screwdriver or monkey wrench, in order to short circuit or disqualify systems of power ... all the better (Foucault, quoted in Brocklesby and Cummings, 1996, p. 749).

Nevertheless, we shall discover in what follows at least two ways in which systems thinking and postmodernism can collaborate. The first is in using various systems models, methods and techniques but in the spirit of postmodernism. The second is in some new methods and tools which postmodernism can provide and which can assist the systems practitioner.

9.2. INTERVENTION IN THE SPIRIT OF POSTMODERNISM - TAKET AND WHITE'S "PANDA"

According to Taket and White (2000), we are entering "New Times" which give rise to a much greater requirement for multiagency working. New organizational forms are coming into being based upon fragmentation, decentralization and networks. Organizational cultures are pluralistic rather than unitary. The "new liberalism" encourages the breakdown of state control and the growth in importance of non-governmental organizations and the private sector. The increasing turbulence of the organizational environment demands co-operation between different enterprises. Whatever the context, in these postmodern times, whether simply the number of choices available to individuals, the variety of stakeholders involved in local decision-making, or the increasing connections between organizations themselves, we seem to be entering an age in which partnership and participation, and decision-making in "multiagency settings" (broadly defined), will be crucial.

Multiagency work, for Taket and White, is

> about 'making things happen' in a complex world. It occurs in an environment productive of different narratives because of the heterogeneity of representations available to the parties involved (2000, p. 35).

Diversity must be encouraged by strengthening the rights of different "clients" or stakeholders to participate and enabling them to explore the possibilities available to them and the constraints limiting them. The multiplicity of available knowledge bases must be protected against the hegemony of "experts" pandering to absolute notions of truth (White and Taket, 1994). It might then be possible to build, out of the various "fragmented rationalities", a local and provisional plan for action.

Multiagency settings, Taket and White argue, are "polyvocal, contingent, dynamic and diverse." Other methodologies and methods frequently employed in multiagency settings, such as "Strategic Options Development and Analysis" (SODA), Strategic Choice, Team Syntegrity, Soft Systems Methodology (SSM) and Total Systems Intervention (TSI), fail to fully respect these characteristics. They draw upon modernist theories of rational action which, with their reliance on rationality, abstraction and verbal competence, can suffocate creativity and spontaneity. Even those approaches which apparently seek to enhance diversity, by encouraging the pluralist use of methods, do so in a totalizing manner which tries to "master pluralism", by showing how different methods are related, rather than "embracing pluralism." Taket and White (2000) wish to promote for multiagency work an approach which is, instead, "unashamedly postmodern/poststructuralist." This approach draws on the work of Nietzsche in emphasizing creativity and reflexivity working together in a "joyful, playful becoming" with no predetermined idea of where such "Dionysian" activity is heading. It respects Foucault's rejection of any guarantees for what outcome might be achieved. Such postmodern practice can be "liberating" but only in the local context and only on the basis of choices made for which those involved and the facilitators must take responsibility. The framework employed to put this postmodern perspective into practice is called, by Taket and White, "pragmatic pluralism."

Pragmatic pluralism is an attempt to work holistically and pragmatically to address the diversity and heterogeneity found in multiagency settings. It rejects prescription based upon totalizing theories and seeks

> guidelines, examples, stories, metaphors for use in planning and interaction, in carrying out the interaction, and in reflecting on it during and afterwards. In moving away from prescription, we seek to maintain an open and flexible stance, capable of responding creatively to the characteristics of a particular moment, continually disrupting the comfort of identification with a fixed theory or view, and seeking instead to mix different perspectives (Taket and White, 2000, p. 69).

Embracing relativism in this way does not mean that "anything goes." Indeed it is important to be "critically reflective." However, it has to be accepted that all knowledge is partial, provisional and contingent. Thus futile questions about "the truth" are replaced by responses to issues such as:

- How does this feel?
- Is this fun?
- Does this do what we want?
- Does viewpoint or action "a" seem better than "b", at least for the moment?

More specifically, for the purpose of intervention, pragmatic pluralism recognizes and tries to respond to pluralism in each of four areas (Taket and White, 2000, p. 67):

- in the nature of the client
- in the use of specific methods
- in the modes of representation employed
- in the facilitation process

Pluralism in the nature of the client refers to the diverse viewpoints held by the various stakeholders in multiagency work – all of which must be acknowledged and respected. This demands attention to the three Cs – "Critical", "Consent" and "Contingent." Being "critical" means ensuring that the widest possible range of viewpoints and values are heard, and that any which are being repressed should be brought to the fore by "strategic essentialism."

"Consent" acknowledges that consensus is often impossible and that all that may be possible is the establishment of a "system of consent." "Contingent" recognizes the importance of time and location, so that the only "truths" are those relevant to the local circumstances of the moment.

Pluralism in the methods employed requires that we "mix and match" methods, adopting a flexible and adaptive stance according to "what feels good" given the particular features of the multiagency setting. To do this well we need to bear in mind the four Ms – "Mix", "Modify", "Multiply" and "Match." Mixing involves using whole methods, or parts of different methodologies, together and at different times during an intervention. Some methods (e.g. brainstorming, nominal group technique, Delphi) lend themselves to convenient use in their entirety. Methodologies (e.g. critical systems heuristics, strategic choice, SSM) usually require "mutilating" in order to break them down into their more usable parts. Modifying asks us to be aware of the need to change and adapt methods so that they become appropriate for the particular circumstances faced. "Multiply" suggests that we can increase our possibilities of success if we try out different methods for the same task. To "match" means to choose methods according to the preferences of the stakeholders and the facilitators and according to the nature of the situation addressed. It is impossible to determine, outside of the local circumstances, which methods are "best" for which situations and this, of course, requires a fresh choice to be made for each intervention and even for each stage of an intervention. Given attention to local circumstances, however, a judicious mix of methods and parts of methodologies can be made which, in that situation, can be regarded as "good enough" (Taket and White, 2000). To achieve a sufficient match of variety with the multiagency settings of their concern, Taket and White are prepared to draw upon the full range of management science and systems methods and methodologies we have been considering in this book, together with methods such as "Participatory Rapid Appraisal" from the development studies literature, as well as particular postmodern methods.

Taket and White note the shift, signaled powerfully in Baudrillard's work, from the notion of "representation" as capturing objects "out there" to representation as capturing only other impressions of the world. This implies that it is no longer technical experts that should be central in any consideration of representation but the actual concerned stakeholders:

> We need to develop modes of representation in OR and systems that are transparent, mutually produced with the participants, are owned by the participants and can be interrogated by the participants. The representations are produced from shared analysis and result in shared meaning between all parties (Taket and White, 2000, p. 86).

The best hope of achieving this is if we consider a range of methods of representation which we can recall using the 3 Vs - "Verbal", "Visual" and "Vital." To ensure equitable participation and learning, therefore, traditional verbal forms of representation, such as encouraged in Team Syntegrity, need to be set alongside visual modes, such as "rich pictures", and vital modes such as sociodrama.

Pluralism is also necessary in the facilitation process,

> in terms of the adoption of different roles and guises ... at different times in the course of an intervention, and of different roles in relation to different individuals/groups involved in the intervention (at the same time) (Taket and White, 2000, p. 82).

The need for facilitators to mix and match different roles and guises is encapsulated in the four Fs - "Flexibility", "Forthrightness", "Focus" and "Fairness." "Flexibility" means a willingness to respond and adapt to the dynamics of the situation. "Forthrightness", or "Forcefulness", suggests that there are times when facilitators need to challenge and intervene. To maintain "focus" requires keeping a sense of purpose, progress and place. Ensuring "fairness", in particular with regard to equitable participation, demands that facilitators continually engage in critical reflection. Recognizing how difficult it is to remain neutral, and accepting the pervasiveness of ethical issues in group decision making, facilitators have to acknowledge and reflect upon their own subjectivity and responsibility during the engagement.

Taket and White give the name PANDA (participatory appraisal of needs and the development of action) to the particular vehicle they approve for putting pragmatic pluralism into effect in multiagency settings. They stress that its application is very much an art or craft and not a science. Of course, this does not mean that detailed advanced planning is not necessary. It is essential to ensure that the facilitators, the participants and the setting are such that opportunities to take maximum advantage of the four aspects of pluralism are facilitated. Nevertheless, once an engagement starts it is all down to flexible improvisation.

PANDA has grown from postmodern roots which involve

> learning to live with uncertainty and change, recognizing and affirming difference and diversity, being comfortable with the notion that contradiction is inherent in what we do (Taket and White, 2000, p. 187).

These roots naturally give rise to certain paradoxes which flower in the application of PANDA, as summarized in Table 9.1 (from Taket and White, 2000, p.187). Once these are grasped, however, PANDA can be described in terms of a fairly traditional structure. Essentially there are four phases (defined by the three Ds - "Deliberation", "Debate", "Decision" - that groups have to go through in multiagency decision making) and nine tasks or foci to be addressed during these phases. Table 9.2 (from Taket and White, 2000, p. 192) outlines this structure. Of course Taket and White make the point that any actual application will require cycling back and forth between the phases and tasks.

"Deliberation I" involves opening a space for discussion, respecting and multiplying diversity, and enabling and facilitating participation. Taket and White (2000) produce a list of their favorite, tried and tested methods for mixing and matching during this deliberation phase. Debate may require more forceful facilitation than Deliberation I because the aim is to deepen understanding of the options under consideration, structure them, lose some and combine others. This requires more systematic appraisal of the options, explicit negotiation over preferences and continued attention to ensuring full and equitable participation. Another list of methods is supplied which Taket and White have found useful in "Debate." "Decision" involves not only debate and discussion about the options to take forward but also the methods to be used in deciding these options. "Deliberation II" sees the monitoring and evaluating of the effects of agreed actions. Lists of favorite methods for "Decision" and "Deliberation II" are provided in Taket and White (2000).

A variety of case studies are described by Taket and White (2000) which show PANDA in action, including five fuller accounts chosen to illustrate its use in a diversity of settings. A brief description of an engagement to assist a development agency in Belize (pp. 117-118) shows attention to pluralism in the nature of the client and pluralism in relation to the use of methods as, at different stages, "participatory rapid appraisal" (PAR), elements of Team Syntegrity and the "shaping" and "commitment package" aspects of Strategic Choice are all employed. There is a longer account of another intervention in Belize, for the Association of National Development Agencies (ANDA), which was designed to help them reach strategy decisions in the face of reduced funding (pp. 205-209). Emphasis on pluralism in the nature

Table 9.1. The paradoxes of PANDA

The only guarantee is that there are no guarantees. The only grand narrative is that there are no grand narratives. Use only what you feel comfortable with … but take risks and expand your boundaries of comfort. Wherever oppression/power is exercised there is the possibility of resistance, empowerment and change.

Theory is dead - long live theorizing.
Have fun - but it will hurt too (or no pain no gain)

Table 9.2. The three Ds and nine tasks or focuses of PANDA

Deliberation I	Selecting participants
	Defining purpose/objectives
	Exploring the situation
Debate	Identifying options
	Researching options (which could include consulting on options)
	Comparing options
Decision	Deciding action
	Recording decisions
Deliberation II	Monitoring/Evaluating

of the client and mixing and matching methods - in this case, cognitive mapping, nominal group technique, a composite causal map, role playing, etc. - is still strong. In this example, however, attention is also paid to pluralism in modes of representation and in the facilitation process. The existence of more powerful groups in the network represented by ANDA, and the lack of facility of other groups with verbal approaches, meant that the facilitators had to work hard, and employ non-verbal forms of representation, to ensure full and equitable participation.

Although, following their postmodern logic, Taket and White are unable to provide any formal "justification" for embracing pragmatic pluralism and employing PANDA, this does not mean that certain principles cannot be upheld. It seems that an engagement can be deemed successful, these are my terms, if it appeals to "exception", "emotion" and "ethics." The aim is to achieve an exceptional result, locally and for the moment, that would otherwise not have come about in the particular multiagency situation addressed. This means working with difference, finding exceptions to taken-for-granted narratives, generalizations and statements, exposing rhetorical devices, and using new and unusual terminology. In doing this it is necessary to trust the emotions. It is possible to do some matching between methods and the specific local context, but it is more essential to do "what feels good" to the facilitators and participants. A method should give those using it feelings of freedom and empowerment. Finally, although there can be no justification provided, this does not mean freedom from ethical choice. Indeed it means that facilitators must be constantly aware of their personal involvement and the ethical choices they are making. Taket and White (2000) are clear that their personal ethics of practice requires them to work to support whichever groups can be identified as disempowered or marginalized in a local context. Taket has described elsewhere (1994) how she was able to exploit the relative power accorded to her expertise to work "undercover" in the service of a disadvantaged group.

There is much of use that can be gleaned from pragmatic pluralism and PANDA whether or not you share a postmodern paradigmatic orientation. Taket and White begin their main text (2000) by stating that it might seem "bitty, fragmented, chaotic, incomplete", but that this is not a flaw, it is part of the (postmodern) point. They end up apologizing for having produced a book that is linear in nature. No need to apologize to this reader. The text argues (il)logically for its postmodern position, is well structured and ordered, and clearly written. There is some original theorizing. For example, their extension of the normal meaning of "pluralism" in management science, to embrace modes of representation and facilitator "guises", is exhilarating and of great utility. The case studies are well presented. There is also much that is attractive in Taket and White's vision of a postmodern OR/systems. The flexibility provided in the employment of methods, the attention given to "local improvement" and the emphasis on the ethical responsibility of facilitators are all to be welcomed.

Critics, however, will wonder whether an approach that appears to work in multiagency settings can be used as successfully in hierarchical organizations where concerns about efficiently and effectively pursuing goals still seem to be paramount. Is there so little need for the expertise embedded in functionalist systems approaches in these settings? The case made for extending the notion of multiagency work to single decision makers and single organizations is a weak one. Critics will also be skeptical about whether doing "what feels good" is a sufficient reason for adopting pragmatic pluralism and PANDA. In reality the sense of "fun" so beloved of Taket and White in theory fails to shine through in the case studies. It seems as though clients, although no doubt hoping to enjoy the projects they are engaged on, value more highly the achievement of other aims and objectives such as improving the functioning of the system or consensus about goals. Does an agency in Belize, hoping to improve the lot of the rural poor, really prioritize "what feels good"? Taket and White argue that other aims and objectives are misleading because they involve "unanswerable" questions. It is a matter of having fun and leaving the rest for ethical resolution. But we are then left dependent on the ethical practice of the facilitators. In this regard, the ethics of working "undercover" for the disadvantaged would be questioned by those who value transparency highly. Isn't the ability, on the part of postmodern practitioners, to recognize disadvantaged and marginalized groups simply another form of unargued expertise? Finally, Taket and White accept our ability to theorize and critically reflect upon local matters such as "which methods engage this group?", "how do we ensure equitable participation?", "how can we challenge existing power relations?", etc., but the absence of a clearly defined methodology, linking the postmodern theory and the pragmatic pluralist practice, makes it difficult to do so in any way that is "recoverable." This critique will be developed further, in more general terms, in the final section of the chapter.

9.3. POSTMODERN SYSTEMS METHODS

In this section we shall consider another way in which systems thinking and postmodernism can collaborate. This involves the appropriation of aspects of postmodern thought into postmodern systems methods which can be used on their own, or in combination with other systems methods, in the course of a systems intervention. This systems intervention might itself be in the spirit of postmodernism or it might be guided by a methodology rooted in another paradigm - in the latter case we would be using the postmodern systems methods "obliquely."

In the previous chapter we witnessed Flood seeking to employ aspects of Foucault's postmodern argument in support of "liberating systems theory." This idea came from a useful contribution by Flood and Gregory (1989), who set out four ideas on the nature of the history and progress of knowledge - linear sequential, structuralism, worldviewism and genealogy - and related these to accounts of the development of systems thinking. The linear sequential model sees knowledge building chronologically and cumulatively. Structuralism represents deeper processes as being at work in history, and uses the "scientific" approach to unearth these and build cumulative knowledge of them. Worldviewism rejects the unilinear perspective and accepts the existence of contrasting and even contradictory knowledges, although there may be periods of settled or "normal" science (Kuhn, 1970). Genealogy, deriving from Foucault's writings, puts emphasis on the effect power at the micro level can have on the formation and development of knowledges. Localized power relations outside of discourse can affect the success or lead to the subjugation of knowledges. In Flood and Gregory's opinion the first three ideas on the history of knowledge are well represented in accounts of progress in systems thinking, but the genealogical view has not yet been exploited. The result has been a neglect of the effect of power at the micro level on the way the subject has unfolded. Obviously, a properly conducted genealogical study could contribute significantly to understanding the history of systems thinking.

Taket and White have developed some specifically postmodern methods to use alongside more standard techniques in the course of interventions based upon pragmatic pluralism. In a case study (White and Taket, 2000), working with an organization responsible for allocating grants to voluntary sector groups, they describe the use of "narrative analysis." Narrative analysis rests on the postmodern notion, derived from Derrida, that "everything can be seen as text." If that is true, White and Taket argue, interventions can be seen as textual and explored using narrative analysis:

> The process involves analyzing surface structures then deep structures which are 'value' or 'belief' systems embedded in the narrative, followed by interpretation and reflection (2000, p. 701).

Surface features of the narrative are analyzed using "actant analysis." This draws on the idea that there are certain roles that need to be filled in any narrative — destinator (determiner of the rules and values), receivers (who receive the values), subject (occupying the central role), object (the goal desired by the subject), adjuvants (entities assisting the subject) and traitors (tricksters or resisters, who try to get in the way of goal attainment). Following actant analysis, the second stage is to reveal the values or deep structure of the text using a process known as "deconstruction." This requires us to expose the particular bias inherent in the text by considering the actual "actants" privileged or ignored:

> Deconstruction uses a series of analytical strategies to examine texts closely and to look for contradictions and ambivalences. The strategies are used to take apart the texts to reveal implicit meaning and unacknowledged biases (Taket and White, 2000, p. 132).

Drawing upon Beath and Orlikowski, Taket and White (2000, p. 105) provide examples of deconstructive strategies which are reproduced in Table 9.4. The final stage of narrative analysis requires taking clients through the previous two stages, revisiting them if necessary, in order to "reflect" on what has been found out.

Table 9.4. Examples of deconstructive strategies

- focusing on marginalized elements
- exposing a false distinction
- looking at claims or assertions which depend on something other than what is clearly stated, especially those that make explicit or implicit recourse to claims of "naturalness"
- examining what is not said or is deliberately omitted
- paying attention to disruptions and contradictions
- examining use of metaphor
- examining use of double entendres

In the voluntary sector example, an early deconstruction revealed that voluntary sector groups themselves were missing from an actant analysis. Further work showed that there was a contradiction between the idea of "partnership", used to describe the relationship between the funding organization and the voluntary sector groups, and the way that the funding organization actually worked - for example using evaluation to exert control. Replacement of the partnership notion by the metaphor of "good enough parenting", to describe the relationship, allowed much richer and more realistic discussion to take place between the relevant stakeholders. The participants in this narrative analysis apparently found it easy to engage with the methods employed:

> The actant analysis is transparent and deconstruction can appear to be a process of critical awareness that is almost natural to the participants (White and Taket, 2000, p. 701).

Taket and White have, elsewhere, used deconstruction in a Community and Mental Health Trust (2000, p. 132) and to analyze various debates in operational research for the presence of oppressive mechanisms (1993). In the former case, the technical scientific meaning attached to the "whole systems approach", a rhetorical device used by one of the doctors, was successfully challenged by the rest of the team and the meaning shifted more to "interprofessional working." In the other example, deconstruction reveals how protagonists in certain debates in OR privilege one term in binary divides such as male/female. They then attach the privileged term to their favored position in order to disparage the alternative. For example, those who prefer hard to soft OR often seek to attach "masculine qualities" such as "machismo", "interventionist" and "potency" to its practice while trying to dismiss soft OR by equating it to "feminine qualities" such as "coy", "effete" and "shy." The particular deconstructive strategy employed here involves revealing the positive pole in a discourse, exposing the hidden negative pole and then "negating the negation" by showing how the positive depends completely on the negative.

Topp (1999), in a highly original Ph.D. thesis, has introduced three further postmodern systems methods which he calls "Knowledge Systems Diagnostics", "Generative Conversation" and "Systems Story." The aim of the thesis, as he states it, is

> to appropriate aspects of postmodern philosophy into systems methods that support new knowledge creation in post-industrial business (p. 3).

In the postmodern world, traditional systems approaches still have a role in helping businesses to achieve goals efficiently and effectively, and in assisting managers to regulate debate. What have become crucial to the success of post-industrial businesses, however, are creating new knowledge and using existing knowledge more productively, and the application of modernist systems methods [for these purposes] can at best only produce new moves in the same game (p. 105).

This, Topp argues, is borne out in his own experience in attempting to change business organizations, when modernist systems interventions were often frustrated by "subtle systemic resistance." There is a need, therefore, for new systems methods appropriate to the creation of new knowledge in post-industrial business. In his search for such methods, Topp decides to follow Churchman's systems approach, in *The Design of Inquiring Systems*, and to look at the world through the eyes of some philosophers. In his case, however, it is the point of view of postmodern philosophers, such as Foucault and Lyotard, that is explored. In designing methods based on their perspective, Topp employs as his giude the four issues identified by Jackson (1991) as being the most important of those raised by postmodernism for systems thinking and practice. These are the challenge postmodernism poses to logic and order; its questioning of progress in terms of both performance and emancipation; the new and enhanced theorizing of power it provides; and its assumption that language is deceptive rather than simply transparent.

Knowledge Systems Diagnostics is a method based on the early work of Foucault, on the "archaeology of knowledge", which seeks to uncover and inquire into the "formative system" operating in any organization. The formative system is a system of "second order" knowledge production which enables and regulates what it is possible for organizational actors to think and express at any point in time. Since the formative system is not usually understood by those it controls, research into how it operates "decenters" the subject. Organizational change can then be seen not as a shifting of individual perspectives but as a shift in the knowledge matrix in an organization which is determining what it is possible for individuals to think:

> Instead of focusing exclusively on the *a priori* concepts and systems ideas of individuals, one needs to understand the formative elements that make it possible for them to say and think new things within specific business contexts. How is new knowledge created or adopted by an organization? What are the sources of the generation or regulation of knowledge? What rules underlie such generative or regulative processes? Why are some concepts and systems ideas adopted and circulated within conversation, while others are discounted and never established as guides for action? (Topp, 1999, p. 50).

Understanding of the formative system is achieved by asking a series of critical questions derived from the work of Foucault. To get a flavor of this, we can list the questions without looking closely at their origins (pp. 53-64).

- What social groupings serve as sources of new object emergence within the organization?
- What groups, individuals or professions represent the organization's "authorities of delimitation"?
- What grids of specification operate within and between bodies of knowledge?
- Who in the organization has the right to make statements within the various bodies of knowledge?
- What are the institutional sites from which individuals make statements within or across bodies of knowledge?
- What positions is it possible for individuals to occupy within a body of knowledge?
- What schemata of dependence, of order, and of succession are regulating individual's articulations within bodies of knowledge?

- What criteria of inclusion or exclusion are visible in the practice of a body of knowledge? (Field of presence)
- What statements from other domains are used as analogies, models, general principles, or authorities within the bodies of knowledge? (Field of concomitance)
- What implicit historical statements are filtering, guiding, and transforming the current bodies of knowledge? (Field of memory)
- What procedures of intervention and transformation are being practiced on statements within the bodies of knowledge?
- What incompatibilities are evident in the active body of knowledge?
- What alternative approaches and theories are evident within the bodies of knowledge?
- Have the alternative approaches developed into coherent theoretical options?
- What economy is at work between the various bodies of knowledge within the business?
- How is the expected function of the body of knowledge affecting the theoretical choices made within it?
- What individuals or groups have access that allows them privileged influence within a body of knowledge? How does this affect the choices made within the discourse?
- What individual or group desires affect the choices made within a body of knowledge?

Once a map of the formative system of a business has been completed, it becomes possible to examine it and aim organizational interventions at the points of leverage likely to have the greatest impact in transforming the first order knowledge of organizational actors. Topp provides, by way of example, his attempt to map the knowledge formation system at work in Life Customer Services, in the Cape Town head office of Southern Life. Examining the map he asks how it might be possible to introduce new knowledge into product design with the greatest chance of success. One of the points of maximum leverage seems to be "outside analogies." The following tactics (p.109) are then considered:

- Increase exposure to possible analogies by having talks presented on the design process used in other industries. Make sure that such analogies have links into the existing classification framework and that they do not intimidate the current authorities of delimitation

- Investigate which analogies are favored by the different authorities of limitation and introduce similar but strategically different analogies to stretch the regulative system

- Increase the spectrum of sites to which authorities have access

- Develop one's own literal site. Design an Intranet site that has information and links to other sites that may support new knowledge creation within the product design body of knowledge

- Challenge the authorities by having the design process go through a benchmark against world-class opposition

An understanding of the formative system of a business is a good starting point for employing the second of Topp's postmodern systems methods - "Generative Conversation." Generative conversations, if successful, can lead to the emergence of new concepts, systems ideas and themes that may guide future action. It is Topp's view that most conversations that take place in organizations are "regulative" in the sense that they do not escape from existing concerns. To ensure generative conversations are successful they need to be supported by a set of heuristics :

> In order to support the creation of new knowledge within organizations one needs to escape the limits of regulative conversations that assume certain stakes and restrict the kinds of moves (utterances) allowed. Such an intervention must free individual subjects to collaborate in the formation of new stakes, patterns and themes. In providing [heuristic] support for generative conversations, the purpose is to increase the probability of participants making creative moves (p. 75).

The necessary heuristics can be appropriated from Lyotard and his key work *The Differend,* which reconceptualizes conversation by focusing on the phrase as a unit of analysis:

> Generative conversations are an attempt at differend resolution through the generation of new links that fuse normally incompatible conversation system-stakes. In generative conversation, the bringing together of different authorities and expertise makes fertile ground for differends. The challenge is to find ethical ways of linking phrases so that new themes and stakes can emerge (p. 74).

The strategy in generative conversation is to replace one "language game" with another in order to create new knowledge. The only rule is that any new phrase brought forth in the conversation must *always link to the previous phrase.* This prevents the recurrence of phrases that take the conversation back to some "higher regulatory business stake." Beyond that certain "guides" can be provided (Topp, 1999, p. 77-78):

* Generative conversation is a game in which we play with ideas, not against each other
* Appoint a facilitator at the start to monitor the application of the "linking rule"
* There is no rush; regulative conversation occurs at speed
* Allow at least three seconds of silence between each phrase
* Watch the pull of habit and pattern. Be aware of the tension to link in a certain way
* Keep a notebook to jot down ideas so that they are not forgotten
* Questions can form part of the conversation but must obey the linking rule
* Make use of creative misunderstanding
* Listen, take a few breaths, think, link
* Remember, silence is a phrase
* Try to link multiple previous phrases

Later analysis of the conversation transcripts should allow the facilitator and participants to identify new themes and stakes that have emerged during the conversation. Topp provides an example of a conversation about organizational management and design which, among other new ideas produced, gave rise to the theme of a CEO as a "facilitator or synthesizer of many different value components" (p. 115).

A third postmodern systems method introduced by Topp requires us to develop and craft any new concepts, systems ideas and themes emerging from generative conversations into a new "business story." This technique, known as "Systems Story", seeks to ensure that original and creative ideas can prosper in the business alongside the traditional stories which govern current business conversations:

> The method synthesizes Bateson's ..... ideas of story, relevance and the difference that makes a difference into a process aimed at integrating the new concepts, systems ideas and themes into narratives of meaning and action. It is argued that story is a useful medium for the development and connection of new knowledge into current local knowledge (Topp, 1999, p. 84).

The case for "story" stems from a number of sources. In an age when all "grand narratives" should be questioned, Topp argues that we need to take responsibility for our own stories. Organizations in the post-industrial era inevitably give rise to very diverse perspectives. Following Lyotard it is easy to see that "narrative" can respect this diversity in a way that the scientific mode of thought does not. Finally, Bateson argues that story is a "pattern which connects." Topp takes from this that it is inherently systemic and can lead to change in the whole pattern of action in a business, not just in individual actions. Topp details a procedure for the development of systemic stories which basically has three phases (Topp, 1999, p. 92):

1. Introduction of the characters and deconstruction of dominant regulative conversations that represent the local current knowledge (guides for action) operating in the area of focus;

2. Identifying and selection of new concepts, systems ideas and themes from generative conversations. These are seen as exceptions and possible beginning points of new knowledge;

3. Construction of an alternative narrative, which allows the development and incorporation of the new concepts, systems ideas and themes into the current regulative conversations.

An example sees a group of individuals, interested in organizational change, rethinking the way they pursue their mutual interest by replacing a narrative based on "sightseeing" by one based on them becoming "tour guides." Story construction is seen as a powerful device for building shared meaning from multiple perspectives.

Topp provides his own analysis of the strengths and weaknesses of each of the postmodern systems methods but, overall, is convinced that the postmodern approach, by decentering the subject and focusing on the micro forces that make up human systems,

> enables one to attempt interventions that are unthinkable using traditional systems methods (p. 133).

A critic would note the significant change in intent between "Knowledge Systems Diagnostics" (KSD) and the other methods. Generative conversation and systems story encourage diversity and creativity in a manner with which we have become familiar from Taket and White's "pragamatic pluralism." KSD, based on the earlier more "structuralist" work of Foucault, seems almost to want to establish objective knowledge about the nature of the discourse taking place in organizations and the way it enables certain statements to come into existence, The tension that exists between the early and later work of Foucault is also one that haunts the whole of postmodernism. It is full of the prescriptions which it denounces when made from any other theoretical position. Topp (p. 75) is aware of this and, using a quotation from Lyotard, captures an aspect relevant to his method of generative conversation:

> The justice of multiplicity: it is assured, paradoxically enough, by a prescriptive of universal value.

9.4. A GENERIC FRAMEWORK FOR THE APPLICATION OF THE POSTMODERN SYSTEMS APPROACH

I have deliberately avoided the word "methodology" in the title to this section as the notion of systematically applying theory in the process of intervention is not one that appeals to postmodern thinkers. From the theoretical side we have seen Foucault referring to his texts as a "tool kit" which people can make use of as they see fit to oppose systems of power. Taket and White (2000), from the practitioner point of view, would like their book to be read as a "cookbook", "where favorite recipes can be tried and variations on themes encouraged." Nevertheless, there are sufficient common themes articulated by the post-modernist writers, and sufficient guidance in the framework that is PANDA, for us at least to attempt to present a generic framework for the application of the postmodern systems approach. This should enable us to determine whether or not intervention is taking place according to the postmodern theoretical rationale and to distinguish this from other forms of systems practice.

I would wish to argue that Table 9.5 captures the essence of the manner in which advocates of postmodernism would like to see their approaches used. Because of the dearth of examples of postmodern systems practice, however, refinements to this generic "framework" are likely, in the future, to be greater than those which will be required to the generic methodologies produced for functionalist, interpretive and emancipatory systems approaches.

We need now to consider in general terms the strengths and weaknesses of the postmodern systems approach.

9.5. CRITIQUE OF THE POSTMODERN SYSTEMS APPROACH

The same pattern of critique is followed as for these sections in the previous three chapters. The postmodern systems approach and the advantages it gives are first discussed in its own terms. It is then subject to a broad critique from the points of view of functionalist, interpretive and emancipatory systems thinking.

If the "grand narratives" of economic growth, emancipation, etc., have inspired human endeavor in the past, it is also true to say that a number of them, such as Nazism and Stalinism, have proved to be extremely destructive ideologies. The skepticism of postmodernism towards all grand narratives has, therefore, much to recommend it. So has, in many ways, its prioritizing of the local and the manner in which we achieve our own identities by engaging in local "struggles." I often find myself in support of local causes which would be difficult to justify on emancipatory grounds but which seem to mean very much indeed. It is good to know that support for the Campaign for Real Ale, and Yorkshire County Cricket Club, together with "fighting" for the East Riding of Yorkshire against the abomination of Humberside, and championing Rugby League against the privileges afforded Rugby Union (and in the world of Rugby League, Hull Kingston Rovers against Hull F.C.), finds understanding at least from the perspective of postmodernism. None of these is probably intelligible without a postmodern appreciation of locality and the formation of

Table 9.5. Constitutive rules of a generic framework for the application of the postmodern systems approach

---

1. Postmodern systems practice is a way of thinking and acting, with an attachment to the postmodern theoretical rationale, that is focused on disrupting real-world problem situations by critically questioning all received opinion and accepted ways of doing things.

2. Postmodern systems practice uses systemic and anti-systemic ideas as the basis for its intervention strategy and will frequently employ methods, models, tools and techniques which also draw upon systems ideas.

3. The claim to have used systems thinking and systems ideas according to the postmodern rationale may be sustained locally according to the following guidelines:

   a. an assumption that the real-world is constructed in such a way through discourse that particular groups and/or individuals are marginalized;

   b. intervention in the problem situation is designed to reveal who is marginalized by existing power/knowledge structures;

   c. diverse forms of pluralism are used to surface subjugated discourses and to allow marginalized voices to be heard;

   d. diverse forms of pluralism are used to allow relevant stakeholders to express their diversity and, possibly, grant a "consent to act";

   e. quantitative analysis is unlikely to be useful except as part of the process of deconstruction;

   f. the process of intervention takes the form of local strategizing and subversion in an endeavor to allow new knowledge to come to the fore;

   g. the intervention is conducted in such a way that conflict is reclaimed and diversity and creativity are encouraged;

   h. facilitators and participants in the intervention take responsibility for any actions on the basis of exception, emotion and ethics;

4. Since postmodern systems practice can take different forms in different situations, and be interpreted differently by different users, each use should exhibit conscious thought and/or an emotional response about how to adapt to the particular circumstances.

5. Each case of postmodern systems practice may yield research findings as well as changing the real-world problem situation. These research findings may relate to the theoretical rationale underlying the practice, to the framework for applying a postmodern systems approach, to the methods, models, tools and techniques employed, to the real-world problem situation investigated, or to all of these.

---

multiple identities. The debunking of pomposity and the constant challenge to cultural élitism and the notion of expertise, which are part and parcel of postmodernism, are also positive aspects of the approach. The original contributions of postmodernism to our understanding of discourse and power, which we have been exploring in this chapter, will not require further elaboration.

At the same time as providing an overall theoretical rationale, postmodernism is able to come up with some distinctive and useful insights and methods. So compelling are these that a number of thinkers and practitioners, who one would normally associate with a different theoretical orientation to postmodernism, seem anxious to incorporate them into their approach. Ormerod (1995), with a background in management consultancy, believes that it is "at least possible that postmodernism offers an underlying philosophical stance that could support consulting practice." Checkland and Scholes (1990), apparently abandoning the allegiance to Habermas expressed in an earlier book (Checkland, 1981), ponder whether "Mode 2" use of Soft Systems Methodology could be regarded as postmodernist. We saw Flood, in the previous chapter, using aspects of Foucault's work in support of a predominantly emancipatory vision. Watson and Wood-Harper (1995) like to see postmodernism as the underpinning to their multi-methodology approach to information systems design - Multiview as metaphor. But perhaps the very promiscuity of aspects of postmodernism should give us pause. Certainly the lack of clear methodological guidance binding postmodern insights, methods and techniques to the overall theoretical rationale (and forbidden by that rationale) makes it difficult to do research on postmodernism. What are the methods and techniques seeking to achieve if they can serve any paradigm? If it is hard to challenge methods like deconstruction, genealogy, systems story, etc., for this reason, we are inevitably driven back to confronting head on the postmodern theoretical rationale in order to establish its limitations. Functionalist, interpretive and emancipatory thinkers do not find this difficult to do.

From the functionalist perspective the theories they produce and test, using the scientific method, clearly relate to some real-world outside of discourse. Moreover, because of the understanding they gain about the nature of reality, functionalists believe that they possess expertise that can be employed to ensure efficiency and efficacy through an enhanced capability to predict and control. As a result they see themselves contributing both to an increase in knowledge and to the progressive improvement of the human condition. Through functionalist eyes it is irresponsible of the postmodernists to question and challenge what has been learned and what has been achieved. It is, of course, this "grand narrative" of progress through performativity which is one of the main targets of the postmodernist critique. However, in attacking it, they open themselves up to the charge that there is a fundamental contradiction at the heart of their own position. Isn't the postmodernist theory that the world is constituted by discourse, or that knowledge is constituted by power, itself a kind of meta-narrative? As Midgley (1994) has it:

> There is ... the contradiction of a meta-narrative which attacks the very foundation of meta-narrative itself (p. 195).

Midgley relies on Rorty to construct a postmodernist response. Rorty would simply answer "so what?" He would see it as an ironic fact of life that it requires a philosophy which is itself based on "certainty" to undermine the certainty of philosophy. We have to live with the irony of employing a meta-narrative to deconstruct certainty and to promote diversity and local, critical thought. Functionalists regard this embracing of contradiction as the road to irrationalism and look on in horror. To them the successes of science and technology and the improvements in society that these have made possible are a serious matter. We all have a stake in these achievements and we must be wary of attempts to denigrate them.

Interpretive systems thinkers wish to promote mutual understanding and learning through the widest possible participation in decision making. They encourage open debate and believe that language is a vehicle which can be used to arrive at a consensus, or at least accommodation, about improvements that can be made to the existing situation. Of course it is necessary to protect against constraints on discussion, but what other democratic alternative is there to rational debate in order to arrive at decisions which can carry the support of the majority? The postmodern injunction to value diversity and conflict above all else seems like a call for anarchy rather than freedom. It is clear, from the interpretive viewpoint, that the constant undermining of order and consensus by postmodernists can only hinder the construction of a better social reality. What is more, it seems that this subversion can sometimes take élitist forms. Rather than being open and transparent about their aims, postmodernists seem willing to work "undercover" and/or use their methods "obliquely" in the service of some cause which they privilege but need not reveal.

Brocklesby and Cummings (1996) see postmodernism, and especially the work of Foucault, as offering an alternative (to the Habermasian) underpinning for emancipatory systems thinking. As we saw at the beginning of this chapter, Nietzsche and Heidegger deny the tradition of the Enlightenment in their pursuit of the means for *self* emancipation rather than *human* emancipation. Brocklesby and Cummings trace this line of thought directly to Foucault and argue that it is emancipatory in three different ways. First, it enables individuals to recognize their own contingency; thrown into history, and shaped and determined by discourse and power structures at the micro and societal levels. In this situation it is the responsibility of each individual to restyle herself, exploiting whatever possibilities are open and forging new ones. Second, it provides methods and tools to be used by individuals, as they see fit, to unmask existing sources of domination and subjugation, and to emancipate themselves from systems of power. Third, skepticism of all "grand narratives" provides its own kind of freedom. We will not fool ourselves that, in communion with our fellow men, we can "flatten" power structures and remake the world on the basis of consensus. Instead we have to employ strategies of individual subversion and self emancipation in order to liberate ourselves to lead an "authentic" existence. Giving up the idea that we can achieve human emancipation through rational agency is not, therefore, a philosophy of despair for postmodernists. Indeed Lyotard (1984) and Jacques (1989) believe that a postmodernist ethics can be constructed from this position. Once we have rejected performativity, emancipation and the other grand narratives, we have to take personal responsibility for our actions - we can no longer hide behind objectivity. We have to live in a world of multiple truths. Just knowing that one does not know everything can be liberating. It opens up a new world of possibilities in which each of us has to take ethical responsibility for the truths we embrace.

None of this is convincing to emancipatory thinkers brought up in the tradition of Marx, the Frankfurt School and Habermas. They share, with the interpretive tradition, the view that postmodernism is more of a recipe for anarchy than for human fulfillment and emancipation. Ormerod's alignment of postmodern philosophy and management consultancy should be warning enough to any self-respecting "radical" postmodernist. And there are worse dangers than that. Diversity is not necessarily a good in itself. Within the variety of human experience lie viewpoints and actions propelled by some pretty nasty forces – racism, for example. It is surely legitimate and justifiable to keep an "emancipatory check" on the emergence of such forces. On a personal level I had, during the 1980s, to call into question my postmodern commitment to Yorkshire County Cricket Club because of apparent racism in the behavior of sections of that club.

There are other arguments against postmodernism, from the emancipatory perspective, that seem even more compelling. Postmodernists see individual subjectivities as created by discourse constituted by power relations. In other words we become what we are in the context of the social structures into which we are born. How then can we restyle ourselves without also remaking those social structures? Emancipatory thinkers, from Marx to MacIntyre to Freire, take the view that humans need to restructure social relations in order, eventually, to restructure themselves. In denying this, postmodernism seems again to be contradicting one of its central tenets. From the emancipatory position, human emancipation is an absolute necessity for self emancipation. This is also the case because emancipation is such a huge task. Many of the ills we face, such as gender, race and class inequality seem to be system-wide. Others are literally global in nature, for example pollution and world poverty. It seems apparent that individual and local resistance are going to be futile in the face of the forces that sustain such ills. A wider coalition of opposition needs to be constructed to have any chance of success in confronting these problems.

The argument between postmodernists and emancipatory thinkers, about the nature of emancipation, puts me in mind of the debate on freedom conducted by Sartre throughout his *Roads to Freedom* trilogy; not surprisingly, perhaps, because it was the tension between existentialist and Marxist versions of freedom that he was exploring at the time. In the third volume, called *Iron in the Soul* (1963), Sartre has Mathieu reflecting on the notion of freedom even as he fires his last rounds against the oncoming enemy. He finds his freedom from "bad faith", and an inauthentic existence, by sacrificing his life to hold up the German advance by fifteen minutes:

> He made his way to the parapet and stood there firing . The world is going up in smoke, and me with it. He fired : he looked at his watch : fourteen minutes and thirty seconds. Nothing more to ask of Fate now except one half -minute. Just time enough to fire at that smart officer, at all the Beauty of the Earth, at the street, at the flowers, at the gardens, at everything he had loved. Beauty dived downwards like some obscene bird. But Mathieu went on firing. He fired. He was cleansed. He was all-powerful. He was free. Fifteen minutes (p. 225).

Meanwhile Brunet, the communist, knowing that this particular battle is lost, gives himself up. He has work to do; lots of work. Within the prisoner-of-war camp he has to organize the comrades, both French and German, for revolution.

It is worth noting, to conclude this chapter, that Habermas (1987), in a series of twelve lectures, has sought to respond to the postmodern attack on his own position and, in the process, has developed a critique of Nietzsche, Heidegger, Derrida, Foucault and others. The nub of his argument is that rather than abandoning the vision of the Enlightenment we need to renew and revitalize it. To do this requires more reason and not less. Against Foucault he points to what he regards as some of the undeniable achievements of the rationalization processes that have taken place in society. In Habermas's view Foucault ignores these and emphasizes only the dysfunctions. Instead of concentrating on the dysfunctions in this way, we should continue to seek to remove them through action based on communicative rationality. Against Nietzsche and Derrida, he argues that while there are discourses, such as the poetic and other literary forms, which are dominated by rhetoric, this is not true of ordinary and scientific communication. In everyday speech, and in specialized scientific discourses, language functions as a means of dealing with problems in the world. Where rhetoric occurs it is "bridled" and enlisted in support of problem solving. It is subordinated to distinct forms of argumentation, the conclusions of which can be tested in the world. Rather than concentrating on the defects in such argumentation, as Derrida does, we should continue to value language and develop communication to increase learning and understanding. Language can be the vehicle through which reason reaches out to the ideals of truth and justice.

Chapter 9 completes Part II of the book, "Systems Approaches." The reader should now have a good understanding of four possible types of systems approach - functionalist, interpretive, emancipatory and postmodern - and of their strengths and weaknesses. A generic methodology has been developed for each type of systems approach and this should assist practitioners to use different models, methods, tools and techniques according to the theoretical rationale, or paradigm, underlying each approach. It will also help researchers to achieve learning, from practical application, about the framework of ideas used, and the methodology and methods employed, as well as about the context of application. Part III seeks to demonstrate how systems thinking can best go forward as a transdiscipline given the variety of apparently competing perspectives, methodologies and methods that exist under its banner. It advocates "critical systems thinking."

III

CRITICAL SYSTEMS THINKING

10

THE ORIGINS OF CRITICAL SYSTEMS THINKING

10.1. INTRODUCTION

Early approaches to using systems ideas in an applied manner, such as operational research, systems analysis and systems engineering, were suitable for tackling certain well-defined problems but were found to have limitations when faced with complex problems involving people with a variety of viewpoints and frequently at odds with one another. Systems thinkers, as we saw in the last part of the book, responded with approaches such as system dynamics and organizational cybernetics to tackle complexity; soft systems methodology and interactive planning to handle subjectivity; critical systems heuristics to help the disadvantaged in situations involving conflict; and pragmatic pluralism to manage diversity. In theoretical terms, the positivism that had dominated systems thinking until the 1970s was supplemented, as a source of support for applied work, by structuralism, interpretivism, "radicalism" and postmodernism. There has been a corresponding enlargement of the range of problem contexts in which systems thinkers have felt competent to intervene. Despite the achievements of the pioneers of systems thinking, and those who later led the break with the functionalist systems approach, I shall nevertheless be arguing that something more was needed if systems thinking was to realize its potential and take its place at the leading edge in the development of the applied disciplines. It has been critical systems thinking that has provided this something more. Critical systems thinking has supplied the bigger picture, has allowed systems thinking to mature as a transdiscipline, and has set out how the variety of methodologies, methods and models now available can be used in a coherent manner to promote successful intervention in complex organizational and societal problem situations.

I shall set out the origins of critical systems thinking, in the next chapter look at the contemporary character of critical systems thinking and practice, and, in Chapter 12, provide three examples of critical systems thinking in action. In structuring the material on origins, in this chapter, I shall discuss the growth of "critical awareness" in systems thinking; the "system of systems methodologies"; the engagement with emancipatory thinking; the developing argument for pluralism; and the preliminary operationalizing of critical systems ideas in the meta-methodology called "Total Systems Intervention" (TSI). In the course of this we will encounter the various landmarks which have served to orientate more recent work in critical systems thinking.

10.2. CRITICAL AWARENESS

Critical systems thinking grew out of the criticisms launched at proponents of particular systems approaches by advocates of other approaches. A reasonable starting point for our discussion, therefore, is the assault launched in the 1970s by soft systems thinkers (Checkland, 1978, 1981; Ackoff, 1979a; Churchman, 1979b) on hard systems thinking. Checkland, for example, argued that the assumptions made by the hard approach severely limited its domain of effective application. Making explicit reference to Burrell and Morgan's work on sociological paradigms, Checkland (1981) showed that hard systems thinking is guided by functionalist assumptions. The world is seen as made up of systems that can be studied objectively and that have clearly identifiable purposes. These systems could be understood and modeled. Thus decision makers can be presented with the means to optimize the operations under their command. The problem for the hard approach, Checkland argued, is that very few real-world problem situations present themselves in terms of systems with clearly defined goals and objectives. At best, therefore, hard systems thinking will prove ineffective in the great majority of problem situations. At worst there will be a temptation to distort situations so that they "fit" the demands of the methodology

A more self-conscious critical approach began to be elaborated when Mingers (1980, 1984) and Jackson (1982) started to ask questions about the social theory on which soft systems thinking was based and how this impacted upon its effectiveness. My own critique of the work of Churchman, Ackoff and Checkland argued that the assumptions made by these authors about the nature of systems thinking and social systems constrained the ability of their methodologies to intervene, in the manner intended, in many problem situations. Soft systems thinking, too, had a limited domain of application. Using Burrell and Morgan's framework, it was shown that soft systems thinking was based upon interpretive (subjective and regulative) assumptions. With Churchman, Ackoff, and Checkland, systems thinking becomes much more subjective, and the emphasis shifts from attempting to model systems "out there" in the world toward using systems models to capture possible perceptions of the world. In Checkland's methodology, for example, systems models of possible human activity systems are used to structure and enhance debate among stakeholders so that an accommodation about action to be taken can emerge. The recommendations of soft systems thinking remain regulative because no attempt is made to ensure that the conditions for genuine debate are provided. The kind of open, participative debate that is essential for the success of the soft systems approach, and is the only justification for the results obtained, is impossible to obtain in problem situations where there is fundamental conflict between interest groups that have access to unequal power resources. Soft systems thinking either has to walk away from these problem situations, or it has to fly in the face of its own philosophical principles and acquiesce in proposed changes emerging from limited debates characterized by distorted communication.

It was now obvious that all systems methodologies had their limitations; their weaknesses as well as their strengths. A series of critiques of different systems approaches followed (e.g. Jackson, 1988a, on organizational cybernetics; and, 1989a, on strategic assumption surfacing and testing), culminating in my (1991) review of five strands of systems thinking - "organizations as systems.," "hard.," "cybernetic.," "soft" and "emancipatory" - from the point of view of relevant social theory.

The significance of the social sciences in enabling "critical awareness" deserves emphasis. Of particular importance has been work that allows an overview to be taken of different ways of analyzing and intervening in organizations. For example, Burrell and Morgan's book on sociological paradigms and organizational analysis, and Morgan's examination of "images" of organization, allowed critique of the assumptions different systems approaches make about social science, social reality and organizations. Habermas's theory of three human interests, the technical, practical and emancipatory, and his warnings about the dominance of instrumental reason (wedded to the technical interest) informed reflection on the role of the various systems methodologies in addressing different human interests. Jackson's (1988c) review of systems methods for organizational analysis and design, Oliga's (1988) look at the methodological foundations of systems methodologies, Ulrich's (1988) program for systems research, and Flood and Ulrich's (1990) examination of the epistemological bases of different systems approaches all drew heavily on this source. Habermas's later work on "communicative competence" and "the ideal speech situation" also permitted critique of the aspirations of soft systems methodologies. Finally, the work of postmodernists, such as Lyotard and Foucault, has led to a questioning of the legitimacy of all "systematizing" and "totalizing" endeavors, and has demanded a response from systems thinkers.

As well as allowing the strengths and weaknesses, and the theoretical underpinnings, of available systems methodologies to be unearthed, the social sciences drew the attention of critics to the importance of the social context in which the methodologies were used. This type of understanding was called at the time (Jackson, 1991) "social awareness;" although I am happy now to see it simply as another aspect of critical awareness. Social awareness involved recognizing that there are organizational and societal pressures that lead to certain systems theories and methodologies being popular for guiding interventions at particular times. For example, it was inconceivable that soft systems thinking could ever flourish in communist Eastern European countries dominated by the bureaucratic, "rational" dictates of the one-party system. With the change toward free-market capitalism and political pluralism, however, the circumstances that allowed hard and cybernetic approaches to "succeed" in those countries have changed and softer methodologies are able to show their usefulness. Postmodern arguments about the relationship between power and knowledge, at the micro-level, have added to our understanding of the importance of social context. Social awareness was also supposed to make users of systems methodologies contemplate the consequences of use of the approaches they employed. For example, the choice of a hard or cybernetic approach implies that one goal or objective is being privileged at the expense of other possibilities. Is this goal general to all organizational stakeholders, or is it simply that of the most powerful? Similarly, the use of soft systems methodologies, which are dependent upon open and free debate to justify their results, might have deleterious social consequences if the conditions for such debate are absent. This form of social awareness was important in Jackson's research (1982, 1985b, 1988a, 1988c, 1989a) and provides the rationale for Ulrich's (1983) demand that the systems rationality of planners should always be exposed to the social rationality of the affected.

Critical awareness, incorporating social awareness, became one of the central principles of critical systems thinking and remains so to this day. The main problem, of course, is that the apparent strengths and weaknesses of any particular systems approach will vary dramatically depending upon the paradigm from which it is observed and judged.

10.3. THE SYSTEM OF SYSTEMS METHODOLOGIES

Once it became clear that different systems approaches had different strengths and weaknesses, it also became apparent that they could be seen as a set with individual approaches, within the set, being more or less appropriate to particular problem situations and purposes. To explore and develop this idea, Paul Keys and I, during 1983/84, initiated a research program, at the University of Hull, aimed theoretically at explaining the relationships between different systems-based methodologies and practically at discovering the efficacy of particular approaches in various problem contexts. I have described the research program, some early practical examples of interventions, and its pedagogical impact, elsewhere (Jackson, 1989b). The theoretical tool at its heart was the "system of systems methodologies" (Jackson and Keys, 1984).

The critical purpose of the system of systems methodologies (SOSM) was the creation of a classification of systems methodologies that would allow for their "complementary and informed" use. Burrell and Morgan's framework of sociological paradigms might have helped with this task as well; however, as was noted in Chapter 5, it was not the easiest of devices to apply in interrogating systems approaches. Jackson and Keys sought therefore to provide, in their SOSM, an alternative framework that would accomplish the critical task mentioned and at the same time be suited to the language, concerns, and internal development of systems thinking.

The formative idea of the SOSM was that it is possible to construct an "ideal-type" grid of problem contexts that can be used to classify systems methodologies according to their assumptions about problem situations. As we saw in Chapter 5, where more detail can be found, the grid is made up of two dimensions, one defining the nature of the systems in which the problems of concern are located and the other the nature of the relationship between the participants who have an interest in the problem situation and its improvement. In later versions of the SOSM (Jackson, 1987a, 1988b, 1990b), systems were classified on a continuum from "simple" to "complex" and participants as to whether they could be said to be in a "unitary.," "pluralist" or "coercive" relationship to one another. Combining these classifications yielded the six-celled matrix of problem contexts shown in Figure 10.1. According to this figure, problem contexts can be seen to fall into the following categories: simple-unitary, complex-unitary, simple-pluralist, complex-pluralist, simple-coercive and complex-coercive. Each of these problem contexts differs in a meaningful way from the others. The existence of these six ideal-types of problem context implies, therefore, the need for a variety of problem-solving methodologies. Important differences among problem contexts should be reflected in different types of methodology. This provided a very convenient means of classifying available systems approaches, especially (see Chapter 5) as the classification of problem contexts was far from arbitrary.

Given the grid of problem contexts, the next step in building the SOSM was to relate existing systems based, problem-solving methodologies to it. Hard systems thinking (classical operational research, systems analysis, systems engineering) was said to assume that problems are set in simple-unitary contexts because it takes as given that it is easy to establish objectives for the system of concern and that it is possible to model it mathematically. Socio-technical, contingency and organizational cybernetic approaches were related to complex- pluralist contexts. They privilege the organismic rather than the mechanical analogy and view systems as complex - made up of elements in close interrelationship, probabilistic, open to the environment, evolving over time, subject to human influence and having purposeful parts. On the other hand, they are weak on procedures for resolving differences of value and opinion, and conflict, in organizations and so depend on a preexisting, unitary agreement among participants about the goals to be pursued. Various soft systems approaches were identified with simple-pluralist and complex-pluralist contexts. Strategic assumption surfacing and testing handles pluralism well, but pays little attention to "systemic" complexity. Ackoff's interactive planning, on the other hand, is an ambitious attempt to handle simultaneously both the complexity of the problem situations facing modern organizations and the pluralism that inevitably follows their serving diverse stakeholders. To tackle the complexity found in and around enterprises in the systems age, Ackoff has long argued that we must abandon the predict-and-prepare

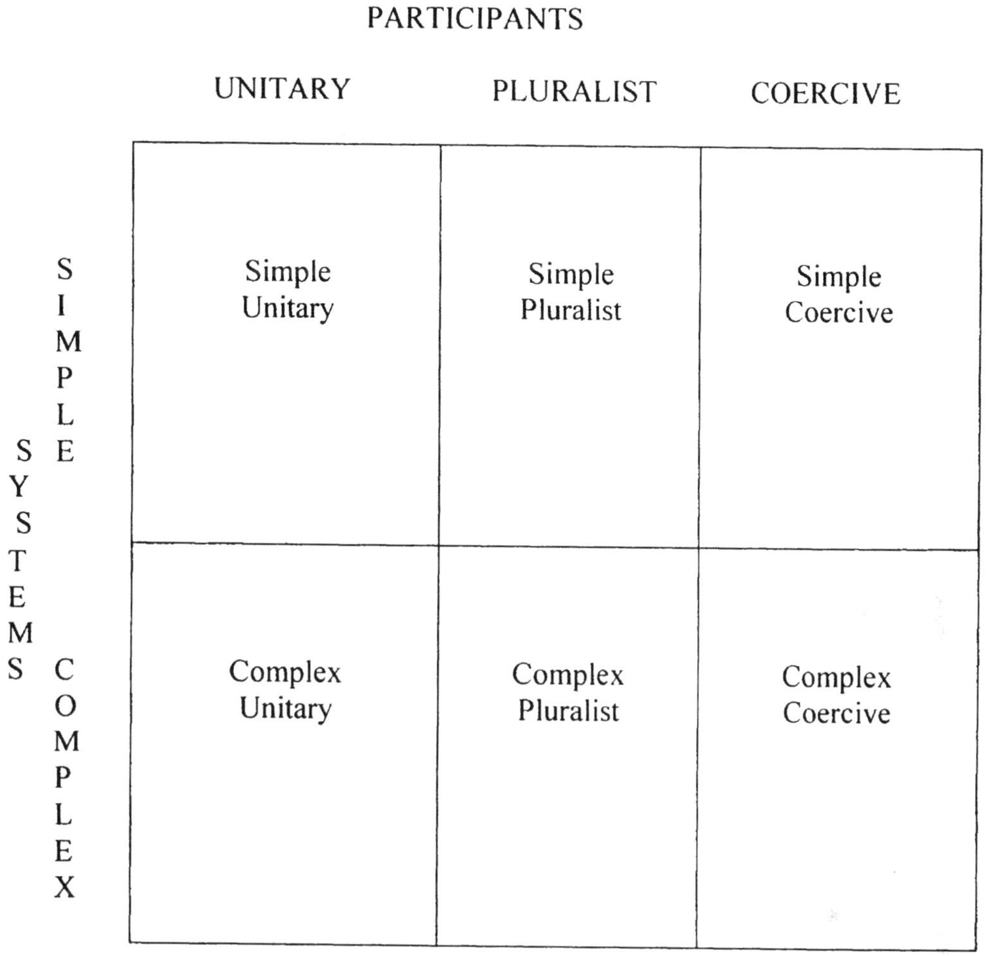

PARTICIPANTS

	UNITARY	PLURALIST	COERCIVE
S I M P L E	Simple Unitary	Simple Pluralist	Simple Coercive
C O M P L E X	Complex Unitary	Complex Pluralist	Complex Coercive

(left axis label: **S Y S T E M S**)

Figure 10.1. Jackson's extended version of Jackson and Keys's grid of problem contexts

paradigm that dominates operations research. The emphasis has to be put on learning and adapting. It is for this reason that he puts forward his "learning and adaptation support system" (see Chapter 7). This should improve the decision makers' power of control over what can be controlled, while increasing responsiveness to what is uncontrollable. Pluralism is accepted as unavoidable by interactive planning and is managed through the participative involvement of all stakeholders at all stages of the planning process. Idealized design seeks to minimize petty differences of opinion between diverse groups by asking them to focus on the ultimate ends they would like to see an organization pursuing. At the time of the construction of the SOSM, in 1984, there seemed to be no systems methodologies based on coercive assumptions. In fact, the major text on the first significant "emancipatory" systems approach, Ulrich's "critical systems heuristics.," had just been published. At a later stage (1987a, 1990b) I argued that if one were forced to place critical systems heuristics in the simple-coercive or complex-coercive box, the argument would go in favor of the former. Critical heuristics does not seek to assist with complexity management along the systems dimension. Evidence of this was adduced from a distinction I made between these two contexts. Simple-coercive contexts are those in which only the "first dimension" of power, as defined by Lukes (1974), operates and the sources of power imbalance are relatively obvious. In complex-coercive contexts, the complexity of the system(s) of concern is likely to mask the sources of power and domination, and to support the operation of Lukes's second and third dimensions of power. Coercion that is embedded structurally in organizations and society cannot be addressed using Ulrich's approach. Something different was needed for complex–coercive contexts. These classifications are summarized in Figure 10.2 (from Jackson, 1991). This work, therefore, provided a "system of systems methodologies" because it demonstrated the interrelationships between different systems approaches and the relationship these have to ideal – type problem contexts. In general terms it did seem that available systems approaches made up a "system" in terms of the assumptions they made about problem contexts.

A number of benefits were claimed to follow from the establishment of the SOSM. First, the SOSM attempted to reveal what was being assumed, in terms of "systems" and "participants.," in using each type of systems methodology. This, it was felt, would enable potential users of systems approaches to assess their relative strengths and weaknesses for the task at hand and to be fully aware of the consequences of employing each approach. It should lead analysts to pause on each occasion they are confronted with a problem situation and ask what methodology is most appropriate in terms of the nature of the context and what the participants are seeking to achieve. Second, the SOSM aids understanding of exactly what goes wrong when an inappropriate systems approach is employed in a particular problem context – soft systems methodology in a coercive context, for example. Finally, and most importantly in the long term, the SOSM opened up a new perspective on the development of systems thinking and management science. Previously it had seemed as if these disciplines were undergoing a "Kuhnian crisis" as hard systems thinking encountered increasing anomalies and was challenged by other approaches (Dando and Bennett, 1981). By questioning one of the underlying assumptions of this analysis - that management science has a well-defined and somewhat uniform subject matter – an alternative future was opened up. Instead of being seen as different strands of systems thinking competing for exactly the same areas of concern (as in Dando and Bennett), alternative approaches can be presented as being appropriate to the different types of situations in which management scientists are required to act. Each approach will be useful in certain defined areas and should only be used in appropriate circumstances. If this perspective is adopted, then the diversity of approaches heralds not a crisis but increased competence and effectiveness in a variety of problem situations. Thus the SOSM, in presenting different methodologies as being appropriate for different types of problem context, offered a way forward from the prevailing systems or management science "in crisis" debates. In doing so it established pluralism as a central tenet of critical systems thinking and encouraged mutual respect between those proponents of different approaches who had previously seen themselves as being at war with one another. The breakthrough made by the SOSM, as recognized by Mingers and Brocklesby (1996), was that it suggested that pluralism could be achieved based on methodologies (hard systems, cybernetic, soft systems, etc) which were developed from more than one paradigm.

It was unfortunate for the immediate prospects of critical systems thinking that the SOSM did not, while it was demonstrating how systems methodologies could be used in a pluralist and informed manner, spend more time on the issue of how the rationalities underlying different strands of the systems movement could also be employed in such a way. This was unfortunate because some have interpreted the SOSM in a functionalist way, implying that it enables us to identify real-world problem situations according to the grid of problem contexts and then to chose appropriate systems methodologies to address these problem situations. The critics (e.g. Kijima and Mackness, 1987; Flood and Carson, 1988) are right to the extent that this would not be a legitimate or fruitful way to proceed. The SOSM would be contradictory if it was associated with any one paradigm. There is, however, no need to see the SOSM in this way. The whole point, indeed, of the SOSM (its critical intent) was to draw upon the strengths of all versions of the systems approach what-

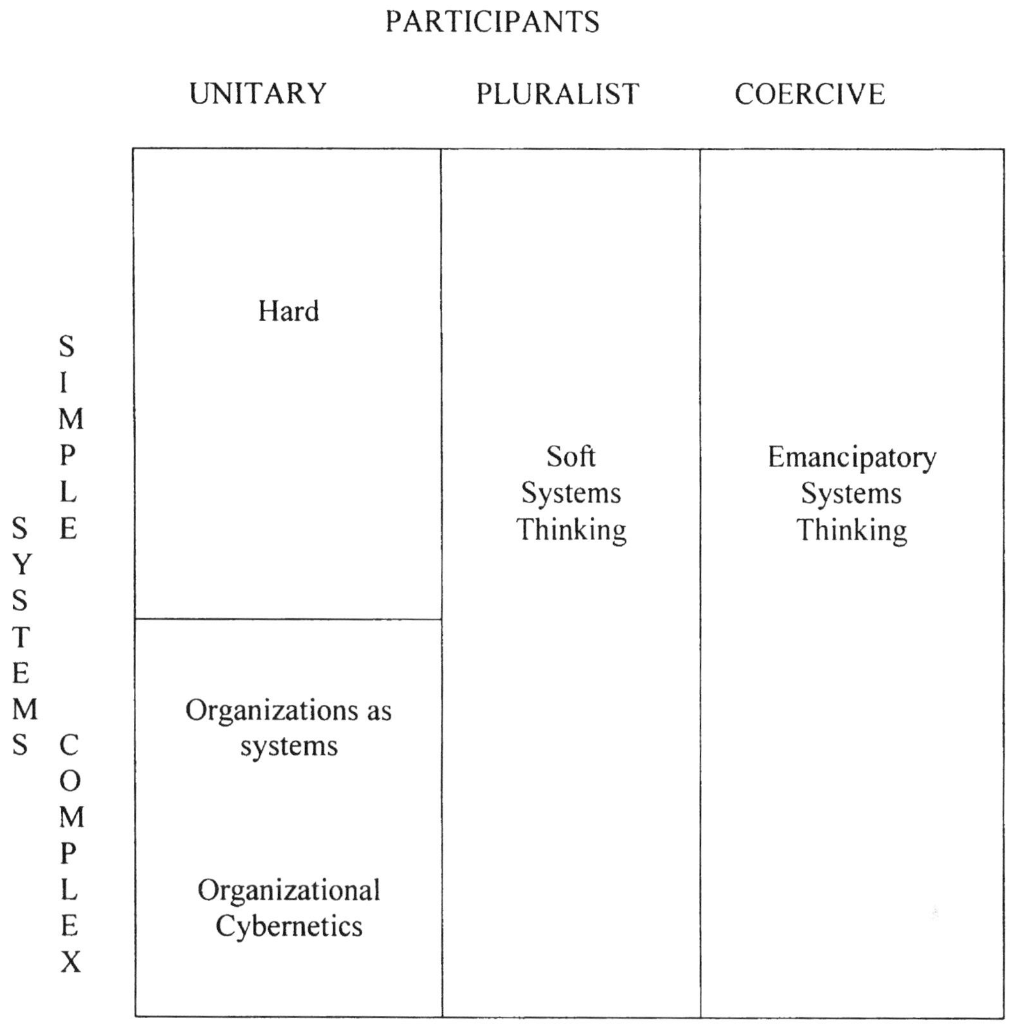

PARTICIPANTS

	UNITARY	PLURALIST	COERCIVE
SIMPLE	Hard	Soft Systems Thinking	Emancipatory Systems Thinking
COMPLEX	Organizations as systems / Organizational Cybernetics		

(SYSTEMS label on vertical axis)

Figure 10.2. Preliminary classification of systems approaches according to the assumptions they make about problem contexts

ever the assumptions on which they rest and the paradigm within which they are located.

While this particular criticism of the SOSM is misplaced, there are some weaknesses that, in retrospect, do need acknowledging. One is that the pluralism embraced by the SOSM is, implicitly, limited to different interventions. The use of different methodologies in the same intervention is not considered. Another weakness is the lack of distinction maintained between "methodology" (relating to the overall theory of method use) and "methods" or "techniques." As a result methods and techniques were not seen as separable from the methodology with which they were commonly associated; if you chose Checkland's soft system methodology you inevitably got rich pictures, CATWOE, etc. as well. In fact, as we have seen, although it is fair enough to pin down methodologies in terms of their theoretical underpinnings, we can be much more relaxed about the purpose to which we put methods, models, tools and techniques. It is also true that insufficient attention was given to different ways of looking at problem contexts. I must, however, quote one passage that does recognize the importance of this and anticipates the later development of "Total Systems Intervention":

The problem solver needs to stand back and examine problem contexts in the light of different "Ws" [*weltanschauungen*]. Perhaps he can then decide which "W" seems to capture the essence of the particular problem context he is faced with. This whole process needs formalizing if it is to be carried out successfully. The problem solver needs to be aware of different paradigms in the social sciences, and he must be prepared to view the problem context through each of these paradigms (Jackson and Keys, 1984, p. 473).

Those interested in the historical contribution of the SOSM to the development of critical systems thinking can consult the references listed in my "researchers guide" (Jackson, 1993c). The SOSM is not just an historical relic however. As employed in Chapter 5, it still offers a coherent way of introducing the developments that have taken place in applied systems thinking over the last few decades. The argument it expresses is that those developments can be seen as responses to the failure of hard systems thinking to tackle extreme complexity, subjectivity, and its own conservatism - organizational cybernetics (for example) aiding the management of extreme complexity, soft systems thinking helping with multiple perceptions of reality, and emancipatory systems thinking designed to free the transdiscipline from serving the status quo. That remains a powerful and defensible position. Nor is the SOSM fazed by the newer developments in systems thinking. Complexity theory, as we described it in Chapter 6, is clearly another development down the vertical (complexity) axis of Figure 5.2. The postmodern systems approach answers, in a sense, the question mark in the lower right hand corner. In the face of the massive complexity, stemming from diverse power/knowledge formations, the proper response might well be not another methodology but the encouragement of diversity and creativity through local strategizing and subversion.

10.4. THE ENGAGEMENT WITH EMANCIPATION

The flirtation of critical systems thinking with "emancipatory systems thinking" was such that, in the early days of the development of both approaches, they could hardly be separated. Indeed, many of those involved in the creation of critical systems thinking were also influential in seeking to develop emancipatory systems approaches. Jackson, Mingers, Oliga and Ulrich all sought to facilitate the emergence of new emancipatory methodologies to tackle problem situations where coercion appeared to reign. This was in part due to the political agenda of the theorists involved. There was also, however, a good academic reason which had been revealed by the SOSM. Once the strengths and weaknesses of existing systems methodologies were better understood, it was possible to ask whether there were problem situations for which no currently existing systems approach seemed appropriate. The most obvious candidates were "coercive" contexts, defined as situations where there is fundamental conflict between stakeholders and the only consensus that can be achieved arises from the exercise of power. Recognition that such contexts were important for systems thinking led to the first explicit call (Jackson, 1982; 1985b) for a "critical approach" which would take account of them. Thus a concern with "emancipation" and the ethics of intervention came to be defining characteristics of critical systems thinking.

The engagement with emancipatory systems thinking predicted in the SOSM became a reality following the arrival of Ulrich's critical systems heuristics. As was stated in the original 1984 article on the SOSM, the unitary - pluralist dimension could be extended to embrace coercive contexts as well (the extension later made by Jackson, 1987a). At the time, Jackson and Keys did not know of any systems methodologies that assumed and acted as though problem contexts might be coercive. From the critical point of view this was obviously a weakness in the capabilities of systems thinking and made the construction of such approaches imperative. Thus, although Ulrich's (1983) critical systems heuristics represented an independently developed strand of critical systems thinking (really emancipatory systems thinking), deriving from Kantian idealism and Churchman's reflections on systems design, when the approach became known in the United Kingdom it was like the discovery of an element that filled a gap in the periodic table. Critical systems heuristics was arguably capable, where soft systems thinking was not, of providing guidelines for action in certain kinds of coercive situation. It enabled systems designs or proposed designs to be carefully interrogated as to their partiality and set down criteria for genuine debates between stakeholders which had to include both those involved in systems designs and those affected but not involved in the designs.

The SOSM benefited critical systems thinking by embracing emancipatory approaches. At the same time it was able to keep emancipatory systems thinking at arms length as far as its becoming a permanent marriage partner was concerned. The appropriate relationship became clearer once critical systems thinking had attached itself to Habermas's theory of three human interests - the technical, practical and emancipatory. It was now possible to define critical systems thinking's "emancipatory commitment" in terms of a much broader dedication to human improvement. Flood and Jackson (1991) saw this as meaning bringing about those circumstances in which all individuals could achieve the maximum development of their potential. This, in turn, meant raising the quality of work and life in the organizations and societies in which they participate. The link to Habermas was that "human improvement" now required that each of his three "interests" should be served by appropriate systems methodologies. So that methodologies that serve the technical interest assist material well-being by improving the productive potential and steering capacities of social systems. Methodologies that serve the practical interest aim to promote and expand mutual understanding among the individuals and groups participating in social systems. Methodologies serving the emancipatory interest protect the domain of the practical interest from inroads by technical reason and ensure the proper operation of the practical interest by denouncing situations where the exercise of power, or other causes of distorted communication, are preventing the open and free discussion necessary for the success of interaction. All human beings have a technical, practical and emancipatory interest in the functioning of organizations and society, Habermas argued. So a systems perspective that could support all these various interests would have an important role to play in human well-being and emancipation. Critical systems thinkers made the point that this was exactly what their approach wanted to achieve. It wanted to put hard, organizations-as-systems and cybernetic methodologies to work to support the technical interest, soft methodologies to work to assist the practical interest, and emancipatory methodologies to work to aid the emancipatory interest.

By 1991, it was possible to state the matter clearly:

> Critical systems thinking recognizes its overall emancipatory responsibility and seeks to fulfill this by adequately servicing, with appropriate systems methodologies, each of Habermas's human interests ... At the same time it perceives a special need, because of previous neglect, to nurture the development of emancipatory systems thinking. In theory, this means encouraging the use of specifically emancipatory systems methodologies suitable for coercive contexts ... In practice it includes supporting initiatives such as Community OR (Jackson, p. 206).

Emancipatory systems thinking was, therefore, narrower than critical systems thinking. It needed to concentrate on providing methodologies that, through critique and the challenging of particular social arrangements, can assist with the emancipation of human actors, putting them more in control of their own destiny. The domain of effective application of emancipatory methodologies is "organizations as coercive systems" or coercive problem contexts. But not all problem situations are usefully regarded as coercive; some are better seen as unitary or pluralist. Emancipatory systems thinking, therefore, just like the hard, organizations-as-systems, cybernetic, and soft approaches, possesses a limited domain for which it is the most appropriate approach. Critical systems thinking was seen as being about putting *all* the different systems approaches to work, according to their strengths and weaknesses and the social conditions prevailing, in the service of a more general project of improvement.

10.5. THE ARGUMENT FOR PLURALISM

The rise of pluralism in systems thinking and practice is inseparable from the emergence of critical systems thinking. We have already noted how the SOSM put the pluralistic use of different systems methodologies on the agenda for systems thinkers. It is now necessary to trace the developing argument for pluralism in more detail if we are to understand the intimacy of the relationship between pluralism and critical systems thinking.

Prior to 1984 most of those who addressed the issue of combining methods or methodologies, in the systems field, did so on the basis of the "imperialist rationale" which we shall explore below. Checkland (1983), for example, divides the area of the systems movement relevant to management science into two parts – hard systems thinking and soft systems thinking – but regards the hard approach simply as a special case of the soft. In 1984, however, Linstone published a book, *Multiple Perspectives for Decision Making*, and Jackson and Keys first publicized their SOSM. These two events independently brought "genuine" pluralism to the fore.

Linstone's form of multiperspective research was aimed at gaining a richer appreciation of the nature of problem situations. The traditional technical (T) perspective, dependent upon data and model based analysis, was to be augmented by an organizational (O) or societal perspective, and a personal (P) or individual perspective. The T, O and P perspectives acted as filters through which systems were viewed and each yielded insights that were not attainable with the others. Linstone argued, in an original way, that the different perspectives were most powerfully employed when they were clearly differentiated from one another in terms of the emphasis they brought to the analysis but were used together to interrogate the same complex problem. Nor, he thought, should one expect consistency in findings; two perspectives may reinforce one another but may equally cancel each other out. A weakness of the approach is that the three perspectives are all employed within the logic of the functionalist paradigm to "provide a three-dimensional view of the real-world system" (Linstone, 1989). Another limitation is that while the manner of employing pluralism to analyze complex problems is explicated, the way in which methods and methodologies might be combined to change problem situations is not thought through. Linstone is continuing to develop his pluralistic vision as part of "unbounded systems thinking" (Mitroff and Linstone, 1993).

Jackson and Keys were motivated, in contrast to Linstone, to explore the relationships between the different problem-solving methodologies that had arisen as guides to intervening in problem situations and to understand the strengths and weaknesses of these different methodologies. We have examined the SOSM and noted that its great strength was that it suggested that pluralism needed to be based on methodologies developed from more than one paradigm. A weakness, in relation to Linstone's work, was that it gave insufficient attention to different ways of looking at problem contexts.

My personal interest in pluralism continued with an effort to view it in the light of "present positions and future prospects in management science" (Jackson, 1987b). This was the first explicit attempt to distinguish the nature of pluralism in the systems field and to argue that embracing pluralism was the best way forward for systems thinking. The paper looked at the breakdown in confidence in traditional management science and the growth of the soft systems, organizational cybernetic and critical systems alternatives to this orthodoxy. A similar argument can be found in Chapter 1, in this book. It suggested that each of the alternatives had a significant contribution to make to the discipline and asked how the relationship between traditional management science and the new alternatives could best be theorized and employed so that management science could make the most beneficial contribution to organizations and society. Borrowing a way of thinking and modifying some terms used in Reed's (1985) account of possible "redirections in organizational analysis.," four developmental strategies for management science were put under the microscope – isolationism, imperialism, pragmatism and pluralism. It is this which deserves our attention.

Isolationists see their own approach to management science as being essentially self-sufficient. They believe that there is nothing to learn from other perspectives which appear to them not to be useful or, perhaps, even sensible. Isolationists were identified as being strong in hard systems thinking and organizational cybernetics. The isolationist strategy would lead to the different strands of systems thinking continuing to go their own ways, developing independently on the basis of their own presuppositions and with minimal contact between the strands. "Paradigm incommensurability" could be adduced in support of the isolationist strategy but, I argued, isolationism should be dismissed because it divided the discipline, forestalled the possibility of "reflective conversation' between the different strands, and discredited the profession in the eyes of clients who did not believe that one method could solve all problems.

Imperialism represents a fundamental commitment to one epistemological position but a willingness to incorporate other strands of systems thinking if they seem to be useful and to add strength in terms of the favored position. Insights from other tendencies will be integrated into the edifice of the favored approach as long as they do not threaten its central tenets. Imperialists believe that they can explain the existence of alternative approaches, and analyze the limited sphere of application of these alternatives, in terms of the approach to which they grant hegemony. Strong imperialist aspirations were identified in soft systems thinking (remember Checkland's view of hard systems thinking), organizational cybernetics and emancipatory systems thinking. This strategy for the development of management science was dismissed, however, because methodologies and methods developed in the service of one paradigm would be "denatured" if used under the auspices of another and so the full potential available to management science, if it capitalized on all the paradigms, would not be realized. It was argued, however, that the imperialist scenario might come to pass if extra-disciplinary, broader, societal influences favored one approach at the expense of the alternatives, squeezing the opportunities available to these alternatives.

The pragmatist strategy is to develop management science by bringing together the best elements of what may appear to be opposing strands on the criterion of what "works" in practice. Pragmatists do not worry about "artificial" theoretical distinctions. They concentrate on building up a "tool kit" of methods and techniques, drawn from the different strands of systems thinking, and are prepared to use them together in the course of problem-solving if the situation warrants it. The choice of techniques and the whole procedure is justified to the extent that it seems to bring results in practice. The attractiveness of the pragmatist option was recognized and its support among traditional management scientists and a few soft systems thinkers detailed. It was dismissed however because it could not support the development of management science as a discipline. Theory, which the pragmatist strategy eschews, is necessary if we are to understand why particular methods work and others do not, so that we can learn from experience, and so we can pass our knowledge on to future generations. Furthermore, pragmatism is dangerous in the social domain – it can lead to costly mistakes which theoretical understanding might have helped us avoid and it can lead to acquiescence in the use of the methods which appear to "work.," but do so not because they are the most suitable for the situation in which they are employed but because they reinforce the position of the powerful, and implementation is therefore ensured.

In contrast to the other three options available to management science, the pluralist strategy was seen as offering excellent opportunities for successful future development. Pluralism would seek to respect the different strengths of the various trends in systems thinking, encouraging their theoretical development and suggesting ways in which they can be appropriately fitted to the variety of management problems that arise. It was argued that a *meta-methodology* would develop which could guide theoretical endeavor and advise analysts, confronted with different problem-situations, which approach is more useful. In these circumstances the diversity of theory and methods in systems thinking could be seen to herald not a crisis (as Dando and Bennett, 1981, had argued) but increased competence and effectiveness in a variety of different problem situations. Jackson and Keys's "system of systems methodologies" was identified as the most formal statement of this pluralist position. Pluralism was defended against the advocates of paradigm incommensurability on the basis that the different strands of management science are necessary as supports for the anthropologically based cognitive interests of the human species, as identified by Habermas – hard and cybernetic approaches supporting the technical interest; soft approaches the practical interest; and critical approaches the emancipatory interest. Pluralism, it was stated

> offers the best hope of re-establishing management science as a cohesive discipline and profession – *and* on firmer foundations than those which supported the traditional version (Jackson, 1987b, p. 464).

A fuller version of these arguments can be found in Jackson (1991).

Following the publication of my 1987 paper, debate about the possibility of "pluralism" in systems thinking began to concentrate at the theoretical level. The main difficulty, as Flood (1989) notes, in accepting that systems methodologies based upon competing epistemological and ontological presuppositions can be brought together in one pluralist or complementarist endeavor, is that the arguments in favor of "paradigm incommensurability" are so strong. For Kuhn (1970), paradigm incommensurability occurs when "two groups of scientists see different things when they look from the same point in the same direction." Burrell and Morgan (1979) support the notion of incommensurability between their sociological paradigms. It would seem inconceivable for proponents of paradigm incommensurability that different systems methodologies, based upon irreconcilable theoretical assumptions, could ever be employed together in some complementarist way. There is the insurmountable difficulty of how it is possible to stand above the paradigms and work with them in this manner. How could such a privileged position be attained?

It was clear enough in what direction critical systems thinking was looking for answers. The preferred vehicle to support critical systems thinking's pluralism at the theoretical level (and, therefore, to give coherence to the system of systems methodologies) was Habermas's theory of human interests. There was a remarkable convergence in the way that three critical systems thinkers used Habermas's ideas in developing their own approaches. Jackson (1985a, 1987b, 1988c) had linked the technical interest to the concern systems methodologies show for predicting and controlling the systems with which they deal, and the practical and emancipatory interests with the concern to manage pluralism and coercion. It followed that the two dimensions of the system of systems methodologies could be justified from Habermas's work and the different systems methodologies represented as serving, in a complementary way, different human species imperatives. Oliga (1986, 1988) argued that Habermas's interest-constitution theory is an important improvement over the interparadigmatic-incommensurability position of Burrell and Morgan, since

> whereas Burrell and Morgan merely explain the different paradigmatic categories, Habermas explains and reconciles the interest categories in terms of their being individually necessary (although insufficient) as human species, universal and invariant (ontological) forms of activity – namely labor, human interaction, and authority relations (Oliga, 1988, p. 97).

Oliga then goes on to conduct his own survey of how well the technical, practical, and emancipatory interests are served by systems methodologies. Ulrich (1988) similarly used Habermas's taxonomy of types of action – instrumental, strategic, and communicative – to specify three complementary levels of systems practice, roughly parallel to the requirements of operational (or tactical), strategic, and normative planning. Different systems approaches were then allocated as appropriate to service operational, strategic, and normative systems management levels.

By 1991 it was possible to suggest that the concern about paradigm incommensurability could be resolved at the level of human interests and that this established the possibility of the complementary and informed use of different systems rationalities at the theoretical level (Jackson, 1991). As a result, the system of systems methodologies could be rescued from adherence to any one paradigm or rationality. Complementarism at the theoretical level provides the justification and basis for complementarism at the methodological level. Understood in terms of critical systems thinking, and not chained to functionalism, interpretivism or radicalism (in Burrell and Morgan's sense), the system of systems methodologies becomes theoretically coherent and an exceptionally powerful tool for guiding practical interventions (see Jackson, 1990b). It can point to the strengths and weaknesses of different strands of systems thinking, both in terms of problem-solving capacity and social consequences of use, and can put them to work in a way that *respects and takes advantage* of their own peculiar theoretical predispositions in the service of appropriate human interests.

As a final point in this section, it is worth noting Flood's (1990) early attempts to strengthen the "pluralism" of critical systems thinking by reference to Foucault's work. In Flood's view, the establishment of the complementarist position in systems thinking, in opposition to isolationist tendencies, represented a first-stage redefinition of the management and systems sciences. The setting up of a tension with complementarism by confronting it with postmodernist arguments, and the extension to embrace "empower" and "transform" (Oliga, 1989c, 1990), leads to a second stage redefinition and the proper establishment of critical systems thinking. Although farsighted in conception, as we saw in Chapter 8 no great second stage redefinition took place. Foucault was robbed of most of the essentials of postmodernism in order to make his arguments fit with those of Habermas. In Flood's hands, at that time, critical systems thinking remained tied to Habermas's project of enlightenment.

10.6. TOTAL SYSTEMS INTERVENTION

The final element in the maturation of critical systems thinking was the operationalizing of its key ideas in a practical meta-methodology which was called "Total Systems Intervention" (TSI) - a product of an intellectual partnership between Bob Flood and myself (Flood and Jackson, 1991). TSI redeemed the pledge in the SOSM (Jackson and Keys, 1984) that pluralism would be based on different views of the problem situation as well as on using methodologies in combination. It fulfilled the prediction, in my 1987 paper, that a meta-methodology would develop capable of guiding practitioners in their pluralist practice. It also employed critique of the different systems approaches and respected the possibility of "coercive" contexts. In other words, it was successful in providing guidelines for the use of all the various critical systems ideas we have been introducing in this chapter.

TSI was said to represent a new approach to planning, designing, problem solving, and evaluation based upon critical systems thinking. It uses a range of (Morgan's) systems metaphors to encourage creative thinking about organizations, and the issues and problems they face. These issues and problems are linked by a framework - the SOSM - to various systems approaches, so that once agreement is reached about which are the most significant for the organization of concern, an appropriate systems-based intervention methodology (or set of methodologies) can be employed. Choice of an appropriate systems methodology will guide problem solving in a way that ensures it addresses what are the main concerns of the particular organization involved. In short, TSI advocates combining Morgan's work on metaphors, the SOSM, and knowledge of the individual systems approaches in an interactive manner that is deemed to be particularly powerful and fruitful. I shall describe TSI, drawing heavily on Jackson (1991), first by looking at its philosophy and principles, and then by considering its three phases.

10.6.1. Philosophy and Principles of Total Systems Intervention

The philosophy and theory that underpins TSI is, as we know, critical systems thinking. Jackson's 1991 account of this sees it as taking its stand on five positions. These are critical awareness, social awareness, human well-being and emancipation, complementarism at the methodological level, and complementarism at the theoretical level. We have been putting in place an understanding of these aspects of critical systems thinking in this chapter. Flood and Jackson's *Creative Problem Solving: Total Systems Intervention* (1991) summarizes critical systems thinking in terms of three postulates - complementarism, sociological awareness, and human well-being and emancipation - and relates these closely to Habermas's work.

There are seven principles embedded in the three phases of TSI. These are:

- Organizations are too complicated to understand using one management model, and their problems are too complex to tackle with quick fixes
- Organizations, their concerns, issues and problems should be investigated using a range of systems metaphors
- Organizational issues and problems highlighted by the metaphors can be linked to appropriate systems methodologies to guide intervention
- Different systems metaphors and methodologies can be used in a complementary way to highlight and address different aspects of organizations and their problems

- It is possible to appreciate the strengths and weaknesses of different systems methodologies and to relate each to appropriate organizational concerns and problems
- TSI sets out a systemic cycle of inquiry with interaction back and forth between the three phases
- Facilitators and clients are both engaged at all stages of the TSI process

The three phases of TSI are labeled *creativity, choice,* and *implementation.* I consider these in turn, looking in each case at the task to be accomplished during the phase, the tools provided by TSI to realize the task and the outcome or results expected from the phase.

10.6.2. Creativity

The task during the creativity phase is to use systems metaphors as organizing structures to help managers and other stakeholders think creatively about their enterprises. The sorts of questions it would be pertinent to ask are:

- What metaphors throw light onto this organization's problems and concerns?
- What are the main issues and problems revealed by each metaphor?
- In the light of the metaphor analysis what issues and problems are currently crucial for this enterprise?

The tools provided by TSI to assist this process are a set of systems metaphors. Different metaphors focus attention on different aspects of an organization's functioning. Some concentrate on organizational structure, while others highlight human and political aspects of an organization. Some examples are:

- The organization as a machine
- The organization as an organism
- The organization as a brain
- The organization as a culture
- The organization as a coalition
- The organization as a coercive system

The main aspects of organizations highlighted and the main problems revealed by each metaphor are disclosed in order to enhance discussion and debate. As well as the metaphors, Jackson and Keys's grid of problem contexts and other theoretical schemata can be used at this stage to gain insight into the organization and its problems.

The outcome (what is expected to emerge) from the creativity phase is a set of crucial issues and concerns, highlighted by particular metaphors, that then become the basis for a choice of appropriate systems intervention methodology. There may be other significant problems that it is also sensible to pursue into the next phase. The relative importance of different issues and problems may, indeed, be altered by later work. If all the metaphors reveal serious problems, then the organization is obviously in a crisis state.

10.6.3. Choice

The task during the choice phase is to choose an appropriate systems-based intervention methodology (or set of methodologies) to suit the particular characteristics of the organization's situation as revealed by the examination conducted in the creativity phase. The tools provided by TSI to help with this stage are the system of systems methodologies and, derived from that, knowledge of the particular strengths and weaknesses of different systems methodologies.

As was demonstrated earlier in this chapter, the system of systems methodologies unearths the assumptions underlying different systems approaches by asking what each assumes about the system(s) with which it deals and about the relationship between the participants concerned with that system. Putting these points together in the matrix of Figure 10.2, it is apparent that systems methodologies can be classified according to whether they assume problem contexts to be simple-unitary, simple-pluralist, simple-coercive, complex-unitary, complex-pluralist, or complex-coercive. Combining the information gained about the problem context during the creativity phase and the knowledge provided by the SOSM, about the assumptions underlying different systems approaches, it is possible to move toward an appropriate choice of systems intervention methodology. For example, if the problem context is characterized by there being clear and agreed objectives (unitary) and by being transparent enough so that it can be captured in a mathematical model (simple) then a methodology based upon simple-unitary assumptions can be used with every hope of success.

On the basis of the SOSM, it is possible to relate individual methodologies to the issues and problems that are particularly crucial for the organization. Bearing in mind the concerns and problems revealed during the creativity phase, and the conclusions of the SOSM analysis, an appropriate choice of systems methodologies to guide intervention and change can now be made.

The most probable outcome of the choice phase is that there will be a "dominant" methodology chosen, to be supported if necessary by "dependent' methodologies.

10.6.4. Implementation

The task during the implementation phase is to employ a particular systems methodology (or systems methodologies) to arrive at and implement specific proposals.

The tools provided by TSI are the specific systems methodologies used according to the logic of TSI. The dominant methodology operationalizes an approach to change which should tackle the major problems faced. The logic of TSI demands, however, that consideration continue to be given to the imperatives of other methodologies. For example, the key problems in an organization suffering from structural collapse may have been highlighted using the metaphors of organism and brain, but the cultural metaphor might also appear illuminating, albeit in a necessarily subordinate way given the immediate crisis. In these circumstances a cybernetic methodology would be chosen to guide the intervention, but perhaps tempered by some ideas from soft systems methodology. Managers in another organization might wish to redesign their information systems but be held back by conflicting views about where the organization should be going, exacerbated by some political infighting. This situation might usefully be understood through the culture metaphor, but with the brain and coercive-system metaphors also illuminating. In this case, soft systems methodology might guide the intervention, but with aspects of cybernetics and critical systems heuristics also being used.

The outcome of the implementation stage is coordinated change brought about in those aspects of the organization currently most vital for its efficient, effective and ethical, etc., functioning.

The three-phase meta-methodology of TSI is set out in Table 10.1. It is important to stress, however, that TSI is a systemic and iterative approach. It asks, during each phase, that continual reference be made back or forth to the likely conclusions of other phases. So, for example, during phase 1, creativity, attempts are made to anticipate the likely consequences of particular choices of methodology for the organization's structure, and information and control requirements. Moreover, participants' views of what are the main problem areas will change and the intervention itself will move the problem situation on. The only way to attend to these matters is to continually cycle around creativity, choice and implementation, changing as appropriate which methodologies are "dominant" and "dependent." This dynamic aspect of TSI is captured in a quotation from the preface to *Creative Problem Solving: Total Systems Intervention*:

> The essence of TSI is to encourage highly creative thinking about the nature of any problem situation before a decision is taken about the character of the main difficulties to be addressed. Once the decision has been taken, TSI will steer the manager or analyst towards the type of systems methodology most appropriate for dealing with the kind of difficulties identified as being most significant. As the intervention proceeds, using TSI, so the nature of the problem situation will be continually reviewed, as will the choice of appropriate systems methodology. In highly complex problem situations it is advisable to address at the same time different aspects revealed by taking different perspectives on it. This involves employing a number of systems methodologies in combination. In these circumstances it is necessary to nominate one methodology as 'dominant' and others as 'supportive', although these relationships may change as the study progresses (Flood and Jackson, 1991, pp. xiii-xiv).

10.6.5. Strengths and Weaknesses of Total Systems Intervention

TSI has attracted a lot of comment both favorable (e.g. Green, 1993) and unfavorable (e.g. Tsoukas, 1993a). Flood (1995) has reacted to this by seeking to further develop and systematize the employment of critical systems thinking. I believe that a more fundamental recasting is necessary. Both Flood's adjustments to TSI and my proposed recasting will be discussed in the next chapter. For the moment I seek only to summarize the main strengths and weaknesses of the earliest version of TSI (1991) as I now see them.

The breakthrough achieved by TSI, noted by Mingers and Brocklesby (1996), is to postulate a meta-methodology for using methodologies adhering to different paradigms in *the same intervention on the same problem situation*. As a meta-methodology, TSI seeks to ensure that pluralism extends beyond the use of different methods and techniques guided by one methodology premised on one set of theoretical assumptions. It seeks to find a way of managing, in a coherent way, very different methodologies premised upon alternative theoretical assumptions. It would be nice to use such different methodologies alongside one another in highly complex problem situations but if this proves to be *practically* impossible, TSI suggests, then the best way to handle methodological pluralism is to clearly state that one methodology is being taken as "dominant" (and others "dependent") for some period of time, being always willing to alter the relationship between dominant and dependent methodologies as the situation changes. One methodology, encapsulating the presuppositions of a particular paradigm, is granted "imperialistic" status - but only temporarily; its dominance is kept under continual review. The other strength of TSI, as we have already suggested, was to bring together pluralism in the creativity phase (looking at the problem situation through different Ws) with pluralism in terms of the management of different methodologies in combination (in the choice and implementation phases).

Table 10.1. The 3-phase TSI meta-methodology

Creativity	
Task	To highlight concerns, issues and problems
Tools	Systems metaphors
Outcome	Dominant and dependent concerns, issues and problems
Choice	
Task	To choose an appropriate systems-based intervention methodology (or methodologies)
Tools	The "system of systems methodologies" and knowledge of the strengths and weaknesses of different methodologies
Outcome	Dominant and dependent methodologies chosen for use
Implementation	
Task	To arrive at and implement specific change proposals
Tools	Systems methodologies employed according to the logic of TSI
Outcome	Highly relevant and coordinated change, improving efficiency, effectiveness, ethicality, etc.

If TSI's great strength was operating at the meta-methodological level, to ensure that methodologies embodying different paradigmatic assumptions were used in combination, operating at this level also led to what, it now seems to me, was one of its weaknesses. As Mingers and Brocklesby (1996) note, TSI (like the SOSM) requires the use of "whole" methodologies. Once an interpretive rationale is chosen as dominant, for example, it seems that you must employ the particular methods and techniques exactly in the manner set out in Checkland's "soft systems methodology" or Ackoff's "interactive planning." There is an unnecessary lack of flexibility here which needs addressing. There is nothing theoretically wrong with using a selection of methods and techniques, as long as they are employed according to an explicit logic, interpretive in this case, and this allows a much greater responsiveness to the peculiarities of each problem situation as it evolves during an intervention. Taket and White (2000) are concerned that the pigeon-holing of methodologies, apparently implied by the SOSM, further detracts from flexibility.

Tsoukas's (1993a, b) critique brings to the fore another problem which TSI leaves unresolved. It grounds its pluralism, or "complementarism," uncritically on Habermas's early theory of human interests. TSI seems to suggest that it can, on the basis of Habermas's three "human interests," stand "above the paradigms," picking out appropriate methodologies according to the particular human interest to be served. As Tsoukas (1993b) notes, however:

> Different paradigms constitute different realities, and as such, they provide answers, either explicitly or implicitly, to *all* three human interests. Positivist problem-solving, for example, is not simply useful for achieving technical mastery over social processes. In attempting to do so, it also provides answers to the inextricably interwoven questions of interaction and power (p. 314).

If TSI claims to stand "above the paradigms" how can this claim be grounded? If it has to abandon this claim, does it mean that TSI, or more properly the critical systems thinking on which it is based, constitutes a new paradigm in its own right? If this is the case what has happened to pluralism? Equally worrying, as Spaul (1997) recounts, is that Habermas himself no longer finds his early human interest theory to be defensible.

Another criticism of TSI centers on the lack of attention given to the process of facilitation. Taket and White (2000) believe there is insufficient discussion, in the literature on TSI, of the "roles" and "styles" that facilitators can adopt. Most detail is provided on the "intervention" phase, whereas they suspect users of TSI have most difficulty with the "creativity" and "choice" phases. They also worry that the emphasis on "rationality" and "abstraction," in approaches such as TSI, leads to the privileging of methods which are verbally based and that this can hinder the participation of some groups.

A further gap in the formulation of TSI is highlighted by those management scientists who give attention to the person actually engaging in the intervention – the subject, agent or user of methodologies. TSI, which demands multi-methodological competence and various ethical commitments, clearly asks a great deal from would-be users, but it does not detail whether or how the relevant competence can be obtained. Ormerod (1997a), by contrast, makes the "intervention competence" of the analyst central to his "transformation competence" approach to multi-methodology and reinforces the argument by setting out the development of his own intervention competence in the course of seven consultancies. Brocklesby (1995) points to cultural constraints in the management science community to the adoption of the multi-methodology approach. He also identifies severe "cognitive difficulties" for individuals in working across paradigms (1997). His conclusion, based on an analysis using the work of Maturana and Varela, is that it is unlikely but by no means impossible for individuals to become multi-methodology literate. Midgley (1997) argues that any new approach to pluralism in systems thinking must take into account the dynamic interaction that occurs between the subject who wishes to take action and the power-knowledge formations which form the identity of the subject. Mingers (1997) also makes the agent the focus of his own preferred version of multi-methodology, labeled critical pluralism. For him, the fact that methodologies carry the critical tag, and prescribe emancipatory practice, cannot guarantee their critical employment – the commitment of the user, embedded in a particular social context, is crucial.

From their postmodern perspective, Taket and White (2000) see TSI as one of the approaches that seeks to "tame" pluralism and diversity rather than embracing them. The emphasis on "rigor" and "formalized thinking" in TSI sets up a tension with the espoused purpose of employing a plurality of methodologies and methods. A "deconstruction" of the language of TSI reveals a contradiction between statements that imply closure and those encouraging an openness to other possible approaches. Another aspect of the emphasis on rationality is that the "feelings" and "emotions" of participants in decision processes get ignored.

Finally, there are those (Tsoukas, 1993a; Taket and White, 2000) who question whether, in practice, TSI lives up to its claims to promote "emancipation." Flood (1995) and Flood and Romm (1996) come under particular scrutiny for being strong on assertion but weak in terms of demonstrating any such commitment. Midgley (1996), developing a variant of this criticism, accuses TSI of partial radicalism. It declares itself for human emancipation but ignores environmental concerns. For Midgley the two are inextricably linked.

We shall leave TSI for the moment but not without a reminder of just how many of these criticisms were anticipated by Flood and Jackson, in 1991, in their self-critique of TSI (see pp. 241-244).

10.7. CONCLUSION

The early days of critical systems thinking saw it providing theoretically informed critiques of different systems methodologies, exploring how to act in coercive contexts, debating the nature of an appropriate pluralism in theory and practice, and engaging closely with social theory, especially the work of Habermas. From these beginnings it developed as an approach for putting all the different systems methodologies, methods and models to work, in a coherent way, according to their strengths and weaknesses, and the social conditions prevailing, in the service of a general project of improving complex organizational and societal systems. This general project embraced efficiency, effectiveness, and the promotion of mutual understanding, at the same time as giving attention to ethics, to empowerment and to emancipation. TSI emerged as a vehicle for pursuing this project in practice. It employs an understanding of a range of systems metaphors, as well as the system of systems methodologies, to interrogate problem situations creatively and to guide choice of appropriate problem resolving approaches.

By about 1991, critical systems thinking had stabilized sufficiently for a number of systems thinkers to try their hand at describing its important characteristics. Schecter (1991), for example, saw it as defined by three commitments: to critique, to emancipation and to pluralism. Jackson (1991), offering the most detailed account of its commitments, argued that critical systems thinking was built upon the five pillars of critical awareness, social awareness, complementarism at the methodological level, complementarism at the theoretical level, and dedication to human emancipation. Flood and Jackson (1991), in developing TSI on the philosophy and theory of critical systems thinking, saw it as making a stand on three positions. These were complementarism, sociological awareness and the promotion of human well-being and emancipation. Finally, Flood and Jackson (1991, eds.), in the introduction to a set of readings on critical systems thinking, recognized the critical systems endeavor as possessing three interrelated intentions – complementarism, emancipation and critical reflection.

The confidence in the nature of critical systems thinking that allowed the formulation of those descriptions was also reflected, in 1991, in the publication of three books which took their inspiration from critical systems thinking. Flood and Jackson's (eds.) *Critical Systems Thinking: Directed Readings* was a collection of papers, accompanied by a commentary, which traced the origins and development of the approach. Jackson's *Systems Methodology for the Management Sciences* sought to provide a comprehensive critique of the different systems approaches drawing upon the social sciences as a basis for the critique. Flood and Jackson's *Creative Problem Solving: Total Systems Intervention* introduced the TSI meta-methodology. Just looking at the examples in that original account of TSI, I can see that the approach was used in interventions to improve quality, in project management, in encouraging participation, in visioning, in crisis management, in planning, in marketing, in organizational restructuring and in policy analysis. In each case, TSI served the purpose of coordinating the intervention and enabling learning to take place.

In a relatively short period of time critical systems thinking and practice had a significant impact on the systems thinking scene. Of course, the approach met opposition and was subject to criticism. Some of the criticism was justified. In the next chapter we see how well it has responded to the criticism and trace the recent developments that have produced a contemporary version of critical systems thinking and practice.

11

CONTEMPORARY CRITICAL SYSTEMS THINKING AND PRACTICE

11.1. INTRODUCTION

The attempt to tell the story of the more recent development of critical systems thinking is fraught with dangers. By 1991 this strand of work was firmly established and research in critical systems thinking took on a dynamic of its own; propelled by an internal logic and by the responses it made to challenges from outside, such as from postmodernism. Ideas arose simultaneously in different places and, although I will try my best, it is often difficult to give precedence to particular theorists in creating new directions for the work. Additionally, of course, there is the usual difficulty of discerning pattern in recent events. The story could be constructed in a variety of different ways, all of which would have some legitimacy.

I shall start by looking very briefly at the three primary commitments of critical systems thinking before constructing my own version of the story around the theme of "towards coherent pluralism in systems thinking." I shall then turn to what critical systems practice would look like if it followed the dictates of coherent pluralism and conclude with a discussion of what more needs doing to improve critical systems thinking and practice.

11.2. THREE COMMITMENTS OF CRITICAL SYSTEMS THINKING

Examining the definitions of critical systems thinking provided at the end of the last chapter, it is clear that three "commitments" dominate the lists that make up the definitions. These are critical awareness, emancipation or improvement, and pluralism.

"Critical awareness" involves, as one of its aspects, critiquing the theoretical underpinnings, strengths and weaknesses of available systems methodologies and the usefulness of the variety of systems models, methods, tools and techniques in the service of different methodologies. It is here that critical systems thinking has drawn most heavily and successfully on social theory and thus helped advance systems thinking as a whole as a field of study. Work of this kind continued throughout the 1990s and the results have been summarized in Part II of this book. Another aspect of critical awareness can be described as a "social awareness" of the organizational and societal "climate" which determines the popularity of use of particular systems approaches at different times, and the kind of impact that use has. As Flood (1990; Flood and Romm, 1995) has insisted, this must incorporate consideration of the effects that power at the micro-level can have on the formulation and development of knowledge. This incorporation derives, of course, from postmodernism and, specifically, the work of Foucault (see Chapter 3 and Chapter 8). A related consideration has been urged on critical systems thinking, from within the tradition, by Brocklesby (1994, 1997). Brocklesby asks that far more attention be paid by critical systems thinkers to the "cultural constraints" preventing easy combination of hard, soft and emancipatory methodologies. He refers to the overall level of receptiveness to culture change in the systems community and how this might hinder acceptance of critical systems thinking. He also worries about the capacity of individual users of methodologies to switch between paradigms and so become "multi-methodology literate." His conclusion, in this regard is that

> the process of transforming an agent who works within a single paradigm into someone who is multi-methodology literate is perhaps an unlikely, although by no means impossible, proposition (1997, p. 212).

Critical systems thinking has, since its inception, made somewhat vague statements about being dedicated to human "emancipation." Putting this item on the agenda by promoting emancipatory systems thinking was a real achievement of the approach. As we saw in the previous chapter the relationship between emancipatory and critical systems thinking was, for some time, so close that there was confusion about their separate identities. Eventually, however (Jackson, 1991), it becomes clear that "emancipation" was only one of three human interests which, following Habermas, critical systems thinking sought to support. Critical systems thinking, therefore, still embraced emancipation but as part of a much broader dedication to human improvement - defined, by Flood and Jackson (1991), in terms of bringing about those circumstances in which all individuals could realize their potential.

These days, following the attack on the "grand narratives" of personal and societal liberation conducted by postmodern thinkers such as Lyotard, critical systems thinkers are much more circumspect when talking in terms of human emancipation. It has been accepted that the Habermasian, universalist position has been undermined and it has become normal to accept the postmodernist argument that the best that can be achieved is "local improvement" (Jackson, 1993b, 1995; Midgley, 1996; Flood and Romm, 1996). In my inaugural lecture, in 1993, I sought to illustrate the point with reference to a Maya creation myth. This recounts how the gods, having created men, become displeased with them because they could see everything and know everything, and decided to do something to restore their advantage. So the gods

> cast a vapor over their eyes which were clouded as when one blows upon a mirror. Their eyes were misted and they could see only what was near. Only that was clear to them. So were destroyed the wisdom and knowledge of the four men, origin and beginning (p. 31).

In 1995, I employed Bob Dylan to make the same point:

> We can no longer believe in a unified systems theory providing unlimited knowledge. The period when we could share that vision and belief stands some time from us. Bob Dylan's refrain, from a 1964 song, is relevant to the state of mind of the systems movement today:

> 'Ah, but I was so much older then, I'm younger than that now'.

> The challenge for systems thinking ... is to continue to progress accepting limited vision ... (p. 41).

This adjustment in the face of the postmodernist challenge does not mean that critical systems thinkers have come to accept the postmodern conclusion that human emancipation is a dangerous fiction and that self emancipation is the proper objective. Rather, they have tempered their arguments to reflect the difficulty of generalizing a notion such as emancipation. Midgley (1997) still seeks "improvement", at least in the local context and I have argued (Jackson, 1997) that pluralism, now more than ever, needs the support of "ethical alertness" if it is to be able to justify the recommendations for improvement it delivers. No rationality on its own carries conviction; in this regard pluralism concurs with postmodern thinking. But different rationalities employed together in the form of different systems methodologies, as recommended by systemic pluralism, will often lead to contradictory possibilities for change. A decision between these possibilities, it seems, can only be made on ethical grounds. Ironically, in new-style critical systems thinking, postmodernism can play a role in ensuring local improvement and promoting ethical alertness.

The third commitment of critical systems thinking is to "pluralism." In fact the three commitments we have identified are closely intertwined. It would be possible, therefore, to tell the story of the recent development of critical systems thinking around any of "critical awareness", "improvement" and "pluralism." I have treated "critical awareness" and "improvement" very briefly, and leave discussion of pluralism until the next section, because I chose to tell the story by concentrating on the struggle to establish a coherent pluralist position in systems thinking. Pluralism will be to the fore in the next section but, because the three commitments are so interrelated, we shall also learn more about the current debate surrounding critical awareness and improvement.

11.3. TOWARDS COHERENT PLURALISM IN SYSTEMS THINKING

Pluralism, interpreted in the broadest sense as the use of different methodologies, methods, models and techniques in combination, is a topic of considerable interest in the applied disciplines these days. There are, perhaps, three reasons which explain why this is the case. One is that critique has taken place, in many of these disciplines, of traditional approaches. In systems thinking, organization theory, information systems and operational research, for example, old ways have been challenged and new perspectives opened up. The relationship between diverse approaches to developing each discipline has to be thought through. A second, related reason is the prevailing fashion for "relativism", preceding postmodernism but now usually associated with it. The spirit of the times is against "totalizing" discourses which claim to know the truth about things. To be in tune with the times we must, according to Lyotard (1984), embrace postmodern thinking which "refines our sensitivity to difference and reinforces our ability to tolerate the incommensurable." The third reason, crucial for practitioners, is that pluralism seems to be necessary. In the information systems field, for example, there is no longer confidence that information systems designed according to traditional structured methods will serve their users and bring competitive advantage. It is inevitable that practitioners will try to buttress traditional approaches with some of the newer thinking. Mingers and Brocklesby (1996) cite the fact that practitioners are increasingly combining different methods and methodologies as a major justification for the need to examine the use of "multi-methodology." It certainly seems to be the case that management consultants have not allowed theoretical niceties to get in the way of "pluralistic practice", if this has seemed appropriate - as apparently it has. Tata Consultancy Services have been working for some time with a "multi-modeling" methodology (Ramakrishnan, 1995). Ormerod (1992, 1996, 1997b) has provided accounts of his own pluralistic practice as a consultant before and after entering academia.

There is, therefore, a clamor for pluralism in methodology use in the applied disciplines. In earlier work (Jackson, 1996, 1997, 1999) I have considered the progress made in pursuing pluralism in organization theory, information systems, operational research, evaluation research and management consultancy. While drawing some lessons from these endeavors, I have concluded that the debates in systems thinking about pluralism have reached a more advanced stage than elsewhere. The reasons for this are many and I have fully enumerated them in the earlier work. For our purposes here, it is enough to note, first, that systems thinking was one of the first applied disciplines to go through a period of crisis when different conceptualizations of the field fought one another for hegemony and, perhaps, the earliest to begin to emerge from this crisis. Second, that systems thinking, of all the applied disciplines, has demonstrated the greatest potential for linking theory and practice. It has used contributions from the social sciences to gain an appreciation of the diversity of viewpoints that exist on the nature of the "systems" it seeks to understand and intervene in, and it has been able, through its leadership in the construction of methodologies to guide intervention, to test in practice the usefulness of the distinctions social scientists make (see Jackson, 1991; 1993). Systems research is, therefore, in advance of organization theory in working out the implications of pluralism for those who wish to actually intervene in problem situations. It is ahead of information systems, operational research, evaluation research and management consultancy in its ability to think through the implications of pluralism at the theoretical level and improve pluralist practice as a result. For these applied disciplines it can supply the theoretical foundations which they lack (see Jackson, 1996).

Convinced, therefore, that the debates in the systems field are the most crucial for the future of pluralism, we must now return to those debates and see how they have progressed. We are back, of course, to the study of critical systems thinking.

11.3.1. The Nature of Pluralism in Critical Systems Thinking

We can re-enter the debates by considering two contributions to theorizing about pluralism in systems thinking which, I think, help to clarify discussion of this topic. The first of these contributions we have already met in the previous chapter. It is my attempt (Jackson, 1987b, 1991) to distinguish pluralism from three other possible developmental strategies for systems thinking - isolationism, imperialism, and pragmatism. The reader will recall that, in contrast to the other options available, pluralism was seen to offer excellent opportunities for future development. The second contribution, originated by Mingers and Brocklesby (1996), provides an overview of the different possibilities that they believe can exist under the label of pluralism. This consists of a table of logical types of "multi-methodology practice", and is adapted and reproduced as Table 11.1. This table, rather confusingly in my view, includes isolationist (A), imperialist (B, D, H), and pragmatist (C, E) possibilities alongside cases of "genuine" pluralism (F, G, I). It is my belief that it is useful to retain these categories as distinct approaches which are different to pluralism. What is extremely useful about this table, however, is the clarification it brings to variations in approach even in the category of what I would call genuine pluralism. In this category Mingers and Brocklesby recognize three possibilities.

The first of these they call "methodology selection." Here the agent employing methodologies regards a variety of different methodologies, based upon different paradigms, as useful and chooses a whole methodology (such as system dynamics or soft systems methodology) according to the problem situation. That methodology, and its associated

Table 11.1. Different possibilities for combining methodologies (adapted from Mingers, 1997, p. 7, in Mingers and Gill, 1997)

	One/more methodologies	One/more paradigms	Same/ different intervention	Whole/ part methodology	Imperialist or mixed	Example	Name
A	One	One	-	-	-	SSM only	Methodological Isolationism
B	More	ditto	Different	Whole	-	SSM | Strat. choice	Paradigmatic isolationism
C	ditto	ditto	Same	Whole	-	Simulation + Queueing Theory	Methodology combination
D	ditto	ditto	Same	Part	Imperialist	Cognitive mapping in SSM	Methodology enhancement
E	ditto	ditto	Same	Part	Mixed	Cognitive mapping + root definitions	Single paradigm multi-methodology
F	ditto	More	Different	Whole	-	Simulation | SSM	Methodology selection
G	ditto	ditto	Same	Whole	-	VSM + Interactive Planning	Whole methodology management
H	ditto	ditto	Same	Part	Imperialist	JSD in SSM	Methodology enhancement
I	ditto	ditto	Same	Part	Mixed	Cognitive mapping + System Dynamics	Multi-paradigm multi-methodology

In the Example column + means combined in the same intervention. | means used in separate interventions.

methods, models and techniques, which best corresponds to the demands of the problem situation will be selected.

The second option is labeled "whole methodology management." In this case again, whole methodologies, based upon different paradigms, are employed by the methodology user but, this time, they are used together in the same intervention. The emphasis shifts to how a variety of very different methodologies can be managed during the process of one intervention. This contrasts with the third possibility which involves using parts of different methodologies (the methodologies owing allegiance to different paradigms) together in the same intervention. Here the whole methodologies are "broken up" and the methods, models and techniques usually associated with each brought together in new combinations according to the requirements of the particular intervention. Mingers and Brocklesby call this "multiparadigm multi-methodology." This option, it seems to me, needs to be operationalized with safeguards to prevent relapse from pluralism into pragmatism or imperialism - a point I will discuss later.

My immediate task is to employ these two theoretical contributions in order to structure the argument during our continuing historical overview of the development of pluralism in systems thinking.

11.3.2. The History of Pluralism in Critical Systems Thinking

We traced the early stages of the developing argument for pluralism in Chapter 10. The first important landmark was established in 1984 with the publication of Linstone's book *Multiple Perspectives for Decision Making* and Jackson and Keys's article on the SOSM. The main weaknesses of Linstone's approach were its functionalist "imperialism" and the fact that, although it emphasized pluralism in viewing complex problem situations, it largely ignored combining methodologies and methods in a pluralist manner to intervene in problem situations. The main weaknesses of the SOSM were its privileging of "methodology selection", in Mingers and Brocklesby's terms, over the use of different methodologies in the *same* intervention, and its failure adequately to distinguish between methodology and methods. These problems notwithstanding, the two pieces of work independently put pluralism firmly on the agenda and, together, made the point that pluralism had to be applied at all stages of an intervention; the analysis stages as well as the action stages.

Total Systems Intervention (TSI), devised by Flood and Jackson, and our second landmark in this account, was also discussed in the last chapter. TSI did seek to operationalize pluralism in each of its three phases - "creativity", "choice", and "implementation." Moreover, it set out a meta-methodology for using methodologies adhering to different paradigms in the same intervention in the same problem situation. Its weaknesses were its uncritical adherence to Habermas's early theory of human interests and its lack of attention to "agents" and the process of intervention. Another serious flaw, noted by Mingers and Brocklesby, is that TSI emphasizes the use of "whole" methodologies. It is, in their terms, an example of "whole methodology management." Because it seemed impossible, from the way TSI was described, to detach methods, models and techniques from the methodologies with which they were most closely associated, TSI lacked a degree of responsiveness in addressing complex, dynamic problem situations.

The flexibility that can be gained by extracting methods, models, tools and techniques from different methodologies, and using them in combination, now seems to me to be so essential that its gradual acceptance should be seen as a third landmark on the way to the establishment of coherent pluralism in systems thinking. Development of this kind of multi-method approach is furthest advanced in practice in operational research, especially among soft OR practitioners, and has received the greatest support theoretically from those influenced by postmodernism.

In OR there has been an increasing willingness to combine various methods, tools and techniques in one intervention. Ormerod (1995) describes Bennett's experiments involving hypergame analysis, cognitive maps and strategic choice; a case study of Matthews and Bennett employing both cognitive mapping and strategic choice; and Bryant's thoughts on mixing cognitive mapping with hypergame analysis. Ormerod goes on to describe a project of his own in which various soft OR methods were used in the development of a new information systems strategy for Sainsbury's supermarkets. This project employed cognitive mapping, soft systems methodology and strategic choice in its various phases, in the context of an overall orientation provided by Ackoff's interactive planning.

The theoretical development that has most encouraged multi-method use has been the alignment of pluralism and postmodernism. This is because (see Chapter 9) postmodernism is opposed to the totalizing endeavors of the "grand narratives" and committed to promoting "difference" in a world which, it is claimed, we can no longer represent with the certainty provided by the old paradigms and in which we can no longer guide action on the basis of the old moralities. As we know, it is a postmodern orientation that underpins Taket and White's "pragmatic pluralism." They have sought to

> find ways of working in situations which have a high degree of variety and in which acceptance and respect for difference is important. Such situations display a high degree of heterogeneity ... The pluralist strategy is based on the acknowledgement and respect of difference, rather than its rationalization (1995, p. 518).

This strategy demands "judicious mix and match" of parts of different OR/systems methodologies and methods in order to fit the requirements of each particular situation as it continually changes. If methodologies are "mutilated" in the process then this is justified in realizing the strategy.

The great merit of unrestricted multi-method use, as practised by some in OR and some who embrace postmodernism, is that it allows practitioners the flexibility to cleave closely to what is appropriate in the problem situation and to the twists and turns taken by the intervention. The weaknesses, however, must also be recognized and are associated with an almost inevitable relapse into pragmatism or an unreflective imperialism. The use of methods, tools and techniques, without reference to the methodology and paradigm supporting their use, means that we cannot learn about the effectiveness of these in supporting interventions conducted under the governance of a particular rationality. The eclectic use of different methods as countenanced by Ormerod (1997a) and Taket and White (2000) means that we cannot ensure paradigm diversity. The sorts of combinations of soft OR methods noted by Ormerod (1995) are all managed under the "imperialism" of the interpretive paradigm. Ormerod describes Bennett's views on the similarities shared by the methods he combines together:

> he suggests that all the methods are designed to help small, relatively autonomous groups of people make non-routine choices ... second ... all the methods ... are designed primarily for a style of working in which consultants work *with* clients, rather than producing analysis *for* them (p. 278).

The creation of such "single paradigm multi-methodologies" (Mingers and Brocklesby, 1996) can be extremely productive and provide great flexibility in an intervention. Without theoretical and methodological guidance, however, mixing methods, tools and techniques can easily relapse into an unreflective imperialism in which one paradigm of analysis is employed in the intervention by default, thus losing the benefits to be gained by exploring what outcomes might be achieved using alternative rationales. Most likely to suffer is any consideration that might be given to "emancipatory practice." Taket and White's (2000) injunction to do "what feels good" hardly provides sufficient safeguard. Under their form of pragmatic pluralism, unless it happens to feel good, pluralism loses its radical potential. Pragmatic pluralism is too easily accommodated to management consultancy. It is hardly surprising that Ormerod (1996) believes that it is "at least possible that postmodernism offers an underlying philosophical stance that could support consulting practice." He cites Foucault's concept of sources of power as multiple and diffuse, Baudrillard's ideas on the collapse of boundaries, and Lyotard's emphasis on plurality and the pragmatic construction of local rules and prescriptives, as postmodern notions that consultants might find easy to accept. It is interesting that he believes consultants will feel much less at ease with the critical systems approach - especially because emancipation might be put on the agenda.

I have now described three landmark contributions to the development of pluralism in systems thinking, although only two of these represent "genuine" pluralism according to the criteria of the previous sub-section. What we have witnessed, in terms of that sub-section, are examples of "methodology selection" (the SOSM) and "whole methodology management" (TSI), together with so-called "pragmatic pluralism" which, in practice, too easily betrays pluralism and lapses into "pragmatism" or "imperialism." I am now in a position to move forward and delimit exactly what critical systems thinkers want from pluralist thinking and practice, and what they think coherent pluralism must look like, if it is to be both theoretically defensible and provide maximum benefit to practitioners.

11.3.3. What do Critical Systems Thinkers want from Pluralism?

In this sub-section, I am concerned with what pluralism can reasonably aspire to and what it needs to avoid. My reading of contemporary critical systems authors (Flood and Romm, 1996; Mingers and Gill, eds., 1997; Midgley; 2000) suggests that pluralism is a response to the many methodologies, methods, models and techniques developed by systems thinkers. This multitude of methodologies, methods, models and techniques is itself a response to the complexity, heterogeneity and turbulence of the problem situations managers (in the broadest sense) face today. The point of pluralist thinking, as part of the critical systems approach, is to make the best use of the methodologies, methods, models and techniques by employing them in a way that increases our capacity to tackle diverse and difficult problem situations while, at the same time, ensuring their continual improvement through research. It seems to me that there are three requirements for pluralism that stem from what critical systems thinkers are trying to achieve with it.

A first requirement is that pluralism must encourage flexibility in use of the widest variety of methods, models, tools and techniques in any intervention. Systems practitioners must be allowed the greatest freedom possible, within pluralism, to tailor their use of methods and tools to the complexities of the problem situation they are seeking to intervene in and the exigencies of the situation as it changes during the intervention. The pluralism needed, therefore, is one that recognizes that methodologies can be decomposed and that the link between the traditional host methodology and the methods, tools and techniques usually associated with it, need not necessarily be a close one. Mingers and Brocklesby (1996) provide the example of a system dynamics model, usually associated with the functionalist approach, being used as a detailed cognitive map for the purposes of enhancing debate in an interpretive framework.

We have to be careful, however, to resist relapse into pragmatism. We cannot afford to allow the theoretically uncontrolled employment of diverse methods, tools, models and techniques that appears to occur in management consultancy and is recommended in "pragmatic pluralism." The reason for this is that we want to learn the value and usefulness of the tools and techniques we employ; we want to do research so that we can improve them. Only by using the methods and tools under the control of a methodology which clearly serves one paradigm can we test them and discover how to improve their effectiveness in supporting an intervention conducted according to that rationality. We can find out if system dynamics models developed originally to serve a functionalist methodology are indeed useful in the context of a soft methodology.

Midgley (e.g. 1989) has long argued that "partitioning" methodologies, and using the methods extracted in a theoretically informed way, could benefit critical systems thinking. Flood and Romm (1996) and Jackson (in this book) have developed the case that all methods, models and techniques can be considered, whichever methodology they were originally developed to serve, as candidates to support functionalist, interpretive, emancipatory, and postmodern rationales. It is this maintenance of clarity about what "generic methodology", and therefore which theoretical rationale, method mixes are being used to serve, at any time, that can save Mingers and Brocklesby's multi-paradigm multi-methodology from relapse into pragmatism or imperialism.

A second requirement of pluralism is that methodologies owing allegiance to different paradigms should be employed in the same intervention unless good reasons are given for temporary relapse into imperialism. It is again the complexity, heterogeneity and turbulence of problem situations that suggest systems practitioners need a pluralism that encourages the use, together, of different methodologies based upon alternative paradigms. We should seek to benefit from what each paradigm has to offer. Pluralism can provide its greatest benefits only in the context of paradigm diversity. This is not to dismiss the usefulness of sometimes employing just one methodology, embodying a particular paradigm, to guide the use of a variety of methods, tools and techniques. Such an approach needs to be followed self-consciously, however, and to permit changes of paradigmatic orientation. If it occurs without due consideration, as tends to be the case in soft OR, it degenerates into imperialism and pluralism is deprived of the vitality it gains from being able to deploy a variety of methodologies, based upon different paradigmatic assumptions, to their true potential. This requirement demands, therefore, a precise understanding of the theoretical underpinnings of different methodologies. If such theoretical understanding is neglected then proper paradigm diversity cannot be guaranteed. Methodologies owing their allegiance to the same paradigm could be employed together in the mistaken belief that "genuine" pluralism was being observed.

In order to protect paradigm diversity to the degree necessary, we have to be extremely watchful. Political, cultural and cognitive (see Brocklesby, 1997) constraints can delimit the range of methodologies it is possible to use and so reduce the potency of pluralism. We have to be particularly careful that pluralism maintains a radical edge to it. Because management scientists often work in a paid capacity for powerful clients, there will be a tendency to employ methodologies that support the status quo. Paradigm diversity demands that pluralism be buttressed against this tendency by requiring it to give proper attention to the development and employment of alternative methodologies based on radical paradigms.

Ormerod (1997a) has argued against an emphasis being placed on the philosophical underpinnings of methodologies. His observation of consultants is that they are quite happy to mix and match methodologies and methods whatever their theoretical origins. Taking his lead from their practice, Ormerod prefers to base any mechanism for choosing between them on their "transformational potential":

> In simple terms the approach (methods and their theories) chosen must support a process of intervention (practice) in a particular context to achieve a desired outcome (p. 49).

While his arguments may be correct, in terms of the short-term demands on consultants, and worthy in that they may lead to short-term benefits for practitioners, they seem to miss the point with regard to the bigger picture. For Ormerod:

> The combination of methods needs to work in the practical sense that the right people (and other resources) need to be involved in a process that results in the desired outcome (1997b, p. 430).

But this takes for granted exactly that which a theoretical orientation allows us to interrogate - who are the "right people"? and what is the "desired outcome"? These concerns are just as "practical" but are of a higher order to those addressed by Ormerod. Further, for researchers concerned to find out why different approaches work, to pass this understanding on to others in systems thinking and to their students, a more theoretical stance is a necessity. There are also, therefore, compelling intellectual grounds for emphasizing the philosophical underpinnings of methodologies. We must understand the relationship between methodologies and their theoretical underpinnings if we are to do research which allows us to operationalize better the hypotheses of particular paradigms and test the conclusions of those paradigms in real-world interventions. Theoretically informed methodologies are essential for ensuring a healthy link between theory and practice in systems thinking.

Methodologies adhering to different paradigms should be used not only in the same intervention but at all stages in the same intervention unless, again, there are good reasons for temporary adoption of an imperialist stance. Mingers and Brocklesby (1996), and Mingers (1997), try to map the characteristics of different methodologies according to their ability to assist four stages - "appreciation", "analysis", "exploration" and "action" - of an intervention. Under pluralism there can be no justification for such a procedure. To functionalists, for example, the "appreciation" stage, carried out according to an interpretive logic, is not "richer"; it is simply misguided. To ensure paradigm diversity, different methodologies should be given consideration at all stages of an intervention.

A third and final requirement of pluralism follows from the need for paradigm diversity. Pluralists must learn to live with and manage a degree of paradigm incompatibility. It is no longer tenable to believe, in the manner of TSI, that paradigm incommensurability can be resolved by reference to some meta-theory such as Habermas's account of different anthropologically based human interests. Or, for that matter, on the basis of his later work (dealing with communicative rationality) on the "three worlds" - as Midgley (1992, 1997) and Mingers and Brocklesby (1996) have occasionally sought to suggest. As Tsoukas (1993a) has it:

> Reality-shaping paradigms ... are not a la carte menus; you don't just pick whatever suits you at any time (p. 315).

In the light of the abandonment of Habermas's "solution" to the issue of paradigm incommensurability, systems thinkers have made a variety of other proposals as to how theoretical pluralism should be handled. The proposals we shall consider are "unreflective pluralism", "pluralism as postmodernism", "pluralism as a new paradigm", and "discordant pluralism."

I introduce the notion of "unreflective pluralism" to close the book , as it were, on Senge. There is a kind of implicit pluralist position running through *The Fifth Discipline*. The "fifth discipline" itself, Senge's version of system dynamics, adheres in his interpretation closely enough to the functionalist paradigm (see Chapter 6). On the other hand the other four disciplines, as we witnessed in Chapter 7, can be regarded as impoverished efforts in support of interpretive thinking. Flood (1999) has even noticed some emancipatory elements in Senge's work:

> Senge goes out of his way to reinforce ideas of openness as a challenge to power and politics in organizations. He expresses sorrow at the many examples of power and politics today ... This 'given' is challenged by learning organizations in a search for openness (p. 26).

If left untheorized this unreflective pluralism can seem all very nice - a case of having your cake and eating it. As I have pointed out, however, (Jackson, 1995), once we take Senge's arguments to the theoretical level it is clear that they are self-contradictory. Systems that we can predict the behavior of using a few archetypes we usually cannot do very much about - the solar system for example. On the other hand, systems that we can do something about, using the other four disciplines, are usually unpredictable using the logic of system dynamics - such as how the politics are going to play themselves out over the next few months in our own complex organizations. There is an awful tension in Senge's book between deterministic ideas of systems governed in particular ways by the interaction of feedback loops, and voluntaristic ideas of our ability to do something about systems. This is not understood by Senge because he does not situate his work in its theoretical background. If he did, he would realize that the discipline of system dynamics fits most readily with functionalism while the other four disciplines are best thought of as interpretive in character. Add a small dose of emancipatory thinking and the "fifth discipline" practitioner is left in a hopeless state.

We have already dismissed the "pluralism as postmodernism" argument (which otherwise, I suppose, might offer some justification for Senge's *mélange*). If paradigm diversity is to be protected, then paradigm incommensurability cannot simply be ignored in the way that Taket and White (2000) propose in their pragmatic pluralism. The eclectic use of different methods, without reference to methodology or paradigm, means that we cannot ensure paradigm diversity. All the methods and models employed may be used according to one implicit paradigm. The easy assimilation of postmodernism, and Senge's work, into management consultancy suggests how it is likely to go.

Recognizing the difficulty of justifying the complementary use of methodologies with contradictory paradigmatic roots, a number of theorists have been tempted to declare pluralism a part of a new paradigm. According to this "pluralism as a new paradigm" solution, a paradigm is embraced and/or developed which is apparently able to house pluralism. Mingers argues that

> although the paradigm incommensurability issue has to be taken seriously in debates about methodology, there are grounds for believing that cross-paradigm research is philosophically feasible. What is required is an underpinning philosophical framework that can encompass the different paradigms, and guidance on appropriate ways to mix different research methods (1997, p. 14).

Walsham and Han (1991) suggest Giddens's "structuration theory" might be a useful meta-theory within which other theories and methodologies can be contained. Mingers and Brocklesby (1996) turn to Giddens and Bhaskar to provide a framework to ground multimethodology work because "both ... dispute the claim that we must chose between the competing realities offered by realist or nominalist thinking." Mingers (forthcoming) has, more recently, come to favor Bhaskar's "critical realism" as an underpinning philosophy. For Walsham and Han, Mingers and Brocklesby, therefore, multimethodology research is not meta-paradigmatic, rather it belongs to a new paradigm. Pluralism can be accommodated within some wide-ranging theory such as Giddens's or Bhaskar's.

Midgley (1995, and 2000) offers what I consider to be a more sophisticated argument for "pluralism as a new paradigm." He wants to defend a version of methodological pluralism consistent with his view of critical systems thinking as a paradigm in its own right. He objects to Flood and Jackson's (1991) claim that critical systems thinking is meta-paradigmatic:

> I have argued that this cannot be the case given that Flood and Jackson make assumptions about human knowledge that are alien to, and incommensurable with, assumptions made by the proponents of other systems paradigms. Far from being meta-paradigmatic, CST is trying to establish the foundations for a *new* paradigm (p. 62).

Midgley's (1992) argument for methodological pluralism is the familiar one that different systems methodologies and methods have evolved to handle the interdependent problems of complexity we face in the modern world. He then insists, however, that "boundary critique", sweeping in the viewpoints of many stakeholders, must be up front in any study. Other methodologies and methods are "subsumed" into this logic and employed for particular aspects of an application. As Midgley (1989) is happy to admit, this is an advanced form of "imperialism." To bring it off, however, Midgley privileges the "emancipatory systems approach" (see Chapter 8), thereby limiting the possibilities of critical systems thinking.

The strength of the "pluralism as a new paradigm" approach is that it resolves the difficulty of having to combine methodologies based upon divergent philosophical and sociological assumptions. A new paradigm is proposed apparently capable of housing pluralism. The obvious weakness is that, unless we accept the new paradigm is capable of containing divergent methodologies, then the power of paradigm diversity is constrained. There are many who could make convincing arguments, from alternative paradigms, against Midgley's version of critical systems thinking, Giddens's structuration theory and Bhaskar's "critical realism." It follows that, in order to protect paradigm diversity, pluralism cannot sell itself to any one paradigm. One paradigm pluralism is simply not pluralism. Another possible disadvantage of the new paradigm version of pluralism is that, depending on the new paradigm embraced, pluralism could lose its radical edge. If the paradigm favored to house pluralism did not give sufficient attention to emancipatory practice, then this possibility would be lost. This is ironic because I suspect (and this is made explicit by Midgley) that the motives of those who argue for the new paradigm approach are often to do with ensuring that pluralism does maintain its emancipatory potential. If it can be associated with the emancipatory paradigm then, necessarily, it will be able to sustain this emphasis. I have every sympathy with those who wish to maintain the emancipatory option by privileging radical paradigms, but this is not the role of pluralism or, in my view, of critical systems thinking. It is an advantage of critical systems thinking, and its use of pluralism, that it ensures protection of the emancipatory option without committing us to emancipatory practice (defined according to the predispositions of the radical paradigms) in every case. To repeat, pluralists must learn to live with and manage a degree of paradigm incommensurability.

Gregory (1992, 1996) has argued for "discordant pluralism" against the "complementarist" version of pluralism, based on Habermas' work, that she sees as dominating TSI. Discordant pluralism suggests that the differences between paradigms should be emphasized rather than "rationalized away":

> To an extent, the main difference between these two pluralist positions is captured in their titles: the complementarist wishes to use theoretical approaches in complementary ways,

> whilst the *discordant pluralist* would allow discordant theoretical approaches to *both challenge and supplement* one another (Gregory, 1996, p. 621).

I see discordant pluralism as a clarification and development of, rather than away, from TSI, and believe that it is the kind of pluralism that can deliver the greatest benefit to systems theorists and practitioners as part of critical systems thinking. In critical systems thinking a meta-methodology (call it "discordant pluralism" or TSI) is required which protects paradigm diversity and handles the relationships between the divergent paradigms. The meta-methodology needs to accept that paradigms are based upon incompatible philosophical assumptions and that they cannot, therefore, be integrated without something being lost. It has to manage the paradigms, not by aspiring to meta-paradigmatic status and allocating them to their respective tasks, but by mediating between the paradigms. Paradigms are allowed to confront one another on the basis of "reflective conversation" (Morgan, 1983, ed.). Critique is therefore managed *between* the paradigms and not controlled from above the paradigms. No paradigm is allowed to escape unquestioned because it is continually confronted by the alternative rationales offered by other paradigms. This argument has been developed by Jackson (1997, 1999) and by Flood and Romm (1996) in relation to their notion of "triple loop learning." Romm (1998) discusses the implications of it in a paper on nurturing the sustainability of organizations and environments:

> The paper was aimed at elucidating ways in which triple loop learning allows for attendance to alternative orientations to nurturing sustainability. Three discourses for addressing concerns with sustainability were explored [structuralist, interpretive and postmodern]. It was argued that the consciousness promoted ... is one which ongoingly develops a propensity for discursive accountability in the light of proffered alternatives. This means that it is attuned to hear news leveled from a range of alternative discourses and to learn from this process. Responsible engagement in situations bears the mark of a consciousness which has taken into account the news it receives, and uses this as a basis for informed understanding-and-action (p. 47).

On the basis of our exploration of pluralism at the levels of methods, methodologies and theoretical positions, we can be bold and provide a definition of the kind of pluralism that recent research in critical systems thinking has demonstrated systems thinking and practice requires. *Pluralism needs, as an approach to managing complex problems, to employ a meta-methodology to take maximum advantage of the benefits to be gained from using methodologies premised upon alternative paradigms together, and also encourages the combined use of diverse methods, models, tools and techniques, in a theoretically and methodologically informed way, to ensure maximum flexibility in an intervention.*

I started this chapter by recognizing that the contemporary history of critical systems thinking could be explored in various ways. I have chosen to tell its story with an emphasis upon the development of a "coherent pluralism." I end this section by alerting the reader to the fact that other accounts are available, although all focused on pluralism, in a useful collection of papers, edited by Mingers and Gill (1997), and called *Multimethodology – The Theory and Practice of Combining Management Science Methodologies.*

11.4. CRITICAL SYSTEMS PRACTICE - TSI REVISITED

We are able to turn now to what critical systems practice should look like if it is to adhere to contemporary critical systems thinking and, especially, the dictates of coherent pluralism. My starting point is that Flood and Jackson's ambitious project to create a meta-methodology, TSI (Flood and Jackson, 1991), was on the right lines, even if the particular theoretical prop provided for TSI's meta-methodology was questionable and even if the description of TSI, at that time, seemed to impose restrictions on flexible multi-method use. In proposing a new form of applying critical systems ideas, I am agnostic as to whether the result is called "critical systems practice" or TSI. I use both phrases here, as do Flood and Jackson in their reworked version of *Creative Problem Solving: Total Systems Intervention* (forthcoming).

The argument that TSI was along the right lines is supported by the fact that the basic philosophy, principles and phases of the meta-methodology (as outlined in Chapter 10) remain intact. The philosophy of critical systems thinking, underpinning TSI, can still be described in terms of commitments to "critical awareness" (including social awareness), "pluralism" (now at the theoretical, methodological and method levels), and "improvement" (now "local" rather than "universal"). The principles need revisiting, as we shall see, to emphasize that metaphor analysis is not the only way of generating "creativity", but otherwise have stood the test of time. The division of an intervention into a "creativity" phase, which surfaces information about the current problem situation; a "choice" phase, which considers alternative ways of addressing important issues; and an "implementation" phase, in which change processes are managed, is as good as anything else that has been suggested.

In considering what developments are now necessary in TSI, or critical systems practice, I shall first consider some of the specific changes suggested in the 1990s, to judge whether they have proved useful or not, before setting out a more fundamental reconstitution based on contemporary critical systems thinking and coherent pluralism.

Following the auto-critique of TSI, which appeared in the original book (Flood and Jackson, 1991), Flood, Jackson and Schecter (1992) followed up by outlining a research program which they felt would address outstanding problems. Four areas were identified as needing attention. The first required researchers to look out for other creativity enhancing devices that could complement or replace metaphor analysis during the creativity phase. The second asked them to consider whether the SOSM should remain the primary vehicle for the choice phase. The third asked, in effect, for a set of "generic" methodologies, clearly related to paradigms, to replace the "specific methodologies" TSI had inherited. The fourth required that more attention be given to the "process" of using TSI. It is arguable that the first two of these tasks were accomplished in the 1990s, that the third has had to wait until the more fundamental reconstitution attempted in this book, and that the fourth remains to be done.

Flood's 1995 version of TSI suggested changes in each of the three phases of the meta-methodology and added two other "modes" in which TSI could be used. At the creativity phase, he suggested supplementing metaphor analysis by allowing participants to create their own metaphors ("divergent" metaphorical examination); helping to enhance creativity through techniques such as brainstorming and idea-writing; and paying attention to the "ergonomics of reflection" – providing people with the time and space to be creative. These are useful additions. In the choice phase Flood argued that SOSM should be abandoned. In his view it was impracticable because it could not be explained to managers easily. To replace this, there should be an ontological commitment to "organizations as whole systems" consisting of interacting parts and with needs in the "four key dimensions" of organizational processes, design, culture and politics. Different systems methodologies can then be related to these needs. I would agree that the SOSM provides only one means of arriving at a "critical awareness" of the strengths and weaknesses of different systems methodologies. Replacing it with "organizations-as-systems" functionalism is, however, not a way forward. Tsagdis (1996) points out that it abandons the greatest strength of TSI – its ability to operationalize a process whereby different rationalities are brought to bear on a problem situation and continually kept under review. Better, as in my 1991 book, to supplement the SOSM by analyzing different methodologies using our knowledge of sociological paradigms, metaphors of organization, Habermas's three human interests, and the modernism – postmodernism debate. With regard to "implementation", Flood insists that the three phases themselves, as well as the whole meta-methodology, are recursive. Midgley (1997) tries to explain:

> So, for example, when we're being creative about the problem situation we should consider the need to be creative about our approach to the creativity task itself, choose an effective creativity-enhancing method, and then implement it (p. 270).

This, and other attempts, to "formalize" the various phases of TSI make the thing incomprehensible and unusable in practice.

The three modes in which TSI can be used (Flood, 1995) are the traditional "problem-solving" mode, the "critical review" mode and the "critical reflection" mode. The critical review mode is nothing new, being a restatement of the need for "critical awareness" about the methodologies employed by TSI. The critical reflection mode sees TSI used to evaluate its own interventions after the event in order to improve TSI itself. This seems to me to have potential, if properly specified, for ensuring that TSI fulfils its obligation to the research element of "action research."

Flood and Romm (1996) seek to give a postmodern twist to TSI, in the form of "diversity management", but in a manner which I find confusing and a language that I find off-putting and opaque. Nevertheless, the notion of setting up a "tension" between three discourses, the emphasis on local rather than universal improvement, and the concept of the "oblique" use of methods are all contributions to critical systems practice which, if not entirely original, receive their first treatment as an integrated set of ideas in this volume.

I can now address some further questions about how critical systems practice should be formulated and operationalized in order to reveal its full potential. We are attempting a more fundamental revision of TSI based upon the contemporary critical systems thinking, embedding coherent pluralism, that was set out earlier in the chapter. This can best be done if we consider in turn the level of methods, models and techniques, the level of methodology and the level of meta-methodology.

At the level of methods, models and techniques, it was argued that, in order to maintain the necessary flexibility, a wide variety of such tools should be made available, from whatever source, to be employed in combination, as appropriate, during each intervention or stage of an intervention. Methodologies can and should be "decomposed" if this seems appropriate. Systems practitioners must be allowed the greatest freedom possible to tailor their use of tools to the complexities of the problem situation they are seeking to intervene in and the exigencies of that situation as it changes. At any moment during an intervention, however, it must be possible to reflect upon and adjust, as required, the particular rationale the tools are being used to serve. They should be capable of being linked to a particular methodology and paradigm. The maintenance of the link between this broad notion of methodology and the use of tools, allows us to learn about the tools. The efficiency and effectiveness of methods, models and techniques for servicing particular rationales can be tested over time. It may be that a system dynamics model does not function well to support interpretive intervention but this will not be ruled out in advance.

The freedom to use the variety of methods, models and techniques in a responsive fashion should, in my view, make critical systems practice (or TSI) more attractive to practitioners. It is for them to decide whether they wish to learn more about these tools by reflecting on their links to methodologies, or about methodologies by reflecting on their links to theory. The argument I now pursue, for the necessity of both these things, is for the benefit of researchers rather than consultants. Researchers, equipped with the theoretical armory I shall outline, will be in a position to learn much from observing the practice of consultants. They will also, with due ethical care, be able to set up "experiments", with tools and methodologies, which are guided by a desire to develop the discipline rather than by a purely pragmatic interest.

I have reached the level of the methodologies which provide principles for the use of different methods, models and techniques. These, as has been argued, must closely reflect different paradigms and are expected to deliver, in the service of pluralism, the benefits inherent in a variety of paradigmatic standpoints. If this theoretical link back to paradigms can be made explicit it will be possible to protect paradigm diversity, as I have argued is necessary, and to ensure emancipatory concerns are always kept on the agenda. It also makes it possible to do research by allowing us to operationalize better the hypotheses of particular paradigms and test the conclusions of these paradigms in real-world interventions. Theoretically informed methodologies are essential for ensuring a healthy link between theory and practice in critical systems thinking.

Following the important distinction made by Checkland and Scholes (1990), methodologies can be used to actually steer the intervention (Mode 1) or to reflect on the normal vicissitudes of managerial decision-making (Mode 2). For either of these things to occur, attention had to be given to specifying the exact nature of generic methodologies representing the functionalist, interpretive, emancipatory and postmodern paradigms, which have all had some impact on critical systems practice. I would want to claim it as one of the achievements of this book that such generic methodologies have been established and that critical systems practice is no longer dependent on the specific methodologies it inherited (see Chapters 6-9). This makes it possible to keep an open mind on the usefulness of the whole set of available methods, models and techniques, and to research what they might be capable of delivering, given sufficient methodological watchfulness, for each paradigm. Further work is necessary to explore whether other paradigmatic positions exist which can usefully be given consideration; to clarify further the generic methodologies serving each paradigm; and to evaluate the success of the methodologies in transferring the propositions of the different paradigms into practice and allowing learning from practice which leads to adjustments in the paradigms.

At the meta-methodological level, critical systems practice requires the kind of meta-methodology which encourages and protects paradigm diversity and handles the relationships between the methodologies, based on alternative paradigms, in order to address the complexity and heterogeneity of problem situations at all stages of an intervention. As we saw in a previous section, the meta-methodology must accept that the paradigms are incompatible and cannot be integrated without much being lost. It has to manage the paradigms not by aspiring to meta-paradigmatic status but by encouraging critique between the paradigms. No paradigm is allowed to escape unquestioned because it is continually confronted by the alternative rationales offered by other paradigms. I am aware, of course, that by reducing postmodernism to just another paradigm, to be incorporated and used by TSI, I shall be accused of propounding a horribly totalizing vision. However, the meta-methodology that TSI now embraces, a critique between the paradigms, seems to me to avoid any dangerous implications. Critique between the paradigms is the sort of game postmodernists can join with gusto. There is need, of course, for further research on how conversation between paradigms can best be orchestrated.

Although the critical systems practice, outlined above, is still in a preliminary form, it is necessary to say something about the guidelines that might be offered for detailed operationalization of the approach. Here I would like to draw attention to three, hopefully helpful notions. First there is the conception of "dominant" and "dependent" methodologies that was present in the original TSI; second is the possibility of Mode 1 and Mode 2 uses of

TSI (analogous to Checkland's Mode 1 and Mode 2 SSM); and third is the attention given to other aspects of pluralism by Taket and White.

In the original version of TSI (Flood and Jackson, 1991), there exists the idea (which can vaguely be traced back to Althusser) that the difficulties associated with multi-paradigm practice can be managed if an initial choice of "dominant" methodology is made, to run the intervention, with "dependent" methodologies, reflecting alternative paradigms, in the background. The relationship between dominant and dependent methodologies can then change as the intervention proceeds in order to maintain flexibility at the methodology level to set alongside the flexibility we have sought at the level of methods, models and tools. This remains, for me, an extremely powerful idea because it allows the intervention to proceed in a theoretically informed way (making research possible), and with less confusion to the participants, while protecting, as far as is feasible, paradigm diversity. There remain, of course, thorny questions about the initial choice of dominant methodology and how to effect changes in status between methodologies once an intervention has started.

Let us take, as an example, the case where the interpretive methodology is taken as initially dominant. Considering this in terms of the phases of TSI, creativity will be conducted on the basis of open discussion employing such techniques as "rich pictures." If models are introduced, at the choice phase, they will be acting as "hermeneutic enablers" to help structure debate about particular issues, rather than being taken as representations of the real-world. If ethical issues arise during implementation they will be for discussion among those involved, not insisted upon as moral imperatives that cannot be flouted. Of course there will be occasions when the models introduced seem to "capture" so well the logic of the situation and its problems that a shift to a functionalist position will seem justifiable; the models will be taken as representations of reality and a shift made which establishes a functionalist methodology as dominant. Similarly, if paradigm diversity is worth a candle, there will be occasions when the ethics of the analyst or relevant stakeholders will be so offended that the shift to an emancipatory rationale becomes clearly necessary. It is the language of moral imperatives that is then talked, not the "business ethics" of making managers more aware. And, finally, it might well be necessary, in the interests of subverting some baneful authority and introducing fun into the intervention, at some stage to adopt a postmodern orientation.

Making explicit the rationality underpinning the methodology with which we are operating, and being ready to switch rationality and methodology, makes the initial choice of "dominant" approach less committing. That said, I can perhaps admit that I find it most comfortable to begin with the interpretive approach as dominant. Embracing an interpretive rather than a functionalist logic, as initially dominant, is attractive because it assumes open discussion and suggests we have the freedom to design our own futures. There are however dangers, and embracing an interpretive rather than an emancipatory logic, as initially dominant, is more difficult to justify. Enough horrors occur in organizations, in our own societies, and at the world level, to give anyone pause. The emancipatory option must remain high on the agenda. As Churchman (1970) argued, and this has a postmodern flavor, the professional management scientist needs to consider whether it is desirable to help certain organizations to commit suicide.

Checkland's notion of Mode 1 and Mode 2 uses of soft systems methodology (see Chapter 7) can, with benefit, be transferred to help us consider how TSI might be employed. An academic, imbued with TSI and in the position to set up a study, is likely to start from the meta-methodological level, choose dominant and dependent methodologies, and operate with a range of methods and models according to the logic of the methodology dominant at a particular time. This allows her, according to her inclinations, to research the process of critique between paradigms, the theoretical assumptions of the paradigms, the robustness of the methodological rules, and the usefulness of certain models or techniques for serving particular purposes. This would be the most formal Mode 1 use of TSI, where the meta-methodology guided the intervention. A TSI–aware manager or management consultant, an academic studying a change process but not leading it, or simply an academic more interested in the "area of application", than the "framework of ideas" or "methodology", would, on the other hand, be more likely to use TSI in the Mode 2 manner. The intervention will be dominated by the pressure and concerns of the immediate organizational situation. The participants will employ whatever methods, tools and techniques happen to come readily to hand. However, the meta-methodology might be used, during the course of the intervention, to help those involved reflect on what was happening and perhaps open up new possibilities. TSI could also be used, after the event, to analyze what had occurred and draw research lessons from the intervention. Most actual applications, as we shall see in the next chapter, lie somewhere between the extremes of Mode 1 and Mode 2.

Third, it is worth reminding the reader of two other forms of "pluralism" which have not been given much attention, in critical systems practice, but which have now been brought to the fore by Taket and White (2000) using their postmodern lenses. These are, as you might recall from Chapter 9, pluralism "in the modes of representation employed" and pluralism "in the facilitation process." TSI is happy to embrace both these additional aspects of pluralism.

11.5. CONSTITUTIVE RULES FOR CRITICAL SYSTEMS PRACTICE

Before considering what more needs to be done to improve TSI, and passing on to the illustrative case studies in the next chapter, we can tentatively, see Table 11.2, set out some constitutive rules for guiding and identifying critical systems practice. These will be somewhat different in form to those presented at the end of each chapter in Part II, because of the need to draw attention to the meta-methodological as well as the methodological level.

11.6. CONCLUSION AND WHAT MORE NEEDS TO BE DONE?

In Chapter 10, I outlined some of the uses to which the original version of TSI was put. In later books (e.g. Jackson, 1991; Flood, 1995) more examples have been provided of TSI coordinating interventions and enabling learning to take place. These interventions have been in many types of organization; big and small, cooperative, voluntary, public and private, as well as in multi-agency situations. Recently, there has been considerable interest in the use of TSI to guide information systems development (e.g. Jackson, 1996; Warren and Adman, 1999; Clarke and Lehaney, 2000).

Today there are critical systems practitioners all over the world - in Australia, New Zealand, Japan, India, China, the Middle-East, South Africa, Tanzania, Mexico, Venezuela, Colombia, etc., as well as in Europe and the United States. The case of China is particularly interesting because Gu and Zhu (2000) argue that they have discovered an indigenous multimethodology approach which can be compared to TSI. The many articles published by these critical systems practitioners can be found in the journals *Systems Research and Behavioral Science* (Wiley) and *Systems Practice and Action Research* (Kluwer/Plenum). Particular attention is being given to the use of critical systems ideas in creativity management, organizational design, organizational learning, evaluation, sustainability, social change and, as noted, information systems design.

Table 11.2. Constitutive rules for critical systems practice

1. A critical systems meta-methodology is a structured way of thinking which understands and respects the uniqueness of the functionalist, interpretive, emancipatory and postmodern theoretical rationales, and draws upon them to improve real-world problem situations.

2. A critical systems meta-methodology makes use of a variety of creativity enhancing methods and techniques to examine the problem situation while ensuring, minimally, that it is viewed from the functionalist, interpretive, emancipatory and postmodern perspectives.

3. A critical systems meta-methodology uses generic systems methodologies, which can be clearly related back to the four theoretical rationales, as the basis for its intervention strategy – often employing the tactic of naming one methodological approach as dominant and others as dependent, with the possibility of this relationship changing during the course of the intervention.

4. The claim to be using a generic systems methodology, according to the particular theoretical rationale it is designed to serve, must be justified according to the principles and guidelines established for the use of each generic systems methodology.

5. The generic systems methodologies called for use in critical systems practice will themselves frequently employ methods, models, tools and techniques which also draw upon systems ideas.

6. The choice of generic systems methodologies and of systems methods, models, tools and techniques will, in part, rest upon an appreciation of their different strengths and weaknesses as discovered during action research

7. In order to ensure responsiveness to the complexity and heterogeneity of the problem situation addressed, attention must be paid to ensuring a pluralism of "clients", theoretical and methodological pluralism, pluralism in the modes of representation employed, and pluralism in the facilitation process.

8. Since a critical systems meta-methodology, and the generic systems methodologies it employs, can be used in different ways in different situations , and interpreted differently by different users, each use should exhibit conscious thought about how to adapt to the particular circumstances.

9. Each use of a critical systems meta-methodology, and the generic systems methodologies it employs, should yield research findings as well as improving the real-world problem situation. These research findings may relate to the relationship between different theoretical rationales, to the theoretical rationales underlying any generic systems methodology used, to the generic systems methodologies themselves and how to use them, to the methods, models, tools and techniques employed, to the real-world problem situation investigated or to all of these.

All this represents a good start for critical systems thinking but much remains to be done. In this chapter I have begun to sketch out a research program which will make the further development of critical systems thinking and practice possible. This includes testing the diversity of methods, models, tools and techniques available, from the systems approach and management science generally, in the service of different rationalities; clarifying the constitutive rules for functionalist, interpretive, emancipatory and postmodern forms of intervention; and learning how to facilitate reflective conversation at the meta-methodological level. Others would insist, and I would agree, that more needs to be said to clarify the process of using TSI, and about the role of the "agent" and the ethical commitments that she brings to the intervention.

Another vital element is the establishment of more educational and training programs that embrace the challenges of critical systems thinking and practice. In this way the "cognitive" and "cultural" constraints preventing adoption of coherent pluralism by individuals, and the systems community more generally, can be overcome. I leave the last word on this to Richard Bawden (1995), who has done perhaps more than anyone to suggest what a "critical learning system" would need to be like in order to produce "systemic individuals:

> The complication ... lies in the fact that to understand the richness of the metaphor of the community as a learning system demands an acceptance of what we can call a systems (or systemic) paradigm. Indeed it demands *a priori* that (a) we accept that we each 'use' particular paradigms to make sense of the world around us; (b) we are able to recognize the nature of those prefered paradigms; (c) that we can recognize and embrace other paradigms in addition to our prefered ones; and (d) that we are especially able to embrace a *systemic* paradigm so that we can make sense of (and make use of) the learning systems metaphor to guide the processes of community development (p. 27).

12

CRITICAL SYSTEMS PRACTICE: THREE ILLUSTRATIVE CASE STUDIES

12.1. INTRODUCTION

In the last chapter I began to sketch out a research program that should make possible the continued development and refinement of critical systems thinking and practice. So far it may appear that the main driver of this research program is theory - but this is, in fact, far from the truth. Critical systems thinking has benefited at least as much from its involvement in practice. In future the continued articulation, operationalizing and reflection upon the theory-practice link, which this book hopes to promote, will be crucial if critical systems thinking is to realize its potential. And one important test of the value of the research program will be its ability to produce results which make a difference in practice. The difference we are concerned about should not, of course, just be for consultants, as implied in Ormerod's (1997b) "transformation competence" approach to multi-methodology. The whole bias of critical systems thinking should ensure that other agents, and affected people, with less of a managerial concern, will be included as well.

In this chapter I consider three illustrative examples of the use of critical systems thinking which, I believe, show the theory-practice link working well and have, therefore, had an impact upon the development and refinement of the critical systems approach. These case studies are located in a large voluntary sector organization, West Newton Council for Voluntary Service; a police district, North Yorkshire Police; and in an engineering company, Kingston Turbines PLC. The range of settings is another factor that influenced the choice of the examples. In each case there is a brief introduction to the organization, discussion of the problem situation and what was done, and theoretical reflection on the example and how it illustrates critical systems practice.

12.2. WEST NEWTON COUNCIL FOR VOLUNTARY SERVICE

12.2.1. The Organization

This study, which is described more fully in Flood and Jackson (1991), was undertaken in a large Council for Voluntary Service (CVS). The contribution of Mary Ashton, as student researcher, was crucial to the success of the project.

Councils for Voluntary Service act as umbrella organizations for the wide variety of other voluntary bodies they have in their membership. They are local development agencies that are non-profit making and non-governmental. There are about 200 such Councils for Voluntary Service in England and Wales. Councils for Voluntary Service aim to promote more and better voluntary action in their areas. West Newton is a large Council for Voluntary Service (CVS); it was founded in 1980 and grew rapidly in size and influence. By the time of the study it had more than 300 voluntary and community organizations under its umbrella and employed around 80 staff.

West Newton CVS had a number of problems, but the one on which the project came to focus concerned certain difficulties faced by its Executive Committee. This committee was experiencing problems trying to oversee and control what was a rapidly expanding organization in a turbulent environment. It continued to operate as it did when the CVS was first founded, meeting every six weeks for a programmed two hours. The committee did not possess the flexibility of means to respond to the needs of the CVS West Newton had become, and was widely perceived to be ineffective.

The Executive Committee was subordinate to a Council in the CVS hierarchy. The Council consisted mainly of representatives of member organizations and met once a year at the Annual General Meeting of the CVS. The Executive was democratically elected by

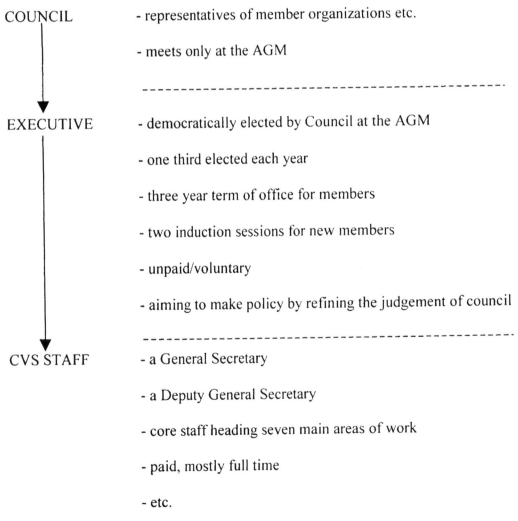

COUNCIL   - representatives of member organizations etc.

                      - meets only at the AGM

EXECUTIVE   - democratically elected by Council at the AGM

                      - one third elected each year

                      - three year term of office for members

                      - two induction sessions for new members

                      - unpaid/voluntary

                      - aiming to make policy by refining the judgement of council

                      ----

CVS STAFF   - a General Secretary

                      - a Deputy General Secretary

                      - core staff heading seven main areas of work

                      - paid, mostly full time

                      - etc.

Figure 12.1. The structure of West Newton Council for Voluntary Service (reproduced from Flood and Jackson, 1991, p. 226)

Council at the Annual General Meeting. Each member of the Executive was elected for a three-year term and one-third of the members were elected each year. Two induction sessions were held for new Executive members. Executive Committee members were, of course, unpaid. The Executive's job was to make policy by representing and refining the broad judgement of the Council and translating this into specific guidelines for action by the CVS. These relationships are shown in Figure 12.1.

The specific structure of the Executive is shown in Figure 12.2. The Executive consisted of a Chair, Vice-Chair, Treasurer, 18 other representatives elected by Council and four co-opted members (a City Councilor, a County Councilor and two direct from Council). The General Secretary of the CVS was minutes secretary and, though he had no voting powers, he exercised a strong influence through his knowledge (as the senior full-time person on the executive) and power of recommendation. Other CVS staff could attend but, again, had no voting rights.

The Executive was supported in its work by a Finance Committee. This had certain delegated powers, also met once every six weeks and provided reports and recommendations for the Executive to consider. It was serviced by the Deputy General Secretary of the CVS, and was made up of five Executive representatives and a voting staff representative. Other *ad hoc* groups were occasionally set up by the Executive to oversee and report on particular developments.

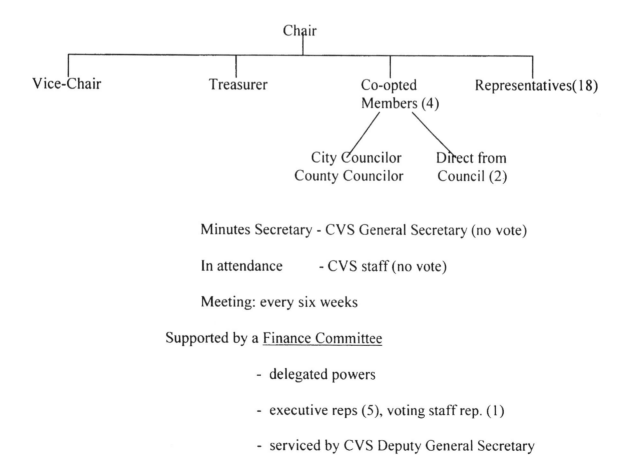

Figure 12.2. The structure of West Newton Executive Committee (reproduced from Flood and Jackson, 1991, p. 227)

Items found their way on to the agenda of Executive Committee meetings from a variety of places. They could emerge from the General Secretary, from the Finance Committee, the *ad hoc* groups, from core-staff members heading areas of work, or simply as Executive submissions (especially from the Chair and Executive members on outside committees). There was some filtering of the items for discussion, usually by the General Secretary, but nevertheless the agenda was severely overloaded. Meetings had become lengthy and acrimonious. It was felt, by both Executive and staff, that the Committee was not providing the direction required. Two-thirds of the issues that came up for discussion concerned "management" rather than the policy matters on which the Executive was supposed to concentrate.

After Executive meetings, minutes would be circulated to all section heads for discussion. The General Secretary and Deputy General Secretary were responsible for monitoring the execution of policy as decided at the meetings.

12.2.2. The Problem Situation and What Was Done

The project began with the gathering of information about the Executive Committee, its structure and role, and the views held of it by both Executive Committee members themselves and the CVS staff. This "creativity" stage of the intervention consisted of lengthy interviews carried out with eight key Executive members and nine staff. Each of these was followed up with a second interview later in the study, with a check made that the interviewer had fully grasped the subject's meaning. The "cognitive mapping" technique developed by Eden, as part of his SODA approach (see Chapter 7), was employed for this purpose. An example of part of one of the cognitive maps is provided as Figure 12.3. Anonymous questionnaires were sent to all other Executive members and to other staff who had recently attended Executive meetings (35 questionnaires in all).

Summarizing massively, the views of Executive members divided into those with an "efficiency orientation" and those with a "suspicion orientation." The efficiency oriented were frustrated by the inability of the Executive to get important business done. They felt that agendas were too lengthy and not prioritised. They wanted each item to come with a clear recommendation. Meetings became bogged down, they thought, because of the massive overload of work, the chronic shortage of time for discussion, and because people attended "cold" without digesting the information. Worse, there was poor committee discipline, with sidetracking and standing orders not enforced. The efficiency orientated felt that the Executive was not concentrating enough on policy. It was wasting time on management issues which the staff should take care of. Unfortunately, some members did not trust the key staff enough to "keep their noses out" of management issues.

The suspicion oriented were generally distrustful of key figures on the Executive and of the Executive's role. They wanted to promote more debate to find out what was going on. They felt that key officers had too much power and that agenda filtering was preventing important issues reaching the Executive. Executive meetings were too formal and hierarchical and this suppressed participation and creativity from ordinary members. The suspicion oriented wanted to know more about what was actually going on in the CVS.

Staff views could also be characterized as falling into two broad types. One group saw Executive shortcomings as having developed as a natural result of the rapid growth in activities of the CVS. They felt that the CVS had grown too rapidly and it was now time to apply the brakes. The Executive was overloaded and could not give enough consideration to staff views. Further, because of bad filtering, staff views did not get through to the Executive. For these reasons it was not surprising if some Executive members felt out of

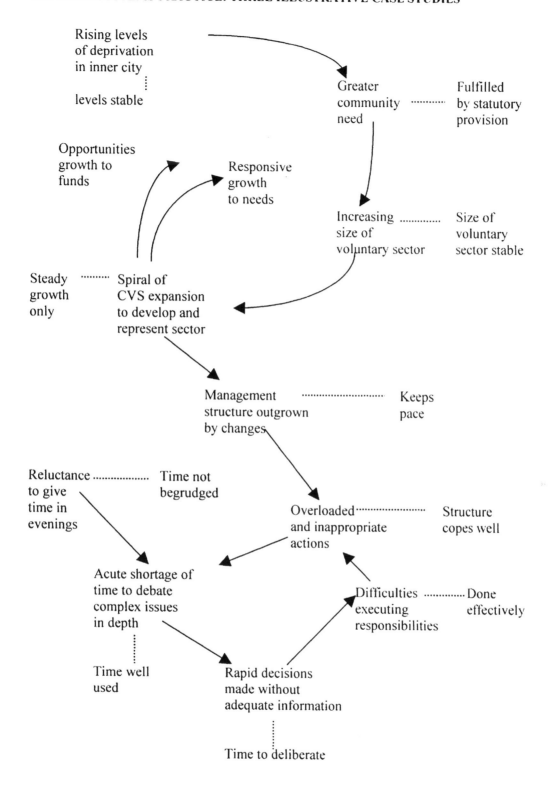

Figure 12.3. Example cognitive map (adapted from Ashton, 1987)

touch. There was a need for more contact between Executive and staff. This could provide learning for the Executive and support for the staff. The second group was much more critical of the Executive and saw its shortcomings as self-inflicted. They thought that the Executive had not adapted to change and was, therefore, a stumbling block to getting things done. It was largely cut off from the reality of CVS work on the ground. More contact with staff was needed to "wake up" Executive members.

From the interviews, cognitive maps and other gathering of information, it seemed that the following were very significant issues that had to be addressed:

- Providing more time for the Executive committee to deal with policy issues
- Increasing the professionalism of the committee's handling of management issues
- Improving the handling of committee business
- Generating mutual respect between committee members and staff
- Making the committee more aware of staff work
- Increasing committee contact with staff
- Increasing staff confidence in the committee

We now entered the "choice" phase of the study. Which systems methodologies, methods, models, etc., would allow West Newton CVS to best manage the problems it faced? The SOSM provided the basis for this. It was easy to see that West Newton had become a "complex" organization which was having difficulty trying to grow at the same time as adapt in a highly turbulent environment. This emphasis on complexity initially drew us toward Beer's VSM. The Executive of the CVS could be seen as the brain of an organism that did not prossess enough requisite variety to control the system is was supposed to direct and manage. It had somehow to be equipped with the various functions of management exhibited by Beer's VSM. As we shall see, this proved a particularly useful metaphor.

We were, however, "critically aware" of the weaknesses of the VSM. Presenting a report based upon viable systems diagnosis might have provided some useful guidelines on how to deal with the structural problems of the Executive Committee, but it would have ignored other very important aspects of the problem context. For the CVS was nothing if not a pluralistic "coalition" of different groups, all with somewhat different interests and ways of perceiving the situation. A way had to be found to generate a consensus for change among the elements of this coalition. What was surely needed was a change in the culture of the organization, so that it was ready to accept change and particularly to rethink the way the Executive functioned. If these matters were not tackled then any "rationalistic" report might fail to achieve improvements because of the opposition it generated or because it failed to gain the commitment and enthusiasm of the most involved agents. There had, in fact, been previous internally generated suggestions for improving the performance of the Executive. These were sound enough and we were unlikely, as outsiders, to discover any magical solutions that had not occurred to those already living in the situation.

The role of the project, therefore, had to be seen as generating a "culture" for change in the organization; and change which did not offend any of the groups in the "coalition." At the same time, we felt, the eventual design had to meet cybernetic criteria of viability. The Executive had to become an effective "brain." This led to the choice of SSM as the dominant methodology. SSM rests upon "complex-pluralist" assumptions and articulates particularly well the concerns of the culture and coalition metaphors in its procedures. There was also likely to be a role for VSD as a supporting methodology, backing up SSM in dealing with complexity because of its uniquely explicit understanding of brain-related issues (learning, forward thinking, etc.).

Finally, it seemed as well to be aware of the significant political aspects to the problem context. These, at times, threatened to take the situation beyond the pluralistic towards the conflict and coercion end of the "participants" dimension of the SOSM. There was conflict between some on the Executive and some staff, and on the Executive between those happy to leave responsibility for "running the show" to the staff and those who tended to suspect the motives of the key officers. The General Secretary's position as an important "broker" between Executive Committee and staff could clearly be threatened by any suggested redesign of the Executive. Particular attention had to be paid to the most influential individuals associated with the various interest groups in order to gain their support and trust. However, in this case, we thought, the political aspect could be handled informally within the bounds of SSM.

Embarking on the "intervention" phase, using SSM, the first task was to build a "rich picture" of the problem situation. In this case it was deemed sufficient to work with the verbal rich picture assembled during the interviews and the cognitive mapping. The next step, therefore, was to consider all this information and to draw from it some insightful ways of looking at the work of the Executive Committee and the problems that it faced. Six "relevant systems" were in fact proposed:

(a) A *policy processing* system: handling policy so that other bodies can execute or be guided by it

(b) A *need-seeking and idea-generating* system: helping the organization to seek and develop new initiatives

(c) A *representation* system: expanding the voluntary sector's voice on other crucial decision-making bodies

(d) A *monitoring and controlling* system: embracing the classical role of a management committee

(e) An *accountability* system: ensuring that the organization is seen to conduct its affairs competently in the eyes of those to whom it is accountable

(f) A *staff support* system: practically demonstrating support towards those appointed to manage the organization

During the course of the work on relevant systems, it occurred to the analysts that there were links between what was emerging and the roles any management or "meta-system" would have to perform in seeking to control a highly complex set of operations. In other words, we were thinking in "cybernetic" terms. It was decided to make this explicit and to see whether our relevant systems "covered the ground" in terms of the functions a meta-system has to fulfill. This was done by locating the function of each relevant system on Beer's VSM. Relevant system (a), *policy processing*, was clearly at System 5 level; relevant systems (b) and (c), *need-seeking* and *representation*, were at System 4 level. Relevant systems (d) and (e), *monitoring and controlling* and *accountability*, were System 3 and System 3* audit functions, respectively; while relevant system (f) *staff support*, operated at the System 3 and System 1 levels. This information is captured in Figure 12.4.

The fact that our choice of relevant systems had this additional cybernetic legitimacy gave us confidence. We were clearly thinking along the right lines if we wanted to provide the Executive with the "requisite variety" to manage the organization. Throughout the study we continued to employ this cybernetic rationality in a subordinate role, thinking about what functions had to be carried out in West Newton CVS. From the outside, indeed, it might look as though we could have taken a short cut through all the information gathering, inter-

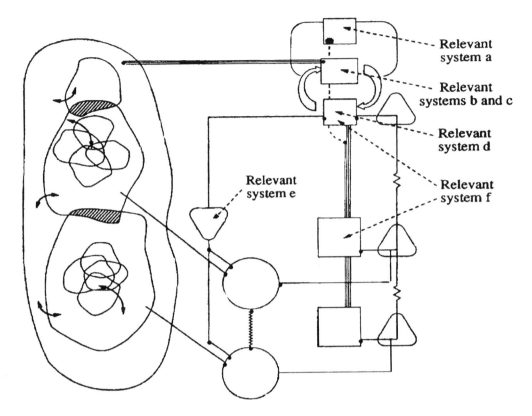

Figure12.4. The six relevant systems related to functions in Beer's Viable System Model for the Council for Voluntary Service example (reproduced from Flood and Jackson, 1991, p. 232)

views and questionnaire survey, by using Beer's VSM directly to pin-point cybernetic faults. This, though, would have been a mistake. We had to engender change in the culture of the organization to create a momentum for "redesign", and we had to hold together the various factions in the coalition, securing the support of each for the proposals. At the same time we had to sidestep and manage the political problems. Only constant working with the people in the organization, so that they were fully involved in generating proposals and came to own the suggested solutions, could address these issues. SSM had to remain dominant if anything was going to change in West Newton CVS. At no time was the "brain" driven logic allowed to take over from the "culture" and "coalition" emphasis supplied by SSM.

A quick preliminary pass through the methodology revealed that four of the six relevant systems were deemed most significant to the main area of concern - the ability of the Executive to control the organization. According to the requirements of SSM these four were then built into "root definitions", and "conceptual models." By way of example, the root definition and CATWOE check for relevant system (a), and the conceptual model derived from this root definition, is supplied as Figure 12.5.

The implications of the four root definitions and conceptual models were then fully discussed with members of the Executive Committee and the staff. Using a set of guiding questions, a comparison was drawn up between the conceptual models and the "real world situation" as expressed in the rich picture. Those interviewed were asked whether the activities in the conceptual models existed in the "real world" or not; if they did exist, "How are they done at present and are they done well?"; and if they did not exist or were done badly, "Are they feasible and how might they be carried out effectively in the 'real world' situation of West Newton CVS?" From the comparisons, an agenda for further and wider

Root Definition (a): A Policy Processing System

"A West Newton CVS owned policy processing system which aims to represent the broad judgment of the Council and is thus able to create, develop and put into effect execution of CVS policy on its behalf; within the constraints of time and resources available to Executive Committee members and the organization."

C = CVS employees, the Council
A = The Executive Committee
T =

| Broad judgement of the Council | → | Created, developed and "put into effect" CVS policy |

W = The Executive Committee carries the ultimate responsibility for committing the CVS to a particular course of action
O = West Newton CVS, that is, The Council (the Membership)
E = Time and resources available to the Executive Committee members and the organization

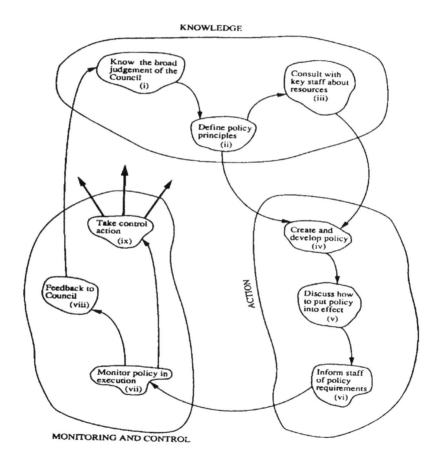

FIGURE 12.5. Conceptual model of the policy processing system (RDa) for the Council for Voluntary Service example (reproduced from Flood and Jackson, 1991, p. 233)

debate was drawn up. By way of example, I can set out the points that emerged from conceptual model (a), *policy processing*:

- the need for more time for the Executive to consider major policy issues and to review implementation

- the need for a better way of consulting core-staff about basic matters of policy implementation
- the need for a sub-structure within which the Executive could improve its knowledge and understanding of the organization they make policy for
- requirements for a method by which the Executive could more closely monitor the execution of that policy and be aware of any necessary control action

On the basis of the discussions that took place around the agenda generated by all four conceptual models, we began to think about possible changes which we felt would help to alleviate the difficulties. Most of the proposals came from suggestions made by various CVS officers in discussion with us. We would then bring these up in meetings with other personnel to gauge their reaction. This was particularly the case with specific suggestions for change, such as one controversial idea to establish a "management committee" to aid the Executive. We were acting as "brokers" between the interested parties, and moving forward only with ideas which seemed to attract general assent or, at least, failed to provoke severe disagreement. The political situation made it simply impossible to bring all the significant actors together, at one time and place, to hammer out an agreed set of proposals. The likelihood of such a meeting breaking up in disarray, and taking the proposals down with it, was too great. We also had our own "expert-driven" cybernetic agenda which contained a set of minimum specifications we felt any changes should meet in order to make the organization "viable." Top of this agenda was to see management issues handled "lower down", thus reducing the "variety" flooding up to the Executive and exhausting its capacity to handle significant policy issues.

Eventually, through a long drawn out and time-consuming process of going back and forth between important Executive members and staff, and constantly modifying the recommendations, we arrived at proposals we believed had general support, and to some degree, met the cybernetic criteria. We were rewarded for this hard work when the recommendations were presented at an Executive meeting. The significant actors had come to own them as their own, and there was no opposition to the setting up of a sub-committee charged to oversee their implementation. The recommendations are set out in detail in Flood and Jackson (1991). They included moving management and auditing tasks down to specialist committees, thus leaving time for policy discussion at the Executive Committee meetings; setting up Committee "support groups" for CVS staff in important areas of work; and providing induction and training sessions for new Executive Committee members. The operating procedures of the CVS Executive Committee were substantially restructured with the help of these recommendations.

12.2.3. Theoretical Reflections

The West Newton CVS intervention, conducted in 1987, used the SOSM as the primary means of operationalizing critical systems thinking. It occurred just before TSI was put into final form although it exhibits several TSI features and has been employed as an example of the TSI meta-methodology in practice (Jackson, 1991; Flood and Jackson, 1991). The "creativity" phase used interviewing and cognitive mapping as its main instruments. The metaphor analysis of TSI had not yet been developed. Looking back later, however (Jackson, 1991), it is clear that we were initially attracted to the "organism" and "brain" metaphors, but eventually allowed the "culture" and "politics" metaphors the primary influence. At the "choice" stage, governed by the SOSM, SSM was taken as the dominant methodology and this remained the case throughout. The VSM, extracted from the organizational cybernetic approach, did however play a strong supporting role. We also had to reflect constantly on the complicated politics of the problem situation, although it did not become necessary to adopt a systems methodology specifically to address these issues. Summarizing, in 1991, I argued that:

> The West Newton case study demonstrates most of the facets of critical systems thinking and practice. It was conducted with constant critical reflection upon the relative strengths and weaknesses of the systems tools being used and with full attention given to the social consequences of their use. Different systems approaches were employed in a complementarist manner at both the theoretical and methodological levels. The project was emancipatory in the outward sense that it was assisting an organization committed to helping the most disadvantaged members of the community (p. 234).

A more detailed examination of the case study can now be achieved by viewing it in the light of our conclusions about contemporary critical systems practice set out in the previous chapter. For the most part the intervention can be seen as taking a Mode 1 form, with the SOSM and early thoughts about TSI running the show. However, later analysis of the case was useful in the development of TSI and took a Mode 2 form.

Let us now proceed to do a comparison with the "Constitutive rules for critical systems practice" outlined in Table 11.2.

1. As the rules require, attention was given to a variety of theoretical rationales and what they could bring to the problem situation.

2. The creativity stage was underdeveloped because of a lack of "metaphor" analysis. Nevertheless functionalist, interpretive and, "political" aspects of the problem situation were surfaced and addressed in the study.

3. It was not possible to use generic systems methodologies as part of a meta-methodological approach because they had not yet been developed. SSM "stood in" for a generic interpretive methodology and was named as the dominant methodology. The intervention started on the basis of the interpretive rationale and this continued to be employed throughout the intervention.

4. No principles or guidelines had, at the time, been developed for generic systems methodologies. Nevertheless, SSM is true to the guidelines that have since been produced, and carried the interpretive rationale through the study.

5. The SOSM and TSI, as early examples of multi-methodology approaches, have often been regarded as inflexible because they were based on "methodology selection" and "whole methodology management" respectively. This case study demonstrates that, in practice, they were used more flexibly than their theoretical expression might lead us to believe is possible. In West Newton CVS different methodologies were used together in the same intervention and "cognitive mapping" and the "viable system model" were extracted from their usual host methodologies and employed as part of other approaches – in the case of the VSM in an "imperialist" manner by SSM.

6. There was reflection on the appropriateness of different systems methodologies and methods given what was known about their particular strengths and weaknesses.

7. Pluralism of "clients" and of methodologies and "methods" was recognized, but little attention was given to pluralism in "modes of representation" and "facilitation."

8. Both the meta-methodology (SOSM) and the methodology used (SSM) were adapted to the particular circumstances.

9. As well as improving the real world problem situation, the intervention generated a number of research findings. Consideration of how to handle the relationship between different theoretical rationales provoked more work which, in time, produced TSI. There was learning about the dominant methodology, SSM; particularly of the need for an early appreciation of the politics of the problem situation and how they might constrain its use. The "imperialist" use of SSM was explored and gave rise to thoughts of generic systems methodologies. New ideas were put forward on how to use cognitive mapping - one of the systems methods employed. A much richer appreciation of the problem situation and the possibilities for change inherent in it were gained. And forgive me if I point to one conclusion, provided by the student-researcher, which points in a postmodern direction:

> Culturally feasible change can very rarely in the 'real world' be based on *true* consensus. It is more often the product of a whole hearted attempt by the consultant to reach a state of heroic compromise with those concerned (Ashton, 1987, p.178).

12.3. NORTH YORKSHIRE POLICE

12.3.1. The Organization

This project, set in the North Yorkshire Police Force, used critical systems thinking to guide information systems development. It was carried out by a Chief Inspector, Steve Green, under my supervision. The original reporting on the project is available to interested readers (Green, 1991) and the case has also been written up as an account of the use of the TSI meta-methodology (Green, 1992). The fullest version (apart from the original reporting) is in Jackson (1996) and I shall follow that version closely in what follows.

North Yorkshire Police is, in terms of geographical area, the largest English, single county force and extends over approximately 3200 square miles. It covers a largely rural area and includes, as part of its territory, the beautiful area of the North Yorkshire Moors shown in the popular television series *Heartbeat* - a series which captures, apparently, what policing was like in the area in the 1960s. Also in its boundaries are urban settlements such as York and Scarborough. In 1991 North Yorkshire Police (NYP) employed some 1400 police officers, supported by 500 civilian staff, and had a budget of more than £55 million for the year. In 1991 it had to cope with almost 170,000 separate incidents of crime, the predominant offences being burglary and thefts of and from motor vehicles.

At the time of the project the North Yorkshire force was undergoing a major reorganization of its structure. Its headquarters are in Northallerton and dealt with matters of policy, finance, personnel, complaints against the police and research and development. Beyond headquarters, it had traditionally been divided into four divisions, centered on York, Harrogate, Richmond and Scarborough, and these divisions then further divided into a total of ten sub-divisions. The reorganization was to see the disappearance of one level in this hierarchy and the amalgamation of a number of sub-divisions, leaving only seven territorial divisions of the force (based at York, Selby, Harrogate, Skipton, Richmond, Malton and Scarborough) reporting to headquarters. These changes were explicitly designed, by the Chief Constable, as a step toward forcing decision making down the hierarchy of the organization. Managers of the various territorial divisions were henceforth to have considerable local autonomy.

The study of communications within NYP which we were undertaking was seen as a part of the overall change program. It was important to ensure that the information that flowed around NYP supported the new structure, and aims and purposes, and not the old. Apart from that most important aspect of the brief, our remit was to produce a workable strategy for communications within NYP which would rationalize information flows, and improve the quality of policy making and dissemination through the provision of accurate and timely information.

12.3.2. The Problem Situation and What Was Done

In relating what happened in North Yorkshire Police, I shall emphasize and highlight those aspects of the project where critical systems thinking seems to have been decisive in determining what occurred. Perhaps because it was in the very early days of trying to use TSI, and because we were very consciously developing and using strategies which later became second nature, the project clearly illustrates a number of the significant benefits that, I believe, derive from taking a critical systems approach. Overall the project was successful but there were some hiccups along the way. Interestingly, at the point where the intervention nearly came to grief, the blame could be laid at our door for *not being critical enough*.

The project began with a series of interviews of a cross-section of individuals at all levels in the organization, civilian support staff as well as police officers, headquarters staff as well as staff from one selected territorial division. This was the start of the "creativity" phase of the intervention, according to the logic of Total Systems Intervention (TSI), which was the specific meta-methodology employed to operationalize critical systems thinking in this study. The interviews were allowed to be fairly general and wide-ranging, but did make some use of the "cognitive mapping" technique and of metaphor analysis.

The impression gained from the interviews was of very general dissatisfaction with the existing communication and information flows. All interviewees recognized that the impending reorganization required new and improved information systems. The higher ranks in the organization were primarily concerned that the spirit of their policy initiatives seemed to get lost in the existing communication system and, therefore, implementation on the ground was never as intended. They could, to some extent, communicate the detail of what they wanted but not why they wanted it. The Chief Constable commented that:

> It is apparent from a number of changes I have made that, frequently, the letter of an instruction is complied with but, clearly, the philosophy has been lost (Green, 1991, p. 42).

He provided the example of an attempt to control vehicle expenditure by imposing a cut in the overall mileage traveled. This was implemented in many sub-divisions by allocating a target mileage to each vehicle on a "per shift", weekly or monthly basis. One officer was instructed to use a Land Rover, which still had mileage to spare, rather than a Ford Fiesta which had exceeded its target miles. The senior ranks were particularly critical of middle managers whom they saw as bureaucratic and unwilling to make decisions.

Middle managers themselves complained about the confusing nature of the various media of communication employed since these seemed to mix up important policy matters with minor administrative details. They also saw the Executive as being secretive and excluding them from decision making but, at the same time, failing to provide them with instructions in a timely and accurate manner. The lower ranks were frustrated by their inability to get what they saw as important information passed upwards and acted upon. Organizational communication in NYP was compared to a game of "snakes and ladders"; information would get so far up the hierarchy but before it reached its destination it would hit a "snake" and tumble down again. Civilian employees saw problems of communication as closely intertwined with their perceived status as second-class citizens in the organization compared to police officers. A final point worthy of note was the feeling among staff representatives that the consultative processes of the force were not useful or meaningful. The staff associations representing the police officers and the trade union (NALGO), representing the civilian support staff, seemed only to be called in once decisions had been taken. They were used to disseminate information about decisions, rather than as bodies to be consulted about the views of staff before decisions were taken.

TSI calls for a problem situation to be analyzed using systems metaphors and this was the next task undertaken. It was clear, and was openly stated by many interviewed, that NYP operated like a bureaucratic machine. There was a functional division of labor at headquarters and in the divisions, a prevalence of charts showing the organizational hierarchy, detailed job descriptions, a formal discipline code, a recognizable "officer class" and, of course, uniforms and badges of rank. Many felt that this form of organization was inappropriate in a situation which required police officers to act flexibly to cope with an increasingly unpredictable and turbulent environment. It seemed, indeed, that the main source of the organization's problems, including communication problems, lay in its adherence to the machine model and machine thinking. As Green (1992) argues:

> Such perceived problems as middle management's adherence to bureaucratic methods and refusal to be more responsive and decisive, the organization's refusal to treat its members as individual human beings, the gulf which existed between the territorial divisions of the force and its headquarters, and the compartmentalization of specialist departments could be explained in terms of the shortcomings of the machine metaphor (p. 585).

Use of the organism metaphor led to reflection on how little attention NYP gave to its environment and to communication with the public it sought to serve. The brain metaphor revealed how little suited were the organization's current information flows to the promotion of local autonomy, and what significant changes would be necessary if decision-making was to be delegated to lower levels, if information was to be conveyed in a manner suitable for learning, and if the organization as a whole were to become responsive in the face of its environment. Cultural analysis tended to support the findings of employing the machine metaphor, especially highlighting the bureaucratic values of middle managers. It was clear enough that changing the culture of the organization, to ensure proper use of information flows based on a more decentralized structure, would be no easy task. The political metaphor revealed no open conflict in NYP about the aims of the organization but drew our attention again to the issue of proper involvement of staff through the consultation process.

What critical analysis allowed us to recognize at this stage was that the kind of improvements sought could not be brought about by designing more efficient and effective information systems on the basis of the machine model. Making NYP a better machine would lead to things getting worse, not better. We were able, using critical systems thinking, to draw in findings from the social sciences to reconsider the nature of the organization for which we were designing the information systems. Instead of making NYP a better machine we needed to rethink it as an "organism with a brain" and put in place information systems that supported local autonomy and decision-making, learning, responsiveness and the ability to adapt. Without critical systems thinking, I would suggest, it would have been easy to fall into the trap of employing an information systems development approach, premised on the machine model, that would not have addressed the real issues; and would indeed have made things worse.

We were now on to the "choice" phase of TSI. Choice is about selecting a systems methodology, or methodologies, best able to deal with the types of problem revealed in the creativity stage. We were aware of the difficulty of changing the organization's culture and aware of the political issues surrounding consultation, but we became obsessed with the notion that rapid progress to improving things could be made if we designed the communication and information systems to support a vision of NYP as an "organism with a brain." This was especially the case since this approach seemed to have senior management support. Critical systems thinking (the system of systems methodologies) told us that Beer's (1985) viable system model (VSM) was exactly what we needed for designing information systems on the basis of the "organism" and "brain" metaphors. We proceeded apace to the implementation phase of TSI and to the application of viable systems diagnosis (VSD) as our "dominant methodology."

Figure 12.6 shows, in very broad outline, NYP pictured as a viable system. The analysis we conducted and the recommendations that we were led to make then became very much standard VSM fare. Each of the seven new territorial divisions was to be given autonomy, developing its own statement of purpose and its own environmental scanning and planning capabilities. In VSM terms, each had to become a viable system in its own right. Figure 12.7 shows the Selby Division as a viable system.

Whereas previously coordination had been achieved by strict adherence to commands from headquarters, this was no longer possible if the divisions were to develop their own identities. The nature of "force orders" was therefore clarified by separating out orders requiring strict adherence, policy guidelines (which the divisions could interpret according to their own local circumstances) and coordination matters. The coordination function should indeed, it was suggested, cease to be controlled by the center. If it could be set up and maintained by the divisions, it would truly be seen as a service to them and not an authoritarian element of command.

Removing direct control from headquarters of so much of the divisions' activities might be seen, by senior management, as a recipe for anarchy unless they could at least be sure of control over the outcomes. To this end, attention was given to the establishment of "monitoring channels" which let senior management know how the divisions were doing in terms of some key performance indicators. Senior management should henceforth exercise control on the basis of goals obtained but would not (generally) interfere in specifying the means used to achieve the goals.

Information on performance, according to the indicators, should also be freely available to the divisions themselves so that they could adjust their own behavior. Finally, it was recommended that policy making at the top level of NYP could best be supported by the creation of a development function which might be formed by merging the current "operational conference", which dealt with internal matters, with the "information technology conference", which showed some rudimentary interest in monitoring external affairs. This was necessary if the organization was ever to be appropriately responsive to the changing environment it faced.

The recommendations outlined were written up in a discussion document, "Divisional Autonomy – The Viable System Perspective", which was circulated to force senior management prior to presentation to members of the Steering Committee overseeing the reorganization, and consisting of the Chief Constable, the Assistant Chief Constable Operations, the Chairman of the Police Authority, representatives of the Staff Associations

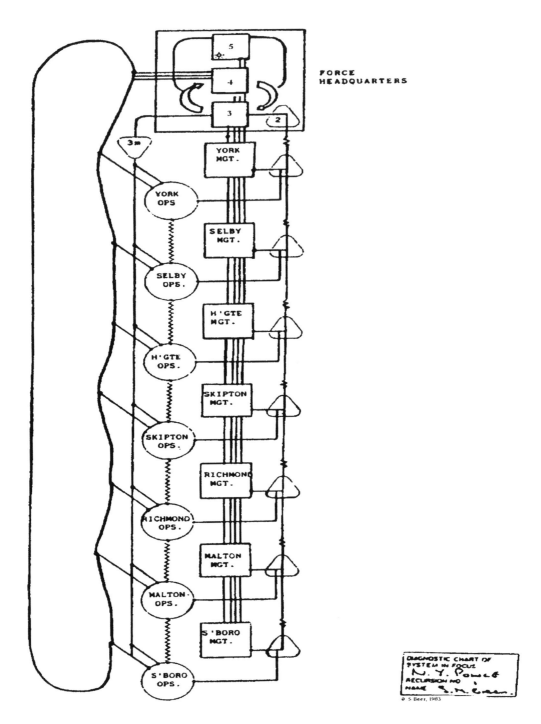

Figure 12.6. North Yorkshire Police as a viable system (reproduced from Green, 1991, p. 135)

and members of the Implementation Team. We were unperturbed at a trickle of feedback before the meeting suggesting that the document had not been well received. We felt that, logically speaking, the VSM provided exactly the information flows NYP needed; giving the divisions autonomy and the information to make their own decisions, ensuring coordination, and providing senior management with the means to ensure proper internal control and to see that NYP was adaptable to external developments. It was disturbing, however, when Steve Green was asked by one middle manager, on the morning of the meeting, whether he had "gone mad."

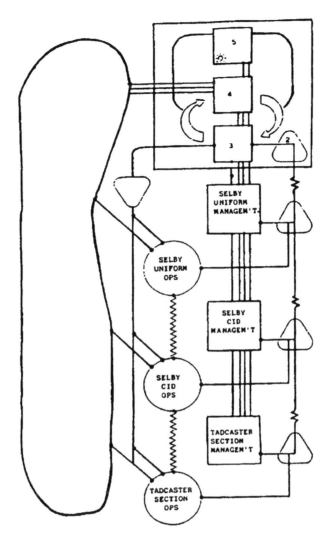

Figure 12.7. Selby Division as a viable system (reproduced from Green, 1991, p. 156)

The project was lucky to survive this meeting. It was clear that there was no general understanding of how local autonomy could work in an organization like NYP, how coordination could be maintained, or why the headquarters meeting structure should be rearranged to ensure responsive policy making as we envisaged it. There was no doubt also that the distrust that had grown up, because of the history of lack of consultation over important decisions, continued to poison the atmosphere. It was probably only the fact that the Chief Constable had not read the report before the meeting, and was impressed by some of the points made in discussion, that saved the day.

As critical systems thinkers we knew about the strengths and weaknesses of the VSM, but we had not been *critical enough* of how its weaknesses would detract from the success of this project. In particular, the VSM did not keep us alert enough concerning whether the changes recommended would be culturally and politically acceptable. The intervention had taken too much of an expert-driven form with insufficient participation from those whose minds had to be won over if change was to be accepted. Furthermore, it had not provided us with the means to address the consultation issue. It was just as well we were forced to think again. Even if we had been allowed to design the information systems suggested, they would have been sabotaged.

Re-entering the choice phase of TSI, we felt we now needed a methodology that would bring about sufficient cultural shift in NYP, through learning, to make feasible the kinds of changes that seemed necessary. We were also determined that it be able to address the consultation issue. To these ends Checkland's (1981; Checkland and Scholes, 1990) SSM was selected. This methodology was followed through in fairly conventional, Mode 1, form. Rich pictures of the problem situation and of important aspects of the problem situation were drawn (see Green, 1991). Four relevant systems were eventually chosen for consideration:

- a system to develop a concept of local autonomy appropriate for implementation in NYP
- a system to provide for the coordinated implementation of policy
- a system to make policy in a manner which balances the demands of the present with the needs of the future
- a system to provide a consultative style of decision-making

Three of these were directed at issues that had troubled participants in the meeting on the recommendations derived from the VSM; the fourth was aimed at improving consultation. Root definitions and conceptual models were constructed. Conceptual models "to provide for coordinated implementation of policy" and "to provide a consultative style of decision making" are included here, as Figures 12.8 and 12.9, for the interest of readers.

Following the philosophy of the new "dominant methodology", SSM, all stages were conducted in as participative a way as possible. The original interviewees (with one or two notable additions) were revisited, the various issues were discussed, on the basis of the root definitions and conceptual models, and the models amended either in the presence of the interviewees or, later, in the light of the discussions. Considerable debate was generated among those involved as they began to learn their way to their own understanding of matters such as what autonomy might mean in NYP. Finally a consultancy report was prepared containing conclusions expressed in simple, real-world, terms. It has to be said that the recommendations in this report were little different from those in the previous one, but the reception of the report was completely different. If anything the response now was "yes, very good, this is obvious, what have you been spending your time doing?" This is a response that is disturbing to inexperienced users of SSM, but is actually just about the highest level of praise an SSM analyst can receive. When something is "obvious" it has become part of the culture of the organization, people act accordingly and things get implemented.

The intervention was successful and brought about considerable change in NYP (see Green, 1992). I am pleased to say that we continued to work with NYP, in the years after 1991, on a number of engagements that stemmed from this original project.

12.3.3. Theoretical Reflection

I have sought to argue elsewhere (Jackson, 1996) that this was a project, in the information systems area, that made full use of critical systems thinking and would not have been as successful if it had not made use of critical system thinking.

The project demonstrated critical awareness of the strengths and weaknesses of the methodologies used, and what they could most appropriately be employed to do - even if, initially, we were carried away with what the VSM seemed able to offer. Had we been more

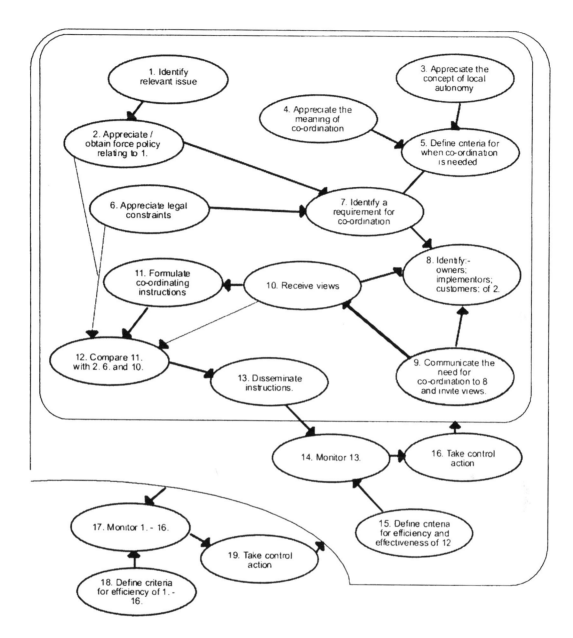

Figure 12.8. Conceptual model to provide for coordinated implementation of policy (reproduced from Green, 1991, p. 229)

socially aware we might have recognized that it was not sensible to try to push through the conclusions derived from the VSM study even if these did seem to command senior management support. There was pluralism in the use of systems methods and models - aspects of cognitive mapping, the VSM and SSM were all employed. There was pluralism at the theoretical level in that two methodologies (VSD and SSM) were at different times chosen as dominant and, once chosen, the distinctive rationale of each was strictly followed. The project should certainly not be read just as a case study on the need for effective participant involvement in change processes (as secured using SSM). The coherence of the recommendations produced on the basis of the VSM diagnosis and design contributed equally to overall success. That said, we were perhaps lucky that the VSM and SSM converged on similar conclusions and we were spared from having to choose between contradictory recommendations derived from alternative rationalities.

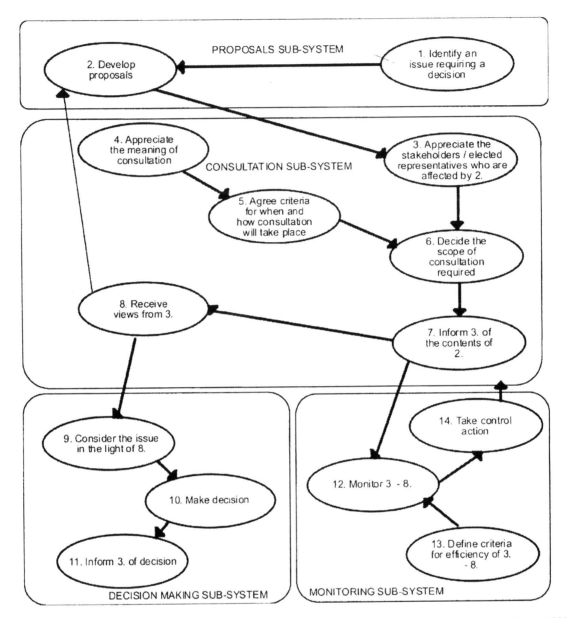

Figure 12.9. Conceptual model to provide a consultative style of decision making (reproduced from Green, 1991, p. 241)

Finally, if nobody was "liberated" or "emancipated" according to any reasonable usage of those terms, then at least attention was given to improving the involvement of ordinary staff in decision-making through new consultative procedures which had the support of the staff associations. Improvement was measured in terms of empowerment as well as against efficiency, effectiveness, elegance and ethicality.

A more detailed examination of the case study will now be provided by examining it in the light of our conclusions about critical systems practice set out in the previous chapter.

In terms of Checkland's distinction between whether an intervention is methodology-driven (Mode 1) or situation-driven (Mode 2), this project was predominantly Mode 1. There were, however, occasions when the demands of the situation took over and reference to the TSI meta-methodology was suspended until the emergency was dealt with. Once the immediate crisis had been overcome, TSI would then be employed in a Mode 2 form to help work out what had gone wrong and what new direction was needed. The prime example was the rethinking of which methodology to take as "dominant" after the failure of the meeting at which the VSM recommendations were presented. We can now refer this intervention for comparison against the "Constitutive rules for critical systems practice" (Table 11.2).

1. Functionalist, interpretive and emancipatory theoretical positions were considered and adopted during the study. There were some distinctively postmodern aspects to the whole thing but these were not recognized as such at the time.

2. The creativity phase was conducted according to TSI as it existed in 1991. Interviews and cognitive mapping were employed to surface significant issues but the main purpose of this was to provide material for a full-blown metaphor analysis. The metaphors were regarded as the vehicle whereby the different theoretical rationalities could be brought to bear to analyze the problem situation.

3. Generic systems methodologies were not available at the time. As a result the intervention was conducted with VSD standing in for the functionalist approach and SSM for the interpretive approach. No emancipatory methodology was used but an "emancipatory gaze" was cast over proceedings. The initial choice of organizational cybernetics as the "dominant" methodology (reflected in the VSM) was perhaps unfortunate. However, the meta-methodology allowed us to change tack and elevate SSM to the position of dominance. The use of specific "stand in" methodologies imposed some constraints on flexibility because the functionalist rationale had to be expressed solely through the VSM, and the interpretive using rich pictures, root definitions, conceptual models etc., when other methods and/or models might have been helpful.

4. There were no principles or guidelines for generic systems methodologies against which the practice could be checked. However, it is apparent that viable systems diagnosis and SSM were adequate in bringing the functionalist and interpretive rationales to bear on the intervention.

5. As stated under 3., the systems methods, models, tools and techniques employed were limited to those usually associated with organizational cybernetics and SSM. The only exception was the use of cognitive mapping in the creativity phase.

6. As previously mentioned, the project demonstrated "critical awareness" of the systems methodologies and methods used.

7. Our account of the intervention did not emphasize it, but there was pluralism in "modes of representation" and "facilitation" as well as in "clients" and "methods." For example, various kinds of visual device, usually variations on rich pictures, were used during the SSM process. Because we did not think to make this explicit, and it was not deliberate, we were unable to reflect and learn from these different forms of pluralism.

8. Both the meta-methodology (TSI) and the methodologies used (organizational cybernetics, SSM) were adapted to the particular circumstances; in the case of organizational cybernetics not sufficiently in the first instance.

9. As well as improving the real world problem situation, the intervention generated a considerable number of research findings. This was one of the first significant

projects to formally use the TSI meta-methodology and Green (1992) was able to reflect on and help develop this approach. Sections in the original reporting (Green, 1991) were devoted to what had been learned about the VSM and SSM. Metaphor analysis, as part of the creativity stage of TSI, was one of the methods about which most was discovered. It began to be seen as important not so much as a replacement for other creativity enhancing techniques, but as an assurance that the ground had been covered in exploring the problem situation. For example, looking at the problem situation through the "coercive system" metaphor ensured that the emancipatory perspective was not forgotten. A good deal was learned about the problem situation in North Yorkshire Police. This both assisted Green in his everyday activities as a manager and facilitated later successful projects.

12.4. KINGSTON GAS TURBINES

12.4.1. The Organization

Kingston Gas Turbines (KGT) has been in the business of manufacturing gas turbines since 1946 and today employs around 2000 personnel. It has had a number of changes of ownership in recent years but is currently the main industrial gas turbine manufacturer in a large European consortium in which General Electric America also has a stake. In 1997, when the study began, KGT was organized as a "matrix", with the primary functional departments of design, sales, production and product support cross-cut by "support" departments such as finance, quality, human resources, information technology, plant maintenance and contracts. Staff from the functional departments and the service units were formed into "working teams" of between 3 to 20 individuals directly responsible for manufacture or providing a service to the customer, whether internal or external. Top management had a vision of "dramatic growth through the excellence of people and products." Their strategy was to "double the business" and clear targets were established (e.g. "design six new products") to ensure that things could be kept on track. To achieve these targets there was to be an internal revolution which, it was hoped, would lead to all staff participating, in interdisciplinary teams, to analyze and solve the company's problems.

The project, which lasted from 1997 to 2000, was carried out by Alvaro Carrizosa, first as an M.Sc. student and then as a change agent/researcher, funded by the company and, at the same time, undertaking a Ph.D. at the University. My role, once I had established the relationship between KGT and the University, was as a supervisor to Alvaro, commentating from a theoretical perspective on what was going on. It was a period of great turbulence in KGT; with new ownership structures, changes in organizational design, and major change programs of all kinds. At times it seemed that the only thing that did remain constant was the existence of our critical systems study exploring purposeful change in KGT.

12.4.2. The Problem Situation and What Was Done

In retrospect (Carrizosa, 2000), the intervention can be divided into five initiatives, which I shall call Projects 1 - 5.

Project 1 started in "Proposals", a part of the Sales Department, and concerned itself with the consequences of the "double the business" strategy for the way that department managed its internal and external relations. It came to involve the Sales Department, more generally, in a restructuring exercise. (Carrizosa, 1997).

Brief flirtations with hard systems thinking and organizational cybernetics as "dominant" methodologies were ended when the SOSM revealed the degree of pluralism in the problem situation. SSM now became the dominant approach and remained so throughout Project 1, although complemented at different stages of the study by metaphor analysis from TSI and the VSM.

The Proposals Department was responsible for working up formal tenders to submit to customers for jobs, once the go-ahead had been given to tender for the work. The various problems and issues faced by this department were unearthed through interviews and informal conversations and captured in a "rich picture." Discussion of the rich picture yielded various themes which demanded further consideration - communication themes, structure themes, uncertainty themes, efficiency themes and roles themes. Metaphor analysis was then used to engender creative thinking about possible futures which would help resolve the problems currently being faced. The metaphors used were the "cover the ground" set from TSI (Jackson and Flood, 1991) but also others, such as the spider-plant metaphor from Morgan's (1993) later work on "imaginization." Participants were also encouraged to develop their own original metaphors. In general terms there was a shift in perception which favored the "organism" metaphor as a way of viewing what the future should be like. It was necessary to be more customer and market oriented in order to survive and prosper in what was becoming a turbulent environment. Inevitably the project now broadened to include the Sales Department and five "relevant systems" were outlined which described structures for the Sales Department which would enable it to react more flexibly to the environment. The VSM was used to inform one of these alternatives. The outcome of considering possible "feasible and desirable" changes were recommendations for changing the structure of the Sales Department to reflect more of a project management orientation.

Reflecting on his experiences in using SSM during Project 1, Carrizosa realized that he had become a critical systems thinker rather than a soft systems thinker:

> In this short period of time I perceived the enormous potential in terms of individual and organizational transformation implicit in the process of developing the study and application of methodologies. I would now feel happy to approach similar problem situations by using several methodologies concurrently and see the benefits, in terms of organizational learning and transformation, which could be thus generated (1997, p. 114).

Fortunately the results of Project 1 coincided with conclusions emerging from preliminary discussions, at middle management level, about restructuring the whole company. He was therefore "hired" by the company and able to put into practice these critical systems ideas.

The middle managers looking at the whole organizational structure were known as the "Process Implementation Team" (PIT group). Carrizosa (2000), therefore, calls Project 2 the PIT Project. The PIT group had been established as a result of dissatisfaction with a previous restructuring exercise which had established the matrix and the various interdisciplinary teams spread across the company. There was a feeling that technical knowledge was becoming diluted because the engineers, for example, were not in as close a contact as they had been. The capacity to transmit information and learning from one part of the organization to another also seemed to be reduced. Moreover, top management seemed to be ready to make things worse by moving to a split site operation. The PIT group was a response to these problems and involved the researcher because they liked the process that had been employed during Project 1.

Project 2 began by looking for solutions in terms of the particular layout of offices and departments. The systems perspective brought by the researcher soon saw its concerns enlarged to communication systems generally, to organizational structures and their relationship to communications and, eventually, to the vision and strategy that needed, in the minds of members of the PIT group, to inform organizational structure. A request to top management to provide a more explicit vision and strategy led to the response that it was middle managers who know more about the market and therefore they could undertake this themselves. The PIT group seized the opportunity provided by this response to focus on those business processes which had a direct link to the market. Five such processes were identified and a new organizational structure proposed which was built around these five processes. The business was now to be viewed and structured in terms of business processes and not in terms of functions, departments and products. Middle managers would be engaged with one significant process rather than having to account to a number of bosses as in the matrix structure.

The new arrangements were presented to top management and, following some minor changes, were approved. Top management then decided that it would reduce anxiety, among those not involved in the PIT group, if the new organizational structure was implemented immediately and without further discussion. Project 3, "The Thinking Space" was born of the realization, by those middle managers charged with implementation, that not all members of the organization understood, let alone agreed with, the changes proposed by the PIT group and now adopted by senior management.

Process 1, which described the key strategic process linking customer requirements to what could be produced, became the center of attention in Project 3. Middle managers wanted to set up a forum for discussion about how this should actually be implemented. They hoped this would help ameliorate any negative consequences that might follow from the autocratic way in which the new structure was adopted and imposed. Emphasis shifted to what characteristics a "Thinking Space" should have in order to permit open discussion of how implementation might proceed. It was thought necessary that it should enable all participants to disseminate their reflections and views on the evolving problem situation. This sharing of multiple perspectives helped to promote and enrich communication, reflection and learning, and eventually encouraged co-operation between those involved. The job of the researcher was to continually bring new perspectives to bear on the issue being discussed. To assist in this, rich pictures, root definitions, conceptual models, the VSM, systems metaphors and system dynamics were all introduced and used. The aim was an increase in the "collective competence" of those directly involved and even among those who were not contributing but nevertheless were interacting with the involved.

Carrizosa (2000) lists the "properties and characteristics" of the Thinking Space as they were co-defined by the researcher and the participants:

- an action language, focusing on "actors" and "activities" in everyday work

- structured conversations which helped the actors address the most relevant issues

- co-equal actors engaging in equal participation and able to freely express their viewpoints

- a systems approach which helps actors define what is important to them

- an activity, a way of doing and acting, not another company program

- the researcher as actor

- a dynamic process

The Thinking Space, established on this basis, played an important role in encouraging participation and learning during the various projects undertaken as the new organizational structure was implemented. Its success led to the idea that it should become a permanent part of continuous learning in the company beyond the implementation activities. Projects 4 and 5 stemmed from this ambition.

Project 4, "The Book", consisted of writing a book about the experiences of participants in implementing the new organizational structure. The book was produced in an interactive manner with different actors contributing their thoughts on change processes and how they could be brought about effectively. The multiple perspectives available from the actual participants were further enriched by discussing Senge's ideas on "organizational learning" and aspects of chaos and complexity theory as they impacted on organizational change and management (interpreted from the work of Stacey). As well as allowing self-reflection and exchange and enhancement of viewpoints, "The Book" permitted issues of power relations and constraints on action to be addressed. Creation of "The Book" allowed the participants to structure and share their thoughts on Project 3 and so consolidate their learning. The new "organization theory" that was then held in common, and objectifed in "The Book", could become the basis for new purposeful action.

Project 5 happened to address the problem of "an integrated business approach" in KGT, but it represented a first attempt to explore an approach to the management of complexity underpinned by knowledge of what was required for a "Thinking Space" and the learning captured in "The Book." Known as "The Wall Workshops" (WW), Project 5 allowed participants to engage in completely open communications about how to deal with complex issues and to decide together how to tackle them. Carrizosa (2000) describes it well:

> On walls, accessible to all actors, systems diagrams and various visual representations were set up as outputs of continuous interaction among participants, who could always express their points of view about the problem situation under analysis, suggesting and exploring options and actions to be taken, new interpretations and perceptions of problems, possible causes and effects of actions, local and global improvements, etc. All were welcome as essential to the WW. Once an issue was raised natural conversation took over which led to a WW if participants considered it appropriate. All this was intended to be founded on the spirit of collaboration, commitment and within the framework of a serious and organized effort, whose progress was visualized on the wall at all stages. Using this device the process was available for scrutiny, validation, revision and feedback (Carrizosa, 2000, p. 8).

By the end of Project 5 this approach had become readily accepted in KGT and continues to be used. Meanwhile, the student-researcher and his supervisor had become even more convinced of the need to employ, in intervention, a pluralism of perspectives and theoretical positions, and to employ methods and models according to the needs of the particular moment.

12.4.3. Theoretical Reflections

The KGT intervention began as a Mode 1 (in Checkland's terms) use of SSM but soon became more Mode 2 in style. This was because the student-researcher was continually having to learn more systems thinking in order to keep up and reflect on what was happening in the problem situation. The situation determined what aspects of systems thinking could be usefully brought to the intervention. At a further step removed from the problem context, I was trying, in a Mode 2 manner, to make sense of what was going on with reference to the critical systems approach. A comparison of what happened in the intervention against the "Constitutive rules for critical systems practice" should bring further insight.

1. Aspects of the functionalist, interpretive, emancipatory and postmodern rationalities are easy to detect in what occurred. Postmodernism asks us to encourage diversity, to challenge power relations and to see improvement on the basis of local knowledge. Much of what happened in Projects 3 to 5, "The Thinking Space", "The Book" and "The Wall Workshops" becomes intelligible from a postmodern perspective. Postmodernism provides the theoretical support necessary to enable us to critically reflect on Projects 3 to 5 with a view to improving the postmodern input to critical systems practice in the future.

2. Various creativity enhancing devices were used to try to understand what was going on in the problem situation. For example, a form of metaphor analysis that went beyond the original TSI set of metaphors was employed. Nevertheless the formal TSI metaphors were also brought to bear on the problem situation so ensuring that it was examined from the point of view of multiple paradigms.

3. Generic systems methodologies began to be used in the intervention itself and have certainly been used to reflect on the intervention. There were numerous shifts of "dominant" and "dependent" methodologies during the project. The project began in a functionalist manner and this rationality reasserted itself during Project 2, which led to the imposition of the new organizational structure. Project 1, once it got into its stride, was governed by the interpretive approach and this was also significant during "The Thinking Space" intervention. Emancipatory concerns achieved, it seems to me, equal status to those of the interpretive approach in "The Thinking Space" project and were also to the fore in "The Wall Workshops." Postmodernism was prominent, as we have noted, in Projects 3 to 5.

4. "The Thinking Space" was run essentially on the basis of a generic interpretive methodology (supported by emancipatory thinking) although the principles and guidelines were not directly employed during the intervention.

5. During the KGT project, systems methods, models, tools and techniques were employed, from whatever source they originally derived, in the service of methodologies reflecting different paradigms, and as appropriate to the particular circumstances - in other words exactly as prescribed by the "rules" of critical systems practice.

6. The project demonstrated "critical awareness" of the systems methodologies and methods used.

7. Attention was given to pluralism of "clients" and of methodologies and "methods." The project was highly original in terms of its pluralist use of different "modes of representation" and "facilitation" approaches.

8. Both the meta-methodology (critical systems practice/contemporary TSI) and the methodologies used were adapted to the particular circumstances in KGT.

9. As well as helping to improve the real-word problem situation, the intervention has had numerous research outputs. A number of these will be apparent from what has already been said but the interested reader should also consult Carrizosa (forthcoming).

We have seen three illustrative examples of critical systems practice, all of which have helped to advance the research program in critical systems thinking. Critical systems thinking provides a basis for "action research" (see Chapter 2) and must continue to develop by enhancing the theory-practice relationship.

13

CONCLUSION

In this conclusion I would like to mention what I think are five achievements of the book, to deal with three possible criticisms, and to suggest in what sense I believe critical systems thinking is "holistic" and in what sense it is "critical."

The first achievement is the review of the emergence of systems thinking in the various disciplines. I think that this recognizes the variety of sources of systems ideas and this, in turn, must indicate the value of systems thinking across the spectrum of intellectual endeavor.

Then there is the pattern imposed on the variety of systems approaches and methodologies. Looking at systems approaches in terms of their functionalist, interpretive, emancipatory or postmodern underpinnings has, I hope, been fully justified and provides for systems thinking a real strength based on "unity in diversity." The pattern also allowed us to be reasonably comprehensive in our treatment of systems methods, models and techniques; while always insisting that these were not locked into the categories employed.

I have tried to build a bridge between the social sciences and systems thinking. The social sciences are essential in developing a critique of the different systems approaches and I hope that I have provided a relatively easy introduction to some issues in the social sciences which are relevant to systems thinkers. From the other side, social scientists have tended to write off systems thinkers as wedded to functionalism and as devoted to the service of one powerful group in society - managers. It is no longer possible for social scientists to do this. Rather, they should see in systems methodologies a means of translating a whole range of social scientific ideas into practical application. This book offers to social scientists an introduction to contemporary systems thinking and a means of making their work usable and useful to all sections of society.

I have mentioned how useful systems thinking has been for theoretical development in the disciplines. Perhaps the main strength of systems ideas, however, is the guidance they offer to practitioners. I trust this has been demonstrated through the many illustrative examples of systems practice. The book promotes "action research." The generic systems methodologies developed in the book, and the "Constitutive rules for critical systems practice" should serve action research by enabling theory to inform practice and vice versa.

The last achievement, I hope, is the establishment of critical systems thinking on the basis of critical awareness, improvement and coherent pluralism. The argument has been a long one, but it has been worthwhile if we now understand how systems thinking can operate as a "transdiscipline" and provide the necessary theoretical and practical support for management and the other applied disciplines.

I pass on from the achievements to the possible criticisms. Two of these I wish to rebut and the third to accept as valid.

I do not believe that critical systems thinking can, even by postmodernists, be represented as some "totalizing" endeavor which, possibly unknowingly, serves the purposes of managerialism. There was a time when systems thinking sought unlimited knowledge but that time has passed. Critical systems thinking is about constantly reflecting on the limitations and partiality of our understanding. We are all much younger now.

I can envisage some trying to work out what critical systems thinking is all about, and coming up with the idea that it is some kind of sophisticated "balanced scorecard" approach. This is true in the trivial sense that it seeks improvement, and evaluates it, on the basis of a whole range of criteria - efficiency, efficacy, effectiveness, ethicality, elegance, empowerment, emancipation, exception and emotion. In a more serious sense, however, it recognizes that an understanding of any of these measures of improvement can only come about through a theoretical awareness of the "paradigms" from which they emerge and within which they make sense. And, of course, these paradigms, and so the measures of improvement, can offer contradictory guidance. When should effectiveness be sacrificed for empowerment? Critical systems thinking makes us aware of such difficult questions.

This leads us to a third line of criticism, with which I have sympathy. If different systems methodologies come up with conflicting advice, how do we choose what to do? Is not critical systems thinking just an elaborate way of delaying choice? To this I would answer that it is an excellent way of informing choice but, yes, in the end it cannot make the choice. That choice is for the human agent using her "ethical awareness." Checkland (1999, p. A44) puts it well when he says that we should never entertain the notion, even for a moment, that a mere "systems approach" or "systems methodology" can ensure that we act in a way that is "fully human."

And, finally, can I justify to you that critical systems thinking is both "holistic" (systemic) and "critical"?

If a man went to his doctor with pains in his stomach, you would expect an holistic doctor, as well as considering relatively trivial explanations such as irritable bowel syndrome, to entertain the possibility of some more deep-seated and dangerous malady, and check for that. I would hope that she would bear in mind the psychological health of her patient. A thoughtful conversation with the patient might reveal that the pains were a symptom of depression. An analysis of what the patient said might suggest that he needed a greater diversity of interests - more fun in his life. Or do the bruises elsewhere on his body suggest that he is suffering at the hands of a violent partner? The doctor willing and able to consider all these alternatives is to my mind an "holistic" practitioner. The critical systems thinker probing his positivist, structuralist, interpretive, postmodern and emancipatory perspectives, is similarly taking an holistic approach to organizational and societal problems.

Is critical systems thinking "critical"? In 1937, Horkheimer (1976) wrote a famous article containing a programmatic statement defining the vision of the Institute for Social Research, the body responsible for the social science version of critical thinking. Horkheimer wrote:

> However extensive the interaction between the critical theory and the special sciences whose progress the theory must respect and on which it has for decades exercised a liberating and stimulating influence, the theory never aims simply at an increase in knowledge as such. Its goal is man's emancipation from slavery (p. 224).

Despite the years between then and now, I like to think this book demonstrates a continuity between Horkheimer's vision and what critical systems thinking is about.

REFERENCES

Ackoff, R.L., 1967, Management misinformation systems, *Management Science*, **14**: 147.

Ackoff, R.L., 1968, Toward an idealised university, *Man. Sci.*, **15**: B121.

Ackoff, R.L., 1970(a), *A Concept of Corporate Planning*, Wiley, New York.

Ackoff, R.L., 1970(b), A black ghetto's research on a university, *Op. Res.*, **18**: 761.

Ackoff, R.L., 1974(a), *Redesigning the Future*, Wiley, New York.

Ackoff, R.L., 1974(b), The social responsibility of OR, *ORQ*, **25**: 361.

Ackoff, R.L., 1974(c), The systems revolution, *Long Range Planning*, **7**: 2.

Ackoff, R.L., 1975, A reply to the comments of Chesterton, Goodsman, Rosenhead and Thunhurst, *ORQ*, **26**: 96.

Ackoff, R.L., 1977, Optimization + objectivity = opt out, *Eur. J. Opl. Res.*, **1**: 1.

Ackoff, R.L., 1979(a), The future of operational research is past, *J. Opl. Res. Soc.* **30**: 93.

Ackoff, R.L., 1979(b), Resurrecting the future of operational research, *J. Opl. Res. Soc.* **30**: 189.

Ackoff, R.L., 1981, *Creating the Corporate Future*, Wiley, New York.

Ackoff, R.L., 1982, On the hard headedness and soft heartedness of M.C. Jackson, *J. Appl. Sys. Anal.*, **9**: 31.

Ackoff, R.L., 1986, On conceptions of professions, *Sys. Res.*, **3**: 273.

Ackoff, R.L., 1997, Beyond total quality management, High-profile lecture, University of Hull, 18 September.

Ackoff, R.L., 1999(a), *Re-creating the Corporation: a Design of Organizations for the 21st Century*, Oxford University Press, New York.

Ackoff, R.L., 1999(b), *Ackoff's Best: His Classic Writings on Management*, Wiley, New York.

Ackoff, R.L., and Emery, F.E., 1972, *On Purposeful Systems*, Tavistock, London.

Ackoff, R.L., and Sasieni, M.W., 1968, *Fundamentals of Operations Research*, Wiley, New York.

Adams, J., 1973, Chile: everything under control, *Science for People*, **21**: 4.

Alvesson, M., and Deetz, S., 1996, Critical theory and postmodernist approaches to organizational studies, in: *Handbook of Organization Studies*, S.R. Clegg, C. Hardy and W.R. Nord, eds., Sage, London, pp. 191-217.

Argyris, C., 1964, *Integrating the Individual and the Organization*, Wiley, New York.

Aron, R., 1967, *Main Currents in Sociological Thought (Volume 2)*, Weidenfeld and Nicolson, London.

Ashby, W.R., 1956, *An Introduction to Cybernetics*, Methuen, London.

Ashton, M.J., 1987, *Direction and control in the modern voluntary sector – a study based on the Executive Committee of the Hull Council for Voluntary Service*, MA dissertation, University of Hull.

Atkinson, C.J., 1984, *Metaphor and Systemic Praxis*, PhD thesis, Department of Systems, University of Lancaster.

Atkinson, C.J., 1986, Towards a plurality of soft systems methodology, *J. Appl. Sys. Anal.*, **13**: 19.

Atkinson, C.J., and Checkland, P.B., 1988, Extending the metaphor "system", *Human Relations*, **41**: 709.

Bailey, K.D., 1994, *Sociology and the New Systems Theory: Toward a Theoretical Synthesis*, University of New York Press, Albany.

Bailey, K.D., 1996, Living systems theory and social entropy theory, *General Systems Bulletin*, **25**: 7.

Baker, W., Elias, R., and Griggs, D., 1977, Managerial involvement in the design of adaptive systems, in: *Managerial Handbook for Public Administrators*, J.W. Sutherland, ed., Van Nostrand Reinhold, New York, pp. 817-842.

Banathy, B.H., 1996, *Designing Social Systems in a Changing World*, Plenum, New York.

Bahro, R., 1978, *The Alternative in Eastern Europe*, NLB, London.

Barnard, C., 1938, *The Functions of the Executive*, Harvard University Press, Cambridge, MA.

Bawden, R., 1995, *Systemic Development: a Learning Approach to Change*, Occasional Paper 1, Centre for Systemic Development, University of Western Sydney.

Beer, S., 1959(a), *Cybernetics and Management*, EUP, Oxford.

Beer, S., 1959(b), What has cybernetics to do with OR?, *ORQ*, **10**: 1.

Beer, S., 1966, *Decision and Control*, Wiley, Chichester

Beer, S., 1972, *Brain of the Firm*, Allen Lane, London.

Beer, S., 1974, *The Integration of Government Planning*, study for the Government of Alberta.

Beer, S., 1975, Fanfare for effective freedom, in: *Platform for Change*, S. Beer, ed., Wiley, Chichester, pp. 423-457.

Beer, S., 1979, *The Heart of Enterprise*, Wiley, Chichester.

Beer, S., 1981a, *Brain of the Firm*, 2nd ed., Wiley, Chichester.

Beer, S., 1981b, On heaping our science together, in: *Systems Thinking*, Volume 2, F. E. Emery, ed., Penguin, Harmondsworth, pp. 409-428.

Beer, S., 1983a, The will of the people, *J. Opl. Res. Soc.* **34**: 797.

Beer, S., 1983b, A reply to Ulrich's "Critique of Pure Cybernetic Reason", *J. Appl. Sys. Anal.* **10**: 115.

Beer, S., 1984, The viable system model: Its provenance, development, methodology and pathology, *J. Opl. Res. Soc.* **35**: 7

Beer, S., 1985, *Diagnosing the System for Organizations*, Wiley, Chichester.

Beer, S., 1990, Recursion zero: metamanagement, *Sys. Pract.*. **3**: 315.

Beer, S., 1995, *Beyond Dispute: the Invention of Team Syntegrity*, Wiley and Sons, Chichester.

Begun, J.W., 1994, Chaos and complexity: frontiers of organisation science, *Journal of Management Inquiry*, **3**: 329.

Beishon, J., and Peters, G., eds. 1972, *Systems Behavior*, OUP, London

Beneder, M., and Chroust, G., eds., 1998, Designing Social Systems in a Changing World (The Ninth Fuschl Conversation), Austrian Society for Cybernetic Studies, Bad Gams.

Bennett, R.J., and Chorley, R.J., 1978, *Environmental Systems: Philosophy Analysis and Control*, Methuen, London.

Berlinski, D., 1976, *On Systems Analysis*, MIT Press, Cambridge, MA.

Bevan, R.G., 1980, Social limits to planning, *J. Opl. Res. Soc.*, **31**: 867.

Blackler, F.H.M., and Brown, C.A., 1980, *Whatever Happened to Shell's New Philosophy of Management?*, Saxon House, London.

Blauner, R., 1964, *Alienation and Freedom*, University of Chicago Press, Chicago.

Bogdanov, A., 1984, *Essays in Tektology: the General Science of Organization*, Translated by G. Gorelik, Intersystems Publications, California.

Bolweg, J.F., 1976, *Job Design and Industrial Democracy*, Martinus Nijhoff, Leiden, The Netherlands.

Boothroyd, H., 1978, *Articulate Intervention: The Interface of Science, Mathematics and Administration*, Taylor and Francis, London.

Boulding, K. E., 1956, General systems theory - the skeleton of science, *Man. Sci.*, **2**, 197.

Bowen, K.C., ed., 1995, *In at the Deep End: MSc Student Projects in Community Operational Research*, Community Operational Research Unit, Barnsley.

Boyd, A., Brown, M., and Midgley, G., 1999, *Home and Away: Developing Services with Young People Missing from Home or Care*, Centre for Systems Studies, University of Hull, U.K.

Braverman, H., 1974, *Labor and Monopoly Capital*, Monthly Review Press, New York.

Britton, G.A., and McCallion, H., 1985, A case study demonstrating use of Beer's cybernetic model of viable systems, *Cybernetics and Systems*, **16**: 229.

Britton, G.A., and McCallion, H., 1994, An overview of the Singer/Churchman/Ackoff school of thought, *Systems Practice*, **7**: 487.

Broad, C.D., 1923, *The Mind and its Place in Nature*, Kegan Paul, Trench and Trubner, London.

Brocklesby, J., 1994, Let the jury decide: assessing the cultural feasibility of Total Systems Intervention, *Systems Practice*, **7**: 75.

Brocklesby, J., 1995, Intervening in the cultural constitution of systems – complementarism and other visions for systems research, *J. Opl. Res. Soc.*, **46**: 1285.

Brocklesby, J., 1997, Becoming multimethodology literature: an assessment of the cognitive difficulties of working across paradigms, in: *Multimethodology: the Theory and Practice of Combining Management Science Methodologies*, J. Mingers and A. Gill, eds., Wiley, Chichester, pp. 189-216.

Brocklesby, J. and Cummings, S., 1996, Foucault plays Habermas: an alternative philosophical underpinning for critical systems thinking, *J. Opl. Res. Soc.* **47**: 741.

Brodheim, E., and Prastacos, G., 1979, The long Island distribution system as a prototype for regional blood management, *Interfaces*, **9**: 3.

Bryer, R.A., 1979, The status of the systems approach, *Omega*, **7**: 219.

Buckley, W., 1967, *Sociology and Modern Systems Theory*, Prentice-Hall, Englewood Cliffs, NJ.

Buckley, W., ed., 1968, *Modern Systems Research for the Behavioural Scientist*, Aldine Publishing, Chicago.

Burns, T., and Stalker, G.M., 1961, *The Management of Innovation*, Tavistock, London.

Burrell, G., 1983, "Systems Thinking, Systems Practice": a review, *J. Appl. Sys. Anal.*, **10**: 121.

Burrell, G., 1989, Postmodernism: Threat or opportunity, in: *Operational Research and the Social Sciences*, M.C. Jackson, P. Keys, and S. Cooper, eds., Plenum, New York, pp. 59-64.

Burrell, G., and Morgan, G., 1979, *Sociological Paradigms and Organizational Analysis*. Heinemann, London.

Callinicos, A., 1976, *Althusser's Marxism*. Pluto Press, London.

Cannon, W.B., 1932, (revised 1939) *The Wisdom of the Body*, Kegan Paul, Trench, Trubner & Co. Ltd., London.

Capra, F., 1975, *The Tao of Physics*. Shambhala, Boston.

Capra, F., 1996, *The Web of Life: A New Synthesis of Mind and Matter*, Flamingo, London.

Caravajal, R., 1983, The impact of a social systems scientist on a country, *Omega*, **11**: 559.

Cardenas, A.R., 2000, *From inquiry to action in complex situations – a sociotechnical approach to interactive management*, PhD thesis, City University.

Carrizosa, A., 1997, *A Systems Approach to Project Management: Structuring the Sales and Proposals Departments in European Gas Turbines*, MSc. dissertation, University of Lincolnshire and Humberside.

Carrizosa, A., 2000, Enacting thinking spaces towards purposeful actions: an action research project, unpublished paper.

Carrizosa, A. and Ortegon, M., 1998, Using systems metaphors to interpret the edge of chaos. In: *Systems Sciences and Engineering* – Third International Conference, Beijing.

Carter, P., Jackson, M.C., Jackson, N., and Keys, P., 1987, Community OR at Hull University, *Dragon*, **2**, special issue.

Chandler, A.D. Jnr., 1962, *Strategy and Structure: Chapters in the History of the American Industrial Enterprise*, MIT Press, Cambridge, MA.

Chapman, G.P., 1977, *Human and Environmental Systems*, Academic Press, New York.

Checkland, P.B., 1971, A systems map of the universe, *J. of Sys. Eng.*, **2**: 2.

Checkland, P.B., 1976, Towards a systems-based methodology for real-world problem-solving, in: *Systems Behaviour*, J. Beishon and G. Peters, eds., Harper and Row, London, pp. 51-77.

Checkland, P.B., 1978, The origins and nature of "hard" systems thinking, *J. Appl. Sys. Anal.* **5**: 99.

Checkland, P.B., 1980, Are organizations machines?, *Futures*, **12**: 421.

Checkland, P.B., 1981, *Systems Thinking, Systems Practice*, Wiley, Chichester.

Checkland, P.B., 1982, Soft systems methodology as process: a reply to M.C. Jackson, *J. Appl. Sys. Anal.*, **9**: 37.

Checkland, P.B., 1983, OR and the systems movement: mappings and conflicts, *J. Opl. Res. Soc.* **34**: 661.

Checkland, P.B., 1985(a), From optimizing to learning: a development of systems thinking for the 1990s, *Journal of the Operational Research Society*, 36: 757.

Checkland, P.B., 1985(b), Achieving "desirable and feasible" change: an application of soft systems methodology, *J. Opl. Res. Soc.*, **36**: 821.

Checkland, P.B., 1987, The application of systems thinking in real-world problem-situations: the emergence of soft systems methodology, in: *New Directions in Management Science*, M.C. Jackson and P. Keys, eds., Gower, Aldershot, pp. 87-96.

Checkland, P.B., 1988, Churchman's "anatomy of systems teleology" revisited, *Syst. Pract.*, **1**: 377.

Checkland, P.B., 1989, Soft Systems Methodology, in: *Rational Analysis for a Problematic World*, J. Rosenhead, ed., Wiley, Chichester, pp. 71-100.

Checkland, P.B., 1994, Conventional wisdom and conventional ignorance: the revolution organization theory missed, *Organization*, 1: 29.

Checkland, P.B., 1999, *Systems Thinking, Systems Practice* (new edition). Wiley, Chichester.

Checkland, P.B., and Casar, A., 1986, Vickers' concept of an appreciative system: a systemic account, *J. Appl. Sys. Anal.*, **13**: 3.

Checkland, P.B. and Holwell, S., 1998, *Information, Systems and Information Systems*. Wiley, Chichester.

Checkland, P.B., and Scholes, P., 1990, *Soft Systems Methodology in Action*. Wiley, Chichester.

Cherns, A., 1976, The principles of socio-technical design, *Human Relations*. **29**: 783.

Cherns, A., 1987, Principles of socio-technical design revisited, *Human Relations*, **40**: 153.

Chesterton, K., Goodsman, R., Rosenhead, J., and Thunhurst, C., 1975, A comment on Ackoff's "The social responsibility of OR", *ORQ*, **26**: 91.

Child, J., 1972, Organizational structure, environment and performance: The role of strategic choice, *Sociology* **6**: 1.

Child, J., 1984, *Organization: A Guide to Problems and Practice*, 2nd ed., Harper and Row, London.

Chorley, R.J., and Kennedy, B.A., 1971, *Physical Geography: a Systems Approach*, Prentice-Hall International, London.

Churchman, C.W., 1970, Operations research as a profession, *Man. Sci.*, **17**: B37.

Churchman, C.W., 1971, *The Design of Inquiring Systems*. Basic Books, New York.

Churchman, C.W., 1979(a), *The Systems Approach*. Dell, New York.

Churchman, C.W., 1979(b), Paradise regained: a hope for the future of systems design education, in: *Education in Systems Science*, B.A. Bayraktar, H. Muller-Merbach, J.E. Roberts, and M.G. Simpson, eds., Taylor and Francis, London, pp. 17-22.

Churchman, C.W., 1979(c), *The Systems Approach and Its Enemies*. Basic Books, New York.

Churchman, C.W., 1982, *Thought and Wisdom*, Intersystems, Seaside, Calif.

Churchman, C.W., Ackoff, R.L., and Arnoff, E.L., 1957, *Introduction to Operations Research*. Wiley, New York.

Clarke, S. and Lehaney, B.,1999, Organisational intervention and the problems of coercion, *Systemist*, **21**: 40.

Clarke, S. and Lehaney, B., 2000, Mixing methodologies for information systems development and strategy: a higher education case study, *Journal of the Operational Research Society*, **51**: 542.

Clegg, S., and Dunkerley, D., 1980, *Organization, Class and Control*, Routledge and Kegan Paul, London.

Clemson, B., 1984, *Cybernetics: A New Management Tool*, Abacus Press, Tunbridge Wells.

Cohen, C., and Midgley, G., 1994, *The North Humberside Diversion From Custody Project for Mentally Disordered Offenders*, Centres for Systems Studies, University of Hull, U.K.

Cook, S.L., 1973, Operational research, social well-being and the zero growth concept, *Omega*, **1**: 647.

Cook, S.L., 1984, *The Writings of Steve Cook* (K. Bowen, A. Cook, M. Luck, eds.), The Operational Research Society, Birmingham.

Cooper, R., and Burrell, G., 1988, Modernism, postmodernism and organizational analysis: an introduction, *Organizational Studies*, **9**: 91.

Craib, I., 1992, *Modern Social Theory: From Parsons to Habermas*, Harvester-Wheatsheaf, Hemel Hempstead.

Dando, M.R., and Bennett, P.G., 1981, A Kuhnian crisis in management science?, *J. Opl. Res. Soc.* **32**: 91.

Davies, L.J., 1998, Understanding organizational culture: a soft systems perspective, *Sys. Pract.*, **1**: 11.

Descartes, R, 1968, *Discourse on Method and the Meditations*, Translated by F.E. Sutcliffe, Penguin Classics, Harmondsworth.

Deutsch, K.W., 1963, *The Nerves of Government*, The Free Press, New York.

Donaldson, L., 1996, The normal science of structural contingency theory, in: *Handbook of Organizational Studies*, S.R. Clegg, C. Hardy and W.R. Nord, eds., Sage, London, pp. 57-75.

Dudley, P., ed., 1996, *Bogdanov's Tektology*, Centre for Systems Studies, Hull, U.K.

Durkheim, E., 1933, *The Division of Labour in Society*, Free Press, New York.

Durkheim, E., 1938, *The Rules of Sociological Method*, Free Press, New York.

Easton, A., 1973, *Complex Managerial Decisions Involving Multiple Objectives*, Wiley, New York.

The Economist, 1993, The flowering of feudalism, March, p.80.

Eden, C., 1989, Using cognitive mapping for strategic options development and analysis (SODA), in: *Rational Analysis for a Problematic World: Problem Structuring methods for Complexity, Uncertainty and Conflict*, J. Rosenhead, ed., Wiley, Chichester, pp. 21-42.

Eden, C., and Ackermann, F., 1998, *The Journey of Strategy Making*, Sage, London.

Eden, C., Jones, S., and Sims, D., 1983, *Messing About in Problems*, Pergamon, Oxford.

Eilon, S., 1983, Dilemmas in the OR world, *Omega*, **11**:1.

Eilon, S., 1987, OR is not mathematics, *Omega*, **15**:87.

Emery, F.E., 1969, *Systems Thinking*, Penguin, Harmondsworth.

Emery, F.E., ed., 1993, *Participative Design for Participative Democracy*, Centre for Continuing Education, Australian National University, Canberra.

Emery, F.E., and Thorsrud, E., 1969, *Form and Content in Industrial Democracy*, Tavistock, London.

Emery, F.E., and Thorsrud, E., 1976, Democracy at Work, Nijhoff Social Sciences Division, Leiden, The Netherlands.

Emery, F.E., and Trist, E.L., 1965, The causal texture of organizational environments, *Human Relations*, **18**: 21.

Espejo, R., 1977, *Cybernetics in Management and Organization*, University of Aston Working Paper 76, University of Aston, Birmingham.

Espejo, R., 1979, *Information and Management: The Cybernetics of a Small Company*, University of Aston Working Paper 125, University of Aston, Birmingham.

Espejo, R., 1980, *Cybernetic Praxis in Government: The Management of Industry in Chile, 1970-1973*, University of Aston Working Paper 174, University of Aston, Birmingham.

Espejo, R., 1987, From machines to people and organizations: A cybernetic insight on management in: *New Directions in Management Science*, M.C. Jackson and P. Keys, eds., Gower, Aldershot, pp. 55-85.

Espejo, R., 1989, A cybernetic method to study organizations, in: *Rational Analysis for a Problematic World*, Wiley, Chichester, pp. 361-382.

Espejo, R., 1990, Complexity and change: reflections upon the cybernetic intervention in Chile, 1970-1973, *Sys. Prac.*, **3**: 303.

Espejo, R., and Harnden, R.J., eds., 1989, *The Viable System Model: Interpretations and Applications of Stafford Beer's VSM*, Wiley, Chichester.

Espejo, R., and Schwaninger, M., eds., 1993, *Organizational Fitness: Corporate Effectiveness through Management Cybernetics*, Campus Verlag, New York.

Espejo, R. and Watt, J., 1978, *Management Information Systems: A System for Design*, University of Aston Working Paper 98, University of Aston, Birmingham.

Espejo, R., Schuhmann, W., Schwaninger, M. and Bilello, U., 1996; *Organisational Transformation and Learning*, Wiley and Sons, Chichester.

Etzioni, A., 1960, Two approaches to organizational analysis, *ASQ* **5**: 257.

Fayol, H., 1949, *General and Industrial Management*, Pitman, London.

Flood, R.L., 1988, The need for a substantive soft systems language, *J. Appl. Sys. Anal.* **15**: 43.

Flood, R.L., 1989, Six scenarios for the future of systems 'problem solving', *Systems Practice*, **2**: 75.

Flood, R.L., 1990, *Liberating Systems Theory: On Systems and Inquiry*, Plenum, New York.

Flood, R.L., 1995, *Solving Problem Solving*, Wiley, Chichester.

Flood, R.L., 1999, *Rethinking 'The Fifth Discipline': Learning within the Unknowable*, Routledge, London.

Flood, R.L. and Carson, E., 1988, *Dealing with Complexity: An Introduction to the Theory and Application of Systems Science*, Plenum, New York.

Flood, R.L. and Gregory, W.J., 1989, Systems: past, present and future, in *Systems Prospects*, R.L. Flood, M.C. Jackson and P. Keys, eds., Plenum, New York, pp. 55-60.

Flood, R.L., and Jackson, M.C., 1988, Cybernetics and organization theory: A critical review, *Cybernetics and Systems*, **19**:13.

Flood, R.L., and Jackson, M.C., 1991, *Creative Problem Solving: Total Systems Intervention*, Wiley, Chichester.

Flood, R.L., and Jackson, M.C., eds., 1991, *Critical Systems Thinking: Directed Readings*, Wiley, Chichester.

Flood, R.L., and Robinson, S.A., 1989, Whatever happened to general systems theory? in: *Systems Prospects*, R.L. Flood, M.C. Jackson and P. Keys, eds., Plenum, New York, pp.61-66.

Flood, R.L. and Romm, N.R.A., 1995, Enhancing the process of choice in TSI, and improving the chances of tackling coercion, *Systems Practice*, **8**: 377.

Flood, R.L. and Romm, N.R.A., 1996, *Critical Systems Thinking: Current Research and Practice*, Plenum, New York.

Flood, R.L. and Ulrich, W., 1990, Testament to conversations on critical systems theory between two systems practitioners, *Systems Practice*, **3**: 7.

Flood, R.L., Jackson, M.C.,and Schecter, D., 1992, Total Systems Intervention: a research program, *Systems Practice*, **5**: 79.

Forester, J., 1992, Critical ethnography: on fieldwork in a Habermasian way, in: *Critical Management Studies*, M. Alvesson and H. Willmott, eds., Sage, London, pp. 46-65.

Forrester, J.W., 1958, Industrial Dynamics - a major breakthrough for decision makers, *Harvard Business Review*, **36**: 37.

Forrester, J.W., 1961, *Industrial Dynamics*, MIT Press, Cambridge, MA.

Forrester, J.W., 1969, *Principles of Systems*, Wright-Allan Press, Cambridge, MA.

Forrester, J.W., 1971, *World Dynamics*, Productivity Press, Portland, Oregon.

Fox, W.M., 1995, Sociotechnical system principles and guidelines: past and present, *Journal of Applied Behavioural Science*, **31**: 91.

Freire, P., 1970, *The Pedagogy of the Oppressed*, Seabury, New York.

Freire, P., and Macedo, C., 1987, Literacy: Reading the Word and the World, Bergin & Harvey Publishers Inc., Massachusetts.

Friend, J., 1989, The strategic choice approach, in: *Rational Analysis for a Problematic World: Problem Structuring Methods for Complexity, Uncertainty and Conflict*, J. Rosenhead, ed., Wiley, Chichester, pp. 1-20.

Friend, J.K. and Jessop, W.N., 1969, *Local Government and Strategic Choice: an Operational Research Approach to the Processes of Public Planning*, Tavistock, London.

Friend, J.K., Norris, M.E., and Stringer, J., 1988, The Institute for Operational research: an initiative to extend the scope of OR, *J. Opl. Res. Soc.*, **39**: 705.

Fuenmayor, R., 1991, Truth and openness: an epistemology for interpretive systemology, *Systems Practice*, **4**: 473.

Fuenmayor, R., and Lopez-Garay, H., 1991, The scene for interpretive systemology, *Systems Practice*, **4**: 401.

Fuenmayor, R., Bonucci, M., and Lopez-Garay, H., 1991, An interpretive-systemic study of the University of Los Andes, *Sys. Pract.*, **4**: 507.

Galbraith, J.R., 1977, *Organizational Design*, Addison-Wesley, Reading, MA.

Galliers, R., Jackson, M.C., and Mingers J.C., 1997, Organization theory and systems thinking: the benefits of partnership, *Organization*, **4**: 269-278.

Gartz, P.E., 1997, Commercial systems development in a changed world, *Transactions on Aerospace and Electronic Systems*, **33**: 632.

Gaskell, C., 1997, *The Management of Change in Prisons*, Ph.D thesis, University of Lincolnshire and Humberside.

Genders, E. and Player, E., 1995, *Grendon: A Study of a Therapeutic Prison*, Oxford University Press, New York.

Gerth, H.H., and Mills, C.W., eds., 1970, *From Max Weber*, Routledge and Kegan Paul, London.

Gibbons, M., Limoges, C., Nowotry, H., Schwartzman, S., Scott, P. and Trow, M., 1994, *The New Production of Knowledge: the Dynamics of Science and Research in Contemporary Societies*, Sage, London.

Giddens, A., 1976, *New Rules of Sociological Method*, Hutchinson, London.

Giddens, A., 1998, *The Third Way*, Polity Press, Cambridge.

Gleick, J., 1987, *Chaos: the Making of a New Science*, Abacus, London.

Gomez, P., and Probst, G.J.B., 1989, Organizational closure in Management: a complementary view to contingency approaches, *Cybernetics and Systems*, **20**: 311.

Gorelik, G.,1975, Principle ideas of Bogdanov's 'Tektology: the Universal Science of Organization', *General Systems*, **20**: 145.

Gorelik, G., 1984, *Essays from Tektology*, 2ⁿᵈ ed., Intersystems, Seaside, Calif.

Gouldner, A., 1959, Organizational Analysis, in: *Sociology Today*, R.K. Merton, L. Broom, and L.S. Cottrell, Jr., eds., Basic Books, New York, pp. 400-428.

Green, S.M., 1991, *Total systems intervention: organisational communication in North Yorkshire Police*, MA dissertation, University of Hull.

Green, S.M., 1992, Total Systems Intervention: organisational communication in North Yorkshire Police, *Systems Practice*, **5**: 585.

Green, S.M., 1993, Total Systems Intervention: a practitioner's critique, *Systems Practice*, **6**: 71.

Gregory, A.J., 1994, *Organisational Evaluation: a Complementarist Approach*, Doctoral dissertation, Department of Management Systems and Sciences, University of Hull, Hull, England.

Gregory, W.J., 1992, *Critical Systems Thinking and Pluralism: a New Constellation*, PhD thesis, City University, London.

Gregory, W.J., 1996, Discordant pluralism: a new strategy for critical systems thinking? *Syst. Pract.*, **9**: 605.

Gyllenhammer, P., 1977, *People at Work*, Addison-Wesley, Reading, MA.

Gu, J., and Zhu, Z., 2000, Knowing *wuli*, sensing *shili*, caring for *renli*: methodology for the WSR approach, *Systemic Practice and Action Research*, **13**: 21.

Habermas, J., 1970, Knowledge and interest, in: *Sociological Theory and Philosophical Analysis*, D. Emmet and A. MacIntyre, eds., Macmillan, London, pp. 36-54.

Habermas, J., 1974, *Theory and Practice*, Heinemann, London.

Habermas, J., 1975, *Legitimation Crisis*, Beacon Press, Boston.

Habermas, J., 1976, quoted in: *The Positivist Dispute in German Sociology*, D. Frisby, ed., Heinemann, London.

Habermas, J., 1984, *Reason and the Rationalization of Society*, Beacon Press, Boston.

Habermas, J., 1987, *Lectures on the Philosophical Discourse of Modernity*, MIT Press, Cambridge, MA.

Hall, A.D., 1962, *A Methodology for Systems Engineering*, D. Van Nostrand Co., Princeton, N.J.

Haralambos, M., and Holborn, M., 1995, *Sociology: Themes and Perspectives*, Collins Educational, London.

Hales, M., 1974, Management science and the 'second industrial revolution', *Radical Science Journal*, **1**: 5.

Hardy, C. and Clegg, S., 1997, Relativity without relativism: reflexivity in post-paradigm organization studies, *British Journal of Management*, **8**: S5.

Harnden, R.J., 1989, Outside and then: an interpretive approach to the VSM, in: the Viable System Model, R. Espejo and R.J. Harnden, eds., Wiley, Chichester, pp. 383-404.

Harnden, R.J., 1990, The language of models: the understanding and communication of models with particular reference to Stafford Beer's cybernetic model of organization structure, *Syst. Pract.*, **3**: 289.

Harvey-Jones, J., 1993, *Managing to Survive*, Heinemann, London.

Henderson, L.J., 1941-42, Sociology - 23 lectures, in: *L.J. Henderson on the Social System: Selected Writings*, B. Barber, 1970, University of Chicago Press, Chicago.

Hickson, D.J., Pugh, D.S., Pheysey, D.C., 1969, Operations Technology and organization structure: an empirical reappraisal, *ASQ* **14**:378.

Hill, P., 1971, *Towards a New Philosophy of Management*, Gower Press, Epping.

Hindle, G.A., and Jackson, M.C., 1997, *SSM within Humberside TEC: the Issue of Sustainability*, Working Paper 13, University of Lincolnshire and Humberside.

Hitch, C.J., 1955, An appreciation of systems analysis, in: *Systems Analysis*, S.L. Optner, ed., 1973, Penguin, Harmondsworth, pp. 19-36.

Ho, J., and Jackson, M.C., 1987, *Building a 'Rich Picture' and Assessing a 'Quality Management' Programme at Thornton Printing Company*, Department of Management Systems and Sciences, University of Hull, U.K.

Holmberg, S., 1995, Living systems applications in Sweden, *Systems Practice*, **7**:47.

Honderich, T., ed., 1995, *The Oxford Companion to Philosophy*, Oxford University Press, Oxford.

Hoos, I., 1972, *Systems Analysis in Public Policy: a Critique*, University of California Press, Berkeley.

Hoos, I., 1976, Engineers as analysts of social systems: a critical enquiry, *J. of Sys. Eng.* **4**: 81.

Horkheimer, M., 1976, Traditional and critical theory, in: *Critical Sociology*, P. Connerton, ed., Penguin, Harmondsworth, pp. 206-224.

Jackson, M.C., 1978, *Considerations on Method*, M.A. dissertation, Department of Systems, University of Lancaster.

Jackson, M.C., 1982, The nature of soft systems thinking: the work of Churchman, Ackoff and Checkland, *J. Appl. Sys. Anal.* **9**: 9.

Jackson, M.C., 1983, The nature of soft systems thinking: a comment on the three replies, *J. Appl. Sys. Anal.* **10**: 109.

Jackson, M.C., 1985 (a), A cybernetic approach to management in: *Managing Transport Systems*, P. Keys and M.C. Jackson, eds., Gower, Aldershot, pp. 25-52.

Jackson, M.C., 1985 (b), Social systems theory in practice: the need for a critical approach, *Int. Journal of General Systems*, **10**: 135.

Jackson, M.C., 1986, The cybernetic model of the organization: An assessment, in: *Cybernetics and Systems '86*, R. Trappl, ed., D. Reidel, Dordrecht, pp. 189-196.

Jackson, M.C., 1987(a), New directions in management science, in: *New Directions in Management Science*, M.C. Jackson, and P. Keys, eds., Gower, Aldershot, pp. 133-164.

Jackson, M.C., 1987(b), Present positions and future prospects in management science, *Omega*, **15**:455.

Jackson, M.C., 1988(a), An appreciation of Stafford Beer's "viable systems" viewpoint on managerial practice, *J. Mgt. Stud.*, **25**:557.

Jackson, M.C., 1988(b), Some methodologies for community OR, *J. Opl. Res. Soc.*, **39**: 715.

Jackson, M.C., 1988(c), Systems methods for organizational analysis and design, *Sys. Res.*, **5**: 201.

Jackson, M.C., 1989(a), Assumption analysis: an elucidation and appraisal for systems practitioners, *Sys. Prac.* **2**:11.

Jackson, M.C., 1989(b), Which systems methodology when? Initial results from a research program, in: *Systems Prospects: the Next Ten Years of Systems Research*, R. Flood, M. Jackson and P. Keys, eds., Plenum, New York.

Jackson, M.C., 1990(a), The critical kernel in modern systems thinking, *Sys. Prac.*, **3**:357.

Jackson, M.C., 1990(b), Beyond a system of systems methodologies, *Journal of the Operational Research Society*, **41**: 657.

Jackson, M.C., 1991, *Systems Methodology for the Management Sciences*, Plenum, New York.

Jackson, M.C., 1992, An integrated programme for critical thinking in information systems research, *Journal of Information Systems*, **2**: 83.

Jackson, M.C., 1993(a), Island ecodevelopment: planning and management issues, *Systems Practice*, **6**: 549.

Jackson, M.C., 1993(b), *Beyond the Fads: Systems Thinking for Managers*, Working Paper 3, Centre for Systems Studies, University of Hull.

Jackson, M.C., 1993(c), The system of systems methodologies: a guide to researchers, *J. Opl. Res. Soc.*, **44**: 208.

Jackson, M.C., 1995, Beyond the fads: systems thinking for managers, *Systems Research*, **12**: 25.

Jackson, M.C., 1996, Critical systems thinking and information systems research, in: *Information Systems: An Emerging Discipline?* J. Mingers, and F. Stowell, eds., 1997, McGraw-Hill, Maidenhead, pp. 201-238.

Jackson, M.C., 1997, Pluralism in systems thinking and practice, in: *Multimethodology: the Theory and Practice of Combining Management Science Methodologies*, J. Mingers and A. Gill, eds., Wiley, Chichester, pp. 237-257.

Jackson, M.C., 1999, Towards coherent pluralism in management science, *Journal of the Operational Research Society*, **50**: 12.

Jackson, M.C., and Alabi, B.O., 1986, *Viable systems all! A diagnosis for XY Entertainments*, Department of Management Systems and Sciences Working Paper 9, University of Hull, Hull, England.

Jackson, M.C., and Keys, P., 1984, Towards a system of systems methodologies, *J. Opl. Res. Soc.* **35**:473.

Jackson, M.C., Keys, P. and Cropper, S., eds., 1989, *Operational Research and the Social Sciences*, Plenum, New York.

Jackson, M.C., and Midgley, G., 1994, *Report for the Community Council of Humberside on the one-day workshop held on Wednesday 19 January 1994*, consultancy report, unpublished.

Jackson, N.V., and Carter, P., 1984, The attenuating function of myth in human understanding, *Human Relations*, **37**: 515.

Jacques, R., 1989, Post-industrialism, post-modernity and OR: Towards a "custom and practice" of responsibility and possibility, in: *Operational Research and the Social Sciences*. M.C. Jackson, P. Keys, and S. Cropper, eds., Plenum, New York, pp. 703-708.

Jantsch, E., 1980, *The Self-Organising Universe: Scientific and Human Implications of the Emerging Paradigm of Evolution*, Pergamon Press, Oxford.

Jenkins, G.M. 1969, A systems study of a petrochemical plant, *J. of Sys. Eng.* **1**: 90.

Jenkins, G.M., 1972, The systems approach in: *Systems Behavior*, J. Beishon and G. Peters, eds., OUP, London, pp. 78-104.

Johnson, J.L., and Burton, B.K.,1994, Chaos and complexity theory for management: caveat emptor, *Journal of Management Enquiry*, **3**: 320.

Jones, S., and Eden, C., 1981, OR in the community, *Journal of the Operational Research Society*, **32**: 335.

Kant, I., 1784, What is enlightenment? in: *Foundations of the Metaphysics of Morals*, I. Kant, 1969 Bobbs-Merrill, Indianapolis.

Kanter, R.M., Stein, B.A. and Jick, T.D., 1992, *The Challenge of Organizational Change*, Free Press, New York.

Kast, F.E., and Rosenzweig, J.E., 1981, *Organization and Management: A Systems and Contingency Approach*, 3rd ed., McGraw-Hill, New York.

Katz, D., and Kahn, R.L., 1966 (2nd edition 1978), *The Social Psychology of Organizations*, Wiley, New York.

Kauffman, S.,1995, *At Home in the Universe*, Oxford University Press, New York.

Keat, R., and Urry, J., 1975, *Social Theory as Science*, Routledge and Keagan Paul, London.

Kelly, G.A., 1955, *The Psychology of Personal Constructs*, Norton, New York.

Keynes, J.M., 1973, The general theory of employment, interest and money, in: *The Collected Writings of John Maynard Keynes, Volume III*, Macmillan, Cambridge.

Keys, P., 1987, Traditional Management Science and the emerging critique, in: *New Directions in Management Science*, M.C. Jackson, and P. Keys, eds., Gower, Aldershot, pp. 1-25.

Keys, P., 1990, System dynamics as a systems-based problem-solving methodology, *Systems Practice*, **3**: 479.

Keys, P., 1991, *Operational Research and Systems: the Systemic Nature of Operational Research*. Plenum, New York.

Keys P., and Jackson, M.C., eds., 1985, *Managing Transport Systems: A Cybernetic Perspective*, Gower, Aldershot.

Kijima, K., and Mackness, J., 1987, Analysis of soft trends in system thinking, *Sys. Res.*, **4**: 235.

Kilmann, R.H., 1983, A dialectical approach to formulating and testing social science theories: assumptional analysis, *Human Relations*, **36**: 1.

Klir, G., 1985, *Architecture of Systems Problem Solving*, Plenum, New York.

Koontz, H., and O'Donnell, C., 1974, *Essentials of Management*, McGraw-Hill, New York.

Kuhn, T., 1970, *The Structure of Scientific Revolutions*, 2nd ed., University of Chicago Press, Chicago.

Lane, D., 1994, With a little help from our friends: how system dynamics and 'soft' OR can learn from each other, *System Dynamics Review*, **10**: 101.

Lane, D., 1998, Interview with Nigel Cummings, *OR Newsletter*, **336**: 2.

Lane, D., 1999, Social theory and system dynamics practice, *Eur. J. of Opl. Res.*, **113**: 501.

Lane, D., 2000, Should systems dynamics be described as a 'hard' or 'deterministic' systems approach? *Syst. Res.*, **17**: 3.

Lane, D., and Jackson, M.C., 1995, Only connect! An annotated bibliography reflecting the breadth and diversity of systems thinking, *Systems Research*, **12**: 217.

Lane, D., Monefeldt, C., and Rosenhead, J., 1998, Emergency – but no accident: a system dynamics study of an accident and emergency department, *OR Insight*, **11**: 2.

Laughlin, R., 1987, Accounting systems in organizational contexts: a case for critical theory, *Accounting, Organizations and Society*, **12**: 479.

Lawrence, J.R., ed., 1968, *Operational Research and the Social Sciences*, Tavistock, London.

Lawrence, P.R., and Lorsch, J. W., 1967, Differentiation and Integration in complex organizations, *ASQ* **12**:1.

Lawrence, P.R., and Lorsch, J. W., 1969, Developing Organizations: Diagnosis and Action, Addison-Wesley, Reading, MA.

Levi-Strauss, C., 1968, *Structural Anthropology*, Penguin, Harmondsworth.

Lilienfeld, R., 1978, *The Rise of Systems Theory: An Ideological Analysis*, Wiley, New York.

Linstone, H.A., 1984, *Multiple Perspectives for Decision Making*, North-Holland, New York.

Linstone, H.A., 1989, Multiple perspectives: concepts, applications and user guidelines, *Systems Practice*, **2**: 307.

Linstone, H.A., 1999, *Decision Making for Technology Executives: Using Multiple Perspectives to Improve Performance*, Artech House, Boston.

Lockwood, D., 1956, Some remarks on "The Social System", *BJS*, **7**: 134.

Lopez-Garay, H., 1991, Guest editorial, *Systems Practice*, **4**: 399.

Lorsch, J.W., 1979, Making behavioral science more useful, *Harvard Business Review*, **57**: 171.

Luck, M., 1984, Working with inner city community organizations, in *The Writings of Steve Cook*, K. Bowen, A. Cook, and M. Luck, eds., Operational Research Society, Birmingham.

Luhmann, N., 1986, The autopoiesis of social systems, in: *Sociocybernetic Paradoxes*, F. Geyer and J. van der Zouwen, eds., Sage, London.

Luhmann, N., 1989, *Ecological Communication*, Polity Press, Cambridge.

Lukes, S., 1974, *Power: a Radical Review*, Macmillan, London.

Lyotard, J.-F., 1984, *The Postmodern Condition: A Report on Knowledge*. Manchester University Press, Manchester.

Mandelbrot, B. B., 1983, *The Fractal Geometry of Nature*, W.H. Freeman and Company, New York.

Marcuse, H., 1968, *One Dimensional Man*, Sphere Books, London.

Marx, K., 1844, Economic and philosophical manuscripts, in; *Marx: Early Writings*. Penguin, Harmondsworth, pp. 279-400.

Marx, K, 1961, *Capital*, Volume 1, Foreign Languages Publishing House, Moscow.

Maruyama, M., 1963, The second cybernetics: deviation-amplifying mutual causal processes, in: *Modern Systems Research for the Behavioural Scientist*, W. Buckley, ed., Aldine Publishing, Chicago, pp. 304-313.

Mason, R.O., 1969, A dialectical approach to strategic planning, *Man. Sci.*, **15**: B403.

Mason, R.O., and Mitroff, I.I., 1981, *Challenging Strategic Planning Assumptions*, John Wiley and Sons, Chichester.

Maturana, H.R., 1975, The organization of the living: a theory of the living organization, *International Journal of Man-Machine Studies*, **7**: 313.

Maturana, H.R., 1986, The biological foundations of self-consciousness and the physical domain of existence, in: E.R. Caianiello, ed., 1987, *Physics of Cognitive Processes: Amalfi 1986*, World Scientific, Singapore.

Maturana, H.R., and Varela, F.J., 1980, *Autopoiesis and Cognition: The Realization of the Living*, D. Reidel, Dordrecht.

Maturana, H.R., and Varela, F.J., 1992, *The Tree of Knowledge: the Biological Roots of Human Understanding*, Translated by J.Z. Young, Shambhala Publications, Boston MA.

May, R.M., 1974, Biological populations with non-overlapping generations: stable cycles and chaos, *Science*, **186**: 645.

McCarthy, T.A., 1973, A theory of communicative competence, *Philosophy of the Social Sciences*, **3**: 135.

McGregor, D., 1960, *The Human Side of Enterprise*, McGraw-Hill, New York.

McLaren, P., and Leonard, P., 1993, *Paulo Freire: a Critical Encounter*, Routledge, London.

Midgley, G., 1989, Critical systems and the problem of pluralism, *Cybernetics and Systems*, **20**: 219.

Midgley, G., 1992, The sacred and the profane in critical systems theory, *Systems Practice*, **5** :5.

Midgley, G., 1994, Ecology and the poverty of humanism: a critical systems perspective, *Systems Research*, **11**: 67.

Midgley, G., 1995, What is this thing called systems thinking?, in: *Critical Issues in Systems Theory and Practice*, K. Ellis, A. Gregory, B.R. Mears-Young, and G. Ragsdell, eds., Plenum, New York, pp. 61-71.

Midgley, G., 1996, Evaluating services for people with disabilities: a critical systems perspective, *Evaluation*, **2**: 67.

Midgley, G., 1997, Mixing methods: developing systemic intervention, in: *Multimethodology: the Theory and Practice of Integrating OR and Systems Methodologies*, J. Mingers and A. Gill, eds., Wiley, Chichester, pp.291-332.

Midgley, G., 2000, *Systemic Intervention: Philosophy, Methodology and Practice*, Kluwer/Plenum, New York.

Midgley, G., and Ochoa-Arias, A.E., 1999, Visions of community for Community OR, *Omega*, **27**: 258-274.

Midgley, G., Munlo, I., and Brown, M., 1996, *The Improvement of Housing for Older People: Developing Services Through an Integrated System of Multi-Agency Working and User Involvement*, Centre for Systems Studies, University of Hull, U.K.

Miller, J.G., 1978, *Living Systems*, McGraw-Hill, New York

Miller, J.G. and Miller, J.L., 1990, Introduction: the nature of living systems, *Behav. Sci.*, **35**: 157.

Miller, J.G. and Miller, J.L., 1991, A living systems analysis of organizational pathology, *Behavioral Science*, **36**: 239.

Miller, J.G., and Miller, J.L., 1995, Applications of living systems theory, *Systems Practice*, **8**: 19.

Mingers, J.C., 1980, Towards an appropriate social theory for applied systems thinking: critical theory and soft systems methodology, *J. Appl. Syst. Anal.*, **7**: 41.

Mingers, J.C., 1984, Subjectivism and soft systems methodology – a critique, *J. Appl. Sys. Anal.*, **11**: 85.

Mingers, J.C., 1989, An introduction to autopoiesis – implications and applications, *Sys. Pract.*, **2**: 159.

Mingers, J.C., 1992(a), Technical, practical and critical OR – past, present and future? in: *Critical Management Studies*, M. Alvesson and H. Willmott, eds., Sage, London, pp. 91-112.

Mingers, J.C., 1992(b), Fuenmayor's interpretive systemology – a critical comment, *Sys. Pract.*, **5**: 335.

Mingers, J.C., 1995, *Self-Producing Systems: Implications and Applications of Autopoiesis*, Plenum, New York.

Mingers, J. C., 1997, Towards critical pluralism, in: *Multimethodology: the Theory and Practice of Combining Management Science Methodologies*, J. Mingers and A. Gill, eds.,Wiley, Chichester, pp. 407-440.

Mingers, J.C., forthcoming, Critical realism as the underpinning philosophy for OR/MS and systems, *J. Opl. Res. Soc.*

Mingers, J.C., and Brocklesby, J., 1996, Multimethodology: towards a framework for mixing methodologies, *Omega*, **25**: 489.

Mingers, J.C. and Gill, A., 1997, *Multimethodology – the Theory and Practice of Combining Management Science Methodologies*, Wiley, Chichester.

Miser, H.J., ed., 1995, *Handbook of Systems Analysis: Cases*, John Wiley and Sons, New York.

Miser H.J., and Quade E.S., 1985, *Handbook of Systems Analysis: Overview of Uses, Procedures, Applications and Practice*, North Holland, New York.

Miser H.J., and Quade E.S., 1988, *Handbook of Systems Analysis: Craft Issues and Procedural choices*, Wiley, New York

Mitroff, I.I., and Emshoff, J.R., 1979, On strategic assumption-making: a dialectical approach to policy and planning, *Academy of Management Review*, **4**: 1.

Mitroff, I.I. and Linstone, H.A., 1993, *The Unbounded Mind*, Oxford University Press, New York.

Mitroff, I.I., Barabba, C.P. and Kilmann, R.H., 1977, The application of behavioral and philosophical techniques to strategic planning: a case study of a large federal agency, *Man. Sci.*, **24**: 44-58.

Mitroff, I.I., Emshoff, J.R. and Kilmann,, R.H., 1979, Assumption analysis: a methodology for strategic problem-solving, *Man. Sci.*, **25**: 583.

Molloy, K.J., and Best, D.P., 1980, The Checkland methodology considered as a theory building methodology, in: *Proceedings of the 5th European Meeting on Cybernetics and Systems Research*, R. Trappl, ed., Hemisphere, Washington, p. 17.

Morgan, G., 1983, Cybernetics and organization theory: epistemology or technique?, *Human Relations*, **35**: 345.

Morgan, G., ed., 1983, *Beyond Method: Strategies for Social Research*, Sage, Beverly Hills, CA.

Morgan, G., 1986, *Images of Organization*, Sage, Beverley Hills, CA.

Morgan, G., 1993, *Imaginization: the Art of Creative Management*, Sage, London.

Morgan, G., 1997, *Images of Organisation*, Sage, London.

Morris, J., 1983, The brain, the heart and the big toe, *Creativity and Innovation Network*, **9**: 25.

Muller-Merbach, H., 1984, Interdisciplinarity in OR - in the past and in the future, *J. Opl. Res. Soc.* **35**: 83.

Munro, I., 1997, An exploration of three emancipatory themes within OR and systems thinking, *J. Opl. Res. Soc.*, **48**: 576.

Naughton, J., 1977, *The Checkland Methodology: a Reader's Guide*, Open University Systems Group, Milton Keynes.

O'Connor, J., and McDermott, I., 1997, *The Art of Systems Thinking*, Thorsons, London.

Oliga, J.C., 1986, Methodology in systems research: the need for a self-reflective commitment, in: *Mental Images, Values and Reality*, J.A. Dillon, Jr., ed., SGSR, Louisville, K.Y., pp. B11-31.

Oliga, J.C., 1988, Methodological foundations of systems methodologies, *Systems Practice*, **1**: 87.

Oliga, J.C., 1989a, Towards thematic consolidation in critical management science, in: *Systems Prospects*, R.L. Flood, M.C. Jackson and P. Keys, eds., Plenum, New York, pp. 109-114.

Oliga, J.C., 1989(b), *Power and Interest in Organizations: a Contingent Relational Review*, paper for the 33rd Annual Meeting of the ISSS, Edinburgh, Scotland.

Oliga, J.C., 1989(c), *Ideology and Systems Emancipation*, paper for the 33rd Annual Meeting of the ISSS, Edinburgh, Scotland.

Oliga, J.C., 1990, Power-ideology matrix in social systems control, *Syst. Pract.*, **3**: 31.

Ormerod, R.J., 1992, Combining hard and soft systems practice, *Systemist*, **14**: 160.

Ormerod, R.J., 1995, Putting soft OR methods to work: information systems strategy development at Sainsbury's, *J. Opl. Res. Soc.*, **46**: 227.

Ormerod, R.J., 1996, Combining management consultancy and research, *Omega*, **24**: 1.

Ormerod, R.J., 1997a, Mixing methods in practice: a transformation-competence perspective, in: *Multimethodology: the theory and practice of integrating OR and systems methodologies*, J. Mingers and A. Gill, eds., Wiley, Chichester, pp. 29-58.

Ormerod, R.J., 1997b, The design of organisational intervention: choosing the approach, *Omega*, **25**: 415.

Ortegon, M., 1997, *A Study of the Application of Systems Methodologies for Approaching Organisations Operating at the Edge of Chaos*, M.Sc. Dissertation, University of Lincolnshire and Humberside.

Ortegon, M., 1999, Unpublished notes on visits to Humberside TEC.

Parsons, T., 1956, Suggestions for a sociological approach to the theory of organizations-1, *ASQ* **1**:63.

Parsons, T., 1957, Suggestions for a sociological approach to the theory of organizations-2, *ASQ* **2**:225.

Parsons, T., 1960, *Structure and Process in Modern Society*, Free Press, New York.

Parsons, T., and Smelser, N.L., 1956, *Economy and Society*, Routledge and Kegan Paul, London.

Pasmore, W., Francis, C., Haldeman, J., and Shani, A., 1982, Socio-technical systems: A North American reflection of empirical studies of the seventies, *Human Relations*, **35**: 1179.

Pearson, A., 1995, You drive for show but you putt for dough: a facilitator's perspective, in: *Beyond Dispute: the Invention of Team Syntegrity*, S. Beer, John Wiley and Sons, Chichester, pp.313-322.

Pepper, S.C., 1942, *World Hypothesis: a Study in Evidence*, University of California Press, Berkeley.

Perrow, C., 1961, The analysis of goals in complex organizations, *ASR*. **26**: 854.

Perrow, C., 1967, A framework for the comparative analysis of organizations, *ASR*, **32**: 194

Perrow, C., 1972, *Complex Organisations: A Critical Essay*, Scott, Foresman and Co., Glenview, IL.

Peters, T.J., and Waterman, R.H., Jr., 1982, *In Search of Excellence*, Harper and Row, New York.

Piaget, J., 1973, *Main Trends in Interdisciplinary Research*, George Allen and Unwin, London.

Plato, 1999, *The Essential Plato*, Translated by B. Jowett, The Softback Preview, London.

Power, M., and Laughlin, R., 1992, Critical theory and accounting, in: *Critical Management Studies*, M. Alvesson and H. Willmott, eds., Sage, London, pp. 113-135.

Prastocos, G., 1980, Blood management systems: An overview of theory and practice, *IIASA Papers*, Laxenburg, Austria, pp. 80-81.

Prigogine, I., and Stengers, I., 1984, *Order Out of Chaos: Man's New Dialogue With Nature*, Bantam Books, New York.

Pugh, D., and Hickson, D.J., 1976, *Organisational Structure in Its Context*, Saxon House and Lexington Books, Farnborough.

Quade, E.S., 1963, Military systems analysis, in: *Systems Analysis*, S.L. Optner, ed., 1965, Penguin, Harmondsworth, pp. 121-139.

Ragsdell, G. and Warren, L., 1999, Learning from Beer – lessons for intervention, *OR Insight*, **12**: 16.

Ramakrishnan, R., 1995, *Multi-Modeling: Intervention as Language*, Working Paper 1, Centre for Systems and Information Sciences, University of Humberside.

Rapoport, A., 1970, Three dilemmas in action research, *Human Relations*, **23**: 499.

Rapoport, A., 1986, *General System Theory*, Abacus, Tunbridge Wells.

Reed, M., 1985, *Redirections in Organizational Analysis*, Tavistock, London.

Rescher, N., 1979, *Cognitive Systematization*, Basil Blackwell, Oxford.

Ritchie, C., Taket, A., and Bryant, J., eds., 1994, *Community Works: 26 Case Studies Showing Community Operational Research in Action*, PAVIC Publications, Sheffield Hallam University.

Rivett, P., 1977, The case for cybernetics, *Eur. J. Opl. Res.* **1**: 3.

Robb, F.F., 1998(a), The application of autopoiesis to social organizations – a comment on John Mingers' "An Introduction to Autopoiesis: Implications and Applications", *Syst. Pract.*, **2**: 343.

Robb, F.F., 1998(b), The application of autopoiesis to social organizations: a comment on John Mingers' reply, *Syst. Pract.*, **2**: 353.

Roethlisberger, F.J., and Dickson, W.J., 1956, *Management and the Worker: an Account of a Research Program Conducted by the Western Electric Company, Hawthorne Works, Chicago*, Harvard University Press, Cambridge (Mass.).

Romm, N., 1998, Nurturing sustainability through triple loop learning: discursive accountability as responsible action, *Systemist*, **20**: 40.

Rosenhead, J., 1976, Some further comments on "The social responsibility of OR", *ORQ*, **17**: 265.

Rosenhead, J., 1981, OR in urban planning, *Omega* **9**: 345.

Rosenhead, J., 1984, Debating systems methodology: conflicting ideas about conflict and ideas, *J. Appl. Syst. Anal.*, **11**: 79.

Rosenhead, J., 1986, Custom and practice, *J. Opl. Res. Soc.*, **37**: 335.

Rosenhead, J., 1987, From management science to workers' science, in: *New Directions in Management Science*, M.C. Jackson and P. Keys, eds., Gower, Aldershot, pp. 109-131.

Rosenhead, J., 1989, Introduction: old and new paradigms of analysis, in: *Rational Analysis for a Problematic World*, J. Rosenhead, ed., Wiley, Chichester, pp. 1-20.

Rosenhead, J., ed., 1989, *Rational Analysis for a Problematic World*, Wiley, Chichester.

Rosenhead, J., 1997, Foreword, in: *Multimethodology: the Theory and Practice of Combining Management Science Methodologies*, J. Mingers and A. Gill, eds., Wiley, Chichester, p. xiii.

Rosenhead, J., 1998, *Complexity Theory and Management Practice*, Operational Research, London School of Economics, LSE Working Paper 98.25.

Rosenhead, J., and Thunhurst, C., 1982, A materialist analysis of operational research, *J. Opl. Res. Soc.*, **33**: 111.

Russell, B., 1961, *History of Western Philosophy*, George Allen and Unwin, London.

Salah, M., 1989, *Structural Prerequisites for the Design of Information Systems: A Cybernetic Diagnosis of a Steel Distribution Organization*, Ph.D thesis, Department of Management Systems and Sciences, University of Hull, Hull, England.

Sartre, J.-P., 1963, *Iron in the Soul*, Penguin, Harmondsworth.

Schecter, D., 1991, Critical systems thinking in the 1980s: a connective summary, in: *Critical Systems Thinking: Directed Readings*, R.L. Flood and M.C. Jackson, eds., Wiley, Chichester, pp. 213-226.

Schein, E.A., 1970, *Organizational Psychology*, 2nd ed., Prentice-Hall, Englewood Cliffs, NJ.

Schoderbeck, P.P., Schoderbek, C.G., and Kefalas, A.G., 1985, *Management Systems: Conceptual Considerations*, 3rd ed., Business Publications, Dallas.

Schumann, W., 1990, Strategy for information systems in the Film Division of Hoechst, A.G., *Sys. Pract.*, **3**: 265.

Schutz, A., 1967, *The Phenomenology of the Social World*, Heinemann Educational Books, London.

Senge, P.M., 1990, *The Fifth Discipline: the Art and Practice of the Learning Organization*, Random House, London.

Senge, P., Kleiner, A., Roberts, C., Ross, R., and Smith, B., 1994, *The Fifth Discipline Fieldbook*, Century, London.

Selznick, P., 1948, Foundations of the theory of organization, *ASR* **13**: 25.

Shannon., C.E., and Weaver, W., 1949, *The Mathematical Theory of Communication*, University of Illinois Press, Urbana.

Sica, A., 1981, Review of "The Systems Approach and Its Enemies", *AJS*, **87**: 208.

Simon, H.A., 1947, *Administrative Behavior*, Macmillan, New York.

Sims, D., and Smithin, T., 1982, Voluntary OR, , *J. Opl. Res. Soc.*, **33**: 21.

Silverman, D., 1970, *The Theory of Organizations*, Heinemann, London.

Skinner, Q., 1985, *The Return of Grand Theory in the Human Sciences*, Cambridge University Press, Cambridge.

Smuts, J.C., 1926, *Holism and Evolution*, Macmillan, London.

Spaul, M., 1997, Multimethodology and critical theory: an intersection of interests?, in: *Multimethodology: the Theory and Practice of Combining Management Science Methodologies*, J. Mingers and A. Gill, eds.,Wiley, Chichester, pp. 323-346.

Spencer, H., 1969, *Principles of Sociology*, Macmillan, London.

Stacey, R.D., 1992, *Managing Chaos*, Sage, London.

Stacey, R.D., 1993, *Strategic Management and Organizational Dynamics*, Pitman Publishing, London.

Stacey, R.D., 1996, *Complexity and Creativity in Organizations*, Berret-Kohler, San Francisco.

Steering Group for the Community OR Initiative, 1986, *Community OR: Notes for Those Submitting Proposals*, Operational Research Society, Birmingham.

Storr, F., 1997, *On Becoming a Learning Company*, Internal Publication, Humberside TEC, Hull.

Stowell, F.A., 1989, Organizational power and the metaphor commodity, in: *Systems Prospects*, R.L. Flood, M.C. Jackson and P. Keys, eds., Plenum, New York, pp. 147-153.

Strank, R.H.D., 1982, *Management Principles and Practice: A Cybernetic Analysis*, Gordon and Breach, London.

Streufert, S., and Swezey, R., 1986, *Complexity, Managers and Organizations*, Academic Press, London.

Swanson, G.A., 1995, Living systems theory and accounting, *General Systems Bulletin*, **25**: 13-14.

Taket, A.R., 1994, Undercover agency? – ethics, responsibility and the practice of OR, *J. Opl. Res. Soc.*, **45**: 123.

Taket, A.R. and White, L.A., 1993, After OR: an agenda for postmodernism and poststructuralism in OR, *J. Opl. Res. Soc.*, **44**: 867.

Taket, A.R. and White, L.A., 1995, Working with heterogeneity: a pluralist strategy for evaluation, in: *Critical Issues in Systems Theory and Practice*, K. Ellis, A. Gregory, B.R. Mean-Young. and G. Ragsdell, eds., Plenum, New York, pp. 517-522.

Taket, A.R. and White, L.A., 1998, Experience in the practice of one tradition of multimethodology, *Systemic Practice and Action Research*, **11**: 153.

Taket, A.R. and White, L.A., 2000, *Partnership and Participation: Decision-making in the Multiagency Setting*, Wiley, Chichester.

Taylor, F.W., 1947, *Scientific Management*, Harper and Row, London.

Thomas, A., 1980, Generating tension for constructive charge: The use and abuse of systems models, *Cybernetics and Systems*, **11**: 339.

Thomas, A. and Lockett, M., 1979, Marxism and systems research: values in practical action, in: *Improving the Human Condition*, R.F. Ericson, ed., SGSR, Louisville, pp. 284-293.

Thompson., J.D., 1967, *Organizations in Action*, McGraw-Hill, New York.

Thompson., J.D., and McEwan, W.J., 1958, Organisational goals and environment: goal-setting as an interaction process, in: *People and Organisations*, G. Salaman and K. Thompson, Longman, London, pp. 155-167.

Tinker, T., and Lowe, T., 1984, One dimensional management science: the making of a technocratic consciousness, *Interfaces*, **14**: 40.

Tomlinson, R., 1984, Rethinking the process of systems analysis and operational research: from practice to precept and back again, in: *Rethinking the Process of Operational Research and Systems Analysis*, R. Tomlinson and I. Kiss, eds., Pergamon, Oxford, pp. 205-221.

Tomlinson,R., and Kiss, I., (eds), 1984, *Rethinking the Process of Operational Research and Systems Analysis*, Pergamon, Oxford.

Topp, W.K., 1999, *Towards Heuristic Systems Methods for Generating New Knowledge in Post-Industrial Business*, Ph.D thesis, University of Cape Town, South Africa.

Tracy, L., 1994, *Leading the Living Organization: Growth Strategies for Management*, Quorum Books, London.

Tracy, L., 1995, Negotiation: an emergent process of living systems, *Behavioral Science*, **40**: 41.

Tranfield, D., and Starkey, K., 1998, The nature, social organization and promotion of management research: towards policy, *British Journal of Management*, **9**: 341.

Trist, E.L., and Bamforth, K.W., 1951, Some social and psychological consequences of the long wall method of coal-getting, *Human Relations*, **4**: 3.

Trist, E.L., Higgin, G.W., Murray, H., and Pollock, A.B., 1963, *Organizational Choice*, Tavistock, London.

Tsagdis, D., 1996, Systems methodologies, reference systems and science, in: *Cybernetics and Systems '96*, R. Trappl, ed., Austrian Society for Cybernetics, pp. 784-788.

Tsoukas, H., 1993(a), The road to emancipation is through organizational development: a critical evaluation of Total Systems Intervention, *Sys. Pract.*, **6**: 53,

Tsoukas, H., 1993(b), 'By their fruits ye shall know them': a reply to Jackson, Green and Midgley, *Systems Practice*, **6**: 311.

Ulrich, W., 1981(a), A critique of pure cybernetic reason: the Chilean experience with cybernetics, *J. Appl, Sys. Anal.*, **8**: 33.

Ulrich, W., 1981(b), On blaming the messenger for the bad news: reply to Bryer's "Comments", *Omega*, **9**: 7.

Ulrich, W., 1983, *Critical Heuristics of Social Planning*, Haupt, Bern.

Ulrich, W., 1985, The way of inquiring systems: review of Churchman's "The Design of Inquiring Systems", *J. Opl. Res. Soc.*, **36**: 873.

Ulrich, W., 1987, Critical heuristics of social systems design, *Eur. J. Opl. Res.*, **31**: 276.

Ulrich, W., 1988, Systems thinking, systems practice and practical philosophy: a program of research, *Systems Practice*, **1**: 137.

Ulrich, W., 1998, *Systems Thinking as if People Mattered: Critical Systems Thinking for Citizens and Managers*, Working Paper 23, University of Lincolnshire and Humberside.

Ulrich, H., and Probst, G.J.B., ed., 1984, *Self-Organization and Management of Social Systems*, Springer-Verlag, Berlin.

Umpleby, S.A., 1990, Comparing conceptual systems: a strategy for changing values as well as institutions, *Cybernetics and Systems*, **22**: 515.

van der Heijden, K., 1996, *Scenarios: the Art of Strategic Conversation*, John Wiley and Sons, Chichester.

van Gigch, J.P., 1978, *Applied General Systems Theory*, 2nd ed., Harper and Row, New York.

Varela, F.J., 1984, Two principles of self-organization, in: *Self Organization and the Management of Social Systems*, H. Ulrich and G.J.B. Probst, eds., Springer-Verlag, Berlin, pp. 25-32.

Varela, F.J., Maturana, H.R. and Uribe, R., 1974, Autopoiesis: the organization of living systems, *Biosystems*, **5**: 187.

Vennix, J.A.C., 1996, *Group Model Building: Facilitating Team Learning Using System Dynamics*. John Wiley, Chichester.

Vickers, G., 1965, *The Art of Judgement*, Chapman and Hall, London.

Vickers, G., 1970, *Freedom in a Rocking Boat*, Allen Lane, London.

Vickers, G., 1973, *Making Institutions Work*, Associated Business Programmes, London.

Vickers, G., 1983, *Human Systems are Different*, Harper and Row, London.

von Bertalanffy, L., 1950, The theory of open systems in physics and biology, in: *Systems Thinking*, F.E. Emery, ed., Penguin, Harmondsworth, pp. 70-85.

von Bertalanffy, L., 1968, *General System Theory*, Penguin, Harmondsworth.

von Foerster, H., 1981, *Observing Systems*, Intersystems Publications, Seaside, Calif..

von Krogh, G., and Roos, J., 1995, *Organizational Epistemology*, St. Martin's Press, New York.

Walker, J., 1990, Diagnosis and implementation: how a large co-operative employed a series of proposals for restructuring based upon the Viable Systems Model, *Sys. Pract.*, **3**: 441.

Walsham, G. and Han, C.K., 1991, Structuration theory and information systems research, *Journal of Applied Systems Analysis*, **18**: 77.

Warfield, J.N., 1976, *Societal Systems: Planning, Policy and Complexity*, Wiley, New York.

Warfield, J.N., 1994, *A Science of Generic Design: Managing Complexity through Systems Design*, Iowa State University Press, Ames.

Warfield, J.N. and Cardenas, A.R., 1994, *A Handbook of Interactive Management*, Iowa State University Press, Iowa.

Warren, L., and Adman, P., 1999, The use of TSI in designing a system for a university IS user support service, *Systems Research*, **16**: 351.

Watson, H., and Wood-Harper, T., 1995, Methodology as metaphor: the practical basis of multiview methodology (a reply to M.C. Jackson), *Info. Systems. J.*, **5**: 3.

Weber, M., 1964, *The Theory of Social and Economic Organization*, Free Press, New York.

Weber, M., 1969, *The Methodology of the Social Sciences*, Free Press, New York.

Weedon, C.R., 1992, *An Interpretive-Systemic Study of Community Operational Research*, MA dissertation, University of Hull.

Weinberg, GM., 1975, *An Introduction to General Systems Theory*, Wiley, New York.

Wheatley, M.J., 1992, *Leadership and the New Science: Learning About Organization from an Orderley Universe*, Berrett-Koehler, San Francisco.

White, L.A., 1994, Let's Syntegrate, *OR Insight*, **7**:13.

White, L.A., 1998, Tinker, tailor, soldier, sailor: a syntegrity to explore London's diverse interests, *OR Insight*, **3**: 12.

White, L.A., and Taket, A.R., 1994, The death of the expert, *J. Opl. Res. Soc.*, **45**: 733.

White, L.A., and Taket, A.R., 2000, Exploring the use of narrative analysis as an operational research method: a case study in voluntary sector evaluation, *J. Opl. Res. Soc.*, **51**: 700.

Wiener, N., 1948, *Cybernetics*, Wiley, New York.

Wiener, N., 1950, *The Human Use of Human Beings*, Eyre and Spottiswoode, London.

Wilby, J., 1995, Book review: Leading the Living Organization: Growth Strategies for Management (by Lane Tracy), *Systems Practice*, **8**: 124.

Willmott, H., 1989, OR as a problem situation: from soft systems methodology to critical science, in: *Operational Research and the Social Sciences*, M.C. Jackson, P. Keys and S.A. Cropper, eds., Plenum, New York, pp. 65-78.

Wilson, B., 1984, *Systems: Concepts, Methodologies and Applications*, Wiley, New York.

Wolstenholme, E.F., 1990, *Systems Enquiry: a System Dynamics Approach*. Wiley, Chichester.

Wood, S., and Kelly, J., 1978, Towards a critical management science, *J. Mgt. Stud.*, **15**: 1.

Woodger, J.H., 1929, *Biological Principles*, Kegan Paul Trench and Trubner, London.

Woodward, J., 1964, *Industrial Organizations: Theory and Practice*, OUP, London

Yolles, M., 1999, *Management Systems: A Viable Approach*, Pitman, London.

Yong Pil Rhee, 1999, *Dynamics and Complexity of Political System*, Ingansarang Press, Seoul.

Zeleny, M. and Hufford, K.D., 1992, The application of autopoiesis in systems analysis: are autopoietic systems also social systems? *Int. J. Gen. Syst.*, **21**: 145.

AUTHOR INDEX

INDEX

Made in the USA